U.S. National Economic Policy 1917–1985

U.S. National Economic Policy 1917–1985

Anthony S. Campagna

PRAEGER

New York
Westport, Connecticut
London

Library of Congress Cataloging-in-Publication Data

Campagna, Anthony S.
 U.S. national economic policy, 1917–1985.

 Bibliography: p.
 Includes index.
 1. United States—Economic policy. I. Title.
 HC106.2.C26 1987   338.973   86-30316
 ISBN 0-275-92426-2 (alk. paper)
       0-275-92907-8 (pbk. : alk. paper)

Library of Congress Catalog Card Number: 86-30316

ISBN: 0-275-92426-2
      0-275-92907-8 (pbk.)

First published in 1987

Praeger Publishers, One Madison Avenue, New York, NY 10010
A division of Greenwood Press, Inc.

Printed in the United States of America

The paper used in this book complies with the
Permanent Paper Standard issued by the National
Information Standards Organization (Z39.48-1984).

10 9 8 7 6 5 4 3 2

For
RUTH
and
ALENA

Contents

part V
Conclusions

My purpose in writing this book was to provide a survey of macroeconomic policymaking over most of the twentieth century, spanning the period when monetary institutions, tax laws, and budgetary procedures, which make economic policy feasible, if not always acceptable, were in place. Over that time span, the U.S. economy was subjected to four hot wars, cold wars, fourteen business cycles (including one major depression), fluctuating growth rates, population and labor-force changes, and shifts and swings in attitudes toward government's role in the economy. Through all of these events, macroeconomic policy was being made, whether consciously or not, willingly or not.

It is my purpose to examine the major policies adopted over the time span that begins with the post-World War I period and ends in 1985 and to trace the evolution of policymaking in the process. For each time period, delineated mainly by political administration, the major economic problems facing the nation are discussed—what was done about them, how successful were the actions taken (or not taken). As part of the evaluation procedure, the policies followed are measured against the prevailing economic orthodoxy, and this requires that the evolution of economic theory be summarized as well. When policy and theory diverge, the cause can frequently be traced to social pressures demanding action, perhaps even prior to theoretical justification and rationalization. The interactions among theory, policy, and social attitudes are very interesting, but only a start can be attempted in this survey.

Clearly this is an ambitious undertaking, and some limits had to be placed on the depth of coverage and the number of policies discussed. For the sake of brevity, many avenues of examination were not followed, and suggestions had to suffice. Yet even the inclusion of just major events resulted in a long book, despite all efforts to restrict it. One self-imposed restraint was to reduce the extent of the analysis in the early years in order to present more detailed coverage of the later years, when data are more reliable and the institutions of policymaking are established and functioning.

Obviously a book of this kind is never finished, for there are always new works to include, new interpretations to consider, and new information available. Equally obvious is that a book of this kind is started and made possible only through the efforts of so many other people who have made contributions in the past, many of whom cannot be properly acknowledged. Either the citations would be too numerous for known contributors or not numerous enough for unrecognized ones. It is not always possible to remember where an idea or phrase came from, and while this problem is ever present, it is especially acute in a book of this kind, where so many sources were consulted and where proper acknowledgment is often difficult or even impossible. Therefore a blanket debt of gratitude is in order to all forerunners without whose work the present book would not be possible.

Those who helped in the preparation of the manuscript can be identified, however, and a special note of appreciation and gratitude can be extended. Sandy Mable of the Economics Department at the University of Vermont typed most of the original draft, and my wife, Ruth Campagna, typed, proofread, and edited the final draft. Ruth went far beyond merely typing the manuscript and helping prepare it for publication. She provided encouragement when needed, understanding when necessary, and support always.

Introduction

Attempting to evaluate past public policy in economic matters is a difficult and humbling task. There is always the historian's problem of trying to interpret the past without using the current period's values and judgments and introducing biases, whether knowingly or not. Then there is the additional problem of choosing a path between the details of policy actions that can overwhelm and obscure, rather than aid in the evaluation, and the general outlines of policy actions that can lead to overgeneralizations and pedantic judgments. No magic formula exists to guide one past the trap of either excess.

Awareness of these problems does not guarantee a solution but can serve to remind everyone of the pitfalls of historical reviews. Furthermore, hindsight should help us understand the past, but should not substitute for wisdom gained with the passage of time and the accumulation of knowledge. Looking back is always easier than looking forward.

With these caveats in mind, the approach taken here is to organize the analysis and the evaluation of public policy around three questions that must be answered: namely, were the policies *justified, successful, and rational*. These categories may seem self-evident, but an elaboration of them may reveal some additional reasons for their selection.

Justification for Economic Policies

Whether or not a particular policy was justified depends upon several factors. First, from an abstract and intellectual perspective, the action taken or forsaken should be judged in relation to the prevailing economic orthodoxy. The prevailing view or paradigm of how the economy works is clearly important in any attempt to discuss the defensibility of any action taken (or equally important, not taken). The options available with the predominant theoretical model may limit the range of problems that could or should be solved by the public sector, as well as the range of solutions deemed acceptable. Of course, ideology plays an important role in the determination of what should or should not be done in the realm of public policy, and ideology cannot be set aside in the search for evidence of what was done.

Given this admonition, it would be appropriate to discuss other viewpoints or alternative approaches. Such a comparison may not only reveal differences but may help us understand the evolution of policies over time; what is unacceptable in one period may be readily accepted in another. Much of our existing social legislation exhibits that pattern of development.

The prevailing view of how the world works or should work can be confining, however, and political and social pressures may build and eventually overwhelm the reluctance to experiment and take action. Political realities may require a response to pressure coming from various constituents to "do something." Conventional wisdom may dictate hesitancy and inaction, but politicians cannot always wait until the new situations or changing conditions can be reconciled with or accommodated by the old ideology, nor can they wait for the more widespread acceptance of a competing paradigm of how the world works.

Thus public attitudes toward social and economic problems may change well ahead of changes in intellectual abstractions and result in demands for action. Indeed, such demands may well inspire the intellectual abstractions, as theoreticians rethink their ideas and respond to pressing concerns. I think actions taken following such demands can be considered justified, although the area is vague and problematic. It could be argued, for instance, that the public does not know what its best interest are and that quick reactions to complex problems are not warranted. This contention would be difficult to refute, but it could also be argued that the risks of democracy cannot be avoided. Without resolving the issue, it seems best to consider policies that emerge from political and social pressures as justified in some larger sense.

In another shadowy area, how are political compromises with ideology to be classified? Suppose a bad economic condition showed signs of becoming even worse and politicians were willing to take some pragmatic actions because of this temporary situation. Would such actions be justified in this case when they would not be in a calmer period, or are they indications that the old orthodoxy was breaking down and these actions are a sign that the new is becoming more acceptable; or are we simply projecting too much into political actions, assuming that politicians are leaders rather than followers and are content to act with or without the niceties of justification? Again, such actions probably should be considered justified, although many more questions arise in this case, questions of intent and legitimacy.

Finally, there is the perennial question of the loss of individual freedom whenever control is transferred to public authorities. The issue is too complex to be discussed here, but several questions may be worth raising. Is there sufficient justification for even trying to manipulate an economic system, given our limited knowledge of its complexities and the nagging suspicion that it might by self-regulating? Indeed, it could be maintained that policies designed to manipulate the responses of masses of people approach the totalitarian idea that a centralized authority knows what is best for everyone. Yet in assessing the justification for economic policies, how much weight should be given to the loss of freedom and how is it to be considered properly—as a benefit–cost problem where the gains to the beneficiaries exceed or are exceeded by the costs to the losers? The calculus is missing to answer these questions, but they must be considered, if not completely answered, as important in an overall evaluation of public policy.

Success of Economic Policies

Questions of justification aside, there is the second problem of determining whether or not the policy adopted was successful. It is not as easy a job as might be first imagined, and definitive answers may never be possible, for one must confront the most basic question: success or failure in relation to what? Is success or failure to be absolute—either total success or total failure? Surely there is room for partial achievements of goals or partial fulfillment of objectives. Yet partial results allow both advocate and critic to claim victory. The advocate points to the partial success, the critic points to the partial failure. Political compromises and hence partial results are routine, however, and this invites confusion over the interpretation of negotiated policies.

Furthermore, there is still no method that allows us to describe what would have happened in the absence of the policies actually followed. Lacking objective criteria by which to gauge success or failure, some criteria, however arbitrary, must be adopted. It follows that any interpretation of past policies must rely on the investigator

xiv   Introduction

and his examination of the evidence and, in the end, on value judgments, intended or not. In the words of Gunnar Myrdal, "All scientific work has to be based on value premises. There is no view without a viewpoint, no answers except to questions."[1] Thus a value-free interpretation of history or a value-free economics appears utopian.

Of course, to make judgments, the goals of public policy must be identifiable and clearly stated. In practice this is not always likely to be the case, but following Richard Musgrave, government policies can be directed at stabilization of the economy, redistribution of income, or alterations in the allocation of resources. These aims can and do result in overlapping in practice, and the results of pursuing one must often be judged on its effects on others as well.[2]

Another problem is that policies actually followed may change the economy by altering its institutions, the behavior of economic agents, and the expectations of all who are affected by them. Economic and social systems are simply not the same following attempts to manage them. For example, a 1930s-style depression is not very likely to recur (in the same way), given the institutional changes that were erected to prevent its repetition. Moreover, people expect protection from such disruptions and have accepted many more modifications of their freedom than might otherwise have been the case. Over time, then, some policies will or will not work, only because the groundwork has or has not been prepared by previous adaptions to public policy.

Clearly there is a cumulative effect here that must be considered. Public policy can rarely be considered in isolation, free from what went before and oblivious to future repercussions. By tracing economic policy over time, some of the cumulative effects will become evident.

Rationality of Economic Policies

Formidable as these problems are, they are typical of studies of this kind. Another problem, however, is seldom confronted directly—that of rationality. Rationality here refers to the pursuit of unstated goals by policymakers, which renders their policies deliberately ineffective or inefficient. For example, in judging the success or failure of policy actions, a conclusion frequently reached is that the policy was ill timed, ill conceived, or ill administered. There is no doubt that many judgmental statements, with varying degrees of truthfulness, include one or more of these ills; indeed partial success or failure can often be traced to the design or administration of the policy.

Sometimes, however, another conclusion emerges: namely, that there are inherent weaknesses in public policy and that the consequences will always be poor policies and inept administration. Critics of public policy have pointed to the evils of bureaucracy, the lag in response to problems, the conflicts of interest and self-serving attitudes, and the compromised solutions, and have succeeded in creating a potent bias against public policy. Like clichés, the problems of policymaking seem to express simple truths, hardly subject to doubt, and with repetition they even become self-evident and harden into implicit value judgments. Fortunately, when such prejudices are fully developed they are easy to recognize and confront.

But what if those who have such a bias are entrusted with guiding, designing, or administering public policy? Perhaps a public outcry demands that something be done, and they are forced into action. Is it not possible that they would develop or devise a policy that would fail? It might even be that they would do so deliberately, since they may have a vested interest—either personal or intellectual—in seeing the policy fail. After all, a successful policy would indicate that the public sector has a role to play in the economic system and that some social problems can be solved (perhaps even efficiently) through public action.[3] The meaning of rationality is clearly ambiguous here; the act is rational for the policymaker but irrational for the society.

Similarly, what of policies that appear ineffective or irrational in attempting to achieve a stated goal but are rational if unstated goals are considered. Policies can be manipulated so that even if they do fail to some extent, another end is achieved. Thus ulterior motives may make current, short-run policies seem ill considered and haphazard, and only the cumulative effects of these policies may reveal the purpose of the actions taken. Mr. Nixon's wage-and-price-control system, as we will see, can be placed in this category. A less obvious example may serve to show the duality of public policies. The investment tax credit was designed to stimulate investment spending, but it also served to encourage the substitution of capital for labor and thus weaken the power of labor in its bargaining with business firms, the recipients of the tax concession.

Policies that are designed to fail or are twisted to achieve other ends are clearly difficult to uncover and "prove," and only a different perspective may reveal them. What may appear rational to one faction may seem irrational to another. Only by viewing the policy through different eyes, from radical to conservative, and by allowing political and social considerations to enter into an evaluation of public economic policies, can more searching and provocative questions be raised concerning rationality.

Methodology

Any analysis of past policies must employ a procedure that will permit an evaluation in terms of the criteria noted above: justification, success or failure, and rationality. Having acknowledged the difficulties involved—and there is no desire to underestimate them—it is necessary to discuss now, if only in general terms, the methodology to be followed.

For the justification criterion, the prevailing, or better, predominant economic theory must be reviewed; then the actual policies proposed or followed can be related to it. This will permit an analysis of just how influential economic theory was in influencing public policy and just how consistent the policies adopted were with the theoretical framework. In some periods it will not be difficult to locate and express the economic orthodoxy that is predominant; in other periods, when the old orthodoxy is under serious attack, it may be necessary to present the conflicting views.

The political and social attitudes, pressures, prejudices, and so on that figure in the justification criterion are much more difficult to determine. It is not difficult to examine economic data for signs of economic and social deterioration and then seek the possible changes in attitudes or pressures for responses, but the reverse procedure is not as easy—to trace the changes in social and political pressures that precede the call to do something. Where is one to look for the signs of change? Evidence can be gathered from the news media, voting records and trends, congressional hearings, public opinion polls, speeches of leading figures, and so on. Such evidence is often ephemeral, however, and caution is required in the interpretation of such information. Nevertheless, any attempt to link and measure the political and social conditions that affect economic policy, no matter how complicated, is better than ignoring altogether the role they play. Economic policy is not formed in a vacuum.

To determine the success or partial success of a policy may be somewhat easier. To satisfy the second criterion it is necessary to find as clear a statement as possible of what the goal was and then attempt to measure how much was achieved by the original policy and any modifications of it. In this regard, it is instructive to follow the original intent of any policy from the initial recognition of a problem through to the passage of any act or final policy as it emerges from the legislative and political bodies. The difference between the original intent and the final version of a policy could be quite revealing, and perhaps more pertinent to the rationality criterion.

Explicit goals or targets are usually found readily enough in official documents, for example, in the *Federal Reserve Bulletins, Economic Reports of the President,* and in the specific acts of Congress. The analysis of economic data should reveal the degree of success in achieving the stated targets and yield some initial conclusions on the attainment of goals.

Thus the steps toward the evaluation of the success criterion run from the description of the problems facing the nation in any one time period, to the recognition of the problems and to the setting of goals and targets and to the formation of policies to meet them, and then to the analysis of the results to determine the degree of success. The next step, if it has not already been taken, is to examine the policy that produced the observed results. Questions about the design, timing, administration, and so on are now appropriate. These more searching inquiries may help explain the results and, more important, may help us understand the limits and constraints of public policy. Finally, some effort must be made to trace the cumulative effects and the long-term consequences of repeated attempts at managing the economy.

To determine the rationality of public policy it is necessary to go beyond the official documents and their statements of goals and targets and intents. It is to unstated goals that we must look. One way to expose unstated goals is to analyze the policy from other viewpoints. Examining the views of critics may uncover ulterior motives, examining alternative solutions to the problem being faced may reveal hidden implications. It remains a difficult task, and, in the end, we are once again forced to examine ideological questions in order to gain a complete picture of policy measures.

It is impossible to go beyond these generalities in this introduction, because each policy action is different and will call for a different approach. I believe it is better to leave the generalities as they are and let the ongoing analyses reveal the specific methodology followed in each case. In outline form, the general procedure can be expressed as follows:

1. Present the facts, known at the time, of economic and social conditions for the period under review. The periods should overlap so that the threads of policy can be traced over time, but the division of time by political administrations should also be recognized.
2. Describe the economic and social problems and concerns and the policies considered and adopted to combat them.
3. Evaluate the policies pursued to determine the degree of success. Analyze the results to ascertain the reasons for success or failure, from official and unofficial perspectives.

4. Review the policies of the period in terms of the criteria of justification, success or failure, and rationality.

One final note on methodology is required on the matter of emphasis. The steps outlined above are necessary, of course, for a full understanding of public policy, but clearly they could also entail a rather long study if each is discussed in considerable detail. It is therefore necessary to place some limitations on the scope of the book. First, not every public policy can be discussed by this procedure. Some choices must be made among them as to which are important enough to warrant the full-scale treatment and which can be treated summarily or even merely mentioned.

Second, even for the more important measures, some condensing is desirable. It seems that any abridgment ought to come at the expense of detailed descriptions of the policy and to some extent in the determination of success or failure from official sources. Getting involved in all the details of a specific policy will be unnecessarily thorough, while determining success or failure for every facet of a policy could get overly tedious. Indeed, much of this has already been done by others, and their work can help reduce the need for further extensive reviews; in other instances, a fresh evaluation must be undertaken to present an alternative interpretation.

What these reductions in the procedures accomplish is to change the focus somewhat to concentration on the aspects of public policy previously ignored or downplayed: namely, the broadening of public policy evaluations to include the questions of justification and, more particularly, rationality.

Purpose and Plan of Book

With these suggestions of the many facets that must be considered in the evaluation of past national economic policies, it is little wonder that the entire subject is so controversial. Nearly everyone, economist and layman alike, has opinions on the matter, which are all too willingly expressed. Yet judgments and evaluations of past attempts to manage the economy may reflect a narrow perspective based on the results of particular episodes or unrecognized value judgments. Some people may be the captives of some ideology or theoretical model learned long ago. At times they may even be near the mark, which only serves to reinforce their predilections; at other times, when their predictions are clearly incorrect, they search for special circumstances that made their forecasts wrong this time. The policy was not carried out long enough, the initial policy was compromised too much in the political process, or some unanticipated event occurred to upset the working of the policy.

Everyone, including this writer, sees the world through eyes that reflect value judgments, and everyone engaged in empirical research, said Bertram Russell, is subject to the error of finding what we set out to find and ignoring the unexpected or unwanted evidence. It is the purpose of this book to help clarify these issues by examining the subject in a systematic way and by challenging single-minded interpretations.

The plan of the book is as follows. Part I presents the overall record of the U.S. economy from the turn of the century to the present. This includes a brief review of the economic conditions of the 1920s. The major emphasis of the study is on the period from the Great Depression to the present, but in order to gain some appreciation for the developing economy after World War I, and to analyze the causes of the Great Depression, it is necessary to go back to the end of the war. Since the Federal Reserve System was created and the income tax was enacted just prior to World War I, this postwar period is the first in which a modern macroeconomic policy was really possible. This is still an arbitrary selection, since to understand the post-World War I economy, it would be necessary to review the economy prior to the war. We must break into history somewhere, however, and the postwar period seems logical enough for most purposes.

Part II covers the Great Depression, World War II, and the post-World War II administration of President Truman. With the Truman administration the analysis becomes more detailed, as economic intervention into the economy becomes more acceptable and economic controversies more open. Part III extends the analysis from the Eisenhower administration to the end of the Great Society of President Johnson in 1968. The reason for the break here will become obvious, since economic policy changed directions. Part IV then takes us to the present, and the analysis becomes even more detailed as we approach the recent past. There is both more interest in the recent past and another shift in policy measures. Finally, Part V presents a summary and conclusions section along with some suggestions of the future of policymaking in the United States and some suggestions as to how it can be improved.

part I

The Record
and Early Years

chapter 1

The Record of the U.S. Economy

Even a cursory glance at the past performance of the U.S. economy reveals two clearly discernible results: growth and instability.[1] That is, the overall record is one of a fairly persistent growth of output, marred by periodic disruptions or business cycles.

The growth of output is usually deemed desirable, since it increases the standard of living of the society. With growth, the number of jobs is increased, the opportunity for upward mobility is enhanced, and the willingness to confront social ills is acknowledged. The goal of continuous economic growth is consistent with the (implicit?) value judgment that more is better. Not until the 1960s was this view seriously questioned. Yet despite all the attention given to environmental concerns, pollution, and the composition of the output, that is, frivolous goods or military hardware, the goal of a steadily rising national output continues virtually unchallenged as one of the principal means by which the success of the economic system is measured.

In this chapter there is no need to discuss the criticism of economic growth as a goal. The criticism will come later, but it is important to recognize at the outset that the growth of output rests on the value judgment that more is better, no matter what is produced or who gets it. Indeed, failure to consider the question of the distribution of the output is responsible for many dissenters from the orthodox view.

3

Growth and the Business Cycle

Selected growth rates for the U.S. economy are given in Table 1.1. The periods covered are arbitrary and are meant only to convey an immediate impression of the past growth rates. More specific analysis of growth and growth rates will accompany the discussion, by period, in later chapters.

It is clear that GNP grew steadily over this time span, although not at uniform rates. For the period 1919–84 the data are certainly better, and here the growth rate was approximately only 3.0 percent. Growth rates, of course, are heavily influenced by the initial and terminal years. Still, there does seem to be a slight decline in the growth rate over time.

One reason for the fluctuating growth rate is the periodic business cycle. Over the time period 1854–1984, the United States has experienced 30 cycles, which are listed in Table 1.2. Just a glance at the table is sufficient to raise some questions about the stability of the economic system. Even before there was an active interventionist government, business cycles occurred with regularity. Causes other than government meddling must be responsible.

Explanations for these cycles range from overinvestment or underconsumption to monetary and psychological causes; they include theories based on fluctuations in agricultural output, overindebted-

Table 1.1   Selected U.S. Growth Rates of Real GNP, 1890–1984

Period	Rate of Growth (percent)
1889–1899	4.3
1899–1909	4.2
1909–1919	2.3
1919–1929	3.4
1929–1939	0.3
1939–1949	4.5
1949–1959	3.9
1959–1969	4.3
1969–1979	3.1
1979–1984	2.1

Source: U.S. Department of Commerce, Bureau of the Census, *Long-Term Economic Growth, 1860–1965* (Washington, D.C: GPO, 1966); and *Survey of Current Business* 65 (July 1985).

ness, and maldistribution of investment. The culprits are usually greedy businessmen, bankers, government in general, and of course, natural phenomena. Since there is no unique or generally accepted theory of the business cycle, there is no point to further discussion, and it will be assumed that each cycle must be explained by itself. This procedure will be acceptable to everyone but those who insist that there is a sole source of business fluctuations.

Furthermore, the crucial point should not be lost sight of here: The economy is simply not stable. Thus there is a case for trying to make it so. Therefore, another goal of an economic system that justifies an active intervention into the economy is stabilization. In the early days of formulating policy, stabilization was interpreted as smoothing out the inevitable business cycle; that is, reducing the amplitude of the cycle. In recent years the goal has been modified to one of closing the gap between potential and actual GNP. Potential GNP can be taken as the estimate of what existing resources are capable of producing if they were utilized fully or nearly so.

Both the gap and the rising trend of GNP since the turn of the century are easily seen in Figure 1.1. The upward trend is periodically interrupted by business cycles that are at times rather severe, as in 1920–21 and the 1930s, while other cycles hardly show up in this ratio chart. Even so, just a cursory look at the chart would suggest that the cycles that do show up must have been crippling to the economy. Yet just how disrupting would not be evident unless some abstract guide were available to suggest what might have happened in the absence of the cycle.

One guide would be a steady growth rate over the period. In Figure 1.1 a growth rate of 3.1 percent is drawn for comparison with the actual experience. While a real growth rate of 3.1 percent is not spectacular, note how often the actual rate is below it, representing the loss of real output. Another abstract guide is potential GNP, which measures the output possible at high rates of resource utilization and hence measures more directly the value of lost output.

The gap between actual and potential GNP measures the output sacrificed because of the failure to employ the existing resources to their capacity. The output lost is gone forever, since there is no way to recover lost man hours or lost machine hours. Idle labor and machines represent lost output estimated to be $265 billion over the period 1952–80—a staggering sum.

The same conclusions emerge from examining the other components of Figure 1.1. In Part b, the variations of industrial production that help explain the business cycle show the same pattern as GNP; in Part c, aggregate hours worked show even more clearly the lost input

Table 1.2 U.S. Business Cycles: Reference Dates and Duration

Business Cycle Reference Dates		Duration in Months		Cycle	
Trough	Peak	Contraction (trough from previous peak)	Expansion (trough to peak)	Trough from Previous Trough	Peak from Previous Peak
December 1854	June 1857	—	30	—	—
December 1858	October 1860	18	22	48	40
June 1861	April 1865	8	46	30	54
December 1867	June 1869	32	18	78	50
December 1870	October 1873	18	34	36	52
March 1879	March 1882	65	36	99	101
May 1885	March 1887	38	22	74	60
April 1888	July 1890	13	27	35	40
May 1891	January 1893	10	20	37	30
June 1894	December 1895	17	18	37	35
June 1897	June 1899	18	24	36	42
December 1900	September 1902	18	21	42	39
August 1904	May 1907	23	33	44	56
June 1908	January 1910	13	19	46	32
January 1912	January 1913	24	12	43	36
December 1914	August 1918	23	44	35	67
March 1919	January 1920	7	10	51	17
July 1921	May 1923	18	22	28	40
July 1924	October 1926	14	27	36	41
November 1927	August 1929	13	21	40	34

March 1933	May 1937	43	50	64	93
June 1938	February 1945	13	80	63	93
October 1945	November 1948	8	37	88	45
October 1949	July 1953	11	45	48	56
May 1954	August 1957	10	39	55	49
April 1958	April 1960	8	24	47	32
February 1961	December 1969	10	106	34	116
November 1970	November 1973	11	36	117	47
March 1975	January 1980	16	58	52	74
July 1980	July 1981	6	12	64	18
November 1982		16	—	28	—
Average, all cycles					
1854–1982 (30 cyles)		18	33	51	51
1854–1919 (16 cycles)		22	27	48	49
1919–1945 (6 cycles)		18	35	53	53
1945–1982 (8 cycles)		11	45	56	55
Average, peacetime cycles					
1854–1982 (25 cycles)		19	27	46	46
1854–1919 (14 cycles)		22	24	46	47
1919–1945 (5 cycles)		20	26	46	45
1945–1982 (6 cycles)		11	34	46	44

Note: Italicized figures are the wartime expansions (Civil War, World Wars I and II, Korean war, and Vietnam war), the postwar contractions, and the full cycles that include the wartime expansions.

Source: U.S. Department of Commerce, Bureau of Economic Analysis, *Business Conditions Digest* supplement, *Handbook of Cyclical Indicators* (Washington, DC: GPO, 1984), p.178.

Figure 1.1 Production and Aggregate Hours (annually; trend, growth rate)

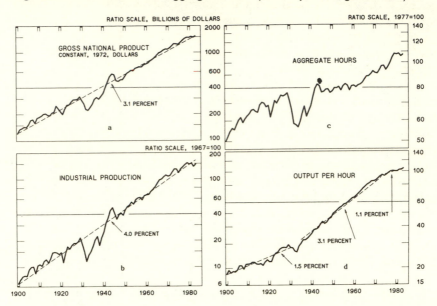

Source: Board of Governors of the Federal Reserve System, *1984 Historical Chart Book*, p. 10.

hours. Finally, Part d depicts the very important measure, output per hour. Although it is not readily apparent in the figure, output per hour does vary with the business cycle, falling during recessions and rising in upswings. Note also the rather low-trend growth rates drawn—1.5, 3.1, and 1.1 percent over the period—and the decreasing actual rate or growth of productivity in the past decade or so.

Unemployment and Price Stability

By definition, closing the gap between potential and actual GNP means reducing unemployment, and hence this becomes one of the major targets of a stabilization policy. Indeed, one of the main indicators of business-cycle trends and one of the principal means to judge their severity is the unemployment rate. The unemployment rate is not only an economic indicator but a social barometer of the health of the society. Increasing unemployment shows up as a major variable in the explanation of many social ills, from crime to the decline of the family. At this stage, however, there is no need to dwell on the importance of unemployment in economic and social concerns. The fact that full employment appears among the nation's goals, along with economic growth and stability, is sufficient to assume its importance for the present.

The unemployment record is given in Figure 1.2. Whenever unemployment rates are graphed, the incredible experience of the 1930s always stands out and dominates the picture. The amount of suffering that occurred in this cycle is almost self-evident from the 25 percent unemployment rate. But it is only a matter of degree, since a similar if less dramatic increase can be seen in nearly every cycle, to be followed by a return to "normal" after the cycle has run its course. This pattern is generally true up until the 1950s, when the unemployment rate seems to edge upwards and does not return to previous levels. This development will have to be explained later. The long upswing of the 1960s is evident in the decline in the unemployment rate, but the 1970s and 1980s saw a return to previous instability.

Figure 1.2 The Unemployment Rate, 1906–84

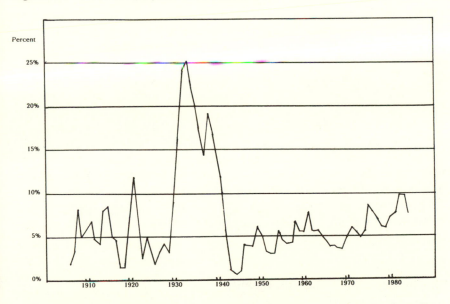

Sources: U.S. Department of Commerce, Bureau of the Census, *Long-Term Economic Growth 1860–1965* (Washington, DC: GPO, 1966); and Council of Economic Advisors, *Economic Reports of the President* (Washington, DC: GPO, various years).

The analysis of these changes in unemployment patterns may help us understand the changes in the structure of the U.S. economy that bring them about. How these shifts affect the usefulness of the unemployment rate as an economic and social barometer also remains to be seen.

In any event, the unemployment rate cannot be viewed in isolation, but must be considered along with other evidence and other goals. One of these goals is price stability. Taken together, full employment and price stability define a stable economy, and achieving these targets has become the object of stabilization policies. Thus all the elements that might be included in the definition of what constitutes a stable economy have often been reduced to these two. In particular, the structure of the economy has been relegated to a secondary concern, if it is considered at all. To see this, consider the behavior of prices over the period.

In the 1960s it became fashionable to refer to the incompatibility of full employment and price stability. Both could not be attained simultaneously, since they varied inversely. There was a trade-off between them, and a move toward full employment meant rising prices, and a policy to control inflation meant higher unemployment rates. A selection had to be made between these two goals. The trade-off apparently was not worrisome, if it existed at all, until the 1960s, and presumably prices, wages, and unemployment behaved as they were supposed to behave over the course of previous cycles.

Without getting ahead of the analysis, some idea of the behavior of prices can be obtained from Figure 1.3. Clearly, consumer prices did fall in the depression of 1920–21 and in the 1930s. Prices also rose following both world wars, as might be expected after wartime financing, shortages, readjustments from war to peacetime economies, and so on. Yet the behavior of prices from the 1950s to the present does not follow past trends, for despite several recessions, prices did not fall. In fact the upward trend of prices is unmistakable. In later periods the rising price level is accompanied by rising unemployment rates, giving us a new condition and a new word for it—stagflation. The coexistence of high unemployment rates and inflation makes the previous existence of a trade-off suspect and poses a dilemma for both economic theory and policy.

Distribution of Income and Wealth

Whatever happens to output, employment, and prices has an impact on another possible goal—an equitable distribution of income and wealth. Economic conditions obviously determine the amounts available to

Figure 1.3   Consumer Prices: All Items and Food (quarterly averages)

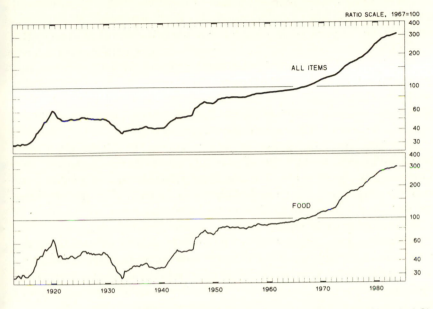

Source: Board of Governors of the Federal Reserve System, *1984 Historical Chart Book*, p. 40.

allocate to the members of the society, but just how the shares are determined and who decides how the gains and losses are distributed are not nearly as obvious.

Economists have long been concerned with what determines an efficient economic system. Economic models have been developed to discover how to maximize output with the minimum use of inputs, for instance. The prevailing models also reach a surprising consensus on how to distribute the output, that is, according to the contribution of those who participated in producing the output. This is the famous marginal-productivity theory of distribution—factors of production are paid according to their worth, their productivity. While there were always dissenters from the marginal productivity theory, the impact of it on distributional questions cannot be overstated. Any or all deviations from the general principles could always be explained as they arose.[2]

Yet what is to be done about the nonproducers—women who work as housewives, children, the aged, the handicapped, and so on? What is their proper share? Furthermore, what can or should be done for the unemployed and the underemployed?

These latter concerns carry over into the realm of social policy, where economic theory is inapplicable or uncomfortable. Similarly, all matters of social justice go beyond the first principles of economic theory to encompass questions on the equality of opportunity, the differential rewards that should or should not accrue to special talents and ability, the inequities that follow from racial, sex, or age discrimination, and so on. Principles of social justice, from utilitarianism to egalitarianism, are not obvious or easily discernible, but appeals to the marginal productivity theory of distribution for answers are likely to be insufficient and unrewarding.

To enter into a discussion of the philosopical problems of defining a just society would certainly take us far away from the purpose of this chapter. Some knowledge of the actual distributions of income and wealth is necessary, however, to help us understand the record of the U.S. economy and prepare the groundwork for later evaluations of public policy for their effects on income and social groups.

One quick impression of how much output is available to the population of the society is possible by looking at per capita GNP. As the name implies, this is the output available to each member of society if it were distributed equally. The first part of Figure 1.4 shows

Figure 1.4   Per Capita Output and Workweek (annually)

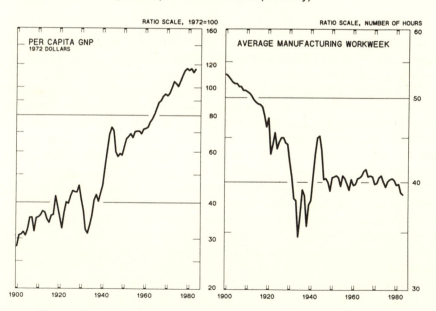

Source: Board of Governors of the Federal Reserve System, *1984 Historical Chart Book*, p. 11.

Table 1.3 Distribution of Money Income of Families and Unrelated Individuals Ranked by Fifths According to Income Received: for Selected Years, 1929–84

Income Rank	1929*	1935–36*	1947	1957	1967	1977	1980	1984
Lowest fifth	12.5	4.1	5.0	5.1	5.5	5.2	5.1	4.7
Second fifth		9.2	11.9	12.7	12.4	11.6	11.6	11.0
Third fifth	13.8	14.1	17.0	18.1	17.9	17.5	17.5	17.0
Fourth fifth	19.3	20.9	23.1	23.8	23.9	24.2	24.3	24.4
Highest fifth	54.4	51.7	43.0	40.4	40.4	41.5	41.6	42.9
Top 5 percent	30.0	26.5	17.5	15.6	15.2	15.7	15.3	16.0

*Data not exactly comparable with other years.

Sources: U.S. Department of Commerce, Bureau of the Census, *Historical Statistics of the United States; Colonial Times to 1970* (Washington, DC: GPO, 1975), p. 301; and *Current Population Reports,* series P60.

the per capita GNP from the turn of the century. Without doubt the trend is generally upward, meaning that aggregate production has outrun population growth, making increasing standards of living possible. There has been a fourfold increase in per capita GNP from 1900 to 1984. The decline in the average workweek, shown in the second part of Figure 1.4, is another indicator of an increase in the general wellbeing of the community. It takes fewer hours of work to earn increasing amounts of output, which attests to the increases in productivity observed earlier. Yet we are still dealing with averages and with the producing members of the society, whose output is measured by the GNP accountants and the Department of Labor statisticians. We cannot infer wellbeing until the actual distribution of income is revealed and the amount available to nonproducers is considered.

Consequently, a more direct look at income distribution is required. The distribution of family income is given in Table 1.3. The degree of stability in income shares is striking. In the words of one who has studied income distributions in considerable detail, using various definitions of income and family status, and so on, "The statistics show no apparent change in income shares for nearly 20 years."[3] Herman

Miller was referring to the period 1941–62. The same could be said for the next 20 years.

The stability of income shares is all the more remarkable when viewed together with the rising GNP, the rising per capita GNP, and the increase in productivity noted above. To be sure, there are difficulties involved in what income to include—money versus non-money income, for instance—and similar problems of how to treat unrelated (or unattached) individuals when analyzing family data. Yet by various definitions and inclusions, the stability remains as Miller found and concluded: "These figures hardly support the view held by many Americans that incomes in our society are becoming more evenly distributed."[4]

Whatever shifts occurred in the distribution of income took place during the 1930s and during World War II in the 1940s. The top 5 percent lost some of its share to the middle and lowest income groups. But the redistributions had virtually stopped until the Reagan administration. Surely some explanation is required as we review the record of the period.

Miller was also careful to point out that these data are only a first approximation to the determination of welfare. Increases in welfare could well have taken place but not been recorded in income data. We have already noted the decline in the workweek, for example, and the increase in leisure time may be considered an increase in welfare. Similarly, better working conditions, better health care, education, housing, and so on are now available to all income groups. In fact, government policies, of the type under review here, may well be responsible for the increase in wellbeing for the lower-income groups. Thus we are prohibited from reading too much about economic wellbeing into these summary income data. Until the reasons for the stability of income distribution are discussed, it is not really possible to understand how the society is affected or how the distribution of power, influence, and control are specified by the disparities.

The data on the distribution of wealth are even less reliable than those on income. Indeed, much less emphasis is placed on the distribution of wealth, and hence fewer data are available. This fact itself is remarkable and indicates a lack of concern over the distribution of wealth and its effects on the economic and social system.

To a large extent, the lack of data attests to the difficulty in gathering the required information. Yearly income data are readily available, while data on wealth are gathered mainly from estate tax returns. Since wealth is not taxed except at death, there is only this source from which to estimate wealth.

Table 1.4   Share of Personal Sector Wealth (Equity) Held by Top Wealth-holders, Selected Years, 1922–56

Year	Top 1 Percent of Adults	Top 0.5 Percent of All Persons	Top 2 Percent of Families*
1922	31.6	29.8	33.0
1929	36.3	32.4	—
1933	28.3	25.2	—
1939	30.6	28.0	—
1945	23.3	20.9	—
1949	20.8	19.3	—
1953	24.2	22.7	28.5
1956	26.0	25.0	—

*Families here defined as all adults less married females.
Source: Robert J. Lampman, *The Share of Top Wealth-Holders in National Wealth, 1922–56,* National Bureau of Economic Research (Princeton, NJ: Princeton University Press, 1962), p. 24.

One notable study was done by Robert Lampman.[5] Using federal estate tax data, he estimated the proportion of wealth held by the top wealth-holders. The results are shown in Table 1.4.

The concentration of wealth among the top 1 percent of wealth-holders is clearly evident, ranging from 36 percent in 1929 to 20 percent in 1949. A similar range is found in the top 0.5 percent of wealth-holders. The top group held about 80 percent of the corporate stock, nearly all state and local bonds, and between 10 and 33 percent of each other type of property, according to Lampman. The trends in the inequality in the distribution of wealth are also very interesting. Inequality rose during the 1920s, fell somewhat in the 1930s, and fell further during World War II. After the war the degree of inequality increased again. Lampman believed that these trends in equality could be explained by decreases in the relative prices of assets held by the rich over the period 1929–49, but the reverse held true over the entire period, 1922–53. Also, the rich failed to save proportionately to their share of wealth, and they also split up their wealth, principally between husbands and wives. Thus the observed decline in inequality would be reduced by half if families were considered. Apparently married women became increasingly important as top wealth-holders.

More recent data gathered by the Federal Reserve System[6] reveal once again the concentration of wealth. Table 1.5 shows both the

Table 1.5a   Distribution of Wealth, 1962: Fifths of Consumer Units Ranked by Wealth, Income, and Age

Fifths of Units	Percent of Total Wealth
Lowest fifth	0.2
Second fifth	2.1
Middle fifth	6.2
Fourth fifth	15.5
Highest fifth	76.0
Total	100.0

Source: Board of Governors of the Federal Reserve System, The Financial Characteristics of Consumers (Washington, DC: GPO, 1962, 1966).

distribution of wealth by dollar amounts and by fifths of consumer units.

The degree of inequality is again striking: From Table 1.5b, 25.3 percent of all units owned only 0.3 percent of total wealth in 1962, and this amounted to less than $1,000! On the other hand, 0.2 percent of units owned 21 percent of total wealth.

The inequality is perhaps more easily seen if the consumer units are ranked by wealth and divided into fifths. Table 1.5a shows the result. The highest fifth owned 76.0 percent of total wealth and the highest two fifths owned 91.5 percent! The lowest three fifths of the units had very little wealth, as can be seen by their share—8.5 percent.

It hardly seems necessary to add that the top wealth-holders owned most of the business assets, stock, and real estate, while the bottom groups held only items of personal wealth—automobiles and liquid assets. The evidence cited here gives only estimates, of course, but there is room for a wide margin of error before the conclusions would have to be altered.

There is no need to belabor the point, but a recent study of consumer finances reveals that there are no signs that the distribution of wealth is moving toward more equality. Tables 1.6a and 1.6b show the basic data for this conclusion. Table 1.6a reveals that 50 percent of U.S. families had a net worth below $25,000 and 5 percent had a net worth of over $250,000. Table 1.6b shows the top 10 percent of families (ranked by income) holding 72 percent of stocks, 70 percent of bonds, 86 percent of nontaxable holdings, 50 percent of property assets, and 78 percent of business assets. The top 2 percent of families owned a

Table 1.5b Distribution of Wealth: Estimates Used to Derive Wealth of Consumer Units

Size of Wealth (dollars)	Consumer Units		Wealth		Cumulative Percents	
	Number (millions)	Percent of All Units	Total Wealth (millions/$)	Percent of Total Wealth	All Units	Total Wealth
All units	57.9	100.0	1,198,404	100.0	(x)	(x)
Negative	1.0	1.7	—	—	1.7	—
Zero	4.7	8.1	—	—	9.8	—
1 to 999	9.0	15.5	3,564	0.3	25.3	0.3
1,000 to 4,999	10.8	18.7	29,387	2.5	44.0	2.8
5,000 to 9,999	9.1	15.7	66,130	5.5	59.7	8.3
10,000 to 24,999	13.3	23.0	213,425	17.8	82.7	26.1
25,000 to 49,999	6.2	10.7	218,184	18.2	93.4	44.3
50,000 to 99,999	2.5	4.3	172,450	14.4	97.7	58.7
100,000 to 199,999	0.7	1.2	92,953	7.8	98.9	66.4
200,000 to 499,999	0.5	0.9	150,178	12.5	99.8	78.9
500,000 and over	0.2	0.3	252,133	21.0	100.1	99.9

Note: (x) = not applicable.
Source: Board of Govenors of the Federal Reserve System, The Financial Characteristics of Consumers (Washington, DC: GPO, 1962, 1966).

Table 1.6a   Distribution of Families by Net Worth, Selected Years (percent except as noted)

Net Worth (dollars)[1]	Current Dollars			Constant (1983) Dollars		
	1970	1977	1983	1970	1977	1983
Less than 5,000	45	39	33	36	35	33
5,000–9,999	11	7	5	6	5	5
10,000–24,999	23	17	12	14	12	12
25,000–49,999	11	17	16	17	15	16
50,000–99,999	7	13	17	14	16	17
100,000–249,999	3	7	12	9	12	12
250.000–499,999	1	1	3	2	2	3
500,000 and above	*	*	2	1	*	2
Total[2]	100	100	100	100	100	100
Memo (dollars)						
Mean	22,154	31,039	66,050	56,781	50,895	66,050
Median	7,189	12,656	24,574	18,425	20,752	24,574

*Less than 0.5 percent.
[1]Excludes major consumer durables such as automobiles and home furnishings, and other items.
[2]Detail may not add to totals because of rounding.
Source: *Federal Reserve Bulletin 70* (December 1984), p. 862.

18

Table 1.6b Selected Characteristics of Asset Owners and Assets, by Type of Asset, 1983

Type of Asset	Percent of All Families Owning	Median Size of Asset (dollars)	Median Income of Owners (dollars)	Median Total Financial Assets of Owners (dollars)	Percent Held by Selected Families Ranked by Income	
					Top 10 Percent	Top 2 Percent
Financial assets, total						
Liquid assets	88	2,850	21,600	3,501	51	30
Checking account	79	500	23,000	4,355	41	23
Savings account	62	1,151	23,580	4,839	26	8
Money market account	14	8,000	33,190	27,360	40	15
Certificates of deposit	20	10,000	26,000	26,750	33	15
IRA or Keogh account	17	4,000	38,170	20,961	48	17
Savings bonds	21	325	29,003	8,782	26	12
Other financial assets						
Stocks	19	4,016	33,438	22,626	72	50
Bonds	3	10,000	42,500	71,952	70	39
Nontaxable holdings*	3	14,125	52,575	115,250	86	71
Trust	4	10,000	32,128	25,395	46	34
Other assets						
Property	19	35,000	31,000	12,036	50	20
Business	14	50,000	32,138	11,300	78	33

*Municipal bonds and shares in certain mutual funds.
Source: Federal Reserve Bulletin 70 (September 1984). p. 689.

19

large proportion of the assets held by the top 10 percent: 50 percent of the stocks, 39 percent of the bonds, and so on.[7]

Indications are that changes in the tax laws in 1981 will hasten the movement toward greater inequality. In the chapters to follow, some explanations can be found for the creation and perpetuation of such large inequalities in the distribution of income and wealth.

Other Economic Goals

Other goals of an advanced capitalist system are easily stated, but not as empirically testable. To many, economic freedom would rank very high on the list of desirable goals. The freedom to produce, sell, consume, choose an occupation, and so forth is highly regarded as part of the capitalist, free-market paradigm. Yet attempts to manage an economic system inevitably interfere with these freedoms of enterprise and choice. The decisions and actions of firms and individuals are heavily influenced by tax laws, public spending plans, the availability of credit, and regulations and restrictions of all kinds.

Clearly the goal of economic freedom can and often does conflict with the goals of stabilization, growth, and an equitable distribution of income and wealth. Policies designed to achieve these goals may involve the sacrifice of economic freedom, if the justification for them is even minimally questionable.[8] How much freedom is lost in the process of managing the economy and how much is gained if the policies are successful? There are no slide-rule answers here and no data to consult for definitive evidence. Hence, the concern for freedom will often be found in controversies over the need or success of public economic policies. Therefore, matters of economic freedom will be discussed in conjunction with these criteria for public policy.

It would appear that one way to preserve economic freedom is to pursue another goal—maintaining competition—yet this goal has seldom, if ever, been a top priority. If it is ignored, however, the structure of the economy changes. Imperfect markets appear or grow stronger, and, as a result, some freedom of enterprise and choice is reduced. As firms spread their influence, there is also the possibility of instability for the system as a whole, along with the possible introduction of inflexibility, as firms fail to adapt to changes in demand, technology, or foreign competition. Consider the automobile and steel industries for prime examples of inflexible markets born out of imperfect competition.

Policies may become ineffective or inefficient in the face of market power, or the enormous impact on the economy may prevent the proper policy from being applied or even suggested. When this economic power is combined with political power, the loss of economic freedom may be "necessary" or in the national interest. Thus public policy has bailed out the Lockheed and Chrysler corporations.

To maintain competition, however, requires an effective administration of antitrust laws. More public policy is required to preserve economic freedom, but more interference in and regulation of the marketplace reduces economic freedom as well. This basic contradiction is recognized at times, and compromises have been made in the enforcement of the existing laws. The result has often been confusion and vacillation, but in the meantime economic power has been sanctioned.

Finally, no economy is isolated enough to avoid some concern for the external balance of trade and balances of payments. External conditions of world trade—that is, relative prices, interest rates, exchange rates, and so on—often dictate in some measure a public policy that may have serious repercussions on the internal economy. A tariff, for instance, imposed on a product like steel, can have adverse effects on the domestic price level. Similarly a monetary policy to keep interest rates high to protect the value of the dollar may seriously affect domestic investment. In short, the attempt to maintain external stability may involve internal instability.

The foregoing goals or targets of public policy are the most generally accepted, although the order of them would prompt considerable controversy. The list is not complete, and others might wish to add other goals, such as a better composition of the output produced—more bread and fewer tanks—compatible ecological and environmental goals, more leisure and less emphasis on material goods, and so on.

Institutional Concerns

Managing the economy, then, is a straightforward task, the results of which are easily assessed only if one is willing to ignore the other goals and the conflicts among them. If the goals of growth and/or stabilization are considered relevant, it is possible to reach the wrong conclusions about the success or failure of public policies. Not only may a stable economy not be growing rapidly enough, for instance, but it may also mask some serious problems in the economic and social systems.

It would seem that determining the priorities among these conflicting goals ought to be the most important task of policymakers. Unfortunately, there is really no institutional mechanism designed to do this essential job. Political elections sometimes are thought to indicate and record the preferences of voters, but the positions of politicians are frequently too vague and inarticulate to be reliable indicators, while the preferences of nonvoters are never registered at all. Most institutions, public and private, are ill designed to formulate coherent policy from the needed macro perspective. This is true of political parties, which are themselves ill defined and too broad, as well as government agencies, congressional committees, and other public institutions that often focus on single issues or areas.

Thus it is not surprising to find that policymakers respond to crises, reacting to events rather than exercising some control over them. Policies so designed are not likely to be well thought out and may not be effective either. In calmer times the analysis of policies issues by outside research agencies may well influence the direction of actual policies adopted whenever a crisis calls for action. These outside agencies may exert more power on the direction of the economy than an uncritical view would reveal. Organizations such as The Brookings Institution, the Committee for Economic Development, the National Bureau of Economic Research, the American Enterprise Institute, and a host of private consultants, lobbyists, and academic advisors play a vital if not always observable role in the formation of public policy.

Lacking an identifiable institution to assume responsibility for public policy means accountability is missing as well. Who will claim success or disown failure and who will judge? Perhaps by following the outline in the Introduction, a systematic analysis of past public policies will help in the understanding of such issues. Answers to some of the questions raised so far might be found, and if we carry out the analysis correctly, new questions will emerge, many of which, I suspect, will require more searching inquiries and some of which may turn out to require new approaches.

This brief survey of the record of the U.S. economy was provided not to answer questions but to justify the raising of them; the data were offered without lengthy explanations because that is the task of the book. The record is the result of management or mismanagement of the economy or of failure to manage at all, hence ignoring fundamental economic and social problems.

The data in this chapter have been juxtaposed against generally accepted goals. The goals have seldom been reached to everyone's satisfaction. Is this because the policies were not needed, ineffectual, or perverse, or is it because the institutional structure of the economy is generally colliding with our ambiguous feelings on the role of the state?

It is time to begin the study against this background of conflicting goals and ambivalent policies.

chapter 2

The Aftermath of War

The United States emerged from World War I a far different country from the reluctant entrant into world affairs. Aside from thrusting the nation into international concerns, the war also transformed the economic and social conditions in the country for years after its conclusion. Then, as always, wars accelerate change, sometimes discernible only in retrospect. Change, however, need not always be forward looking, but could, as in this case, reverse prior directions.

For instance, before the war the Progressive movement was seriously questioning the generally accepted economic and social doctrines. Led intellectually by Herbert Croly[1] and politically by Theodore Roosevelt, Robert La Follette, and many others, the Progressive movement called attention to matters of social justice so often neglected by risk-averting politicans. Calling for a redistribution of privilege from the property-owning class to the wage-earning class, they advocated more public intervention into the economic and social life of the nation to ensure adequate standards of health, education, and economic security. In the words of Croly, a new program was needed to "impose upon the industrial system certain minimum standards of security, health, education, and remuneration which are necessary to the enjoyment of wholesome human life."[2]

The individual worker was comparatively helpless against the employer and needed assistance in organizing for more economic power and protection by society against accidents of work and exploitation. Indeed, Croly urged the extension of democracy into the workplace, as ideas on industrial democracy followed from his notions of democratic ideals generally. The justification for public intervention was found in the evolution of industrial capitalism. Capitalism is a system of privilege, but that privilege is not evenly distributed, and the New Nationalism sought to add more privilege to the worker's share. More abstractly, Croly wanted to transform democratic ideals from historic straightjackets: that is, to take the Jeffersonian democratic ideals, based on equal rights and opportunities but a weak government, and combine them with Hamiltonian ideals, based on a strong government willing to intervene to alter economic relations, and achieve by this merger Jeffersonian ends by Hamiltonian means.[3]

In practice, what emerged from these ideals was a progressive platform or program that included such policies as a minimum wage for women, a federal child labor law, a federal workmen's compensation law, federal mediation in labor disputes, a health and conservation program, and tariff legislation to protect workers. In addition to these areas of social concerns, the New Nationalism also embraced and exploited the long-held belief that big business controlled the economy and had to be brought under federal control. The idea that economic power was concentrated in the hands of large giant corporations (or an eastern establishment, in other expressions) was not particularly innovative, nor was Roosevelt's record in achieving the dismantling of them very impressive, but the constant railing against them must have had its effect in molding public opinion.[4]

These ideas obviously caused considerable debate in general and even influenced Woodrow Wilson, who was forced to modify his basic conservative philosophy and become a vague progressive. Wilson won the election of 1912, of course, but the progressives under Roosevelt polled over 4 million votes, 65 percent of Wilson's tally. While Roosevelt failed to win over the progressive Democrats, the progressives in both parties were numerous enough to exert considerable influence on the course of future directions and legislation.

The progressive influence is easily seen in the battles they waged over some important institutional changes that were made in this period. For instance, progressive Democrats were able to restructure the original income tax bill to increase the rates of taxation, so that higher-income groups would bear a larger burden and some redistribution of income could take place. They were also able to block passage of the original bill to establish a central bank. The original bill, drawn up by Paul M. Warburg, provided for a central bank with branches controlled by member banks. The central bank would have been run by the branch banks. In effect, the banking system would be under private control. This plan was modified by progressives who favored government control over the banking system, particularly over the money supply. The Federal Reserve Act that emerged from the compromise retained private ownership with government control, and while the progressives were not satisified with it, they clearly won a partial victory against some powerful interests.[5]

For those who argued passionately for fundamental changes in the economic and social structure of the nation, political compromises and partial victories are not causes for celebration. How much more distressing to find crucial elements in the movement's platform defeated or watered down, especially since all presidential candidates in 1912—Wilson, Roosevelt, Taft, and Debs—represented various shades of progressivism. Expectations of far-reaching changes could easily be justified.

Yet organized labor failed to win an outright exemption from the Sherman Antitrust Act and later from the Clayton Act. Farmers failed to get government support for long-term credit arrangements or a land-bank program. In the social sphere, no progress was made on a child-labor law or on women's suffrage. Wilson, needing the support of sourtherners who helped elect him, even acquiesced to widespread segregation practices in the federal government. Blacks were appalled at this shameful and shocking retrogression and felt betrayed.

The attack on big business, giant corporations, and economic concentration also failed, as the Clayton Act was so watered down from its original contents that it became virtually useless in confronting economic power. The same fate was in store for the Federal Trade Commission. Holders of economic power had little to fear from these statutes or the antitrust attitude of this administration. Wilson was indeed a vague and uncommitted progressive.

Yet the above examples indicate that political discussions and debates must have raised the consciousness of many to progressive concerns. Even in losing battles, the progressives were providing a different view of economic and social conditions. They pointed out the failures of laissez-faire doctrines in a rapidly changing world. They revealed the evils of economic power and control by the few and exposed the problems of labor in an industrial society. They called attention to the problems of blacks, women, child laborers, immigrants, farmers, and others. Indeed, the commercial philosophy of capitalism with its glorification of individualism and laissez-faire and with its emphasis on monetary success, particularly in business, seemed to be disintegrating in favor of the battle for social justice and equity.

It could reasonably be expected that economists would have responded to such ferment by revising their theoretical models of the economy. Such was not the case. Despite the clamor for change, traditional economic theory remained impervious. Based on a laissez-faire, self-regulating and competitive economy, there was no room for societal intervention to change the outcome of market decisions. Free markets, individualism, and competition determined the prizes and punishments, and the rules of the game ensured beneficial results for the community.

The clash of reality with the theoretical models of it did not cause widespread disaffection with these abstractions. Only minor modifications were introduced, while the main conclusions of the classical economic theory continued unaltered. In the long run, flexible wages, prices, interest rates, and so on, derived from competitive markets, determined the distribution of privilege in the society. Attempts to interfere with the results would be foolish, at best, and possibly quite destructive of the functioning of the system, at worst. Seldom in economics are facts and contrary evidence allowed to discredit a theoretical model. The reigning paradigm had remarkable tenacity.

For example, during World War I many of the prohibitions against government intervention had to be overcome, of necessity. Since the United States was woefully unprepared for the conduct of war, many controls and planning boards had to be instituted. One of the most powerful and successful was the War Industries Board under Bernard Baruch. It had enormous power to allocate scarce resources, redirect investment to ensure supplies, determine production and distribution priorities, and so on. In short, it functioned as a massive planning agency. In the words of Baruch, hardly a radical, "WIB (War Industries Board) had demonstrated the effectiveness of industrial cooperation and the advantage of government planning and direction. We helped inter the extreme dogmas of laissez-faire, which had for so long molded American economic and political thought. Our experience taught that government direction of the economy need not be inefficient or undemocratic, and suggested that in time of danger it was imperative."[6] This was probably the first time that the economy had to marshal its resources and coordinate economic activity in order to achieve some national objective. Accordingly, some 5,000 agencies were created to do the job. Not all of them functioned properly or efficiently. Yet consider the kinds of programs attempted: There were price controls under a separate committee of the War Industries Board (due to the resistance of business to price controls), food controls under the Food Administration headed by Herbert Hoover, shipping controls and a Railway Administration to run the railroads, a War Finance Corporation to guarantee capital to war industries, and so on.[7]

Moreover, there were parts of the programs that called for public housing, recognition of the rights of women—equal pay for equal work—and provisions recognizing the rights of unions to exist and bargain. These and countless other disconcerting provisions were tolerated as necessary for the war, but not apparently for the peace.

The point of suggesting the type and extent of government intervention in World War I is not to make a case for an active and powerful public sector. Rather, it is to question why the experiences of the war years did not affect the postwar economy more than they did. Some of these war agencies did a marvelous job, which would ostensibly mean more societal acceptance of governmental planning and coordination. Even economic theorists might have been impressed with the results of some free-market restrictions. But the pendulum was to swing in the other direction.

Effects of the Wartime Economy

Before turning to the postwar economic and social conditions, it might be very instructive to take a brief look at some of the lasting effects of the wartime economy. Wars and the mentality they foster often permit radical changes that were previously resisted, or they disturb existing institutional arrangements not previously under attack. In such periods some far-reaching changes can go unnoticed or unappreciated. In this section some of these changes in the economic and social structure are only suggested, but the effects will be seen as the analysis progresses.

Aside from the previously mentioned transgressions against laissez-faire—the price and wage controls, the allocation of resources of government, and the tendency toward planning in general—there were other developments that would seriously affect the working of the economic system. They can be outlined briefly as follows:

1. The War Industries Board standardized products and processes, reduced the number of sizes and styles of goods, and encouraged the interchangeability of parts. Chairman Baruch was quite proud of these achievements as inducing efficiency.

2. Scientific-management techniques were introduced and personnel management became possible.

3. Mass-production techniques were introduced by Henry Ford. National advertising was soon to follow.

4. The various agencies responsible for labor management adopted standards of wages, hours, and working conditions based on union standards. Thus unions were given a boost in importance and recognized in contractual relations. For instance, the War Labor Board adopted the basic 8-hour day,

40-hour week; the principle of equal pay for equal work for women; and protection of children in employment. After the major strikes at Lawrence, Massachusetts, in 1912 and Paterson, New Jersey, in 1913 and after the violence connected with the formation of the International Workers of the World (IWW), such recognition was a considerable advance for the labor movement. Moreover, the U.S. Employment Service was set up in the Department of Labor to coordinate job openings and applicants.

5. The bargaining power of labor increased, as did money wages, as the demand for labor exceeded the supply. Despite, however, the increased strikes that occurred as workers responded to speed-up practices of firms and the rising living costs, the Socialist movement suffered because of its opposition to the war.

6. The industrial structure changed as some industries grew and others declined. The automobile industry grew rapidly, setting off a boom in investment that spread to many allied industries, including road building. Iron and steel, copper, petroleum refining, and rubber industries were among the big gainers, while housing, lumber, and construction industries were among those losing shares of output. Since the gainers were in industries characterized by large corporations, substantial economic power was transferred to the already powerful.

7. The agricultural sector boomed as it sold foodstuffs to the allies and as the Food Administration, under Hoover, undertook a program of price guarantees for its output without controlling production. Agricultural controls succeeded in increasing the economic wellbeing of farmers and the nation generally, but their continuation after the war proved unthinkable.

8. Finally, exports to the allies as well as their borrowing in the United States reversed the debtor position of the United States in international affairs. As discussed later, the United States became a creditor nation, but was totally unprepared for that role.

The Postwar Boom

Following a war that so clearly disrupted the trend of economic and social movements in the United States, severe economic dislocations would have appeared likely if forecasts had been made using the prevailing classical economic model. The dismantling of the public sector, the return of the armed forces, and in general the conversion from a wartime to a peacetime economy should have been causes for economic problems that could be solved only over a long time period. Given sufficient time, resources would flow back to their traditional uses and the prewar economic structure would be restored. Only if people's tastes had changed, or if new products had altered the structure of demand, and so on, would the private postwar economy differ from the prewar one; only if the government's wartime role had become accepted as the norm, would the public sector retain its position and influence.

Indeed, there were forecasts of a depressed economy subject to stagnation, and there were considerations of public-works projects to relieve the problems. Instead of a depressed economy, however, there was a postwar boom that lasted until 1920. The questions become, What happened to the problems and what caused the boom? From a policy viewpoint, can it be inferred that the absence of problems was the result of forecasts based on faulty theory, or can the boom be attributed to the return to the mainly free-market economy that is closer to the theoretical model?

The ever-present conflicts among ideology, theory, and pragmatism and the contradictions they provide are evident here in the first examination of policymaking in this survey. The idealism and reformist spirit found in the Progressive movement were two of the many casualities of the war, and after the war, "People were tired. In particular their public spirit, their consciousness and their hopes were tired."[8] Combine this mood with the disillusionment of returning servicemen, and it may be easier to understand the general wish to put the war, with all its horrors, behind their collective backs and with it the moral sentiments of reformism, in favor of relaxation and immediate gratifications. This general mood helps to explain the immediate postwar sentiment, but even more the culmination of such feelings that became more widespread in the 1920s.

This desire to shed the effects of war can also be seen in the rapidity with which some portions of the wartime machinery were dismantled. Little thought was given to reconversion, as over 600,000 servicemen were released immediately, war-agency offices closed quickly and the staff personnel scattered hastily, and some price controls were removed almost immediately after the Armistice was signed, and war contracts were quickly canceled.

Such actions are consistent with the desire to return to private enterprise, of course, but how many of them emanated from the desire to retreat from a wartime society with all of its negative connotations? For some, no doubt, ideology played a part, but for others an explanation of the haste might better be found in exasperation and frustration with the confinements of wartime society. Still, whatever importance society's mood had on the function of the economy, it was overshadowed by the policy actions of government.

The monetary and fiscal policies of the federal government were responsible for much of the postwar boom and for the problems associated with it. The paradox here is that the government pursued policies more appropriate for a theoretical model developed by Lord

Keynes decades later. In the meantime, lacking a theoretical basis, pragmatism overruled the prevailing orthodoxy; without a theoretical foundation, public policy is free, or better, is forced to extemporize.

The main stimulus to economic activity can quickly be located in governmental finances. Table 2.1a shows that the federal government ran up some large deficits in its budgets. From a small deficit of $401,000 in 1913, the total rose to over $13 billion in 1919. The only exception occurred in 1916 when income taxes were increased dramatically. Not only were tax rates increased, some even doubled, but the distribution of the tax burden was adjusted to place a higher burden on high-income groups. The progressive infuence was still in evidence at this time.

Taxes increased in each year of the war, and the changes in rates were striking. For example, the lowest rate on taxable income between $2,000 and $4,000 rose to 6 percent in 1918 from zero in 1916, while the rate on taxable incomes of $1–1.5 million rose from 13 percent to 77 percent over the same period.

The tax increases were not sufficient to cover the growing war expenditures, however, and deficits resulted. How these deficits were financed can be seen in the rise in public debt, which increased by 2,036 percent from 1913 to 1919. To compound matters, government borrowing was financed in such a manner that the money supply increased rapidly.

The Federal Reserve System, as many have noted, began operations at a time when the conditions that gave it birth no longer existed. Prior to U.S. entry into the war, the increased demand for U.S. exports resulted in the inflow of gold and transformed the United States into a creditor nation. The Federal Reserve was powerless to offset the gold inflow, since it had no assets to sell and had no power to alter bank reserves. As soon as the United States entered the war, it subordinated whatever power it had to the Treasury's need to finance the war. As a result of this agreement, the Federal Reserve surrendered virtually all control over the money supply.

The Treasury first tried to raise funds without increasing the money supply by selling Liberty Bonds to the public, but the proceeds proved insufficient. It then began selling short-term securities to commercial banks and of course increased the money supply.

More puzzling, in retrospect, was the policy of the Federal Reserve System as the demands for funds by Treasury continued to grow. The Federal Reserve began lending to commercial banks at a rate below the discount rate, so that the banks could relend the funds to enable the public to buy bonds. Not only did the commercial banks make a profit on this transfer, but the Federal Reserve in the process

Table 2.1a   Federal Government Finances, 1913–19 (in millions of dollars)

| Year | Expenditures | | Receipts | | Surplus or Deficit (−) | Public Debt |
	Total	National Defense	Total	Individual Income Tax		
1913	714.9	335.4	714.5	28.3	−0.4	1,193.0
1914	725.5	348.0	725.1	41.0	−0.4	1,188.2
1915	746.1	343.9	683.4	67.9	−62.7	1,191.3
1916	713.0	337.0	761.4	173.4	48.5	1,225.1
1917	1,953.9	617.6	1,100.5	691.5	−853.4	2,975.6
1918	12,677.4	6,148.8	3,645.2	1,127.7	−9,032.1	12,455.2
1919	18,492.7	11,011.4	5,130.0	1,269.6	−13,362.6	25,484.5

Source: U.S. Department of Commerce, Bureau of the Census, *Historical Statistics of the United States, Series Y* (Washington, DC: GPO, 1975), pp. 1104–14.

Table 2.1b Money Stock and Gold Stock, 1913–19 (in billions of dollars)

Year	M1 (Demand Deposits + Currency)		M2 (M1 + Time Deposits)		Gold Stock
	Amount	Percent Change	Amount	Percent Change	
1913	—	—	15.73	—	1.88
1914	—	—	16.39	4.2	1.88
1915	12.48	—	17.59	7.3	2.00
1916	14.70	17.8	20.85	18.5	2.48
1917	17.08	16.2	24.37	16.9	3.11
1918	18.96	11.0	26.73	9.7	3.16
1919	21.79	14.9	31.01	16.0	3.13

Source: U.S. Department of Commerce, Bureau of the Census, *Historical Statistics of the United States*, Series X 410-419 (Washington, DC: GPO, 1975), p. 992.

Table 2.2   Consumer and Wholesale Price Indexes, 1913–20 (1913 = 100)

Year	Consumer Price Index	Wholesale Price Index		
	All Goods	All Commodities	Raw Material	Manufactured Goods
1913	100.0	100.0	100.0	100.0
1914	100.8	98.2	98.7	97.8
1915	100.5	102.8	104.2	102.0
1916	116.4	129.1	127.9	129.4
1917	158.6	171.2	174.4	169.4
1918	190.6	195.7	188.9	198.4
1919	207.7	203.4	196.1	206.1
1920	228.3	227.9	202.2	239.5

Source: Frederick C. Mills, *Prices in Recession and Recovery* (New York: National Bureau of Economic Research, 1936), pp. 491, 493.

simply abandoned all control over credit and the discount rate (which in practice became the lower rate at which banks could borrow, secured by government securities under an amendment to the Federal Reserve Act, and which was pegged to the rate set on government securities determined by the Treasury).

Of course, the money supply rose dramatically, twofold over the period. Table 2.1b shows the increases in both M1 (currency and demand deposits) and M2 (M1 plus time deposits).

As might be expected, this combination of monetary and fiscal policies put enormous pressure on price levels. Consumer prices were fairly stable until 1916, when they increased by over 16 percent from the base period of 1913. In 1917 they rose even more dramatically, by over 36 percent over 1916 and 58 percent over 1913, and by 1918 they had almost doubled from 1913 levels. By 1919 consumer prices had more than doubled over 1913 and the index stood at 207.7. Prices for both manufactured and nonmanufactured goods rose by roughly the same magnitudes.

Table 2.2 presents the data on prices developed by Frederick Mills. While these data are not nearly as accurate as current estimates (in fact none of the data in these early years are), they do permit some approximation of the changes that occurred.

The sharp rises in wholesale prices are also evident, as again there is a 29 percent increase in 1916 over 1913, a 71 percent increase in 1917, and so on, to the doubling of prices in 1919 over 1913. The increases in manufactured goods were greater than those in raw materials, particularly in the later war years. This latter result can be attributed to the success of price controls on raw materials imposed by the War Industries Board. The success of price controls in other areas and particularly in consumer goods is not so evident and probably reflects the lack of commitment to them.

Aside from the stimulus given to the domestic economy by monetary and fiscal policies, there was also the boost given to foreign trade by governmental actions. As previously mentioned, exports increased steadily during the period of U.S. neutrality and during the course of the war. Much of this increase was made possible by loans and credits given to our allies.

This impetus to exports continued after the war, as additional loans and credits were granted mainly by government, although some private concerns were involved as well. Both foodstuffs and manufactured goods were in demand, so that the boom in exports had widespread repercussions throughout the economy. Table 2.3 shows the exports by stage of processing.

Many of these exports were stimulated by governmental actions. The American Relief Administration erected under Mr. Hoover in 1919 and the U.S. Grain Corporation, already in existence, were entrusted with selling relief supplies and making loans for foodstuffs

Table 2.3   Indexes of Unit Value of Exports, 1913–29 (1913 = 100)

Year	Total	Crude Material	Crude Foods	Manu-factured Goods	Semi-manu-factured Goods	Finished Manu-factured Goods
1913	100.0	100.0	100.0	100.0	100.0	100.0
1914	97.7	87.9	114.5	103.3	97.6	94.3
1915	105.1	86.0	133.8	106.5	113.2	100.9
1916	135.5	115.5	144.2	118.4	156.5	130.6
1917	177.0	166.8	214.8	170.5	198.4	150.4
1918	206.1	219.0	234.6	214.2	202.8	169.7
1919	215.7	241.3	241.7	237.4	199.5	174.4
1920	232.5	285.3	268.2	217.2	210.5	197.7

Source: U.S. Department of Commerce, Bureau of the Census, *Historical Statistics of the United States,* Series U 225-248 (Washington, DC: GPO, 1975), p. 892.

Table 2.4   Gross National Product, 1913–20

Year	GNP Current Dollars	Billions of 1929 Dollars				
		GNP	Govern- ment	Consump- tion	Investment	Net Exports
1913	39.1	63.4	4.5	46.7	12.0	0.3
1914	36.4	58.6	4.8	46.1	7.8	−0.2
1915	38.7	60.4	5.0	45.3	7.6	2.5
1916	49.8	68.9	4.7	49.4	10.7	4.0
1917	59.9	67.3	7.0	48.3	8.3	3.6
1918	76.2	73.4	16.5	48.1	6.7	2.1
1919	78.9	74.2	9.7	50.2	10.7	3.5
1920	88.9	73.3	5.6	52.7	12.8	2.3

Source: U.S. Department of Commerce, Bureau of the Census, *Long-Term Economic Growth* (Washington, DC: GPO, 1966).

to our allies in the war. As is evident from Table 2.3, exports in nearly every stage of processing had doubled from prewar levels at war's end.

Turning to other sectors in the economy, it is apparent that the private sector played some role in the boom, but a lesser role than might have been expected.

We have already seen the hand of government in its direct stimulus to the economy and in its role in increasing exports. Part of that stimulus can be seen in Table 2.4, where the importance of government as a sector in the national output is shown once again.

Households did not suffer very much during the war. Goods were not rationed, and although shortages did occur, they were not the type that would result in pent-up demand following the war. If coal was in short supply during the war, one did not burn twice as much to make up for it after the war. Also, the consumer-durables industries were not extensive at that time, and thus there was not the sacrifice associated with a cessation of their production for the war effort. Therefore consumers did not rush out to buy goods of which they had been deprived and did not spend the balances available from bond holdings. Except for housing, increases in consumption cannot be credited with causing the boom.

This may be better understood if it is realized that real wages did not increase significantly over this period. In fact, there is evidence that the inflation caused much resentment among workers, which resulted directly in strikes or in reactions against strikers. These events occurred during the latter part of the period under review and will be covered in the next section.

Private investment also contributed to the postwar recovery, as housing shortages and the revival of automobile demand stimulated activity. There were increases in plant and equipment and in inventories, but much of the increase could be traced to the speculative actions that were occurring.

With rising prices there were profits to be made just by speculating in inventories. Inventory profits stimulated more production and investment in more productive facilities. Speculation in stocks and securities was also widespread at this time, and the Federal Reserve felt compelled to issue warnings (the first was in October 1915) about the dangers of speculation and to remind member banks that loans made for speculative purposes were not permitted by the Federal Reserve Act. The Federal Reserve was more sanguine about the possibility of ending inflation and proposed no direct solution, but advocated greater economy and greater productivity.[9]

The Federal Reserve also lamented that repeated warnings over speculation had done little good in the past. This time, however, it was in a bind. It was prevented from using its major weapon, raising the discount rate, because it was pledged to support the Treasury's operations. As we saw earlier, the Treasury was in effect setting the discount rate by setting the interest rate on bonds, and clearly the Treasury preferred a low interest rate.

Only after strong inflationary pressures became alarming and speculation widespread, did the Federal Reserve force its way out of its agreement with the Treasury. The Treasury objected, as might be expected, but its needs had clearly decreased; it gave way in November 1919, and the Federal Reserve finally was able to push up the discount rate to around 4.5 percent.

In the second quarter of 1920 the prolonged inflationary boom came to an end, and the economy entered into a downswing. Before analyzing the reversal, it is necessary to pause and examine some social upheavals that just preceded it.

The Labor Movement

During the war unions were recognized by the various war agencies and their right to exist was given a boost. Employers, too, went along with unions as necessary for the war effort, but looked forward to resisting them after the hostilities eased. Thus, after the war ended and the war agencies were dismantled, whatever experiments were used to promote peace came under increasing question.

The postwar inflation reduced real wages and was responsible for the first overt conflict. While by 1919 prices and the cost of living had doubled over prewar levels, real wages in manufacturing and in the coal industries had increased by only 17 percent, and in the building trades and teaching they had actually declined by nearly 19 percent.[10] True, the unemployment rate had declined from a prewar high of 8.5 percent in 1915 to 1.4 percent in 1918, but workers were not content with this improvement and sought more direct rewards.

For one thing, working conditions had not improved, and those that had improved during the war period faced cutbacks or elimination. In the steel industry the conditions were poor indeed. Living in shacks, workers were forced to endure a 12-hour workday. In the coal mines conditions were equally bad. There was a great deal of resentment in this "boom" period, as prices rose dramatically, filling the pockets of business with profits, while wage increases and improvements in the workplace lagged behind.

Despite the opposition to them, unions were not terribly strong, nor were they expanding. Organizers had failed to make inroads in the industrial organizations, and the labor movement had failed to produce the unity for nationwide actions or for a political force. Yet the recent Russian Revolution had created apprehension in the United States, and Socialists were no longer accorded the respect they previously commanded. Even though there was a rift between the Socialists and the newly organized Communists and even though the small number of Communists were divided into two warring parties, the Red scare had begun.

The U.S. public, already upset with inflation and the postwar society, looked with concern at the Third Communist International in March 1919, at Communist uprisings in Eastern Europe, at radicals in the United States who hinted that the revolution would soon be imported to the United States, and finally at a wave of strikes that occurred in major industries. In January 1919 Seattle shipyard workers struck for higher wages, and labor organizations supported the strike by calling for a general strike. Without any real basis, the strike was attributed to the rising Red menace.

There followed a series of bombings, probably by anarchists, but blamed on Communists. A bewildered public became fearful, and then the Boston police strike occurred following the dismissal of 19 policemen who had joined the AFL. Violence broke out, and both President Wilson and Governor Calvin Coolidge condemned public-service strikes and emerged as heroes. In September there was a steel strike, and again the Red menace was evoked—this time by a top U.S. official, Attorney General A. Mitchell Palmer. In March 1920 John L. Lewis led his mine workers, who had not had an increase in wages, out on strike, but was met with injunctions, since coal was necessary for the "war" effort. Each of these strikes gained practically nothing for the strikers, but cost the labor movement a great deal. In the words of the noted historian, William E. Leuchtenburg,

> By the autumn of 1919 millions of Americans had come to believe that the country was faced by the menace of revolution, although genuine revolutionaries constituted almost no threat of any kind and the great strikes were for the most part expressions of legitimate grievances. Political careerists, reactionary employer groups, and monomanical faddists stirred up new alarms and exploited the sense of panic, in part out of ignorance, in part to serve their own ends.[11]

The country was ready, however, for action against the radicals. Attorney General Palmer started his campaign to rid the country of troublemakers. Trampling on the civil rights of the suspected, he began his raids against aliens, Communists, and anyone else who resembled a radical. He appointed J. Edgar Hoover to head the antiradical division in the Department of Justice. Private homes, meeting halls, and union headquarters were invaded and many arrests were made. Aliens were detained for deportation, and some actually were deported, paving the way for new immigration laws in 1921. This shameful period came to an end after a forecast great uprising failed to materialize in May 1920.

Perhaps the last episode was the case of the anarchists, Sacco and Vanzetti, who were accused of murdering a paymaster in a robbery attempt in South Braintree, Massachusetts, in May 1920. Found guilty and executed, they became the subject of many analyses over their guilt. More important, their case raised the specter of people being persecuted for their political beliefs or for their alien backgrounds. The implications of their case raised it to a symbol of the ugly side of feelings evoked during this period.

If the labor movement suffered under this barrage of setbacks, the nation lost as well. Political dissent became less tolerable, civil rights became limited to only those who deserved them, and class distinctions based on ancestry became ingrained. Thus postwar

economic conditions contributed to social upheavals that were justified on other grounds or found expression alongside economic complaints.

The Business Cycle of 1919–21

The Red scare is another manifestation of the decline of progressivism
or reformism in the postwar years. The general public, weary of
preaching and longing to escape from foreign entanglements, sought to
reconcile itself to changing economic and social conditions. The nation
faced many conflicts between the old and new conditions and values,
and, as will become apparent, the result was a good deal of confusion.

After the armistice of November 11, 1918, President Wilson faced
a rejection of his moralistic views of society and was now engaged in
the battle to promote his views of peace and internationalism. He
became preoccupied with his mission to promote the League of Nations
and pushed himself to the extent that he suffered a stroke in
September 1919. Lacking a leader, the movement for the league
floundered, but it might have done so in any case. Did the economy
flounder for the same reason or did events overtake the ability to
prevent economic fluctuations?

The National Bureau of Economic Research (NBER) designated
the postwar peak of the business cycle as August 1918, followed by a
mild decline to a trough in March of 1919. This cyclical designation
seems rather arbitrary, since economic activity was only mildly
affected, and the upswing really continued into the first part of 1920.
Indeed, the NBER lists the next peak as January 1920, followed by a
really sharp depression that reached a trough in July 1921. Again,
data for this period are not very reliable, nor are the dates of turning
points, but some idea of the magnitude of the decline is possible from
later works, and however imprecise they may be, some data are
necessary to judge policy actions.

GNP in current dollars had reached its peak of $91.5 billion in
1920 and dropped a phenomenal 24 percent in 1921. GNP in 1958
dollars reached its peak in 1918 at $151.8 and then fell by 3.6 percent
in 1919, 4.4 percent in 1920, and 8.8 percent in 1921; the total decline
was approximately 15.8 percent from the peak in 1918.

Since GNP in current dollars continued to rise in 1919, clearly
prices had to be increasing in 1919, despite the slight decline in that

year. This is confirmed by a look at the data. Wholesale prices continued their rise until 1920, when they fell sharply. Prices for all commodities fell by 34 percent from 1920 to 1921, and for farm commodities the drop was 38 percent. Prices for manufactured goods fell less, about 30 percent, as production plans were altered. In general, though, wholesale prices fell between 30 and 40 percent.[12] Consumer prices fell much less, something like 11 percent, while the GNP implicit price index fell approximately 31 percent.[13]

Industrial production fell by over 23 percent from 1920 to 1921, and the unemployment rate, which had reached a postwar low of 1.4 percent in 1919, now climbed to 5.2 percent in 1920 and to 11.7 percent in 1921.[14] Clearly this was a sharp depression and a quick turnaround from the postwar boom. Can the swift reversal be explained by events or incorrect policies?

One of the main factors in the reversal was the steep decline that took place in exports. The total value of all exports fell by over 32 percent from 1920 to 1921, while the quantities sold fell by only 20 percent in the same period. This greater fall in the value of exports obviously reveals the severe drop in prices occurring at that time. The effects of deflation are even more apparent in food and material exports. The value of crude foods exported fell by 42 percent, while quantities sold fell 32 percent; crude materials fell by over 45 percent in value, but only 4 percent in quantities. Similar magnitudes are found in manufactured foods. Only in manufactured goods is the result different, as quantities sold fell more than the value of exports.[15]

These trends in exports reveal somewhat the recovery of the European economies in both manufacturing and agriculture. Now U.S. surplus farm commodities were competing with increased European agricultural output. The result was falling prices and eventually the steady decline of U.S. agricultural exports from earlier prosperous periods.

The other components of aggregate demand remained stable. Both consumption and fixed-investment expenditures were fairly constant. Industrial production fell drastically, however, and by 1921 was at the same level as in 1913. Since gross private domestic investment fell sharply over this period, while fixed investment remained stable, the difference must be due to other elements of investment spending.[16]

Both inventories and construction spending declined to account for the overall decline in gross private investment. Construction also declined to prewar levels, as builders feared the deflationary period and mortgage funds became scarce. Even though shortages kept the prices of houses and rents high, the construction industry did not or could not respond.

Inventory profits were also a thing of the past, as falling prices meant inventory liquidation to repay bank loans or as part of bankruptcy proceedings. Forced sales clearly reinforced the trend of falling prices and deflation.

Fiscal and Monetary Policies

Turning to the fiscal policy of the federal government first, a sharp reversal took place. Instead of the huge deficits of the recent past, the budget registered a surplus; from a deficit of $13.3 billion in 1919, the budget showed a surplus of $0.3 billion for 1920 and a surplus of $0.5 billion for 1921. Much of the shift from a deficit to a surplus can be traced to the reductions in national defense spending.

Total federal government expenditures decreased by 66 percent from 1919 to 1920 and by 20 percent from 1920 to 1921. Reductions in national defense expenditures for those same periods were 79 percent and 25 percent. Only interest on the public debt increased from 1919 to 1920 (by 65 percent), but even interest payment fell from 1920 to 1921 (by 2.1 percent).

While federal tax receipts rose from 1919 to 1920 by 30 percent, they fell by over 16 percent from 1920 to 1921. Most of the changes can be attributed to the effects of inflation and deflation on tax collections. Tax rates were increased for corporations in 1921, but individual tax rates were stable or even falling over the period 1919–20.[17]

Clearly the fiscal policy of the federal government contributed a great deal to the onset of the depression. Reductions in national defense spending were warranted, of course, by the cessation of the war. There being no commitment by the federal government to maintain economic stability, nor any great consideration given to the effects of reconversion, the fiscal policy of the period is consistent with prevailing orthodoxy. The goal was a balanced budget that would, it was thought, keep the fiscal actions of government as neutral as possible in the economic system.

From mid-1919 on, the Federal Reserve System finally had the opportunity to act independently and utilize its powers of control over monetary conditions. Yet it permitted monetary expansion by keeping its discount rate below market interest rates, presumably to support the Treasury's deficit. But the deficit disappeared, and their motivation appeared to change to the support of the Treasury's refunding of the debt and the prevention of the fall in value of government bonds in the hands of commercial banks. The Federal Reserve also believed that rising prices and demand pressures were responsible for the increase in the money supply and did not feel the necessity to react to them by policy actions.[18]

The Federal Reserve did not act until pushed to do so by Benjamin Strong, president of the New York Federal Reserve. Strong finally managed to increase the discount rate in New York in November and December 1919. In December all reserve banks had matched those of the New York branch at 4.75 percent.

By then the increases were a little late, since the peak of the cycle was in January 1920. Yet in January and February the rate was pushed up to 6 percent, which was justified by the Federal Reserve as necessary, since the gold reserve ratio had fallen close to the legal minimum.

Still, banks found it advantageous to borrow, and the Federal Reserve increased the rate still further to 7 percent on June 1, 1920. The increase in the discount rate came at the time the economy was nearing the trough and prices were collapsing. This was hardly appropriate timing in the face of the steepest decline in prices in the nation's history.

The money supply still increased slowly until September, but the monetary policy of the Federal Reserve scarcely seems rational in retrospect. Yet the Federal Reserve had no real experience with controlling credit conditions; its poor performance in its first test is understandable.[19] There is also evidence to suggest that the Federal Reserve did not understand that the discount rate could be safely lowered in a deflationary period. In this view the money supply was excessive, because production had not kept pace, and the proper relationships between money, prices, and production had to be restored. This monetary model called for "liquidation" of government securities held by banks; this condition was causing the money supply to increase, and only when the public purchased the securities would the increases stop and the proper relations be restored.[20]

That monetary policy was perverse in this period is clear, but the question is why. Inexperience in handling matters is an answer, but Elmus R. Wicker and others point to a money model that the Federal Reserve was following as a better one. The Federal Reserve was accomplishing what it set out to, only what it wanted to accomplish was basically incorrect.[21] Of course, both reasons for inappropriate monetary policy could and probably were occurring simultaneously.

The Changing Economic Structure

Thus both fiscal and monetary policies were conducted to a large extent to fit the theoretical perceptions and judgments of the time. It is doubtful if the authorities were capable of anything else. Neither fiscal nor monetary authorities were committed to stabilizing the economic system, and both were simply trying to go back to some relations that existed prior to all the disruptions; to return to balanced budgets and fiscal sanity; and to reestablish some previous relations between prices, money, and production.

In this sense their actions appear rational, if not appropriate. They were striving to achieve old goals and would have justified their actions accordingly. With hindsight and using the later goal of stability, their actions appear nonsensical. The theory that might have influenced their actions was a long way off, however, and one can hardly blame their ignorance for their failure to follow it.

Yet even if we accept the conclusion that stabilization was not a goal at the time and therefore failure to achieve it was understandable, we can still ask if policy actions to restore an old order actually made things worse in terms of the economic (and social) structure. And in making things worse, would it appear that they were successful in achieving what they sought—moving back to laissez-faire conditions— when in fact they may have moved the economy away from the competitive one they sought? If so, they may also have made future economic policy more difficult to implement and less likely to succeed. One important avenue to altering the economic structure is through the disappearance of firms via bankruptcy. As might be expected in any depressed period, the number increases, and this is true for this period as well; the number of bankruptcies rose a phenomenal 40 percent from 1920 to 1921 and another 40 percent from 1921 to 1922.[22] The numbers for voluntary bankruptcies were 47 percent and 74 percent for the same periods.

Since the monetary and fiscal policies of the federal government contributed to the causation of the depression, they probably have some responsibility for the number of bankruptcies that developed. There is, of course, no way of determining how many bankruptcies were caused directly by government policies. All that can be inferred from the data is the suggestion that there may be some connection, and that is sufficient for the present.

Another way that firms disappear is through mergers. Mergers occur for a variety of reasons, one of which is weak financial conditions of one of the firms that has declared or is near bankruptcy. Another reason is obviously to secure a larger share of the market and curtail competition. In many cases the end result of a merger is diminished competition in an industry. For this reason mergers have been monitored, sometimes carefully and at other times with neglect bordering on indifference.

As will become apparent, the probusiness attitudes that prevailed in this period resulted in rather lax enforcement of the antitrust laws. Moreover, the recently established Federal Trade Commission (FTC) was equally unsuccessful in preventing anticompetitive practices and was under repeated political attack for even trying. In short, there was little in the government's actions or attitudes that would have discouraged mergers or the reduction of competition that might result.

For whatever reasons, the number of mergers increased by some 74 percent from 1919 to 1920 and then dropped by 36 percent from 1920 to 1921.[23] Unfortunately, the data do not permit any analysis of how competition was affected or how the structure of the economy was changed; nor do they reveal how the concentration of industries was affected. The merger movement began in earnest around the turn of the century, and the concentration of resources in the hands of fewer and fewer large firms accompanied it. That this trend continued in this period is probable but not demonstrable.

There is evidence to suggest that industries dominated by fewer numbers of large firms, such as steel, copper, meat packing, lumber, and oil, made huge profits during the war and were encouraged to form trade associations by the War Industries Board. Despite an excess profits tax, government policies probably encouraged concentration as well in its desire to encourage efficiency and a reliable supply of war materials.[24] After the war the share of corporate net income received by the largest 5 percent of corporations rose from 76.7 percent in 1919 to 78.9 percent in 1920; thereafter it declined slightly until 1923.[25]

Again, these bits of evidence do not and perhaps never could show the direct connection between government economic policies and the economic structure. They do indicate, however, that the observed changes or inferences are not inconsistent with the thesis that government actions and inactions helped alter the economic structure; if the changes in economic structure make future policy actions less effective, then government itself must share the blame for the loss of control.

It is not possible to go much beyond these generalities for the period under review. Only suggestions as to the changing economy and society are permissible. In the next chapter these changes can be documented more fully and seen more clearly, for there is no question that the economy and society were about to be transformed in many ways, both small and far-reaching.

chapter 3

The Convulsive 1920s

Some historians have used Hamlet's words, "The time is out of joint," to describe the 1920s.[1] Some writers of the period referred to themselves as "the lost generation," while others refer to the 1920s as "roaring." Each of these seemingly contradictory descriptions captures a part of the truth and, together, perhaps most of it.

Surely the times were out of joint, as the 1920s saw the rejection of many values and traditions and much of inherited wisdom. From the reaction against Puritanism and Victorian mores to the decline in religious fervor, the desire for change appeared evident. Tired of war, tired of meddling in European affairs, tired of reformers, and tired of a confining society, people simply wanted relief.

Just as surely, they were lost. Having rejected so many of the standards of society, those givens that cement the foundations and bind successive generations, and further, having ridiculed them, there was nothing to put in their places. The movements were led by the young, but eventually the older generations came to emulate them, and, in fact, youth was elevated to the prominent position it retains to this date. Surely it was a roaring time as well, if by roaring one means the release from the traditional constraints in favor of immediate gratification, experimentation, and challenges to cherished beliefs.

Not everyone, however, was enchanted by the changes taking place, and some attempted to halt them or even reverse them. Amid the turmoil brought about by quick and profound shifts from past values, there were those who objected and attempted to reestablish what they held to be essential fundamental principles. First there was the movement to fundamentalism in religion illustrated by the famous Scopes trial, which represented, in microcosm, some of the sharp divisions in society that were occurring as the break from the old was being carried out in sensitive areas.

Less amusing than the Monkey Trial was the resurgence of the Ku Klux Klan. These white supremist, anti-Jew, anti-Catholic groups also could not adjust to the rise of their victims in the cultural and economic standings and fought back with their perverse means.

The third reaction to changing conditions was in the demand to restrict immigration from southern and eastern Europe and prohibit immigration of Orientals altogether. This racist policy was fought by industrialists as long as they wanted cheap labor, but now, with labor-saving technical advances, there was no longer that excuse. The result was the National Origins Act of 1924, which fixed immigration to annual quotas on the basis of the proportion of descendants of each nationality resident in the country in 1920.

Finally there was the 18th Amendment of 1919—prohibition. Designed to legislate morality and reduce the evils attributed to the consumption of alcohol (and drink was blamed for everything), it proved to be disastrous and impossible to enforce and encouraged disrespect for the law in general.

Industrial Growth

In the industrial world the automobile industry really boomed. What better symbol of liberation can be found than the automobile, particularly the closed automobile? It not only facilitated the change in sexual mores but transformed the face of the nation as well. Its rapid development required roads and traffic signals, and soon hot-dog stands and service stations followed; then traffic engineers and mechanics, and even small buildings to shelter it were required. There simply is no way to overstate the repercussions of the growth of the automobile industry on all facets of life in the United States.

While the automobile was the most dramatic product of the times, other new products emerged as well. From cigarette lighters and wristwatches to oil furnaces and reinforced concrete, the new products were quickly accepted, thanks to the prevailing hedonistic mood; if that proved insufficient, the booming advertising industry stood ready to assist. Mass production required mass consumption, and advertising and other marketing activities became necessary.

Other industries were growing as well. The chemical industry introduced new synthetics such as rayon; the radio part of the communications industry was taking off, and the construction industry followed the population into the suburbs (in their automobiles) and built skyscrapers for those who remained to work in the cities.

In truth, this was the age of business, and businessmen were elevated to the top of the list in prestige. Business was glorified by all segments of the society and worshiped by the politician—for example, Coolidge: "The man who builds a factory builds a temple, the man who works there worships there." As we shall see, this attitude is partly responsible for the business excesses that were condoned. The trend toward concentration continued in the period as corporations grew larger; trusts flourished; banks merged and grew branches; and chain stores, such as Woolworth and A&P, began to dominate in retail markets.

The boom was not for everyone, of course, as will become apparent later, but there was the feeling expressed by both Coolidge and Hoover that the free-enterprise, capitalist economy was on the verge of eliminating poverty in the United States. The second industrial revolution would mean prosperity for everyone, including workers who would find their wages, working conditions, education, health care, safety, and so on improving along with the profits of firms. There was undeniably a feeling of optimism in the business world that contrasted in many ways with the negativism expressed in other areas of life. Perhaps Hamlet said it best after all.

Institutionalism

Some economists also responded to the changing social and economic structure, but their influence and impact was much less than might have been expected. Led by Thorstein Veblen but including W. C. Mitchell, S. H. Slichter, G. C. Means, W. E. Atkins, and John R. Commons, a group of economists fashioned a rather genuine U.S. contribution to economic thought, labeled institutionalism or evolutionary economics. While their work extends to the periods before and after the 1920s, it can logically be included here, when their ideas really found cohesion.

They differ in many ways, of course, but they generally viewed man as acting out of habit and instincts, motivated by forces that cannot always be measured, including custom. Thus they rejected the neoclassical model based heavily on abstractions and deduction and its conclusions based on self-interest as a motive and static equilibrium as an analytical device. Economics as a positive science seemed beyond realization; the proper study of economics should revolve around the growth and evolution of institutions, together with behavioral patterns more in keeping with what was being postulated by sociologists and psychologists. Forget the hedonism and rationality found in conventional theory; neither in the real world nor in a properly constructed model would actions reach "optimal" results so common in neoclassical reasoning. The neoclassical economists were not observing the actual workings of the economy, but were involved with their own clever abstractions.

Had they confronted reality, they would have noticed the tendency toward disequilibrium rather than equilibrium. The institutions that man erects out of instinct, custom, habit, property rights, technical methods, and so on become fixed and unable to adjust to changing experience and evolutionary gradations. Thus there is a cultural lag between existing institutions, representing the embodiment of past instincts and current behavior. (It is easy to see why this expression was more readily accepted in the 1920s.) When people pursue their own self-interest, they block institutional change and indeed profit by doing so. Without going into analytical detail, this kind of behavior might easily explain or account for the price fixing, supply restriction, planned obsolescence, and so on that the economists saw in the real world but not in the idealized results of abstract reasoning.

One segment of the group, led by Wesley Clair Mitchell, thus began to employ statistical methods to actual data to study the business cycle in an attempt to find recurring patterns in economic activity. Mitchell, who founded the National Bureau of Economic Research, gave a further boost to quantitative economics, but was later accused of pursuing measurement without theory.

Other members, such as Gardiner Means and Sumner Slichter, were not content merely to study the workings of the economy, but sought to control the economy by setting social goals and by accepting state intervention into the economy to modify or control the institutions that compose it. Using the textbook written by Slichter (*Modern Economic Society*, 1928), based on evolutionary economics, some idea of the proposals for social control can be made explicit. In his last chapter entitled "Some Constructive Suggestions," he listed the following topics:

The control of population
The provision of more adequate market information
Providing industry with more accurate cost accounting
Improving the regulation of public utilities
The creation of more public utilities
Making economic fortune less of a gamble
Greater recognition of needs in the distribution of income
A greater voice for labor in the direction of industry
A greater voice for consumers in the direction of industry
A planned economy
Making management neutral instead of partisan

     Clearly many economists in the 1980s could subscribe to several or all of these suggestions. Therefore the subject of the influence of these institutionalists, though difficult to measure, is obvious in that the criticisms continue in the same vein, but critics of their contribution contend that similar criticisms were made before and only new terminology was added ("leisure class," "pecuniary employments," for example). Their critics insisted that they had produced no new theory to replace the old theory and were thus merely repeating familiar criticisms of neoclassical economics in obscure jargon. Eventually their brand of economics was pejoratively labeled "descriptive economics" and dismissed. In the words of one critic, "Let the Institutionalist describe our institutions—even let him change them—but let him not forget such laws as supply and demand, diminishing utility, and diminishing returns. The laws of economics work through institutions, but they are more fundamental than institutions."[2]

     Their observed influence can be seen in the boost given to quantitative economics in general, and to the more systematic study of the business cycle in particular, and later in their contribution to policymaking in the 1930s under the New Deal of President Roosevelt. In more subtle ways their unobserved influence can be traced, with patience, to the anticipation of both theoretical and policy insights of J. M. Keynes and to the recognition of economic problems still existing today.

The Harding Administration

If the time was out of joint, it may not be surprising to learn that the times did not produce "first raters."[3] This was the judgment by

Connecticut Senator Brandegee of the newly selected Republican candidate for the presidency in 1920—Warren Gamaliel Harding. Running on a favorite-son ticket for state political reasons, the senator from Ohio was way down the list of potential candidates, but after the convention became deadlocked, Harding was selected by a group of party leaders in a smoke-filled room (a reporter's phrase) to break it. The next day he was cleverly maneuvered into position to be acceptable to the convention as a whole. The convention then went on to demand Calvin Coolidge as the vice-presidential candidate. Coolidge, the governor of Massachusetts, had attained fame for his handling of the Boston police strike; there was, he said, "no right to strike against the public safety by anybody, anywhere, any time."

From all accounts, Harding looked the part of a president and was a warm, affable, friendly man. By his own later admission, however, he was not well equipped for the job—a job he did not seek and did not want. In a Boston speech in May 1920, he uttered these now famous words asking the nation to return to, "not heroism, but healing, not nostrums, but normalcy." (Harding had difficulty with suffixes.)[4] After a lackluster campaign Harding easily beat his Democratic opponent, James M. Cox, former governor of Ohio, who in the public mind became identified with Wilson. Since the nation was busy repudiating Wilsonian ideals, this identification hurt Cox, who won only 34.1 percent of the popular vote (127 electoral votes) and captured only 11 states.

Harding enjoyed handing out government posts and rewarding his friends, but he was ill served by them. After his death the vast corruption of his administration was revealed in the famous Teapot Dome scandal in which Albert Fall, secretary of the interior, had leased government oil reserves at Teapot Dome, Wyoming, receiving compensation in cash and cattle. Fall was fined and was the first cabinet member to be jailed; Harding's appointment of a casual acquaintance, Colonel Charles R. Forbes, to head the Veterans Bureau turned out to be disastrous, as Forbes condemned carloads of hospital supplies and then sold them in return for part of the proceeds. The sale of German chemical patents for minimal amounts led to the conviction of Thomas Miller and eventually led to Attorney General Daugherty himself. Daugherty was forced to resign after he refused to testify, hinting by his refusal that the Hardings were touched by scandal, although no one ever accused Harding of any wrongdoing; he was a very honest man by all accounts.

Other members of his administration were involved in wrongdoing as well, but it must not be inferred that Harding made only poor choices for government posts. His appointment of Charles Evans

Hughes, for instance, as secretary of state was an excellent choice. The scandals, however, often overshadow his positive achievements.

Harding has received much condemnation from historians, stemming from his laziness, gullibility, or downright incompetence.[5] Yet his administration was not without achievements: The Bureau of the Budget was initiated, giving the United States its first formal budgeting institution; civil rights for blacks were given a boost as Harding opened up jobs for blacks and made a startling speech declaring that he wanted to see the time "when black men will regard themselves as full participants in the benefits and duties of American citizenship"; the workday for steelworkers was reduced from 12 to 8 hours after he met with industry leaders and demanded action. More fascinating for late twentieth-century readers was the naval disarmament conference he convened that eventually banned construction of capital ships by the United States, Britain, and Japan for ten years, and provided for the destruction of some existing warships. The long-term results of the conference were to prove disappointing, but the very idea of disarmament and of Harding's renouncing of armaments and war showed some promise for his administration in world affairs.

In the economic realm Harding would be remembered as ushering in the age of business. ("The business of America is the business of everybody in America.") For Harding, and after him Coolidge and Hoover, prosperity for the nation was not possible without prosperity for business. For progress, the nation should look to the corporate boardroom, and for the means the nation should look to business practices. The Republican party came to be identified with business interests, and business leaders were quick to take advantage of their elevated stature and, as will be seen, demanded more favorable treatment.

So pervasive became the identification of progress and business that everyone copied business practices and adopted the jargon. Indeed, when the scandal cases were being tried, the press excoriated those who prosecuted more than they condemned the acts themselves.[6] The excesses of businesses did not seem to affect their power and prestige, and they continued to be entrusted with the nation's prosperity.

Harding's choices for some key posts also reveal his probusiness inclination: Andrew Mellon, the richest man in the United States, for secretary of the treasury; Herbert Hoover for secretary of commerce, and crony David Grissinger as comptroller of the currency and later head of the Federal Reserve Board, and so on. The stage was set for the decade of business.

Fiscal Policy in the 1920s

When Harding took office on March 4, 1921, the economy was
approaching the trough of the cycle (July 1921) that had reached a
peak in January 1920. The expansion would continue throughout most
of the decade at a 6 percent growth rate, interrupted twice by minor
recessions in 1923–24 and 1926–27.

What is also striking in this decade is the remarkable price
stability and steady unemployment rates for the years following the
trough year of 1921. Consumer prices actually fell by 4 percent from
1921 to 1929, while wholesale prices fell by 2 percent; the unemployment rate fell from a high of 11.7 percent in 1921 to 3.2 percent in
1929. Only the recessions of 1923–24 and 1926–27 interrupted the
steady decline in the unemployment rate, and, even then, the rates
were only about 5 and 3.5 percent, respectively. Clearly, rapid growth
with price stability is remarkable for any decade and must be
explained. What, if any, of the explanation can be traced to macroeconomic policies?

Turning to the fiscal policies of the federal government over the
decade, it is clear that they reflect the values of the conservative
leadership. Limited governments and balanced budgets were the
counterparts to the reverence for private enterprise. Thus no new
spending programs were introduced, and total spending by the federal
government remained exceptionally stable. This stability is one of
the reasons that the budget showed a surplus in every year of the
1920s.

There was also the feeling that the federal debt ought to be
retired to preserve the credit worthiness of the government and
demonstrate its commitment to sound finance. The federal debt did
decline from a high of $25 billion in 1919 to $16 billion in 1920. Paying
off the debt was desired in order to release funds to the private sector,
reduce interest payments to facilitate the reduction in taxes, and
reduce the dangers of inflation.[7]

The real story of fiscal policy in this era, however, was the drive
to reduce taxes and, as a result, government involvement in the
economy. Indeed, one of the major confrontations of the decade pitted
Andrew Mellon, secretary of the treasury, against the last remnants of
the Progressive movement, and the battleground was over taxation
and which groups should bear the burden.

During the last years of the Wilson administration, Carter Glass,
secretary of the treasury, began the movement for the removal of the
excess profits tax, which he regarded as undesirable in peacetime.

Businessmen picked up the cry in 1920 and added the demand for a reduction in surtax rates. Many felt that a sales tax would be preferable to income taxes anyway and fought for its substitution. Organizations were formed and funds raised to promote business interests. In opposition, Socialists and the farmer-labor party were urging that the tax system be used to promote social policies that they favored, while other farm groups, the AFL, and some business groups fought the sales-tax proposal. The tax system seemed sure to change and political power would determine the direction.

No actions were taken until Harding took office and in a special session of Congress that he called, the Emergency Tariff Act of May 27, 1921 (later made permanent) emerged, which levied high duties on agricultural imports in the attempt to rescue farmers from falling prices. This standard Republican policy failed to work in practice, but it not only was the outgrowth of the usual protectionist arguments but also reflected the feelings of nationalism and the desire for self-sufficiency. The revival of world trade took a blow, of course, and world tensions developed that would prove one element leading to World War II.

After venting its emotions on the tariff issue, the overwhelmingly Republican Congress turned its attention to taxation. Andrew Mellon urged the repeal of the excess profits tax; an increase in the corporation income tax (to appease farmers); reduction in surtax and normal tax rates to 40 percent for 1921 and 33 percent thereafter; repeal of some luxury taxes; retention of excise taxes on transportation, tobacco, admissions, and so on; and a new stamp tax on automobiles.[8]

The House went along with these proposals, but the Senate, where midwestern Republicans and Democrats united, balked at the program. Especially troublesome was the proposal to reduce surtax rates for the wealthy—from 65 percent to a maximum of 25 percent after 1921. Mellon and his followers argued that reductions in tax rates for the high-income groups were necessary in order to stimulate initiative, rechannel funds from unproductive tax-exempt securities to productive business capital, and encourage new capital formation that would "increase the number of jobs and at the same time advance general prosperity."[9] In short, the argument is the same one that has come to be called the "trickle-down effect" and, in the 1980s, supply-side economics.

The struggle over tax changes ended in the passage of the Revenue Act of 1921, which repealed the excess profits tax, reduced substantially the surtax rates, and provided a special treatment for capital gains, hereafter to be taxed at a maximum rate of 12.5 percent. No provision for limits on capital losses was provided, however, and soon the capital gains were wiped out by writing off capital losses against them. In addition, corporate taxes were increased from 10 percent to 12.5 percent.

The reduction in surtax rates was not as drastic as that recommended by Mellon—down to a maximum rate of 50 percent on net incomes over $200,000. The surtax rates began at 1 percent on incomes over $6,000 and increased by 1 percent for each $2,000 income bracket up to the $98,000–100,000 bracket at 47 percent. Then the brackets became much larger. Thus the "wild asses of the desert," the insurgents, won a partial success, but the victory was only temporary, for the Revenue Act of 1921 turned out to be a major turning point in the determination of the distribution of economic power in the United States. This result will become evident as the decade unfolds.

As a concession, the personal exemption for heads of families was raised and the allowance for dependents was increased from $200 to $400 per dependent. Thus the tax load for lower- and middle-income groups was reduced as well. But the Revenue Act of 1921 pleased no one. Passed near the end of the special session of Congress, it was not the final word on taxation. After Harding's death in August 1923, Coolidge was in turn dominated by Andrew Mellon, who once again came forward with a new tax plan. Since there were budget surpluses and reductions in the public debt despite falling tax revenues, the time appeared ripe for another round of tax reductions.

Recall that 1924 was an election year, and Republicans had to win friends and recover the public trust following the Harding scandals. Tax reductions are always popular, and Mellon was prepared to continue the trend in taxation developed over the postwar period. Once again, he advocated a reduction in the surtax rates from a maximum rate of 50 percent on incomes over $200,000 to 25 percent on incomes $100,000 and over. In addition, there would be a reduction in normal tax rates from 4 and 8 percent to 3 and 6 percent, a reduction in the federal estate tax, the elimination of some excise taxes, and a host of refinements to the tax code.

What emerged after heated debates was the Revenue Act of 1924, which was more extensive than intended by the administration and Coolidge nearly vetoed it. There was a 25 percent reduction in taxes in 1924 on 1923 incomes, a normal-tax-rate reduction to 2 percent on the first $4,000 (from 4 percent), a 4 percent on the $4,000 and 6 percent on incomes over $8,000 (from 8 percent on incomes over $4,000), a reduction in surtax rates to 1 percent on incomes in excess of $10,000, rising gradually to a maximum of 40 percent on incomes of over $500,000 (from 1 percent on incomes over $6,000 to a maximum of 50 percent for incomes $200,000 and over).

While large-income recipients benefited greatly from these reductions, the gains were well spread out over all income groups. It was an election year, to be sure, but the widespread benefits also attest to the Progressive and Democratic alliance. They managed to increase the estate tax and added a gift tax as well.

Another interesting innovation was the provision for a reduction of 25 percent on "earned" income up to $5,000 for low-income groups and $10,000 for high-income groups. This followed the British precedent and helped gain the support of labor for the tax package that favored high-income groups even more. To illustrate, while many excise taxes were reduced or repealed, those that fell most heavily on lower-income groups were not (tobacco, admissions, jewelry, and automobiles).

Calvin Coolidge, running on the usual Republican platform of high tariffs, reduction of government involvement, and continued tax reductions, easily beat John W. Davis, an attorney for J. P. Morgan. The Democrats ran on an opposite platform promising a more equitable distribution of taxes. Only Robert La Follette and his third party, Conference for Progressive Political Action, promised anything new or dramatic. They advocated an attack on monopolies and trusts; public ownership of natural resources, railroads, and water power; continued high surtax rates on upper-income groups and new excess profits taxes; large estate taxes; and repeal of excise taxes. La Follette made a great showing, and for a time it appeared that a farmer-labor movement would be possible.

That was not to be, however, and the party dominated by business emerged the easy victor and immediately began to consolidate its strength and continue its undermining of the public sector. Almost immediately Coolidge pressed for the repeal of gift, estate, and excise taxes, and the reduction of surtax rates. Opposition to these plans was in disarray now, as both Progressives and Democrats lost ground in the election and strong leadership was lacking.

Thus the Revenue Act of 1926 was easily passed in February 1926. The act continued to reduce and shift the tax burden away from high-income and wealthy groups. Surtax rates were reduced for incomes over $26,000 and rose to a maximum of only 20 percent on incomes over $100,000 (down from 40 percent on incomes over $500,000). Justification for such sharp reductions was the usual need to shift funds from nonproductive, tax-free securitites to productive capital and to provide incentives. The lack of evidence for these assertions did not appear to hinder the expression of them.[10]

Furthermore, the gift tax was repealed and the estate tax weakened as the maximum federal rates were reduced, allowing the states to increase their rates. Any desire to reduce economic power or pursue equity in the distribution of wealth was sacrificed, as those with power used it unabashedly. The taxation of wealth in the United States never revived as a serious rival of income for tax purposes.

To secure passage of the bill, normal tax rates were also reduced slightly and personal exemptions were increased. The earned income credit was retained for all, but the maximum income to which it applied was increased to $20,000 from $10,000—a useful move to win the support of middle-income taxpayers. Excise taxes were reduced on items such as tobacco, admissions, and the like, but repealed for luxury goods consumed by the wealthy. Also, the corporate income tax was increased slightly.

The last of the Coolidge–Mellon tax proposals made in 1927 once again asked for reductions in surtax rates, repeal of the estate tax, and a reduction in the corporate income tax. No longer in command of Congress, the Republicans did not make substantial gains in the tax bill passed in May 1928. The corporate income tax was reduced, and the earned income credit was increased to incomes of $30,000 from $20,000. Congress, however, repealed the excise tax on automobiles, reduced that on wines, and exempted more events from admissions taxes.

Thus ended one of the most prolonged and successful assaults on the taxation of wealth and privilege in the history of the United States. Principles of equity in the distribution of the tax burden—whether of income or wealth—were set aside in favor of the unverified contention that progress and prosperity required a lower tax burden for the rich so that they would use their wealth productively and have the incentive to do so.[11]

Attitudes toward the taxation of wealth were formed in this period and became ingrained, and with them went any serious attempt to tax wealth in the United States. Income became the major tax base thereafter, particularly when tariff revenues declined. Yet certain types of income were to be taxed differently: Capital gains were given special treatment without regard to their being productive or not; rules regarding the taxation of trusts were formed here, and rules governing the taxation of corporations versus their stockholders began to change in this period.

This restructuring of the tax burden had profound effects on fiscal policy. Having to turn to incomes for government revenues meant greater reliance on current economic conditions rather than on changes in economic positions over time. Government revenues would now fluctuate more and the budget would become less controllable. And aside from the principles of equity and justice involved, the virtual abandonment of wealth as a base for taxation meant that a privileged class was allowed to develop unhindered; the result was economic power that eventually could be joined to political power. The threat to democratic principles is obvious; the threat to economic stability remains to be spelled out.

It follows from the foregoing that fiscal policy was complying with ideological beliefs and was not undertaken for stabilization purposes. Mellon did insist, however, that his policies would promote economic growth and development.

On the expenditures side, government spending was reduced and the role of government in the economy minimized. Table 3.1 shows that after the sharp reductions in national defense spending in 1920–22, expenditures remained relatively stable. The tax reductions are also evident in the years 1921–23 and 1925.

Whether or not these tax cuts actually worked to stimulate the economy and provide the incentives to productive investment and capital formation cannot be determined from the data available, but at least one contemporary observer felt that not all the growth in

Table 3.1 Federal Receipts and Expenditures, 1919–29 (percent change)

Year	Budget Receipts	Budget Expenditures	Surplus or Deficit (−)	Public Debt
1919	40.7	45.9	47.9	104.6
1920	29.6	−65.6	102.0	−4.7
1921	−16.2	−20.4	74.8	−1.3
1922	−27.7	−35.0	44.7	−4.2
1923	−4.3	−4.5	−3.4	−2.7
1924	0.5	−7.4	35.2	−4.9
1925	−6.0	0.5	−25.6	−3.5
1926	4.2	0.2	20.7	−4.3
1927	5.7	−2.5	33.5	−5.8
1928	−2.8	3.6	−18.7	−4.9
1929	−1.0	5.6	−21.8	−3.8

Source: U.S. Department of Commerce, Bureau of the Census, *Historical Statistics of the United States* (Washington, DC: GPO, 1975), p. 1104.

revenues could be attributed to the tax cuts. If that were the case in 1922, he wrote, then how could one explain the recession of 1924 (and later 1927) when even lower tax rates were in effect.[12] The early evidence did not support the view that funds were diverted from tax-exempt securities to productive investment. Later in the decade, when speculation was flourishing, it would be even more difficult to suggest such a transfer. Only a more detailed look at investment spending (later) will help answer the question.

Note that the public debt decreased steadily over the period, which is consistent with conservative views, but repayment of the debt also furnished funds for the private sector, as did the tax cuts. Note also the large surpluses in 1923 and 1926–27, years of recession. This suggests that government may have aided in bringing about those downturns by its fiscal actions.

Before turning to monetary policy and the analysis of the private sector, one final observation on government spending is necessary. While the federal government was busy reducing the role of government in the system and boasting of this effort, state and local governments were increasing their involvement dramatically. Data are lacking for this period, but some idea of the magnitudes involved is possible. Comparing the data available for 1922 with 1927, state and local governments' expenditures increased by 3,812 percent, taxes increased by 51.6 percent, and their debt had risen by 47.2 percent. It appears that economizing at the federal level of government was achieved at least partially at the expense of state and local governments. Great demands were placed on those governments for roads, education, police and fire protection, and welfare, functions that were left to them by the Constitution.

Thus, whatever fiscal stimulus was provided by the federal budget may have been partially offset by the fiscal actions of states and localities. With the lack of data, it is impossible to be more precise.

Monetary Policy in the Early 1920s

As mentioned earlier, the United States became the financial center of the world following World War I. Not only was it ill prepared to play that role under the old monetary system, but with the collapse of the gold standard during the war, the rules of the game were changing as well. Furthermore, the Federal Reserve System had little opportunity to organize its operations and learn from them, since their powers were subordinated to the needs of the Treasury. Thus the Federal Reserve had yet to develop policy guidelines in theory or in practice.

Still, it is doubtful if it would have devised policy actions even if it had had the opportunity. With the monetary theory that it appeared to hold, no policy actions were required anyway. The System was prepared to furnish credit to business for working capital or to meet the seasonal or emergency demands for credit and was not concerned with long-run or cyclical problems.[13] The function of the System under this interpretation (a real-bills variant) was to preside over this fund of self-liquidating loans and serve as the intermediary in the saving–investment process.

This function does not require that the Federal Reserve manipulate the reserves of banks, for this takes place automatically. Presumably the operation of the gold standard provided for both long-term needs and cyclical variations. Thus, if bank reserves are not a focus of attention, there is no need for a monetary policy, nor a concern for the quantity of money in existence.

The postwar inflation, followed by the sharp depression of 1920–21, and the growth of the federal debt during the war, soon forced changes in the Federal Reserve's theoretical and operating beliefs and procedures. This is not to say that the System learned quickly and agreed on the proper courses of action. In fact, the record is replete with sharp disagreements, incomprehensible statements about monetary affairs, and, often, rather confused ideas of the nature of monetary problems and what to do about them. For example, the Federal Reserve System finally admitted government securities into bank portfolios as an asset, rather than as a source of inflation or as a signal of excess credit in the system. This reversal now paved the way for open-market operations—the buying and selling of government securities to manipulate bank reserves. No longer would the gold standard alone change bank reserves and determine monetary conditions. (Of course, the Federal Reserve has as yet little notion of how open-market operations worked and actually learned by accident.)

Also contributing to the need to revise the operations of the Federal Reserve System was the influx of gold in this period. Since the United States was the only major country on the gold standard, there were no automatic offsets to gold movements. Hence the increase in the gold stock, if left unchecked, would have threatened the nation with more inflation.

Lacking the rules of the game provided by the gold standard, however, it was necessary to devise new ones to help guide Federal Reserve policy. In the now famous *Tenth Annual Report* (1923), the

Federal Reserve tried to spell out its new approach until the gold standard was restored. It would supply the necessary credit for productive uses as before—the so-called qualitative test—and it would tie the amount of credit to the nation's aggregate output—the so-called quantitative test. The appropriate amount of credit would be determined by changes in real output. When prices rose and real output was stable, this would signify excess credit in the economy; however, as long as real output was rising, even if prices were, too, credit would not be deemed excessive.[14]

For the remainder of the decade, the Federal Reserve would attempt to achieve from its new approaches the following objectives: maintaining price stability consistent with a high and stable national output, preventing the use of bank credit for speculative purposes, and restoring the gold standard. These goals are not listed in any order, and conflicts and confusion over them were to complicate Federal Reserve policymaking over the decade.

Monetary policy was rather passive in most of 1922, as output expanded. The accompanying price increases were regarded as acceptable, since output had not reached its maximum. Discount rates were actually lowered slightly in several Federal Reserve banks including New York, which lowered its rate to 4 percent. The System did buy bonds—not for stabilization purposes, but to protect their earnings. The New York Bank also began selling securities late in the year to offset (sterilize) the inflow of gold.

Discount rates were increased in the New York and Boston Banks in early 1923, as the System began to sense that production was nearing capacity and some restraint was called for. No further changes were made for the year, however. In March 1923 the Open Market Investment Committee was established, which formalized a major institutional change that had actually been initiated earlier. Despite the formation of the committee, the effects of open-market operations were still not fully understood by all board members. In fact, the Treasury wanted the Federal Reserve to sell off all of its government securities, fearing uncoordinated actions by member banks. One of the first actions of the newly formed committee was a decision to sell a small amount of bonds, but just why remains unclear.

The upswing in economic activity that began in April 1921 continued until May 1923. The mild decline from this peak would continue until July 1924. What were the monetary policies following the creation of the Open Market Committee?

The Federal Reserve did not react to the downturn in economic activity and in fact was still selling securities in June 1923. Toward the end of the year it began buying securities, but again not for stabilization purposes, but to rebuild its portfolio of assets. Discount rates for the New York Bank were reduced to 4 percent in April 1924 and fell in steps to 3 percent later in the year. Only after the recession was a year old did the Federal Reserve begin to pursue open-market operations in earnest, as it increased its holdings of government bonds by nearly $400 million over the year.

The actions of the Federal Reserve during this period are subject to various interpretations and, of course, disagreements. The monetary ease suggested above would certainly be appropriate to combat the recession, but it would also be appropriate if the Federal Reserve wanted to see a restoration of the gold standard. This confluence of goals was propitious for the policy followed, but which one would have been pursued if the goals had conflicted?[15] It is well known, for instance, that Benjamin Strong of the New York Bank wanted to see Britain return to the gold standard, and his influential voice was calling for interest rates in New York to be below rates in London. With this interest-rate differential, gold would not be flowing so readily to New York, and with low rates in New York, Great Britain could pursue monetary ease as well. The British economy, so stimulated by easy money, could revive and eventually return to the gold standard. Thus a policy of easy money served two ends: It was beneficial in stimulating the U.S. economic recovery from recession, and it helped pave the way for the return to the gold standard.

There was, however, a negative aspect to low interest rates and easy money—stock-market speculation. Since 1915 the Federal Reserve had been concerned that banks were making loans for speculative purposes and had warned banks to stop the practice. Lacking effective sanctions and always mindful that too much interference in the banks' affairs was to be avoided, the Federal Reserve did little more than jawbone. From 1924 to the end of the decade, stock-market speculation was a problem for the monetary authorities, and the root of the problem can be traced to their easy-money policy. Banks at that time kept their excess reserves on deposit with other large banks. When the rate of return on these deposits fell below the loan rate to the stock-market participants, the banks naturally shifted their excess reserves to the stock market. This made credit tighter for other borrowers and obviously helped fuel speculation.

The economy recovered in the summer of 1925 and seemed to be progressing nicely, with GNP growing and unemployment falling. Stock-market speculation, however, continued to increase. Banks increased their loans on securities by 24 percent from 1924 to 1925 and by another 9 percent in 1926. Call rates on stock-exchange loans began to climb as well.

The Federal Reserve debated the problem, but decided not to raise discount rates for fear of hurting Britain. Not until February 1925 did it sell some securities and raise the discount rate in New York to 3.5 percent. The System was reluctant to go further, since it feared that it might abort the recovery or interfere with Britain's progress. Yet, after Britain raised its bank rate, the New York Bank increased its rate to 4 percent; later, when stock-market activity slackened in 1926, the rate was again lowered to 3.5 percent, and some securities were bought. It is clear that stock-market activity, not the domestic economy, was governing the policies of the Federal Reserve during these stable years between recessions.

In the summer of 1926 the Federal Reserve policy once again turned to restraint, as the discount rate was again increased to 4 percent in New York, and open-market sales of approximately $90 million were made. This policy of restraint remains curious, since there was no apparent need for it other than perhaps psychological.

Monetary Policy, 1925–29

While the U.S. economy was expanding, Great Britain returned to the gold standard in April 1925. In a rather chauvinistic move the pound sterling was given its prewar gold content, which made the exchange rate over $4.87. The pound was simply overvalued, and Keynes excoriated the then chancellor of the exchequer, Winston Churchill.[16] As a result, exports—on which Britain depends highly—were in trouble, and soon the entire economy was floundering. Britain would have clearly benefited from a policy of low interest rates, but low rates would also have encouraged the outflow of gold to New York.

Gold did begin to flow into the United States again in early 1927, following the interest-rate increases in late 1926. To protect the gold standard, the Federal Reserve would have had to purchase bonds and reduce interest rates. Such a policy would have conflicted with its desire to prevent excessive credit from threatening price-level stability and to prevent further stock-market speculation. Consequently, it did little for the first quarter of 1927.

Once again, as in 1924, a recession in the United States beginning in 1927 made the easy-money policy appropriate for both international and domestic stabilization. Unfortunately, easy money also contributed to stock-market speculation, which began to accelerate.

This brief recession from October 1926 to November 1927 was a mild one, with GNP and consumer prices falling about 2 percent. Unemployment, however, increased dramatically, so that the rate for 1927 was 83 percent greater than for the year 1926 (3.3 percent versus 1.8 percent). In the summer of 1927 the Federal Reserve began to act and employ its open-market operations for the second time.

The monetary policies were undertaken after Governor Strong had convened a meeting with officials from Britain, France, and Germany in an extraordinary effort to secure cooperation among the world's leading banking centers. There seems little doubt that international stabilization was determining the Federal Reserve's policies, even though they may have had some beneficial effects on the domestic economy as well.

Following the historic meeting, discount rates were lowered to 3.5 percent, and open-market purchases of securities were begun. Interest rates fell quickly, and the easy-money policy achieved its aims of internal and external stabilization; the gold flow was reversed, and other countries were free to revitalize their economies.

The situation in 1928 was perplexing. The economy was drifting downward, as unemployment rose to the high rate of 4.2 percent, although prices and real GNP remained relatively stable. Yet while the economy was stagnating, the stock market became bullish in the spring of the year. Soon stock prices were spurting ahead, gaining 5, then 10 points, and so on. Week after week the trend was generally upward, and more and more people entered the market, bent on getting rich. The speculative orgy had begun.

The monetary authorities were also understandably perplexed. Raising discount rates to prevent speculation would be bad for the domestic economy and would also hurt the European economies that were struggling as well. Yet the stock-market activity was alarming. The Federal Reserve chose restraint, as it sold securities between January and June of $415 million, leaving its holdings of bonds at a very low level. In February the New York Bank raised its discount rate to 4 percent; in May it rose to 4.5 percent, then to 5 percent in July, and eventually to 6 percent in August 1929.

Interest rates on government bonds rose slowly, but brokers' loan rates rose sharply to over 8 percent and eventually to 10, 12, and 20 percent in 1929. The policy on restraint resulted in perverse effects: It may have adversely affected the domestic economy (the Federal Reserve denied it), but it did little to stem the stock-market activity. (The Federal Reserve was not ready to label the increase in activity speculation.) In fact, the high rates of interest began to attract more funds into the market. Now financial intermediaries, corporations, and foreign investors began or increased their activity in the market. Table 3.2 shows the flow of funds to brokers from nonbank sources that fueled the speculation. Meanwhile, holders of domestic government bonds were being demoralized.

The Federal Reserve never acknowledged that its policy of restraint was actually adding to the funds available to the stock market, while at the same time it was becoming concerned over the domestic economy. The policy of mild ease followed for the latter half of 1928 did nothing to correct the situation. It turned then to jawboning—"direct pressure" or moral suasion—to warn banks of making loans for purposes of speculation. In a letter to all Federal Reserve Banks it stated, "The Federal Reserve Act does not, in the opinion of the Federal Reserve Board, contemplate the use of the resources of the Federal Reserve Banks for the creation or extension of speculative credit. A member bank is not within its reasonable claims for rediscount facilities at its Federal Reserve Bank when it borrows either for the purpose of making speculative loans or for the purpose of maintaining speculative loans."

As a result of its letter, the Federal Reserve hoped to reduce interest rates, as banks would reduce loans to the stock market and make funds available to other borrowers. It did not work, as interest

Table 3.2　Loans to Brokers (in millions of dollars)

Date	Total	By New York City Banks	By Outside Banks	By Others
Dec. 31, 1924	2,230	1.150	530	550
Dec. 31, 1925	3,550	1,450	1,050	1,050
Dec. 31, 1926	3,290	1,160	830	1,300
Dec. 31, 1927	4,430	1,550	1,050	1,830
June 30, 1928	4,900	1,080	960	2,860
Dec. 31, 1928	6,440	1,640	915	3,885
Oct. 4, 1929	8,525	1,095	790	6,640
Dec. 31, 1929	4,110	1,200	460	2,450

Source: Board of Governors of the Federal Reserve System, Banking and Monetary Statistics (Washington, DC: GPO, 1943), p. 494.

rates continued their upward climb. The rise in stock prices did break, however, and continued in a rise-and-fall pattern for a few months until the summer of 1929, when prices spurted again. The failure of the direct-pressure policy became obvious to all, but the Federal Reserve did nothing else, either in changing discount rates or open-market operations, from August 1928 to July 1929. The Federal Reserve System, of course, had no control over margin requirements, no authority to use credit controls or credit rationing, and no real knowledge of how to or even whether to control the stock market. They were committed only to controlling credit to the stock market, but not to controlling or making judgments on stock prices. Economists were of no help either, as Irving Fisher, the leading economist of the times, was talking about a permanent high plateau of stock prices, and others were counseling investment in people's capitalism.

Stock-Market Speculation

Speculation was not confined to the stock market. In 1925 there was the Florida land boom, one extreme example of real estate speculation that spread to California and North Carolina. Promoters, swindlers, schemers, and con artists were everywhere in the 1920s, taking advantage of the mood of the country. Everyone was promising riches and continued prosperity and each had a special route to follow. And people went along, from bankers to cab drivers, from gamblers to the cautious; everyone, it seems, wanted in.

This mass psychology was nowhere more evident, of course, than in the stock market. Everyone heard of someone who had made a fortune without any special knowledge, and news of market activity was front-page material. The small investor could participate by trusting his or her funds to an investment trust that would pool these funds and invest them. Holding companies pyramided assets until a relatively small outlay controlled vast sums. Propelled by greed, few were inclined to weigh the risks involved in these institutions. The few who did question these and other practices were derided and easily dismissed. Risk there was, but it seemed remote; as long as prices were rising on stocks of well-known and respected companies, as long as financial leaders led the way, where was the need for restraint and caution? Indeed, just a glance at the change in stock prices over the period is sufficient to understand the euphoria that prevailed. When stock prices did fall, as they did occasionally, it was regarded as a

Table 3.3   Selected Stock Prices

Stock	March 3, 1928	September 3, 1929*	November 13, 1929
American Can	77	181⅞	86
American Telephone & Telegraph	179½	335⅝	197¼
Anaconda Copper	54½	162	70
General Electric	128¾	396¼	168⅛
General Motors	139¾	181⅞	36
Montgomery Ward	132¾	466½	49¼
New York Central	160½	256⅜	160
Radio	94½	505	28
Union Carbide	145	413⅝	59
United States Steel	138⅛	279⅛	150
Westinghouse	91⅝	313	102⅝
Woolworth	180¾	251	52¼
Electric Bond and Share	89¾	203⅝	50¼

*Adjusted for stock splits and stock rights.

"technical adjustment"—a temporary setback; nothing could dispel the underlying optimism.

Table 3.3 shows the rise in prices of selected stocks for the period. The periods chosen are the beginning of the real spurt to the high point and back to the low point in the cycle of price movements.

Breaks in stock prices did occur periodically in September and October 1929, prior to the final crash on Black Tuesday, October 29, 1929. There were also attempts to prevent the crash by brokers, led by J. P. Morgan and Exchange officials, but they ultimately failed. When prices fell, margin calls went out, and since many investors lacked cash, they sold securities to obtain more funds, further depressing stock prices, inducing further margin calls, and so on. Finally the whole thing collapsed like a house of cards.

So much has been written about the stock-market crash that it would be indeed superfluous to recount once again the events leading up to the final disaster.[17] The bubble burst, and with it went the dreams and fantasies of many people who got caught up in the folly. The crash signaled the end of an era that began in and ended with disillusionment.

The Federal Reserve Bank of New York reacted (without authority) quickly by purchasing over $130 million of government securities to relieve the strain on money markets. Corporations and interior banks began clamoring for their money that was loaned out as call loans. This contraction would have reduced the money supply dramatically, if not offset. From late October into December, the Open Market Committee purchased still more securities and then it stopped buying bonds until March 1930. Also, the New York Bank lowered its discount rate from 6 percent to 5 percent to 4.5 percent in mid-November 1929. Interest rates began to fall as a result of these actions and, probably more important, of the precipitous decline in the demand for funds for speculative purposes.

In retrospect, the Federal Reserve's actions appear timid and hesitant in the face of this shattering episode. Yet the System had no experience with such occurrences and lacked knowledge of how to confront them. It reacted as it had to the recessions of the mid-1920s and did not foresee the possiblity of a much greater depression in the offing.

The Boom of the 1920s

What, then, caused the boom of the 1920s, and how were the gains distributed? Just a glance at Table 3.4 is sufficient to reveal the source of the boom; both consumption and investment spending led the way. Consumption of semidurable and durable goods increased substantially, while perishables and services remained stable or declined. Since a large portion of the national income is devoted to consumption expenditures, it follows that much of the growth of the national output can be traced to this source.

Consumption spending increased steadily over this period, even in the cyclical downswings. In the last cycle of the decade, however, 1925–27, the rate of increase in consumption spending fell drastically, reflecting the decline in expenditures on consumer durables. By this time the automobile was no longer a novelty, for instance, and the market for new buyers was certainly diminishing. After 1927 consumption would not play the role of supporting growth as it did in the first half of the decade.

Similarly with investment spending, residential construction was important in the boom, but it, too, followed its own cycle, going from its trough in 1920 to a peak in 1925 and declining thereafter. The decline was not due to an overabundance of adequate housing but rather to the supply catching up to the effective demand for housing for those able to buy. Incidentally, public construction was stable throughout the period and did counterbalance the decline in the private sector.

Changes in business inventories are always observed as a phenomenon of—if not an explanation for—the business cycle. Both recessions in the 1920s clearly conform to expectations. Inventories collapsed in the downswings and rose in the upswings, but they never recovered to the level existing during the boom that began the decade.

Finally, investment in producers' durable goods should also exhibit the same procyclical behavior as was the case for the change in inventories. Again this is true of the 1920s. Yet overall, gross investment increased by over 51 percent from 1919 to 1929. In fact, with the exception of the 1920–21 cycle, spending on plant and equipment rose rather steadily and/or remained stable after 1923. Together with public construction spending, this boom helped to mask what was happening in the housing and consumer durable markets.

Table 3.4   Components of GNP, 1919–39

	GNP (in billions of 1929 dollars)					
Year	GNP	Consump-tion	Gross Investment	Foreign Sector	Govern-ment	Per Capita GNP
1919	74.2	50.2	10.7	3.5	9.7	481
1920	73.3	52.7	12.8	2.3	5.6	495
1921	71.6	56.1	7.4	1.5	6.5	517
1922	75.8	58.1	10.6	0.7	6.4	528
1923	85.8	63.4	15.6	0.5	6.3	567
1924	88.4	68.1	12.4	1.0	6.9	597
1925	90.5	66.1	16.4	0.7	7.4	571
1926	96.4	71.5	17.1	0.4	7.4	609
1927	97.3	73.2	15.6	0.7	7.9	615
1928	98.5	74.8	14.5	1.0	8.2	621
1929	104.4	78.9	16.2	0.8	8.5	648
Percent change, 1919–29	40.7	57.2	51.4	−77.1	−12.4	34.7

Sources: U.S. Department of Commerce, Bureau of the Census, Long-Term Economic Growth 1860–1965 (Washington, DC: GPO, 1966); idem, Historical Statistics of the United States (Washington, DC: GPO, 1975).

Total capital formation as a percent of national income increased sharply from 6.6 percent in 1922 to 11.5 percent in 1923. It fell in the recession year of 1927 to 7.7 percent and then resumed the 1923 rate or slightly lower until 1929.[18] The same trend is true for producers' durables, although there is much more stability over the years. Hence, the evidence does not support the assertion that tax reduction funds would flow into productive uses. In fact, there was considerable excess capacity in the U.S. economy in the 1925–29 period, amounting to about 20 percent.[19] Thus it is not surprising to find that the share of national income devoted to producers' plant and equipment remained stable during the same period.

On the other hand, individual saving helped to finance about one-half of the capital formation, while government contributed about one-sixth and business one-third. Yet these proportions were true before the tax cuts as well, and individual behavior did not change as a result of them. The available evidence is not overwhelming, and the actual effects of the tax cuts may never be fully known. It would appear, however, that much of the tax savings may have found its way into consumption expenditures and speculation. This can be surmised by examining the income share of the national income.

The issue of the tax-cut effects is intertwined with the larger question of who benefited during the period. Did the 1920s roar for everyone? One piece of evidence is that output per man hour increased over the period 1919–29 by over 26 percent and by over 72 percent for the manufacturing sector, but real wages rose by only 25 percent,[20] meaning that in many sectors, especially manufacturing, costs of production must have fallen. The evidence is scanty but does show the trend.[21] Since the consumer price index (CPI) did not fall nearly as much (−1 percent), it is clear that profits must have risen.

These trends, while hardly conclusive, are nevertheless consistent with more reliable evidence of the period. A look at GNP shares by income recipients reveals that property incomes rose dramatically over the period, by nearly 23 percent. Indeed, the share going to stockholders in the form of dividends increased by 60 percent from 1919 to 1929.[22] Meanwhile, employee compensation increased by only 3.6 percent.

Unfortunately, there are no data to construct a distribution of income by income classes in order to ascertain a corresponding trend in inequality. A highly regarded study of the incomes of the period does conclude, however, that "There has been a tendency, at least during the last decade or so, for the inequality in the distribution of income to be accentuated."[23] That is to say, while the incomes of the masses of the people were rising during this period, the incomes of those in the upper income levels increased with greater rapidity.

Summary and Conclusions

By any definition the 1920s was certainly a fascinating period. In so many areas one finds experimentation competing with regression, creating a period that will always be difficult to interpret. For the economist, the lack of data that are comparable to present data in both accuracy and detail often prohibits searching analysis, and whatever results are obtained are frequently impressionistic. Yet enough information is available to permit some conclusions and judgments concerning the changes in the economic system that occurred during that era and to suggest some of the consequences.

First, it is crucial to note that the economic system was functioning in a manner most favorable to the capitalist model. It would be difficult to find a period that was more receptive to the capitalist ideology. Government was not a problem but a help. There were few regulations on business; taxes were reduced; the budget showed surpluses; and the national debt was being retired. Indeed, the public sector championed the cause of a free enterprise, laissez-faire economy, and openly embraced the businessman and his ethics. Whenever the free-enterprise model faltered, government came to the rescue, as in the case of protective tariffs.

Private attitudes reinforced the public attitudes, confidence in the system was very high, and the hopes for the future were bright. Profits rose and were accepted as necessary for economic progress; wages also increased, productivity increased even faster, and costs fell. Prices were stable and posed no problem for economic agents.

Under these conditions the supply of resources was abundant and did not hinder economic growth. Unions were declining and becoming less militant. Funds were available to finance capital expenditures, and optimism was so pervasive that the new inventions that poured forth could find financial backing. Raw materials were readily available and at reasonable prices.[24]

In short, these are ideal conditions for the smooth functioning and development of the capitalist system. Any failures or shortcomings would be caused by the malfunctioning of the system itself and not by artificial restraints or unwarranted government interference and meddling.

Yet the economy did stumble in the 1920s and finally collapsed shortly thereafter. Despite the considerable gains achieved in elevating the standard of living in the United States, the economy fell victim to its own excesses. Thus the 1920s allowed a glimpse of the potential gains that could be achieved but also reminded us of the losses that always threaten to reverse them. The scourge of economic fluctuations, so easily forgotten in the euphoria of the boom, was not so easily removed.

With this background in mind and in keeping with the brevity of the discussion, let us examine the major macro policies of the era in terms of the questions posed in the introduction: Were they justified, successful, or rational?

The major public policy of the period was undoubtedly tax reduction. The tax cuts pushed through by Andrew Mellon would have been justified, given the prevailing economic orthodoxy of laissez-faire. Tax reductions return economic power to the private sector, diminish the control exerted by the public sector, and preserve the principle of maintaining economic freedom. The economic model of the times clearly would have sanctioned the shifts of control over economic resources.

In addition, the economic paradigm would have approved the resistance to unions, the repayment of the public debt, and the basic trust of monetary policy for much of the period. All efforts to remove restraints of trade and all attempts to make the system function smoothly would have been applauded. The model would not have approved of the protective tariff that once again was enacted. Free trade was the prevailing attitude toward international transactions.

There were no great social pressures to enact the tax cuts or to impose trade barriers. The pressures for these policies came from the business sector, which, as we know, had gained influence and power throughout the period. Indeed, the voices of the less fortunate were stifled, and they found their efforts at organization inhibited, sometimes by violations of their civil rights. Union meetings were disrupted, labor laws affecting women and children were reversed, and attempts at political control through a third party were thwarted.

The 1920s also saw the slow demise of the Progressive party that had championed the cause of equity and justice in the United States. With its disappearance went the hope of using the public sector to redress societal ills. Thus government spending was stable over the period and no major new programs were initiated. True, the economic model advocated a limited role for government spending and hence the failure to initiate new avenues for public involvement could be justified. Yet there was pressure in the early years for new health, education, and labor programs. The power to push these programs through was lacking, and the political system did not respond. Government was more responsive to the needs of the business sector. For example, to facilitate the use of the automobile, large expenditures were made on road building.

How successful were the policies followed? We have already seen that the tax cuts did not result in significant increases in investment expenditures. Surely some of the tax cuts aided some industries and thus contributed to the industrial boom. Yet much more was promised than helping marginal firms. The promised rechanneling of funds from unproductive to productive uses was not as robust as had been anticipated. No doubt much of the funds released from taxation found their way into speculation and conspicuous consumption.

Still, even the partial success of the tax cuts contributed to the feelings of optimism and of progress. Perhaps much more important than the policies themselves was the favorable climate provided by the political administrations of the period. Business firms were at least assured of a proper hearing and obviously were aware of the prevalent favorable attitudes toward the business sector. Combine these attitudes with the timely appearance of some far-reaching inventions and developments, such as the automobile and communications, and there would be sufficient grounds for an industrial boom, whatever government policies were pursued.

Furthermore, the knowledge of the business sector that whatever gains were achieved would not be eaten up by new social programs or meddling regulations must have been encouraging and worth the risks involved in any undertaking. The resistance to pressures for social programs made the business climate even more propitious.

The same can be inferred concerning the protective tariff. No doubt it, too, worked to protect domestic industries, at the expense of a revival of world trade, but even more, the tariff legislation once again confirmed the probusiness attitude of the government and reinforced the belief that business would find a helping hand whenever needed.

Monetary policy, ambiguous at times and perverse at others, also did little to dispel the probusiness attitudes. Nor did it act with vigor to reduce speculation or try to confront the excesses of banks that promoted it. The Federal Reserve's easy-money policy added fuel to the fire that was already out of control. The resulting low interest rates, deemed necessary to restore the gold standard, may have also induced firms to overexpand, and this overexpansion would later turn into excess capacity and help reverse the boom.

If we are now asked to examine the rationality of policies followed, it must be admitted that the policies adopted, even if they did not work exactly as predicted, still created the conditions and climate necessary for the desired results. The question is, Was this climate an intentional outcome or a byproduct of the policies? Clearly the evidence would support the conclusion that the creation of a favorable climate was deliberate. The policies, successful or not, added to the confidence of business leaders that the attitudes would be backed up by actions.

In terms of rationality the tax cuts can be viewed as necessary to convince business that the administrations meant what they said. The fight against estate and gift taxes really showed that the various administrations were committed to seeing that whatever gains were made would be permanent—embedded in an unequal distribution of wealth.

The attack on estate and gift taxation may have been the crowning achievement for Andrew Mellon and the one with the most far-reaching consequences. From that time on, the taxation of wealth in the United States has never been burdensome. Mellon's repeated attacks eventually removed the issue of wealth taxation from serious consideration as an alternative base for raising revenue. Mellon's assaults on wealth taxation could have forced the dwindling opposition to concentrate on income taxes, thereby achieving a possible unstated goal: the removal of wealth taxation from further debate for a long time. One can only speculate about his motives, but the results are not debatable. More simply, he may just have wanted to reduce taxes—all taxes—as an end in itself.

Yet the consequences of his efforts go well beyond the question of his motives. The concentration of the federal government on income as the base for raising revenue virtually assured that fiscal policy would become controversial. With an income tax, revenues now depend upon the state of economic activity, rising in booms or inflation, and falling in recessions and deflation. The fluctuations in tax revenues can be an asset, since they help stabilize the economy automatically. This automatic stabilizer would limit booms by transferring funds to the federal government from the private sector and would help cushion downswings by taking less out of the private sector. Private expenditures on goods and services were thus either curtailed or enhanced by a tax that varied with the level of economic activity.

This beneficial result of income taxation was appreciated as long as government expenditures were tightly controlled. Later, when expenditures on wars and on social programs grew and became entrenched, any slowdown in economic activity resulted in budget deficits. Since a sanguine view of budget deficits was never a part of the conservative economic model, one argument against government spending was easily provided. Fiscal policy would forever operate with this handicap and at times would be subject to attack on this score alone.

Had wealth become a major part of our taxation base, revenues may not have fluctuated so much and a more rational view of government spending may have emerged. Government programs would have been evaluated on their merits rather than on the effects on the budget; government planning would have been more feasible, since revenues would have been more stable; and, finally, more justice and equity would have been achieved in taxation that included wealth as well as income.

Permitting more rational government spending is not what an economic conservative wants, of course, since that would admit a useful role for the public sector. Making government revenues unstable would serve to limit and restrain politicians from expanding that role. Without overstating the case, there was a fundamental decision made in the 1920s in regard to the base for taxation that was to have repercussions for generations thereafter.

part II

The Great Depression
and World War II

chapter 4

The Great Depression

The 1920s began and ended in economic turmoil; the 1930s repeated that experience, but added political disruptions as well. The stock-market crash and its aftermath began the decade, and the push toward World War II ended it. In the United States, and indeed for most of the world, economic conditions came to dominate the concerns of everyone, overshadowing all other facets of life, and preoccupation with economics always signals severe disruptions.

The 1930s, unlike the 1920s, showed no sign of optimism of belief in progress. Instead, the belief in both the economic and political systems was severely shaken. Unable to reconcile or even account for the steady deterioration in the economy, many turned to alternative "isms" in the hope of finding a more secure and humane system; others began to realize the inherent instability brought about by advanced capitalism and industrialization and became bewildered. The very foundation of belief in how the world works was crumbling, and no one knew why or how to correct it.

At times like this a nation looks to its leaders for direction and inspiration. They look also to the institutions that were developed in better times to respond to fundamental and drastic changes in conditions. Instability is always difficult to live with, and it appears natural to look to the existing structure of society to resolve the conflicts between what has been and what is happening.

The economic decline was a national problem and affected every region of the country. Therefore the burden fell primarily to national leaders and institutions to respond and furnish direction. In the White

House was Herbert Hoover, the easy winner in 1928. Hoover was well respected as a self-made man, a mining engineer with a genius for administration and management and a worshiper of efficiency. He had handled food relief for Belgium and Europe prior to World War I admirably and then after the war became the director general of relief for the allies and food administrator for the American Relief Administration. He had gained a worldwide reputation for his humanitarian efforts on behalf of war victims.

Hoover was also a conservative but far from the stereotype image. As a Quaker, he found voluntary cooperation among people to be a sound guiding principle, and yet his family had embraced a variant of Quaker belief that stressed and favored individualism.[1] Thus cooperation and individualism would coexist in Hoover, sometimes making his policies appear contradictory. As secretary of commerce for most of the 1920s, he advocated farm cooperatives, public-works programs to combat unemployment, orderly development of radio airways without government ownership, censorship in advertising, reduction of the workweek and better treatment of labor, and, finally, better collection and organization of statistical information. All these programs (and more) were designed so that individuals would function better and make the economy more productive and efficient. As a technocrat, he followed the Veblen dictum that engineers could best run the economy and that managers simply made a mess of things. As a true conservative, he concluded that there was nothing wrong with capitalism, except for the capitalist: He was too greedy.

In the words of a biographer,

> Progressive American individualism, he [Hoover] said, meant the guarantee to all of equality of opportunity—the "fair chance" of Abraham Lincoln—so that the individual's place in the world would be determined by intelligence, character, ability, and hard work at the emery wheel of competition. To keep the system open, to discourage the formation of classes, and to protect the infirm, Americans also practiced "neighborly obligation and a higher sense of justice ... self-sacrifice and ... public conscience." Private enterprise worked as a vital, innovating force; but government had to eliminate greed and assure social justice.[2]

This is but a brief sketch of the complex man who sat in the White House promising the alleviation of poverty, but who was to preside over the most serious economic decline in U.S. history and the sharpest increase in the number of poor.

Economists were not very helpful either, as the prevailing economic paradigm did not include a reasonable response to a crisis of this kind. Hoover, who was fond of appointing special commissions, received the report of the President's Conference on Unemployment, *Recent Social Trends in the United States*, in early 1933. The scholars who contributed to the report revealed a great deal of uncertainty over the course of the depression and appeared reluctant to propose remedies. They did state, however, that governmental actions were required to combat the effects of this serious depression.[3]

Congressional leadership also appeared lacking. Not only were some senators, like Reed Smoot of Utah, tied up with other matters (tariffs), but progressives like Norris often pressed beyond the limits of Hoover's brand of progressivism. Hoover did not relish congressional politics and made scant effort to woo its practitioners. He became annoyed at Congress for its foot dragging and contrariness in regard to his policies. At other times, when Congress showed some initiative, such as in proposing relief programs, he became stubborn, intransigent, and defensive.

In short, the political leadership of the period was ill prepared for such a crisis and was not helped by the confused intellectual voices of the era. This situation must be constantly kept in mind in the evaluation of the responses to the onset of the depression. It is easy in retrospect to condemn this action or that or to puzzle over the resistance to one policy or another, but the economic and social upheavals were different from the experiences of past fluctuations. The timid or inappropriate responses that now appear obvious must be measured against the prevailing economic theory and orthodoxy, in which such an economic decline could not happen, and gauged against a social philosophy that espoused individual responsibility in the face of societal disruptions.

Economic Profile of the 1930s

Before turning to the actual policies adopted to meet the crisis, a brief profile of the decade is necessary. The economy reached a peak in August 1929 and then fell to a trough in March 1933. The slow recovery took the economy to a new peak in May 1937 when the "recession within a depression" caused national income to fall to the trough of June 1938. Another recovery took the economy to the wartime peak of February 1945.

Table 4.1 shows the dramatic drop in output over the period 1929–39. The peak level of GNP in current dollars occurred in 1929 and was never matched again in the decade; GNP in 1958 dollars did

Table 4.1   Gross National Product, 1929–39

| Year | Actual GNP | GNP in 1958 Dollars | | Per Capita GNP in 1958 Dollars |
		Amount	Percent Change	
1929	103.1	203.6	—	1,671
1930	90.4	183.5	−9.9	1,490
1931	75.8	169.3	−7.7	1,364
1932	58.0	144.2	−14.8	1,154
1933	55.6	141.5	−1.9	1,126
1934	65.1	154.3	+9.0	1,220
1935	72.2	169.5	+9.9	1,331
1936	82.5	193.0	+13.9	1,506
1937	90.4	203.2	+5.3	1,576
1930	84.7	192.9	−5.1	1,484
1939	90.5	209.4	+8.6	1,598
Percent change, 1929–39	−12.2	—	2.8	−4.3

Source: U.S. Department of Commerce, Bureau of the Census, Long-Term Economic Growth 1860–1965 (Washington, DC: GPO, 1966).

return to the 1929 level, reflecting the increase in output in 1939. Real GNP fell steadily to the low in 1933, a drop of over 31 percent. Then it increased by over 38 percent in the recovery period until the recession of 1937–38, after which it increased by enough to surpass the initial 1929 level by some 2.8 percent.

The tragic loss of output over this period and some sense of the deprivation involved can be observed by noting the decline in per capita GNP of over 4.3 percent from 1929. The population increased at a rate of 7.5 percent, while real GNP grew by only 2.8 percent. In 1929 the U.S. population was 121.9 million, and by 1939 it had grown to 130.9 million.

Even more troublesome was the growth of the labor force in the same period. The labor force grew from 49.4 million in 1929 to 55.6 million in 1939, an increase of over 12.6 percent. With output fluctuating while the population and labor force were growing, it is clear that the impact on workers was bound to be severe. Table 4.2 shows the essential details.

The severity of the decline in economic activity is clearly revealed by the unemployment rate. From a low of 3.2 percent in 1929, the rate climbed to a staggering 25 percent of the labor force in 1933. The unemployment rate declined thereafter, except for the temporary setback in 1939, but still it stood at 17.2 percent in 1939; using just the unemployment rate as an indicator, the depression was certainly not over in 1939.

It is also interesting to note that in the face of such massive unemployment, output per hour in manufacturing continued to rise until, by the end of the period, it was 25.8 percent above the rate in 1929. Obviously the most productive workers were retained, and working with the most efficient capital goods, they were able to increase output per hour worked. The threat of unemployment might have worked to enhance the efficiency of those who remained employed; they must have been pressured to produce and might have willingly acquiesced, for the alternative was all too visible. Yet this

TABLE 4.2   The Labor Force, Productivity, and Unemployment, 1929–39

Year	Labor Force (millions)	Unemployment Rate	Output per Hour in Manufacturing (1929 = 100)	Union Membership as a Percentage of the Labor Force
1929	49.4	3.2	100.0	—
1930	50.0	8.7	100.7	6.8
1931	50.7	15.9	103.9	6.5
1932	51.3	23.6	97.1	6.0
1933	51.8	24.9	105.7	5.2
1934	52.5	21.7	110.4	5.9
1935	53.1	20.1	117.6	6.7
1936	53.7	16.9	118.5	7.4
1937	54.3	14.3	116.9	12.9
1938	55.0	19.0	114.9	14.6
1939	55.6	17.2	125.8	15.8
Percent change, 1929–39	12.6	437.5	25.8	132.4

Sources: U.S. Department of Commerce, Bureau of the Census, *Long-Term Economic Growth 1860–1965* (Washington, DC: GPO, 1966); and idem, *Historical Statistics of the United States* (Washington, DC: GPO, 1975).

fear may not have been the whole explanation, since the same increase in productivity is found in the agricultural sector—19.5 percent over the same period.

The inferior position of labor is also evidenced in the decline in union membership. Organized labor had been set back in the 1920s as aggressive employers sought to break union strength and began the movement to substitute capital for labor in the production process. Led by old-time leaders of the AFL, unions began to lose membership, and the trend continued into the depression. The reason the decline in numbers is not greater is that some unions, representing teachers, office clerks, and actors, were gaining in membership and offsetting the declines in construction, transportation, and textiles. In 1935 the decline was reversed, and union membership increased steadily until it stood at 132.4 percent above its 1930 level.

The reversal was fostered by the New Deal in its National Recovery Act (NRA) codes that encouraged collective bargaining and also by the birth and growth of the Congress of Industrial Organization (CIO), which began about that time. The discussion of these institutions is better left to responses to the depression and was inserted here so that some comparisons of the growth of union membership can be made with the growth of unemployment.

The effects of the depression on wages and prices are given in Table 4.3. Looking at wage rates first, the decline mirrors the pattern of all other series, falling (by 21.4 percent) to lows in 1932 and 1933, and thereafter rising, with some retardation in 1937 or 1938. Over the period, however, average hourly earnings of productive workers in manufacturing increased by 12.6 percent. All prices fell to lows in 1932 or 1933; the implicit price index or GNP deflator fell by 22.3 percent, the wholesale price index (WPI) by 31.7 percent, the CPI by 24.5 percent, and stock prices by 73.5 percent. Prices rose during the 1937–38 recession and afterwards fell slightly. In brief, prices and the wages of at least one important segment of the labor force followed the cyclical behavior observed in many other series.

To complete this profile of the depression, it is necessary to note only that most series conformed to the cyclical behavior shown above: That is, they reached lows in the 1932–33 period, gradually returned to previous levels or rates, were disrupted again by the recession of 1937–38, and again were returning to previous norms when the decade ended. This is true for gross investment, industrial production, the stock of money, corporate profits, and, to a lesser extent, net exports, mergers, and the industrial failure rate. It is not true for the federal budget, federal debt, private debt, or bond yields. These latter series may reflect the pursuit of public policies and will be discussed in the next section.

Table 4.3   Wages and Prices, 1929–39

Year	Average Hourly Earnings in Manufacturing	Implicit Price Index (1958 = 100)	WPI (1957–59 = 100)	CPI (1957–59 = 100)	Stock Prices (1941–43 = 100)
1929	0.56	50.6	52.1	59.7	26.0
1930	0.55	49.3	47.3	58.2	21.0
1931	0.51	44.8	39.9	53.0	13.7
1932	0.44	40.2	35.6	47.6	6.9
1933	0.44	39.3	36.1	45.1	9.0
1934	0.53	42.2	41.0	46.6	9.8
1935	0.54	42.6	43.8	47.8	10.6
1936	0.55	42.7	44.2	48.3	15.5
1937	0.62	44.5	47.2	50.0	15.4
1938	0.62	43.9	43.0	49.1	11.5
1939	0.63	43.2	42.2	48.4	12.1
Percent change, 1929–39	12.6	−14.6	−19.0	−18.9	−53.5

Sources: U.S. Department of Commerce, Bureau of the Census, *Long-Term Economic Growth 1860–1965* (Washington, DC: GPO, 1966); and idem, *Historical Statistics of the United States* (Washington, DC: GPO, 1075).

The Hoover Administration's Response to the Depression

In general, the slide into the cyclical trough of March 1933 corresponds to the latter half of the Hoover administration. It is time to look more closely into that descent and the administration's response to it.

As real GNP fell by 9.9 percent in 1930 and by 7.7 percent in 1931, and as the economy slowly sank into the depths of the depression, Hoover's actions seemed contradictory. Perhaps his native optimism prevented him from accurately assessing the extent of the downturn following an equally unpredicted crash in the stock market. He first attributed the economic decline to overoptimism as to profits in the period of progress, and this mood carried over into the stock market, where overspeculation occurred. As speculation continued, capital was diverted from productive uses to the stock market. When the bubble burst, consumption fell, unemployment increased, and so on.

Clearly, this situation would reverse itself in time, and this temporary disruption would be corrected. The temporary nature of the decline was to be a recurring theme in Hoover's pronouncements. Combine this forecast with his deeply held conviction that there would be a movement toward voluntary cooperation, which was always desirable to make capitalism function properly and humanely anyway, and it is easy to appreciate his initial reactions.

He responded quickly and convened the Conference for Continued Industrial Progress, made up of leaders from business, finance, utilities, agriculture, labor, and the Federal Reserve. He presented this group with four areas where cooperation was necessary: no strikes, no reduction in wages until consumer prices fell (to help keep consumption high), work sharing where possible, and employer-sponsored relief programs where possible. In short the first shock should fall as much as possible on profits. This scheme for voluntary cooperation had some impact, mainly because the nation's leading business leaders endorsed it.[4] It could not survive the drastic decline that followed.

To bolster confidence, he asked Congress for additional appropriations for public works and at the same time asked the states and localities to speed up their capital projects. Always a believer in cooperation, he also appealed to corporations to increase their outlays for capital goods, and even homeowners were encouraged to make home repairs.

Yet confidence was the very thing he never could inspire. He had a poor relationship with the press, caused by a basic sensitivity and shyness that made him wary of confrontations. His public stances on matters relating to the depression seemed cold and casual. In his first message to Congress in December 1929 he appeared to treat the matter in an offhand manner by barely mentioning it directly and then only to point to the initiatives made to restore confidence. He reiterated the need for a balanced budget and his belief that the federal government should not get involved in the provision of social services, but should leave those actions to localities and private philanthropy. His relationship with Congress was also uneven, and he frequently distrusted it. Unable to deal with political controversy, this efficient engineer preferred to work independently in solving problems. Often he became stubborn, even in the face of incontrovertible evidence.

Perhaps his intransigence and stubborness is no more evident than in the matter of relief for suffering families, many on the brink of starvation. At times he simply refused to acknowledge that people were starving. "Nobody is actually starving. The hoboes, for example, are better fed than they have ever been. One hobo in New York got ten meals in one day."[5] And at other times he believed that neighbors would help each other out by volunteering their money and efforts to solve these private concerns. Government-sponsored relief programs would ruin the sense of community and destroy personal liberty, as happens whenever private obligations are transferred to the state.[6]

Here was the acknowledged world's expert in administering relief programs, in Europe and Russia, and also an acknowledged humanitarian who labored so diligently in the cause of the unfortunate, now denying any program for domestic residents. He was not alone in his distaste for the public dole, but when things deteriorated, he continued to resist a relief program and even accused a group of senators who were pressing for one in December 1930 of "playing politics at the expense of human misery." Hoover's ambivalence on the relief issue remains an enigma, but perhaps some explanation can be found in the distinction he may have made between relief programs to aid the victims of war and those designed for economic breakdowns. Governments may have a greater degree of responsibility for wartime tragedies, while people as individuals must bear the burden of providing aid when the source of the difficulty is domestic.

The ideology of laissez-faire embraced by Hoover and twisted in his peculiar reconciliation of it with voluntary cooperation did not extend to questions of free trade. In June 1929 he called a special session of Congress to deal with the possibility of some limited revisions in duties on agricultural goods. He suggested that duties be raised on agricultural commodities and possibly some manufactured goods as well. The special session lasted until December, when it merged into the regular one, and eventually the tariff bill that emerged, known as the Hawley–Smoot Tariff Act, was passed in June 1930.

There was no pressure for a tariff revision, and it was not an issue in the 1928 campaign. Coolidge and Hoover, however, had opposed export bounties to farmers in prior bills, and their opposition had caused great bitterness and anger. Given this opportunity for relief, Congress seized the chance to play politics. Led by Senator Reed Smoot of Utah and Senator Joseph Grundy of Pennsylvania and others, the two branches of Congress vied with each other in destroying the meaning of "limited revisions" to tariff duties.

The duties on agricultural products were increased without regard for costs, as provided in other tariffs; without regard for society, as in the case of hog duties, since hogs were mainly exported; and without regard for effects, since sugar duties were increased dramatically despite the fact that most farmers were consumers of the product, not producers.

Not to be outdone, congressmen from manufacturing states began to protect their interests, and duties on many manufactured goods were imposed without regard as to whether those industries were depressed. In a shameless display of logrolling, duties on some goods were granted provided duties on others were granted. The end result was that the conference committee reconciled two bulky bills filled with amendments, and the monster they finally produced was simply a disaster. Agricultural duties went from 19.86 percent in 1922 to 33.62 percent in 1930, cotton from 40.27 percent to 46.42 percent, and among many curiosities—men's straw hats went from 60 percent to 150 percent, fireworks duties were 135 percent of value, women's gloves went from 70 percent to 140 percent, and so on.[7]

Mr. Hoover, who failed to give direction to Congress, was now forced to sign the measure or risk political problems later. Economists, represented by 1,000 members of the American Economic Association, voiced opposition to the tariff bill, but were not heard in the frenzy of protectionism.

The result was soon evident. The United States as a world leader had shown the way (even when imports were falling). Its example was followed by many other nations with a wide variety of protectionist measures, and gradually world trade began to break down. The depression would become worldwide, thanks in no small measure to the Hawley–Smoot Tariff Act. Yet Hoover might also be responsible for the protectionist mood, for by this time he was blaming the depression on other countries of the world. They had overproduced (raw materials) according to him, and their subsequently depressed economies were unable to buy from others, thus transmitting their depressed condition to others.

Thus did the United States contribute to the spread of the depression, but failed to grasp the importance of one of the causes of the depression in the first place. Following World War I, when the United States emerged as a world financial leader, unwillingness to import meant that other countries had difficulty repaying their war debts and rebuilding their economies. Struggling to maintain or reestablish the gold standard, many nations were forced to depreciate their currencies and enact tariffs, quotas, and other trade barriers to reduce the outflow of capital. The passage of the Hawley–Smoot Tariff Act continued the perverse U.S. trade policy and doomed worldwide cooperative action.

Yet the ever-ambivalent Hoover was capable of heroic acts of leadership. However much the Hawley–Smoot Tariff Act had embarrassed him, he showed his ability to understand when innovative moves were necessary. With the depression it became clear that

European countries could not pay their war debts, even after they had been reduced by the Young Plan in 1929. To add to the repayment problem, funds were being withdrawn from European banks in search of safer areas for investment. The potential financial collapse was nowhere more evident than in Austria and Germany. In Austria the largest bank, the Kreditanstalt, declared it could no longer maintain operations, and despite attempts to rescue it, was forced to reorganize. The result was panic as fears of more bank defaults spread. In Germany the situation became critical. Forced to borrow short-term at high interest rates to finance reconstruction, many banks could not repay their loans and creditors refused to renew them. Widespread default would have had massive repercussions in general on British and U.S. loans in particular.

In June Hoover acted and proposed a one-year moratorium on all intergovernmental loans, war debts, and reparations. He considered this move for some weeks before overcoming his own fear that the money saved would go for armaments.[8] Besides, there was the popular notion, which he shared, that war debts should be repaid, and thus he risked political capital as well. This bold move was hailed, however, and Congress ratified the decision in December. Panic was averted for a while, and only France was worried that the German reparations would not be resumed and had to be talked into a "standstill agreement" that delayed short-term repayments of Germany from July 1931 to February 1932. The standstill agreement extended the moratorium to private loans by private bankers.

Timely as Hoover's actions were, they could not prevent the failure of a large German bank (Danatbank) and the German reaction to it. Germany declared a policy of bank protection (similar to our bank holiday), which severely curtailed banking activities.[9] Now bank failures in Hungary, Romania, and soon Amsterdam followed. Banks in Amsterdam had invested heavily in Germany, and they began to draw heavily on London banks. Then London came under attack, as anticipated devaluations resulted in speculation in gold and eventually to withdrawals of gold when Britain sank into depression.

Despite attempts by the United States and France to rescue Britain and the plea of Prime Minister Ramsay MacDonald to halt the damaging practices, Britain was forced off the gold standard on September 20, 1931.[10] Within six months 42 countries followed, and only a handful, including the Unites States, remained on the gold standard. Now the race was on for each nation to increase tariffs and compete in exchange depreciation to bolster their exports. Private loans between countries had to be renegotiated in this mutually destructive atmosphere.

Attention also shifted to the United States, and the raid on the dollar began. The United States lost gold in the process and also some of its ability to export in a world with rapidly depreciating currencies. Later we can examine the Federal Reserve's response to these events. Once again the subject of war debts and reparations became critical. The Lausanne Conference in July 1932 absolved Germany from reparations, following fears that unless this were done, Germany might fall into dictatorship. France continued to balk, but England was willing to agree, providing war debts to the United States were also forgiven. The agreement at Lausanne was never ratified, in view of U.S. intransigence on war debts. When Hoover left office, only a few countries were current on their war-debt installments, with many others (hoping for Hoover's defeat), including France, in default.

The Problem of Agriculture

In the presidential campaign Hoover promised to address the problem of agriculture. The chronic problem of agriculture for most of the decade of the 1920s was overproduction, and now at the onset of the depression, demand was falling still farther. In addition, most farms in the nation were of the family type, and many of these were barely at the subsistence level. Indeed, the Census of 1930 revealed that "49 percent of our 6 million farms yielded only 11 percent of the total farm product which was sold in the market. On the other hand, a bare 1.5 percent of our farms at the top of the list produced 18 percent."[11] There apparently was a good deal of excess capacity in agriculture, and over half a million farm laborers were redundant. Clearly these factors spelled the decline in agriculture and farm incomes, and Hoover promised some relief.

Table 4.4 tells the agriculture story. While farm production, productivity, and population remained steady or grew slightly, income from farming began to fall by two-thirds from 1929 to 1932. Furthermore, the prices paid by farmers fell slowly over this period, by over 30 percent, while prices received by farmers fell even more, by 56 percent. Wholesale prices of farm products fell over 54 percent from 1929 to 1932 and never did recover to the 1929 level in the decade of the 1930s. Exports collapsed as well, due in part to the effects of tariffs and other trade restrictions, and in part to the increase in competition in world markets.

The relief came out of the same special session that produced the Hawley–Smoot Tariff Act; the Agricultural Marketing Act was signed

Table 4.4   Agricultural Sector, Selected Series, 1929–39

Year	Prices Received by Farmers (1957–59 = 100)	Prices Paid by Farmers (1957–59 = 100)	Farm Production (1957–59 = 100)	Farm Output per Man Hour (1957–59 = 100)	Farm Population as Percent of Total Population	Net Income per Farmer ($)	Wholesale Price Index: Farm Products (1926 = 100)	Exports of Crude Food (millions of dollars)
1929	61	55	62	28	25.2	945	104.9	270
1930	52	52	61	28	24.9	651	88.3	179
1931	36	44	66	30	24.9	506	64.8	127
1932	27	38	64	30	25.2	304	48.2	89
1933	29	37	59	28	25.8	379	51.4	48
1934	37	41	51	27	25.5	431	65.3	59
1935	45	42	61	31	25.3	775	78.8	59
1936	47	42	55	29	24.8	639	80.9	58
1937	51	45	69	33	24.2	905	86.4	105
1938	40	42	67	35	23.8	668	68.5	249
1939	39	42	68	35	23.5	685	65.3	111

Sources: U.S. Department of Commerce, Bureau of the Census, *Historical Statistics of the United States* (Washington, DC: GPO, 1975), pp. 200, 889; and U.S. Department of Agriculture.

into law on June 15, 1929. This remarkable piece of legislation not only revealed the perpetual battle within Hoover over the role of government but served as a model for many of the New Deal programs that were to follow. In the realm of public policy, this was truly a revolutionary change.

The act created the Federal Farm Board, which was to assist farmers in restructuring the marketing system for farm output. Specifically, it encouraged the formation of cooperatives that would be voluntary arrangements to rationalize farm marketing. Hoover's ideals were clearly embodied here in the operation as well. There were to be no fees or taxes on farmers; the government would not directly buy, sell, or fix prices, and would not encourage increasing output.[12] The cooperatives themselves would stabilize prices and reduce output by their distributional practices—purchasing, storing, and processing.

The act appropriated $500 million to be used as a fund for making loans to cooperative organizations. Farmers were quick to join, as loans or advances were promised equal to 90 percent of the crops' current market value pending final sale. Gradually the cooperatives gained control over commodities. When the stock market crashed, the Farm Board was promised enough in loan funds to stabilize the prices of cotton and wheat. It then went on to stabilize the other major crops as well.

As part of its mission, the board wanted to stabilize all aspects of farm production and encourage regional and national organizations of cooperatives. The Farmers National Grain Corporation and the Cotton Stabilization Corporation were two of the leading examples, but there were others in wool and live stock. These organizations were forerunners of those envisioned in the National Recovery Act (NRA) of the New Deal.

The difficulty with the program was that it encouraged farmers to join the co-ops, but then stabilized prices above the equilibrium price, and the result was to encourage output and soon surpluses began building up. Despite attempts to reduce farm production by tying loans to acreage reduction, little was accomplished in reducing supply. Buying up land and retiring it was a solution, but there were no funds, and the cooperatives began losing some control over supply as the depression deepened. Even the severe drought in the Middle Atlantic States and in the Ohio and Mississippi valleys did not reduce output sufficiently to matter very much. As prices fell, dumping the surpluses would have made things worse. Surplus wheat and cotton were given to the Red Cross; some wheat was sold to China and Germany in exchange for bonds; and some wheat was exchanged for coffee from

Brazil. On August 31 the board began to advocate the plowing under of cotton and perhaps the killing of pigs as well. (Hoover agreed.)

The depression was simply too much for the concept of cooperatives to deal with in the initial stages of their development. That they worked for a time is evidenced by the profits made by the Grain Corporation and in the salvation of some farms. The Chamber of Commerce and Bernard Baruch denounced the scheme as Communistic, but for Hoover it was a realization of the dream of the marriage between voluntarism and capitalism. That is, private organizations operating with public funds did not conflict with his notion of laissez-faire and government intervention. Perhaps he never let such conflicts arise in his thinking.

Whether or not a fully developed scheme of cooperatives and national organizations would have worked better had they developed in an era different from the early 1930s is problematic. In this period they were not successful in stabilizing prices or rationalizing output. The depression never gave them the opportunity to experiment or grow with experience.

Life on the farms became increasingly difficult, as farmers borrowed more heavily on mortgages and as property taxes became more burdensome. Congress approved more funds to allow farmers to borrow from agricultural credit companies that received funds from the RFC. Still, the rate of forced sales of farms increased from 19.5 per 1,000 farms in 1929 to 54.1 per 1,000 farms in 1933. The value of farm real estate fell by one-third, and the real burden of their increasingly mortgaged farms went up. Early promises of relief were evaporating and prospects for the future in farming appeared bleak.

The Reconstruction Finance Corporation

Another extraordinary example of Hoover's basic philosophy of voluntary cooperation clashing with the will of those unwilling to cooperate can be found in the evolution of the Reconstruction Finance Corporation (RFC). Hoover naturally did not want to see government bailing out private-sector firms, but sincerely desired industry leaders to erect their own institutions to address their own problems.

Thus he asked New York's financial leaders in October 1931 to design a private system of insuring deposits before the government was forced to do so. A government-sponsored scheme apparently was what the bankers really wanted, however, and the threat fell on deaf ears. Whether or not the bankers considered Hoover naive, they did manage to construct a private organization called the National Credit Corporation with funds enabling loans of up to a billion dollars to banks in difficulty. The private agency failed in very short order, because it initially was unnecessarily conservative in its policies, and when it became more liberal with its funds, it was too late. The corporation was reluctant to make loans to small banks and with its limited funds was unable to cope with the downslide in the economy as the end of 1931 approached.[13]

Putting aside his personal fears of business entering into government and of its subverting representative government and individualism, Hoover asked Congress to resurrect the War Finance Corporation (WFC) that worked so well (to allocate funds) in World War I. The name was later changed to the Reconstruction Finance Corporation, perhaps to emphasize the emergency nature of the institution. The RFC Act was passed in January 1932, giving the corporation $500 million in capital with the power to borrow $1.5 billion (later increased to $3.5 billion) in securities fully guaranteed by the federal government.

The RFC was originally empowered to lend to banks, insurance companies, savings and loan associations, agricultural credit institutions, and railroads. Later it was authorized to lend to state and local governments, and then to other institutions as well. The loans were supposed to be self-liquidating and very businesslike, which would obviously meet with Hoover's approval.

The RFC was criticized by many as an experiment in "state socialism" or fascism, or as an abuse of federal power. Even Hoover remained uneasy with this new institution, but it had the potential for helping an economic system in distress. A more disturbing criticism that bothered Hoover was the charge that the RFC was a "breadline for business," while the deprivation of the unemployed and starving went unnoticed. Hoover replied that it was necessary to get the economy moving again and this method would succeed. Yet he continued making speeches denying that starvation was actually occurring or that the suffering was a bad as purported. The efficient technician simply could not confront the human consequences of the breakdown in the economic system.

The RFC was headed by Eugene Meyer, whom Hoover had appointed to the Federal Reserve Board, and included Charles Dawes as chairman and others as members of the governing staff. In retrospect these may not have been the wisest choices, since both were involved with the banking industry, and (after he had resigned from the board) a bank that Dawes had developed received a loan from the RFC. Although perfectly legal, the episode created the atmosphere of a scandal and tainted the RFC.

The RFC granted loans of over $1.4 billion in the period of Hoover's presidency and nearly all of it, $1.1 billion, was loaned to banks, trust companies, and savings and loan associations. Obviously the RFC felt its main goal was to rescue the banking system by providing needed credit so that more loans could be made to business and consumers. The loans might have slowed down the rate of bank failures, but, as will be seen, they could not prevent the eventual collapse.

Thus the RFC seemed willing to socialize the losses of business in the hope that the benefits would trickle down to aid the general public. The New Deal, which was to continue the RFC, socialized the losses of individuals for the preservation of the society. In any case, the losses were too much for the private sector, and nowhere was this more evident than in questions of direct relief.[14]

The architect of several relief programs, Hoover still insisted that private charity must come to the aid of the distressed, lest the handouts deprive the poor of their incentive to help themselves. Anyway, federal programs would destroy any possibility of a balanced budget. Private philanthropy must do the job, or lacking that, the states and localities must shoulder the burden. As the economy sank, it soon became evident that private philanthropy would be insufficient for the task. With massive unemployment and with few social programs in place, private charity was woefully inadequate. States and localities did attempt to meet the deteriorating conditions by providing public-service jobs, but lack of funds, mostly from nonpublic sources anyway, soon curtailed the effort. Similarly, local welfare offices, jammed with applicants, tried to keep up with the demand with limited funds. Social workers were in despair and pleaded for federal relief funds. Relief was spread thin; some received nothing at all and many blacks and minorities were forced to fend for themselves.[15]

Still, the administration and Congress continued to deny the extent of the suffering and managed to defeat the Costigan–La Follette bill for federal relief in 1932. Perhaps the hunger marches on Washington in December 1931 had some effect, for some actions were taken on the relief front in 1932. The Farm Board dispersed surplus wheat to the unemployed as a first step toward federal relief. Then Hoover replaced Meyer as head of the RFC with a Democrat, Atlee Pomerene. The Democrats were urging the RFC to get involved with direct relief. Thanks to the efforts of Senator Robert Wagner, the RFC was granted $300 million to make loans to states for relief and public works, including slum clearance and low-cost housing. The funds were slowly disbursed, and when Hoover left office, only $210 million had been spent.

The same can be said of efforts to create jobs through public-works projects. From the San Francisco–Oakland Bay bridge to Jones Beach on Long Island, and other projects such as sewage systems, railway bridges, and electric transmissions lines, only $20 million had been loaned. How many jobs were created to ease unemployment was questionable, especially compared to the costs of direct relief.

Prompted mainly by the plight of farmers, Hoover pressed for some sort of mortgage discount banks to lend to savings and loan associations and savings banks with home mortgages as collateral to prevent foreclosures. The Federal Home Loan Bank bill emerged after some time with $125 million in RFC funds. Again excessive caution resulted in a high interest rate on loans, 7 percent, and as a consequence, only $37 million had been loaned during Hoover's tenure.

Hoover also attempted to rationalize the operations of the railroad industry by consolidating them into four lines (systems). The plan was resisted by all factions, and what finally developed was simply $300 million in RFC funds for the Railway Credit Corporation.

This pattern continued throughout Hoover's tenure: He would make bold proposals (for him), but little more than RFC loans was accomplished. There is no need to catalog every attempt to respond to problems. Suffice it to say that all of his efforts fell short and counted for little in the general evaluation of his performance as president. The general perception of him at the time and subsequently was that he favored the rich and ignored the poor, that he remained indifferent to the widespread suffering of the many, but responded to business concerns and business interests.

Remarkable as his programs were and pathbreaking as they would become in retrospect, he was simply unable to break out of his intellectual binds to propose equally bold social programs. This shy man, with his peculiar brand of individualism that included voluntary cooperation, was not prepared for the severity of the crisis. Since no one else was either, Hoover was and has been much maligned for not doing more.

Yet the depression was not his fault, and he did respond within the limits of his personal philosophy, as well as within the generally accepted economic and social wisdom of his time. He became a convenient scapegoat for the unprecedented conditions that had everyone bewildered. It is time to follow the general confusion to its impact on fiscal and monetary policies.

Fiscal Policy

In keeping with the administration's predictions that the downturn was only temporary, Hoover and Mellon proposed a tax cut on 1929 incomes for taxes payable in 1930. The individual normal rates were temporarily reduced from 1.5, 3, and 5 percent to 0.5, 2, and 4 percent, and corporation income tax was reduced from 12 to 11 percent. These fiscal moves were acceptable to the administration because the budget showed a surplus and because higher expenditures were not antici-pated. Congress quickly passed a bill in December 1929 with only a few dissenting.

Apparently this move toward stimulation was tolerable as long as the balanced-budget philosophy was not being challenged. About a year later Secretary Mellon was back, warning that these temporary reductions could not be continued in the face of the continued downslide in the economy. Congress ignored his warnings and adjourned in March 1931, as usual, without acting on matters of taxation.

The administration's complacency was not shattered even when tax receipts from the depressed economy fell by 40 percent from a year earlier and expenditures were $300 million over estimates. The projected deficit, it was argued, could be controlled, if Congress agreed to keep expenditures down and ignore pleas for assistance. The Treasury could finance its budget by short-term loans, and everyone accepted the premise upon which this policy rested, namely, a short-lived depression.

As the months passed, the prospect of a larger and more distressing budget deficit confronted the administration. First, Secre-tary Mellon, and then his successor, Ogden Mills, began to urge a tax increase in order to balance the budget. The fiscal year 1931 was about to end with the first deficit in 11 years of close to one-half million dollars. The federal debt would increase rather than fall, as it had over the same 11 years. Since the balanced budget was financial dogma in this year, something had to be done.

Urging expenditure reductions, the administration began press-ing for a general sales tax, since the small income tax was paid by only a few and was subject to fluctuations according to business conditions. One should recall that it was this administration and the previous one that had reduced the income-tax rates and had tried to eliminate wealth as a tax base. In any case, an excise tax was proposed to make up for the shortfall in tax revenues. The deficit must have been a major concern, for 1932 was an election year, and tax increases in hard times are never popular. Thus the administration continued to resist higher taxes, even as the deficit mounted, but was testing the waters by proposing a sales tax.

Members of Congress reacted as might be expected, with some—for example, Senator David Reed of Pennsylvania—advocating a general sales tax, while progressives, such as Congressman Fiorello LaGuardia of New York, urged income-tax increases and excise taxes on luxuries. When Congress convened again in December 1931, some tax increase appeared inevitable, although Hoover's message made no specific proposals.

By this time the estimated budget deficit for 1932 was over $2 billion. Secretary Mellon continued to press for excise taxes, small increases in income and estate taxes, and an increase in postal rates. Later, as budget-deficit forecasts continued gloomy, the administration added consumption taxes on gasoline, telephones, and electricity and a small increase in corporate income taxes.

The House Committee on Ways and Means, despite widespread opposition, decided to recommend a general sales tax along the lines of the manufacturing sales tax levied in Canada, rather than impose excise taxes on specific commodities. The full House later rejected the sales tax overwhelmingly and instead opted for excise taxes closer to the administration's wishes. It also agreed on a tariff on coal and oil imports that was pushed by representatives from states where these commodities were important. The Senate also wrestled with the tariff and the sales-tax questions. Despite prolonged debate, the bill that emerged was close to the House version, and the conferees had little difficulty in reconciling the two.

Individual income-tax increases saw a return to nearly wartime rates as the base for taxation was widened. From a normal rate of 1.5 percent on the first $4,000 and gradual increases thereafter, the rate jumped to 4 percent on the first $4,000 and 8 percent thereafter. The surtax began at 1 percent in excess of $6,000 and rose in steps to a maximum of 55 percent on incomes over $1 million. The total maximum rate became 63 percent (8 percent normal and 55 percent surtax) on net incomes over $1 million, up sharply from the 1928 maximum rate of 25 percent. Personal exemptions were reduced from $1,500 to $1,000 for single individuals and from $3,500 to $2,500 for married couples.

The corporate income tax was increased slightly from 12 percent to 13.75 percent, and some exemptions and deductions were removed. A graduated estate tax that nearly doubled the rates was imposed, revising the act of 1926. To prevent the escape from high estate taxes, a gift tax was imposed with a flat-rate deduction of $50,000 and rates ranging from 0.75 percent on net gifts in excess of $10,000 to a

Table 4.5   Federal Government Finances, 1928–39

Fiscal Year	Budget Receipts	Budget Expenditures	Surplus or Deficit (−)	Federal Debt (calendar year)
1928	3,900	2,961	939	17,604
1929	3,862	3,127	734	16,931
1930	4,058	3,320	738	16,185
1931	3,116	3,577	−462	16,801
1932	1,924	4,659	−2,735	19,487
1933	1,997	4,598	−2,602	22,539
1934	3,015	6,645	−3,630	27,053
1935	3,706	6,497	−2,791	28,701
1936	3,997	8,421	−4,425	33,779
1937	4,956	7,733	−2,777	36,425
1938	5,588	6,765	−1,177	37,165
1939	4,979	8,841	−3,862	40,440

Source: U.S. Department of Commerce, Bureau of the Census, Historical Statistics of the United States (Washington, DC: GPO, 1975), p. 1104.

maximum of 33.5 percent on amounts in excess of $10 million. The 72nd Congress was accused of trying to "soak the rich" by these measures, but the Revenue Act of 1932 clearly extended the tax base as well. The act, when it was signed into law and became effective on June 6, 1932, produced the largest tax increase in peacetime in the nation's history to that date.

Unfortunately, the depression saw to it that there would be no balanced budget, as tax receipts continued to fall. Tax receipts from the tax bill were clearly overestimated. Table 4.5 shows what happened to budget receipts, expenditures, and the national debt.

Following 1930, budget receipts fell short of budget expenditures, and inevitably deficits rose, as did the national debt. Hoover and Mills continued to urge the necessity of a balanced budget, since excessive borrowing by government would depress bond prices (both government and eventually private) and thereafter threaten banking stability. Since income taxes were not yielding the desired revenue, they both began to advocate a general sales tax and further expenditure reductions.

In November the electorate expressed its disapproval of the Republican administration and its programs. Hoover and many members of the 72nd Congress became lame ducks and presided over the government until March 1933. Hoover's plan for a sales tax was all but ignored, and his plan for expenditure cuts was impossible to achieve, as only a small portion of federal expenditure was available for reductions. The remainder was accounted for by defense spending, interest payments, veterans' expenses, and money appropriated for fighting the depression—perhaps as much as 75 percent of the budget was accounted for by these items.

Hoover became more and more isolated, still working long hours, still proposing schemes for recovery, but both the Congress and the president-elect, Franklin D. Roosevelt, ignored him. The country was waiting for something new.

Monetary Policy

The response of the monetary authorities to the stock-market crash has been the subject of a good deal of criticism and controversy. That they were slow to act and timid when they did is fairly well accepted. The question is, Why?

In the beginning it was likely that the Federal Reserve Board viewed the downturn as temporary, as did many others, and acted on the premise that this downturn would resemble those in 1924 and 1927. They had no experience to contradict that forecast, and the fall in production did not occur until late in the year. The situation improved early in 1930, and even the stock market rallied and showed confusing signals.

In addition, there is considerable evidence to indicate that board members still were uncertain as to how monetary policy worked and doubtful of its effects in stimulating an economic system.[16] Thus, over the next year and a half to May 1931, the New York Bank managed to reduce the discount rate to 1.5 percent from 4.5 percent, but only after considerable delay and many misgivings. Similarly, increases in the money supply through bond purchases were also resisted. In November and December of 1929 the Federal Reserve purchased $355 million in securities and then added a little more in March and June of 1930 ($70 million in total), and after an August purchase of $120 million, it had purchased nearly $600 million. Short-term interest rates declined steadily over the period to a low of around 2 percent for prime commercial paper in the summer of 1931, but long-term rates held steady.

The Federal Reserve System continued its reluctance to act, even in the face of growing bank failures that were occurring toward the end of 1930. The Bank of The United States, and many banks associated with it, failed. The Bank of The United States had grown by merging with other banks and had extended itself into so many areas, some illegal, that it was in a fragile condition and unable to withstand the downswing. Other banks failed as the cotton market collapsed and agricultural loans were defaulted.[17]

One consequence of the bank failures was an increase in hoarding, as the public became wary of further failures. According to Milton Friedman and Anna J. Schwartz,[18] the Federal Reserve's failure to act at this stage turned the recession into a depression. The decline in deposits followed by the banks' excessive demand for excess reserves meant that the money supply was bound to fall. As the money supply fell, people sold securities and other financial assets to obtain funds, but as they did so, these prices fell and interest rates rose. Seeing falling prices, some sold other nonfinancial assets, depressing their prices as well and discouraging new production of these assets. Some of these assets were real investment goods or housing, and, with high interest rates, their production was curtailed. The end result was a fall in the level of incomes and the price level.

The Federal Reserve System could have stopped all this by supplying credit in the form of reserves for the banking system. By buying bonds the Federal Reserve could prevent the scramble for funds. At the time of the bank failures, the amount of Federal Reserve credit was declining rather than expanding—offsetting the inflow of gold that was contributing to credit availability. Thus the Federal Reserve reacted incorrectly to the banking crisis and caused the downturn to become more severe than was necessary. Its failure to increase the money supply becomes the major cause of the Great Depression, according to this view.

From Table 4.6 it is clear that the money supply fell over this period. From 1929 to 1933 the basic money supply (currency plus demand deposits) fell by $6.9 billion, or by 26 percent. A similar decline occurred in the velocity of money. Declines in the money supply that includes time deposits fell by even greater amounts—about one-third. Clearly, the direction of change for Federal Reserve credit was the wrong one.

Others contend that the demand for money fell more than the supply of money and thus attribute the depression to nonmonetary factors. The question becomes, What caused the demand for money to fall? Peter Temin[19] attributes the fall in demand for money to an (unexplained) decline in consumption spending. This drop in consumption spending occurred after the stock-market crash (wealth declined) and merely made the recession of 1929 much worse. The initial decline

Table 4.6   Money Supply, 1929–39 (billions of dollars)

Year	M1 = Demand Deposits + Currency		M2 = M1 + Time Deposits	
	Amount	Velocity	Amount	Velocity
1929	26.4	3.90	46.2	1.95
1930	25.5	3.55	45.3	1.70
1931	23.8	3.19	42.0	1.47
1932	20.7	2.81	35.0	1.28
1933	19.5	2.86	30.9	1.38
1934	21.4	3.05	33.2	1.52
1935	25.4	2.85	38.1	1.52
1936	29.0	2.84	42.7	1.60
1937	30.4	2.98	45.0	1.67
1938	29.9	2.83	44.8	1.53
1939	33.4	2.71	48.5	1.52

Source: U.S. Department of Commerce, Bureau of the Census, Long–Term Economic Growth, 1869–1965 (Washington, DC: GPO, 1966), p. 209.

cannot be adequately explained, but it is clear that the capital-goods boom had come to an end before the crash; the housing market was depressed; exports fell, and so on. Money markets were also tight until the crash, but afterwards individuals and firms began to refrain from borrowing from the banking sector.

For all these reasons the demand for money fell as people reduced their money balances, as incomes and spending declined. This explanation is also consistent with the observed decline in interest rates. (The monetary explanation would have required that interest rates rise as people sold assets and bonds to secure the desired money balances.) There is no dispute that the Federal Reserve acted unwisely over this period; rather, the dispute is over the cause of the sharp contraction. Despite the obvious decline in the money supply, it is more likely that the drop in the demand for money played a larger role in causing the declines in income and output.

In November and December 1930 alone, 608 banks failed, and the public began to lose faith in the banking system. They began to withdraw funds. The trend would continue over the next few years until the bank holiday of 1933. Thus the banking system was already in trouble when Britain went off the gold standard on September 20, 1931.

The Federal Reserve responded to the declaration according to how it was supposed to respond, given the rules of the gold standard. To prevent a gold outflow, the Federal Reserve increased the discount rate in New York in early October from 1.5 to 2.5 percent and a week later to 3.5 percent. Still, by the end of October the gold outflow totaled $608 million. Increasing discount rates in the midst of a downturn is the "wrong" monetary policy by almost universal agreement. The defense of the gold stock was deemed necessary, however, because there would soon have been insufficient collateral to back the Federal Reserve notes. This concern was a legitimate one later on, but not at this time. Apparently the real concern of the Federal Reserve was to maintain European confidence in the dollar and stem domestic hoarding as well.[20]

Indeed, the problem of the amount of free gold for backing the Federal Reserve notes did not affect policy until February 1932, when the Glass–Steagall Act was passed allowing government securities to be used as collateral for notes. In any event, the Federal Reserve did not offset the gold outflow by purchasing securities, but allowed interest rates to rise.

In February and March 1932 the Federal Reserve began to purchase government securities in the attempt to pursue monetary ease. The prevailing view of monetary ease was the extent of Federal Reserve credit, not changes in the money supply or interest rates. Now however, the Federal Reserve confronted something new—excess reserves. Banks' demand for liquidity following the bank failures meant that purchases of securities by the Federal Reserve ended up in excess reserves of banks. Arguing that a glut of excess reserves would do no good but might result in a loss of confidence, the Federal Reserve tried to establish some target level for excess reserves. A target of $500 million was determined, but not without disagreement, as some wanted to sell securities to reduce excess reserves.

Excess reserves were reduced as economic conditions worsened and more banks collapsed. People began to withdraw cash, and by mid-February excess reserves began to fall below the target level. On February 14, 1933, the governor of Michigan declared an eight-day bank holiday, and the panic quickly spread to other states, until by March 4 every state had declared a bank holiday and deposits were frozen.

The Federal Reserve did not react to the Michigan declaration of a bank holiday by restoring the now rapidly declining excess reserves. By this time it had begun to let political considerations determine policy. Roosevelt had won the election of 1932, and rumors as to his ideas of monetary policy (devaluation) had become widespread. The Federal Reserve decided to wait and became extremely cautious. Hoover attempted to initiate some actions and asked the Federal Reserve to consider some form of guarantee of bank deposits, a federal clearing house in problem areas, and the possibility of a national bank holiday.

The Federal Reserve refused to initiate new policies or expand on the old ones. It became passive. Not wishing to entertain bold initiatives by the lame-duck President Hoover and not informed of the new president's plans, it simply stood pat. It finally advocated a national bank holiday, but waited until the evening of March 3 to advise Hoover to issue a proclamation. Hoover had doubtful authority at this time, and Roosevelt cagily refused to cooperate in a joint resolution.

Thus political considerations, exacerbated by the extremely long lame-duck period, prevented any real attempt at rational monetary policy. Instead, the nation witnessed the inevitable collapse of the banking system, as the Federal Reserve refused the power that was handed to it by default and preferred to resist all efforts to assume the necessary authority to turn things around.

The Campaign of 1932

Hoover managed to antagonize all factions and all groups: from those selling apples on street corners or standing in breadlines, to doctors and lawyers with few clients who could pay; from those living in cardboard boxes and makeshift shanties in "Hoovervilles" or riding the rails searching for jobs, to bankrupt stockholders now forced to reduce their living standards drastically; from the homeless, living in parks and scavenging in garbage cans behind restaurants for food, to charitable organizations that now lacked the contributions to continue their work. In short, everyone and every institution was affected by the depression: Homeowners lost their homes; farmers lost their farms; banks lost their credibility; colleges lost their enrollment; and corporations and Wall Street lost their luster.[21]

Someone had to be blamed, and Hoover became the convenient scapegoat. People forgot his attempts to reverse the tide and his far-reaching programs and proposals that anticipated the New Deal: agricultural, public works, the RFC, and so on. Yet, it was Hoover's failures that made the New Deal possible. His deep commitment to his ideals made radical change more acceptable. His dogmatic insistence on laissez-faire principles and his rigidity on balanced budgets and toward relief programs were perceived as cruel, unjust, and passive.

Under these conditions anyone could have beaten Herbert Hoover in 1932, and the Democrats were regarded as shoo-ins. After some tough battles and near deadlock, and after Huey Long delivered Louisiana and John Garner delivered Texas (in exchange for the vice-presidential slot), the Democrats chose the ex-secretary of the navy and two-term governor of New York, Franklin Delano Roosevelt, over Al Smith, who wanted another chance. So to the strains of "Happy Days Are Here Again," curiously published just days following the stock-market crash, the Democrats nominated an aristocrat to lead them to victory. Breaking all tradition, which he called foolish, FDR flew to Chicago to accept the nomination and aver, "I pledge you, I pledge myself, to a new deal for the American people." The phrase "new deal"—not an original one—became the rallying cry for this important Democratic campaign.[22]

What kind of man did the Democrats and finally the nation select to lead the country out of this terrible depression? Clearly he was an experienced public servant, knowledgeable in governmental operations. As governor of New York he had instituted an unemployment relief system, worked for conservation causes and public power, and generally was regarded as progressive. Still, there was little in his background to suggest any radical proposals or even modest programs or ideas for dealing with the current crisis.

He was not particularly intellectual, but practical and pragmatic. A shrewd politician, he learned from past campaigns how to appeal to an electorate. In his campaign he spoke of trying things, of remembering the "forgotten man," and even of compromises between the ideal and the practical. In a speech at Oglethorpe University he said, "The country needs and, unless I mistake its temper, the country demands bold, persistent experimentation."

His words were bold, his voice confident, and the audiences were inspired by his sincerity. What he was saying was virtually indistinguishable from what Hoover, the Republican nominee, was saying. His words were inspiring, but his policies and ideas were vague, ambiguous, and undeveloped. He believed in the gold standard, in balanced budgets, and in unregulated free markets, while only occasionally hinting at programs that would later be a part of the New Deal: regulation of Wall Street and public utilities and federal relief, if absolutely necessary. Other parts of the New Deal were not mentioned for two reasons: First, the programs simply did not exist at this stage and, second, because it was important to win first, and this meant not alienating any group or sector of the electorate. Even in the area of civil rights he took no chances of being labeled left-wing and chose instead to make speeches that "aroused hope without arousing opposition."[23]

Anyway, prohibition was a large issue in the campaign, perhaps too large, and FCR was a "damp" and Hoover was a "dry." Important as they were, economic issues were sometimes overshadowed by peripheral ones and by the personalities of the candidates. The stern and moralistic Hoover, who disliked making speeches, and the warm, friendly Roosevelt, who reveled in them, made a striking contrast. Hope was what the public wanted, and the victim of infantile paralysis who stood on braces to speak provided it by personal example and by inspiring words.

There simply was no contest, and FDR won easily, securing a 472–59 margin in the Electoral College and winning 42 of the 48 states, while capturing over 58 percent of the popular vote. Equally significant, the Democrats seized control of the Senate by gaining 12 seats for a total of 57 of the 96 seats and also got control of the House by gaining an additional 97 seats for a total of 313 out of the 435 seats. The Democratic victory was complete and devastating.

chapter 5

The Great Depression: The New Deal

Roosevelt surrounded himself with liberals who favored more direct government action in reviving the economy and in reforming its operation. In the cabinet were Cordell Hull (secretary of state), Henry Morgenthau (secretary of the treasury), Henry Wallace (secretary of agriculture), Frances Perkins (secretary of labor), and Harold Ickes (secretary of the interior).

Moreover, the promise of experimentation brought large numbers of academics, largely from Columbia and Harvard, to the Roosevelt administration. These "Brain Trusters," as they were called, were liberal in outlook and energetic in battle. Among them were Raymond Moley, Rexford Tugwell, Felix Frankfurter, A. A. Berle, Harry Hopkins, and Isador Lubin. While hardly radical by later standards, they seemed so at the time, as they cut through established bureaucracy and pushed through the New Deal programs.

If Roosevelt had no concept of economic theory, some of his followers did. Marriner Eccles and Lauchlin Currie of the Federal Reserve were heavily influenced by John M. Keynes and advocated the concept of compensatory finance, whereby the federal government must unbalance its budget to meet economic conditions: It should incur deficits during recessions to stimulate aggregate demand, and surpluses in recoveries to dampen it. In addition, A. A. Berle, together with Gardiner Means, had described the changing economic structure of the U.S. economy, due in large measure to the growth of large corporations where ownership and control had become separated. Thus new economic models of the economy were receiving a hearing and finding their way into policymaking, and the short-run concerns of Keynesian economics would soon come to dominate the long-run emphasis of classical economics. Clearly the latter's conclusions that the economy is basically stable and tends toward full utilization of its resources were bound to be questioned in this period. On the other hand, the Keynesian model sought to explain the basic instability of the economic system, due largely to the instability of investment spending and the unlikelihood that the economy would reach full employment unaided, except by accident.

This was the message that the New Dealers wanted to hear. Not all of them were followers of Keynes, of course; they may simply have found support for what they wanted to do anyway. Therefore the influence of Keynes on the "New Economics," as it was later called, must not be overestimated, for the time was ripe for experimentation, regardless of theoretical justification. Keynes's ideas were certainly timely, but their general acceptance came later. Nevertheless, the old orthodoxy was being questioned anyway, as it simply could not explain the economic collapse, and the obvious contradiction between its conclusions and reality gave new voices the opportunity to supply explanations.[1]

So the New Dealers set about restoring and reforming the system without a theoretical foundation or a blueprint for action. All we had to "fear was fear itself" were the reassuring words of FDR as he pledged to provide a plan for recovery. The restoration of the banking system was the obvious choice of where to begin. On March 6, under the Trading with the Enemy Act, a four-day national bank holiday was proclaimed. A special session of Congress was convened on March 9 to deal with the banking crisis, and that very same day the Emergency Banking Act was passed, empowering the RFC to buy capital stock of distressed banks and the Federal Reserve to make loans to nonmember banks and businesses. The act also provided a plan for the reopening of banks. Generally, banks considered to be sound were allowed to reopen on March 15, after the bank holiday was extended to six working days. Other banks faced restrictions on their operations, and about 5 percent of the banks never were allowed to reopen.

Many of those banks that were allowed to reopen were still in bad shape. The market value of their loans was well below the actual value, and many loans had to be readjusted downward; interest charges or repayment periods had to be adjusted to permit the debtors to repay. The restructuring of the loans took time, and the scaling down of debts risked damaging creditors. The whole process was not as easy as the New Dealers claimed, and there was considerable concern that a new panic would develop if confidence faltered.

The public responded, and confidence returned quickly, as currency of nearly $1.2 billion flowed back into banks by the end of March. The inflow of funds continued even as many banks continued to operate under restrictions. Gold and gold certificates also were turned in on orders of the government. Later, when the Federal Reserve supplied $600 million of reserves to banks, the system appeared on the road to recovery.

Yet there was a clamor for more inflation to make the adjustments in restructuring debts less painful for all. The president, too, favored a policy of rising prices (and wages) and effectively took the nation off the gold standard in April by forbidding the export of gold unless it was in the national interest. So intense was the desire for lifting prices that Congress gave the president some sweeping powers under Title III of the Emergency Farm Relief Bill, sponsored by Senator Elbert D. Thomas of Oklahoma. The amendment transferred a great deal of control over monetary matters to the president and away from the Federal Reserve System. Thus on May 12, 1933, the president, or at his direction the Treasury, was authorized to

1. Direct the Federal Reserve to purchase $3 billion of government securities and release the banks from any penalties if their reserves fell below the required amounts. This part was inserted in the hope of increasing bank lending. (It was never used.)
2. Issue a maximum of $3 billion in U.S. notes or greenbacks, which could be used as legal tender.
3. Fix the relative weight of gold and silver and reestablish a bimetallic standard.
4. Establish the gold value of the dollar, but the value should be reduced by more than 50 percent.
5. Accept silver in payments due to the United States at not more than 50 cents an ounce (up to a maximum of $200 million). The silver thus acquired was to be used as backing for the issuance of silver certificates or coined into silver dollars.
6. Let the Federal Reserve control the reserve requirements of banks.

Such broad powers given to the president obviously show the intense atmosphere in the Congress. Those who clung to the old gold standard or wished to reestablish some earlier international monetary relations had reason to be concerned.

World trade was contracting steadily, and by the time FDR took office, the volume had fallen by 67 percent. In the attempt to restore world trade and stabilize currencies, a world Monetary and Economic Conference was called to meet in London in the summer of 1933. Many countries were anxious to restore the old gold standard and, with currencies stabilized, to resurrect international trade. Roosevelt was at first committed to these negotiations, but increasingly was moving to revive the U.S. economy before worrying about currency stabilization. Thus, he expressed a desire for a rising price level in the United States, which would have meant a depreciating dollar. A fall in the value of the dollar would have damaged British and French exports, and thus the conference was thrown into a panic.

Finally Roosevelt demolished the conference entirely by sending a message stating that the United States was not concerned with the purpose of the meetings—stabilizing currencies—and wished to restore the domestic economy first. "The sound internal economic system of a nation is a greater factor in its well-being than the price of its currency in changing terms of the currencies of other nations." Keynes called the action "magnificently right," but others saw the possibility of more economic distress for the world community. Whether or not the conditions were right at this time for international agreements was and is debatable. Nothing may have come out of the conference, anyway. What is undeniable is that FDR served notice to the world that the United States was determined to restore its economy first, as he turned away from internationalism to focus on domestic concerns.

Devaluation of the Dollar and Silver Prices

The London Economic Conference did produce an agreement by silver-producing and consuming countries to raise the price of silver, which had fallen drastically in value. Led by Senator Key Pittman, the silver interests in the United States pushed the reluctant FDR to ratify the agreement and, under powers granted to him by the Thomas amendment, to restore the price of silver to its earlier relation to gold. The old ratio was 16 to 1, so that with gold at $20.67 per ounce, the price of silver would be $1.29. FDR objected to paying this price, however, and offered to buy at 50 percent of this value ($0.6464 per ounce) and retain the other half as seigniorage.

The president ordered the purchase of newly mined silver, while fixing the price of old silver at $0.50 per ounce. Unhappy with the price set for silver, the silver-mining interests pushed through the Silver Purchase Act of June 19, 1934, which had followed a presidential message directing the Treasury to purchase silver, both domestic and foreign, until the price had reached $1.29 or until the silver stock reached one-third of the monetary value of the gold stock. Later the president nationalized all silver, and the public was forced to surrender its silver holdings to the U.S. Mint at a value of $0.50 per ounce.

Silver mining increased substantially, and since the price paid by the Treasury was greater than the market price, silver producers earned a handsome subsidy. Furthermore, silver consumers purchased their silver from foreigners at the lower price, and thus silver flowed into the country. The inflow of silver helped to supply dollars to foreigners and probably reduced the inflow of gold, and "purchases of silver were to some extent a substitute for gold purchases."[2]

Thus the main effect of this silver program was a huge subsidy to domestic silver interests. The increase in the money stock through the issue of treasury silver certificates and silver dollars was small relative to the other components of the money supply. From 1934 to 1940 silver certificates and silver dollars amounted to $1.3 billion. These amounts were too small to result in the promised and hoped-for increase in the domestic price level. Thus the unnecessary addition to the money supply did nothing domestically but increase the economic wellbeing of silver miners.[3]

Recall that Roosevelt had wrecked the London conference by his insistence that the needs of the United States would come first and stabilization of world currencies could await economic recovery. What was needed to restore the value of output to predepression levels, according to FDR and to many others as well, was inflation. He now began to pursue this goal. By October most of the gold had been called in, and the nation really was off the gold standard. In April 1933 Congress had to abrogate the gold clauses in all contracts. Inserted to protect creditors in the first place, they now could not be honored, since there was not enough gold to go around. Later it would be clear that another reason was the contemplated increase in the price of gold, which would have hurt debtors obligated to pay in gold or dollars.

The stage was set for FDR to raise the price of gold in terms of the dollar. Despite arguments to the contrary, he accepted the monetary theory of one of his advisors, Professor George F. Warren, who argued that an increase in the price of gold would raise the domestic price level. Presumably an increase in the value of the money stock would increase the price level through some unexplained version of the quantity theory of money. Reasoning from past correlations between money and prices led to this curious proposal.

In a "fireside chat" on October 22, 1933, FDR expressed another rationale for his upcoming policy: the overvalued dollar.

> The effect of this had been to contribute to the serious decrease in our foreign trade, not because our own prices, in terms of dollars, had risen, nor because our products were of inferior quality, nor

because we did not have sufficient products to export. But because, in terms of foreign currencies, our products had become so much more expensive, we were not able to obtain our fair share of the world's trade. It was, therefore, necessary to take measures which would result in bringing the dollar back to the position where a fair amount of foreign currency could again buy our product.

A few days later he instructed the RFC (the Federal Reserve refused to help) to begin purchasing gold, domestic gold at first and, when that was not sufficient, foreign gold as well. The first price of gold determined by FDR and other staff members, mainly Morgenthau, was $31.36, up from the market value of $29.80. Gold prices were determined daily and were set above the previous ones until they had bid up the price of gold to $34.45 on January 31, 1934.

Prior to this, on January 15, Roosevelt had sent a message to Congress asking for a devaluation of at least 60 percent and requesting that gold "profits" from devaluation be put into a fund to stabilize foreign exchange rates. The Gold Reserve Act of 1934 was passed on January 30, 1934, giving the president the authority to fix the gold value of the dollar at between 50 and 60 percent of the old level. The act also nationalized all gold, ended the coinage of gold, and authorized the Treasury to regulate all gold matters. It also created the stabilization fund, worth about $2 billion for stabilization of exchange rates.

The president established the price of gold at $35 per ounce, giving a profit to the Treasury of $14.33 over the old price of $20.67, for a total of $2,805 million. Only $200 million was ever used for stabilization purposes. These actions clearly affected international exchange rates, as the dollar depreciated against other currencies on the gold standard. In fact, other countries protested the exportation of the U.S. deflationary problems and later were forced into deflationary actions; eventually they were forced to abandon the gold standard.

Banking Reform

Banking reform was also high on the agenda following the failure of the banking system in the economic crisis. Both Senator Carter Glass and Congressman Henry Steagall had been conducting hearings before their respective banking committees on the problems of the Federal Reserve System. The hearings before the Senate Committee on Banking and Currency had been filled with cases of financial abuses, immoral and possibly illegal acts, and numerous examples of deceit on Wall Street, particularly on the part of investment bankers.

The Banking Act of 1933, signed into law in June 1933, attempted to meet some of the problems in the banking structure by divorcing investment banking from commercial banking, by regulating bank holding companies, and by limiting bank branching to intrastate boundaries where allowed by states. To help restore confidence in the banking system, now at a low level, the act provided for government insurance for private depositors through the Federal Deposit Insurance Corporation (FDIC). Thus one of Hoover's ideas became law, but only after considerable debate over the propriety of bailing out one sector of the private economy. Yet it worked, and after the passage of the act, the number of bank failures was reduced dramatically.[4]

Other provisions of the act prohibited banks from paying interest on demand deposits and gave the Federal Reserve the power to fix interest rates on time deposits. Clearly, more power was transferred to the Federal Reserve System. Further shifts of power were given later in the Banking Act of 1935. The revised board of governors was to serve for 14 years without members of the executive branch (the secretary of the treasury and comptroller of the currency). Open-market operations were centralized, and securities would be purchased in the open market and not from the Treasury. The Federal Reserve was also given a new tool—the power to determine reserve requirements.

The financial abuses of Wall Street brought to light by the Senate Banking Committee also spurred Congress to react to the growing disenchantment with financial markets. The Securities Act of 1933 and later the Securities Exchange Act of 1934 created a regulatory body, the Securities and Exchange Commission (SEC), to oversee the stock market. Primarily, the SEC was designed to insure that stock offers would be registered and that the information given to prospective buyers would be accurate and truthful. The concern for preventing fraud grew out of the states' "Blue Sky Laws" (to prevent sellers from selling the blue sky itself) and recently uncovered abuses.[5]

To help regulate the availability of credit for stock purchases, the Federal Reserve was given the power to set margin requirements on security loans. Much of the excessive speculation in the 1920s can be traced to the small amounts of cash needed to purchase stock, and, when the bubble burst, the loans, which were secured with stock as collateral, could be repaid. Falling stock prices meant that the value of the collateral diminished, and the brokers called the borrowers for additional funds. Often funds were lacking, and the brokers were instructed to sell the stocks, resulting in further reductions of stock prices, and so on, and so on. The Federal Reserve, acting independently of Wall Street, was now empowered with a tool to limit speculation and with a signal to express its displeasure: It could set the minimum amount of cash required to obtain a stock-secured loan.

Agricultural Programs

Another area crying out for attention was agriculture, and the administration promised quick action. Haste was certainly demanded, as many farmers were losing their farms, while others banded together to prevent losses; judges who sanctioned foreclosures were threatened, and some states had to pass mortgage-moratorium laws. Falling prices saw farmers destroy their crops rather than sell at such prices, and dairy farmers emptied their milk cans on the roads.

Henry Wallace, the secretary of agriculture, did call a meeting of farm leaders to hammer out a policy from the many proposals being offered by various groups. What eventually emerged and passed on May 12, 1933, was the Agricultural Adjustment Act (AAA). It represented a compromise, but the main feature was to raise farm prices to a level that would yield the same purchasing power of farm goods that existed in the base period 1909–14, the golden age of agriculture.

The act provided means to accomplish a rise in farm prices and incomes. There were crop limitations to be achieved by allocating each farmer a share in total output, marketing agreements among farm producers and distributors to maintain prices, and income payments to farmers who agreed to participate. The funds for the program would be raised by a tax on processors.

Again, the precedent of the Hoover administration is evident in the New Deal farm program. Also evident was the commitment to the "rehabilitation of a system that depended on scarcity."[6] At a time when millions of people were hungry, crops had to be plowed under to reduce supplies and pigs had to be slaughtered. Crops had to be reduced, no matter the means or the morality of acts designed to accomplish the ends. The consumer would pay twice for support of farmers: They would have less supply and would eventually pay the processing tax as well; this at a time of mass hunger, malnutrition, and falling incomes.

The chronic problem of overproduction was made worse over the period by several factors. High tariffs erected to preserve U.S.

industries served only to reduce trade and limit the demand for U.S. agricultural goods. Our former trading partners simply revived their own agricultural sectors. Dumping agriculture produce overseas was also becoming a less realistic outlet.

In addition, farm mechanization was proceeding and increasing productivity on the farm. New tractors, reapers, and harvesting machines, especially in cotton, meant increased output for those farmers who could afford the equipment, and increasing misery for the small farmer who could not and who was driven off onto very marginal land. Underemployment rose. Moreover, better fertilizers and more hybrids were developed, as extension services of federally supported colleges of agriculture began to inform farmers of better farming methods.

Also, the structure of demand changed among the more affluent in the 1920s, away from cereals and grains to meat products.[7] This natural shift was made worse by the invention of synthetics—rayon and nylon—as substitutes for cotton and in many ways superior to it. Finally, the falling birth rate and slowing immigration meant that the number of mouths to feed was also declining.

Thus, in the face of these trends, the Agriculture Adjustment Administration had an enormous job in curtailing output and raising prices. It chose to concentrate on certain "basic" commodities, some 16 in all, including grains, hogs, tobacco, dairy products, peanuts, sugar cane, and potatoes. The program, seemingly so beneficial to farmers, was resisted by many who wanted to be free to plant more, once prices rose. Even those who signed on to participate had some notions of planting more intensively, retiring inferior land, and switching to alternative crops on the land taken out of production. Farmers had to be coerced into joining by taxing schemes embodied in later farm bills, such as the Bankhead Cotton Control Act of 1934 and others.

Another incentive for farmers to join allotment programs was the existence of the Commodity Credit Corporation. If prices were not high enough, the farmer could store his output and receive a low-interest loan from the Commodity Credit Corporation. If prices rose, the farmer could reclaim his output and sell it; if prices fell, the farmer could choose not to pay back the loan, in which case the government took the crop in payment. It was a "heads I win, tails you lose" proposition; the farmer tossed the coin. The potential problem of perennial surpluses became evident in the case of cotton, which was threatened by synthetics.

The potential for surpluses to accumulate was diminished by allowing dumping abroad and by the distribution of farm output in federal relief programs. The former benefited foreign at the expense of domestic consumers, and the latter helped mitigate against the effects of the farm program. It is also true that the severe droughts of 1934 and 1936 helped to reduce output. The droughts and dust storms blew away the topsoil and darkened the skies, causing many farmers to migrate to the west coast from Oklahoma and Arkansas, a movement so eloquently described by John Steinbeck in *The Grapes of Wrath*.

The results of the AAA were mixed, and even successes were unspectacular.[8] The experiment with crop management was disrupted, however, by the Supreme Court, when in January 1936 it declared the AAA unconstitutional: The crop control and the processing tax were held to be an invasion of state powers. The New Deal quickly responded with the Soil Conservation and Domestic Allotment Act of February 1936 and later the revamped AAA of 1938.

The emphasis in the new laws switched to the restoration of the same purchasing power of income that existed for the farmer in the 1909–14 period. Payments were made to farmers for soil-conservation practices from a fund of $500 million. In the AAA Act of 1938, crop allotments were reinstituted to bolster prices and ensure surpluses in good years to be available for use in bad years—Wallace's "ever normal granary." The new programs did not work very well, and even World War II in the early stages was not able to rescue the farmers from distress. Only when the United States entered the war would the picture improve.

Thus, a welter of farm programs were initiated by the New Deal in an attempt to rescue a declining sector. They were not terribly successful, born as they were out of humanitarian feelings rather than out of economic analysis. Quick responses could not substitute for unhurried long-range planning. In other areas the planning concept found more favor, but in agriculture the fundamental problems were never addressed, and, as will become evident, these same problems continued to plague agricultural policy in the United States for many years thereafter.

National Recovery Administration

If the AAA represented an attempt at planning in agriculture, the National Industrial Recovery Act (NIRA) of June 16, 1933, was its counterpart for industry. While not specifically mentioned in the act, national planning clearly was the interest of a strong and vocal group of presidential advisors and now they had their tool for achieving it.[9]

Briefly, what the act did was to create the National Recovery Administration (headed by General Hugh S. Johnson), a government agency that was to enforce the business agreements designed to regulate prices, production, investment, marketing, and selling practices. The agreements were called "codes of fair competition" and drawn up largely by business, with little input from labor or consumers. In effect, the act legalized cartels, and the government stood ready to enforce the provisions of the codes. Business would be self-regulating and free at last from cutthroat competition and the antitrust laws of the past.

Roosevelt clearly believed that the NRA would rationalize the industrial sector of the U.S. economy. How else to explain such a bold venture into state capitalism? There were precedents, however, for the move and also events that helped prod the action along and make it more acceptable. For instance, there was the War Industries Board of World War I, which pioneered industrial cooperation and coordination by government.

Moreover, there were many trade associations in existence, and even the FTC had sanctioned "fair trade practice conferences" in which codes of fair competition had been drawn up.[10] Senator Hugo Black of Alabama was calling for a shorter workweek and Secretary of Labor Frances Perkins was urging the emulation of some state laws for a minimum wage. Business was ready for anything that would lessen the rigors and confinements of free competition and provide for more orderly conditions.

As might be imagined, the codes were slow to develop, and much confusion was evident. While bargaining over provisions of the codes was provided for, the actual development of them was dominated by business and mainly big business at that.[11] Labor and consumers had little voice in their construction. Aside from fair-competition practices among firms, the codes did specify that labor must be given the right to bargain collectively—the famous Section 7(a) of the NIRA—must provide for shorter hours and wage payments not lower than they were and, if possible, higher, and gave the direction for inclusion of minimum wages.

Near the end of July 1933 the president, concerned with the slow pace of the NRA, asked firms to come under a blanket code that he developed. The Re-employment Agreement eliminated child labor, provided for a 40-hour week in some cases and a 40-cent minimum wage for 35 hours maximum in others, and proscribed unnecessary price increases. The president was quite successful in stimulating code agreements, and the Blue Eagle became the symbol of compliance and also a means of coercion for joining. More important, however, was the fact that firms had to agree to restrictions for their activities without getting the rewards of freedom from competition and the antitrust laws.

The Blue Eagle was displayed in storefronts, and parades were held in demonstrations for support of the NRA. No doubt morale was lifted as a result of the program, when it appeared that something was being done. Yet the results of the NRA were clearly mixed. The codes did end some grossly unfair business practices and helped pave the way for more government involvement in labor matters. There may even have been a slight boost to output, employment, and prices in 1933, attributable to the initial reactions to the codes. But such effects were short-lived, and soon compliance with the codes diminished and violations and grumbling became routine. So when the NRA was declared unconstitutional by the Supreme Court on May 27, 1935, in a unanimous decision, no one was really shocked. What went wrong with this attempt by government to rationalize the industrial sector?

A grave mistake was made right in the beginning, when responsibility for recovery was divided into two uncoordinated branches: the administration of industrial recovery under General Hugh S. Johnson, and the control of public works under Secretary of the Interior Harold L. Ickes. Public-works programs developed very slowly under Ickes, while Johnson was headstrong and energetic with his part.

The provisions for labor under the codes became the source of severe conflicts. The elimination of child labor and the special treatment of women in the labor force were welcome, but the provisions for hours, minimum wages, and collective-bargaining rights caused much labor unrest. Workers sought to retain the old wage differentials that had developed within an industry—the so-called wage contours of later labor-market theory. Employers resisted, as formerly high-wage employers sought either to make wages uniform or depress them to enhance profits. Both firms and workers were unhappy with the wage adjustments, and conflicts arose. In the words of one harsh critic,

[The NRA] set terribly low minimums, restrained workers on strike for higher wages, and cut real wages by the inflationary rise in prices. [T]he minimum wages tended, moreover, to become the maximum, a complaint made again and again by labor leaders, who did little about it. ... Strikers were put in the position of fighting the government, as limits were fixed by the government apparatus of the NRA. The codes were framed by representatives of capitalist government and capitalist industry.[12]

The provision of the right to bargain collectively appeared as a concession to organized labor and was so viewed by labor leaders and liberals. The NRA ruled, however, that a company union would satisfy this requirement of Section 7(a). Firms hastily initiated company unions over the objections of trade unions. Many strikes ensued, but, as was seen, strikes were also subject to control, and thus this great victory of unions for collective bargaining turned out to be a hollow one.

The fixing of prices also caused great difficulties and eventually encouraged violations of the codes. Prices were fixed somewhat arbitrarily and usually at a level higher than market conditions would have dictated. Yet fixing prices in an industry that was subject to wide differences in quality, numerous types of output, sizes, grades, and so on, left many inequities that invited violations. The enforcement rules were inadequate, and the rules seemed unjust anyway. Add the controls over the investment spending, inventories, and production quotas to the pricing problems, and the possible inequities are multiplied. Under these conditions cartels are likely to break down, whether or not they are government sponsored.

When the end came for the NRA, Bernard Baruch, who initially supported the resurrection of his ideas of the War Industries Board (including the insignia of the Blue Eagle), wrote later, "There are not many who were overly upset when the Supreme Court declared it unconstitutional."[13] Nor were others, not as sympathetic, who viewed this flirtation with European ideas and fascism with some dismay. Many intellectuals welcomed the experimentation with other economic arrangements and institutions, particularly with long-range planning, as an answer to the growing misery attributed to capitalism.

Lacking an economic theory that could explain events, the administration simply resurrected some old programs that worked somewhat in World War I and, with an eye to European experiments and planning in the Soviet Union, hastily put together a bold program for recovery. As Baruch put it, "Many men in the new administration seemed to think that recovery could be decreed."[14]

While the Keynesian influence was present in this administration, his basic message was not heard clearly enough: It is necessary to stimulate total spending before recovery can begin. The administration and later the NRA wanted to increase costs (wages) and prices first, but this was hardly the way to stimulate aggregate demand. Most economists would concur with the conclusions of the Brookings Institution study:

> The rise in prices prevented the increase in the total real purchasing power of labor expected to accrue from wage raising ... on the whole price and wage rate levels both moved to considerably higher ground without material change in their relative positions. ... In trying to raise the real purchasing power of the nation by boosting costs and prices the NRA put the cart before the horse. Raising the prices either of labor or of goods is not the way to get a larger volume purchase.[15]

The failure to increase total spending at stable costs and prices led the authors to conclude "that the NRA on the whole retarded recovery." To what extent it was detrimental, no one can say with much assurance.[16]

Organized Labor

The NRA may not have contributed to recovery, but it certainly contributed to the growth of organized labor in the United States. Section 7(a) provided collective-bargaining rights, and accordingly union membership began to increase. The early years of the depression saw union membership decline from 3.6 million in 1930 to 2.9 million in 1933, a decline from 6.8 percent of the labor force to 5.2 percent.

The NRA codes reversed the slide, and in 1934 the number increased to 3.2 million or 5.9 percent of the labor force. The right to bargain collectively, however, was often abridged, as already noted, by the growth of company unions and by the slow pace of code formation, during which time speedups occurred and real wages fell. There were many strikes as workers contested these conditions and tested their strength: Strikes against the Fisher Body Company, against poor working conditions in San Francisco, and against textile plants were the most notable. The National Labor Board of the NRA was used to mediate, but special labor boards, such as the Automobile Labor Board, were necessary in certain cases.

The National Labor Board was slowly weakened by its procedures and by special boards and was replaced by FDR with the National Labor Relations Board. When the NRA was declared illegal shortly thereafter, the National Labor Relations Board became an important part of the bill proposed by Senator Robert F. Wagner that came to be known as the National Labor Relations Act. The Wagner Act, its other name, attempted to preserve the provisions of Section 7(a) by providing that "employees shall have the right to self-organization, to form, join or assist labor organizations, to bargain collectively through representatives of their own choosing, and to engage in concerted activities, for the purpose of collective bargaining or other mutual aid or protection." Unions would have free elections to determine their own bargaining units, free of employer interference, and employers would be prohibited from engaging in any unfair labor practice, including the formation of company unions.

FDR was originally opposed to the Wagner Act, but reversed himself and signed it into law on July 5, 1935. Both the Roosevelt switch and the ease with which the bill was passed remain unexplained. One result of the NLRB was the growth in union membership. From 1935 to 1940 union membership grew from 3.7 million to nearly 9 million, representing a growth of from 6.7 percent of the labor force to 15.5 percent in 1940.

Of course, the formation of the Congress of Industrial Organization (CIO) added importantly to the growth of union membership. Begun in 1935, the CIO unions were expelled from the American Federation of Labor (AFL) in 1936. The AFL, organized along individual craft lines, was rapidly becoming obsolete for unionization in the mass-production industries. The CIO set about filling this void and organized the steel, rubber, textile, and automobile industries. In perhaps its most dramatic success, it challenged General Motors by the sitdown strike, as workers occupied plants. General Motors conceded, and the open-shop concept, whereby workers were free to join a union or remain outside its ranks, began to fall in the process.

The CIO, led by John L. Lewis of the United Mine Workers, could not make its peace with the AFL, and their quarreling inevitably hurt the cause of organized labor. Despite the wrangling, or perhaps because of it, union membership continued to grow and change direction. Under the CIO the right to bargain collectively was only the first phase, and the union soon embarked on political activity to insure labor's voice in national policymaking. Even if labor did not speak in unison, it was still finding a voice that began to demand a hearing.

The Drive for Security

As will become apparent in the next section, the New Deal did not restore full employment, and, impressive as its programs were, the truly unemployable were really ignored in the recovery plans. The

aged, the handicapped, and the sick were not brought into federal
programs and were made the problem of the states, which were ill
equipped to handle their special circumstances, even if they had the
desire to do so. Sensitive to this criticism of New Deal policies, FDR
appointed a cabinet committee on economic security in 1934, headed by
Frances Perkins. The charge was to develop a social insurance system.

What emerged from the committee's report eventually became
the Social Security Act of August 1935. The act provided for old age
through annuity-like payments made from a fund that accumulated
from a payroll tax on covered employers and employees. The retirement age was set at 65, when the payments would begin, to workers for
their lifetimes and later to their survivors. Other provisions of the act
addressed the problem of the blind and handicapped, but sickness
insurance was omitted. This latter omission and the failure to cover
many workers made the insurance scheme subject to criticisms, as did
the regressive tax used to finance it. Roosevelt admitted that the
taxation scheme might have been a mistake, but, in his famous
remarks, he revealed the wisdom of the policy: "Those taxes were
never a problem of economics. They are politics all the way through.
We put those payroll contributions there so as to give the contributors
a legal, moral and political right to collect their pensions and their
unemployment benefits. With those taxes in there, no damn politician
can ever scrap my social security program."

Perhaps not so well known today are rival plans to the Social
Security System. One of these plans became very popular in this
period, that of Dr. F. G. Townsend of California. His proposal would
have given a pension of $200 per month to every person over 60 years
old who promised to retire and spend his or her pension within a month
of receipt. The plan was to be financed by a 2 percent tax on business
transactions. It was claimed that adoption of this plan would solve the
problem of the aged, the problem of unemployment as the old made
way for the young, and the problem of insufficient spending as the
pensioners quickly spent their allotment.

The Townsend Plan caught on, and hundreds of Townsend Clubs
were formed. These Townsend meetings discussed more than just
recovery and pension plans, and they came to resemble religious
meetings denouncing current mores. The Social Security Act deprived
the Townsendites of one of their main issues, but "Dr.Townsend
unleashed a new force in American Politics: the old people."[17] Another
voice found expression in the debate over national economic policy.

There were also precedents for the provision of unemployment
compensation. In New York and in Wisconsin a state unemployment
scheme had been devised. Other states, however, were fearful of taxing

employers, lest they move to states that refrained from providing unemployment relief at the expense of the employer.

The Social Security Act cleverly coerced the states into adopting unemployment compensation funds by levying a 3 percent federal tax on employers, but then allowing a 90 percent tax credit for employers who made payment to a federally approved state unemployment insurance fund. The state insurance fund would not cost the employer any additional tax, and thus the fear of losing business was removed.

The states quickly signed up for this "costless" insurance scheme, which would collect 2.7 percent of payrolls, with the remaining 0.3 percent available for administration expenses. All payroll taxes would go into a common fund, out of which workers would make claims when they were unemployed for acceptable reasons and after a waiting period. The act required that all disbursement be made by a public agency, and the states then created employment departments to deal with the cases.

This, then, was the first recognition by the federal government that it had some responsibility for reducing the pain caused by unemployment. Furthermore, there was the implied recognition that people became unemployed through no fault of their own, but by the operation of the economic system. For the economy's failure, society must accept its social responsibility to mitigate the hardships. Also included in the act was a merit system to recognize employer responsibility for unemployment. Those employers who seldom created unemployment would receive a reduction in their tax rate, and those who habitually created unemployment would pay the maximum rate.

In addition, the act stipulated that workers could not be forced to take jobs and lose their benefits, if the refusal was due to the fact that the job was in a nonunion plant, in a situation when there was a labor dispute, or in which the wage and hours were below standard for that type of work. The rules of operation and the extent of coverage of workers have all changed over time, but the principle remains that workers be given some relief from the loss of income due to unemployment until they can find another job somewhat comparable to the one they lost.

Fair Labor Standards Act

The Fair Labor Standards Act of June 1938 was the final major reform for labor in this period. Once again the NRA codes supplied the precedent for the measures relating to child labor, maximum hours, and minimum wages. The act set the maximum workweek at 44 hours, to fall to 40 hours after two years, and set the minimum wage at 25 cents per hour with exceptions at 40 cents an hour. The minimum wage could be changed whenever desired.

The act excluded many workers, particularly farmers, and really represented only a beginning to the regulation of hours and wages. The attempt to control hours and wages met with bitter opposition from the time of its introduction by Senator Hugo Black in May 1937. Conservatives generally and southerners particularly opposed the bill, the former in opposition to New Deal measures in general, and the latter to protect the low wage differentiation enjoyed by southern employers over their northern counterparts. Their opposition finally crumbled when Claude Pepper won election to the Senate from Florida, based on his support for the wage-and-hour bill. These New Deal programs that introduced the nation to the welfare state were resisted; they were controversial then, and they have remained so ever since.

Relief Programs

As previously noted, the massive numbers of unemployed put a real strain on states and localities to supply relief. They had neither the funds nor the staff to handle the task, and in the case of blacks, they also had little inclination. While neither the Hoover nor the Roosevelt administrations had any commitment to direct relief programs, the amount of suffering demanded that some action be taken. Yet the dole, it was thought, would rob the recipient of dignity, weaken the work ethic, and diminish the skills of the nation. Despite the objections, Congress finally authorized $0.5 billion to be given in grants to the states that would actually set up the payments machinery. State agencies would be developed and under federal guidance would preserve some minimum standards.

The Federal Emergency Relief Administration was headed by Harry Hopkins, who had worked for FDR in New York and who persuaded Frances Perkins to advance the cause of relief directly to FDR. This most unusual man, who apparently would have looked more at home at a race track than in the White House, set to work immediately and spent $5 million dollars in the first hours on the job, operating from a desk in the hallway of the RFC building.[18]

Hopkins, reacting to charges of socialism or to pleas to consider the long-run consequences of this relief, expressed his views succinctly:

Table 5.1   Direct Relief Payments by Federal and State and Local Governments, 1929–40 (millions of dollars)

Year	Federal	State and Local	Total
1929	—	71	71
1930	—	105	105
1931	—	176	176
1932	—	317	317
1933	—	558	558
1934	—	745	745
1935	2	954	956
1936	20	635	655
1937	36	787	823
1938	23	965	988
1939	22	1,024	1,046
1940	63	1,013	1,076

Source: U.S. Department of Commerce, *National Income and Product Accounts of the United States, 1929–1976* (September 1981), p. 146.

In Congressional testimony he said, "People don't eat in the long run, Senator. They eat every day." His early motto was "hunger is not debatable."[19] Still, the funds available were clearly insufficient and provided at most for food and fuel, while other household expenses went unmet. Picket lines now appeared, replacing breadlines, with slogans like "no money for toilet paper."[20]

In January 1935 FDR had had enough of direct-relief programs and wanted to end them by substituting public-works employment for the employables and leaving the unemployables for the states and localities to handle. Federal obligation for welfare was abandoned and the responsibility turned over to the states; another opportunity for shifting the obligations under federalism was lost in the process.

The amounts of direct-relief payments by both the federal and state levels of government are shown in Table 5.1.

Public Works

Aside from direct relief, always subject to criticism, another way to stimulate aggregate demand and employment is through expenditures on public works. The New Deal began its programs for public works in

November 1933 with the creation of the Civil Works Administration, which replaced the small amounts spent under the Federal Emergency Relief Act of 1933.

In operation from November 1933 to July 1934, the CWA spent nearly a billion dollars on a variety of projects, from roads, school buildings, parks, and airports to programs for artists, writers, and opera singers. The CWA also kept many schools in operation by paying for teachers for both children and adults. Employment under the CWA rose from 1,532,000 in November 1933 to a maximum of 4,311,000 in January 1934. Generally, the CWA tried to pick labor-intensive projects that were of short duration. The sacrifice of expenditures on capital goods led to inefficiency, of course, but it did put to work large numbers in a hurry.[21] Paying minimum wages in general, the CWA paid out over $718 million in earnings to people employed on its projects.

The CWA was popular with everyone except the president, who was concerned over the increasing costs of the program and the possibility of its become too popular and hence a permanent feature of the economy. He ordered the elimination of the program, and by April 1934 most of the employed were released. Winter was over, and the CWA had done its job.

The unfinished work was taken over by the Federal Emergency Relief Administration (FERA), which not only continued the same type of program but experimented with new ones as well. The FERA built thousands of public buildings, constructed bridges, and repaired waterways. It also continued to spend on education, and one adult program led to the derogatory term "boondoggling" for its output—boondoggles, belts, and linoleum-block prints.[22]

By the end of 1934 the New Deal programs had spent nearly $2 billion on direct relief alone and had furnished earnings on public-works projects of another $1.5 billion. FDR was determined to cut the relief rolls and to shift even more spending to the public-works programs, where people were working, at least. Accordingly, in January 1935 he proposed a huge program of public-works spending totaling some $5 billion. In March Congress finally passed a measure, the Emergency Relief Appropriations Act of 1935, that gave the president a blank check of nearly $5 billion to allocate as he wished. Congress relinquished its control over the spending of a large portion of the budget and entrusted the president with additional powers.

The act created the Works Progress Administration (WPA), renamed in 1939 the Works Projects Administration after it merged with the Public Works Administration, to provide employment on public works and reduce direct relief. The WPA was headed by Harry

Hopkins, and the advisory Committee on Allocations was chaired by Harold Ickes. This arrangement set the stage for one of the more interesting battles between New Deal philosophies.

Hopkins wanted to maximize employment in small projects and to do so quickly. Ickes preferred the large-scale projects where assets of value were created without the emphasis on maximizing employment or limiting capital expenditures. The latter's plans would have aided the long-term recovery of the economy, but they suffered from long delays in getting projects started and completed. Hopkins simply wanted to put people to work and reduce relief rolls, even if the end project did not yield a return to society over many years and was considered make-work.

Hopkins won most of the battles, as nearly 89 percent of funds spent by the WPA were for labor. The WPA had to operate under certain conditions: that the project have local sponsors, be useful, be completed in one year, be on public property, and not interfere with private employment.

With these (and more) conditions, the list of the WPA's achievements is astounding. The WPA really started in August 1935 when it employed 220,163 people, a figure that rose to a high of 3,334,594 in November 1938 and gradually diminished until it disappeared in 1943. Over that period it constructed 651,087 miles of highways and roads; 77,965 new bridges and viaducts; 35,064 public buildings, as well as parks, stadiums, pools, golf courses, tennis courts, and so on. Through March 1943 the WPA had spent over $10 billion, and sponsors had spent nearly $3 billion. About 77 percent of the expenditures were for construction projects.[23] Even more interesting are the amounts spent on "public activities" ($7.64 million): on education, music, recreation, writing, libraries, art works, and museums, and on "research and records" ($435 million).[24]

It is clear that the New Deal did not achieve full employment, since at best it employed 3 million out of roughly 10 million unemployed. Many remained on the dole. One group hit hard by the depression was youth, and they bore a disproportionate burden of unemployment. One-third were unemployed, and of those who had work, one-fifth were working part time. Females and poor youth suffered most.

The New Deal tried to meet this problem by designing programs for the young. The first, the Civilian Conservation Corps (CCC), was limited to people 17–25 years old for work on public projects. Working out of camps in every state, the young men worked on roads, bridges, and fire towers, on forestry improvements and recreational facilities, on erosion and flood-control projects, and on conservation projects.

Over the years over 2 million men entered the CCC, with the maximum strength being in the late summer of 1935 when nearly 500,000 were enrolled. Many came from the cities and regained or improved their health in addition to learning new skills on the job. Some learned academic subjects as well. The pay was minimal, about $1,000 per year, and the desertion rate was high. Toward the end of the program, the instruction became semimilitary in character.[25]

The other program, the National Youth Administration (NYA), was part of the Federal Emergency Relief Appropriations Act of 1935. It had two facets: for those in high school and college and for those out of school and living at home.

For those in school the NYA provided funds to the school, which then would design projects to be undertaken. The jobs were part time with limits on the number of hours that could be worked. High school students (about one-half million) received $6 per month, while college students (about 600,000) received $10–20 per month, with amounts rising to $20–30 for graduate students. They did a great deal of clerical work, but there was an attempt to fit a job to the student's interests.

The out-of-school youths worked on public projects similar to those found in other public-works programs: road work, repairing schools, construction work in general, and so on. They worked longer hours than those in school and, of course, earned more income— approximately $225 per month. Over 2.6 million youths were involved with this part of the NYA.

Other New Deal Programs

By now, the types of programs advocated by the New Deal should be familiar. There is no need to spell out the other programs in detail, but they should be mentioned, if only in brief, for they indicate the range of New Deal initiatives over all facets of economic life.

One of these programs finally settled the Muscle Shoals controversy that had gone on for years. The Tennessee Valley Authority Act of 1933 was passed to address the problems of flood control, reforestation, power generation and sale, and, in general, planning for land use for the whole region. Despite the opposition from private power companies, the TVA survived all attacks on it and went on to demonstrate the feasibility of public enterprise and large-scale planning.

Another program was designed to rescue the owners of homes when their mortgages were in jeopardy and at the same time aid the banking industry as well. The Home Owners Loan Corporation (HOLC) was created to purchase home mortgages from banking institutions, thereby providing them with funds while the mortgages were being scaled down or postponed for the homeowner. Moreover, the HOLC authorized federal charters for the building and loan associations and savings and loan associations that became the main mortgage lenders. To restore confidence and permit orderly growth of the industry, an act of June 1934 created the Federal Savings and Loan Insurance Corporation (FSLIC), which insured the first $5,000 of each account. The same act created the Federal Housing Administration to insure long-term mortgages on private dwellings by taking over some of the functions of the HOLC that were gradually phased out.

The Federal Land Banks and the Federal Farm Mortgage Corporation did much the same thing for the farmer, while the RFC was engaged in activities on behalf of businesses. Thus the rehabilitation of each sector was attempted by similar though different agencies.

Having outlined the major New Deal programs on a sectoral basis, it is now appropriate to look at the national monetary and fiscal policies of the Roosevelt administration. This is not to say that the two types of programs, sectoral and national, are entirely separate from each other and did not interact. They are treated separately for the present until the evaluation of the New Deal is attempted.

Monetary Policy, 1934–40

Monetary policy became passive for the most part from 1934 to 1940. The Federal Reserve System stood by and watched the gold and silver inflow do its job of affecting the volume of bank reserves. Gold inflows rose from $ −173.5 million (valued at $20.67 per ounce) to $1,133.9 million in 1934 after devaluation, and for the period 1934–40 totaled over $15.7 billion. The stock of gold rose from $4 billion in 1934 to over $22 billion in 1940. Similarly, silver inflows amounted to over $1 billion in the period 1934–40.

While banks used some of these increases in reserves to finance new loans, much of the inflow merely served to create excess reserves. Excess reserves began to increase rapidly after 1934, posing a new problem for the Federal Reserve System. As indicated, the System played no part in creating the excess reserves; in fact, Federal Reserve credit was virtually constant over the period. Obviously, banks did not have to borrow from the Federal Reserve, and the discount rate was not altered after 1935, when it was lowered to 1 percent in New York and Cleveland and 1.5 percent in other areas.[26]

While monetary ease was appropriate for the times and while the Federal Reserve was committed to contributing toward a recovery, the system began to view the buildup of excess reserves with increasing concern. Federal Reserve officials worried that the existence of excess reserves posed a threat to the monetary authority if it tried to use its weapons of open-market operations to control bank reserves. Prices were rising, and using restraining policies later, which might become necessary, would be made more difficult if banks held such large excess reserves.

The Federal Reserve decided to reduce the excess reserves to make open-market operations feasible in the future. The question was, How? To sell bonds might have indicated a switch in policy of the Federal Reserve and reduced bank earnings. The system did not desire to do either. Besides, the amount of securities held by the Federal Reserve was not sufficient at the time to absorb the excess reserves through open-market sales. Also, the discount rate was useless as a tool in this situation.

So the Federal Reserve chose to utilize the latest weapon in its arsenal—the power to alter reserve requirements. In August 1936, after much debate, the Federal Reserve increased reserve requirements in three steps, until by May 1, 1937, reserve requirements would be doubled. The reserve requirement rates were 13 percent on demand deposits in major cities and 10 percent and 7 percent in other areas; time deposits carried a rate of 3 percent. By May 1, 1937, these rates had doubled to the maximum rates permitted by law.

The Federal Reserve made a survey to determine whether many banks would be affected seriously by this move and concluded that no major disturbances would result. The excess reserves, then, were regarded as superfluous. So the August action increased reserve requirements by 50 percent without creating hardships. Yet bank excess reserves were still large (over $1.8 billion), and gold inflows were continuing.

Alarmed, the Treasury began "sterilizing" the gold inflows in December by purchasing the gold with new issues of interest-bearing bonds instead of issuing gold certificates to the Federal Reserve and creating a deposit from which to make payments. Moreover, the Federal Reserve once again increased bank reserve requirements in January 1937 by 50 percent, effective in halves on March 1st and May 1st. No further increases were possible without changes in the law.

Now, however, the banks did not respond by giving up their holdings of excess reserves, but instead acted to preserve them. The excess reserves were performing a function for the banks and were not regarded as superfluous. The banks' demand for excess reserves was to satisfy their desire for liquidity.[27] Perhaps they feared the risks attendant to making loans, with interest rates so low anyway. Yet even with the low interest rates, private investment was not stimulated by businessmen seeking capital.

Thus banks sold securities to augment reserves, increasing interest rates and eventually decreasing the money supply. The Federal Reserve's actions might have been understandable if viewed with concern for rising prices and the fear of inflation, but the magnitude of the action was clearly inappropriate for this purpose. Short-term interest rates rose from 0.17 in January to 0.56 in April 1937, before the Federal Reserve forced them down again by swapping short-term securities for long-term bonds. The money supply that had risen by over 53 percent from April 1933 to March 1937 now began to fall slightly, by 2 percent in the following year.

These results of the Federal Reserve's and Treasury's actions, as well as the uncertainties they created, may have helped bring about the recession within a depression that began in the spring of 1937 and lasted for about a year. If the Federal Reserve was mistaken in its policies on reserve requirements, it was also slow to respond to the conditions it helped to create. Only in September 1937 did it buy any securities and then relied on the Treasury to desterilize gold stocks to pay bills and create monetary ease. In the following April the reserve requirement was lowered by one-third, and the Treasury stopped sterilizing gold inflows.

The result was that interest rates fell again as excess reserves were allowed to increase. By 1940 the excess reserves were over $6 billion, with gold continuing to flow into the United States. According to Friedman and Schwartz, monetary measures were deemphasized in the 1930s in favor of fiscal policies, and the view that "money does not matter" became widely accepted.[28] If true, this helps explain the passivity of monetary actions. The Federal Reserve switched its behavior to prevent disorderly markets, as the shift of power within the Federal Reserve moved from New York to Washington after reorganization.

Federal Reserve motivations may be debatable, but their actions can be judged by the facts. Clearly the Federal Reserve's monetary policies were inappropriate for this period and may have made things worse. After the recessions of 1937–38 and its response to them, the

Federal Reserve System did little until forced to by the demands of
World War II.

Fiscal Policy in Roosevelt's First Term

In the presidential campaign Roosevelt reprimanded Hoover for not
balancing the budget, the sure sign of sound fiscal principles.
Presumably his commitment to a balanced budget was stronger.
Probably he did remain faithful to the balanced-budget concept,
although in his second term he may have relented a bit.[29] In any case,
he never achieved a balanced budget while in office. Table 5.2 shows
the federal budget figures, as well as their effect on the national debt.
    Of course, the continuous deficits worried Roosevelt, more for
political than economic reasons. For instance, he even separated the
budget outlays between regular expenditures and emergency outlays
in order to try to convince the public that the budget was balanced for
regular items. (Hoover's would have been, too.) He may not have been
swayed by Keynes, but neither was he deterred by the principles of
fiscal orthodoxy: Pragmatism and necessity would win, whatever
struggle developed. Just before World War II, the Roosevelt administration was reaching for budgetary reforms that would have separated
current from capital items and would have advised balancing the
budget over the business cycle, as the Swedes had done.[30]

Table 5.2   Federal Fiscal Operations, 1933–40 (millions of dollars)

Fiscal Year	Receipts	Expenditures	Surplus or Deficit (−)	Federal Debt at End of Year
1933	1,997	4,598	−2,602	22,539
1934	3,015	6,645	−3,630	27,053
1935	3,706	6,497	−2,791	28,701
1936	3,997	8,422	−4,425	33,779
1937	4,956	7,733	−2,777	36,425
1938	5,588	6,765	−1,177	37,165
1939	4,979	8,841	−3,862	40,440
1940	6,361	9,456	−3,095	42,968

    Source: U.S. Bureau of the Census, Historical Statistics of the United States
(Washington, DC: GPO, 1975), pp. 1106–17.

The first year of the Roosevelt administration was dominated mainly by monetary and reform measures that tend to overshadow fiscal moves. For instance, the Economy Act of March 21, 1933, restrained the federal bureaucracy, reduced spending on veterans' pensions, and reduced government employees' salaries. Also, the NIRA of June 1933 contained a provision for a $3,300 million public-works program. The act also contained a plan to raise taxes to pay for interest and sinking-fund requirements. The president gave the Committee on Ways and Means just one week to find the necessary taxes. The sales tax was proposed and rejected, as were increases in income-tax rates, following the revelation that J. P. Morgan and others had paid no income tax the preceding year. It would have been unfair to tax lower-income recipients after that fact became known.

The Senate Finance Committee scrapped the additional income taxes and other House-backed provisions and came up with the following program, later adopted by the Conference Committee: (1) a capital stock tax of $1 for each $1,000 of declared value of the capital stock of corporations; (2) an excess profits tax of 5 percent on the portion of net income in excess of 12.5 percent of the declared capital stock value; (3) an additional tax on gasoline of one-half cent per gallon; (4) a 5 percent tax on dividends received by individuals; (5) changes in the tax laws designed to collect more taxes from private bankers and partnerships; (6) a 50 percent penalty tax upon undistributed corporate surplus to prevent individuals from evading taxes.[31]

In addition, the Agriculture Adjustment Act included processing taxes on domestic products grown in excess of quotas, and certain customs duties. These taxes were passed on to the consumer and amounted to a billion dollars before they were discontinued. Also, Prohibition was repealed in December 1933, and taxes were quickly imposed on liquor.

The tax increases were accepted by the business community without much complaint. Perhaps Roosevelt was still trusted to balance the budget and pursue the principles of sound finance. Besides, the banking sector was being revitalized, and this was not the time to protest.[32]

Tax increases in a depression were defended on the ground that the changes reduced the inequities in the tax system. Then, too, there were those deficits. Alvin Hansen, however, blamed the taxes on consumption for delaying the recovery.[33] On the expenditure side, Roosevelt was known to be suspicious of public-works programs as recovery vehicles; first, because there probably were not enough useful projects to undertake; and, second, he doubted whether these outlays would have multiplier effects. That is, expenditures on public works created incomes for these (labor-intensive) projects, and these incomes were spent on consumer goods, creating more income, and so on. He did not understand or believe in the multiplier concept made famous by Keynes.

Alvin Hansen, on the contrary, felt that public-works expenditures were too small for the task of recovery.[34] Perhaps Roosevelt also underestimated the duration of the depression and hence did not want to undertake public-works projects that were long-term.

Thus, in the first year the New Deal was increasing taxes on business and embarking on a public-works program as to which it had serious reservations. When the strong upturn in mid-1933 petered out, so did any hope of a quick rebound.

The fiscal year 1934 gave the New Deal the opportunity to produce a budget that would reveal its philosophy. Roosevelt promptly began to use the budget as a political weapon. He apparently deliberately overestimated the planned expenditures ($10.6 billion), so that the actual expenditures ($6.7 billion) would put his administration in a favorable light.[35] Moreover, the estimated deficit of $7.3 billion would look dreadful compared to the actual deficit of $3.6 billion.

Once more the budget totals were generally accepted as necessary, particularly when faith in a balanced budget was continually expressed. Perhaps the Revenue Act of May 10, 1934, helped to convince those inclined to be skeptical. This revision of the tax code was originally intended to reduce inequities and hence reduce tax avoidance. The Committee on Ways and Means went beyond mere tinkering and produced a bill that the Treasury found necessary to modify. The income tax was made more progressive, as the normal tax was made a flat 4 percent and the surtax rates were graduated from 1 percent on income over $4,000–6,000, to 59 percent on incomes in excess of $1 million. The earned income credit was restored at a rate of 10 percent on incomes of less than $14,000. Capital-gains taxation was revised, and gains and losses were calculated on the length of time the assets were held, from 100 percent for not more than one year to 30 percent on assets held more than ten years. The remaining gains were then taxed at regular rates.

A tax was imposed on the improperly accumulated surplus of any corporation, and the capital stock and excess profits taxes were continued. Finally a tariff was put on coconut and other edible oils to protect U.S. dairy farmers. The proceeds from the tax were collected in a fund to be paid to the Filipinos who were the main exporters to the United States.

These and other provisions helped reduce tax avoidance and permit the tax codes to reflect social concerns for equity. They did not, however, produce great amounts of revenue, nor did they seriously challenge the positions of high-income recipients.[36]

Perhaps the tax changes were acceptable for that reason, but some were beginning to question the timidity of the New Deal proposals. Despite the overwhelming Democratic victory at the polls in 1934, the New Deal was not developing new ideas and proposals, but seemed to be floundering or content to bolster its existing programs. As it paused, the critics became more vocal.

In the Senate the progressives, led by La Follette and Frank Norris, continued to press the administration to propose new, daring programs to foster social justice, and every New Deal bill was attacked by them for not going far enough. The economy was not rebounding with the speed that everyone had hoped. Conditions had improved, but much remained to be done.

Other critics of the administration were also finding a voice. Senator Huey Long of Louisiana had developed his share-the-wealth plan and had attracted many followers. Originally a backer of Roosevelt, Long grew increasingly impatient with the New Deal, and when his criticisms became too strident to be ignored, Roosevelt decided to break away from further associations with him, whatever the political risk in doing so.[37]

Long maintained that since wealth was unduly concentrated in a few hands, a new tax should be imposed. Anyone could accumulate up to $1 million without penalty. On every million beyond that, however, there would be a "capital levy tax." On the second million the rate would be 1 percent; on the third, 2 percent, and so on in progression, up to $8 million, when the tax would become 100 percent.[38] Inheritances were limited to $1 million, with the remainder going to the government. Similarly, income in excess of $1 million per year would all go to the government.[39]

Concern for the aged found a champion in Dr. Francis E. Townsend, who devised the Townsend Old Age Revolving Fund. The plan that involved the payment by the government of a pension to the aged has already been described in connection with the New Deal's response to it with the Social Security Act. His followers numbered in the millions, and while they were involved in a narrow program, they still demonstrated the range of discontent to be found in the country and the ease with which it could be mobilized.

Perhaps the most unconventional analysis of the depression came from the radio priest, Father Charles Coughlin. Originally on the radio to raise money for the church, his Sunday sermons turned increasingly political, until his popularity destroyed him. "In his weekly radio sermons and in his speeches and writings, he created an explanation of the crisis that was in many ways illogical and occasionally dangerously distorted. But it was, nevertheless, a message that reflected some of the oldest and deepest impulses of the American people, a message that raised fundamental questions about the structure of the nation's economic life."[40] In his famous mellow voice, he railed against banks and banking institutions, calling for a revaluation of gold, the remonetization of silver, and the creation of a Bank of the USA to replace the Federal Reserve System.

In November 1934 Coughlin decided to channel his growing radio audience into an organization, the National Union for Social Justice, to be an organized lobby to pressure government to pass legislation it felt desirable. Millions listened to his Sunday sermons, and many responded to his new organization and presumably agreed to the following principles: liberty of conscience and education, a just and living annual wage, nationalization of a new central bank, congressional control of coinage, equity in taxation, and simplification of government.[41]

Meanwhile, the Socialists, led by Norman Thomas, were berating these demagogues and their movement toward fascism. Despite the similarity of some of their programs, the Socialists rejected the two organizations. Yet the Socialists were losing support, as potential sympathizers were moving toward Long and Coughlin and away from the "radical" ideas of the Socialist program. People preferred the more limited (they felt) proposals for change to be found in the less revolutionary organizations of the Kingfish and the radio priest.

Thus Roosevelt found himself struggling to keep together the coalition of his administration, but he seemed to fear radical elements more than conservative ones. The spring of 1935 brought to the administration a reawakening. In May the Supreme Court struck down the NRA as unconstitutional. One cornerstone of the New Deal was now missing. Also in May the Chamber of Commerce broke with the New Deal and began its criticisms of Roosevelt and his programs. Now the business part of the coalition was breaking away.

Roosevelt, shaken out of his irresolution, began to act, and, as previously outlined, the "second hundred days" saw the enactment of the Social Security Act, the Wagner Act, the Banking Act of 1935, and the Revenue Act of 1935. To what extent Roosevelt was prodded by his critics can never be known with certainty, but his response was swift and dramatic.

On June 19, 1935, Roosevelt sent a surprise tax measure to Congress that included these introductory words: "Our revenue laws have operated in many ways to the unfair advantage of the few, and they have done little to prevent an unjust concentration of wealth and economic power." Progressives and Long (who uttered "amen" upon hearing these words) seized the opportunity to push this bill through Congress, despite the late date of submission before adjournment and the far-reaching changes that it contained.[42] Roosevelt was proposing an inheritance and gift tax, increases in surtax rates, graduated taxes for corporations, taxation of dividends received by corporations, simplification of corporate structures, and a constitutional amendment to tax state and local securities. Conservatives branded it a "soak-the-rich" scheme, but liberals and progressives embraced it, complaining only later, after compromises, that it did not go far enough. Even Long favored it at first and claimed credit for the direction. Incredibly this complex bill was pushed through and signed into law on August 30, 1935, giving the president most of what he wanted.

The key provisions of the bill were as follows: an increase in surtax rates for income brackets of $50,000 and over, with the rates increasing to a maximum of 75 percent on incomes over $500,000 (instead of 59 percent on incomes over $1 million); a graduated corporation income tax with rates of 12.5 percent on net income less than $2,000 to 15 percent on net income in excess of $40,000; an increase in the tax on capital and in the capital stock tax; an increase in the estate tax (the inheritance tax was rejected) by reducing the exemptions from $50,000 to $40,000 and increasing the rates to 2 percent on the first $10,000 to 70 percent on amounts over $50 million; similarly, an increase in the rates on gift taxes, 1.5 percent on gifts in excess of $10,000 up to 52.5 percent on gifts in excess of $50 million. Excise tax changes and penalties for failure to file returns were also included.

Critics complained that the bill was passed merely to please the administration—the revenue-raising features were weak. It is estimated that the revenues raised, one quarter of a billion dollars a year, reduced the concentration of wealth by one-half of 1 percent of the national income at the time. What went unexplored by both critics and advocates alike was that the progressive features of the act would be cancelled by the Social Security tax. The Social Security tax was a regressive tax burdening the low-income taxpayer in whose name the soak-the-rich tax bill was justified.[43]

Actual federal expenditures for fiscal year 1935 and those estimated for 1936 did not reveal any dramatic changes, and thus attention was focused on taxation policy. After the tax changes in 1935 the president could therefore say to Congress that except for relief, the budget was "in balance" and no new taxes were required in 1936.

Three days later the Supreme Court ruled the Agriculture Adjustment Act unconstitutional, and this threw the budget out of balance. The processing tax of the AAA was estimated to yield $0.5 billion, and on the expenditure side $ 0.5 billion was now needed to provide farm relief. To add to this budgetary problem, Congress passed the soldiers' bonus, overriding the president's veto. The bill called for an immediate payment of $2.2 billion in 1936 instead of in 1945 as scheduled.

Accordingly, on March 3 the president sent a special message to Congress, asking for additional revenues of $617 million annually for nine years and $517 million for the next two or three years. Ostensibly leaving the source of the additional revenue to Congress, he suggested that a tax on undistributed corporate profits would not only raise the revenue but contribute toward tax reform as well. The individuals who owned the corporation would not be able to escape taxation by letting the corporation accumulate earnings. He wanted a rate that would yield almost the same revenue that would be obtained if corporate profits were distributed to stockholders. In return, the excess profits tax, capital stock tax, and the 1935 tax on corporate income would be repealed. To meet the need for temporary tax revenue, he suggested a windfall tax on processors who had shifted the taxes collected under the AAA, and an excise tax on the processing of agricultural products.

As might be imagined, these tax suggestions brought out all the arguments over the taxation of corporations as opposed to individuals and partnerships. After much debate Congress passed the Revenue Act of 1936 on June 27, 1936.

The main provisions of the act were the imposition of a normal tax on corporations, ranging from 8 percent on income less than $2,000 to 15 percent on the excess over $40,000 (banks and insurance companies would pay a flat 15 percent); a new surtax on undistributed corporate profits, graduated from 7 percent of undistributed net income not in excess of 10 percent of "adjusted net income" to 27 percent of undistributed net income not in excess of 60 percent of adjusted net income; a reduction in the penalty tax rate on corporate accumulated surplus by 10 percent; and a reduction in the capital stock tax to 1934 rates.[44]

The tax on undistributed profits created a good deal of controversy, as opponents argued that it increased economic instability, meddled in the internal affairs of the corporation, delayed economic recovery, affected large and small corporations differently, and so on, while proponents stressed the release of excessive corporate savings that would aid the recovery by increasing consumer spending. Not many were pleased with the act that emerged and probably preferred to raise the needed revenue through more conventional sources.

Fiscal Policy Changes after the Election of 1936

The landslide victory of Roosevelt over Alfred M. Landon in 1935 is well known, of course—he carried every state except Maine and Vermont. Winning by over 11 million votes, the president also saw the Congress continue to shift to an overwhelming Democratic rule.

In his campaign he attacked the "economic royalists" and promised to keep fighting the money changers for the general welfare, yet there were no startling innovative schemes for a second New Deal. Still, he managed to forge a new coalition of progressives, labor, blacks, lower-income groups, urban dwellers, and so on, and with the invaluable help of Mrs. Eleanor Roosevelt, the Democratic victory was assured.

The Socialists, Communists, and the messiah groups of Long, Coughlin, and Townsend did not present any serious threats. They lost their following as the New Deal met many of their concerns over failures in the U.S. economy—social security, unemployment compensation, collective bargaining rights, and so on. Huey Long was gone, Townsend declining in power and influence, and Coughlin's third party was floundering.

What is more interesting about the 1936 election is the movement toward party affiliation by class. The "economic royalists" were furious with Roosevelt and the New Deal tax policies, particularly the tax on undistributed profits. Many of these people had supported Roosevelt in 1932 and even made contributions to his campaign. Now the campaign contributions went to the Republican candidate, so that the Republicans outspent the Democrats by 2 to 1 or $10 million to $5 million. Bankers, brokers, big industrialists, publishers, and so on backed the Republican Landon against "that man in the White House." Not all members of these groups supported Landon, of course, but it is clear that the Democrats had to rely on their new coalition for most of their financial support. U.S. politics began to reflect class interests to a larger extent in this campaign.[45]

Hardly anticapitalist, as claimed by his critics, FDR did acknowledge that institutions must change when necessary. Furthermore, the job was not done with the completion of the first term, for in his second inaugural speech he revealed, "I see one third of a nation ill-housed, ill-clad, ill-nourished. In our seeking for economic and political progress as a nation, we all go up—or else we all go down—as one people."

The attack on economic royalists continued with a tax message sent to Congress on June 1, 1937. Roosevelt asked for legislation to close loopholes in the tax laws that allowed individuals and corporations to evade taxes. Secretary Morgenthau enumerated the devices for evasion of income taxes used by the economic royalists: foreign holding and insurance companies, domestic personal holding companies, family partnerships, multiple trusts for relatives and dependents, and pension trusts.[46]

The House drafted a bill largely attacking the personal holding company, with some provisions to curb multiple trusts abuses and alter the taxation on nonresident aliens. The Senate readily accepted the House version, and the Revenue Act of 1937 was signed into law on August 26, 1937. New rules were made on the taxation of personal holding companies. The main provision raised the tax rate on undistributed net income of personal holding companies from 8 to 65 percent on income not over $2,000 and from 48 to 75 percent on amounts over $2,000. Other provisions did close some loopholes, but the act left so many remaining that little effort was needed to continue escaping taxes.

Meanwhile Roosevelt developed his scheme for packing the Supreme Court to prevent the dismantling of the entire New Deal. The Court had already struck down the NRA and the AAA, and other New Deal programs were being considered. The press pointed out that this tax measure was not achieving any purpose except perhaps to smear economic royalists or divert attention from the Supreme Court issue.[47] The press was hostile and blamed the administration for failure to rewrite the tax laws that encouraged evasion and for failure to estimate revenues accurately, so that new sources were always needed.

The economy in 1937 was still far from robust, and unemployment was still hovering near 15 percent, with considerable slack in capacity usage. Yet the administration decided to retreat from the goal of full employment, protesting that the attainment of full employment went beyond government's responsibilities. Besides, prices began to rise at both the wholesale and consumer levels.

So Roosevelt reverted to his previous position regarding balanced budgets as sound finance. While he probably never abandoned his belief in balanced budgets, he had sanctioned deficits, justifying them as necessary for emergencies. Now he was told that with some fiscal restraint in 1937, a balanced budget was possible in fiscal 1938.[48] Receipts were expected to grow from income tax and excise tax increases, as well as from the inflow of Social Security taxes. Expenditures were expected to fall, because of decreases in the soldiers' bonus and the fall in relief and recovery expenses.

When receipts fell behind production, FDR pressed all agencies to hold down expenditures. They were unsuccessful, and the promised balanced budget for fiscal 1938 evaporated. Yet there were budget shifts taking place, as receipts were growing (due to Social Security taxes) over the calendar year 1937, while expenditures were falling as the soldiers' bonus was ended. Thus the budget was registering restraint and moving toward balance.[49]

Along with these fiscal trends, recall that the Federal Reserve was busy in March and May of 1937 increasing the reserve requirements of member banks. Concerned with inflation and the ability of the Federal Reserve System to manage monetary conditions with the excess reserves that banks held, the Federal Reserve's actions resulted in increasing interest rates and falling bond prices. The banks desired the excess reserves and simply sold bonds to recapture them. The Federal Reserve refused to reverse the slide in bond prices by buying bonds and advised the Treasury that a balanced budget was necessary first.

The result was a recession that began in May 1937 and lasted until June 1938. This sharp recession within a depression jolted the administration, which was unprepared for this set-back to New Deal recovery policies. Roosevelt was advised to spend more to stimulate the economy or to spend less to balance the budget; to reverse antibusiness attitudes and reduce business taxes, especially the hated tax on undistributed profits; to go back to some version of the NRA or to attack economic power; and so on. Clearly the advice was conflicting, and for a time after the recession was fully recognized (August 1937) the administration did little, which meant moving toward a balanced budget.

The lack of response to the recession continued for most of the first quarter of 1938, interrupted only by pressures to spend more on relief programs. In early April Roosevelt was suddenly convinced of the need to spend more, even if deficits followed. Keynes had urged this route, and Harry Hopkins, Leon Henderson, Beardsley Ruml, and Aubrey Williams managed to convince the president over his own and other advisors' objections. This was spending for its own sake to stimulate the economy through increases in consumption, not the pump-priming kind to stimulate production.

The new approach, made public on April 14, called for a reversal of the cuts in recovery programs and for additional spending of $1,550 million for fiscal year 1939 for New Deal programs; for an easing of credit by increasing the money supply and reducing reserve requirements, and by new public-works spending and additional federal loans for housing.

Critics of the spending program, mainly business and conservatives generally, preferred to discard the New Deal and unleash the business sector from burdensome taxation. Businessmen saw nothing in the spending plan to change their opinion of the New Deal, only the

continuation of deficits and the centralization of power. Indeed, they
had reason to fear the New Deal, since FDR had attacked them, then
wanted cooperation via some variant of the NRA, and now in April
1938 had sent a message to Congress asking for an investigation into
the concentration of economic power. Congress established the Temporary National Economic Committee (TNEC) to look into the issue.
This sharp reversal by the administration obviously did little to
mollify business or to advance the recovery.

Yet the complaints of businessmen did gain a hearing in
Congress that established in August 1937 a subcommittee of the House
Way and Means to consider a tax revision bill. While the administration was pondering its response to the recession, the tax issue was
being debated in Congress. What emerged was a comprehensive tax
law, the Revenue Act of 1938, which became law on April 26, 1938,
without the president's signature.

The main provision of the act reduced the rate of taxation on
undistributed profits to 2.5 percent (down from 27 percent) for
corporations with incomes over $25,000 for 1938 and 1939. Corporate
tax rates were changed, as was the penalty tax on improperly
accumulated surplus. The only major tax revision for individuals
altered the tax treatment of capital gains. The net effect was to
increase the tax paid on the sale of assets held less than 18 months and
reduce the tax liability for assets held more than 18 months. The
maximum rate of tax became 20 percent for short-term gains and 15
percent for long-term gains.[50]

Business scored a victory and might have been encouraged to aid
in the recovery effort, but Roosevelt threatened a new assault in 1939.
Despite the confusion and conflicts, the economy began to recover in
May and June of 1938. The threatened tax bills to reverse business
gains did not occur. Instead, the Revenue Act of 1939 repealed the tax
on undistributed profits, imposed a flat tax rate of 18 percent on
corporate net income, and liberalized the treatment of capital gains.[51]
Thus, while the TNEC was examining economic power, Congress was
being told by Undersecretary of the Treasury John W. Hanes, "that it
is the intention of the government to establish a tax system which
preserves and increases the incentives that are essential to the
perpetuation of a system of free enterprise in a nation of free men."[52]

The only tax measure that suited FDR was the Public Salary Tax
Act of 1939, which permitted federal taxation of salaries of state
employees and federal judges. It did not include one of his long-time
irritants, the taxation of tax-exempt securities. While the recovery
began in the summer of 1938 and continued into the fall of 1939, the
upswing was a weak and irregular one. The administration, although

committed to fiscal policy, proposed no large increases in federal spending. Opposition to deficit spending and to the New Deal had been growing, and FDR himself appeared hesitant once again in proposing deficits in a period of recovery. He did finally propose a scheme to have the RFC borrow $3.8 billion to spend or lend to finance self-liquidating investment projects to stimulate the sluggish economy. The plan was scrapped in the House as too radical and contrary to principles of sound finance (that is, balanced budgets).

In January 1939 the president submitted a budget message for fiscal year 1940 that estimated over $9 billion in total spending and included a substantial increase in defense and relief spending. (Later in the year Congress would increase these amounts for the coming year, but that move will be covered in the next chapter.) The same budget message was notable for its discussion of when budgets should be considered balanced; which government expenditures, ordinary or extraordinary, should be balanced against current receipts; and at which level of national income the expenditures should be measured. This latter discussion paved the way for measuring the impact of government on the economy by a high- or full-employment surplus.[53]

Discussions about the budget were made even more relevant when Roosevelt forwarded the recommendation of the President's Commission on Administrative Management to Congress on January 12, 1937. Anticipating trouble, he included in his message the idea that he was not asking for more power, but only seeking to make the method of managing the fiscal operations of the government more efficient and rational.

The plan to reorganize the Budget Bureau met with great opposition, as it aroused the fear of dictatorship. It was finally passed on April 25, 1939, establishing the Executive Office of the President and transferring to it the Bureau of the Budget (from Treasury) and the National Resources Planning Board (from Interior).[54] To assist the president in the preparation of the budget and to advise him on all matters relating to the process of budget making, the act went a long way in revitalizing the Bureau of the Budget and in introducing economists to high advisory positions. This latter trend would continue over the years.

Reorganizations and budget discussions aside, the year 1939 saw the economy far removed from full employment or rapid growth. True, money GNP had increased, back to its 1937 level, and real GNP had actually increased over the 1937 level. Clearly, prices were still weak or falling. Yet the unemployment rate stood at 17.2 percent, down from the 19.0 percent rate of 1938, but hardly indicating a healthy economy. Many question what all those deficits and New Deal programs had accomplished. At this time, however, the specter of a world at war took some attention away from the functioning of the domestic economy. World War II eliminated the need for the evaluation of the new Deal, since it elevated the economy out of the depression.

Distribution of Income

If the New Deal was not successful in solving the unemployment problem, did it at least remember the forgotten man it championed? If the size of the national income pie was shrinking, did the lower-income group get a larger slice? Again the data on income and wealth are not as detailed or as accurate as one might wish. With this admonition, what data are available are given in Table 5.3.

The data in Table 5.3 give the distribution of family incomes by fifths. The data are incomplete but can be used to give an impressionistic view of where changes occurred. From 1929 to the mid-1930s, the shifts in income distribution are from the highest fifth and top 5 percent to the fourth fifth and the lowest two fifths. The shifts reduced the degree of inequality, and later shifts in the early 1940s continued that trend (only data for 1941 are shown in the table). Yet the shares of those at the bottom, the lowest 40 percent, remained unchanged.

What these data show is that in the 1930s there was some redistribution of income from the top fifth to the middle fifth but no sweeping redistribution of income. The result is not surprising, since the New Deal did not embark upon a path that would have transformed the economic system and altered the distribution of rewards. Indeed, the New Deal programs that aided the low-income groups—relief, public-works employment, youth programs, and so on—did little more than provide for the basic needs of those at the bottom. The New Deal programs certainly posed no threat to the economic royalists, who complained bitterly but who benefited from many of the administration's efforts to revive the economy. The banking sector was rescued from collapse, and many private firms were called up for public-works projects. The existing distribution of capital ownership was not seriously disturbed or undermined.

Data on the distribution of income are generally regarded as more reliable than are those for the distribution of wealth. One attempt to analyze the concentration of wealth, cited in Chapter 1, was done by Robert J. Lampman for the National Bureau of Economic Research. Using federal estate-tax data, his estimates for the concentration of wealth are as accurate as one is likely to get from any system

Table 5.3   Distribution of Family Personal Income Received by Each Fifth and Top 5 Percent of Families and Unattached Individuals, Selected Years

Year	Lowest Fifth	Second Fifth	Third Fifth	Fourth Fifth	Highest Fifth	Top 5 Percent
	Percent Distribution of Aggregate Family Personal Income					
1929	12.5		13.8	19.3	54.4	30.0
1935–36	4.1	9.2	14.1	20.0	51.7	26.5
1941	4.1	9.5	15.3	22.3	48.8	24.0

Source: U.S. Department of Commerce, Bureau of the Census, *Historical Statistics of the United States* (Washington, DC: GPO, 1975), p. 301.

that estimates wealth holdings in retrospect. A brief summary of his findings were given in Table 1.4.

It is clear from Table 1.4 that the inequality of wealth increased substantially in the 1920s, as the top 1 percent of adults increased their share of wealth from 31.6 percent to 36.3 percent; the top 0.5 percent of all persons (including children) shows, of course, a lower percentage of wealth held by the top group, but the same trend is evident for the 1920s. During the 1930s the inequalities in wealth holdings fell for both measures in the depths of the depression in 1933, but by 1939 the inequalities were returning to predepression levels.

Clearly the depression erased or reduced many property values (particularly real estate), as assets were revalued and portfolios rearranged. Again, however, the New Deal does not appear to have affected the distribution of wealth to a significant extent. The basic structure of capital ownership remained intact, as did the basic framework of capitalist production. While this is hardly a revelation, it may still be necessary to repeat the obvious, if only to counter the belief that somehow the New Deal was able (and aimed) to alter the economic system, away from pure capitalist principles. Judging from its programs, the structure of production, the ownership of wealth, and the distribution of income, it made no such attempt, nor was it successful in affecting the distribution of economic power.

Causes of the Great Depression

Before attempting to evaluate the national policies of the depression years, it is appropriate first to try to summarize the causes of the depression in the first place. What made this depression so severe? Why did not this cycle follow the previous experiences—say of those downturns in the 1920s?

It is fair to say that scholars do not and cannot agree on the answers to these questions. Indeed there were so many factors that seemed to converge in this period that it is possible for some to stress one or two of them, while others stress another set. Disagreement over the causes is certainly understandable, but what may emerge is the disconcerting idea that we may never know what ultimately set this cycle apart from others and may never be able to isolate "the" cause.

As a consequence, anyone interested in examining the causes of the Great Depression is forced to reproduce a list of possible causes or contributing factors and then stress those considered most important. Accordingly, a list of causes follows, ranked in a general way by the order of importance:[55]

1. The capital-goods boom created excess capacity in many areas. Buoyed by high profits and increases in labor productivity, there was a tendency to overinvest in anticipation of demand. Investment spending contributed to the boom of the late 1920s, but when the economy slowed, the existence of excess capacity reduced the need for investment demand and postponed recovery. Aggravating the decline was the slowdown in residential construction, which began in the mid-1920s.

2. The same observation can be made about inventories, which also were allowed to accumulate beyond demand, leading to cutbacks in production in the summer of 1929.

3. High interest rates did not encourage investment spending, although inflated capital values offset somewhat the reluctance to borrow.

4. The propensity to consume fell in 1929 by over 2 percent, reacting adversely on (1) and (2).

As many have noted, these factors were sufficient to cause a downturn, but are not sufficient to explain the severity of it. Add to these objective factors the amorphous ones, and the situation is made more complex.

5. The euphoria of the 1920s that resulted in the stock-market boom, get-rich-quick schemes of all kinds, and the general mood that downgraded all risk were shattered by the decline of the economy and replaced by pessimism. First, short-run expectations were reversed, and then long-run expectations, as the economy sank deeper. The toll of disillusionment was costly.

6. The stock-market crash obviously contributed to the reversal of expectations and to the collapse of investment spending and the further reduction in consumption spending. Yet the market's crash went far beyond

the immediate impact, as it created panic, fear, uncertainty, and led to a type of paralysis for many and bewilderment for most.

The downturn in the economy interacting with adverse expectations for the future and the fear and bewilderment caused by the collapse of the hallmark of capitalism, the stock market, are sufficient to ensure confusion and possibly inaction as well. Now combine these conditions with the institutional weaknesses in the economy, and a genuine crisis of undetermined length is likely.

7. The Banking system was ill equipped to handle the downturn. When loans, many unwise in retrospect, turned sour, assets were frozen. The failure of one bank affected others, as depositors rushed to withdraw funds upon hearing the news. Again, bank failures are a crushing blow to a society where banks (and bankers) are regarded as very stable and trusted institutions. Confidence, the lifeblood of the banking industry, was simply devastated.

8. Similarly, the existence of holding companies meant that failure of one firm had repercussions on a number of firms, often in diverse industries. Like a house of cards, the removal of one sent the whole structure down. Investment trusts, some legitimate, others on paper only, were vulnerable to declines in one area spreading to other areas, until the whole edifice collapsed.

9. The rigid banking industry and the fragile corporate structure clearly destroyed faith in existing institutions. Still another weak institutional reality was the inequitable distribution of income in the United States. When the stock market crashed, the incomes of those who indulged in the market fell and so did those of all industries that were dependent upon their consumption, namely, luxury and durable goods. Again the fall in consumption reacts unfavorably on (1) and (2).

These institutional deficiencies combined to make the downturn a severe one: What made the depression a lengthy one was the response of governmental institutions to it.

10. As recited in this chapter, neither monetary or fiscal authorities acted in a timely manner to cushion the fall, nor did they devise the appropriate policies for the longer term. The Hoover administration and the Federal Reserve System failed to act promptly and blundered when they did. They simply were unprepared for the task by lack of knowledge of how the economy functioned and by ideological commitments.

Finally, there are other factors to be considered in the list of contributing causes of the depression. While not directly responsible for the depression, their existence helped to make it worse or prolonged it.

11. The perennial problems of agriculture, overproduction, fluctuating farm incomes, and low prices were addressed by the New Deal. The dust storms and droughts, however, brought new concerns that policies to control output and prices could not handle. On top of falling prices, bank foreclosures, and loan denials, many farmers had to face a new threat to their survival. Many did not make it.

12. The decline in foreign trade due to the increases in tariffs hurt the agricultural sector, and as the economy sank into the depression, the United States reduced its lending abroad. Worldwide trade fell and caused problems with the balance of payments, debt repayment, capital movements, and so on, which probably contributed to the prevention of economic recovery. In this regard, in the aftermath of World War I, reparations, war debts, national rivalries, and so on must also be counted as contributing factors in the depression, as seen in the fragility of the international financial system and the worldwide spread of the depression once it started.

The list of causes could probably be extended, but little would be served by doing so. The multiple factors interact and form their own house of cards. It is likely to prove impossible to assign a particular emphasis to each, and in the end this is what accounts for the controversy over what actually caused the depression—a question of emphasis.

Evaluating Roosevelt's Economic Policies

Let us now turn to an evaluation of the Roosevelt administration's economic policies in terms of the three avenues for judgment: Were the policies justified, successful, and rational?

There is no point in seeking justification for New Deal policies in the economic orthodoxy of the times. As noted earlier, the classical economic paradigm, wherein full employment and stable growth would return if the free market were unhindered, had little to offer the policymaker seeking immediate solutions. The paradigm of the Hoover administration surely demonstrates this. Indeed, it is a wonder that any traditional economist could be taken seriously, and, clearly, they were not. Economists had few answers, and their training in the classical model left them ill prepared to respond with fresh ideas.

It is not surprising, under these conditions, that the message of John M. Keynes became increasingly acceptable; yet Keynes' influence on New Deal policies was minimal at first and only slowly gained favor among a few administration economists later in the decade, when deficit spending met with greater, although still reluctant, approval.

The depression and the New Deal responses to it led to the rejection of the old economic model and began the process of adapting to the new economic model of Keynes. In the coming years the process would be complete, and the Keynesian revolution would have profoundly altered and revised attitudes toward economic public policy.

The New Deal had to act before the process was completed and the converts were unified. Lacking a theory of the cause of the depression, not to mention the cures, the Roosevelt administration was forced to take actions without a sound justification for doing so. Rather, the justification for the New Deal policies came from pressure—political and social—to do something, and do it quickly. In the face of massive suffering, widespread fear, despair, and disillusionment, theoretical vindication of the need to act would simply have to be deferred. "This nation asks for action, and action now" were the inaugural words of FDR.

Roosevelt was not an intellectual and cared little for the theoretical niceties or ideological consistency. He acted more out of humanitarian concern, mixed with a touch of paternalism and noblesse oblige, than out of commitment to fixed ideals.[56] His anti-intellectual attitude made him pragmatic and willing to experiment; paradoxically, it also made him partly responsible for the more general acceptance of the new economic theory of J. M. Keynes.

Imagine, then, how an orthodox economist must have looked upon the New Deal policies. Government was intruding into all areas of economic life, controlling, regulating, licensing, guiding, and coercing economic agents. The free-market ideology was crumbling, and with it went the loss of economic freedom. Some government agency was always telling you what you could do, should do, or would do. Besides, this administration, led by FDR, rejected the notion of business wisdom and efficiency and alienated itself from this progressive force.

The radical ideas of the New Deal, those entertained and those put into practice, did pay little attention to the loss of economic freedom so dearly cherished by free-market economists. What justification was there for this indifference to a fundamental right, without even the customary cautious reserve for such sweeping changes?

Perhaps unhindered by ideological shackles, FDR and some of his advisors claimed that much of the free market had already disappeared, turning the economic system even more into a system of privilege, a system that had provided economic freedom for only a few. He railed against the concentration of economic power and argued frequently along these lines: "The struggle against private monopoly is a struggle for, and not against, American business. It is a struggle to preserve individual enterprise and economic freedom."[57] He spoke frequently of his belief in individualism, private property, and personal freedom. Yet he saw these values threatened by institutional changes that favored the few.

What justified his actions, then, was his belief that he was providing more economic freedom to more people. The New Deal policies perceived that this could be done by responding to the clamor for more security and more protection from the vagaries of the economic system. The desire for security replaced unbridled economic freedom in the hierarchy of wants for many people bewildered by weaknesses in the economic system that they did not understand. Of what use are economic freedoms when they cannot be exercised? In his State of The Union message of January 4, 1935, FDR said, "We do assert that the ambition of the individual to obtain for him and his a proper security, a reasonable leisure, and a decent living throughout life, is an ambition to be preferred to the appetite for great wealth and great power."

The desire for security, even if the sacrifice of some economic freedom was the price, furnished the justification for many New Deal programs. The fact that many of them still exist is testimony to the strength of the desire for security and protection. Almost any government, given time, would have had to respond to the human misery involved and, moreover, would have felt justified in doing so; a government that did not would have found itself replaced.

Yet even if we grant the humanitarian impulse as sufficient justification for the New Deal programs, there is still the question of whether or not they were successful. The question would be easier to answer if explicit goals were expressed, but the character of the New Deal did not permit such a coherent approach. Obviously, the Roosevelt administration hoped to right the economy and restore full employment and healthy economic growth within the framework of capitalism and democracy.

If we are to judge the New Deal strictly by its success in restoring full employment or stable economic growth, then it was only marginally successful. As will become evident in the next chapter, World War II accomplished what the New Deal left unfinished. The New Deal did manage to reduce the unemployment rate, but not far enough; it did increase the growth rate for the entire period compared to previous decades, but the rate had begun to fall in the second term, and the distribution of income became only slightly less inequitable. Thus the judgment of marginal success. Yet it did manage to alter the allocation of resources, largely from the private sector and from the state and local government sectors to the national government. The federal government became "the" government, as the locus of power, influence, and control shifted to Washington.

Without doubt, however, the New Deal did not reach all the economic goals it would have liked to achieve. Yet the success or failure of the New Deal cannot be gauged solely by the criteria set out in the beginning, and to do so would miss its character and its pursuit of noneconomic goals.

It did, for instance, try to bring into government participation many segments of the society and to try to give each a voice. It tried to provide security and protection against exploitation and future business fluctuations. It did all these through a series of reforms and institutional changes that virtually transformed the face of U.S. capitalism. Consider what was accomplished in just 100 days in 1933 during a special session of Congress.

In that short period of time government took upon itself the obligation to stabilize agriculture, the commitment to cooperate formally with industries, the task of providing for the unemployed, the responsibility for preventing home and farm foreclosures, the revamping of the banking industry and the dismantling of the gold standard, and the regulation of Wall Street.

In the "second hundred days" the list was extended to provide for retirement, disability, unemployment compensation, and so on in the Social Security Act; for labor rights in the National Labor Relations Act; for regulation of utilities in the Public Utilities Holding Company Act; for improved operations of the Federal Reserve System in the Banking Act of 1935; and for better distribution of the tax burden in the Wealth Tax Act.

It would indeed be difficult to exaggerate the attempted transformation of the society and its institutions. The reforms did succeed in providing more security to individuals, as the government took on and accepted the responsibility for the ills that befall an economy. It thereby acknowledged that people suffered, through no fault of their own, by the operation of the economic system. Also, it acknowledged that the system had to be regulated, that it was not free of abuses, and that it could not be left alone; government had to ensure that the game of business was played by the rules, rules that it deemed necessary to impose.

Surely all economic institutions, including individual behavior, were greatly altered by these fundamental changes in the operation of the U.S. economy. It would be impossible to account for all of them in this space, but since most of the institutional changes and reforms still exist, perhaps an overall judgment of the success or failure of the New Deal can best be determined as the historical record unfolds. Viewed in this wider perspective, the success of the New Deal becomes even more difficult to assess, since all manner of value judgments of what constitutes a good society now become more important to consider. What is the function of the public sector under this modified capitalist system? What constitutes public responsibility as opposed to individual responsibility? To ask the questions is to reveal the source of the interminable controversy raised by the New Deal programs.

The same questions were relevant to the New Deal thinkers as well, and it is now time to ask if their answers and their programs were rational. As to rationality, the New Deal started at a disadvantage, owing to the type of administration tolerated by FDR. In attempting to bring all interests into government policymaking, he sought balanced and representative views. Instead, he often got deep divisions and disagreements. All too often, the interest that screamed the most or was more powerful got its way.

Thus, FDR acted as a broker among interests and presided over a balkanized administration. To bring all interests into government participation was a laudable aim, but the people who were attracted to the New Deal and its openness were headstrong, forceful, and action oriented. It is not surprising that clashes were frequent among these diverse people with different philosophies and goals.

If rational decisions were made difficult by these internecine struggles, they were exacerbated by the general New Deal aproach advocated by FDR of experimentation and improvisation. The pragmatic, nonideological approach to problem solving meant shifts from one policy to another, depending upon short-run performance. Again the desire for immediate action prevailed over more calculated and cautious plans.

Never sure what precisely it wanted to achieve or how to do it, the New Deal often lacked consistency. In the first New Deal, the reform movement prevailed, as FDR reached for a more rational economy and a more just society. He even reached out to business to form a partnership with government to rationalize production and employment.

After the first reform measures were passed and the NRA had been struck down, the administration paused and retreated into inaction. When the economy faltered and rising protests were heard against New Deal policies, the administration abruptly changed direction.

Instead of a partnership, the second New Deal began the attack on business, launching the TNEC to investigate market power and anticompetitive practices. The New Deal rushed out to embrace the competitive economy so dear to the classical model of laissez-faire. The attack on economic royalists signaled a reversal of policy, just as the Keynesian prescription of deficit spending and a managed economy were becoming acceptable within the administration.

The administration's ambivalent attitudes toward business reflect its same ambivalence toward capitalism. The reform phase signaled the need to modify and soften the effects of capitalism. The opportunity to overhaul it and perhaps replace it was not taken, and the initial attack subsided. After a while the economic system entered into its recovery phase, but now responsibility for its harsher side effects would be diffused. FDR, always basically conservative, began to relax his modifications of the system. When recovery lapsed, he again turned to radical language but conservative action, that is, restore free enterprise.

To see the bias of New Deal policies designed to reach unstated goals, consider a few examples. The reform measures, however just they were, could also have been used to forestall unrest and radical uprisings. Programs that put youth to work also kept them off the streets and out of trouble; programs that put people to work on public projects also exploited a generous supply of cheap labor; programs that fostered collective bargaining, unemployment compensation, and the like also robbed labor radicals of their rallying cries and took the steam out of more radical movements and organizations; programs that aided agriculture in supply limitations and crop developments also resulted in quieting this powerful bloc, while plowing under crops in the midst of massive hunger, keeping welfare recipients grateful for their handouts; programs for agriculture preserved farming for large farms while inhibiting the growth of cooperatives; programs to insure bank deposits also freed bankers from accountability; and so on down the list of New Deal actions.

Of course, the Roosevelt administration was aware of events in Europe and in the Soviet Union and of the interest shown by intellectuals in this country to alternative systems. Just how much these events influenced New Deal policies cannot be precisely determined. Yet it would be naive to deny that some programs were proposed with an eye toward halting the internal threat of challenges to the system or to limiting the growth of organizations that might have presented threats to existing institutions.

The New Deal was not rational, but it was effective. Its reforms did yield more economic security; its policies did preserve capitalism and democratic principles, and its methods did insure a greater role for government in national affairs—remarkable achievements for experimentalists. Still, much of the credit must go to Herbert Hoover, who paved the way and made the New Deal possible by his policy suggestions and by his ineptness and intransigence.

Finally, the question remains as to whether the proper fiscal and monetary policies would have achieved as much or more than the shotgun approach of the New Deal. That is, if Keynes had been listened to, would the recovery have been swifter and more complete, regardless of what can be said about the reforms of the New Deal?

Probably most economists would answer in the affirmative. Proper monetary and fiscal policies would have done a better job than the trial-and-error approach to policy actually followed. It is also interesting to note that Keynes's attack on the classical economic prescription for restoring full employment was correct. The classical economists argued that a cut in money wages would restore full employment, for as costs fell, the demand for labor would rise. In this view, labor had priced itself out of the market.

Keynes argued that this argument essentially would be applicable for only one firm at a time. If all workers cut their wages, aggregate demand would fall, inventories would pile up, and eventually prices would fall as well. If costs (wages) were to fall but prices fell in proportion, there would be no incentive for firms to hire more labor. The reduction in money wages would result in no reduction in real wages (money wages corrected for price changes), and nothing would happen to unemployment.

All that would happen is a period of deflation in the economy. In the period 1929–33 this is precisely what happened: Wages and prices fell proportionally about 22 percent in the implicit price index. The self-correcting mechanism to restore full employment under classical economics did not work. Direct action by government to stimulate spending was required. To the extent that the New Deal was doing some of this pump priming, Keynes was approving, although he was critical of other parts of the New Deal and was certainly against the basic philosophy of FDR on balanced budgets.

chapter 6

The Economy in World War II

For obvious reasons, domestic economic matters dominated the discussion of the 1930s, with only a hint at how foreign political developments were influencing domestic policy. In 1933 the United States was concerned with getting its economy in order and seeing to domestic problems first.

Of course, the rise to power of Adolph Hitler in 1933 did not go unnoticed, and surely many were concerned for the future of Europe. The recognition of the Soviet Union in the same year also added to feelings of unease and uncertainty about future relations. Yet the United States was in no mood to become entangled in the affairs of other nations. The isolationism of pre-World War I was back, but this time it was made worse by the actual experience of World War I, by Wilson's League of Nations, and by distrust of former allies.

Roosevelt, not an isolationist, appeared in step with the general mood when he wrecked the London International Economic Conference of 1933, claiming that the needs of the domestic economy came before the restoration of stable exchange rates. Characteristically of this administration, it seemingly reversed itself shortly thereafter, when Roosevelt signed into law the Reciprocal Trade Agreement Act of 1934. The act empowered the president to negotiate tariff reductions, presumably to increase employment and speed recovery. At first the act accomplished little but to remove trade barriers of mass-production industries, now gaining political as well as economic strength.[1] Later the act was renewed (in 1937 and 1940), and some gains were made in increasing world trade.

Roosevelt also expressed the desire to be a "good neighbor" to South America. At least in principle, the United States was pledged not to intervene in the affairs of another state. The isolationists, however, were in command. In 1934 the Johnson Debt Default Act of 1934 prohibited loans to any government that was in default on prior loans to the United States. The Neutrality Act of 1935 prohibited the export of munitions to any of the belligerents and was designed to legislate the United States out of war. In 1937 the act was used to ban the export of munitions to nations involved in civil war, and the Fascists won in Spain as a result. Also in 1937 Congress prohibited passage on any ship of a country involved in war. All these steps were designed to keep the United States out of war and to remove the provocations that might entice it into taking sides.

Roosevelt feuded with the isolationists, but made no headway until after Germany invaded Poland on September 1, 1939, and Britain and France declared war on Germany two days later. Even after these events the isolationist sentiment was unshaken. A Roper poll taken in September 1939 revealed that nearly 80 percent were opposed to any involvement in the war, and of these, a surprising 30 percent did not even wish to trade with any warring country.[2] Roosevelt, however, requested Congress to repeal the Neutrality Act and finally succeeded on November 3. The United States could now sell its munitions, but only on a cash-and-carry basis.

Yet the year 1940 saw Britain virtually alone against Germany, as Denmark, Norway, Holland, Belgium, and France had fallen to the German war machine. In a moving letter to FDR, Churchill wrote of the dismal prospect for 1941 and informed the president that "the moment approaches when we shall no longer be able to pay cash for shipping and other supplies."

In response FDR conceived a plan to circumvent the isolationist acts, to aid Britain without entering the war. He would send her munitions without charge and be repaid after the war, not in dollars but in kind—the Lend-Lease Program. Hailed by some—even Wendell Willkie, the man FDR defeated for the presidency in 1940 supported it—but denounced by many as well, HR 1776 (an ingenious number) was finally passed and signed into law on March 11, 1941. Roosevelt immediately asked for $7 billion to carry out the law.

Mobilization for War

Throughout this period FDR hesitated, waiting for public opinion to catch up to him and hoping that Hitler would commit some act that would provoke the United States into action. Despite the isolationists, however, there was a growing recognition and acceptance of an eventual entrance of the United States into the conflict. The question then becomes, How was the administration preparing to mobilize the economy for war?

It had ample time. It even had a mobilization plan of sorts that had been developed in 1931 by the War Department and revised into final form in 1939.[3] This was the plan that was scrutinized by a special committee of the U.S. Senate to investigate the munitions industry. Senator Gerald Nye, its chairman and an isolationist, found the munitions industry to be "merchants of death." Still, there was a plan, modified to meet congressional criticism, in existence during the "phony war" period of 1939–40.

Thus when FDR appointed The War Resources Board in August of 1939, he appeared to be following the dictates of the mobilization plan. The board was designed to provide advice to the armed services industrial mobilization planners and, if war did come, to become another War Industries Board similar to that of World War I. Bernard Baruch was delighted, since he had been advocating such a body for some time.[4] Others protested that the board, made up of industrialists and headed by Edward R. Stettinius, Jr., chairman of the board of U.S. Steel, was unrepresentative and would assume vast powers that could destroy democracy. Roosevelt ignored the criticism and also the report of the board, and it was abandoned.

Roosevelt still wanted to do most of the mobilization job himself, was still wary of economic royalists, and was still hoping to convince the nation that he was not planning for war. At about the time the Germans were crossing the border into France, he created another agency, the Advisory Commission to the Council of National Defense (NDAC). A throwback to 1916, the NDAC had no legal standing and no authority and no head. FDR did manage to attract some prominent men to this advisory commission: Edward R. Stettinius for industrial materials, William S. Knudsen of General Motors for industrial production, Sidney Hillman for manpower problems, and Leon Henderson, the New Dealer, for materials and prices. Toward the end of the year 1940, the commission itself urged a stronger, more structured replacement.

So in early 1941 the president created the Office of Production Management (OPM), headed by Knudsen, Hillman, Stettinius, and Knox. Knudsen and Hillman, representing management and labor, tried diligently to run this agency, but it failed, too, as it tried to wrestle with an economy not fully recovered, several major strikes, and the loose organizational structure of the agency itself for setting priorities. It gave way in August 1941 to the Supply, Priorities and Allocation Board (SPAB).

The SPAB was another stopgap agency that functioned no better than the OPM that it subordinated. Meanwhile Congress was delaying any bill to control wages and prices. The mobilization effort was stalled, as production of munitions, aircraft, and essential minerals had actually begun to fall in the latter half of 1941.[5] The poorly functioning war management organizations were partly to blame, but in reality they lacked power, direction, and leadership. Senator Harry Truman's special committee to investigate the defense program was finding all kinds of problems with mobilization and was urging a change in organization.

Pearl Harbor was bombed on December 7, 1941, and a few days later Congress declared war on Germany, Italy, and Japan. In his State of the Union speech on January 6, 1942, Roosevelt began to set high production goals for war goods—planes, tanks, guns, ships, and so on. He was also forced to face up to the inadequacy of the organizational structure to achieve the production quotas he had set. A few days later he established the War Production Board, chaired by Donald M. Nelson, which brought in the members of the SPAB, which was dismantled, and the OPM. This time, however, the chairman was given broad powers of direction over all phases of war procurement and production—a czar of production. The establishment of the War Production Board was followed by the National War Labor Board to deal with labor problems.

Roosevelt had established the Office of Price Administration (OPA) in April 1941, but it had no formal authority and acted on an ad hoc basis. Now that FDR was asking labor to hold down wage demands, accept long hours of work, and forego strikes, it was essential that prices and profits be kept down also to ensure labor's cooperation. The Economic Stabilization Act finally was passed and signed into law in October 1942, nine months after the other parts of war mobilization were in place. The bill giving legal status to the OPA narrowly passed, and even FDR was unhappy with it, since it included special provisions for farmers, among them a price ceiling at 100 percent of parity.

Now at least the basic machinery for mobilization and control over the domestic economy were in place. They did not function smoothly by any means, and frequent problems emerged and personalities clashed. It is not our purpose to review the operations of these agencies or describe their evolution. Indeed, the discussion of their development was intended primarily to reveal the state of preparedness of the society when it had time to adjust, the mood of the society toward involvement in the war, and the peculiar brand of leadership exhibited by FDR in this period.[6]

Wartime Resource Requirements

A nation at war or on the verge of it must somehow transfer resources from private to public use. Some industrial output must shift from the production of consumer or investment goods to the production of war material, and the same shift must take place in the case of labor and raw materials. The conversion period can be lengthy and hence damaging to the pursuit of military objectives. In the case of World War II, there was time enough for conversion, but it did not proceed smoothly.

In the so-called "defense period," that is, pre-Pearl Harbor, private firms were reluctant to invest in plans to produce war goods when the entrance of the United States into the conflict was in doubt. Lacking any tradition, government ownership of arsenals was resisted by most businessmen, but eventually was made necessary in certain cases. Thus in June 1946 the RFC was given the power to make loans or purchase the capital stock of a corporation for plant construction, for acquiring essential materials, for the provision of working capital, or for the creation of a corporation to produce necessary goods, and so on. In brief, the RFC was given wide power to embark upon a program to overcome manufacturers' fears and insure the necessary production of essential goods for national defense. It quickly set out to use its powers by setting up corporations for essential rubber and metals.

Still there was controversy, and firms were accused of a "strike of capital" until they got their terms regarding amortization of war plants; they were also accused of campaigning against the NLRB. The heated issues were solved by the government granting accelerated depreciation for defense-related plants, but making them subject to an excess profits tax. Labor was assured that its gains would not be eroded by defense contracts.

Defense contracts in 1940 amounted to "only" $10.5 billion (but nearly nine times the amount spent on defense in fiscal year 1938), but the process of war conversion was under way. Later, as U.S. stocks were depleted by supplying Britain and France, production orders came pouring in, giving U.S. industries the opportunity to gear up for later heavy demands.[7]

When war production stepped up in 1941, the Supply, Priorities and Allocations Board was forced into making allocations of resources among military, domestic, and foreign users. To insure the necessary resources for military users, civilian production had to be curtailed. Limitation orders on the production of automobiles, refrigerators, vacuum cleaners, metal office furniture, and typewriters were announced in the fall of 1941.

Obviously, the limitation orders caused problems in the economy, but one of the major criticisms voiced throughout the war was made by small businesses. The defense procurement process favored the large firms, and the small ones were ignored. "Of the more than $11 billion in price contracts awarded by the Services during the seven months from June through December 1940, 60 percent went to 20 firms and 86.4 percent to only 100 companies."[8] Thus, war would continue the trend toward concentration of industry. Whether intentional or not, such favoritism would have long-term consequences for the operation of the economy, long after the war was concluded.

Toward the end of 1941 defense expenditures were accelerating by nearly 225 percent from the beginning of the year. Thus, while the United States may have entered the war far behind the Germans in war goods, the machinery was in place to increase military output when the heavy demands followed. When war was declared, we were already devoting about 15 percent of our industrial production to war.[9]

After war was declared, Congress acted quickly to appropriate huge sums for war contracts, so that procurement officers could place orders. In the first six months of 1942, $100 billion were appropriated and another $60 billion in the next four months. These appropriations soon became contracts of $100 billion in the first half of 1942, with another $40 billion in orders already in process. These huge sums (GNP for 1941 was $124 billion) caused some severe problems, since the orders exceeded our industrial capacity. All kinds of imbalances occurred in the composition of our war goods; bottlenecks developed, large amounts of waste resulted, as plants converted to war goods that should not have; new facilities were built that were not needed; and conflicts over priorities occurred.[10]

These problems were eventually confronted by organization changes, and with time the percentage of the industrial capacity devoted to war production increased from 15 to 33 percent within a period of less than one year.[11] The rapid buildup was necessary for war production, but had some adverse consequences on the rest of the economy, as will become evident.

By 1942 the nation had apparently solved its production problems to meet wartime demands. In 1943 it appeared that there was excess capacity in existence, and raw materials became insufficient for

Table 6.1 GNP by Type of Expenditure, 1939–45 (billions of dollars)

Year	GNP	Con-sump-tion	Invest-ment	Net Exports	Total	Government National Defense	Government Percent of GNP
1939	90.5	66.8	9.3	1.1	13.3	1.2	1.3
1940	99.7	70.8	13.1	1.7	14.0	2.2	2.2
1941	124.5	80.6	17.9	1.3	24.8	13.8	11.1
1942	157.9	88.5	9.8	—	59.6	49.4	31.3
1943	191.6	99.3	5.7	−2.0	88.6	79.7	41.6
1944	210.1	108.3	7.1	−1.8	96.5	87.4	41.6
1945	211.9	119.7	10.6	−0.6	82.3	73.5	34.7

Source: Council of Economic Advisors, *Economic Report of the President* (Washington, DC: GPO, 1967), p. 213.

production. Later in 1943 the materials problem disappeared, and the trouble came from intermediate goods, such as the proper metal fabrications. Again raw-material problems reappeared, this time in nonmetallic areas—lumber, leather, textiles, and so on. Finally, in 1944 manpower shortages became a problem that continued until the end of the war.[12] These structural problems were troublesome but not insurmountable.

The enormous increase in productive capacity (about 50 percent over the period 1939–45, concentrated in munitions industries, of course) made it possible to produce the necessary munitions. Labor productivity increased as well, in part due to longer hours, and in part due to superior capital goods. In short, despite the wastes involved, the organizational problems, bottlenecks here and excess capacity there, the economy managed to achieve the high production goals set for it by the president.

The composition of our national output is shown in Table 6.1. The shift toward government and war-related activity is obvious and will be discussed in detail later. Briefly, national defense rose from 1.3 percent of GNP in 1939 to 41.6 percent in 1943 and 1944. From 1939 to 1944 consumption declined from 73.8 percent of GNP to 51.5 percent, and investment declined from 10.3 percent of GNP to 3.4 percent.

In any economy gearing up for war, manpower problems can often be a serious limitation. As the most productive age group of men (and some women in this period) enter the armed forces, labor shortages are inevitable. In the situation of an economy emerging from a serious depression, however, an acute labor shortage is not an immediate problem.

In 1939 over 9 million people were unemployed, or over 17 percent of the labor force. By the summer of 1940 the number of unemployed was estimated at between 5 million officially and up to 11 million who might have been available should the need arise. Within this reservoir of available workers there would still be a likely shortage of skilled workers. Sidney Hillman of the President's Advisory Commission attempted to initiate enough training programs to remedy the possible future shortage. Some upgrading of vocational schools was begun, and a training-within-industry job program was started, financed by a special appropriation of $91 million in October 1940.[13] By the end of 1941 some 2 million workers had been trained on the job and another 2.5 million had been trained in vocational and engineering studies.[14]

Thus when war broke out, there was no labor shortage in sight; in fact, the number of women in the labor force was less than the previous year. Shortages that did develop were handled by training programs and by employers simplifying the production process to overcome the shortage of skilled workers. The simplifying of the production process that helped meet the immediate need continued in the later years, but after the war this expedient would have severe repercussions. In order to increase output, the production process was broken down into easily mastered tasks. The trouble is that the jobs became boring and dehumanizing, and the worker became a mere appendage to the machine, as Marx so aptly described it. How much labor unrest of later years can be traced to this source cannot be determined with accuracy, but it may explain a considerable portion. The needs of war may supply the problems of peace.

Now that war was declared, the estimates for the armed services were revised upward. Still, the problem was not in the supply of labor but in its location; the war plants and the available labor were in different geographical locations. High wages did work to encourage migration, causing housing and transportation problems in some areas. There was no cause for concern, however, and officials were more occupied with shortages of facilities and materials.[15]

In 1942, then, labor shortages were not a pressing problem. The possibility, however, of strikes in defense industries had to be confronted. In January 1942 a National War Labor Board was established to arbitrate all disputes in essential industries. Also in 1942 the War Manpower Commission was created to oversee labor supply problems and act as a national employment service for both civilian and military needs.

As the war progressed, additional demands for military personnel were made necessary. The Selective Service System Act was passed on September 16, 1940 (at a crucial time in the presidential campaign, but FDR dismissed the controversy it provoked), and by December 7, 1941, 17 million men aged 21 to 35 were registered and about 1 million had been inducted; by 1942, 30 million men, now 18–45, had been registered and more than 5 million had been inducted.

To this date, the problem of labor supply was manageable. By the fall of 1943, however, the situation changed. The forecasts of military manpower needs ranged from 7.6 to 10.6 million. While the needs were overestimated (actual military needs for 1943 were more like 9 million and rose to 11.4 million in 1944 and 1945), a serious labor shortage loomed.

The labor supply began to affect production. There were shortages in the nation's mines, textile mills, lumber camps, foundries, and in general whenever and wherever wages or working conditions were below standard. The West Coast, particularly, felt the labor shortage in all industries, and a special plan for allocating the available supply was instituted there and extended to other areas later.[16] By the fall of 1943 the huge reservoir of available labor had been virtually exhausted. The unemployed had been put to work (the rate was now 1.9 percent); 7 million new workers, mostly women (about half) and men who had postponed retirement, teens who left school early, and the previously unemployables, including many blacks, made up the difference. In addition to the added numbers of workers, the workweek had been increased by about eight hours per week.

In fact, in 1943 people were leaving the labor force, anticipating an early end to the war. At the time war production was increasing, military demands were growing, and turnover rates were at an all-time high. "In September 1943 the monthly quit-rate reached a peak of 6.29, while total separations were 8.16—a rate of almost 100 percent per year."[17]

The problem was met by a labor-budgeting scheme of Bernard Baruch to allocate the scarce supply and encourage economy of it by encouraging employers to hire only those who had a certificate from the Employment Service (now more involved in the problem), and by publication of occupations given preference for deferments, thereby encouraging people to stay in their jobs or move to them from nonessential ones.[18] One of the basic problems not addressed was that pay rates were not attractive enough for free mobility of labor (housing and transportation were problems, too), but adjusting pay scales to encourage mobility was never seriously considered, as will be seen later in the discussion of wage controls. Also, the problem really was not with the overall supply, but with its allocation. Shortages were acute in some areas, even in defense establishments, but the problem was generally analyzed in terms of total numbers needed.

The conversion from peace to war also resulted in dislocations due to the shortage of raw materials. At first defense orders were superimposed upon civilian production, but as defense orders rose, some system or priority usage had to be devised. The first priority system, devised by the Office of Production Management, became effective on March 22, 1941, requiring producers of raw materials to give preference to defense orders. Affected were producers of aluminum, copper, nickel, rayon, rubber, and silk; others were brought in later.

Eventually some civilian uses of these raw materials had to be prohibited entirely. As more defense orders competed with civilian goods, the production of automobiles, refrigerators, and other consumer durables had to be curtailed or eliminated. Similarly, private investment had to be curtailed in nonessential areas to conserve scarce materials. Exports were also brought under control to preserve essential materials and to prevent shipments to enemies. Thus early in the defense period, the nation was shifting resources from civilian to military uses. The composition of GNP changed over the next few years, as consumption and investment declined and the public sector's share rose (see Table 6.1).

When the slack in the economy was eliminated in mid-1942, and raw materials really became a problem, it was not unusual to have production in some industries cease for want of supplies. These cases always revived the controversy over whether the military or civilians ought to be in charge of managing the war economy. The military pushed for control and made significant gains, but were unable to convince Congress of the need for total control.

Instead, the situation was usually solved only after much confusion and delay.

In every case the history was the same: A serious shortage with its attendant confusion would develop, the columnists and the public became alarmed; officials with conflicting authorities or ideas each proposed his own solution, or failed to present immediately a clear simple plan of action; Congress often commenced to investigate; and sooner or later someone would come forward with a dramatic plan for solving the particular issue by giving one man all the power necessary to do the job.[19]

The men became known as "czars" and were directors over rubber, petroleum, solid fuels, and food. These czars were supposed to be given authority to allot the supplies among competing uses. They created more publicity than action, however, and the War Production Board really took control of production in 1943, following its reorganization in November 1942.[20]

Agricultural production and distribution also became problems for the U.S. economy. Accustomed to large surpluses of wheat, corn, cotton, and so on, the United States was unprepared for the loss of foodstuffs that normally came from the Pacific. One year after war was declared, shortages began to appear in meats, fats, oils, dairy products, and canned food.

Shortages occurred for several reasons: expanding military requirements; demands on the United States to help feed our allies, who were experiencing even more critical shortages; expanding domestic consumption as U.S. citizens (armed with higher incomes and limited areas in which to spend them, as consumer durables disappeared) chose to eat better. And, as the war progressed, demands were placed and accepted by the United States to help feed the liberated peoples.[21]

After the customary wrangling over the administration of the farm program, as in the areas of rubber, aluminum, and so on, the president finally designated the secretary of agriculture to oversee food production and allocation. The Office of Price Administration (OPA) would still be responsible for determining farm prices. Farm output rose, but the Department of Agriculture was only partially successful in getting farmers to produce essential foods. Many farmers, the smaller ones, continued to produce the crops they were accustomed to growing, even though such crops were in excess supply (cotton) or nonessential (watermelons). It also proved difficult to predict the food requirements of the military and of foreign demand.

Farmers continued to benefit from the power of the farm bloc in Congress. Farm laborers were deferred for military service; fertilizer could be imported; the Commodity Credit Corporation was still in operation, and so on. They were even successful in securing high prices for foodstuffs.

In May 1941 Congress raised the lowest rate for basic commodities to 85 percent of parity, and a year later, in the Economic Stabilization Act, rates were raised to 90 percent of parity. In July

1941 nonbasic commodities were raised to 85 percent of parity and later to 90 percent by the Department of Agriculture. Thus high prices for agricultural goods were assured over the course of the war.

Tying production to parity prices meant not only high prices but inefficient allocation of resources to the crops most wanted. A cotton farmer, for instance, was guaranteed 90 percent of parity; to induce him to switch to another more essential commodity, it would have to far exceed 90 percent of the new crop, before the farmer would take whatever risk was involved. Furthermore, as prices rose in the economy, many farmers switched to those goods (such as watermelons) or diverted fruits to nonessential uses (such as ice cream), and away from much needed canned goods.

Thus the usual pricing mechanism, designed for surpluses, conflicted with proper food management in a period of scarcity. Higher prices did not adjust production and distribution. Neither did they fit into the goals of the OPA for price stability.[22]

Rationing and Price Controls

In a wartime economy the demand for resources generally outstrips the supply, especially in a global war where responsibilities extend far beyond national borders. In a free-market economy, prices would rise to ration the available supply according to who was willing and able to buy the output. Clearly, the free-market solution is inappropriate under wartime circumstances. First, as will shortly become evident, inflation is also a companion of war, and efforts must be made to control it. Second, rising prices would allocate the short supply to the wealthiest members of the society, and this would surely create undue hardship on lower-income groups and surely damage morale—so often necessary for war production—especially since personal privation is likely to be the case in other areas.

One solution is to limit the demand to supply by nonprice rationing. The remedy, however, became "the most common social irritant to afflict the home front during the war."[23] Many accepted the hardships as necessary for the war effort, but many were involved at one time or another in the black market. Some participation in illegal activities came to be regarded as the norm, and perhaps the black market served as an outlet for the frustrations that built up from self-denial.

Among the goods rationed were sugar, meat, coffee, butter, dairy products, fats, processed foods, gasoline, tires, fuel oil, typewriters, and shoes. Clearly, these are essential goods in a household's consumption plans, and if you combine them with the lack of consumer durables, it is easy to understand why consumers were bothered by rationing and controls. For many of them, wartime incomes were far above their past earnings, but there was little to spend them on.

Often the goods that did exist were inferior, since the superior ones went to the military. This was the case, for instance, with cuts of meat and cigarettes. Basically, the program was administered by the OPA, but it did not decide which goods were to be rationed; these orders came from the War Production Board.

By itself, however, rationing would not control prices, but could only try to promote equity in the distribution of available supplies. Prices and wages would have to be regulated as well, but despite the recognition that war and inflation are constant companions, there was a reluctance to institute direct controls. The economy had some breathing room in the defense period, as idle resources were available to forestall inflationary pressures. As production increased, however, there was growing concern that prices would soon begin to rise as well. Recall that in May 1940 Roosevelt resurrected the World War I organization, the National Defense Advisory Commission. One part of the commission was an office on price stabilization, headed by the ardent, energetic New Dealer, Leon Henderson. Henderson issued many price schedules, but was forced to rely on voluntary cooperation, since there were no sanctions against violators.

Later the same procedure was employed when the Office of Price Stabilization became the Office of Price Administration and Civilian Supply (OPACS), and still later the Office of Price Administration (OPA), before it was legislated into law by Congress in December 1942. When war came in December 1941, there were more than 70 such voluntary price schedules in effect, but the administration was not really controlling prices, nor did it have the power to do so. Thus wholesale prices rose by 23 percent from August 1939 to November 1941, and increases in the cost of living in 1941 averaged nearly 1 percent each month. Food prices in 1941 increased by about one-fourth and wages rose by about one-fifth.[24] After war was declared and defense needs calculated, economists estimated that consumer demand would outstrip supply by $17 billion in 1942.[25] Clearly something had to be done to stabilize the economy.

In the fall of 1941 Congress was wrestling with a price-control bill that would have placed price ceilings on selected commodities only when they were needed as a way to hold down costs. Baruch argued that the special-interest groups would appear to argue their case for exemption from controls. He proposed a general ceiling on all goods and services and argued against the piecemeal approach to controls: "I do not believe in piecemeal price fixing. I think you have first to put a ceiling over the whole price structure, including wages, rents, and farm prices up to parity level—and no higher—and then to adjust separate price schedules upward or downward, where justice or governmental policy requires."[26] In other words, find some period when prices, wages, and so on were normal—set by supply and demand—and make this the base period. Then roll back current prices to the base period. If necessary, adjustment could then be made for abnormal situations. Baruch also stated that price controls could be established only as part of the whole plan for wartime finances, which included taxation, trade, production controls, and so on.

On December 9, 1941, Leon Henderson finally presented the administration's proposal for price-control legislation, and on January 30, 1942, the Emergency Price Control Act of 1942 was signed into law. The act embodied the piecemeal approach, giving the price administrator (Leon Henderson) the power to set maximum prices on commodities whose prices were rising too fast for economic stability. He was also given the power to control rents in areas of heavy defense buildups and to ration items in short supply.

Yet, as Baruch predicted, there were glaring omissions in the act. First, wages were not controlled. The president had indicated that he expected labor to cooperate in restraining demands, once it saw that the cost of living and profits were being constrained.[27] Second, the farm bloc managed to secure special considerations. The act required that no action could be taken by the OPA without prior approval of the secretary of agriculture. Furthermore, the OPA was limited to price regulations according to the highest of (1) 110 percent of the parity price of the commodity; (2) the market price prevailing as of October 11, 1941, or December 15, 1941; (3) the average price for the commodity during the period July 1, 1919, to June 30, 1929. If food prices and wages were not effectively controlled, what hope was there for combating inflation?[28]

Although the price-control machinery was in place and working as well as could be expected, it was handicapped by the lack of controls over food and wages. Labor had agreed to a "no-strike, no-lock-out pledge" for the duration of the war, and the mediation of labor management disputes was put in the hands of the National War Labor Board, composed of members from labor, management, and the public. Still, there was no wage standard, and very soon cases began piling up. Impatient with delays and seeing the cost of living increase, workers went out on wildcat strikes, breaking their earlier pledge.

In March 1942 the president finally turned his attention to economic stabilization of the economy and instructed the director of the Bureau of the Budget to develop an anti-inflation program.[29] The final report was filled with sweeping measures, including a ceiling on all prices, wage controls,and a compulsory savings plan. Committee members were clearly alarmed by the price data: From December 1941 to March 1942, food costs rose 4.9 percent and clothing prices 7.7 percent.[30] Something had to be done fast.

The president, however, merely sent a seven-point program to Congress, a program that was vague and very general. One of the seven points was a ceiling on all prices. On April 28, 1942, the OPA acted. Calling this the "most important date in the history of wartime economic policy," J. K. Galbraith, in charge of price controls at the time, was forced to concede that Baruch was right. On these data all prices were fixed for the duration of the war by the General Maximum Price Regulation or General Max. The ceiling price was set at the highest price charged in March for each commodity.[31]

Meanwhile, the War Labor Board was still struggling to devise some sort of wage formula that would satisfy another of FDR's seven points and at the same time earn labor's cooperation. In July 1942 the WLB developed a formula that came to be known as the Little Steel formula. The WLB proposed to raise wage rates only in a case where wage increases had fallen behind the 15 percent rise in the cost of living between January 1941 and May 1942. Workers accepted the formula, but the OPA worried that tying wages to the cost of living would complicate the task of maintaining price ceilings.

The OPA was correct, as farmers sought higher prices, too, but higher food costs would mean higher living costs and a call for higher wages, and so on. Throughout the summer of 1942 the president became increasingly concerned with the rising cost of living. Yet with an election coming up, congressmen were reluctant to impose price ceilings on farm output or levy higher taxes.[32]

On September 7, 1942, FDR sent a message to Congress stating that while he had the power to impose controls, he was loath to exercise it, but if Congress failed to act, he would. Farm prices had to be stabilized: FDR wrote, "You cannot expect the laborer to maintain a fixed wage level if everything he wears and eats begins to go up drastically in price." Congress passed the necessary legislation (the stabilization act) on October 2, 1942, after considerable debate, empowering the OPA to control rents; the secretary of agriculture to set farm prices at parity or comparable prices or the highest prices received between January 1 and September 15, 1942; and the WLB to set wage rates at the highest levels paid between the same dates as for farm prices.

Now a full set of controls was in place. The Office of Economic Stabilization was created and headed by James F. Burns, who resigned from the Supreme Court in order to take the top economic job. In return for passing the act, Congress demanded the head of the pesty Leon Henderson, and he was sacrificed and replaced by Prentiss M. Brown and still later by Chester Bowles. For the next three years, prices and wages were stable, and the nation achieved a victory over domestic inflation. Consumer prices increased by only 10 percent— from 1942 to 1945—and wholesale prices increased only 7 percent over the same period.

Paying for the War

Price and wage controls, rationing, and resource allocation programs were clearly necessary for economic stabilization, but they would not have been sufficient. Additional policies were needed to sop up the excess purchasing power generated by the defense buildup. In Keynesian terms, a large inflationary gap existed, and unless some method of curbing spending were found, the inflationary pressures would have been too great for the existing controls. How to finance the war without wrecking the economy was from the beginning a very controversial issue.

The question of how to limit spending generated a number of proposals that were given consideration by the Treasury. Michael Kalecki had a scheme labeled "purchasing power rationing."[33] This type of expenditure rationing would limit the amount of spending on scarce goods and services and thus prevent the upward pull in their prices. Expenditures on other, unrestricted goods would continue as always, with market forces determining their prices. In the aggregate, purchasing power rationing would prevent a general rise in the price level. In addition, it would be possible that some of the income not spent on restricted goods would be saved or held in cash. Either way, that portion would not be spent. While the plan was considered attractive, it was rejected for administrative reasons.[34]

Another scheme proposed was the spendings tax. A spendings or expenditure tax would be levied on total expenditures on all goods by individuals. The tax could be graduated easily enough to discourage consumption: after some exemption level, a 25 percent tax, say, on the first $1,000, a 50 percent tax on the next $1,000 of spending, and so on.

Again, total spending would be reduced, but the administrative problems would still remain. Households would have to calculate their net worth at the beginning and end of each period, since in reality an expenditure tax is a tax on the change in net worth. The Treasury decided to accept a spendings tax in 1942, and it was actually proposed to the Senate Finance Committee, where it was quickly rejected.[35]

Another interesting proposal was made by J. M. Keynes and summarized in his book *How to Pay for the War*.[36] Keynes advocated a form of compulsory saving (or alternatively, compulsory lending, or deferred pay, or forced saving), in which "a percentage of all incomes in excess of some minimum income will be paid to the Government, partly as compulsory savings and partly as direct taxes." The savings part would be deposited in some savings institution from which the government would borrow.

These forced savings would not be available (except in emergencies) until after the war was over. The blocked savings would earn interest and when released would be available to avoid a postwar slump. Since income-tax rates are progressive, the higher-income groups would be credited with smaller savings deposits (and pay more in taxes), and the lower-income groups would be forced to save a higher than normal proportion of their incomes. This is a powerful tool to reduce total spending, while ensuring social justice after the war is over. (There would be some redistribution of wealth.) On the other hand, compulsory saving might well come from income that would have been saved anyway. Also, there is nothing to prevent the wealthy from dipping into past savings to maintain their previous spending habits.

In the United States the term "forced savings" caused bitter opposition. Voluntary saving was deemed more compatible with democracy. Thus the Keynes plan fell victim to emotional responses, rather than serious analysis. Incidentally, Germany also seriously considered the Keynes plan, but rejected it also on the grounds that Germans "save automatically," and rationing can do a better job. Thus "the authoritarian German government emphasizes the 'constriction of the pantry,' democratic Professor Keynes prefers the 'constriction of the pocket'."[37]

Having rejected alternative plans to control spending, the United States was forced to choose the more conventional ways—taxation and/or borrowing. Still, the choice between taxing and borrowing is not as straightforward as might appear. Both taxation and borrowing divert incomes to the government, but they affect the economy differently.[38]

In terms of fairness, taxation may be preferable, since it distributes the cost of the war while it is being fought and prevents the burden from being passed forward to future generations. Part of the income being taxed is artifically higher, however, since some of that income would have been used for repairs, maintenance, and investment that were prohibited during the war. Also, to secure the necessary revenue to conduct the war, heavier (regressive) taxation on lower-income groups would be unavoidable.

In terms of inflation control, taxation also has the edge. Taxation leaves individuals with less disposable income out of which they may continue to save a portion. Borrowing may leave the individual with the feeling that he or she has already saved enough and no further saving is desired. Also, borrowing results in the buildup of liquid assets, which may threaten to exacerbate the inflationary tendencies in the postwar period.

In terms of production incentives, borrowing is preferable to taxation. Heavy taxation may discourage the incentive to produce, but borrowing leaves the worker with an asset. In the first case, the worker feels poorer; in the other case, richer. If there are any psychological limitations or boundaries to patriotism, borrowing is less likely to test them. Besides, workers with newly earned higher incomes would clearly prefer the chance to enjoy their gains in the postwar period, if not the present.

These, and still other considerations make the choice a difficult one, particularly when the extent and cost of the war are unknown at the time of the decision. In the end, politicians who are held accountable later must decide the limits of taxation and borrowing. The choices actually made are given in the next section.

After much discussion among Treasury officials, members of the Federal Reserve System, and economists, voluntary borrowing was chosen as the primary method to reduce spending. The major reasons for the choice were the flexibility of borrowing to reach all segments of the society and the fact that borrowing provided production incentives, whereas taxation had serious shortcomings in both areas. It should be understood, however, that the "voluntary" way must be interpreted quite loosely, since there was a great deal of pressure and coercion by government, employers, and patriotic groups to buy bonds for the war effort.

In the attempt to reach all classes of investors, the Treasury, with the Federal Reserve concurring, decided to issue securities to meet the needs of different investors. In World War I only Liberty Bonds were issued, regardless of the wishes of investors.[39] Thus the Treasury, defying tradition, decided to finance a large part of World War II by issuing short-term securities. Short-term securities permitted greater shifting among assets, greater liquidity, and a means to avoid many market strains. Of course, long-term securities were issued as well for those who preferred this type of asset.

To reach the small investor, Series E Savings Bonds (later F and G as well) were issued. This series of bonds was designed to overcome the difficulties experienced with the small investor in World War I. They contained the following features, lacking in their World War I counterparts: They were redeemable in cash after 60 days, according to a schedule on the back of the bond; they were registered in the name of the purchaser and thereby replaceable; they paid interest on maturity to avoid the administrative nightmare of payment on small amounts (the $18.75 bond was the lowest denomination) and to avoid upsetting the structure of market interest rates. These small-denomination securities could be purchased by a payroll deduction scheme to facilitate their purchase by workers. Even children could purchase savings stamps to paste into coupon books until $18.75 had been accumulated to convert into a bond.

It is interesting to note that the redemption of these small bonds varied according to the prospects of the war's end. Redemptions as a proportion of sales for Series E Bonds were 2 percent in 1942, 8 percent in 1943, 18 percent in 1944, and rose to 33 percent in 1945. Postwar problems can easily be forecast (in retrospect) from these data. After some initial organizational difficulties and an issue of bonds that got into trouble in October 1942, the Treasury finally agreed to follow the policy of war-loan drives. The Treasury resisted this World War I technique, but after some wrangling Victory Fund committees were set up to supervise the marketing of securities. Over the course of the war, seven War Loans and a final Victory Loan were initiated. The results of these loans are shown in Table 6.2.

How successful were the bond drives in reducing spending, or better, in channeling available savings into bond purchases? In 1943, of the amount available for the purchase of government securities, 44 percent was so invested. The figures for 1944 and 1945 were 56 percent and 43 percent, respectively. Corporations other than savings institutions did better; their investment percentages for the same years were 67, 100, and 67.[40] Clearly, corporations had profits that could not be reinvested in plant and equipment, nor could repairs and maintenance activities be conducted. As their funds became available, but restricted, the corporations were limited to financial investments.

The success of the Treasury's plan to reach all classes of investors can be seen in Table 6.3. The banking sector clearly exceeded all others as investors in government securities. This was to be expected, given

Table 6.2 Total Sales in the Seven War Loans and the Victory Loan, by Investor Group and Type of Security (billions of dollars)

Investor Group	All Issues	Savings Bonds (issue price) E	F and G	Savings Notes	Bills	Certif- icates	Notes	Bank- Eligible Bonds	Bank- Restricted Bonds
Individuals	43.3	19.9	4.1	1.3	—	2.6	0.6	6.1	8.7
Insurance companies	22.1	—	0.1	*	—	1.0	0.4	4.1	16.5
Savings banks	12.4	—	*	*	—	0.6	0.3	4.9	6.6
Savings and loan associations	1.9	—	*	*	—	0.1	*	0.4	1.3
Other corporations and associations	53.5	—	1.6	15.2	—	22.3	1.7	5.0	7.6
Dealers and brokers	4.2	—	—	*	—	1.6	0.2	1.4	1.0
State and local governments	8.2	—	0.2	0.6	—	3.5	0.3	0.8	2.9
Treasury investment accounts	1.2	—	—	—	—	*	—	0.2	1.1
All nonbank investors	146.7	19.9	6.0	17.1	—	31.6	3.5	22.9	45.7
Commercial banks	10.2	—	—	—	1.7	4.3	—	4.2	—
Total	156.9	19.9	6.0	17.1	1.7	35.9	3.5	27.1	45.7

*Less than $50 million. Source: H. C. Murphy, The National Debt in War and Transition (New York: McGraw-Hill, 1950), p. 154. Reprinted with permission.

the large amount of excess reserves they possessed. Individuals came next in importance, accounting for 25 percent of the total. The U.S. government agencies and trust funds came next, as they channeled the tax funds they collected directly into government bonds—an example of forced savings. Insurance companies and mutual savings banks again used the increase in assets and earnings to buy government bonds, and the states, using their surpluses, were more inclined to reduce their indebtedness, rather than buy federal securities, so their proportion is relatively modest.

The total net amount borrowed, $215 billion, represents 55 percent of the total expenditures of the federal government from 1940 to 1946. The remaining 45 percent needed to fund expenditures came from taxation. With this broad presentation of the fundamentals of

Table 6.3   Net Amounts Borrowed during the Defense and War Periods (June 30, 1939 to June 30, 1946) from Each Principal Investor Class

Investor Class	Billions of Dollars	Percentage of Total
Commercial banks	60.2	28
Federal Reserve banks	21.2	10
Total banking system	81.4	38
Individuals	53.9	25
Insurance companies	19.1	9
Mutual savings banks	8.5	4
Other corporations and associations	22.8	10
State and local governments	6.1	3
U.S. government agencies and trust funds	23.2	11
Total nonbank investors	133.6	62
Net amount borrowed	215.0	100

Note: Net amounts borrowed are the increases in estimated amounts of government securities held between June 30, 1939 and June 30, 1946, by each class of investor, except that the excess of total borrowing over the deficit is subtracted from the increase in government securities held by commercial banks (where most of such excess was held as government balances). Estimates for the period June 30, 1940 to June 30, 1946 are from the *Treasury Bulletin* for December 1948, p. 30. Estimates for the period from June 30, 1939 to June 30, 1940 are by the author, on the basis of data contained in the *Annual Report of the Secretary of the Treasury for 1940*, pp. 95–99. *Source:* H. C. Murphy, *The National Debt in War and Transition* (New York: McGraw-Hill, 1950) p. 259. Reprinted with permission.

borrowing during the period, it is now appropriate to look more closely at the monetary and fiscal policies followed and their consequences.

Monetary and Fiscal Actions during the War

On page 1 of the *Annual Report of the Board of Governors* (of the Federal Reserve System) for 1941, there is the following statement that set the objective of the Federal Reserve System for the duration of the war: "The System is prepared to use its powers to assure that an ample supply of funds is available at all times for financing the war effort and to exert its influence toward maintaining conditions in the United States Government security market that are satisfactory from the standpoint of the Government's requirements."[41] For the first several months of 1942, the Federal Reserve System set about making this broad statement operational. In addition, the Federal Reserve did recognize that it had a secondary role to play in containing what appeared to be inevitable inflation.

As the "phony" war was coming to a close, the Federal Reserve was once more concerned over the large volume of excess reserves of member banks. On November 1, 1941, it raised the reserve requirement to its maximum rate of 26 percent and reduced the volume of excess reserves from $4.7 to $3.5 billion. The existence of these large excess reserves led to a pattern of interest rates, as follows: On short-term, three-month securities the rate was ⅜ of 1 percent; on nine- to twelve-month securities, it was ⅞ of 1 percent; on five-year maturities, it was 1.5 percent; on ten-year maturities, it was 2 percent; and on long-term issues, it was 2.5 percent.

During 1941 the Federal Reserve began to argue that the 2.5 percent on long-term issues should be established as the rate to finance the emergency and eventually the war. To this rate the Treasury agreed in February 1942; there was also agreement that the decision be announced publicly. It never was announced, but became established by common knowledge in the market. The rate was chosen because it represented the rate determined in the prewar marketplace by the demand and supply of funds and was reasonably in line with other long-term interest rates. Besides, a higher rate, favored by some, would have meant or at least indicated a form of profiteering.[42]

There was less agreement on short-term rates. The Treasury wanted, as always, to keep interest rates as low as possible to minimize interest costs. They wanted the 90-day rate to equal the actual rate at the time of about 0.25 percent. The Treasury was determined to maintain the 2.5 percent rate, and it thought that was possible only if market conditions that determined it were kept unchanged: namely, those excess reserves. (Later, Treasury officials would state that banks ought to invest heavily in government securities, which is, of course, contradictory.) The Federal Reserve wanted more short-term securities issued, with a higher rate than existed. The Federal Reserve feared an unsound rate structure with a low short-term rate and promised to ensure that the long-term rate of 2.5 percent would not be disturbed.

An agreement was finally reached with the Treasury in March 1942 to support treasury bills at ⅜ of 1 percent and to maintain the existing structure of interest rates. The Federal Reserve policy, known as "pegging," would simply direct open-market policy objectives to maintaining the structure of interest rates and maintaining an adequate supply of reserves.[43] To maintain the prices of government securities and their yields, the Federal Reserve simply stood ready to buy all securities offered to it at the stated prices and yields.

This, of course, meant that the Federal Reserve monetized all government securities, accepting a security in exchange for high-powered money—cash or reserves—and was forced to abandon all control over the money supply. Also, by keeping interest rates low and stable, it encouraged private borrowing. Not surprisingly, the stock of money grew by 195 percent from 1939 to 1945, and the main cause was the growth of holdings of government securities both by banks and by the Federal Reserve System.

Other problems with interest rates developed. The Federal Reserve "posted" the treasury bill rate at ⅜ of 1 percent on April 30, 1942, to encourage investment and stabilize the short-term market. Later in the year, in August, the Federal Reserve announced that it would repurchase any bill sold at the stated rate—the pegging policy. In essence, the treasury bills became excess reserves, since the bank could transfer between bills and reserves with ease. Moreover, on October 30, 1942, the discount rate was reduced to 0.5 percent on loans secured by government securities collateral, and the reserve requirement was reduced to 20 percent, where they remained for the duration. Why would banks hold excess reserves, when they could hold interest-bearing securities that were highly liquid?

Moreover, why would anyone hold a short-term security at ⅜ of 1 percent, when a security yielding 2.5 percent was available? One could obtain 2.5 percent for three months by simply acquiring a long-term security and selling it after three months. Consequently, the irrational rate structure meant that the Federal Reserve was forced to buy a great deal of short-term securities that investors began to shun as they "played the rates." The Treasury and the Federal Reserve argued over what to do about the structure of interest rates. The Federal Reserve wanted to increase short-term rates, and the Treasury wanted to introduce more uncertainty into the market, making the holding of short-term securities more reasonable. The issues went unresolved until the end of the war.

Other measures taken by the monetary authorities included Regulation W, which empowered the Federal Reserve to set the terms of consumer credit, fixing the maximum loan and the repayment periods. This selective control was designed to help reduce consumption and limit spending. The Federal Reserve also instructed banks to be very selective in making loans and to reduce loans for nonproductive purposes, especially real estate loans.

FDR was elected to an unprecedented third term in 1940, easily defeating the Republican candidate, Wendell Willkie. In the campaign and in the phony war, the New Deal gradually was put aside, as FDR turned his attention to international affairs. It was not that he had given up on it or thought that all had been accomplished. In fact one of his reasons for running for a third term was to protect the gains made against possible dismantling by a conservative Republican.[44] When queried about the disappearance of the New Deal in the midst of war, FDR responded by enumerating the past accomplishments and suggesting that the New Deal would be resurrected in the postwar period.[45]

The shift in emphasis was reflected in federal government budgets that began to be weighted toward international matters and away from domestic concerns for social justice. Similarly, the undisputed need for higher taxes to pay for the increasing involvement in the war in Europe would have to be considered in relation to who should bear the burden of higher taxes. The answer would not only involve matters of social justice during the war but possibly extend beyond it to affect the tax burden and the distribution of income for years thereafter.

Thus, the interruption of the New Deal by World War II could have significant impact on the economic structure of society and the distribution of power and influence. If the New Deal was set aside, who would benefit from the financing of the war? Would the benefits be temporary or long-lived? To ask the question is to show the dilemma of New Dealers and progressives who sought to protect the gains already made and prevent any assault on them. The attacks had already begun and were growing, as manufacturers joined the financial community in deserting FDR. Did the New Deal have the strength and social acceptance to withstand the assault by these powerful groups who could find ready allies in the large number of conservatives, both Republicans and Democrats, in the halls of Congress?

Keeping these broader questions in mind, it is necessary to review the record of the decade and the decisions made year by year, to see how they accumulated to affect the economy and the society over the long run. Table 6.4 contains the record of how the federal government was financed during the period.

Obviously the explosion in government expenditures came from national defense spending. The increase in the period 1930–45 is a whopping 7,290 percent. Expenditure on all other functions increased as well, but the total amounted to only 48 percent. The record of the change in social spending is mixed in the period 1940–45, with expenditures on income security falling by 20 percent, while spending on natural resources fell by 35 percent; spending on housing and community activities actually became negative in 1945, by $191 million. In education and health, however, there were increases of 222 percent and 281 percent, respectively.

Increased economic activity brought about by the war, together with tax increases (discussed below), accounted for the rise in tax receipts. From 1939 to 1945 receipts increased by over 804 percent, with taxation of individuals increasing by 1,740 percent and of corporations by 1,272 percent. Still there were deficits. In 1939 the deficit was $3.9 billion, and in 1943 it rose to $54.9 billion and declined to $47.5 in 1945. As indicated earlier, taxation accounted for only 45 percent of the war financing, leaving the rest to be financed by borrowing. The result is clear in Table 6.4, as the public debt rose from $40.4 billion in 1939 to $258.7 billion in 1945, an increase of some 540 percent. The increase in the public debt of over $200 billion during the war has always troubled many people, because of the alleged burden on future generations to repay it. Without debating the merits of the case, one powerful argument can be made against it by pointing out that the real burden was on consumers at the time, a burden born out of a real sacrifice of resources that were diverted from the production of consumer goods to military goods.

When FDR submitted his budget for the fiscal year 1941, he estimated a deficit of $2.8 billion, with spending on national defense of $1.9 billion. In June 1941 defense expenditures were revised upward to $3.25 billion and in August to over $14 billion. Secretary Morgenthau became concerned over the $45 billion debt limit, and the administra-

Table 6.4 Federal Government Finances, 1939–1945 (unified budget in billions)

Fiscal Year	Expenditures			Receipts				Budget Surplus or Deficit (−)	Gross Public Debt at Year End
	Total	National Defense	Other	Total	Taxation		Other Receipts		
					Individuals	Corporations			
1939	8.8	1.1	7.7	5.0	1.0	1.1	2.9	−3.9	40.4
1940	9.5	1.5	8.0	6.4	1.0	1.1	4.3	−3.1	43.0
1941	13.6	6.1	7.5	8.6	1.4	2.0	5.2	−5.0	49.0
1942	35.1	24.0	11.1	14.4	3.2	4.7	6.5	−20.8	72.4
1943	78.5	63.2	15.3	23.6	6.5	9.6	7.5	−54.9	136.7
1944	91.3	76.8	14.5	44.3	19.7	14.7	9.9	−47.0	201.0
1945	92.7	81.3	11.4	45.2	18.4	15.1	11.7	−47.5	258.7

Source: Tax Foundation, Inc., *Facts and Figures of Government Finance,* 1979.

tion finally persuaded Congress to consider a modest tax increase. Even before that could be done, higher defense requests were made, and a new tax bill was quickly designed.[46]

On June 25, 1940, the president signed into law the first Revenue Act of 1940. The act made some "permanent" income tax changes and some "temporary" (five years) defense taxes and authorized $4 billion of defense obligations. The income tax changes reduced the amount of personal exemptions and increased the surtax rates on net incomes over $600 and not over $100,000. These changes meant that the base of taxation was lowered, making more people required to file a return and increasing taxes for lower-income groups already paying taxes. In addition, corporate taxes were increased by 1 percent in a graduated structure, beginning at 13.5 percent on the first $5,000 of net income and ranging to 19 percent on net income in excess of $25,000.

What angered the progressives, and made Senator La Follette label it "the most inequitable tax bill enacted by congress in the last decade," were the "temporary defense taxes."[47] These five-year taxes were mainly increases of 10 percent on individual and corporate incomes, gifts, estates, excess profits, capital stock, and personal holding companies. A flat 10 percent tax merely exacerbated the already existing inequities in taxation; high incomes, over $100,000, were barely affected.

In addition, 43 excise taxes were increased from 10 to 50 percent, and others (wine, cigarettes, liquor) were raised from 8 to 30 percent. These temporary taxes were to be collected in a fund to retire $4 billion in public debt with a maturity less than 5 years.[48]

Senator La Follette had been pushing for an excess profits tax to prevent war profiteering. Defeated in the first tax bill of 1940, he picked up support, and on July 1, 1940, FDR sent a message to Congress asking for a steep excess profits tax. An excess profits tax already existed, however, on government contracts for ships and planes. The revised Vinson–Trammell Act of 1934 limited the profits on government contracts exceeding $25,000 to 12 percent for planes and 10 percent for ships. In June 1940 Congress further restricted such profits to 8 percent.

These were pure profits, with all costs covered by contract. Still the defense contractors were unhappy and in effect went on strike and refused government contracts. They were also reluctant to invest in plants and equipment that would be useless after the emergency had passed. Thus, of the 4,000 planes authorized in June, contracts for only 33 were completed.[49]

FDR relented somewhat and promised to reconsider these items in a new tax measure. The result was the Second Revenue Act of 1940, signed into law on October 8, 1940. The act suspended the 8–12 percent profit limitations of the Vinson–Trammell Act, increased the normal tax rate to 24 percent on corporations with net incomes over $25,000, provided for the amortization of "emergency facilities" to be reduced to 60 months instead of normal depreciation time schedules, and enacted an excess profits tax.[50] The act was fairly complicated and generally was generous toward existing large corporations, but could prove burdensome for new or growing firms. Again, wartime measures aided the trend toward concentration, whether recognized or not.

Along these lines, the chairman of the War Production Board was given the authority to issue certificates exempting firms from antitrust laws. More than 200 certificates were handed out during the war.[51] Moreover, antitrust actions against large firms were postponed if a war agency requested it. The potential for abuse is obvious in these measures, although documented evidence of actual abuse has not really been established.

Returning to the record of taxation changes, several additional revenue measures were enacted during the war. The Revenue Act of 1941 increased the surtax on individuals to a new range of 6 percent on the first $2,000 to 77 percent of the excess over $5 million. Again, personal exemptions were lowered, continuing the trend of reaching down into the income structure to collect more taxes. In addition, excise taxes were again increased. The normal tax on corporations with net incomes in excess of $20,000 was increased from 24 to 31 percent, and the excess profits tax rates were increased by 10 percentage points in each bracket (now 35 to 60 percent).

The Revenue Act of 1941, passed in the fall of 1942, increased the normal tax rate on individuals from 4 to 6 percent, and surtax rates were graduated from 13 percent on the first $2,000 to 82 percent on income over $200,000. Again, personal exemptions were lowered, with the same result of making this a mass tax. Moreover, a victory tax at 5 percent of net income over $624 was imposed, with a postwar provision for credit (an example of forced saving). Tax rates for larger corporations rose from 31 to 40 percent, and the excess profits tax structure was replaced by a flat rate of 90 percent.

In June the Current Tax Payment Act of 1943 was passed, providing for a 20 percent withholding tax. The withholding of taxes obviously facilitated the collection of taxes and increased the tax yield, as it certainly fostered greater tax morality from a basically self-administered tax system.

In February 1944 Congress overrode a veto of FDR, and the Revenue Act of 1943 was passed. Congress, with an eye toward the election year, reduced the victory tax from 5 to 3 percent, increased the excess profits tax rate to 95 percent, and increased the excess profits tax exemption from $5,000 to $10,000. Other changes were made in excise taxes, but this was certainly not a bill designed to increase tax revenues or reduce inflationary pressures.

Finally, in May of 1944 Congress passed a measure, the Individual Income Tax Act, that was designed to simplify the income tax without affecting its yield. This was accomplished by abolishing the victory tax, reducing the normal tax rate from 6 to 3 percent, and increasing the surtax rates from a range of 13 to 82 percent to a range of 20 to 91 percent. Personal exemptions were fixed at $500 per person, and earnings of minor children were no longer taxed to parents.

Assessing War Financing

Looking back over the success or failure of wartime financing, one treasury official appeared satisfied—"All in all it was a job well done."[52] Admittedly, improvements were possible, particularly in the proportion of war financing assumed by taxation. More taxation would surely have reduced the burden of price controls, rationing, and debt servicing, and the postwar attempt to control inflation would have been easier without the large amounts of liquid balances.

The Federal Reserve was less satisfied with the war record. There the feeling was that higher interest rates, particularly on short-term securities, were necessary and that long-term securities should have been nonmarketable in the same manner as Series E Bonds. Failure to do this resulted in an irrational structure of interest rates and in profiteering on the purchase and sale of securities.

Also, the Federal Reserve considered the Treasury's view of easy money to be too sanguine when it came to questions of inflation and too shortsighted when it came to postwar problems. According to one Federal Reserve official, we should not have tried to freeze the rates of interest that existed at the start of the war, because these rates reflected the depression conditions that were quickly changed. In short, the Federal Reserve asked for more flexibility in monetary policy than it had the chance to employ, due to the Treasury's intransigence.[53] The same criticisms of wartime finance can be found in the writings of the Federal Reserve chairman, Marriner S. Eccles: "It was the policy of establishing and maintaining a set pattern of interest rates that was the primary source of difficulty in financing the war."[54]

The discussion of war finance would be incomplete without reference to plans for managing the postwar economy. No matter how successful war financing was, it would be deemed shortsighted without the provisions for postwar economic problems. As early as 1943, when the tide began to turn, the Senate established the Special Committee on Postwar Economic Policy and Planning, which conducted hearings on war contract cancellations, surplus property disposal, and industrial reconversion. The War Production Board had begun to consider the matter, and the OMB initiated a study by Bernard Baruch to examine the question of reconversion. Other agencies were involved, as well, in one or another facet of the problem.[55]

The details of the reconversion plans and actual policies, while very interesting, would require more space than is warranted in a survey of this kind. Suffice it to say that special agencies were set up to deal with the many problems of reconversion, from the termination of war contracts to the timing of reversion to civilian goods with an adequate supply of labor and financing to make the transition smoothly. The more interesting question is, What were the forecasts for the postwar economy? What problems of economic stabilization would the termination of hostilities present? What plans were made to deal with the aggregate economic problems?

The Federal Reserve, and those knowledgeable about money markets, were concerned with inflation: "We had no adequate fiscal and monetary policy laid out in advance to deal with the inflationary potential that might ravage the economy when the war ended."[56] The postwar economy would find billions of liquid assets that had built up as a result of government borrowing. While the war was on, there was little to buy with the high incomes being earned, but after the war this pent-up demand would seek to be satisfied. Businesses, too, would seek to repair or add to their capital stock. The backlog in the demand for goods could lead to demand-pull inflation—inflation that would rob the household sector of the value of the savings and demean the sacrifice involved.

The proper policy in this view[57] would be to keep intact the network of wartime controls until civilian production had recovered and could supply the output to meet the demand. Irksome as the controls might be, they were necessary for an orderly reconversion. This analysis seems reasonable enough, but there was an opposing view that emerged at the same time. In this view the forecast was for a postwar depression. The Office of War Mobilization issued a report, typical of this viewpoint, that the cancellation of war contracts would cause large-scale distortions in the economy, and the returning servicemen would drive the unemployment rate back to prewar levels. Reconversion would take too long, and the transition from a war to a peacetime economy would be too devastating to deal with effectively. Alvin Hansen wrote of a possible "post-defense slump."[58]

A postwar depression would call for a policy of dismantling the wartime machinery and controls rather quickly. Nothing should stand in the way of a quick return to private decision making. Of course, Hansen proposed a postwar budget that would have kept public expenditures high: "We must rebuild America for peace no less than for defense. Express highways, modernized urban transportation systems, reforestation, soil-erosion control, flood control, hospitals, slum clearance, together with the accumulated backlog of ordering public works held in abeyance during the defense effort, will call for large expenditures."[59] This liberal program of public spending would combat any slump, countenance the unmet needs, and prevent the economic stagnation that appeared to have plagued the U.S. economy since the onset of the depression.

In addition to these diametrically opposite forecasts and their attendant economic policies, other voices could be imagined arguing: for and against the continuation of the New Deal policies and philosophy, for more planning, for retaining the war machinery for fear of another war on the horizon, for resisting all caution in the haste to put war out of sight or consideration. On balance, then, the preparations for a peacetime economy were not nearly so farsighted and comprehensive as might appear from looking at reconversion plans. Many of these plans were necessarily involved with industrial problems or with surplus items to be disposed of.

Forecasts for the aggregate economy were obviously less consistent and hence less solvable. With the end of the war in sight, the confusion over the postwar economy continued, but the issue was still secondary to the successful conclusion of the war. In the next chapter the results of the contradictory views will be explored.

Evaluating Wartime Policies

In order to analyze the extent of success, rationality, or justification of wartime macro policies, the standards for evaluation clearly must be changed. The primary aim was to win the war, and many voiced the opinion that finances must not be allowed to interfere with the attainment of that end. Financial matters were considered important, but definitely subsidiary to the main goal. Still, a separate analysis of wartime economic policies can be both instructive and possibly illuminating.

So it is that the question of whether or not the wartime policies were justified becomes somewhat irrelevant. In periods of war almost anything can be justified. Beyond that generality, however, it has been observed that all kinds of interferences with and disruption of business as usual are tolerated, sometimes welcomed. Rationing, wage and price controls, resource-allocation schemes, excess profits taxes are but a few of the constraints on private actions that are justified as necessary for the war effort. Similar constraints imposed without an apparent emergency would elicit screams of protest and widespread resistance.

Similarly, the transfer of power to the national government is also accepted as essential, due to wartime requirements. The national government is allowed to control the economy and to engage in planning for the duration of the war and even for the immediate postwar period. Take away the emergency and the rationale for national actions, and government planning is questioned. No matter how effectively government does the job, after the war it is held to be incompetent to perform the same function in a peacetime period. No matter how contrary the evidence, ideology resumes its influence, whereby government is inefficient and private enterprise is efficient.

Hence, after the hostilities, the return to private enterprise and the dismantling of the controls was very hasty. As will become apparent, only a few voices were heard in opposition to the quick reversal of power and control from the government to the private sector. Was it because the public sector was really learning how to control the economy efficiently? Was there a danger that people would begin to accept the wartime shifts of power and control?

These questions cannot be answered with assurance now. There was widespread dissatisfaction with controls by both households and firms, but these objections measured unhappiness due to scarcities. Consumers were grumbling about the lack of gasoline, meat, sugar, and so on. With time, the shortages would have disappeared and so would the grumbling. Whether more acceptance of governmental allocation of resources would have followed is uncertain—but certainly possible. The same sort of argument can be made about firms. If government planning and resource allocation were given an opportunity to work in peacetime, it is not unreasonable to suggest that firms might have come to accept this substitute for prewar productions methods.

At the end of World War II, progressives were in no position to raise these larger issues. The successful conclusion of the war brought an enormous sense of relief to the population, and in the period of rejoicing it is doubtful whether anyone would have listened anyway. With the war out of the way, there was a genuine wish to return to normal again, a wish born out of emotional release. Few were prepared to make or listen to intellectual arguments to the contrary.

Whatever other lessons World War II yielded, the economic one is that many restraints on private behavior are possible if they are deemed required for an emergency period. If restraints are perceived as temporary, extensive justification for them is unnecessary. If war can be justified, designing wartime policies should pose no problems.

Similar evaluation problems arise in the assessment of the success of wartime policies. Obviously the war was won, democracy was maintained, and the economic system survived. The goals were achieved, but the question is basically whether they could have been achieved at a lower cost or with less sacrifice.

One of the problems in gauging success is that the degree of success varied over the course of the war. In the phony-war period, when the nation was slowly shedding its isolationist stance, the economy was able to shift resources to supply the necessary munitions for our future allies. The United States was "fortunate," however, to have such a sluggish economy, with excess capacity and a large volume of unemployment to meet the challenge. The buildup under these conditions allowed output to increase without significant pressure on wages, prices, or capacity. Also, there appeared to be sufficient time, since there was great uncertainty over whether the United States would even enter into the conflict. In short, pressures were minimal in the "defense period," but only because of the great depression having preceded it.

After the United States entered the war in 1941, there were huge sums appropriated for the conduct of the war, but the institutions required were still evolving. Again, there was lack of preparation prior to the formal declaration of war, and more time was allowed to elapse before real controls and management systems became effective. It was not until mid-1943 that most of the institutions were in place and had the purpose and the authority to carry out their missions.

While the federal government was learning how to design the management systems, from 1940 to 1943 prices were rising by over 29 percent, wages by 45 percent, corporate profits by 54 percent, and so on. Meanwhile, managers were voting themselves large salaries, labor was becoming envious, and an attitude of "get all you can at government expense" was allowed to develop. Firms delayed conversion to war production, in effect going on strike, until their demands for guarantees were met, and labor began to flex its muscles, so long dormant.

Of course, much of the problem could be traced to the uncertainty over how long the war would last. Many of the delays in devising management systems can be attributed to this source. Still, the costs of inaction or belated actions mounted up. Some of these costs were inevitable, unless detailed plans were available for a world war on two fronts. Perhaps democracies are not well suited for the mobilization for war when free speech, controversy, and voting rights are maintained. In fact, the Bureau of the Budget felt that the Germans and the Japanese counted on the inability of the United States to act decisively and mobilize quickly enough.[60] Whether or not autocracies are better suited than democracies for war mobilization is probably a misleading comparison, since, as just discussed, democracies are quite capable of relinquishing enough of their character in periods of crises to do the necessary job.

Once the machinery was in place, the United States managed to produce the necessary munitions, manage its economy, including the civilian sector, with controls and restraints, and finance the cost of the war. Whatever was required was sanctioned by the democratic process. Furthermore, after 1943 there were no significant alterations in the management systems, and thereafter things went more smoothly.

Nevertheless, the evolutionary process took a long time; objectives changed, and uncertainty was endemic. As the Bureau of the Budget put it, "The tasks were unique, the problems not well understood, the resources not well inventoried, the necessary objectives not always clearly visualized, the methods to attain them untried."[61] On the whole, though, it concluded, "The record is one in which the American people can take pride. It was not without error, and while it contains much experience in administration that can profitably be studied, it does not contain a finished blueprint for government arrangements for future crises."[62] Much the same conclusion can be found from an examination of the War Production Board record.[63] The record of postwar planning is left for the following chapter.

Wage and price controls worked as well as could be expected, once they were fully instituted and responsibility for them clearly assigned. They did not—and could not—work perfectly: There were bogus job promotions and padded costs. Still, the consensus is that controls worked fairly well and certainly helped control the inflationary pressures. Rationing also worked to allocate the scarce commodities as equitably as possible. True, there were black markets in some goods, counterfeiting of stamps in others, and in general many schemes to avert the rationing procedures. Whatever the problems involved, it would be difficult to devise an alternative scheme for the distribution of goods on such a wide scale. With rationing, as with wage and price controls, there is likely to be a group of people who take them as a challenge and devise ways around them for their own benefit. To expect otherwise is to seek utopia.

More pertinent to our inquiry is the success and failure of monetary and fiscal policies. These more impersonal policies have less emotional content than do the direct controls. The choice between borrowing and taxing to finance the war has already been discussed at some length. The view from the Treasury was that the choices made were, in general, correct. Henry Murphy points with pride at the proportion of expenditures covered by taxation in World War II (45 percent) as an improvement over World War I (30 percent from 1917–1919, or 42 percent, if 1920 is included). "There were no financial bottlenecks to the mobilization of the country's human and industrial resources. The financial markets were orderly, and the credit of the government was never questioned in the slightest. We should all be well content to let World War II stand, forever as the high watermark in our development of the techniques of war finances."[64]

Members of the Federal Reserve, as we have seen, would disagree. They wanted higher taxation and more flexibility in managing interest rates, particularly the short-term ones. Furthermore, borrowing set the stage for postwar inflationary problems, as the availability of these liquid assets would encourage spending. On balance it would appear that the Federal Reserve was correct. Higher taxation could have been pursued without damaging incentives during the war and would have limited inflation after the war. Still, given the forecasts of a postwar depression that determined the Treasury's view, the degree of borrowing does not seem excessive. The differences between the Treasury and the Federal Reserve can be traced to disagreement over the incentive effects of taxation and the opposite postwar forecasts that framed their views.

In the end it is difficult to judge the success of wartime fiscal and monetary policies. During an all-out war, the standards of success are blurred by the overriding concern for victory. It is true that money markets were stable, but only because the Federal Reserve abandoned all control over the money supply and reserves and pegged interest rates. It is true that taxation did increase, but only by making more people subject to taxation.

Yes, the overall system of war financing worked. The question we must ask now is, Was it equitable and rational?

The bias toward free enterprise in the management of wartime production has already been noted. Thus it is not surprising that the mobilization plans called for production to be carried out by large corporations. Profits, however, were held down somewhat by the excess profits tax. Still, the large corporations became further entrenched in the economy, and their power grew.[65] Suspension of antitrust laws during the war again signaled the desire to win the war rather than consider longer-term consequences. This concern with the short-run objectives and the disregard of long-run consequences recurs frequently in the analysis of wartime management.

After the war, government agencies scrambled around to ensure the availability of working capital, labor supplies, and resources to furnish to larger corporations (particularly the automobile industry) favored in the reconversion process.[66] Smaller firms would have to wait for the general economic recovery, and many firms driven out of business because of wartime conditions would receive little if any help at all.

Another example of the encouragement of concentration can be found in the working of the excess profits tax. All firms that made profits over the exemption paid the tax, but the small, dynamic, growing firm got caught in the formula for calculating the tax. Taxes calculated on the basis of a percentage of capital meant heavy taxation on a small firm, taxes that could limit its growth. Here a tax structure designed to prevent profiteering brought about unforeseen consequences. Furthermore, the tax applied to all profits of the corporation. Thus, a large defense contractor could earn exhorbitant profits on war contracts and below or average profits on nongovernment production, reduce or pull down the average profit rate, and possibly escape the excess profits tax that was calculated on some base-year profit. The corporations having failed to prevent the levying of an excess profits tax altogether did manage to have it written so as to minimize its impact and to inhibit the growth of potential rivals.

World War II also spelled the decline of the New Deal. Congress continuously pressured the administration to reduce nondefense spending as war expenditures grew. Yet nondefense spending was quite minimal compared to defense spending and contributed little to the problems of public finance. The real message was dissatisfaction over the New Deal social programs, disapproval of FDR pursing third and fourth terms, and more retreat from liberal ideas, now that conservatives had gained more power. Ostensibly concerned with deficits and the public debt, many really wanted to undo the New Deal programs before they became entrenched in the social consciousness and accepted as entitlements. The trend would continue into the postwar period.

One example of irrationality must remain incomprehensible— advertising. Advertising was allowed to continue during the war, despite the need to reduce spending and the obvious shortage of goods. What purpose was served, other than to keep the names of larger corporations before the public to ensure their survival? Why did the taxpayers have to subsidize the efforts of advertising (expenditures were tax deductible) when taxation could have caused disincentive effects? Again, this free-enterprise tactic became sacrosanct, even when it was clearly irrational.[67]

Evaluating economic policies in terms of rationality, as applied elsewhere in this study, refers to the designing of policies or institutions that may appear irrational and yet be consistent with some unstated goal or ulterior motive. It also refers to policies designed to fail for one reason or another, perhaps to comply with some ideological bias.

While some of this usage of rationality can and has already been applied to the World War II experience, it is again evident that this criterion for judging economic policy is not always appropriate for this period. Instead, the primary objective of winning the war was allowed to obscure the longer-term consequences of wartime actions. Hence, in the following discussion of rationality it is not so much unstated goals that are the issue, but simply failure to recognize and act on the profound changes that were occurring as part of the wartime programs. Without pausing to examine each in detail, here are some examples of challenges to the society that went unrecognized or unmet.

1. The workplace was transformed. In the desire to increase output as rapidly as possible with inexperienced workers—women, blacks, teenagers— the production tasks were drastically simplified. The result was an increase in output, but the jobs became boring, repititious, and dehumanizing, and the worker became further subordinated to the machine. After the war, the simplified production process was continued in the name of efficiency, but worker discontent grew.

2. Women were brought into the production process and into the armed forces in large numbers. They proved themselves capable and refuted the previous assessment of their ability. More than destroying the stereotype, they gained in self-esteem, in independence, and in the desire for additional self-expression and fulfillment: Female liberation was given a substantial boost, but postwar conditions were to frustrate the movements; society was not ready for drastic change.

3. Similarly, blacks were brought into the mainstream of postwar activity. Previous discrimination limited their participation in primary jobs,

but now they, too, had proved equal to the challenge of functioning on a level with any other group. The stereotype of a lazy, inefficient worker was found wanting, but again the society was not ready for change. Segregation continued, even in the armed forces, despite the honorable performance of the black units, and after the war the old patterns of behavior continued for years.

4. Internal migration to where the high-paying defense jobs were located altered the population distribution. The cities and large metropolitan areas gained and the countryside lost. Aside from the immediate social problems and the alleged decline in moral standards, the overcrowded cities would experience many problems that did not disappear at war's end. In fact they are still evident.

5. For the women, blacks, teenagers, and elderly who entered into productive employment for the first time, or from the unemployed ranks, or from part-time work, and so on, rising incomes were greeted with rising expectations. For many this was their first real opportunity to gain access to jobs that paid well and were steady and secure. Low-income groups were able to increase their living standards, even with rationing and the scarcity of consumer goods. Rising expectations meant that the prewar economic conditions would never again be tolerable. The economic gains would translate into political demands.

6. The distribution of both income and wealth became more equal over the course of the war. Workers' real incomes increased, while property incomes remained stable.[68]

The top 1 percent of the population received 11.8 percent of the income in 1939, but by 1945 the share had decreased to 8.8 percent; the top 5 percent of the population's share for the same period dropped from 23.5 percent to 17.4 percent. Similar shifts occurred in the percentage of income received by upper-income families compared to low-income families.

Moreover, the top 0.5 percent of the population held 28 percent of the total wealth in 1939, but by 1945 their share had declined to 20.9 percent. Similar shifts in the distribution of wealth can be found in looking at the top 1 percent of wealth-holders—from 30.6 percent to 23.3 percent in the same period.

Lower-income groups did begin to accumulate wealth as a result of buying government bonds and by accumulating assets out of their higher real incomes.

These gains were partially offset by the broadening of the tax base and somewhat by the withholding of taxes. (No withholding was made on interest, dividends, or profit receipts.) The trend toward greater equality is interesting, since it began to stabilize after the war.

chapter 7

The Truman Administration

After failing in health for some time, FDR died on April 12, 1945, in Warm Springs, Georgia. While the nation and the world mourned his loss, there was no time to assess his contribution to the nation, for the war was approaching a critical stage. In this early phase of his fourth term, the nation was preparing for peace, but still anxiously awaiting the end of the conflict. In January he had begun his fourth term, having bested Thomas E. Dewey in the 1944 campaign. Growing noticeably haggard, he attended the conference at Yalta in February. He did not live to see the establishment of the United Nations that he so fervently advocated.

Harry S Truman, former senator from Missouri, was Roosevelt's running mate in 1944 and immediately assumed the presidency on the day FDR succumbed. Like Harding, Truman had been filled with self-doubts all through his political career; unlike Harding, he overcame them to earn the respect of many contemporaries. Truman, the former country judge, farmer, haberdasher, and senator, was indeed ill prepared for the role he was now assigned. His main contribution had been the formation and leadership of a special committee to investigate the defense program. It exposed countless examples of waste in defense spending that could have been eliminated without hindering the conduct of the war. He earned respect for his integrity and thoroughness, and his record on the New Deal revealed him to be a loyal Democrat.

Now approaching 61 years of age, he became the thirty-third president of the United States. To him was given the task of presiding over one of the most troublesome and disrupting periods in U.S. history. The social, moral, political, and economic worlds were about to shift, both for the nation and the world. With the use of the atom bomb, mankind had taken a giant step toward the possibility of human annihilation, and every facet of life would be forever changed.[1]

The Keynesian Revolution

The field of economics, too, was undergoing a revolution—the Keynesian revolution. In the latter half of the 1930s and all through the war years, John Maynard Keynes's *General Theory* was gaining adherents. His influence was seen in the New Dealers, and now his theory found support at Harvard, as Alvin Hansen became a convert who taught a generation of students who would explain and extend the model and ensure its continued acceptance. Included among them was Paul Samuelson, who would write the first and enormously influential textbook that included the teachings of Keynes as interpreted by Hansen.[2]

Meanwhile, Simon Kuznets was developing a system of national income accounting, organized along the lines suggested by the theoretical model of Keynes. We now would collect the data according to his breakdown of the economy into sectors of demand, but more important in the long run, the success or failure of the economic system would henceforth be judged by the resulting summary figures of national income and output. The Keynesian model was truly a revolution in the sense that it altered the way we look at ourselves, and, in use, it set the criteria for determining the degree of success or failure of the economy.

What was the essence of the Keynesian revolution? Briefly, Keynes showed that a less-than-full-employment equilibrium is possible. The cause was an insufficiency of aggregate demand, mainly due to the instability of investment demand. There were no automatic forces in the economy to return it to full employment, once a disturbance upset it. Left alone, the economy would result in unemployment when aggregate demand was insufficient and inflation when aggregate demand was excessive.

This was the early interpretation of the Keynesian model, and the early remedy was compensatory finance by government for the woes created by inappropriate levels of demand. Abba Lerner and others had begun to illustrate that if aggregate demand were insufficient, the only sector capable of working in the national interest, the federal government, would have to increase its own spending or reduce taxes in order to close the gap; when aggregate spending was excessive relative to aggregate supply, the government would have to reduce its share directly or increase taxes to reduce the spending of the other sectors. If the gap was not completely closed by government actions, at least the amplitudes of the business cycle could be reduced, making fluctuations in the level of economic activity less destabilizing.[3]

Not only were swings from recessions to prosperity often painful and frustrating, but they threatened capitalism by encouraging the search for an alternative system free of such fluctuations. Thus the message of Keynes's *General Theory* was a conservative one—the rescue of capitalism rather than its overthrow, as often alleged. Why not give the economy a steering wheel, asked Lerner, and keep the car traveling on a straight course?[4]

In any case, the Keynesian theory was expounded at the right time, explaining as it did the depression and approving in theory what had already occurred in practice. Government intervention in the economy had begun in World War II, expanded with the New Deal, and continued in World War II war agencies. Government was now regulating industries, helping to rationalize production in them by planning schemes (not called that, of course), investing in research and development to stimulate them, changing the tax laws to accommodate them, building an infrastructure to help them grow, awarding contracts to larger firms to control competition, and protecting them where necessary from foreign competition. Indeed, the free-enterprise system became a theoretical ideal, but in practice the government and the industrial managers were aware of the need for government to stabilize the economy and to rationalize the output decisions of private firms to avoid overproduction and the business cycle.[5]

In the household sector, government had already stepped in to provide economic security and protection from the fluctuations of economic activity. The New Deal had provided Social Security and unemployment compensation, regulation of food production, insurance for bank deposits, and so on.

Thus the role assigned to government by the Keynesians was not foreign to the U.S. economy in the 1940s. Government had already assumed the responsibility for a more rational industrial sector and a more humane and just society. Not that these trends had been accepted by everyone, to be sure, and subterfuges were employed to conceal the obvious, but at least the society was prepared when the call came to make the government commitment more formal.

Formal recognition of government responsibility came in January 1942 from the National Resources Planning Board in a report that called for a program of postwar economic expansion and later in 1943 went further to declare that government should underwrite full employment and high levels of economic activity. In Britain Sir William Beveridge argued for a national budget that would attain full employment along the lines of a Keynesian-type fiscal policy.

Another proposal for a national policy to achieve full employment was developed in December 1944 by a subcommittee of the Senate Military Affairs Committee, including Senators Murray from Montana and Truman of Missouri. This proposal became the basis for the Full Employment Bill of 1945, introduced in the Senate on January 22, 1945. The bill provided that full employment be made a national goal, and that, if necessary, the government should provide the necessary expenditures and investment to assure its attainment.

The bill proposed a National Production and Employment Budget, developed annually by the president, in which estimates of the actual levels of aggregate demand and estimates of the full-employment level of aggregate demand were to be included. If the actual anticipated level was less than that needed for full employment, the president was to initiate programs to close the gap. Obviously a measure of planning was introduced by this bill, and, just as obviously, it was denounced by business groups and economic conservatives. Senator Robert A. Taft (R., Ohio) saw the possibility of unlimited spending and deficits and proposed balancing the budget over a longer period, say eight to ten years. Other senators tried to introduce weakening amendments, but failed.

The House was more successful in slashing its version of the same bill. It was completely rewritten, taking out the "right" to work, and substituting "high" for "full" employment. Gone, too, was the National Budget, and in its place the president was required to submit an annual report with the aid of a three-member Council of Economic Advisors. The report would go to a Joint Economic Committee with no legislative authority. The bill was sent to a conference committee, but not acted on until 1946.[6] In February 1946 the conferees emerged with a bill close to the House version that was entitled the Employment Act of 1946. With little debate the original backers of a full-employment bill yielded, and it was signed into law on February 20. The preamble is worth quoting in full, for with all the qualifying phrases and escape clauses, the act was so watered down as to represent a travesty of the original intentions.

The Congress hereby declares that it is the continuing policy and responsibility of the Federal Government to use all practicable means consistent with its needs and obligations and other essential considerations of national policy, with the assistance and cooperation of industry, agriculture, labor, and state and local governments, to coordinate and utilize all its plans, functions and resources.

(1) For the purpose of creating and maintaining, in a manner calculated to foster and promote free competitive enterprise and the general welfare, conditions under which there will be afforded useful employment opportunities, including self-employment, for those able, willing, and seeking to work, and

(2) To promote maximum employment, production, and purchasing power.

Truman nominated Edwin G. Nourse as chairman of his Council of Economic Advisors, and Leon H. Keyserling and John D. Clark were nominated to serve with him. Yet, like Roosevelt, Truman really did not appreciate abstract thinkers or intellectuals and accordingly tended to ignore the council.[7]

The Employment Act of 1946, parody or not of the original draft, did reveal more faith in the ability to manage the economy, and, more important, did reveal the growing acceptance of government involvement in the economy. The debate over the act did much to educate everyone on the possibilities of fiscal policy. Given the knowledge and presumably the commitment, it is now time to observe how the act was used in the postwar economy.

The Truman Program

After the hostilities ended, there was the understandable collective wish to put the war behind and return to fewer restraints on personal actions. The nightmare of war, both at the front and at home, was now over, people wanted to restore some order to their lives, and that meant getting back to business as usual—not back to the depression days, but back to individual freedom with their newfound increases in economic wellbeing.

Roosevelt's last budget message left no doubt that when the war was over he wanted to strengthen the gains made in the New Deal. Truman also wished to continue the New Deal, with more emphasis on full employment. In his delayed message to Congress in September

1945, he made 21 recommendations, but emphasized the following areas for congressional action.[8]

1. Full employment—He strongly endorsed the Employment Act (in its initial form) being considered by Congress.
2. Public works—He called for Congress to provide funds for highways and grant-in-aid to states for construction of hospitals, airports, and other public works.
3. Housing—He urged Congress to provide funds for slum clearance and urban development and subsidies for public-housing projects.
4. Research—To encourage progress through scientific developments, he asked for a federal research agency.
5. Taxes—To promote the transition to peacetime economy, he asked for a limited amount of tax reductions.
6. Jobless benefits—He requested the extension of the law to workers not covered and asked for supplemental benefits to assure weekly benefits of $25 for up to 26 weeks.
7. Minimum wage—He also asked that the minimum wage to extended to cover workers in agricultural processing industries and that the rate be raised to $0.40 per hour.
8. Economic controls—He urged the retention of wartime controls to prevent postwar inflation.

Mr. Truman was not popular with Congress, where many viewed him as not up to the job. Republicans and southern Democrats teamed up to resist most of his proposals. Later, in the election of 1946, the Democrats would lose control of Congress and make Truman's job even more difficult.

Accordingly, his New Deal-like proposals got nowhere. There was a tax bill enacted in November 1945 that reduced taxes by $6 billion for 1946. This act repealed the capital stock and excess profits taxes, and corporate and personal income tax rates were reduced slightly; the range for personal taxes became 20–91 percent, down from 23–94 percent, and corporate surtax rates were reduced from a range of 10–16 percent to 6–14 percent. These tax reductions came at a time when inflation was an administration concern, and the 1946 budget was estimated to have a deficit of some $30 billion! (It should be remembered here that the Federal Reserve was still pegging interest rates on government bonds and was not in a position to counter any inflationary threat from the fiscal policies adopted. Monetary policy could be of little help.)

The attack on the disliked price controls came from most segments of the society and was building in 1945. The administration asked for an 18-month extension of the Price Control and Stabilization

Acts due to expire on June 30, 1945. Heeding the farm bloc, Congress reluctantly extended them for one year, to June 30, 1946. Other wartime controls were dismantled quickly, but the administration wanted to retain some war powers to deal with items like sugar and tires that were still in short supply. It asked for an extension and got one to June 30, 1946, but many of the powers were deleted. Clearly, then, 1946 would be the real test year for policymaking. The policies of 1945 show some ambiguities, but considering the postwar forecasts, some allowances must be made.

Postwar Inflation

In the winter of 1945–46, one of the liveliest topics was whether peacetime controls were necessary. The Office of Price Administration (OPA) was always under attack by some group or other, but its existence was always justified by the need to cooperate for the war effort. Consumers were always upset, producers felt frustrated, and even Congress was always railing against "the professors and economists" at OPA. Now, with rationing virtually over, controls on wages removed, and limitations on raw materials and transportation lifted, attention turned to the last highly visible major restraint of World War II—price controls.

Chester Bowles, price administrator of OPA and later director of the Office of Economic Stabilization, led the fight for retention of price controls. He argued for an orderly removal of price controls when supply and demand had been brought into balance for each industry. Gradual removal would fight inflation and keep the lid on wages, which would tend to rise if living costs went up.[9]

Marriner Eccles, chairman of the Federal Reserve System, also advocated the retention of price controls and looked on with dismay at the rapid abandonment of all wartime controls. Inflation was the main postwar problem to him, and he worried over actions that would exacerbate the inflationary pressures. He was also acutely aware that the Federal Reserve would do little in the way of monetary policy to combat it.[10]

No doubt many others supported the retention of price controls, but they were no match for the opponents. Again, many households were fed up with rationing and shortages and might have blamed the OPA. When farmers and cattlemen, however, were led to believe they had not gotten their share during the war and held back supplies, driving up prices, many consumer and women's groups demanded that

OPA be fully restored. In April 1946 a march on Washington by housewives to protest rising prices and artificial scarcities brought the battle to Congress.

Meanwhile, the National Association of Manufacturers and the Chamber of Commerce were conducting a massive lobbying campaign against this "socialistic" program that was inhibiting production and employment. Congressmen, too, echoed this concern, and the influential Senator Taft added the loss of freedom to the list of problems caused by continued interference by government. Harold G. Moulton and Karl L. Schlotterbeck of the Brookings Institution analyzed the situation and concluded that price controls were unnecessary and impractical. "Without wage stabilization and without rationing, the OPA is not in any case in a position to hold the price line"[11]—and did not have to, for agricultural and raw materials were abundant and only consumer durables posed any problem.

When Congress acted to restore the "natural, divine, God-given law"[12] of supply and demand, it produced a price-control bill so watered down that President Truman vetoed it and was sustained. Congress tried again and produced another bill, which the president signed into law in July with reluctance, that was again so riddled with exceptions and special provisions that although controls were extended to June 30, 1947, by fall they were virtually inoperative. Only rent controls remained effective: Over the entire period 1939–48, rents rose by only 12.8 percent.

Not unexpectedly, prices rose dramatically at both the retail and wholesale levels. From June to December 1946 consumer prices rose by 15 percent and wholesale prices by 25 percent. Food prices rose by 28 percent at the consumer level and by 42 percent at the wholesale level; food was allegedly in abundance, and Moulton and Schlotterbeck foresaw no price problems there![13] All prices rose, including the raw materials, which were also held to be in abundance, until August 1948, when they either leveled off or fell. (Table 7.1 gives the data for this period and other important dates as well.) Another way to view the dramatic increases in prices is to note that over the period 1939 to August 1948, consumer prices rose by 76 percent and wholesale prices by 120 percent. However, 45 percent of that increase came after controls were removed from consumer prices and 40 percent in the case of wholesale prices.

Despite the sharp price rises and the administration's continued pleas for reinstatement of controls, Congress balked. An exception was made only in the case of rent controls, which continued in effect until July 1953, after Truman had left office. This long history of rent controls attests to the acute housing shortage after World War II. The

Table 7.1 Percentage Changes in Consumer and Wholesale Prices, 1939–48

Item	1939 to June 1946	1939 to August 1948	June to December 1946	June 1946 to August 1948
Consumer prices				
All items	34.1	75.6	15.0	30.9
Food	52.9	127.5	27.7	48.8
Apparel	56.4	98.7	12.3	27.0
Rent	4.0	12.8	n.a.	8.5
Wholesale prices				
All commodities	46.4	119.8	24.8	50.4
Food	60.4	169.2	41.8	68.1
All other	29.9	88.3	18.1	45.2

Source: Compiled by author from Council of Economic Advisors, *Economic Report of the President* (Washington, DC: GPO, various years).

lack of construction during the war, together with the increased demand, put a strain on existing structures, but until the supply caught up to the demand, some restraint on the housing sector was allowed. Even the Supreme Court accepted the constitutionality of the controls, over the objections of the real estate industry.

Labor Problems in the Postwar Period

Another postwar problem quickly developed after the removal of wage controls and the no-strike pledge—labor unrest. Almost immediately after the cessation of hostilities in mid-August 1945, President Truman removed these wartime controls as no longer necessary, since there was "no longer any threat of an inflationary bidding up of wage rates by competition in a short labor market." Once again there is the appearance of contradictory forecasts for the postwar period, since a depressed economy would not need to be concerned with rising wages, but still there is the hint that inflation might still be lurking in the wings. Yet, if inflation was a serious concern, why were wage controls removed so swiftly, while price controls were being defended as necessary in the postwar economy? Economically, price controls without wage controls made little sense; politically, there may be a rationale. On the surface it would appear that these acts were an admission that wage and price controls were poorly administered, shortchanging labor while letting profits grow by permitting prices to rise faster than wages. Indeed, organized labor felt this to be the case. The gains that labor had made during the war were now thought to be threatened by attacks, first from business and gradually from the public and finally from a hostile, antilabor Congress that was ushered into office in 1946.

Accordingly, the postwar period showed a sharp rise in labor unrest along with congressional attempts to curb organized labor's power. Union membership had soared during the war, rising from 6.7 million workers or 15.5 percent of the labor force in 1940 to nearly 15 million or 24 percent of the labor force in 1947. Thereafter it grew slowly and then stabilized for the next decade. Observing the attack on collective-bargaining rights, organized labor sought to solidify them and protect its wartime gains. One method was the strike, and work stoppages grew from 2,508 in 1940 to 4,985 in 1946, representing 116 million man days of idle time![14]

Labor, in addition to cementing bargaining rights, also feared rising unemployment rates and falling wages, now that the workweek would return to 40 hours from the wartime 52 hours. It sought to retain the same pay for a reduced workweek, feeling that business had the ability to pay these higher wages out of swollen profits without raising prices. Unemployment also became a worry, as the unemployment rate fell to a low of 1.2 percent in 1944 but began climbing in the reconversion period to 1.9 percent in 1945 and 3.9 percent in 1946.

Labor militancy did not extend to the protection of workers drawn into the labor force by wartime requirements. Females, who left their households and were suddenly able to perform the tasks that were previously denied them, were forced out of the labor force by returning males. Some 5 million of them joined the labor force from 1940 to 1945, and by 1946 half that number were out of it. Many chose to leave, of course, but many indicated a desire to remain in their jobs.[15] Woman's role was still in the home, and pressure was exerted to return her there. The same was probably true for the minorities who were drawn into war jobs, although the data are not available to show it.[16]

However justified labor felt in its actions, it was not able to convince the general public and certainly not the 79th and 80th Congresses. The hostility toward labor began in 1941, as labor sought to unionize the defense establishment, and later widespread strikes and the failure of the collective-bargaining process resulted in calls for industrial peace. The no-strike pledge of 1942 restored some goodwill toward labor, and, despite some wildcat strikes, most disputes were settled by the National War Labor Board.

The real trouble came in 1943, when strikes in the coal mines really stirred up the general public. The government was forced to seize the mines, but gave in to wage increases that broke the wage formula. The public was irritated with John L. Lewis, head of the United Mine Workers, who was viewed as arrogant, selfish, and concerned only with the wellbeing of his miners. Coal was essential at that time and hence highly affected the public interest.

As a result, Congress passed the Smith–Connally Act, over the president's veto, that gave the president the power to take over war plants engaged in labor disputes. The act also provided that unions had to give notice of a strike and submit to a strike ballot in defense industries. Labor branded it a "slave" act and promptly began issuing strike notices, only to withdraw them later. Public hostility grew, as workers voted for strikes they did not intend to carry out as a method of strengthening their bargaining position.[17]

Still, the number of strikes continued to grow in 1944 and 1945. Truman generally had a favorable record on labor matters and was a loyal New Dealer. Yet shortly after he sent his special message to Congress on September 6, 1945, reasserting his desire to continue FDR's request for an Economic Bill of Rights,[18] a strike was called (September 17) in the oil industry. The main demand of the oil workers was the same pay for a 40-hour week that they had earned in 52 hours at straight time. No amount of government negotiation was able to settle the issue, and Truman ordered the Navy to seize and operate the refineries after severe shortages occurred. The workers returned quickly and submitted to a growing mechanism for settling disputes— the fact-finding board.

The wave of strikes spread to workers in the United Clerical, Technical, and Supervisory Union; the Lumber and Sawmill Workers; the United Brotherhood of Carpenters and Joiners; the Federation of Glass, Ceramic, and Silica Sand Workers; and from the Shipyard Workers in San Francisco to the longshoremen in New York City to the Textile Workers in New England.[19] Reacting to the growing concern, Truman called a conference in October 1945, convening representatives from labor, business, and government to examine the whole issue of labor–management relations. The conference discussed many issues in labor disputes, including more use of fact-finding boards and "cooling-off periods," but in the end it achieved very little, since neither labor nor management was prepared to give any ground. The most dramatic strike during the reconversion period came as the conference was in session and debating the means of settlement for such cases. On November 21, 1945, some 200,000 United Auto Workers struck the giant General Motors Corporation. The immediate issue was a union demand for a 30 percent wage increase plus other provisions. GM offered only 12 percent. The union contended that GM had the "ability to pay" the higher wages, while GM wanted price and profit issues excluded from negotiations.

President Truman appointed a fact-finding board that recommended a 19½-cent wage increase in January 1946 and reinstatement of the contract. The union accepted the terms, but General Motors agreed to raise its offer to only 18½ cents. Talks dragged on until March 13, 1946, when agreement was reached after 113 days, giving the workers the 18½-cent increase and other contract items. The 18½-cent-per-hour increase became the magic number and the standard for other contracts in the automobile industry, in the steel industry, in the mining industry, and so on. Both the company and the workers were hurt by the long strike, and the public, starved for cars, was irritated by the production delay and the higher prices it foresaw. Truman began to advocate methods to settle labor disputes that heavily affect the public interest—fact-finding boards.

The drive for higher wages continued in 1946, as the United Steelworkers of America struck the steel mills and again accepted the recommendations of Truman, after he received a report from a fact-finding board appointed by him. The wage increase recommended was 18½ cents, but it was not accepted by the steel firms. In the spring of 1946 the United Mine Workers went on strike for a health-and-welfare fund. The parties could not reach an agreement, and Truman ordered the mines seized and operated by the secretary of the interior, Julius A. Krug. The two-month strike was finally settled by a recommendation by Krug of the 18½-cent wage increase and the health-and-welfare fund.

Finally, the last major strike occurred in the railroad industry. Some of the railroad unions had agreed to arbitration, but the Engineers and Trainmen did not. The latter groups rejected the arbitrator's proposals and planned to strike. Truman ordered the seizure of the railroads, but the unions postponed the strike. Further negotiations broke down, however (again the 18½-cent increase was included), and Truman went before Congress to ask for emergency legislation to prevent strikes that destabilize the economy. Union officials capitulated at the last moment.

The reconversion strikes continued until the summer of 1946, but they gradually settled down to a pattern involving smaller numbers of workers. Yet the damage to organized labor had been done. In the elections of 1946 many supporters of labor were ousted from office, as a Republican majority was achieved in both houses of Congress. Truman himself began proposing ideas to give labor–management relations more structure to avoid upsetting the economy.

The public, too, was aroused by the inconvenience caused by strikes and the propaganda campaign against organized labor waged by the NAM and the Chamber of Commerce. These organizations called for reforms to the Wagner Act, which they claimed had created an "imbalance" in favor of labor, for "right-to-work laws," and any regulation to curb the power of labor. The public was confused even more by the antiunion campaign and by union practices and issues they did not understand, such as the closed shop, the boycott, discrimination against minorities, output restrictions, union financial conditions, and, of course, the Communist role in the labor movement.

The result of public pressure and the antiunion sentiment was the huge number of bills introduced in Congress to curb labor's power—73 bills in the House from 1945 to 1947 and 45 in the Senate from January 1946 to April 1947.[20] Most of them never got out of committee, but they do reflect the concern over the breakdown of collective bargaining. They called for compulsory arbitration, fact-finding boards, waiting or cooling-off periods, expulsion of Communists and racketeers, strike prohibitions in certain services, and elimination of the closed shop. Organized labor adamantly resisted all these provisions.

The Case bill, incorporating many of these provisions, did manage to pass both houses, but was vetoed by Truman in June 1946. The Case bill brought out all the discussion of labor problems to that date, with labor bitterly opposed to the solutions. The veto was sustained, but one section of the bill on antiracketeering was salvaged and became the Hobbs Act, the only labor bill passed into law by the 79th Congress.

When the Republican-controlled 80th Congress convened in January 1947, bills on labor matters again flooded the docket. What emerged was titled the Labor-Management Act of 1947 or, more popularly, the Taft–Hartley Act. This time the act easily passed both chambers, and Truman's inevitable veto was easily overridden. It was one of the most sweeping pieces of labor legislation in quite some time. It bore more than a passing resemblance to the Case bill and provoked the same response from labor—it was denounced as the "slave labor act."

The right to collective bargaining won with the passage of the Wagner Act was not questioned, but the procedures for collective bargaining and the content of the agreements were brought under government regulation. In brief, the act banned the closed shop and imposed limitations on the union shop; imposed an 80-day cooling-off period in strikes that imperiled the national health and safety; banned unfair labor practices, such as secondary boycotts, jurisdictional and other organizational strikes, featherbedding practices, and discrimination against employees, and prohibited the charging of excessive dues and fees; forbade the use of funds for contributions for political purposes by both unions and corporations; prohibited Communists from holding office in a union and required affidavits to that effect; and in general gave more power to and enlarged the NLRB.

In operation the Taft–Hartley Act appeared to be less destructive than organized labor had feared. Still, labor fought it and remained bitter right up to the 1948 elections, when Truman would be the beneficiary of their discontent. Others saw this act as a turning point in labor relations, the culmination of the all-out attack on unions by all segments of the society. Collective bargaining, they assert, never had a chance to develop into routine procedures that come with experience. The propaganda campaign was orchestrated to prevent labor from solidifying the gains that it made in the New Deal. There was sentiment in the House to repeal the Wagner Act entirely, bring labor under antitrust laws, and basically repeal all of labor's gains.[21]

Taking the abuses of a few unions as evidence for all unions, the act capitalized on a few excesses to tie up the union leadership in litigation over procedural matters. Union membership growth came to an abrupt halt and stabilized, and much of the militancy went out of the labor movement. True collective bargaining also suffered in the process.

The real mistake in dealing with postwar labor–management relations must be assigned to the haste in dismantling the National War Labor Board. Wages were held down during the war by the Little Steel formula that permitted average wage increases of 18 percent in manufacturing and in some industries only 15 percent. After the war, labor pressed for wage increases, and it was expected that employers would grant them without price increases or work stoppages. Some firms did just that, but when important firms balked, there was no agency to help settle the disputes.

Labor, seeing OPA threatened, corporate excess profits taxes reduced, the hours in the workweek falling, prices rising, and unemployment rising, had reason to fear the loss in its economic share. Unions came to the bargaining table equipped with these data and could support their demands; Walter Reuther of the UAW challenged GM to refute his data. The challenge went unanswered, since the

Table 7.2   Percentage Changes in Money and Real Average Weekly Earnings, Selected Industries and Periods

Industry	Percentage Change in Average Weekly Money Earnings		Percentage Change in Real Weekly Earnings	
	August 1939 to March 1947	March 1945 to March 1947	August 1939 to March 1947	March 1945 to March 1947
All manufacturing	+100.8	+0.7	+26.7	−18.3
Durable goods	+88.9	−5.5	+19.2	−23.3
Nondurable goods	+106.4	+15.3	+30.2	−6.5
Selected industries				
Basic steel	+71.1	−7.7	+7.9	−25.2
Automobiles	+57.5	−5.9	−0.6	−23.6
Cotton manufactures	+179.9	+41.1	+76.6	+14.5
Bituminous coal	+112.4	+24.2	+66.4	+0.7
Retail trade	+65.1	+29.8	+4.2	+5.4

Source: Closton E. Warne et al. (eds.), *Labor in Postwar America* (New York: Remsen Press, 1949), p. 130.

company refused to negotiate on these grounds. Table 7.2 may help illustrate the postwar history of wage changes.

While most workers were able to achieve substantial money and real-wage increases in the period 1939–47, note the reversal for the postwar period, 1945–47 (before wage increases in the steel and automobile industries). Indeed the loss in real wages in the postwar period was beginning to erode the gains made in the 1939–45 period. In particular, note the conditions in the automobile and steel industries, where workers were essentially no better off (in real terms) than they were prior to the war.

Without serious bargaining and an agency to settle disputes, the unions turned to their ultimate weapon, the strike. Firms used the opportunity to isolate labor as the culprit in delaying consumer goods to the waiting public, while instituting an advertising campaign to turn public opinion against the unions involved. What better time to mount an assault on unions, union leaders, and collective bargaining? That they succeeded and dealt a severe blow to organized labor is seen in the passage of the Taft–Hartley Act.

Truman versus Congress in an Unstable Economy

Labor problems were only one factor responsible for the confusing economic picture in 1947. Prices had risen throughout 1946, with the CPI increasing by over 18 percent from January to December 1946. Prices continued to rise in the spring of 1947, then leveled off, only to resume the rise once again in the fall.

Some of the price increases could be traced to (or attributed to) wage increases, but the backlog of demand from consumers, business, and importers continued to exert its pressures on the price level as well. All sectors of demand were competing for the available supply, which had not sufficiently recovered to moderate prices. The administration accordingly continued to express its concern for demand-side inflation.

These factors were listed in the first *Annual Economic Report of the President* in January 1947 as favorable for a prosperous year ahead. There were hints, however, that if certain things went awry, a recession toward the end of the year 1947 was possible. The Council of Economic Advisors (CEA) feared that the price increases that reflected shortages would not be reversed when the shortages disappeared. Hence, consumers would be unable to purchase the output, once their liquid assets had been depleted. If consumer demand faltered as a result, the economy could turn downward. If prices remained fixed, output and employment would fall: Some prices had to be adjusted, in the council's view, and a shift was necessary in the distribution of income toward consumers and away from profit takers. Excessive wage demands must, however, be avoided.

Business investment would also slow down if its demands were satisfied, if inventory requirements were met, and if labor–management strife had created too much uncertainty.[22] Thus the council had one eye on inflation and the other on recession. The economic outlook for 1947 was uncertain, but the administration was basically optimistic.

President Truman continued to press for extensions of rent controls and coverage of the Fair Labor Standards Act to workers currently excluded. He also asked for revisions in Social Security benefits, a long-range housing program, regional development projects, public works, public health, nutrition, and educational programs, and so on. Against this call for an extension of social programs, Truman maintained that "sound public finance" called for a surplus— "In the postwar situation, it is clear that it would be unsound fiscal policy to reduce taxes."[23]

Congress had other ideas. The elections of 1946 had given the nation a right-wing Congress, controlled by Republicans but supported by southern Democrats in many areas. Their work has already been noted in the Taft–Hartley Act, but they also had designs on the dismantling of the New Deal as well. They took their revenge on FDR by passing the Presidential Succession Act in July 1947, limiting a future president to two terms.

First, however, came the item of tax reductions. What they had in mind, true to conservative principles, was an income-tax reduction. Thus, when Truman proposed an extension of excise taxes, Congress quickly complied; indirect, regressive taxes were acceptable. Yet when Truman opposed a reduction in income taxes, the hostile Congress just as easily passed tax-reduction bills.

Two tax bills were passed by Congress in 1947, and both were vetoed by Truman. Both bills were weighted toward greater tax relief for the higher-income groups. The apparent inequities were defended on the grounds that there was a need to increase the supply of venture capital and increase managerial incentives. Despite the fact that little evidence had ever been found to support these arguments and that none could be produced in this period either, the Republicans continued to justify their tax proposals on these grounds. When reminded that a tax reduction in times of inflation would exacerbate the problem, they responded that the increase in supply would reduce the demand-pull pressures; when reminded that a tax reduction would run counter to the Republican aim of reducing the national debt, they responded by stating that debt retirement in the face of a possible recession would be inappropriate.

If the tax reduction was to forestall deflation, however, there were as yet no signs that the economy was headed in that direction. Besides, if a recession were anticipated, a tax reduction weighted toward lower-income groups would be more appropriate. These and other contradictions make it difficult to credit short-run fiscal policy as the motive for a tax reduction. More likely, such proposals were meant to force the administration to reduce public expenditures by reducing revenues, that is, to dismantle the New Deal programs. The Republicans were content to force a reduction in public spending over a long-run period, while at the same time pushing for tax cuts for the upcoming election period.[24].

Truman vetoed both bills and was sustained in both cases. He objected to the inequitable tax reductions and to the fact that inflation would be made worse. Nor did the administration see a recession ahead to justify tax reductions to forestall it. If a recession did occur, it was not likely to be a serious one in any case, and the automatic stabilizers could handle it. For Truman, it was "the wrong tax reduction at the wrong time."

When the inevitable attack came on the expenditure side of the budget, Congress found that 75 percent of the budget was uncontrollable—for national defense, veterans' services, and interest. Nevertheless, it recommended a total cut of $6 billion out of the $35.5 billion budget, but was able to achieve a reduction of only $1.8 billion. The cuts in social programs were partially restored, and the alleged superfluous government employees could not be found. Expenditure cuts were made in the administrative budget, in national defense (18 percent), and in international affairs and finance (30 percent). The administrative budget showed a surplus of $8.4 billion, which was consistent with Truman's hold-the-line stance on inflation (see Table 7.3). A tax cut would most likely have aggravated inflation, and thus the administration was basically correct in its attempt to combat the economic problem it most feared.

In October 1947 President Truman called Congress into a special session to consider an aid program for Europe and an anti-inflation program. Congress was asked to provide aid for European recovery, which came to be known as the Marshall Plan after the secretary of state who announced it. Originally estimated to require some $17 billion, it ended up with a bill closer to $12.5 billion. Hailed by many as a savior of Europe, it was also evident that the aid helped to stimulate the U.S. economy (about to slow down) and benefited U.S. firms as well.

The Marshall Plan was to prove acceptable to Congress in 1948; the anti-inflation program was not as successful. It called for the

Table 7.3   Federal Government Finances, 1945–52 (billions of dollars)

Fiscal Year	Receipts	Expenditures	Surplus or Deficit (−)	Public Debt at End of Year
1945	44.4	98.3	−53.9	259.1
1946	39.7	60.3	−20.7	269.9
1947	39.7	38.9	0.8	258.4
1948	41.4	33.0	8.4	252.4
1949	37.7	39.5	−1.8	252.8
1950	36.4	39.5	−3.1	257.4
1951	47.5	44.0	3.5	255.3
1952	61.3	65.3	−4.0	259.2

Source: Council of Economic Advisors, *Economic Report of the President* (Washington, DC: GPO, 1967), p. 284.

restoration of consumer credit controls, regulation of commodity speculation, more export controls, more rent control, rationing of selected goods, price ceilings on selected products in short supply, and control over the allocation of scarce commodities affecting the cost of living and limiting production. This last item would have authorized industries to enter into voluntary agreements (free of antitrust actions) for allocating scarce commodities and regulating speculation. Congress made these agreements voluntary, but they were not to involve price fixing and were to expire March 1, 1949. Export controls, too, were authorized until that date.

The rest of the program (Senator Taft called it a "police state") was ignored or enacted in 1948. Apparently Congress was not as fearful of inflation as was the administration, despite the fact that it had or was about to authorize huge increases in foreign aid and was still entertaining the idea of a tax cut.

In his State of the Union message and in the *Economic Report of the President* in 1948, Mr. Truman changed his mind and presented his own version of a tax cut. What prompted this turnaround? It was not the lessening of inflation, for the administration held that "inflationary pressures are a major threat to the stability of the American Economy,"[25] but in the next paragraph it proposed a cost-of-living tax reduction of $40 for each taxpayer and each dependent.

The tax cut was not an admission that revenues were excessive, for corporate taxes were to be increased to make up for the lost revenues. In fact, there was little in the economy of early 1948 to call for a tax reduction: GNP was rising; unemployment was stable; and although there were faint signs and even forecasts of a future downturn, the administration was asking for the reinstitution of regulations of consumer credit and for a consideration of a Federal Reserve idea that reserve requirements be raised to curb bank credit.

It is difficult to escape the conclusion that the administration was responding to social and political pressure to reduce taxes. It was a popular idea, and this was an election year anyway. The increase in corporate taxes and the reintroduction of the excess profits tax would be popular politically, but risky in terms of corporate responses. The tax reduction for individuals would also be popular, appealing as it did to matters of equity, but in terms of combating inflation, it would have adverse effects. Predictably, however, the Truman plan for tax changes got nowhere.

The budget submitted by Truman in January for fiscal 1949 showed estimated expenditures at $39.7 billion and receipts at $44.5 billion, yielding a surplus of $4.8 billion. Again Congress set out to reduce spending and called for a reduction of $2.5 billion in expenditures. Also, the Committee on the Legislative Budget accused the administration of underestimating receipts by $3 billion, and, with the recommended budget cuts, this would put the surplus closer to $10 billion. Clearly a tax cut was easily affordable.

Since debate had already begun on a tax-reduction measure and since nearly all members of Congress were eager for a tax-cut bill, such estimates fell on receptive ears. In the House there was no attempt to relate the tax measure to inflationary effects on the economy. Members simply repeated the slogans about increases in incentives and increasing supply. They did not acknowledge that the tax reduction would also increase demand.[26]

The Senate did consider the possibility of a recession more seriously and did observe some softening in food prices and did consider forecasts of investment declines. Still, members may have been receptive to such information because it supported what they wanted to do anyway.

The Congress would not be denied and passed a tax measure over Truman's veto on April 2, 1948. It provided for an increase in the exemption to $600, gave a $600 additional exemption for the blind, permitted married taxpayers to split their incomes equally, increased deductions, and reduced income tax rates. Rates on the first $2,000 fell about 13 percent, rates to $137,000 fell about 7.4 percent, and rates on incomes above that amount fell about 5 percent.

The act also extended the interspousal exemption to the estate tax. This marital deduction for estate purposes, together with the income-splitting provisions of the income tax, benefited higher-income groups and offset the lower income-tax-rate reductions they received. Thus the measure increased inequities in the distribution of tax burdens.

In any case, the Revenue Act of 1948 was passed, not for stabilization purposes but for political and ideological ones, but "if there was ever a case of broadly sound economic measures being taken in very good time through good luck rather than good judgment, this was it."[27] The tax cut turned out to be the correct policy taken for the wrong reasons, for shortly thereafter the inflationary boom slowed down, as consumers had caught up with their postwar demand, and the CPI reached its peak in August 1948.

The tax reduction of approximately $5 billion helped to maintain consumption spending for a while, but personal saving shot up in mid-1948, after which the tax cut added neither to demand nor to price pressures.[28] In mid-year industrial production began to fall off, and inventories began to increase. The signs of a slowdown were on the horizon.

In the *Mid-Year Economic Report of the President*, the CEA appeared to place most of its emphasis on the problem of inflation, which had not been defeated, and only occasional vague references to deflationary tendencies were made. The economic situation was not all that clear, nor was past experience much of a guide. Yet President Truman, now a candidate for reelection, called a special session of Congress on July 27, 1948, to consider an anti-inflation program. According to Nourse, the *Mid-Year Economic Report* now served little purpose; the relationship between the CEA and the president was becoming even more uncertain.[29] Mr. Truman was setting policy as he gave the special session his eight-point program for combating inflation: rent control extension, consumer credit controls, price and wage controls, rationing, an excess profits tax, and so on.

Again Congress rejected the president's call for more controls and regulations, opting instead for the reinstitution of consumer credit controls (Regulation W), effective September 20, governing the terms in installment credit (for example, one-third down and 15–18 months to repay for automobiles). Also, Congress authorized the Federal Reserve Board to raise member-bank reserve requirements to 7.5 percent (from 6 percent) on time deposits and to 30 percent on demand deposits in New York and Chicago; reserve requirements rose to 24 percent in reserve cities and to 18 percent for country banks. Both powers were to end on June 30, 1949.

Chairman Eccles had advocated reserve requirement increases for some time, and his plan appeared in a different form in the *Annual Report* for 1945. Eccles had wanted a special reserve for banks, consisting of treasury bills, certificates, and notes, or cash. This plan would have permitted the support of government securities and at the same time restrained bank credit.[30]

The special session accomplished little that was not already being considered, but it gave Truman some ammunition for the upcoming election campaign. The session was politically inspired, for there was little chance that Congress would authorize such controls, any more than it was willing to consider the special programs submitted by the president. Later, however, he could run against the fiscally irresponsible 80th Congress, with its tax bill for the rich and unconcern for either inflation or social justice.

The First Postwar Recession

The recession, according to the NBER, began in November 1948 and lasted until October 1949, making it a brief downturn of 11 months. It was also a fairly mild contraction, with GNP falling about 3.4 percent, unemployment rising from 3.0 percent to 5.7 percent, and prices falling

Table 7.4   GNP by Type of Expenditure, 1945–52 (billions of dollars)

Year	GNP in Current Dollars	GNP in 1958 Dollars				
		GNP	Consumption	Investment	Net Exports	Government
1945	213.6	355.2	183.0	19.6	−3.8	156.4
1946	208.5	312.6	203.5	52.3	8.4	48.4
1947	231.3	309.9	206.3	51.5	12.3	39.9
1948	257.6	323.7	210.8	60.4	6.1	46.3
1949	256.5	324.1	216.5	48.0	6.4	53.3
1950	284.8	355.3	230.5	69.3	2.7	52.8
1951	328.4	383.4	232.8	70.0	5.3	75.4
1952	345.5	395.1	239.4	60.5	3.0	92.1

Source: Council of Economic Advisors, *Economic Report of the President* (Washington, DC: GPO, 1967), p. 213.

slightly. (Table 7.4 provides the national income data for the Truman years.)

This first postwar recession has been labeled an inventory recession, and with some justification, as the inventory component of gross investment fell from $9.0 billion in the fourth quarter of 1948 to $ −1.5 billion in the fourth quarter of 1949. Investment in plant and equipment also fell some $4 billion over the same period, and these declines account for the fall in GNP. Other sectors of demand were stable or increased, helping to make the recession a modest one.

This was the first recession following the passage of the Employment Act of 1946 and the first opportunity to observe the government's commitment to stabilization policies. In the beginning of 1949 the president was still concerned with inflation and sought a budget surplus. To achieve it, he asked for tax increases on corporate profits and upon estates and gifts. In addition, he recommended an increase in Social Security taxes. This is scarcely a countercyclical fiscal policy, but would seem more appropriate if inflation were viewed as a threat. Moreover, he asked that the powers given to the Federal Reserve to regulate consumer credit and to impose higher reserve requirements be extended beyond their expiration date of June 30, 1949.

Yet, paradoxically, he asked for a continuation of the Federal Reserve's support of government bonds at the low rate of 2.5 percent. Increased spending on Social Security, public assistance, a national health program, housing, aid to education, urban redevelopment, and increases in the minimum wage were also proposed. These spending increases were balanced by the request for wage and price controls, rent controls, and export controls.

Proposals for a tax increase in the midst of a recession seem perverse, and there were many who felt he was not serious, since the proposals were vague.[31] There was also the possibility that a tax increase was in response to the cold war, for in April 1948 the Soviet Union had instituted a blockade of West Berlin, and Truman had responded by airlifting food and fuel to that beleaguered city. Uncertain defense expenditures and hence higher taxes for the future could have prompted some provision for this contingency. In addition, NATO was soon to be a working institution (in April 1949), and, again, larger defense expenditures might have been anticipated.

The incorrect policy could not really be attributed to political ends. Truman had defeated Governor Thomas E. Dewey for the presidency in a stunning upset victory. The disenchantment with Truman was not strong enough to break the usual Democratic coalition. Of course, Truman in his masterful whistle-stop campaign was quick to point out the fiscal irresponsibility of Republicans who passed tax cuts for the wealthy in times of inflation, of their antilabor stance as evidenced by the Taft–Hartley Act, of their thwarting of social programs, and so on. This much-analyzed campaign is best left to others for elaboration, but it is interesting to note how Truman exploited the economic issues in it.[32]

The CEA was also concerned with inflation, since the current price declines could be interpreted as signaling the end of inflation. Prices had dipped before, only to resume their increase later. Besides, the council was unsure whether prices were changing because the structure of demand was changing or whether they were signs of softness in the economy. It was also concerned with the structure of investment, for housing had fallen off and other industries appeared to have caught up with their capacity desires. Still other industries, such as steel, were behind and posed a bottleneck problem.[33]

The council was cautious, concerned for inflation, but warning of possible deflation if these structural problems should worsen. The economy continued to decline until it was clear to all that a recession had begun some time earlier. In his *Mid-Year Economic Report* the president acknowledged that a decline had taken place, and his tax-increase proposal was withdrawn in favor of raising estate and gift-tax rates, the elimination of excise taxes on transportation, and the allowing of greater loss carryovers for corporations.[34] He still insisted on some of the social programs of his earlier report and acknowledged that a federal deficit must be accepted for the time being and that a balanced budget was desirable and just around the corner.

The CEA also acknowledged the recession, but had little to offer in the way of actual policies to reverse it. Both the president and the CEA stated that the situation did not call for large-scale public works because the economy was basically sound and would recover largely on its own through the efforts of the private sector. The response to the recession was timid and in the end proved correct.[35] The fortuitous tax cuts of 1948 and the increases in national defense spending helped to smooth out the downturn and make it a modest one.

Meanwhile, Congress had given the president little of what he requested in his budget for FY 1950. The budget showed an increase in spending of $1.7 billion for that year to cover increases in defense, public works, and social programs. A deficit of $900 million was projected. Congress refused Truman his anti-inflation controls and his tax increase, but granted extensions of rent controls and the voluntary allocation-of-scarce-commodities scheme. The recession made the actual deficits $1.8 billion for FY 1949 and $3.1 billion for FY 1950.

Congress wanted to cut expenditures, now that receipts were down, in order to pursue sound financial policy. The right wing of Congress was still pursuing its goal of reducing expenditures, no matter what was happening in the economy, while those on the left did not object to the meek antirecession measures of the administration. In general, there was little understanding in Congress of the principles of compensatory public finance, so that any action it did take on the budget was not for stabilization purposes.[36] Congress did manage to cut national defense spending by over $1 billion and reduce spending on public works as well. In the social area only a housing bill was passed for low-rent public housing, slum clearance, and farm housing.

Monetary policy during this first postwar recession was hampered by the pegging policy of the Federal Reserve. Twice in 1948 the Federal Reserve raised the discount rate, up to 1.5 percent in August. These were symbolic gestures, since banks were not forced to borrow from the Federal Reserve System. When the Federal Reserve was given the power to raise reserve requirements for time and demand deposits, it promptly did so, but, again, the move was not very effective; banks simply sold bonds back to the Federal Reserve.

The Federal Reserve's monetary policy did not permit more active intervention in money markets, but the pegging policy of the period might have been expected to add fuel to the inflation. It is interesting to note along with Friedman and Schwartz that "the foremost monetary puzzle of the immediate postwar period is why the money stock did not grow at a very much more rapid pace."[37] Gold was flowing in from Europe and neutral nations to add to our high-powered money. Moreover, the velocity of money exhibited very little rise from 1946 to 1948. Friedman and Schwartz attribute the low rate of increase in the money stock to the public's willingness to hold large amounts of liquid assets. Thus the Federal Reserve was lucky, for if the public had decided to spend these balances, it would have sold securities, driving up their yields, and the Federal Reserve would have been forced to step in to buy securities and thus contribute to high-powered money and presumably later to higher price rises.[38]

So the monetary authorities were "lucky" with the money-stock growth, just as the fiscal authorities were "lucky" in a tax reduction and defense buildup that came at the right time. It would seem that discretionary monetary and fiscal policies to stabilize the economy were meager, while fortuitious events made them unnecessary. In this sense the recession turned out to be mild, but without these unplanned actions, the downturn could have been much worse. Certainly there is nothing to indicate that government officials and Congress either understood compensatory public finance or were willing to act if they did.

The Fair Deal

In the last quarter of 1949 the economy recovered somewhat, led by consumption and a housing boom. The Housing Act of 1949 had authorized the FHA to issue mortgages, and together with the direct purchases of the Federal National Mortgage Association (Fanny May) stimulated a housing boom. This act of the liberal 81st Congress in part achieved a goal on Truman's shipping list of New Deal extensions. The 1948 elections had returned both houses of Congress to the Democrats and had given them a "liberal" cast.

Accordingly, President Truman continued to press for enactment of his proposals, now known collectively as the Fair Deal. In his *Economic Report* of January 1950 he repeated his requests for a new housing bill, a new farm program to protect farm incomes, extension of Social Security, aid to education, a health insurance bill, improved unemployment compensation, grants-in-aid to states for public construction, and extension of rent controls. From time to time the Fair Deal included requests for standby authority for price controls, rationing, and credit controls. Also, there was a strong push for legislation to end racial discrimination in jobs, Jim Crow laws, and other vestiges of a segregated society. Truman had ordered the desegregation of the armed forces, and that was slowly occurring. On other civil rights proposals he faced a hostile southern contingent bent on preserving the old ways.

Truman's budget for fiscal 1951 showed an increase in defense spending and decreases in foreign aid, veterans' payments, and agriculture. Still, the projected deficit was $5.1 billion, down from $5.5 billion for FY 1950, but still a deficit in supposedly prosperous times. Chairman Nourse of the CEA resigned his post in protest, and there were howls from conservatives generally. The acceptance of a planned deficit by the administration was a remarkable step to take for the times. True, all discussions of budget deficits were accompanied by statements that balanced budgets were preferable or were coming eventually.

The CEA also saw the economy recovering nicely and restoring some balance to postwar structural problems. Inventory disinvestment had begun to be reversed; only investment in plant and equipment showed signs of weakness, having fallen throughout 1949. The council was still concerned that the economy was operating below its capacity and dismissed the popular notion that a resurgence of inflation was approaching. The council foresaw no shortage of funds for capital investment and maintained that there was no need for a tax cut at this time, particularly in view of the deficit.[39]

The president, however, was asking for a tax increase. This at a time when the federal budget, together with the automatic stabilizers, was beginning to exert a restraining force;[40] this at a time when unemployment was close to 7 percent and industrial production was well below prerecession levels. Since the president was proposing an increase in corporate tax rates, the inference is that part of the tax proposal had nothing to do with the current economic situation, but was a long-term measure.[41] Other features of the bill would have reduced or repealed excise taxes, increased estate and gift taxes, reduced depletion allowances, and so on. Again, these are matters of equity or allocation, not stabilization. Truman warned Congress not to focus on tax reductions alone and not to cut his expenditure requests.

On June 25, while Congress was still grappling with the budget, war broke out in Korea. The cold war, with all its shades of hysteria, paranoia, and military posturing, had become hot. The economic situation was instantly transformed; the societal transformation took a little longer to recognize.

No one knew how long the "police action" would last, and the uncertainty caused consumers to prepare for the worst. Accordingly, they rushed out to buy and hoard all the goods that were rationed or in short supply during World War II: sugar, automobile tires, nylons, household linens, and meat. Such panic buying brought on the very shortages that were feared; it was a self-fulfilling prophecy. The CEA, in its January 1951 *Economic Report of the President*, reported that the brief consumption outburst did not require government action, but it did have some lasting effects.[42]

The effect was on prices, as consumer prices rose 1.7 percent from June to July 1950 and 5.1 percent from June to the end of the year. Consumption expenditures on goods jumped 10.5 percent from the second to the third quarter of 1950. The surge in consumption triggered off a series of repercussions: Inventories fell, and retailers rushed to replenish them, causing some speculation in raw materials; the WPI rose 12 percent from June to December 1950, and higher wages were demanded and in many cases granted. The return of controls was probably in the minds of many who tried to protect themselves.

Some estimates of the cost of national security were finally made in the January 1951 *Economic Report of the President*. The figure was put at $140–150 billion. In July the president asked for $10.5 billion for defense and $4 billion for military aid, and in December he asked for an additional $20 billion. These increases were promptly approved, but were not entirely responsible for the immediate postinvasion inflation. In the second quarter of 1950 national defense expenditures totaled $12 billion, and in the third quarter the sum had risen to $14.1 billion, a 17 percent increase. Yet together with the increases in consumption, they touched off a boom. Add to this the recovery of investment spending in the second quarter of 1950, and inflation became a real menace.

Truman asked for the wartime powers of control over scarce commodities, of regulation and control of the civilian economy, including credit controls and, if necessary, wage and price controls. Congress was reluctant to grant such sweeping powers, but was swayed by the influential testimony of Bernard Baruch and finally passed the Defense Production Act of 1950, giving the president most of what he requested, including wage and price control authority.[43]

In addition, the Federal Reserve, using its newly restored powers, reissued Regulation W on September 8, 1950, and strengthened it in October 1950. Regulation W required minimum deposits on installment credit (33⅓ percent for cars, 25 percent for consumer durables, and 15 percent for furniture) and maximum repayment periods of 15 months. These stringent requirements significantly helped curb consumption spending, as consumption fell by 4 percent from the third to the fourth quarter of 1950. Moreover, Regulation X of October 1950 set minimum down payments on housing, from 10 percent up to 50 percent on homes costing in excess of $24,250.

The Federal Reserve also increased the discount rate in August to 1.75 percent from 1.5 percent and allowed short-term interest rates to rise. It was still bound, however, to support the Treasury's operations and was forced to rely more on moral suasion than explicit actions. Fiscal policy would have to play the major role in this period.

Both the president and the council agreed that increases in expenditures would have to be met with pay-as-you-go tax increases. The necessity for a tax increase was well recognized in Congress, and the administration's tax proposal was generally well received. The main issue was the introduction of an excess profits tax in the Senate. The bitter debates over taxes on excess profits brought out the usual arguments pro and con, and eventually this controversial measure had to be separated (passed later in January 1951) from the main tax bill in order to get a tax increase through at all.[44] The Revenue Act of 1950 was regarded as a stop-gap measure and was hastily enacted in September. The need for a tax increase to prevent inflation was well understood, and the speed of passage probably prevented special-interest groups from marshaling their forces to combat it.[45]

The act provided for an increase in individual tax rates; some loopholes were removed, and some excise taxes were extended or maintained. Corporate tax rates were restructured to eliminate the graduated rates and in effect raised the rate to 45 percent for net incomes exceeding $25,000.

The Korean War and Macroeconomic Policies

The quick response by the administration and Congress to the possible economic disruptions due to the Korean War could be taken as a good sign in the evolution of macroeconomic policy. Despite other considerations, equity and New Deal sentiments and so on, the anti-inflation policies still showed some sensitivity to the needs of the national economy. The initial responses to the emergency situation, however, were helped along by the entrance of the Chinese into the conflict, and now that the war was recognized as a longer-run affair than originally anticipated, it was time for more thoughtful policies.

Yet as the Korean War settled down to a stalemate, public frustration set in, and the controls and restraints on economic actions that would have been more acceptable in an "all-out" war became irritating and burdensome. Policymakers were fortunate in one sense, since the scare buying by consumers ended in the beginning of the year, and consumption spending stabilized. This decline in an important source of demand-pull inflation helped to make the job of stabilization easier.

Consumer prices rose moderately, 4 percent for the year 1951, while wholesale prices actually fell by over 1 percent in the same period. Credit controls, wage and price controls, and higher taxes kept the lid on inflation for the year. The boom continued, as GNP increased to $329 billion in 1951 from $258 billion in 1950, an increase of 15.6 percent in current dollars (7.5 percent in constant dollars). The unemployment rate dropped to an average of 3.3 percent for the year, down from 5.3 percent the year before.

The boom was considered a threat to price stability, and further increases in defense-related activities posed additional problems. The president's budget of January estimated that the share of national output going into defense would increase to 18 percent in 1951, from 7 percent in 1950. He urged higher taxes to continue his pay-as-you-go policy for war mobilization.

Truman's budget for fiscal 1952 estimated a $16.5 billion deficit with the existing tax structure. He asked for increases in taxes of $10 billion to cover the increase in spending that in total was scheduled to rise to $71.6 billion from $47.2 billion. The administration's efforts to get a tax increase in 1952 were hampered by two things: The projected deficit for FY 1951 turned into a surplus of $3.5 billion, caused by a lag in defense spending and rising income tax receipts due to the boom, and the movement in Congress to cut expenditures, particularly on "socialistic" schemes of the Fair Deal.

Although it could be shown that the proportion of the budget devoted to social programs actually was below the previous year's, that did not stop congressional conservatives from demanding cuts in spending.[46] The continuing refrain, now becoming familiar to all, was that the government should not and could not spend on unnecessary items. Equally predictable, the actual budget cuts turned out to be rather small, on the order of 3 percent from a requested budget of $81 billion. Across-the-board budget reductions were debated and finally enacted, thus saving Congress from having to grapple with individual programs.

Congress did grant an extension of the Defense Production Act for another year, and most credit controls were also extended. In January the economic stabilization chief, Eric Johnston, had announced a general price–wage freeze and later issued price roll-back orders. Congress began to chip away at the powers it had granted by exempting commodities from price controls or protecting them with individual formulas. Organized labor withdrew from representation on mobilization boards in protest over wage freezes and business dominance of the agencies. The weakening of controls fortunately coincided with the moderation of inflation referred to earlier.

The administration's far-reaching tax bill to fight inflation and avoid a budget deficit also received the hostility of Congress and special interest groups. Conservatives and business interests attacked it as punitive and suggested a sales tax; labor applauded high taxes on corporations, and so on, to familiar and oft-repeated stances on taxation. What finally emerged in the Revenue Act of 1951 was a slight increase in individual tax rates, an increase in the corporate tax rate to 52 percent on net incomes over $25,000, a new excess profits tax ceiling, and many other small changes in tax provisions unrelated to revenue considerations.[47] The act was estimated to yield $5.7 billion or about half the administration's original request.

The Korean War and the boom it created also resulted in a heating up of the feud between the Treasury and the Federal Reserve over the latter's pledge to support the government bond market through its system of pegging. The long-standing feud developed in the post-World War II period, and in 1949 the Federal Reserve expressed concern over its inability to affect monetary conditions. In the recession the Federal Reserve wanted to pursue an easy-money policy, but buying securities to increase bank reserves drove down interest rates, and then Federal Reserve purchases to maintain interest rates absorbed bank reserves. The Federal Reserve was helpless to combat either recession or inflation. The boom in mid-1950 created inflationary pressures stemming from excess demand. If the Federal Reserve continued its policy of pegging, this would keep interest rates stable all right, but it would also feed excess demand and exacerbate the inflationary tendencies. The Federal Reserve began its push to be free of the restraints imposed by the Treasury's operations. The Treasury understandably did not wish to abandon support for its operations, at least "not now." Truman ordered a halt to the debate that had now become public and confrontational. Finally, after frequent discussions in early 1951, the following joint statement was released on March 4, 1951: "The Treasury and the Federal Reserve System have reached full accord with respect to debt management and monetary policies to be pursued in furthering their common purpose to assume the successful financing of the Government's requirements and, at the same time, to minimize monetization of the public debt."[48]

The accord, as it came to be known, returned monetary policy to the Federal Reserve, which was now in a position to control bank reserves, while still assisting the Treasury finance its operations.

These were the general aims, but the problem quickly became how to implement them. Not since the 1930s had the Federal Reserve maintained any real control over reserves or monetary policy. The inexperience of the Federal Reserve was matched by that of bankers, and the general public that was not accustomed to flexible interest rates. Following the accord, the Federal Reserve did little, as it watched the development of a free market. During this period the Federal Reserve was still groping for a proper guide for monetary policy, as all investors had to adjust to the new conditions.

One immediate feature of the accord was the issuance of a 2.75 percent nonmarketable bond to replace the 2.5 percent ones. Holders of the 2.5 percent bonds could exchange them for 2.75 percent bonds, and in this way one of the main problems of pegging was removed from the market. Furthermore, as the demand for funds rose in the boom, the Federal Reserve simply let banks reduce their excess reserves and let the market rates of interest rise. Despite many predictions to the contrary, the market adjusted to the new conditions without undue disruptions.

On March 29, 1952, Harry Truman made public a decision he had made in the early part of 1950: He would not seek reelection.[49] If his relations with Congress were strained before, they now became worse. The stalemate in Korea, the accusations of Communists in government and the unwillingness of Democrats to do anything about it, the "loss" of China, the resentment of isolationists over foreign aid and the Marshall Plan, and the dissatisfaction with federal budget priorities, and so on made his chances for another term rather improbable anyway, but he still had to work with Congress for the remainder of his term.

In January 1952 he presented his budget calling for large increases in national defense ($12 billion) and international affairs ($3 billion), giving a level of spending of $85.4 billion and revenues of $70.9 billion. The deficit of $14.4 billion for FY 1953 would follow a deficit of $8.2 billion for FY 1952. He asked Congress to come up with tax increases, largely by closing loopholes, to close the gap between the tax-increase request of the previous year ($10 billion) and the taxes raised by the Revenue Act of 1951 ($5.7 billion). Clearly the requested tax increase was insufficient to cover the deficit, and hence the pay-as-you-go scheme was being abandoned. So, too, was the Fair Deal, although Truman continued to ask for spending for education, health, unemployment compensation, and so on. Congress was in no mood to grant the president anything on his wish list.

Instead, Congress ignored the tax-increase request and proceeded to cut spending. National defense expenditures were reduced by about $5 billion, foreign aid by $1.7 billion, and the number of government employees was reduced (always a favorite target), along with their travel allowances and overtime pay. In the end the budget deficits turned out to be $4 billion for FY 1952 and $9.4 billion for FY 1953.

Truman also asked for a two-year extension of the Defense Production Act without the amendments of the previous year. After considerable debate he did receive an extension, but in a weakened form and only to June 30, 1953. Other extensions of wartime powers were also limited: to April 30, 1953, for rent controls in critical defense areas and for wage and price controls; to September 1952 for general rent controls; and to June 30, 1952, for credit controls. Again he had infuriated Congress by seizing the steel mills in April to avert a strike. The Wage Stabilization Board had approved a wage increase for steelworkers (endorsed by Truman), but opposed a price increase for steel. When the steel firms balked, Truman seized them as a vital output necessary for national defense. The Supreme Court, however, ruled the action unconstitutional. A long steel strike followed (54 days) and was ended by a substantial increase in wages.

The economy, however, was able to withstand the loss of 20 million tons of steel and continued strong. The unemployment rate continued to decline in 1952, and the average for the year was 3.1 percent. GNP rose 5.5 percent over the year (3.4 percent in constant dollars), while the CPI rose slowly, and the WPI continued its decline.

Both Truman and the CEA seemed concerned with the problem of a defense buildup and domestic economic stability. As the Truman administration came to an end, the stability seemed threatened by congressional actions that restrained the executive branch's efforts to gain more direct controls over the economy. As the year wore on, however, political considerations moved to the forefront, and all actions taken in this period are colored by political posturing and hysterical anticommunism, as evidenced by Senator Joseph McCarthy's (R., Wisconsin) hearings and the witch hunt of the House Unamerican Activities Committee (HUAC).

Evaluating Economic Policies of the Truman Years

It might appear obvious that whatever fiscal and monetary policies were pursued could be justified by the Employment Act of 1946. In that act, and in the long debates that preceded its enactment, governmental responsibilities for active intervention in the economic system were acknowledged. Memories of the depression were still fresh enough to make any return to prewar conditions unacceptable. Besides, the government-led increases in demand during the war had demonstrated the success of policies with this Keynesian-type solution that was now receiving increasing theoretical justification as well.

Thus there were political and social pressures for the public sector to assume more responsibility for managing the economy. Most people just wanted to avoid the prewar situation and felt that the government should do something to ensure that such an economic breakdown would never recur. Their concerns reflected a desire for economic security.

The concern of economists was to explain the breakdown. The classical model of the economy clearly would not help, since it precluded the breakdown they had to explain. Thus the Keynesian model gradually found more and more subscribers, since it allowed for economic instability and suggested a cure as well. The theoretical view of how the economy functioned was also concluding that the public sector had an active role to play in advanced capitalism.

Clearly, all the elements needed to justify a change in economic policymaking were converging in this period. The path toward a new economic awareness seemed assured, and that new awareness would rescue capitalism at the very time when it faced the growing threat from real and imagined adversaries.

Yet such sweeping changes seldom occur in a smooth, orderly progression. Many theorists, politicians, and citizens questioned the need for any change and resisted the lure of government as the savior of the economy. They saw the sacrifice of economic and political freedom in the surrender of power to government officials. The resistance to deficit spending, the attempt at dismantling the New Deal and preventing the Fair Deal, and the perennial attempts to reduce government spending, regardless of the economic situation, all attest to the deep-seated sentiments held by many about the role of government in the society. Clashes in ideology and in economic paradigms, and hence in views toward the efficacy of economic policy, were inevitable in this period, as they would be whenever traditional and received learnings are threatened.

The success or failure of postwar macroeconomic policy must be determined with these fundamental disagreements in mind. Also, it should be noted that the publication of economic data on which policies are made was not nearly as timely as is the case today. The lag in policy decisions due to lack of information is always a problem, but it was a more severe one in the postwar era. To add to the barriers to timely policy, forecasting was rather primitive at this time, but was receiving a boost from those who saw the need for predictions if policymaking was to be successful. In fact, quantitative analysis in general was fostered both by the need to test theoretical formations and the desire to make predictions. Along the way the need for more accurate and reliable data was recognized and addressed. These contributions would be welcome regardless of their effect on actual policymaking.

The actual postwar policies adopted show an increased awareness in Washington of economic matters, but at the same time reveal that the thoughtful prescribing for the economy had a long way to go. In the immediate postwar years, inflation was a major stabilization problem. With consumers laden with liquidity and eager to consume, cutting income taxes can hardly be said to be a wise policy. The same can be said for business taxes. Granted that forecasts of a postwar depression were common, once the true situation was revealed, why the continuation of the tax-cut policy?

In view of the obvious inflationary pressures, why did the administration resist the Federal Reserve's request to be released from the policy of pegging? Understandably, the Treasury wanted to keep its costs low and protect bondholders, and so on, but it clearly waited too long, so that inflation was worsened by the pegging policy. Add to this the fact that dismantling all controls over wages and prices so quickly meant that the goal of stabilization was either ignored or misunderstood. Again, some excuses can be made in that the responses to a forecast depression would be understandable, but the same responses continued long after the depression scare was obviously inappropriate.

When the recession did come in 1948, the only really effective policy to combat it was the tax cut passed earlier, when no one had recession in mind. It was plain good luck, not timely policy responses to economic conditions. Furthermore, there was considerable strength in Congress to cut expenditures in order to avoid a deficit in the budget. Although the cuts were small in the end, the drive for a balanced budget in a recession again indicates that ideology was taking precedence over economic judgments. Fortunately for the economy, increases in national defense and in foreign aid helped to moderate the economic decline.

So the first postwar recession to which the principles of the Employment Act of 1946 could be applied ended up being limited by a fortuitous tax cut and exogenous increases in spending caused by world events. The automatic stabilizers did the rest. The recession turned out to be a mild one—not due to the wisdom of policymakers.

The response record to the crisis of the Korean War was far superior. The tax increases and the regulations on consumer credit surely helped contain the inflationary tendencies so quickly anticipated. In other aspects, however, monetary policy remained subservient. The containment of government expenditures other than national defense also helped to moderate the inflation.

When the accord was reached, monetary policy was still passive, and the primary reliance upon fiscal policy continued. Yet there was growing resistance to tax increases, and the bill passed in 1951 was far below the administration's request. Finally, tax resistance stiffened even more to deny the administration another increase in 1952. Meanwhile, Congress continued the attempt to decrease spending, not for stabilization purposes, but to deny the president his Fair Deal. The inflation had to be restrained by wage and price controls and other wartime powers. Again fortuitously, prices moderated in the early 1950s, as consumption fell and inventory speculation relaxed.

In conclusion, economic stabilization owed more to good fortune than to conscientious policymaking. Although a number of congressmen and administration economists demonstrated their knowledge of proper policies, there were a number of their opponents who continued to argue and vote out of economic dogma of the past: balanced budgets, minimal government, and free markets. Their influence over economic policy in this period was still considerable.

In other areas the concern for economic growth was not translated into direct policy. Some would argue that tax reductions were meant to bolster economic growth, but they were not really enacted for that purpose. Nor was there any attempt to reduce income inequalities. In fact, the inequities in the distribution of income and wealth were made greater. In the allocation of resources, there was the attempt to return more economic activity to the private sector. The Fair Deal did manage some successes, however, in public support for slum clearance, housing programs, extensions of Social Security, hospital construction, public works, flood control, rural electrification, and even the establishment of the National Science Foundation. Still, Congress was able to fight the "socialist" programs on health, aid to education, and civil rights, and to resist attempts to repeal the Taft–Hartley Act.

Perhaps the rearmament program took precedence, which it did, but nevertheless there was considerable opposition to additional government programs. The Fair Deal got lost in the Korean War and in the antagonisms between Congress and the chief executive.

In conclusion, the successes of postwar macroeconomic policymaking are few and mainly confined to the responses in a wartime atmosphere where the ranks are closed. Beyond that instance, the overall policy record, including that in the business cycle of 1948–49, is poor. The clashes of ideology, the commitment to long-held convictions and the political struggle between Congress and the president prevented more "appropriate" responses.

The foregoing suggests that economic policies were not only inappropriate but irrational as well. By present standards they seem perverse. What is rational, however, depends upon who is making the determination. What may appear irrational when applied to the goal of stabilization or allocation of resources may not be irrational if other or ulterior motives can be uncovered.

The postwar period was the first opportunity for those who lost some of their share of the national pie to try to recover it; it was the first chance to undo the horrors of the New Deal and all notions of the welfare state or collectivism of any shade in the United States.

Thus, to reduce taxes in the face of apparent inflation is to court irrationality. Yet if the taxes could be cut so as to favor upper-income groups, the gain in income shares is worth the risk of the inability to find protection from inflation. For corporations to lobby for the repeal of the excess profits tax in the name of the need for an incentive to produce, to increase employment, to prevent deflation, or to protect small corporations seems to be specious now and was thought so then.[50] Repeal of the excess profits tax favored the large, financially secure corporations and would allow them to maintain their position in the struggle over market shares. It would also strengthen their hands against the demands of organized labor, demands that were sure to follow, since they were provoked by the corporations themselves.

With labor treasuries full, with demand strong, with no fear from the smaller concerns, it is difficult to conjure up a need for incentives to produce. A return to private-sector controls to them meant a return to earlier positions of private power and privilege. Power could permit a return to precollective bargaining positions vis-à-vis labor, and that contest has already been described.

The calls for cuts in government spending in the name of sound financial policy—that is, balanced budgets—were attempts at dismantling the New Deal and denials of the Fair Deal. Many of these programs, however, were popular and politically sensitive; hence the hiding behind the balanced-budget principle. When war came, cuts in nondefense programs were easier to justify. Also, it was convenient to label them "Socialistic" or "Communistic" in order to have the cuts in spending accord with prevailing scourges of the day.

When tax increases were in order, as was the case in the rearmament period, Congress correctly saw the necessity for increased revenues, but it preferred sales or excise tax increases. Liberals had a difficult time combating the sales tax scheme and finally prevailed with income tax increases. At least before disillusionment with the

Korean War set in, tax increases were accepted; when the war turned into a stalemate, such acquiescence to tax increases vanished. The initial proper stabilization policy was acceptable as long as the war was, but when the war came under question, so did the proper policy of paying for it; economic stabilization gave way to political expedience.

When the cold war was building, conservatives wanted a strong defense, no tax increases, and a balanced budget. The inherent contradiction of these aims apparently escaped them. True, they wanted to decrease government spending as well, but they never accomplished much, despite the blustering and political posturing. When war came, the tax increases to pay for the arms buildup were passed over their objections, but the final bill included items that had little to do with stabilization but appealed to special interests— liberalization and extension of depletion allowances, for instance. Conservatives had fought and won the battle over exclusion of interest and dividends from withholding, as well. If tax increases were to be had, they would come only at the expense of equity, while favoring special-interest groups. What better time to use political power when the need for a tax increase was seen as urgent?

Meanwhile, liberals, including Truman, pressed for increases in social programs long after any hope of getting them passed had vanished. This may or may not have been a shrewd political move, but after a while the budgets that were submitted including these programs were less than realistic and gave erroneous impressions.

In short, the budgetary process was used by both sides for political purposes. While this is scarcely surprising, it is again noted here as an indication of what developed after the passage of the Employment Act of 1946 and as an indication of the degree of rationality surrounding the whole process of policymaking. If more thoughtful, calmer, and more rational policymaking was to follow the Employment Act, there was little evidence of it when the Truman administration came to an end.

part III

The Postwar Years
and New Directions

chapter 8

The Eisenhower Administration and the 1950s

Dwight D. Eisenhower already had a long and distinguished career as supreme commander of allied forces in Europe, president of Columbia University, and commander of NATO forces, when he was persuaded to run for the presidency as a Republican. The Democrats also wanted him, but he apparently chose the party closer to his political beliefs, although his interest in politics was scant prior to his selection as a presidential candidate. It is easy to see why he was pursued: He was a war hero with a kind, benevolent demeanor, reminding everyone of a friendly and helpful grandfather. Above all, he seemed so stable and reliable.

His opponent, Adlai E. Stevenson, was an articulate intellectual who spoke from a loftiness that confused the general voting public. Where Eisenhower inspired confidence and trust, Stevenson generated skepticism and uncertainty. Eisenhower won the 1952 election easily, receiving 442 electoral votes from 39 states. The victory helped the Republicans regain control of both houses by slight margins, but the 83rd Congress could be expected to reduce the hostility between the executive and legislative branches.

The campaign did not elicit any innovations in economic matters. In fact, economic issues played a secondary role, as they simply did not warrant attention when compared to the Korean War and the cold war. Eisenhower did reveal a basic fiscal conservatism when he promised to "maintain security with solvency," and stop the "wild spending" and the inflation that inevitably followed from budget deficits. This much was to be expected, but he also promised not to roll back the welfare state and not to stand idly by if a recession threatened.[1]

The pledge to use all levels of government to combat recessions, while continuing with the security provisions of the welfare state, was something new for conservatives. True, there was talk of reliance upon the private sector, of the elimination of all controls, and of ending the unnecessary meddling in the economy. True, his cabinet appointees gave the administration a probusiness aura: George M. Humphrey, a steel executive, for secretary of the treasury; Joseph M. Dodge for director of the budget; and Sinclair Weeks for secretary of commerce. All of these appointees to economic posts held similar views of the proper economic policies of balanced budgets and economy in government spending.

Still, no one was rolling back the clock to the 1920s, and, in fact, Republicans were sensitive to the charge of repeating Hoover's mistakes and bringing on another recession. Quite simply, with the Eisenhower administration there was the tacit recognition that we could not go back to that world ever again. No one would undo the welfare state, and no one would abide another depression. Rhetoric and ideology aside, this was a significant step in the evolution of advanced capitalism.

Economic conditions were not a major factor in the Eisenhower victory. In the declining months of the Truman administration, prices were stable; unemployment had fallen to 2.2 percent in December 1952, and GNP, both real and money, had increased in the third and fourth quarters, after being stationary for the first two quarters. Only the increase in projected public spending and another large budget deficit could be open to criticism from fiscal conservatives. So once again it appears that the vote was for Eisenhower as a personality and his promise to end the war in Korea.

Eisenhower was influential in ending the conflict soon after taking office in July 1953. Peace was restored for the time being, and the United States began to seek stability in international relations, as John Foster Dulles, secretary of state, sought to build alliances around the world to maintain the status quo and combat the spread of communism or roll it back.[2]

Moreover, U.S. might would be employed to see to it that U.S. corporations could be free to expand their markets abroad. In his State of the Union message Eisenhower spoke of "a serious and explicit purpose of our foreign policy ... the encouragement of a hospitable climate for investment in foreign nations"[3]: thus, the CIA-inspired coup that overthrew Mossadegh in Iran in 1953 to preserve U.S. oil-company interests; thus, the overturning of the Arbenz government in Guatemala that had tried to institute social reforms and purchase land from United Fruit Company; thus, the turning away from Ho Chi

Minh in Vietnam, and so on, through the history of U.S. domination of the Third World.

In other areas the Eisenhower administration was the beneficiary of previous conflicts over power and control. In the field of labor–management relations, the strident, bitter conflicts were settling down to routine relations. Management won its right to exclusive control over decision making in production, work assignments, financial and marketing concerns, while labor earned collective-bargaining rights, security, and higher pay and gave up its fight for a greater say in how the corporation was run. A kind of truce was declared and a kind of peace settled over the whole area of labor–management concerns.

Thus the rise of corporate power,[4] fostered by the public sector that encouraged international expansion and that guaranteed the welfare state, and aided by the labor-management truce, was to give an aura of stability and calm to the Eisenhower administration. Throughout the 1950s there would be this feeling of tranquility and security, born out of the unobtrusive use of power. Beneath the surface of serenity, however, were developing trends that would continue to plague the U.S. economy for decades. These, too, will warrant further analysis after the record has been unfolded.

The Eisenhower Administration's Initial Policies

Even before Eisenhower took office, the conservatives in Congress began to assert themselves. In their dislike of outgoing chairman Leon Keyserling and his politicizing of the Council of Economic Advisors, they managed to appropriate funds for the CEA for only nine months instead of the usual twelve months. Before leaving office Truman asked for additional funds to pay salaries until June 30. Congress, instead, gave him only enough for an economic advisor and his staff.[5] Clearly Congress, irked by Keyserling's open advocacy of the Fair Deal programs, was in a punitive mood. Moreover, Keynesian economics became identified with the New Deal in general and with the Democratic party in particular, and soon the "New Economics," the welfare state, and the liberal Democratic party got amalgamated; the mixture was labeled Unamerican, Communistic, and so on, and problems were traced to the evils of deficits.[6]

When Eisenhower appointed Arthur Burns chairman of the CEA on March 6, 1953, Burns literally became the sole economic advisor. Eisenhower decided to rescue the original composition of the CEA and submitted a reorganization plan that gave administrative responsibility to the chairman. He also revealed his intention to name an advisory board on economic growth and stability, to be headed by the chairman. Congress never did act on the organization plan, but it did provide the funds for it for the fiscal year 1954.

The appointment of Arthur Burns to chair the CEA seemed to signal the sincerity of Eisenhower's pledge to avoid another depression and to combat any downturn with public policy. Having helped to establish the NBER, Burns was an expert on business cycles, and his advice would be likely to be carefully framed, cautious, and valuable, given the economic conditions and the inchoate economic philosophy of the president.

When Eisenhower took office, he inherited a budget from Truman that showed increases in federal spending to $78.6 billion and a deficit of $9.9 billion. He had opposed both of these budgetary trends in the campaign, and, accordingly, the first order of business was to reduce both. Eisenhower cut $8.5 billion from the January appropriation request, with the largest cuts in defense ($5 billion) and mutual security ($2.5 billion), and smaller cuts in the Atomic Energy Commission and in the Departments of Interior and Commerce. The 83rd Congress, delighted with the expenditure cuts, easily granted them and proceeded to cut another $4.6 billion.[7]

Despite the budget cuts, the backlog of huge sums ($81 billion) that were appropriated in the past but unspent meant that Eisenhower's efforts to balance the budget were unsuccessful, and the budget ended up with a $9.4 billion deficit for FY 1953. Congress went along with the budget cuts, but was not so readily appeased when the tax cuts that were promised were delayed.

In fact, one of the first bills of the 83rd Congress was introduced by Congressman Daniel Reed (R., New York), chairman of the Ways and Means Committee, to move up by six months a scheduled tax reduction for individuals, originally planned for January 1, 1954. (The reduction was built into the Revenue Act of 1951.) Eisenhower indicated that he was opposed to tax cuts as long as budget deficits existed and asked Congress, in a special message on May 20, 1953, not to move the tax reduction forward, but leave it as scheduled. Again Congress went along, with some grumbling, but resistance grew when Eisenhower also asked for an extension of the excess profits tax, due to expire on June 30, 1953. The administration won in the end on this issue and on delays in excise tax and corporate tax rate reductions, as well; for "simple justice," the postponement in the scheduled Social Security payroll tax rate increase was also honored.

Clearly, fiscal policy would be strongly deflationary with large spending cuts and the continuation of high taxes. The spending cuts satisfied the ideological bias of fiscal conservatives who always want to see government spending reduced; the continuation of high taxes could always be justified by the necessity to curb the growing budget deficit. Neither facet of fiscal policy appears to have been guided by stabilization requirements or geared to national economic conditions.

If excuses had to be made for the contractionary fiscal policy, none were necessary for the elimination of wage and price controls. Declaring that they "have proved largely unsatisfactory or unworkable," Eisenhower revealed in his State of the Union address that he had no intention of renewing them when they expired on April 30, 1953. He maintained that prices could be contained by the more acceptable means of fiscal and monetary policy. By the end of March the controls were gone, and, despite efforts by some in Congress to grant the president the power to impose emergency wage and price controls, the House refused to include it in the extension of the Defense Production Act, which authorized only an extension of rent controls, along with the power to control the allocation of scarce resources. Clearly, inflation was not a major concern of the administration at this time, or if it was, controls were not deemed to be a proper response to it.

Inflation, however, was on the minds of Federal Reserve officials. In January the discount rate was increased from 1.75 percent to 2 percent, and bank reserves were allowed to fall as gold exports rose. The result of these actions was a dramatic rise in interest rates to record highs: In April three-month treasury bills were yielding 2.2 percent; long-term treasury bonds, 3 percent; corporate bonds over 3.25 percent, and the prime rate stood at 2.4 percent. Just five years earlier these rates had been over 1 percent lower. These high interest rates also reflected the Treasury's actions in exchanging maturing certificates: In February it exchanged the 1⅞ percent certificates for 2.25 and 2.5 certificates, and in April it offered $1 billion of 30-year bonds paying 3.25 percent. Exchanging certificates made the bondholders— especially banks—wealthier and interest costs higher, and the issuance of 3.25 percent bonds upset the market unduly. Unaccustomed to a free market, investors expected interest rates to climb still higher and borrowers hastened to secure funds before that happened. Interest rates were increased on FHA and veterans' home mortgage loans in May, further indicating credit stringency. The Federal Reserve System, initially responding to meager signs of inflation in rising stock prices and rising inventories that were regarded as speculatively inspired, and the Treasury, acting to restructure its bonds, brought on a tight monetary policy that was misinterpreted by the marketplace. Arthur Burns maintains that the monetary policy was not as restrictive as indicated, but that federal officials underestimated the market's response to monetary actions.[8]

Still, the monetary tightness, together with the contractionary fiscal policy, brought about or at least exacerbated economic uncertainty, and the economy entered into its second postwar recession. By May 1953 it became apparent that inflation was not going to be the problem, but that an economic slowdown was beginning. The NBER selected July as the peak of the cycle that began in October 1949, and the decline would continue until August 1954, a period of 13 months.[9]

The recession turned out to be a rather mild one, with GNP falling about $5 billion or about 1 percent, and real GNP falling $8 billion or about 2 percent. The unemployment rate rose from 2.4 percent in July 1953 to 5 percent at the trough in August 1954. Interestingly, both consumer and wholesale prices showed virtually no change over the period, again attesting to the mild decline.

Macroeconomic Policies
in the Second Postwar Recession

Thanks to the accord, the Federal Reserve System was now free to use its powers to help stabilize the economy. This was the first recession in which monetary policies could be effective, and so it is appropriate to inquire into how the system used its freedom to act. Earlier, in March 1953, the Open Market Committee adopted a set of rules to guide its actions, and later in December a fourth rule was added. Briefly, they were as follows:

1. It would confine its actions to the short end of the market and deal in short-term treasury bills only ("the bills-only doctrine").
2. It would not support any pattern of prices and yields in the government securities market and would not engage in swap operations to influence the prices of yields of long- versus short-term securities.
3. It would not buy any new treasury security at the time it was issued.
4. It would not buy any security from outstanding issues of comparable maturity to those being offered.[10]

Clearly the Federal Reserve was more interested in restoring a free market and ensuring order than it was in stabilization policies. Abandoning direct control over the long-term interest rates meant that it put the improvement in the government securities market ahead of its primary function of monetary policy. The Federal Reserve was now committed to intervene in the government securities market as little as possible and to affect the structure of interest rates as little as possible, while maintaining an orderly market. The new policy guidelines were the opposite of those in effect before the accord.

In May 1953, when the slowdown became apparent and the scramble for liquidity was under way, the Federal Reserve reacted rather quickly and began buying short-term government securities. Between May and June it added $1.2 billion to its holdings. Bank excess reserves increased by $200 million as a result, but interest rates remained stable, as investors were uncertain over future Federal Reserve actions. To show its intentions, the Federal Reserve lowered reserve requirements in July from 24 to 22 percent on demand deposits in central cities and by 1 percent in other areas. Additional purchases of securities further released reserves and ended the tightness in credit markets. In February 1954 discount rates were lowered from 2 percent to 1.75 percent and in April to 1.5 percent. In the summer of 1954 reserve requirements were again reduced on demand and time deposits. By mid-year 1954 the Federal Reserve had succeeded in easing money and credit conditions and in reducing interest rates. Treasury-bill yields were less than three-fourths of 1 percent in June, down from the 2.25 percent of a year earlier, and long-term rates were 2.75 percent, down from 3.25 percent. In this same period the money supply had risen about $8 billion, and excess reserve continued to climb.

Clearly the Federal Reserve used its newfound powers to combat first an inflation that did not materialize and then reversed its policy of credit stringency to provide monetary ease and combat the real problem of recession. Indeed, the CEA found reason to extol government officials and their policies that "should inspire confidence among all citizens in the capacity and readiness of Government to respond promptly to changes in economic conditions."[11] It is likely that the easy money policy helped the economy climb out of the recession. The impact on the housing industry alone was significant. There were critics, however, who warned that credit conditions had been made too easy and that there was too much liquidity in the system. The recovery would bear close scrutiny for its possible inflationary possibilities.

Fiscal policy in the early years of the Eisenhower administration can only be characterized as irresolute. On the one hand, there was enormous pressure to prevent the recurrence of a 1929 depression. Eisenhower made that a campaign promise and was very sensitive to the issue throughout the downturn. In cabinet meetings he frequently reminded his members of his unwavering commitment to that pledge.[12] As was the case with the welfare state, combating recessions gradually became proper public policy, rather than a Democratic or Republican issue.

There was pressure also from vocal Democrats, such as Senator Paul Douglas of Illinois, the highly respected economist, who badgered the administration for its hesitancy in proposing solutions, and from organized labor leaders such as Walter Reuther, who called a labor conference to examine the growing problem of unemployment. These are only examples of the prevailing mood that would not countenance another depression or tolerate government denial of responsibility in times of economic difficulty.

On the other hand, one should not exaggerate the conversion of many in Congress and in the administration to an activist fiscal policy. Eisenhower himself had pledged to stop meddling in the economy and balance the budget, and so on, while his chief economic advisor George Humphrey, secretary of the treasury, viewed with horror any deficit incurred to combat a recession and threatened to resign if one were proposed. Arthur Burns, chairman of the CEA, also was cautious in his advice and inclined to put a favorable light on economic trends.

In its *Economic Report* for 1954, the CEA blamed the decline on "an imbalance between production and sales,"[13] causing an inventory buildup, with the result that producers curtailed operations to bring sales in line with output. They based their analysis on the change in inventories from the first quarter of 1953 to the second quarter—a change from $4 billion to $7 billion—concentrated in the durable-goods industries. Little mention was made of the decline in defense expenditures as a cause of the imbalance between production and sales. The decline in consumption was explained by the fact that personal income was outpacing purchases on goods; a few pages later, however, the CEA explained that installment credit expanded by a phenomenal $4.6 billion in the year ended June 30, 1953.

Later, when the inventory accumulation total was revised downward to only $4.0 billion, Burns admitted that defense cuts probably affected consumption spending and contributed to the inventory accumulation. Curiously, however, the defense cuts were never really given as a contributing cause of the recession. They were justified on the basis of economy—more bang for the buck—but the relationship between defense budget cuts and the level of economic activity was not openly discussed. This is surprising, since the economic decline after 1953 can be attributed largely to defense reductions, as is easily seen in Table 8.1, where the quarterly totals are brought together.

According to Wilfred Lewis, the actual decline in defense expenditures in 1953 understates the impact of the cuts, since defense orders had begun to decline earlier and dropped dramatically in this period.[14] By the fourth quarter of 1954, the change in inventories rebounded to a +$0.8 billion, while defense spending fell to an annual rate of $38.4 billion. Thus, even as production and sales were coming into balance, the reductions in national defense spending continued and probably accounted for most of the decline in 1954.

Table 8.1   Components of GNP at Annual Rates (billions of dollars)

	1953			1954		
	Second Quarter	Third Quarter	Fourth Quarter	First Quarter	Second Quarter	Third Quarter
GNP	368.8	367.1	361.0	360.0	358.9	362.0
Consumption	233.3	234.1	232.3	233.7	236.5	238.7
Investment	52.9	51.1	45.2	46.6	47.2	48.8
Change in inventories, nonfarm	4.0	1.5	−4.3	−2.8	−3.2	−2.8
Government purchases	83.3	82.7	83.5	79.4	74.4	74.1
National defense	50.5	49.3	47.6	44.8	41.5	40.0

Source: U.S. Department of Commerce, *U.S. Income and Output,* (Washington, DC: GPO. 1958), Table I-3, pp. 120–22.

According to Arthur Burns, "In its new role of responsibility for the maintenance of the nation's prosperity, the federal government deliberately took speedy and massive actions to build the confidence and pave the way for renewed economic growth."[15] Let us examine these "massive actions" a little more closely. First, Burns mentioned the Federal Reserve's actions in May 1953 to ease credit conditions. True, the Federal Reserve's actions may have helped to cushion the fall in economic activity, but no mention was made of the Federal Reserve's earlier restrictive actions that may have contributed to the decline in the first place.

Next there is the matter of the tax cut scheduled to take effect on January 1, 1954. The reductions in individual tax rates and the expiration of the excess profits tax amounted to over $5 billion and again may have helped cushion the fall in economic activity. Yet these tax reductions were scheduled for that date, and the administration would have had a difficult time postponing them further. Again, little mention was made of the fact that the tax cuts had already been postponed by the administration from June 30, 1953, to January 1, 1954. Had the administration not postponed the tax cuts, the economic decline would have been less. Thus the fact that Secretary Humphrey assured the public in September that the tax cuts would be honored on January 1 hardly serves as an active countercyclical policy; the fact that the balanced budget was pushed aside hardly serves as notice of recognition of the federal government's responsibility for the nation's welfare.

The only tax measure of 1954 was the result of a thorough revision of the Internal Revenue Code that had been in process since 1952 and was concerned with tax reform and equity. This revision was not concerned with stabilization, although it did result in a tax reduction of over $1 billion and thus fortuitously helped in the economic recovery. (This tax reduction, however, was partially offset by an increase of $1 billion in the Social Security tax.) For the administration to claim credit for this tax measure as a countercyclical policy or even for various provisions of the revision is misleading. In fact, the administration fought the reductions in excise taxes that eventually passed and the Democratic move to increase the amount of personal exemptions in the income tax, which was not enacted. Pressure for tax cuts came from Congress, not the administration.

Indeed, what the administration did propose was far less dramatic than that suggested by Burns. In May 1954 the administration moved to speed up expenditures for the next six-month period. Plans for each agency were formulated to ascertain where speedups could occur, but before much could be accomplished in this area, the recession was over, and thus not much credit can be given to this fiscal-policy move. There was also some attempt to rationalize expenditures on public works, both for their own sake and for their effect on the recession, but the delays in the stabilizing effects of spending on public works became evident, and little was accomplished.

In an effort to stimulate home building, the administration did see the Housing Act of 1954 pass, which authorized the FHA to insure mortgages with smaller downpayments and longer payback periods. New housing started under FHA financing increased by 10 percent from 1953 to 1954, and under the VA (Veterans Administration) it nearly doubled. Some of the boom in housing can be traced to the Housing Act of 1954 and was beneficial to economic recovery; however, some of the increased housing activity can also be traced to the Federal Reserve's policy of monetary ease.

Other programs that the administration claimed helped in the recovery phase were the modernization of the commercial tanker fleet and the stockpiling of zinc and lead to aid the mining industry. Beyond these minimal measures, little else was achieved that would warrant the boast of massive actions.[16] The automatic stabilizers were just as effective as the discretionary actions of the administration, since the antirecession measures taken had little effect until late 1954.

It is difficult to contest the assertion that "discretionary counter-recession expenditure actions were slow to be initiated, were not all announced to the public, and were modest in scope—being limited at first to a within-year shift of government expenditures."[17]

In summary, the administration's response to this second postwar recession was cautious and timid. It refused to call it a recession, but referred to the downturn as a "rolling adjustment" from a war to a peacetime economy. Still, there was the recognition of responsibility of the federal government for the nation's economic health and the willingness, however grudgingly, to set aside the balanced budget and laissez-faire philosophy to accept the need for government intervention. In this first Republican administration in over 20 years, the development is significant and represents a victory for the advocates of a Keynesian-type view of the need for governmental actions.

The Strong Recovery and Inflation

As expected, the Democrats took control of both houses of Congress in 1954 but by surprisingly small margins: 1 seat in the Senate and 29 in the House. At a postmortem cabinet meeting no one blamed the reversal of control on the recession. In fact, there was little concern for national economic matters in the election, and defeats were blamed by Vice-President Nixon on local conditions, weak candidates, and so on.[18]

One of the reasons the Democrats were unable to exploit the downturn was that the economic recovery began in the summer of 1954 just prior to the election. Until the summer of 1957 the economy would expand once again, a period that would also cover the next presidential election in 1956. Thus the economy would not be a major issue in national politics until later in the decade. To emphasize the point, federal budgets were more stimulative in off years than in election years, and hence economic conditions were not permitted to influence the policymaking of the Eisenhower administrations in order to win votes.[19] This is not to imply that economic criticisms were lacking, but only to point to the secondary role of economic conditions in the Eisenhower victories.

The recovery was led by the private sector, as the federal government did not pursue an active fiscal policy. Even national defense expenditures stabilized over the period. The boom was led initially by consumer spending on consumer durables and housing. Expenditures on housing increased by 40 percent from 1953 to 1955, but toward the end of 1955 they began to slow down. Both the increases and the reversal can be partially explained by the actions of the

Federal Reserve System in encouraging mortgage loans and by the operation of the FHA and the Housing Act of 1954. The boom was also fed by the demand by the public for 1955 automobiles. Automobile factory sales increased by over 42 percent from 1954 to 1955, and to pay for them installment credit for automotive loans increased by over 40 percent. Again, automobile purchases fell in late 1955 and 1956, as did spending on housing.

What makes this boom remarkable is that when expenditures on consumer durable items were falling, they were first increasing on construction in the commercial sector and then on investment goods in the manufacturing sector. In the words of the *Economic Report of the President 1956*, "With sales rising, profits improving, depreciation reserves increasing, and more and more shortages of facilities emerging or impending, established firms were both willing and able to risk increasingly large sums on the expansion or modernization of plant and equipment."[20] Moreover, new incorporations were increasing by over 19 percent from 1954 and 1955, and new businesses of all types were increasing by over 11 percent in the same period.

Thus in the second quarter of 1955, just as consumption spending was leveling off, investment expenditures offset the decline and began to rise sharply. From the $20.5 billion spent on plant and equipment in the first quarter of 1955, investment rose to $28.2 in the last quarter of 1956, an increase of over 37 percent; thereafter investment spending stabilized until the fourth quarter of 1957, at which time the economy was headed into another recession. (See Table 8.2.)

The administration hailed the recovery and pointed to the fact that its policies were appropriate, since the private sector was responsible for the upswing and little government intervention was necessary. While this assertion is basically correct, it is still necessary to indicate the role of national defense in this period. The Office of Civilian and Defense Mobilization decided to encourage investment for national-security purposes, as in World War II, by allowing firms to write off the cost of their assets for tax purposes in only five years. From January 1, 1954, to June 30, 1955 some $3 billion in investment spending qualified for this special amortization schedule, and from July 1, 1955, to April 1956 another $5 billion so qualified.[21] The investment was concentrated in utilities and transportation and provided additional stimulus, but when the program was stopped in 1956, it contributed to the eventual downturn.

The CEA also commented favorably on the increase in consumer spending: "Consumers were of a mind to buy better things and increase their spending. This pervasive attitude, combined with the willingness of women and young people to take on jobs so that their families might better approximate the plane of living they wished to attain, has been

Table 8.2   Characteristics of the Recovery, August 1954 to July 1957 (percent change)

Item	From 1954 IV to 1955 IV	From 1955 IV to 1956 IV	From 1956 IV to 1957 III
GNP	10.3	5.3	3.5
Consumer durables	17.4	−0.8	2.3
Producers' durables	27.6	11.0	−0.7
GNP in 1954 dollars	8.4	1.5	0.5
Consumer durables	17.7	−3.8	0.3
Producers' durables	22.6	2.9	−4.4
Implicit price index	1.7	3.7	3.0
WPI	1.5	3.4	2.3
CPI	0.2	1.9	3.2
Unemployment rate	−20.9	8.5	5.4
Capacity utilization rate	9.6	−2.6	−5.6

Source: Compiled by author from U.S. Department of Commerce, *U.S. Income and Output* (Washington, DC: GPO, 1958), pp. 120–25.

an outstanding feature of recent experience. These factors were basic, and they were reinforced by aggressive selling efforts of businessmen, who sought out customers more energetically than had become customary in recent years."[22] Societal values were altered significantly, however, as advertising took a sharp turn in this period. Advertising expenditures continued to rise until they amounted to over 2.3 percent of GNP, and now there was the new medium to use—the television set that trapped people in their living rooms. It should come as no surprise to learn that consumer-durables spending rose in this boom period; those are the types of products that TV promoted heavily—automobiles, refrigerators, dishwashers, and, of course, television sets. The point, however, is not whether or not TV advertising is effective, but the slow commercialization of the society and the invasion of public relations and motivational research people into all aspects of everyday life. To quote just one critic among many, "Throughout the decade tastelessness and vulgarity shrieked out from billboards and TV screens."[23] Soon the PR people would intrude into every sphere—politics was a likely fertile ground—and Robert Montgomery, the actor, would soon be coaching Eisenhower in public speaking.

Getting back to the cyclical analysis, it is clear from the data in Table 8.2 that 1955 was the best year in the recovery period; GNP increased in both money and real terms; prices remained fairly stable, especially in the CPI; and the unemployment rate fell sharply. The annual rate of change in the WPI index does, however, obscure the offsetting price changes that were occurring and causing alarm. While crude materials and foodstuffs were falling over the period from August 1954 to the end of 1955 by 7.8 percent, intermediate goods, materials, and supplies were rising by 3.9 percent (but by 7.9 percent for materials for durable-goods manufacture and 6.5 percent for materials and components for construction). Finally, firms added to their capacity at a rate of 4.5 percent and actually used 9.6 percent more of their capacity over the period.

In 1956, however, the situation changed. In the middle of the boom, GNP began to slow down and grew at half the first-period rate in money terms, but fell by 82 percent in real terms. Clearly prices must have been rising, and that is borne out by the data in Table 8.2. Prices in all indexes began to rise, and this time the price increases were across the board for all commodities. At the same time unemployment began to increase, and firms used less of their capacity even as they added to their total productive capacity. Furthermore, these trends continued right up to the peak of the cycle in the summer of 1957.

The change from 1955 to 1956 and into 1957 is significant. During the early expansion phase, economic magnitudes behaved as expected, but as the recovery proceeded, they exhibited deviations from the predictable. Thus, as the rate of growth of GNP was falling, prices continued to rise and unemployment began to rise, even before the peak was reached. It would appear that this peculiar boom requires closer inspection. In 1956 we know that housing expenditures, consumption of durables, and eventually construction began to fall. Later investment in plant and equipment also tapered off, and thus there should have been less pressure on prices, not more. If the price increases in 1955 can be explained by excess demand pressures, what accounts for the price rises in the absence of demand pressures?

Surely there was the productive capacity to meet the demand in 1956, for, as seen in Table 8.2, firms added to their capacity and throughout 1956 began utilizing less and less of it in the production process. Supply was not the problem. Nor was the excess demand explainable by looking at productive incomes. During 1955 wages and hours worked increased as expected, but in 1956 average weekly hours began to fall again. The same can be said for corporate profits. Thus if aggregate demand was falling and aggregate supply was rising, at least from capacity data, how can prices rise?

This inexplicable price behavior caused some reexamination of the source of inflation. What emerged is the explanation now labeled "cost-push" or sellers' inflation. In this "new" inflation, prices and wages are administered prices; that is, they are determined without due regard to economic circumstances, but with a view to increasing or altering income shares. Thus wages are pushed up (by unions?) in expansions, but do not fall in downswings; prices are set by reference to a desired profit margin or markup over costs, regardless of the ability to sell the output. The era of flexible wages and prices responding to demand and supply signals appeared to be over. Moreover, the world of competition was recognized as gone, being replaced by monopolies or oligopolies that were able to exercise market power to impose their price and wage demands on the buyers. Thus if wages were arbitrarily pushed up, firms could simply pass on the added costs to the buyers.

Analyzing the wage-price spiral in the postwar period, Otto Eckstein expressed it succinctly in an early view of the phenomenon: "Much of the concern about the price trends in our economy has been prompted by the wage–price spiral, in which wages are pushed upward regardless of circumstances, productivity does not keep pace with wages, and business is content to pass the resultant wage costs on in higher prices, perhaps adding a little markup of its own."[24] Other economists contributed to the analysis of cost inflation: Abba Lerner and Gardiner Ackley tried to explain the inflation of 1955–57 in terms of problems on the supply side.[25] The latter showed the possibility of excess demand in one sector, and hence rising prices, affecting prices and wages in other sectors where excess demand was absent. Inflation could begin as demand inflation in some areas and spread to other sectors, where it would reappear as cost-push inflation.

If these economists were correct, policies designed to combat demand inflation would be useless in fighting cost-push or sellers' inflation. Policies designed to reduce demand to fight excess-demand inflation would result in reductions in output and employment in a world where prices and wages were inflexible, administered prices were widespread, and market power existed. Only if the reductions in aggregate demand were enormous and unemployment massive, would there be any appreciable effect on wages and prices. Only better antitrust policy, direct controls, or more government involvement in steering the economy can be effective in a world where market structure is the main problem.

Inexplicable price behavior becomes another attribute of this peculiar cycle. Never again would inflation be viewed as emanating from excess demand alone, and there would always be the recognition that inflation was a more complex phenomenon than previously suspected. Not everyone accepted—or does accept even now—the cost explanation for inflation, and hence it has remained controversial to the present.

Monetary and Fiscal Policy in the Recovery

The Federal Reserve became concerned about inflation and reversed its policy actions of 1954. In the latter half of 1954, the money supply was allowed to grow at an average rate of 4.7 percent—recall that there were criticisms of its too easy money policy; in 1955 the Federal Reserve System permitted the money supply to grow at an average rate of only 2.6 percent; in 1956, 2.2 percent; and through August 1957 by −4.9 percent. Since the rate of growth of nominal or money GNP was over 20 percent for this period, it is clear that the Federal Reserve's restrictive monetary policy forced other changes, to accommodate the income growth.

In early 1955 the Federal Reserve sold securities of about $1 billion, forcing banks to reduce their excess reserves and begin borrowing from the Federal Reserve. Free reserves (excess reserves minus borrowings from the Federal Reserve) fell from $772 million in July 1954 to $ −491 million in November 1955 and remained negative until 1958. The banks also sold government securities to raise funds to make private loans, over $7 billion in 1955 alone, as they scrambled for funds to finance the growing demand for money.

In addition, the Federal Reserve raised the discount rate from 1.5 percent to 3 percent in steps of 0.5 percent increases in April, August, September, and November of 1955 and April and August of 1956. A final increase was made in August of 1957, bringing the rate to 3.5 percent. These rates did not discourage bank borrowing from the Federal Reserve, since market interest rates were generally above them.

The income growth was therefore financed by an increase in income velocity of money, as people found ways to economize on money balances and banks converted idle balances to active balances by selling securities to depositors who held idle funds. Of course, interest rates shot up to record highs, as three-month treasury bills, which yielded three fourths of 1 percent in July 1954, were yielding 2.5 percent at the end of 1955 and rose to 3.4 percent in August 1957; the prime rate rose from 1.5 percent to 4 percent over the same period.

The Federal Reserve's concern for inflation and its consequent policies would appear designed to curb the boom. Still, prices rose despite the tight money policy, and investment continued despite the high interest rates. Perhaps monetary policy restrained the boom, but it was not able to halt it, and the question of whether the boom would have been more vigorous with an accommodating monetary policy is, of course, unanswerable. The monetary policy described above could not be expected to affect investment in national-defense projects that

Table 8.3   Federal Budgets, 1954–57 (billions of dollars)

	1954	1955	1956	1957
Fiscal year basis:				
Expenditures	67.8	64.6	66.5	69.4
Receipts	64.6	60.4	68.1	71.0
Surplus or deficit	−3.1	−4.1	1.6	1.6
Calendar year basis:				
National income accounts:				
Expenditures	69.4	68.9	72.0	79.3
Receipts	64.0	72.5	78.2	83.3
Surplus or deficit	−5.4	3.6	6.2	4.0

Source: Council of Economic Advisors, *Economic Report of the President,* (Washington, DC: GPO, 1958), pp. 173, 176.

would not be discouraged by the high costs of borrowing. Nor would the high interest cost deter consumption of durable goods, if those items were regarded as necessities. In fact, installment credit rose from $22 billion in August 1954 to $33 billion in August 1957, an increase of an astounding 50 percent. Moreover, the increases in margin requirements, from 50 percent to 60 percent in January and then to 70 percent in April 1955, reduced the rate of growth of stock-market credit only slightly, and the index of stock prices continued rising until July 1957.

There is no question that monetary policy was expected to play the dominant role in the administration's plan. Still, the actual monetary policy followed elicited much criticism. High interest rates, rising prices, and falling real output gave the critics of the Federal Reserve much to complain about, and in general monetary policy came under attack for its perverseness.

Fiscal policy was to take a back seat in the Eisenhower administrations. The stabilization of the economy through the federal budget was not part of the administration's idea of proper budgetary considerations. Fiscal conservatism, on the contrary, dictated a balanced-budget philosophy, that whatever government spends must be justified on the basis of actual need and not the conditions of the national economy. Just a glance at Table 8.3 is enough to see the drive toward sound public finance.

Clearly fiscal policy became more and more restrictive and acted as a brake on the recovery. This can be seen, of course, in the usual fiscal-year budget for 1956, but much more clearly in the national income accounting budget in 1955. Since taxes are recorded as they accrue in the national income accounting budget, it is apparent that receipts were increasing in the boom of 1955, acting as a drag on the economy unless they were spent. (The term "fiscal drag" would be used in the 1960s to describe this tendency. Also the full- or high-employment budget surplus developed in the 1960s moved from a deficit in 1954 to surpluses in 1955 through 1957. The high-employment budget measures what the surplus or deficit would have been, had the economy produced according to its potential with no automatic stabilizers operating.)

Thus for any budget concept, fiscal policy turned restrictive during this boom period, and the question is, Why? Despite a nod at using fiscal policy for stabilization, there was much more emphasis on economy in government and therefore reducing expenditures and limiting the tax burden. The budget surplus in 1956 was hailed, for "this achievement was the culmination of persistent efforts since 1953 to bring the Federal budget into balance without impairing national defense or other essential Government services."[26]

When the idea of a surplus emerged, there was the hope that taxes would be reduced. The Eisenhower administration would not consider one, however, and in fact postponed the scheduled reductions of corporate and excise taxes due on April 1, 1955, and repeated that postponement annually for the next three years. The reason given was the loss in revenue that would unbalance the budget. Thus the administration paid only lip service to the stabilization function of the federal budget—the balanced budget and the reduction in the public debt would take precedence.

Still, fiscal conservatives called for additional expenditure cuts, but after the reductions of national-defense spending were completed, there was no further drive to reduce spending by the administration. When defense expenditures came under question, the administration balked at further reductions. Secretary Humphrey did not help matters when he suggested that there was room for budget cuts, and later Eisenhower also challenged Congress to find areas to cut. Congress did not find the areas, but the administration was forced to reduce the rate of spending on national-defense contracts in 1957, because it had failed to revise upward the debt-limit ceiling and was now forced to reduce spending on the major controllable item in the budget. The drop in defense spending came at a most inopportune time, as the economy fell into another recession in the summer of 1957. Clearly, national economic policy had been a restraining influence rather than a stimulating one, and now the economy slid slowly into its third postwar recession.

The Recession of 1957–58

Before examining the record of this cycle, it might be worthwhile to pause and note some events that had taken place—or were doing so—that might have influenced the mood of the society or affected economic actions. First, Eisenhower suffered a heart attack on September 24, 1955, and government operations understandably stagnated. He made a complete recovery and decided to run for reelection in 1956, hesitantly agreeing to Nixon as his running mate. They won again, defeating Stevenson again by an even wider margin than in 1952. The composition of the Congress, however, changed very little, with the Democrats winning two seats in the House and one in the Senate. Eisenhower had won on a platform of peace and prosperity and now felt justified in the policies followed in his first administration.

In 1957 the Treaty of Rome was signed, out of which would come the European Economic Community (Common Market) of six European nations. At the time the event received little attention, but another event did: the USSR had succeeded in launching an earth-orbiting satellite—called Sputnik—in October 1957. The United States, accustomed to being first in technological advances, now found itself embarrassed and humiliated. The administration tried to belittle the feat, but the rest of the world took note of the advances made by Soviet scientists. Suddenly we were behind in a new race—the technological one—and there was considerable anguish over what had happened to U.S. supremacy in science. While everyone had an answer and everyone was pointing a finger, the outcome was that education, particularly in mathematics and science, was held to blame. The renewed interest in education brought about the National Defense Education Act of 1958 to provide federal aid to improve teaching in mathematics, science, and foreign languages. In the same year the National Aeronautics and Space Administration (NASA) was created to catch up in space exploration. Federal aid to state and local governments for education increased from $345 million in 1950 to $727 million in 1960. The rush was on to close the education gap.

Therefore 1957 was not a good year for a recession. There was widespread fear of the USSR following Sputnik and general anxiety over the loss of technological supremacy. When the economic-growth race began to heat up, the U.S. economy was sliding into another recession. The society was shaken, and it demanded the proper responses. Before viewing these responses, a recounting of the data in the downturn is necessary.

Table 8.4   Changes in Economic Magnitudes during the Decline, July 1957 to April 1958

Item	Percent Change from Third Quarter 1957 to 1958, First Quarter
GNP	−4.4
GNP in 1954 dollars	−5.6
Consumption	−2.3
Durables	−10.1
Investment	−26.0
Producer durables	−19.2
Change in inventories	−339.1
Net exports	−89.2
Government	2.4
Federal	0.0
GNP implicit price index	1.3
WPI	0.9
CPI	2.2
Unemployment rate	78.6
Capacity-utilization rate	−11.7

Sources: Council of Economic Advisors, *Economic Report of the President* (Washington, DC: GPO, 1959); and *Federal Reserve Bulletin* 62, No. 11 (November 1976), p. 903.

Once more the contraction was a short one. The NBER established the peak then at July 1957 (revised to August later) and the trough at April 1958, a period of nine months. Though short in duration, the recession of 1957–58 was sharp and more severe than the previous postwar recessions. Table 8.4 gives the profile of the decline.

It is clear from Table 8.4 that one of the major reasons for the decline was the remarkable turnaround in inventory accumulation, going from $2.3 billion in 1957 to $ −7.8 billion in the first quarter of 1958. The inventory disinvestment, of course, is just symptomatic of other causes that made for the decline. For instance, the slowdown in the consumption of consumer durables is an obvious contributor. Not surprisingly, the growth of consumer debt slowed from 1957 to 1958 and showed virtually no increase.

Another contributor to the decline was the drop in investment spending. Apparently the capital investment boom of 1955 resulted in overbuilding of capital stock, and now excess capacity became a problem. The capacity-utilization rate fell dramatically (over 11 percent) and in fact never returned to previous highs until the 1960s.

The overinvestment led to a period of mild stagnation that would characterize the economy until the boom of the 1960s. Also, the decline in defense expenditures, already mentioned, contributed to the recession, perhaps by more than indicated, since defense orders fell even more than expenditures.[27] Although the drop in defense spending was not as severe as in 1953, it was enough to contribute to the overall decline in economic activity.

Finally, there was the drop in net exports of some 89 percent during the decline, while imports remained stable. Part of the decline in exports is artificial, since exports had risen during the Suez crisis (when the French and British invaded to recapture the canal from Egypt), especially for petroleum and cotton, and now export of these commodities fell back to normal. Still, there were strong declines in coal, automobiles, and iron and other metals. Economic recovery had been achieved in Europe, and now its production of coal and metals made it self-sufficient; in fact, excess capacity appeared, as did falling prices. U.S. producers suffered from both aspects. The decline in automobiles and parts reflects in part the desire for smaller cars being produced in Europe. Imports of these cars also began to erode the automobile market in the United States.

In addition to these trends in exports and imports of merchandise, new issues of foreign securities increased dramatically from the second half of 1957 to the first half of 1958. Meanwhile, direct foreign investment abroad returned to pre-1957 levels, after reaching a peak in the first half of 1957. Balances of payments with industrialized countries now began to turn into deficits, and these areas, especially Western Europe, Canada, and Japan, began to accumulate gold and dollars, as the United States experienced difficulty in competing because of price disadvantages in exports and heavy importing. While the flow of dollars certainly helped to finance international trade after World War II, the volume of dollars was building up in foreign banks and soon would present a problem for the international community. While Europe and Japan were rebuilding their economies, the availability of dollars stimulated world trade, but now that these economies had recovered, the excess dollars were no longer needed. Here, then, is another problem emerging during the Eisenhower years that would persist for decades. At the time the problem was not regarded as severe, and little thought was given to policies designed to strengthen exports or to deal with the incipient world trade problems that were becoming evident.

This was the first time in many years that the foreign trade sector contributed to an economic decline. In the *Economic Report* of 1959,[28] the CEA recognized the problem, but offered no solutions and seemed relatively complacent. Some of these trends were apparently considered temporary.

Together, the declines in demand managed to push the unemployment rate from 4.2 percent to 7.5 percent, an increase of 79 percent.
This sharp increase illustrates the severity of the recession, but the
interesting thing about this decline is that the rate never fell below 5
percent again until the mid-1960s. The economic stagnation alluded to
earlier resulted in excess capacity and excess labor for years after the
recession was over. Even in recovery the economy would not regain its
previous levels of employment of either capital or labor. This, too, was
something new, although signs of it could be seen in the previous
postwar recessions.

To confound the issues even further, prices continued to rise
during the downturn, with the implicit price index increasing by 1.3
percent, the WPI by 0.9 percent, and the CPI by 2.2 percent. Here
again, cost-push elements might have been responsible for this
development. In terms of policymaking the Eisenhower administration
began to fear inflation, and its policy recommendations would be
constrained by inflation considerations, even in the midst of a
recession that was exhibiting signs of longer-run stagnation. The
economic system was not behaving properly, making the analysis of it
more difficult and policymaking more perplexing.

Macroeconomic Policy
in the Third Postwar Recession

The recovery began in May 1958 and would last until May 1960, a total
of 25 months from the trough of April 1958. The expansion was both
brief and weak, adding to the fears of economic stagnation accompanied by inflation.

Looking at the contribution of macroeconomic policy in getting
the economy moving again, the record is not inspiring. The Federal
Reserve did not act until late October 1957, when it hesitatingly began
some open-market operations to ease market conditions. In mid-
November the discount rate was lowered to 3 percent from 3.5 percent,
but this action was four months after the cyclical trough. Later, in
January, March, and April, the discount rate was reduced until it stood
at 1.75 percent in April 1958. Interest rates fell almost immediately:
Three-month treasury bills fell from 3.3 percent in November to 1.1
percent in April 1958; the prime rate fell from 4.1 percent to 1.9
percent; and high-grade corporate bonds fell from 4.1 to 3.6 percent. In
late 1957 the Federal Reserve did increase the money supply

cautiously, but by the end of the period the stock of money slowly fell back to its original level of July 1957. Still, banks were able to reduce somewhat their borrowings from the Federal Reserve by these purchases of securities, but more directly when the Federal Reserve reduced the reserve requirements. In February, March, and April 1958 the reserve requirements were reduced by 2 percentage points, and reserves were lowered by about $1.4 billion. By the spring of 1958 banks had excess reserves again, instead of being in debt to the Federal Reserve.

While these measures probably helped ease short-term money-market conditions, the Federal Reserve continued to cling to its bills-only doctrine when events in the long-term market required some attention. Both the Treasury and state and local governments were involved in borrowing in the long-term bond market to repay short-term debt. These actions decreased the availability of funds for private-sector borrowing and increased long-term interest rates. Since private investment is primarily geared to long-term rates, the Treasury was competing for funds at a time when private investment should have been encouraged. Critics explain that the Treasury should not have been floating long-term bonds in the first place, but when it did, the Federal Reserve should have stepped in to buy them and abandon its bills-only stance.[29]

Thus, long-term interest rates fell from 3.5 percent in November, when the Federal Reserve acted to ease monetary conditions, to 3.1 percent in April 1958. This slight drop was thereafter followed by steady increases up to the first quarter of 1960, to 5.0 percent, and stood at 4.2 percent at the next peak in May 1960. These high interest rates over the period were the cause of much unrest and criticism by Democrats, and the Eisenhower administration frequently had to defend them as necessary to fight inflation.

The profile of the expansion is given in Table 8.5. In addition, the subsequent downturn to February 1961 is also provided, in part to show comparative data and in part to show the quick turnaround from the 1960 peak.

The recovery, while hardly robust, did exhibit the normal V-shaped cycle typical of postwar cycles. By the spring of 1959 most components of demand had recovered to their previous peaks in 1957. Investment spending on producer durables recovered at a somewhat slower pace than did consumption, and that was probably due to the greater stability of consumer incomes, thanks to the transfer payments that propped up personal income. The change in inventories rebounded quickly, however, and by the third quarter of 1958 had moved from $ −5.0 billion to $0.3 billion. Net exports continued to be a concern, as they deteriorated steadily in 1959 and regained their former levels

Table 8.5 Changes in Economic Magnitudes over the Cycle from April 1958 to February 1961

Item	Trough, 1958 II or April	Peak, 1960 II or May 1960*	Percent Change from 1958 II	Trough, 1961 I, February 1961	Percent Change from 1960 II
GNP (bill)	438.3	504.7	15.1	503.6	−0.2
GNP (bill of 1958 dollars)	439.5	489.7	11.4	482.6	−1.4
Consumption	287.5	317.7	10.5	316.2	−0.5
Durables	37.0	45.6	23.2	41.7	−8.6
Investment	56.0	73.5	31.2	62.4	−15.1
Producer durables	24.6	30.5	24.0	27.3	−10.5
Change in inventories	−5.0	3.8	76.0	−3.4	−89.5
Net exports	2.5	3.9	56.0	6.4	64.1
Government	93.6	94.7	1.2	97.6	3.1
Federal	53.4	51.0	−4.5	52.2	2.4
Implicit Price Index (1958 = 100)	99.7	103.1	3.4	104.3	1.2
WPI (1947–49 = 100)	119.3	119.7	0.3	120.0	0.3
CPI (1947–49 = 100)	123.5	126.3	2.3	127.5	1.0
Unemployment rate	7.5	5.1	−32.0	6.8	33.3
Capacity-utilization rate	72.4	81.3	12.3	73.8	−9.2

*The date of the peak has subsequently been changed to April 1960.

Source: Council of Economic Advisors, *Economic Reports of the President,* (Washington, DC: GPO, various years); *Federal Reserve Bulletin* 62, No. 11 (November 1976); p. 903; U.S. Department of Commerce, *Survey of Current Business* 49, No. 8, Supplement (August 1966).

only in late 1960. As before, prices continued to rise, but in the recovery, of course, unemployment fell; still, the trends were disturbing, for prices did not fall in the recession and unemployment did not fall back to the previous rates in the recovery.

For policy purposes, note what happened to federal expenditures in the expansion. Federal government expenditures declined steadily over the course of the recovery, and at the peak in May 1960 were actually lower than they were in the trough in April 1958. Over the same period state and local government spending increased by nearly 9 percent. Once again the recovery was led by the private sector.

True to its philosophy, the administration saw no need to meddle in the economy unnecessarily. In its *Economic Report of the President* of January 1958, the administration suggested that "the decline in business activity need not be prolonged, and that economic growth can be resumed without extended interruption."[30] The decline did not need to be prolonged, since the administration saw an increase in defense spending, more state and local expenditures, reversal of inventory liquidation and plant and equipment deferrals, consumption spending being upheld by the stability of personal incomes, and finally the planned rebound in the housing sector. The only contractionary force would come from exports. Hence, the economy was undergoing a mild readjustment and there was no need for government intervention on a massive scale. Besides, the administration was acutely aware of the problem of inflation and did not wish to aggravate it by unwise government spending.

Accordingly, the president proposed no tax changes, even after acknowledging the decline in economic activity and even though others in Congress and elsewhere were calling for a tax reduction to revive the economy faster. In fact the administration continued to ask for postponement of the scheduled tax reduction for corporations and on excises, as it had for the previous years and would continue to do in the future. The only tax change was the repeal of the excise tax on freight transportation. Senator Douglas of the JEC, Arthur Burns, Walter Reuther, and even Richard Nixon favored a tax reduction, but their views ran counter to those of the new secretary of the treasury, Robert Anderson, who worried over the loss of revenue and was opposed to countercyclical fiscal policy anyway.[31]

The administration did not abandon tax reductions as a fiscal tool, but saw that policy as correct only when the recession became severe. Until then inflation was the main problem over the long run, and tax reductions might only exacerbate this problem, making it more difficult to combat later on. The debate over tax reductions continued into the spring of 1958, as the administration was pressed to act to reverse the downslide. As noted above, it never responded, but allowed the recession to continue its course until the decline stopped and tax cuts were no longer needed.

Yet it did little to increase expenditures, either. The reductions in defense spending that it ordered in 1957 were reversed in January 1958, when the administration asked for a supplemental defense budget increase of $1.3 billion and declared that a balanced budget must not be accomplished at the expense of national security. Sputnik had aroused all kinds of fears of lagging behind the Soviet Union in technology and defense capability.

Prodded by critics in Congress, the administration finally moved to increase expenditures. It ordered a speedup of expenditures on public works, the release of funds for mortgages, the award of defense contracts targeted to heavy unemployment areas, and a liberalization of lending rules by the Federal Home Loan Bank to savings and loans associations. It also asked Congress to suspend the limitations on expenditures for highways to permit additional spending of $2.2 billion over three years, and an extension of unemployment compensation payment periods by 50 percent.[32]

Congress went farther than the administration recommended. It passed the extended unemployment compensation measure, authorized the speedup of expenditures, and authorized the changes to the Highway Act of 1956, permitting more funds to be spent and increasing the amounts of federal contributions. Finally the Housing Act of 1958 reduced the downpayment for FHA-insured mortgages and made some liberalizing changes in VA-guaranteed loans as well.

The results of the administration's actions on the speedups of spending were not very effective, nor were efforts to use national defense spending as a countercyclical tool any more successful. The actions taken in the housing field were not as effective as those taken by Congress. The reduction in the downpayment for loans and the increase in interest rates for VA mortgages were more effective than the release of a small amount of funds and the liberalization of rules. The latter were more appropriately viewed as measures to avoid direct federal loans by substituting guarantees.[33] Yet together with the changes made by Congress and the monetary policies of the Federal Reserve, expenditures on housing made a strong rebound and helped lead the economy out of the recession.

Actions on the highway program also helped to bolster the economy. The original highway program, from the Highway Act of 1956, was justified in terms of the amount of economic activity that was dependent on the nation's highways and on the requirements for national defense. To use increased expenditures now for pump-priming purposes not only belied the administration's disavowal of pump-priming schemes but also illustrated the administration's approach to fiscal policy. Both the highway and housing programs were easily reversed, once the crisis had passed—just the type of policy favored by this administration. Thus the impact of the highway program was greatest in FY 1959, fell somewhat in FY 1960, and became negative in FY 1961, when spending returned to pay-as-you-go plans. For the housing program, again the major effect was felt in FY 1959, fell sharply in FY 1960, and disappeared in FY 1961.[34]

In any case, the administration was pushed into action and eventually responded. The response was timid, however, and the amounts involved did little to influence the economy. Without question, the built-in stabilizers did most of the job of turning the economy around and cushioning the decline. Thus, from the peak in 1957 to the trough in 1958, the automatic stabilizers contributed $10.9 billion to cushioning the decline, while deliberate policy actions contributed nothing. In the following three quarters of 1958, the automatic stabilizers contributed some $27 billion, while discretionary actions contributed $2 billion.[35] Clearly, the response to this recession by fiscal actions was not encouraging. The administration was cautious and concerned about inflation; it was not helped by some confusing signals given off by the economy, nor by the controversies surrounding the appropriate policies when the extent or duration of the downturn was in doubt.

Nevertheless, the Eisenhower administration's budgets were unnecessarily restrictive, and officials frequently spoke of the need to curb government spending. Thus, even as the recovery was just beginning in 1959, one finds this approach to fiscal policy as stated in the *Economic Report of the President*: "When the Nation is prosperous, as it is today, with production, employment, and incomes rising, the most appropriate fiscal policy is one that provides a sizable excess of Federal revenues over Federal expenditures. In the economic circumstances now prevailing and expected in the near future, a budgetary surplus used to retire debt would be a powerful aid in helping to restrain inflationary pressures and to promote sound growth."[36]

The restrictive nature of fiscal policy can be seen by examining the budgets over the period in question. Table 8.6 supplies the necessary data.

Note the surpluses in fiscal years 1956 and 1957, followed by deficits in the recession year of 1958 and in the recovery year of 1959. In fact, the deficit in FY 1959 turned out to be the largest in peacetime in the history of the United States up to that time. Of course, deficits are to be expected in periods of recession, as tax receipts fall off and transfer payments increase.[37] Some of this experience can be observed by looking at the budget as it is recorded in the National Income Accounts, which includes the trust fund accounts, puts taxes on an accrual basis, and records expenditures when delivery is made. On this basis the federal budget was very restrictive in the calendar years of 1956 and 1957, and the large deficit occurs in 1958 instead of 1959. Again, on either basis the 1960 budget shows the restraining force of the federal budget.

Table 8.6   Federal Budgets, 1956–61 (billions of dollars)

Period	Receipts	Expenditures	Surplus or Deficit (−)
Fiscal Year			
1956	68.2	66.5	1.6
1957	71.0	69.4	1.6
1958	69.1	71.9	−2.8
1959	68.3	80.7	−12.4
1960	77.8	76.5	1.2
1961	77.7	81.5	−3.9
Government receipts and expenditures on a national income accounts basis (calendar year)			
1956	77.5	71.8	5.7
1957	81.7	79.7	2.0
1958	78.5	87.9	−9.4
1959	89.4	91.2	−1.8
1960	96.0	92.8	3.3
1961	97.9	101.4	−3.6

Source: Council of Economic Advisors, Economic Report of the President, (Washington, DC: GPO, 1962), pp. 272, 275.

Clearly, fiscal policy took a holiday in the Eisenhower administrations. True, the Eisenhower administrations made price stability the number-one goal and constantly worried about inflation. Yet from the trough of 1958 to the next peak of May 1960, wholesale prices were constant and consumer prices rose at a modest 2.3 percent over the period (see Table 8.5). The administration did worry about the burden of the debt, and, after the horrible deficit of 1959, Eisenhower warned of burdening our grandchildren with an enormous federal debt. Yet all but a small proportion was held internally, and thus the burden was overstated, since our grandchildren would also inherit the bonds as well as the debt. In short, it is difficult to avoid the conclusion that the administration simply did not believe in countercyclical fiscal policy, although it frequently declared that it would take all the necessary steps to combat severe recessions.

Interestingly, this very statement made fiscal policy even less apt to be used. An administration that disavowed fiscal actions unless the situation was serious would feel its actions constrained, lest it spark a psychological panic that would make the situation even worse.[38]

The administration managed to secure a budget surplus for FY 1960 and argued that a surplus was needed to fight inflation. Democrats argued that greater economic growth was needed, that this was not the time for caution. Not everyone concurred with the administration's position that inflation was the main enemy of the economy.

Perhaps the administration was made more apprehensive by the 116-day steel strike that started on July 15, 1959, and caused some havoc in the economy, as firms stocked up on steel prior to the strike and then used the stocks during the strike. The change in inventories from the first half of 1959 to the second half was striking, building up to $10.4 billion and then falling to zero in the last quarter.

The economy righted itself after a time, but the administration remained concerned over labor–management relations. It began to jawbone for price and wage restraint on the part of both parties. In its *Economic Report of the President for 1960*, the administration declared:

> And leaders of business and labor have a joint responsibility for facilitating economic growth through the conduct and results of collective bargaining. This responsibility is especially great in industries that are basic to the Nation's defenses and economic health. ... disputes in basic industries should be settled promptly ... on terms that are fair [but] ... do not contribute to inflation.

The analysis goes on to recommend a guidepost policy of voluntary wage controls that would reappear in the Kennedy administration.

> Settlements should not be such as to cause the national average of wage rate increases to exceed sustainable rates of improvement in national productivity. ... Hourly rates of pay and related labor benefits can, of course, be increased without jeopardizing price stability ... [However] it would be a grave mistake to believe that we can successfully substitute legislation or controls [for] the complex relationships cannot be fixed by law.[39]

Here is an administration so concerned about inflation that it overcame, at least in words, its distaste for government interference in the economy to suggest a system of voluntary wage and price controls. The suggestion went unnoticed, but the remarkable thing is that it was made at all.

The executive branch was not alone in its concern about inflation. The Federal Reserve began a move toward restraint in May 1958, just one month after the expansion began. Perhaps it was determined not to repeat its mistake following the previous recession of keeping monetary ease too long; it certainly was alarmed at the outflow of gold (some $2.3 billion in 1958 alone), and, like others, it saw the failure of prices to fall in recessions and became concerned over the possibility of perpetual inflation.[40]

In 1958 and 1959 the Federal Reserve decided to offset the gold outflow. Once again the loss of gold elicited the traditional response, as the Federal Reserve purchased securities on the open market and restored most of the bank reserves lost by the gold outflow. The money supply remained fairly stable, which was the intention of the Federal Reserve's policy of "leaning against the wind." Still, banks lost reserves and had to borrow from the Federal Reserve System. Free reserves (excess reserve minus borrowing from the Federal Reserve) went from $493 billion in April 1958 to $ −424 billion by the end of 1959 and to $ −33 billion at the peak of the cycle in May 1960.

The restrictive monetary policy, together with the increased demand for funds as the recovery proceeded, drove interest rates to levels not seen since the 1920s: Three-month treasury bills rates rose from 1.13 in April 1958 to over 4.5 percent at the end of 1959; long-term rates rose from 3.12 percent to 4.27 percent in the same period, while the prime rate rose to nearly 5 percent.

Accordingly, the discount rate was increased in September 1958 and in four steps to a high of 4 percent in September 1959. Also, margin requirements were raised to 70 percent in August 1958 and to 90 percent in October 1958. Only after the recession had developed did the rate return to former levels of 70 percent in July 1960.

Clearly the Federal Reserve was overly restrictive, if domestic considerations were paramount, since the recovery was not strong enough to seriously threaten price stability. Indeed, the Federal Reserve was beginning to feel constraints on its ability to make policy with only the domestic economy in mind. Now it had to consider its policy for the effects on the balance of payments and gold and capital outflows. While keeping interest rates low would have aided the recovery, such a policy would have hastened capital outflows and made the deficit in the balance of payments even worse.

The balance of payments had showed deficits for some time (see Table 8.7), but after World War II they were welcomed, since they furnished the liquidity for the resumption of world trade. Now, at the beginning of the 1960s, huge dollar balances had accumulated in foreign hands, and there was growing concern that the United States would abandon the fixed exchange rates that had given rise to the deficits and allow the dollar to depreciate. Holders of U.S. claims were understandably nervous over either devaluation or depreciation of the dollar. They were also upset with the deficits causing inflation in their countries, as excessive liquidity replaced scarcity of reserves.

Of course, the Federal Reserve could have refrained from offsetting the gold outflow and allowed bank reserves to fall, thus restricting credit. This alternative the Federal Reserve declined to follow, since that would have meant severely restraining the economic recovery, or, worse, keeping it depressed until the terms of trade had been reversed. This the Federal Reserve was reluctant to do, but the dilemma of what policy to pursue would continue for another decade. No longer would the Federal Reserve be free to pursue whatever policy was necessary for domestic purposes; it would now have to consider the international implications of its actions. Keeping interest rates high might discourage capital outflows, but such a policy would not encourage domestic economic growth.

It will be necessary to return to these issues as the record unfolds, but before leaving the topic, note the private capital outflows in Table 8.7. The increases in private-capital outflows from 1955 to 1956 are phenomenal: 137 percent for direct foreign investment, 150 percent for long-term flows, and 170 percent for short-term flows. Moreover, the higher levels remain, except for some variations in short-term flows, for the period under review. As will become apparent later, this trend was part of a larger revolution in the structure of the U.S. economy.

The Recession of 1960 and the Legacy of the Eisenhower Era

The peak of the expansion that began in April 1958 was reached in May 1960, some 25 months later. The economy then began another slide that would last until February 1961, a period of only nine months. From Table 8.5 it is clear that the recession was a mild one, with GNP falling by only 0.2 percent (real GNP by 1.4 percent). Again, investment expenditures account for most of the decline, with the change in inventories dropping 89 percent from the peak. Prices continued to rise, however, for both the implicit price index and the CPI; wholesale prices remained remarkably stable. The unemployment rate failed to fall significantly in the expansion and in May stood at 5.1 percent; as the downturn continued, the rate rose to 6.8 percent by February 1961. The failure of prices to fall in recessions and the

Table 8.7 U.S. Balance of Payments, 1950–61 (millions of dollars)

Year	Balance on Goods and Services	Overall Balance (R – L)	Change in Reserve Assets (R)	Change in Liquid Liabilities to Rest of World (L)	Gold Stock (@ $35 per oz.)	U.S. Private-Capital Flows Direct Invest-ments	Long-Term Portfolio	Short-Term
1950	1,779	-3,580	-1,743	1,837	22,820	621	495	149
1951	3,671	-305	53	358	22,873	508	437	103
1952	2,226	-1,046	379	1,425	23,252	852	214	94
1953	386	-2,152	-1,161	991	22,091	735	185	167
1954	1,828	-1,550	-298	1,252	21,793	667	320	635
1955	2,009	-1,145	-41	1,104	21,753	823	241	191
1956	3,967	-935	306	1,241	22,058	1,951	603	517
1957	5,729	520	798	278	22,857	2,442	859	276
1958	2,206	-3,529	-2,275	1,254	20,582	1,181	1,444	311
1959	134	-3,743	-731	3,012	19,507	1,372	926	77
1960	3,769	-3,881	-1,702	2,179	17,804	1,694	850	1,348
1961	5,444	-2,370	-741	1,629	16,947	1,598	1,011	1,541

Source: Council of Economic Advisors, Economic Report of the President, (Washington DC: GPO, 1964); and U.S. Department of Commerce, Bureau of the Census, Historical Statistics of the United States (Washington, DC: GPO, 1975).

unemployment rate to improve significantly in expansions is again evident in this phase of the cycle.

The Federal Reserve recognized that the expansion was coming to an end and took action before the peak of May 1960. In March it began to purchase securities and move toward a policy of ease. Interest rates that had begun to fall in January, due to the lack of demand for funds, now began to fall further. They fell continuously until August and then stabilized. Three-month treasury bills, for instance, fell from 4.57 percent in December 1959 to 3.39 in May and 2.29 in August. This was the first time that interest rates had fallen prior to the peak of the business cycle.[41] The Federal Reserve, however, did not reduce the discount rate until June—by 0.5 percent to 3.5, and again in August to 3.0 percent. The discount rate was thus above market rates since the beginning of the year and could not help in checking the downslide. In September and December reserve requirements for central reserve city banks were lowered for additional monetary ease.

The Federal budget for fiscal year 1961 showed a surplus of $4 billion, as estimated in January 1960, but the recession pushed it into a deficit of nearly the same amount. In its *Economic Report of the President for 1961*, the administration showed no great concern for the recession and declared its belief that "an increase in general economic activity should not, accordingly, be long delayed."[42] It expected the private sector to lead the way, aided by the actions of the Federal Reserve authorities.

According to Richard Nixon, Arthur Burns approached him in March 1960 to report that there were some disturbing signs in the economy and evidence of a future slowdown. He advocated easing up on credit and increasing spending on national defense to avert the recession. Nixon reported this advice to the president, but in a cabinet meeting the proposals were rejected: first, because Burns's prognosis was not shared, and, second, because even if correct, there was no sentiment for using government fiscal or monetary policy to affect the economy, unless the situation was severe.[43]

By this time Nixon, by his own admission, "was more sensitive politically" than the others and more attentive to the advice. Nixon was well aware of the importance of pocketbook issues, especially in October of an election year. Unfortunately for Mr. Nixon, Burns's predictions were correct. In October the unemployment rate stood at 6.3 percent and was rising from 5.7 percent in the previous quarter; the CPI jumped by 0.5 percent from September or by about 6 percent at an annual rate. The economy was in the middle of a recession, which is no time for a member of the administration in power to run for office. Writing of the rise in unemployment, Nixon noted, "All the speeches, television broadcasts, and precinct work in the world could not counteract that one hard fact."[44]

The Eisenhower era was over. It has been characterized as apathetic, intellectually dull, stable, calm, and uneventful. It has even been suggested that the lull in activity was beneficial, since the society was given a breathing spell. Apparently World War II, the Korean war, and the initial phases of the cold war had proved exhausting and the accelerated pace of change too bewildering for the society to cope with over the short time span.

In rapid succession society had been dragged through a depression and two major wars, had seen the world divided into two camps dominated by the two superpowers, had witnessed the domestic revolution led by the automobile, TV, airplane travel, and so on, and had experienced the anxiety of being defended by atom bombs. Perhaps society longed for a period of peace and stability to allow it to catch up to the events that had shattered its institutions and traditions.

Perhaps this accounts for part of the reason this generation accepted so passively the trend toward conformity. Row upon row of identical houses were constructed; clothing styles showed few innovations; movies and TV made little use of their potential. Even college students became complacent, content to secure a degree and fit into society with a job and a split-level house. People moved to the suburbs in their automobiles and sought stability and peace in their unattractive dwellings.

Yet the move toward conformity had another explanation, an economic one. Many in this generation had matured in the Great Depression and World War II, and this was the first time that they had the opportunity to own homes and cars. Mass-produced houses became affordable and were willingly purchased. The movement toward materialism can be explained by the consumption of many who had little for many years and now wanted their chance at enjoying the fruits of their progress. The GI Bill of Rights, which gave to the returning servicemen an opportunity to attend schools for all kinds of training, was more revolutionary than envisioned and fostered the upward movement of social classes. Those who were moving upward were experimenting with new goods and consumption habits, and the trend toward conformity is understandable in this context.

Whether or not the Eisenhower years invited conformity and apathy in the social world must be left for others to decide. If the judgment is that they did, it would be doubly indicting, considering the events that were taking place in those years. Some of these events have already been mentioned and others will be mentioned later. Yet whatever the verdict on stability in the rest of society, in the economic world the generalization is simply incorrect. Beneath the tranquility some fundamental changes in the economy were taking place or about to surface. Some of these have already been discussed. To reiterate:

1. There was a leap toward a more commercial society. Promoted by advertising, TV commercials, and so on, consumption rose and was encouraged by the phenomenal increases in consumer debt, over 147 percent for total credit and over 180 percent for installment credit alone. The public relations atmosphere spread to all facets of life, from politics to business to sports.

2. Inexplicable price behavior became the norm, as prices failed to fall in recessions and then even rose during one. Cost-push inflation coming from the supply side became an explanation for the unusual price behavior.

3. The inability to utilize resources fully also became evident in the 1950s. Excess productive capacity became commonplace and unemployment remained high by historical standards, even in recovery from recessions. The tendency toward economic stagnation should have been apparent, but was overlooked or ignored in the cycles over the decade.

4. The balance of payments became a problem, and weaknesses of the Bretton Woods agreements began to surface. International repercussions of Federal Reserve monetary policy began to constrain the system's policy actions.

5. The trend toward concentration continued as the merger movement accelerated. The structure of industry was fundamentally altered in the process.

6. Foreign investment abroad increased, as multinational corporations stepped up their direct investment abroad and private capital sought higher returns.

These are some of the major economic changes that were altering the economy in the 1950s and for years to come. If you add to these the potential problems of the merger of the AFL–CIO, the slowdown in the rate of economic growth (some of which can be explained by the foregoing), the emergence of the Common Market, and the looming problems of environmental damage and pollution concerns, the period looks anything but stable and tranquil. Most of these emerging problems have already been discussed in the process of describing the record of economic policy over the period. Items 5 and 6, however, require further comment.

Looking first at the total number of mergers, Table 8.8 supplies the aggregate data. The number of mergers had been increasing steadily since 1949, but began to take a real jump in the mid-1950s. In 1954 mergers increased by almost a third from the previous year, and in 1955, the year of the capital-goods boom, they increased by over 76 percent. When the capital-goods boom was falling off and during the ensuing recession, mergers fell off, only to resume again in the recovery. From 1961 until the mid-1960s, the number of mergers would again stabilize.

Table 8.8   Recorded Mergers in Manufacturing and Mining, 1951–61

Year	Recorded Mergers	Percent Change from Previous Year
1951	235	7.3
1952	288	22.6
1953	295	2.4
1954	387	31.2
1955	683	76.5
1956	673	−1.5
1957	585	−13.1
1958	589	0.7
1959	835	41.8
1960	844	1.1
1961	954	13.0

Source: U.S. Department of Commerce, Bureau of the Census, *Historical Statistics of the United States*. Series V38–40 (Washington, DC: GPO, 1975), p. 914.

The total number of mergers, revealing as it is, does not tell the whole story. To judge the movement toward concentration, it is necessary to consider which firms were merging and what types of mergers were involved. First, many of these mergers were undertaken by large firms. The top 100 firms accounted for 44 percent of the assets of large manufacturing and mining companies acquired over the period, and the top 200 accounted for 64 percent. In fact, the acquisitions of the top firms accounted for over 20 percent of their growth over the period.[45]

There was a huge increase in merger activity in the mid-1950s, followed by a trailing off until a decade later, when the merger movement was again revived. Clearly the trend toward concentration is evident in that the top 200 largest corporations increased their share of corporate manufacturing assets from 42.4 percent in 1947 to 54.1 percent in 1960. Of this increase of 11.7 percentage points, 5.6 points were attributable to mergers, and, over the entire period to 1968, mergers accounted for an increase of 15.6 percentage points in the share of total assets.[46]

Second, the character of the merger movement was changing. Early mergers were characterized as horizontal, that is, mergers between companies that produced similar goods for a geographical market. Over the period the decline in this type of merger is pronounced, from over 75 percent of all mergers in 1926 to 8 percent in the late 1960s. Vertical mergers increased somewhat over the period, but were falling at the end of the period. Vertical mergers combined companies that had a buyer–seller relationship before the merger—for example, a copper-mining firm with a fabricator of copper products. The really remarkable change, however, occurs in the conglomerate form of merger. Conglomerate mergers are of three types: geographic-market-extension types combine firms that manufacture the same products but sell them in different markets; product-extension types combine firms that produce related products not in direct competition with each other—for example, soap and bleach; and all other types combine firms that do not sell or produce the same products or functionally related ones—roofing products and shoes, for example.

Conglomerate mergers increased markedly over the period. In 1929–30 only 19 percent of all mergers could be so classified, and by 1968 the figure was 82 percent. Of particular interest is the increase in "other" types of conglomerate mergers; in 1948–51 there were no such mergers, but in 1968 they accounted for 44 percent of all mergers.

Why would firms wish to diversify? The obvious answer is to increase profits, but how is that achieved? First, firms might wish to take advantage of economies of scale, but being limited by rivals in one market, they may reach out into another market. This reason is particularly applicable if the firm expands in a related-product market and can take advantage of economies in distribution, management, marketing, warehousing, and so on.[47]

Another reason for diversification is found in the case of a firm moving into a higher profit area. Its own capital having become immobile, it can expand or exit from an industry only by diversifying into another by acquisition. Still another reason for diversification is to enable a firm to exercise its market power. A firm can use its market leverage to secure advantageous conditions in another market. Or a firm can use market power gained in one market to subsidize the operations of an acquired firm in another market and damage competition in that market. Obviously this latter reason is of greater concern in the breakdown of competitive markets.

One final reason for diversification is to escape antitrust limitations on growth within an industry. Too great a share of the market could bring about antitrust actions.

Despite the rationales for diversification, the Subcommittee on Antitrust and Monopoly found little support for claims that such mergers were made necessary for the reasons stated. It concluded that these mergers "pose a serious threat to America's democratic and social institutions by creating a degree of centralized private decision making that is incompatible with a free enterprise system, a system relying upon market forces to discipline private economic power."[48] It

Table 8.9   U.S. Investments Abroad, 1951–60 (billions of dollars)

Year	Total	Total Private	Private				
			Long-Term			Short-Term	U.S Govern-ment
			Total Long-Term	Direct	Other		
1951	56.4	20.8	19.2	13.0	6.2	1.7	35.6
1952	59.1	22.7	21.0	14.7	6.3	1.7	36.4
1953	60.2	23.8	22.2	16.3	5.9	1.6	36.4
1954	62.4	26.6	24.4	17.6	6.7	2.2	35.8
1955	65.1	29.1	26.7	19.4	7.4	2.4	35.9
1956	70.8	33.4	30.4	22.5	7.9	2.9	37.4
1957	76.4	36.9	33.7	25.4	8.4	3.2	39.5
1958	79.2	41.1	37.6	27.4	10.2	3.5	38.1
1959	82.2	44.8	41.2	29.8	11.4	3.6	37.4
1960	85.6	49.3	44.5	31.9	12.6	4.8	36.3

Source: U.S. Department of Commerce, Bureau of the Census, *Historical Statistics of the United States,* Series U 26–39, (Washington, DC: GPO, 1976), p. 869.

advocated stricter interpretation of antitrust laws to prevent further erosions of competition.

For our purposes, that there was a trend toward concentration and diversification is evident, along with the restructuring of the U.S. economy; the potential for the exercise of market power seemed to be growing, and a major step forward was made in the presumably uneventful 1950s.

The industrial structure of the U.S. economy was also altered by the movement of direct investment abroad. In 1951, $13 billion went abroad as direct investment; by 1960 the amount had grown to $32 billion, an increase of over 145 percent. The multinational corporations were finding it advantageous to invest in foreign countries and not at home. Mergers do not add to productive capacity, nor does investment in plants and equipment abroad. Again, private long-term investment abroad shows a steady increase during the 1950s, as can easily be seen in Table 8.9. Yet the mid-1950s again witnessed a sharp increase in private investment abroad. A higher rate of return abroad can explain some of the movement, as can a reaction to the Common Market in later years, but direct investment can also be viewed as another manifestation of the growing market power of U.S. corporations seeking to control world markets for their output.

Space does not permit the elaboration of the economic consequences of the trends toward conglomeration, concentration, and multinational expansion. The point of raising these developments along with the others listed above is to refute the notion that the Eisenhower years were stable, tranquil, and uneventful. At least in the economic sphere, there were fundamental changes taking place. Some were noted at the time; others went unnoticed or were underestimated. Unmistakably, though, the 1950s saw some trends developing that would affect the economic system for decades to follow. The breathing spell, so often lauded, gave the opportunity to those who were in a position to use it a chance to maneuver and improve their economic condition.

Evaluation of Eisenhower Administration Policies

Perhaps the decade of the 1950s was a still night, interrupted only by the shrieking of the whippoorwill. What concerns us is that there was very little shrieking for a change in economic policy; there was little if any social pressure for any change in policy, even in recessions. Despite the warnings and advice of professional economists and from members of Congress (Senator Douglas and other Democrats), the general public appeared to be rather apathetic to calls for more government involvement in the economy and more direct action to avert or modify economic fluctuations. Was this complacency or ignorance? Was it gratitude that no depression had followed the wars, or was it that memories of worse times forced a kind of conservatism on those old enough to remember, or were the new toys of civilization simply too enticing to worry about creating better times for all or building new dreams? It is no easier to answer these questions than it is to characterize the period. Perhaps the times were more carefree, simple, and innocent, and the temporary setbacks of (mild) business cycles seemed only a slight irritant before the resumption of progress.

Lacking any real social pressure, the administration felt justified in pursuing its economic policies. The underlying belief in the strength of the private free-enterprise system was not fundamentally shaken by the recurrence of recessions. Recessions were only temporary interruptions in the growth of economic activity, and the private sector could be expected to lead the way out of any disruptions. The administration never abandoned its belief in the soundness of a balanced budget, nor did it seriously consider any enlargement of the public sector for any reason.

Thus the automatic stabilizers were forced to provide whatever countercyclical spending occurred. When discretionary fiscal actions were undertaken, they were often dictated by other than fiscal-policy purposes. Thus the post-Sputnik defense buildup helped stabilize the economy, but that was not the impetus for the spending increases. If the variations in expenditures were not related entirely to stabilization, the variations in taxes were nonexistent.

There is no necessity to belabor the point made often enough in the discussion of the Eisenhower administration: Fiscal policy took a holiday. In retrospect, the recessions turned out to be mild ones, but not because of enlightened economic policies. Thus the administration was lucky in that its policies do not appear to have hampered the recoveries, and it could claim some credit for not overreacting.

The administration seemed determined to return to a more orthodox relationship between the federal government and the national economy. In the first recession of the decade, 1953–54, the administration had to demonstrate that the first Republican administration since Hoover would not sanction another depression. Having weathered that storm, it was more relaxed about such accusations in the second and third recessions of the decade. The administration no longer had to prove that Republicans were not insensitive to the effects of the business cycle and certainly did not approve of a complete laissez-faire philosophy. In its confidence, however, it may have invited an unnecessary corollary: In its repeated claims that it would not intervene in the economy until conditions really warranted it, it faced the possibility that when it did take action, the public would interpret the situation as being really bad, and their reactions might make it worse. Any administration has to consider how its actions will be viewed by the general public and would be at pains to prevent panic, but an administration that promised to take action only when the situation was serious would risk giving out the wrong signals.

The Federal Reserve did appear to learn from experience in the recessions. In the first, it reversed policies when the recession became apparent, and in the last, it seemed to act prior to the cyclical peak to reverse policies. Just as it was learning its lessons, however, and reacting to criticisms of its past policies, the economy changed; always concerned with inflation, it now found that prices did not fall in recessions and thus monetary ease might make inflation worse. The Federal Reserve became hesitant and reluctant to pursue easy-money policies. Adding to its policy constraints was a new development, a new worry: the balance-of-payments problem. In the latter half of the decade, monetary policy had to be conducted with an eye on international economic conditions, and easy money and low interest rates to aid recoveries had to be weighed against their effects on the balance-of-payments capital flows.

Thus the concern for inflation, balanced budgets, and balance of payments all converged to give the administration an excuse for doing what it wanted to do anyway—as little as possible. With assurances that the private sector would be relied upon to correct any pause in economic activity, the administration retreated to more traditional Republican ideology. Since this section of the analysis is usually concerned with an explanation of how the administration in power justified its policies, we have had to analyze how this administration justified inaction. Apparently the Eisenhower administration grew increasingly confident, after a major recession had been averted, in returning to traditional orthodoxy.

How successful was it in this endeavor? Judging from the lack of pressure to change them, the administration's economic policies must be judged at least partially successful. It did manage to force a return to more traditional approaches to economic policy. It was not entirely successful, of course, as the business cycle kept getting in the way. Yet even when the administration was goaded into action by a Congress controlled by the opposite party, it managed to resist wholesale intervention and to delay action until congressional pressure built up and threatened to challenge the administration's desire to revert to a laissez-faire view of government.

Again, success here means not the achievement of particular ends by economic policy but the resistance to calls for more involvement. The administration became the defender of free enterprise against those who would destroy it by trying to save it. With this attitude the aim became to prevent the further erosion of the free-enterprise system by those who had lost faith in its ability to function as promised. The system would stabilize itself, grow at the proper rate if left alone, and distribute the rewards justly without government interference. There was no need for Truman-like policies that encouraged the federal government to step in and make adjustments where shortcomings were found.

This attitude was not lost on those who sought to enlarge their economic power or influence. The trend toward concentration stepped up as the merger movement accelerated. If the allocation of resources was also to be left in the hands of the private sector, then those who could benefit from greater private control took action to guarantee their rewards. Apparently the protectors of free enterprise did not view the concentration of power as anything to be alarmed about. Nor did they view with concern the movement back to a more unequal distribution of income and wealth. They simply looked away, since they were determined to restore the pre-New Deal orthodoxy. The New Deal programs could not be dismantled; it was too late for that, but additional, similar programs could be forestalled.

Thus the Eisenhower administrations were pursuing a rational program, and they were open about it. Rationality to them meant the reestablishment of the old order—if not completely, then as much of it as possible. Cautious at first, the administration gained in confidence and, after a second term was won, became more aggressive. Eisenhower became the first president since Hoover to resist the demands for more spending and more government involvement.[49]

Whether such policies are considered rational has more to do with value judgments than economic policymaking. True, the administration was aided in its plans by rather mild recessions and could afford to cling to ideological beliefs. Had it been forced to react to severe recessions, some of its beliefs would have been brought into question. As it was, the last recession did turn out to be more severe than the previous ones, and already there were calls to abandon the hands-off attitude that had developed. The sluggish economy would testify that the private economy was not capable of righting itself and allow others to suggest that more could be done to help the economy grow and prosper. At the end of the decade such criticisms could be heard with more frequency.

Whether such criticisms would have eventually forced the Republicans to modify their economic policies, as suggested by Nixon, is problematical. History tells us only that many appeared to agree with Nixon on many matters, but on the economy they chose to vote with their pocketbooks. Eisenhower was a popular president, but he was unable to return the economy to the free-enterprise vision that appeared to dominate his administrations. In the end, what was rational to him was not so readily accepted by the nation.

chapter 9

John F. Kennedy and the New Frontier

In his inaugural address the new president stated that "the torch has been passed to a new generation of Americans," and later he presented the philosophy of the New Frontier when he challenged Americans to "ask not what your country can do for you; ask what you can do for your country." That the torch was passed to a new generation turned out to be an understatement, for the 1960s would be the opposite of the 1950s; where tranquility and conformity had been the rule, turbulence and variety would take their place. This sharp reversal affected all facets of life in the United States, including the social and economic, and if changes in economic policy are to be understood, it is necessary to view them as being partially determined by the conditions out of which they emanated.

The 43-year-old president received the torch from a president born in the nineteenth century, but it was not passed willingly by Eisenhower, who at first regarded Kennedy as a "young whippersnapper."[1] Nor was it passed with enthusiasm from the public, for the margin of victory over Richard M. Nixon was only 118,550 votes out of over 68,000,000 cast. Despite allegations of election fraud, Nixon declined to demand a recount, fearing the months of delay that would face the nation and the possible bitterness that such a long process might engender.[2]

The closeness of the vote does indicate that the new president took office without any real mandate for change. In fact, the Democrats lost ground in Congress, and their majority was reduced in both houses. Even with a majority, the president would have to confront many Democratic conservatives in Congress, who could be expected to resist the programs of their new liberal leader. Thus, if Kennedy hoped to introduce anything innovative, he would have to proceed slowly and be forced to sell his ideas to his somewhat reluctant legislative colleagues.

The campaign, however, produced no great innovative ideas, anyway. Kennedy spoke of a missile gap (that did not exist), of our falling behind in the technology race, in the economic growth race, in educational achievements, and so on. There were no new proposals or central focus to indicate any radical change.[3] Aside from the liberal concerns for unemployment, national health matters, education, and so on, Kennedy introduced only the concept of the Peace Corps. Nixon, on the other hand, was saddled with a recession to explain and resorted to references to Eisenhower to capture some goodwill from that name. Otherwise, he was put on the defensive, having to justify policies of the previous administration to which he belonged but of which he did not always approve.

In general, Nixon was regarded as the more experienced of the candidates and better known than the wealthy, inexperienced, young Catholic.[4] Unfortunately, religion was an issue in the campaign and may have influenced the indifferent voter. Ironically, Kennedy was known to be an indifferent Catholic.

The candidates debated the issues on national television, thanks to a law signed by Eisenhower that relieved the TV networks from granting equal time to fringe parties. Eisenhower, however, advised Nixon against the debates. That turned out to be sound advice, as Kennedy projected a forceful image, serious and handsome, while Nixon appeared weak, defensive, and less attractive. These impressions, formed largely at the first debate, were maintained, despite the actual content of the candidates' remarks. From these first TV debates to the present, the TV cameras would play a vital role in U.S. politics. Physical appearance and charisma would become more important than the ideas expressed, and the public-relations contribution that began with Eisenhower would assume enormous importance. Thus television in the 1960s would transform elections in the United States without anyone's endorsement.

The New Frontier and the New Economics

Kennedy had just 72 days to staff his administration and get it into operation. If the mark of a good leader is the caliber of the people he selects to advise him or help him administer the organization, then Kennedy deserves some high grades. The liberals, so weary of the dullness of the Eisenhower administrations, cheered as Kennedy raided the universities for advisors and searched for talent from previous public servants, so long on the sidelines. The eggheads from Cambridge, Massachusetts, together with the "Irish Mafia" from anywhere, gave the administration and Washington an intellectual excitement not felt since the New Dealers.

Among his choices for the cabinet were Dean Rusk from the Rockefeller Foundation for secretary of state; Robert S. McNamara, president of the Ford Motor Company, for secretary of defense; Stewart Udall for secretary of the interior; and the most controversial appointment of all, Robert F. Kennedy, the president's brother, for attorney general. For the top economic posts, Kennedy selected the highly respected Republican from Wall Street, C. Douglas Dillon, for secretary of commerce; Arthur J. Goldberg for secretary of labor; and Abraham A. Ribicoff for secretary of health, education, and welfare. In addition, his Council of Economic Advisors was composed of three very capable economists—Walter Heller, James Tobin, and Kermit Gordon. Moreover, Paul Samuelson helped shape the economic policies before and after the campaign and, along with J. K. Galbraith and Seymour Harris, was always available for advice and consultation. Of course, many others were involved both directly and indirectly in the new administration.[5] The building of the staff was soon over, however, and the hectic days of transition came to an end. It was time to put the New Frontier into action.

The economic situation facing the administration was certainly challenging. The nation had been in a recession since May 1960 and was about to change direction: in February 1961 the economy began the longest recovery in history. Of course, that fact was not known to the administration; as Kennedy complained in his State of the Union message, "We take office in the wake of seven months of recession, three and one-half years of slack, seven years of diminished economic growth." In January 1961 the unemployment rate stood at 6.6 percent, manufacturing firms were operating at 74 percent of capacity, wholesale prices were stable, and consumer prices and the implicit price index were increasing slightly. The rate of growth of real GNP during the Eisenhower years had declined to 2.4 percent, a full percentage point below the rates following World War II and below the average of 3.2 percent for the decade 1950–60.[6] President Eisenhower left a budget that was in balance for FY 1961 and showed a surplus of $1.5 billion for FY 1962. These budget estimates were either hopelessly optimistic or, according to the new administration, deceitful. They were based on revenue from a robust recovery, reductions in programs that would surely be continued (housing, airport development), underestimations of expenditures (farm support programs), and recommendations for programs for which no funds had been provided. Monetary policy, meanwhile, moved toward ease over the year, and interest rates declined. The money supply declined by $1 billion in 1960, and interest rates as of December 1960 stood at 2.2 percent for three-month treasury bills, 3 percent for the discount rate, and slightly over 3 percent for the prime rate.

The picture is one of economic stagnation that presented an opportunity for bold initiatives in policymaking, for even if recovery were imminent, there was no assurance that the upswing would not leave the economy still floundering, with large, unused resources. What new ideas did the New Frontier have to meet the challenge of economic stagnation, and which of these was it prepared to advance?

Being "Keynesian" economists, they would naturally seek to reverse the ideology of the Eisenhower administrations. Containing government expenditures and pursuing "sound finance," meaning balanced budgets, would not be likely to appeal to the new generation of economists. Paul Samuelson provided the general direction for economic policy in his task force report. The emphasis was on fiscal rather than monetary policy, compensatory public finance, public-works programs, and the like, to stabilize the economy when necessary, and an active government to promote growth when needed. The commitment of the New Economics came from the general belief, held by most administration economists, that the public sector should intervene in the economy to ensure that the goals of the Employment Act of 1946 would be achieved. It would not be enough to know how to manage the economy without the commitment to utilize this knowledge to reach attainable goals, particularly full employment and sustainable growth.[7]

To implement the basic Keynesian prescription and to make policy more rational in operation, these economists began to add methods of analysis to try to understand just where the economy was operating and to measure the impact of various proposals. They turned to the developing subdisciplines of econometrics and mathematical economics for help in answering these questions. To prescribe for an economy, it is necessary to know at what level it is functioning, forecasts of where it is likely to be heading, and the likely impact of policies designed to influence it. The quantitative side of economics was surely given a boost, and soon new techniques were developed to fill the gaps in our knowledge. The process continues to the present, regardless of ideology or even in spite of it.

New analytical devices were conceived or old ones used in imaginative ways. Samuelson wrote of an "output gap," the difference between what an economy was producing and what it was capable of producing at full employment. The aim of policy became to close the gap, thereby increasing employment and output and encouraging economic growth. To close the gap required actions by the federal government, meaning usually fiscal policy. The gap concept would gradually replace the notion of smoothing out the cycle as the proper guide or goal of public policy.

The concepts of a potential GNP and a full-employment surplus led to another idea—fiscal drag. As the potential GNP grows, the tax system produces increases in revenues, which, if not offset, will act as a brake on the economy. The recovery can be stalled long before GNP reaches its potential, before the gap is closed, and before full employment is reached. The "fiscal dividend" of rising revenues must be offset before the drag sets in, if a slowdown is to be avoided. In this connection it was thought necessary to stress that rising output (direction) is different from the level of output, and policymakers must be vigilant not to confuse the two and abandon policies in periods of rising GNP before the economy has reached its potential.[8]

To these general approaches to the analysis of policymaking, there were also added specific policy innovations. To stimulate both aggregate demand and economic growth, the investment tax credit was developed. Firms that purchased capital goods would be allowed a credit against their federal tax liability, thus reducing the cost of capital and increasing the rate of return. Such a policy should stimulate investment spending and, when combined with the liberalization of depreciation allowable, should result in more capital-stock accumulation and greater potential economic growth.

Not content with direct policymaking measures, the Council of Economic Advisors (CEA) undertook to educate the public, labor, and management about the economic effects of wage and price decisions made by firms or industries acting independently. Without direction the private wage and price decisions can be inflationary, particularly with the growing attitude of workers, then developing, that employers can grant whatever wage increases are demanded and then pass on the higher costs in the form of higher prices. Indeed, in the late 1950s there was growing evidence that this was occurring.

Yet even if that were not the case, the successful implementation of fiscal policy requires that no adverse effects (inflation) follow whenever government spending increases or tax reductions are incurred in order to manipulate the economy. The closer the economy gets to full employment, the more likely are inflationary pressures to develop. Thus the CEA introduced the concept of guideposts, that is, tying the rate of wage increases to the rate of growth of labor productivity.[9] If wage increases were equal to labor productivity increases, then costs would not rise and neither would there be a cause for prices to rise. The increase in wages could be granted without inflation and still benefit business firms. This is because wages constitute only three-fifths of total compensation, so that if wages are equal to productivity, there is still the gain in productivity to be shared with the remaining two-fifths—property incomes.

If a national standard could be set at the long-term rate of growth of productivity, then at 3.2 percent, both workers and employers would be aware of the noninflationary rate of wage increases. A wage–price spiral in which no one wins could thus be averted. Overall price stability called for prices to fall in industries where productivity exceeded the national average and for prices to rise when the reverse was true; on balance, they would cancel out, and price stability would be assured.

This guidepost concept would thus be a useful adjunct to fiscal policy. The guideposts were not mandatory and so avoided the pitfalls of wage and price controls. Being voluntary, however, there were no legal sanctions if they were violated and no way to enforce them if they were ignored. Being voluntary, they were politically more acceptable and palatable. They also had the virtue of being costless if they did not succeed—the administration could hardly be blamed for good intentions. In addition to the ideas generated within the administration, the president and his advisors were quick to embrace the policies that were proposed by the Commission on Money and Credit, a group of independent scholars and leading citizens sponsored by the Committee for Economic Development (CED).[10] Among their proposals, the administration chose to adopt three immediately:

A standby capital improvement authority. The president would be granted standby authority to initiate up to $2 billion of public investments any time that the unemployment rate rose in at least three out of four months or by at least 1 percentage point higher than four months earlier. The federal government would spend the funds either directly or through grants to states and localities. In either case, the projects would have already been approved by Congress. These projects would be selected for their ease in starting up and their short-run duration.

A standby tax reduction authority. The president would be granted the authority to reduce tax rates across the board by no more than 5 percentage points, to take effect 30 days after submission and remain in effect for six months, unless revised or renewed by Congress. This temporary authority is obviously a powerful weapon in the hands of the president, for it removes the inevitable lag in fiscal-policy measures and makes fiscal policy much more responsive to economic conditions. Of doubtful constitutionality, the standby tax policy was and probably always will be resisted by Congress, which has always been reluctant to give up its power over the purse strings.

Improvement of the unemployment compensation system. The proposal here was for a federal program to extend for as much as 13 additional weeks the unemployment compensation benefits payable to workers who had exhausted their benefits. Also included was a proposal to extend coverage of the system and raise the amounts payable in benefits.

These ideas and others quickly became known as the New Economics, often put in quotation marks by critics, but they were hardly new. These economists simply built on the structure provided by Keynes as they attempted to make his (and others') ideas operational. They were to give a new look to economic policymaking and stamp a generation of economists with their views. Influential they were, but how effective were they in applying their ideas to actual policies?

The Kennedy Program
and New Directions in Policy

With the economic situation facing the administration in mind, and with some appreciation for the general philosophy of its members, along with some of the new policy approaches being discussed, it is time to record the responses actually made. Administration economists and outsiders alike agree that little progress was made in the New Frontier economic programs in 1961.[11]

President Kennedy, sensitive to being labeled an "irresponsible spender," did not push for a sizable budget deficit, which appeared necessary to his advisors. He was not fully convinced of the benefits of deficit spending and had to be educated by his advisors into accepting this element of the New Economics. Indeed, the budget for FY 1961 turned from the small surplus estimated by Eisenhower to a $3.9 billion deficit. Kennedy publicly blamed Eisenhower for his fraudulent budget and appeared to put some distance between himself and the deficit.

While the charge that the Eisenhower budget was deceitful has some justification, Kennedy appeared to want the credit for the economic recovery without acknowledging that increased government spending did help to increase the deficit. Federal government expenditure increases were $5 billion over FY 1960, while tax receipts remained stable.

Even had Kennedy embraced the logic of deficit spending, he would still have faced the resistance of others nurtured in the balanced-budget philosophy. Thus, Samuelson, acknowledging this reality, wrote:

> Had President Kennedy come out boldly for the sizeable deficit which objective economic analysis called for, he would have run into severe opposition in the divided Congress; and by becoming tarred with the assinine label of an "irresponsible spender," the President might have put all his new programs in jeopardy. Here then, was one of those reminders that politics is the art of the feasible; while it is always easy for expert advisors to urge that the Head of State exercise his "leadership," he must ever deliberate on how best to spend and conserve his limited bank-balance of leadership.[12]

It is apparent that the economic advisors were being educated, just as they were educating the president.

The education process takes time, and in the meantime the increases in government spending were predictable in view of the administration's liberal slant. In his February 2 economic message to Congress, Kennedy announced that action was being taken, or about to be, on plans to accelerate or speed-up procurement and construction projects: post office construction, a release of federal aid for highway funds, an advance pay-out of veterans' life insurance dividends, surplus food distribution, reduction in interest rates by federal agencies, additional farm loans, and a pilot program for food stamps. In addition to these speed-up steps, he also asked Congress for six major antirecession measures, all of which were approved.

1. *Temporary extended unemployment compensation.* An extension of up to 14 weeks of unemployment compensation for those who had exhausted their benefits. The advance of $1 billion to states to finance the increased benefits was to be made up by an increase in payroll taxes in 1962 and 1963. Approved in March.
2. *Aid to dependent children.* Extended to children of the unemployed the same aid available to children deprived of support by reason of desertion, disability, or death. Passed in April with estimates of a cost of $200 million.

3. *Social Security.* Increases in Social Security minimum benefits, an earlier retirement age for men, and increased benefits for widows were included in a bill passed by Congress in June. The estimated cost of $800 million a year was to be financed by an increase in FICA taxes.

4. *Minimum wage.* In May the minimum wage was increased to $1.25 per hour, and coverage was extended to an additional 3.6 million workers.

5. *Area redevelopment.* The Area Redevelopment Act was passed in May to assist areas with large and persistent unemployment. The act provided for loans to private firms, loans and grants to communities, urban renewal, and so on, to erect facilities of various kinds in order to increase employment. Also, the act provided for manpower training. As enacted, the program gave the administrator the authority to borrow $300 million from the Treasury.

6. *Housing.* The Housing Act of 1961, passed in June, committed $2.5 billion over four years for urban renewal, low-interest loans for nonprofit rental and cooperative housing, public housing, and housing for the elderly.

Congress took no action on

- Major revision of the Unemployment Compensation System.
- Manpower training.
- Youth Employment Opportunities Program.
- Federal aid to education programs.
- Health program and medical care for the aged.

Finally, there was the buildup in national defense. In response to the USSR threat to turn East Berlin over to the East German government and limit or deny Western access to the city, Kennedy and the allies chose to respond with a show of force. Kennedy sought over $3.2 billion in national defense expenditures to build up our defenses and demonstrate our resolve to resist the Soviet move. In June of 1961 Kennedy had met in Vienna with Soviet Premier Nikita Khrushchev, who had announced the Soviet intentions. In July the president asked for the necessary funds to shore up our defense of West Berlin. Kennedy had managed to defuse the issue of Laos (Vietnam, however, was lurking in the background) and had even managed to explain the invasion of Cuba by a group of exiles under CIA direction. The operation, known as the Bay of Pigs, after the landing site, was planned in the Eisenhower administration, but President Kennedy failed to stop it, and the result was an absolute fiasco. These scattered events probably helped prepare the public to accept the necessity for additional defense spending. At first Kennedy wanted to finance the increase in defense spending with an additional tax. His economic advisors, in consternation, led by Walter Heller, managed to talk him out of any tax increase by arguing that a tax increase at this time would abort the recovery.

Still, there was the sense that the president had been bested in Vienna by the bullying Khrushchev, and still there was that missile gap to account for. Upon taking office the Kennedy administration found that no real gap existed, although miscalculations, conflicting numbers, and so on surely clouded the issue.[13] Ambiguities aside, the Kennedy administration proceeded to create a gap, but the advantage would be held by the United States. In his March defense message the president began his plan for, in Ted Sorensen's words, "[the] build-up of the most powerful military force in human history—the largest and swiftest build-up in this country's peacetime history, at a cost of some $17 billion in additional appropriations" over three years. The Polaris and Minuteman missiles would provide the necessary deterrent against attack. As usual, both sides spoke of peace and planned for war. The caution of Eisenhower was giving way to bold activism.

On military Keynesianism the economic advisors were silent, but spending would be beneficial for the economy in any event. Being basically liberal, the administration sought to improve the lives of the disadvantaged as well, as can be seen in the above spending requests. The tug between domestic programs and militarism would continue for the rest of the decade, but for now the contest was not too severe, as the economy began to recover.

On the revenue side the president asked for the enactment of an investment tax credit of 8 percent to stimulate private investment. He also asked for withholding on interest and dividends and for some minor tax reforms. Congress postponed action on this "little tax bill" until 1962.

Surprisingly, the business community opposed the investment tax credit feature, apparently wanting an accelerated depreciation scheme instead.[14] Moreover, businessmen were wary of Kennedy and could not accept the fact that he had proposed a program for their benefit. They managed to block any tax measure in 1961. Business animosity toward the president would last throughout his administration, despite Kennedy's repeated efforts to overcome it.

We have already seen how deficits in the balance of payments had begun to restrict the Federal Reserve's actions on domestic affairs. The Kennedy administration was also concerned that monetary policy would be unable to aid in the recovery. Clearly, low interest rates would be desirable for domestic purposes, but might encourage further capital outflows contributing to the balance-of-payments problem and adding fuel to the fears of those abroad who held dollars or dollar assets that the dollar would weaken.

Accordingly, on February 20, 1961, the Federal Reserve abandoned its "bills-only doctrine" in order to push short-term interest rates up relative to long-term rates. This policy, called "Operation

Twist" or "Operation Nudge," was accomplished by the Federal Reserve selling short-term securities and buying long-term ones. The Treasury aided in the effort to affect interest rates by also buying long-term bonds for its investment portfolio and by issuing more short-term securities in its new offerings, by swapping treasury bills for longer-term obligations, and so on.

The underlying assumption of Operation Twist was that domestic investment was influenced by the rate on long-term maturities, while capital flows were conditioned more by short-term rates. Accepting this contention for the present, it is still not clear whether the attempt to manipulate interest rates was successful or not. Long-term rates did decline slightly, from 3.89 percent in February to 3.73 percent in May, but they climbed slightly to 4.06 percent in December of 1961. Short-term rates varied little and ranged within a span of 2.408 in February to 2.617 in December. On balance, Operation Twist could be considered only a very modest success at best.

The stability of interest rates was partly the result of monetary ease, as the Federal Reserve added about $1 billion to member-bank reserves and the money supply increased 3 percent over the year for currency and demand deposits. In addition, time deposits grew by over 11 percent for the year, as the public shifted its assets from securities to savings and loans and other financial intermediaries, further adding to the liquidity of the banking sector. The monetary ease fostering stable interest rates led the CEA to observe that interest rates do not have to rise in periods of economic recovery.[15]

Two other examples of actions taken in 1961 indicate the concern over the balance-of-payments problem. In March the Treasury, and one year later the Federal Reserve, began to engage in foreign exchange operations to attempt to discourage the movement of funds abroad. By buying and selling currencies in the spot and forward exchange markets, the monetary authorities could affect the exchange value of the dollar, influence expectations of future rates, and perhaps increase the risk of speculation. The second action, taken in December of 1962 but effective on January 1, 1963, was an increase in the maximum rate that could be paid on time deposits, from 3 to 4 percent. This action, too, was partly motivated by the desire to reduce the outflow of funds.

The Slow Recovery

The results of the policies followed were encouraging to the administration. From the trough of the cycle in February 1961 to the end of the year, real GNP increased by 6.7 percent. Real gross investment rose by over 30 percent, as producer durables rose by over 10 percent, and there was a huge tunaround of inventories of 175 percent. As the council suggested, the role of government spending was also substantial, with federal purchases increasing by 9 percent. Net exports, however, were disappointing, falling by over 52 percent in the three quarters of the upswing. (See Table 9.1.)

The recovery was not marred by inflation, as wholesale prices fell by 0.4 percent in 1961, consumer prices rose by 1.1 percent, and the GNP deflator rose by 1.3 percent. Unemployment fell by over 10 percent, from 6.8 percent in February to 6.1 percent in December. The small decrease in unemployment was attributed to the increase in productivity that allowed increases in output without additional labor input. The increase in productivity was over 6 percent in the recovery, and thus the increase in output was achieved without the need for additional employment.[16]

Still, the CEA calculated the potential GNP on the premise that a 4 percent unemployment rate was obtainable and should be made the benchmark for calculating the full-employment output. The output gap stood at $51 billion in the first quarter of 1961, and by the last quarter of 1961 the gap was reduced to about $28 billion.[17] The administration economists rejected the view that structural unemployment prohibited a decline in the 4 percent unemployment rate. Structural unemployment refers to situations where the job openings cannot be filled by the unemployed; they may have the wrong skills, be in the wrong place, or lack mobility. Increases in demand, therefore, may not reduce this type of unemployment at all. Since the administration was banking on increasing aggregate demand to stimulate the economy, it had to answer this criticism. Heller and others found no evidence to support the hypothesis that structural unemployment had been increasing and posed a threat to their analyses.[18] Administration economists would not be moved from their position that the output gap could be closed by policies that would provide for sustained economic growth. The current stage of the business cycle was not important. What was important was to create the conditions for the economy to grow in a self-sustaining way.[19]

One final piece of evidence supplied to support the contention that government spending had contributed significantly to the recovery was that the full-employment surplus had declined over the year from an annual rate of $12.5 billion in the latter half of 1960 to $8.25 billion in the latter half of 1961. Still, there was the matter of the fiscal drag that would sap the recovery before full employment was reached. The CEA still had to persuade the president of the necessity to prevent this development. Heller was at work arguing for a tax cut, while other advisors, namely, J. K. Galbraith, were arguing for increases in government spending to alleviate the condition of "private affluence and public squalor." In either case, the budget was to be used as a stabilizing device and its impact measured in a more sophisticated form than from simple totals. This approach was becoming more acceptable, as even the Committee for Economic Development (CED), a nonprofit group composed of 200 leading educators and businessmen, recommended that "it should be the policy of the government to set its expenditure and tax rates so that they would yield a constant, moderate surplus under conditions of high employment and price stability."[20]

The outlook for 1962 was for continued economic expansion. The CEA was optimistic that the recovery would continue, and the administration was prepared to help it along with its fiscal policies. The new economists were growth-oriented, and while the economy was moving in the right direction, a better rate of growth was still necessary to fulfill the promises of the administration made during the campaign. The nation had come to believe that other countries were growing at a faster pace and that the United States had fallen behind in the growth race. Particularly irksome was the perception that the Soviet Union had been growing at a faster rate in the 1950s. To an administration that had pledged to get the country moving again, more had to be attempted.

The year 1962 did not live up to expectations. While the expansion continued, it was not as steady or as fast as predicted. GNP was expected to grow by 9 percent, to about $570 billion for the year, but the actual growth turned out to be more like 7 percent, to $554 billion. The slowdown occurred throughout the year, but began right in the beginning, as the rate of growth of GNP fell from 1961, then really slumped in the summer of 1962, and thereafter climbed slowly back to the rates of the early part of the year. The slump in the summer revived fears of another recession, and the administration took some steps to remove such apprehensions.

The events leading up to the summer slump and often listed as causes of it were Kennedy's confrontation with the steel industry in April (discussed later) and the stock-market collapse in May. On May 28, 1961, the stock market took its most severe short-run plunge since 1929. To his dismay, Kennedy was blamed for it, and it became the "Kennedy market." Actually, the stock market had been declining for some time, and now with inflationary psychology broken, many who had been expecting capital gains that follow from rising prices, simply sold and went into bonds. Yet at times like these, the technicalities do not really matter, and the administration considered responding with a presidential talk to calm fears and with a reduction in the margin requirements. The fireside chat never materialized, with the president opting for opening remarks at a press conference.[21] Margin requirements were not reduced immediately, lest that in itself signal an unwarranted crisis. The rate was reduced from 70 percent to 50 percent some six weeks later, in July.

The talk of a recession and the increasingly gloomy forecasts by Heller, Samuelson, and other economists sparked the discussion of a quickie tax cut to avert the pending slowdown. The president hesitated, being also advised that a tax cut could not be enacted by Congress and the economic signals were mixed anyway. In addition, the president feared a larger deficit and did not wish to exceed Eisenhower's largest deficit.[22] Besides, if Congress did pass a temporary tax cut and it turned out that it was not needed, he would risk not being able to get a tax bill when it really was needed. Being unconvinced that a tax cut was really necessary, he waited, and then in August finally announced that he would not press for a tax cut at that time, but would ask for one in 1963.

The proposed tax cut, to take effect on July 1, 1963, would reduce individual tax liabilities by some $6 billion at first, and further reductions would follow in 1964 and 1965, eventually bringing the rates down to a range of 14–65 percent from 20–91 percent. Corporation taxes would also be reduced in stages, with an eventual total of some $13.5 billion at annual rates, and tax rates would fall from 52 to 47 percent.

In the meantime other tax changes were initiated that would help stimulate investment spending. In July the Treasury issued new guidelines for depreciation, allowing firms to write off the cost of their capital goods at a much faster rate. For example, manufacturing-asset lives were 32 percent shorter for tax purposes than they were under the old rules. In October Congress passed the Revenue Act of 1962, allowing an investment tax credit of 7 percent against the cost of new capital goods purchases. While these tax changes would not have had much of an effect in 1962, they could have provided the stimulus of raising expectations for the future and hence possibly averted the type of actions that might have been taken in a recessionary mood. Estimates of the effectiveness of these tax policies, made by experts from The Brookings Institution, Robert E. Hall, Dale W. Jorgenson, and Charles W. Bischoff, reveal that they were effective. For accelerated depreciation, the estimates range from $0.64 to 0.9 billion in 1962 and from $0.67 to 1.1 billion in 1963; for the investment tax credit the range is from $0.9 to 0.22 billion in 1962 and from $1.51 to 2.2 billion in 1963.[23]

These data are for gross investment, as the law intended. The CEA and other economists, however, argued unsuccessfully for the credit to apply only to net additions to capital stock and not to investment goods that were bought for replacement purposes. For firms merely replacing capital stock, this was simply a subsidy that would increase profits without increasing productive capacity and hence potential economic growth.[24]

Still, gross private domestic investment remained remarkably stable through 1963. As a percent of GNP in real terms, it stood at 13.7 percent in 1960, fell to 12.8 percent in 1961, and climbed back to 13.7 percent for both 1962 and 1963. Producers' durable equipment remained at 5 percent throughout the same period. If growth was a main goal, then the constancy of investment spending must have been discouraging. So, too, would be the data on capacity utilization. After growing from 74 percent to 81 percent in 1962, it remained constant throughout 1962 at about that amount. The economy still had a good deal of excess capacity to eliminate. The CEA blamed the sluggishness of investment spending on the long period of inadequate demand that made businessmen cautious in expanding their facilities, particularly with the existence of excess capacity. The council looked to the future, for "plainly, a decisive upward adjustment in the economy's underlying expansionary forces was needed, and it is this the President's 1963 tax program is designed to supply."[25]

New Economics in Practice:
Tax-Cut Proposals, Guideposts, and Trade Policies

As part of the defense buildup of over $3 billion in mid-1961, Kennedy promised to balance the budget when he submitted his first budget six months later. Accordingly, in January 1962 he estimated that a deficit of $7 billion in fiscal year 1962 would be reversed by a surplus of $462 million in fiscal year 1963. The improvement was to come about mainly from an increase in tax receipts following the tax proposals the administration was making, thus giving a boost to GNP of nearly $50 billion for the year. Hopes for a surplus began to fade when the economy faltered in mid-1962, but Kennedy in his now famous speech at the commencement ceremony at Yale Univesity declared his conversion to Keynesian economics and emancipation from the balanced budget shackles of previous administrations. "In our own time we must move on from the reassuring repetition of stale phrases to a new, difficult, but essential confrontation with reality." Yet Heller reminds us that the conversion was not complete, and the president began to waver on his tax proposal in December 1962.[26]

In January all doubts were gone, and he submitted a tax measure that would reduce taxes at a time of an apparent deficit. The talk of balanced budgets was also gone, as was the issue of tax reform. What began in the campaign as a tax-reform movement, including items to revamp the tax treatment of dividends, capital gains, cooperatives, mutual insurance companies, and foreign income now was being billed as a tax-reduction measure.

Wilbur Mills, chairman of the House Ways and Means Committee, was opposed to any tax measure, but particularly one that promised to reduce taxes in the face of a deficit and when no recession was imminent. Mills did favor tax reform, and the president slowly got him around: "Initially Mills agreed to a major tax reform bill, with a little tax reduction to help pass it. When presented, it was a tax reform and tax reduction bill. In testimony it became a tax reduction and tax reform bill. And when it was finally reported out by Mills, the president had his major tax cut bill with a little tax reform."[27] The House passed the bill in October 1963 by a vote of 271–155, but many members were voting for a tax-reduction bill and probably remained unconvinced of Keynesian economics. The Senate was not prepared to act until 1964—too late, of course, to be witnessed by Kennedy.

The Federal Reserve continued its policy of relative monetary ease as the money supply rose in 1962 by 1.5 percent for currency and demand deposits and by 7.5 percent including time deposits. For 1963 the same increases were 3.7 percent and 8 percent, respectively. The Federal Reserve and the Treasury also continued Operation Twist, which together with relative price stability and a slack economy allowed interest rates to remain stable. Short-term rates rose slightly from 2.746 to 2.856 for the year 1962 and then began to climb, until by the end of 1963 they stood at 3.523, an increase of over 23 percent from the start of the year. Long-term rates actually fell in 1962 from 4.08 in January 1962 to 3.87 in December, but again they climbed as well to 4.14 by December of 1963.

In general, the Federal Reserve followed a policy of accommodating the fiscal actions of the executive branch. At first the Federal Reserve, under its chairman, William M. Martin, balked at financing the tax-induced deficit, but later it acquiesced in accommodating the president.[28] It provided the needed liquidity to the banking system, banks continued to have sizable free reserves, and the public built up its stock of liquid assets.

Still, concern over the balance-of-payments problem led the Federal Reserve to increase the discount rate in July 1963 from 3 percent to 3.25 percent and increase the interest rates on time deposits payable in 90 days to one year. Banks could not, presumably, compete with foreign banks for funds that might otherwise go abroad. In any case, the deficits in the balance of payments continued rising to $3.6 billion in 1962 and to $3.3 billion in 1963. Military expenditures, government grants, and both long- and short-term capital outflows were causing the imbalance. President Kennedy sent a special message to Congress in July 1963, proposing an interest-equalization tax on U.S. purchases of foreign securities, which was designed to add approximately 1 percentage point of additional interest cost to the seller. Low interest rates in the United States (the proper domestic policy) made it a target country to raise funds at favorable terms.

In addition, he proposed a policy of "tying" foreign aid to U.S. goods to reduce the dollar outflow from aid programs, military expenditures abroad, and government purchases of material abroad, and he included a program of "See America Now" to encourage travel to the United States.[29] These steps were carefully taken so as not to interfere with the domestic expansion, but in reality were not strong enough to affect the imbalance seriously.

Another attempt to deal with the balance-of-payments problem came from the Trade Expansion Act that was signed into law on October 11, 1962. Hailed as the most important tariff legislation since 1934, the act allowed the president to decrease by 50 percent (or more in special cases) the duty existing on July 1, 1962. The act was aimed at the tariff walls being erected by the European Economic Community (EEC) or Common Market, particularly those for agricultural commodities.

Many firms had invested in Europe to overcome the Common Market's preferential treatment for countries within the bloc, and the resulting capital outflows had adversely affected the balance of payments. These outflows were expected to decline if tariff reductions could be negotiated. Thus, the administration's goals were to reduce capital outflows, encourage domestic investment instead, and alleviate a source of balance-of-payments disequilibrium. Yet the tariff walls of the EEC were slow to fall, and not much progress was made by the "Kennedy Round" of tariff negotiations in 1963.

Critics of the administration's policy saw this act as basically contradictory, since it tried to discourage U.S. capital outflows abroad, while still trying to extend U.S. influence and promote U.S. interests worldwide.[30] Moreover, this liberalization of trade was inconsistent with Keynesian domestic economic policy, as already noted. The drive for full employment would require low interest rates, but they tended to encourage capital outflows. In brief, international liberalism seemed incompatible with domestic liberalism and with the aim of extending U.S. interests abroad.

The recognition that free trade might injure U.S. industries led to a provision in the act that provided for direct assistance to firms and workers seriously injured by tariff concessions. Financial aid, technical assistance, and tax concessions were available to firms, and trade allowances for workers for up to 50 weeks were included to pacify organized labor and to insure passage of the bill.

Trade discussions did instigate a move to review the operation of the IMF, with particular emphasis on the reassessment of the system of fixed exchange rates established at Bretton Woods in 1944. The leading industrial countries—the "Group of Ten"—agreed to study the international monetary system in October 1963. The United States found itself unable to live with the rules of the game, and its deficits were putting strains on the entire system. It was the beginning of many discussions leading up to the eventual abandonment of the Bretton Woods system ten years later.

The Council of Economic Advisors was quick to point out that the gap between potential GNP and actual GNP had remained the same since 1962, namely, about $30 billion. Macroeconomic policies had failed to bring the economy closer to its potential, and again the slowdown was evident. Moreover, the full-employment surplus had risen in 1963 over 1962, indicating that fiscal policy was becoming more restrictive in the face of economic slack. The full-employment surplus rose from about $6.5 billion in 1962 to over $8.5 billion in 1963. Clearly the government was contributing to the slowdown, and the fiscal drag was in operation. The CEA, looking forward to 1964, predicted, "The tax reductions of 1964 will be a giant step to remove a burdensome fiscal restraint *before* the economy levels off or goes into a recession and to provide a framework for continued economic growth."[31]

Other indicators of the performance of the economy were also not encouraging. The unemployment rate that had fallen from a high of 7.0 percent in May 1961 to a low of 5.3 percent in October 1962 began to rise again to 6.1 percent in February before stabilizing in the 5.6 percent area. Unemployment was reflecting the slowdown in the economy, and so was the capacity-utilization rate of manufacturing

Table 9.1   Selected Economic Series, 1961–63 (billions of dollars)

Item	1961	1962	1963	Percent Change, 1961 to 1962	Percent Change, 1962 to 1963
GNP	518.2	554.9	585.0	7.1	5.4
GNP (in 1954 dollars)	447.7	474.8	493.0	6.1	3.8
Consumption	303.6	317.6	329.1	4.6	3.6
Investment	57.5	65.2	67.7	13.4	3.8
Net exports	2.3	1.8	2.5	−21.7	38.9
Government	84.3	90.2	93.8	7.0	4.0
Federal	44.8	49.0	50.6	9.4	3.3
State and local	39.5	41.2	43.2	4.3	4.9
Unemployment rate	6.7	5.6	5.7	−16.4	1.8
Manufacturing output as a percent of capacity-utilization rate	77.6	81.4	83.0	4.9	2.0
Average hourly wage rate in manufacturing	2.32	2.39	2.46	3.0	2.9
Prices					
GNP implicit (1954 = 100)	115.7	116.9	118.7	1.0	1.5
WPI (1957–59 = 100)	100.3	100.6	100.3	0.3	−0.3
CPI (1957–59 = 100)	104.2	105.4	106.7	1.1	1.2

Source: Council of Economic Advisors, *Economic Report of the President (Washington, DC: GPO, 1964).*

firms. While the rate continued to climb, there was still too much excess capacity to encourage investment spending. (See Table 9.1).

Prices remained stable over the period, which may again be a reflection of the slack in the economy. Still, the reduction in wholesale prices was remarkable. Wage rates, at least in manufacturing, maintained a steady rate of growth, well below the rate of growth of productivity in this period, further contributing to the observed price stability. In addition, the wage and price guideposts were still in effect as far as the administration was concerned, as it repeated its commitment to them.

Were the guideposts working? To test such a policy is nearly impossible, since no one knows what the rate of wage increase would have been in the absence of the guidelines. Besides, other explanations could always be offered to explain the price and wage stability. For instance, the fear of inflation and the inflationary psychology could have been broken by the previous recession; there was also increasing competition from foreign trade and foreign competitors, and the pace of the expansion was even and balanced, thus eliminating any bottlenecks. After examining these arguments and the empirical evidence of direct tests of the guideposts in operation, John Sheahan concluded, "They add up to a convincing case that wage behavior in manufacturing became more restrained in the four years following presentation of the guideposts than it had been in the preceding decade."[32] Just precisely how restraining they were is more difficult to answer, but the range in the estimates for combined wage and price effects runs from a low of 0.8 percentage points to about 1.6 percentage points over the period 1962–65.[33] These modest results are not surprising; what is surprising is that the administration would even suggest such a national policy at a time when there was relative price and wage stability. Surely the relationship between wages, productivity, and prices was not a new discovery, but in fact had been around since the time the marginal productivity theory had been developed. What was new was the "official presentation of a more specific set of principles, consistent with efficiency and pointing toward a more active role by the government in shaping the evolution of prices and wages."[34]

One indication of this resolve was made clearly evident in the not very subtle confrontation with the steel industry. The steel industry had long been regarded as the bellwether of inflation—what happened to steel prices determined the overall direction of prices. In September 1961 President Kennedy wrote an open letter to the 12 major steel companies, asking them to forego or restrain price increases after October 1, the date of the automatic wage increase negotiated earlier. The CEA had informed him that the wage increase could be absorbed by the firms without a price increase. Meanwhile, Secretary of Labor Arthur Goldberg had been busy persuading the steelworkers to accept a noninflationary wage increase. Originally they had requested a 17-cent-per-hour increase, which would have been above the wage increase that would have matched the productivity increase in the industry—that is, 12 cents per hour to match the 3 percent productivity increase.

Responding to the administration's pressure, the union agreed to a 10-cent-per-hour increase, which was about a 2.5 percent increase in hourly compensation. On March 31 the contract was signed by the union and the industry. The president was elated and hailed the parties' statesmanship. On April 19, 1962, the United States Steel

Company announced a $6-a-ton increase in the price of steel—a 3.5 percent increase. This move set in motion one of the most interesting confrontations between politicians and businessmen in the annals of U.S. history.

Roger Blough, U.S. Steel chairman, appeared in the late afternoon in Kennedy's office to apprise him of the price increase, news that was soon to be released to the general public. Kennedy was apparently stunned, since no hint of any pending price increase was ever given and other industry leaders were stating that this was not the time to increase steel prices. Competition from abroad was getting troublesome, and profits were high and recovering anyway. At the time Kennedy said only that U.S. Steel was making a mistake, but as the affront to the presidency set in, his anger grew.

Bethlehem Steel Company, one of those previously eschewing price increases, and four other large firms joined in identical price increases. It was difficult to believe that these firms would act so openly without regard for different cost structures, different product mixes, and so on, and in the face of an apparent flouting of the antitrust laws. Still, the guideposts had no legal standing, and other legal actions against the firms appeared inappropriate. In addition, the issue was further clouded by the fact that U.S. Steel was losing market shares and was also losing more profits than its competitors, so that the situation for the industry as a whole was not the same as for U.S. Steel. What was true for the industry in terms of labor productivity and profits was not true for one firm in that industry—the one that raised prices first.

The guideposts were silent about a situation of this kind. In fact, if it were not for the typical "follow-the-leader" pricing of the steel industry, the administration would have found it difficult to justify actions against one firm in an industry. Of course, the actions in the steel industry were just the kind that the guideposts were designed for.[35]

The administration reacted quickly. It threatened antitrust actions, switching of steel suppliers by defense procurers, and, more controversially, letting the FBI investigate to learn what actually happened at the press conference of Bethlehem Steel Company when no price actions were deemed warranted.[36] In addition, administration officials friendly with the steel companies that had not followed the price increase began to pressure them not to do so. Inland and Kaiser Steel Companies were the main targets.

Public opinion was also courted. In a press conference Kennedy's opening statement read in part, "The American people will find it hard, as I do, to accept a situation in which a tiny handful of steel executives whose pursuit of private power and profit exceeds their sense of public responsibility can show utter contempt for the interests of 185 million Americans." These are strong words for a president, but, as he said later, "There is no sense in raising hell and then not being successful." The prestige of the presidency had been tarnished, and Kennedy felt betrayed by the steel executives.

All of these actions combined to coerce the steel industry to back down. First, Inland and Kaiser announced that they would not increase prices. Bethlehem Steel followed by announcing that it would rescind its price increase, and then U.S. Steel rapidly followed in rescinding its price increase in order to meet competition, and others fell in line. The episode was over, but business relations had been badly damaged, despite Kennedy's attempt to be conciliatory.[37]

The larger question remained: What would happen if the guideposts were ignored? Would the spotlight of public opinion be sufficient to bring errants into line? What other threats would or could be made to ensure compliance? If businessmen grew wary, if not hostile, they could hardly be blamed. Still, the question of how a voluntary program was expected to work remained unresolved and posed an obvious limit to further usage, as will become evident in later years.[38]

Other Kennedy Administration Initiatives

On other economic matters, the Kennedy administration made little headway. No action was taken by Congress to give the president standby authority to cut taxes or to give him his standby public-works program. Nor did he receive any permanent improvements in the unemployment compensation system, a mass transit program, a Youth Conservation Corps, higher minimum wages, additional aid for depressed areas, and some new agricultural subsidy programs. Whether or not progress would have been made on these programs in the following year cannot be known, of course, but continued administration efforts might have seen the passage of a few of them.

Yet even before these programs were enacted or the tax-cut bill passed, Kennedy turned his attention to another problem that had been virtually ignored in the 1950s—poverty. Toward the end of 1962 he instructed Heller to collect the data on poverty in the United States in order to tackle the things still to be done.[39] According to Arthur Schlesinger, Kennedy had been heavily influenced by two books, J. K.

Galbraith's *The Affluent Society* and Michael Harrington's *The Other America*, a moving and indignant book on poverty in the United States. "He [Kennedy] was reaching the conclusion that tax reduction required a comprehensive structural counterpart, taking the form, not of piecemeal programs, but of a broad war against poverty itself."[40] The foundation was laid for the war on poverty that was to start in the Johnson administration. Still, the necessary economic analysis was begun in 1963 and appeared in the *Economic Report of the President* of 1964.

Environmental concerns were also growing in the late 1950s and early 1960s. Kennedy signed a water-pollution-control bill that had been vetoed by Eisenhower. Kennedy, however, was not in the forefront of the environmental movement, but was clearly more receptive to recognition of federal responsibility and willing to spend federal dollars on environmental protection. Senator Edmund Muskie of Maine and Representative John Blatnik of Minnesota, both Democrats, took the lead in pressing for more federal involvement in water-pollution controls.

Soon air-pollution-control bills would be debated, and in December the Clean Air Act of 1963 was passed. Bills to protect wildlife areas and provide more recreational facilities were also introduced. The federal government slowly began to assume responsibility for the nation's environment. Indeed, this was the main contribution of the Kennedy administration in this emerging national problem. The nation was aroused, however, not by the debates in Washington but by Rachel Carson's book, *The Silent Spring* (Boston: Houghton Mifflin, 1961), in which the horrors of the careless use of pesticides were exposed.

If the nation had to be educated in the problems of poverty and pollution, it had to be jolted into recognizing the plight of its minorities. In February 1960 four young black students denied service at a lunch counter refused to leave the premises. The nonviolent protest of sit-ins had begun. Soon the tactic would spread to kneel-ins, sit-downs, and so on in the attempt to desegregate facilities and institutions. The nonviolent protests captured the imagination of everyone, and new organizations, such as the Congress of Racial Equality (CORE), led by James Farmer, and the Student Nonviolent Coordinating Committee (SNCC), joined the NAACP and Southern Christian Leadership Conference, headed by Roy Wilkins and Martin Luther King, Jr., respectively. These groups led protests of all kinds, ranging from sit-ins, marches, pray-ins to the freedom riders who rode buses to the South to desegregate public facilities. The Kennedy administration's reaction to all this was minimal, but the civil rights movement gained momentum and forced itself upon the administration and the general public.

Concern for the poor was also growing, domestically and internationally. The Kennedy administration initiated two projects that were sources of pride for it and for Kennedy in particular. The first, the "food for peace" program, saw the United States distributing surplus food to poor nations, sometimes giving it away, sometimes loaning it, and sometimes accepting local currency in payment. The second was the Peace Corps. Marshaling the idealism of thousands of Americans, mostly young, the Peace Corps sent these volunteers into many countries to use their skills in projects that directly helped the poor. They built schools, helped in land improvements, and so on. Many felt the program to be largely symbolic, but its head, Sargent Shriver, was enthusiastic and mobilized many who responded to Kennedy's call to give of themselves for the benefit of others.

In addition, Kennedy's concern for Latin America found expression in his program born out of a campaign speech that came to be labeled the Alliance for Progress. The United States promised assistance to Latin America for technical assistance, long-term development loans, stabilization of export prices, programs of land reforms, and support for democracy. The August 1961 agreement called for the United States to supply $20 billion for economic development, while 19 other nations agreed to increase their own contributions for economic and social development and for domestic reforms.

Perhaps these Kennedy initiatives were more symbolic than substantive, more idealistic than reasoned responses, and soon other challenges would occupy the administration. The first would prove embarrassing. The Russians had orbited a man around the earth, and the administration, seeking at first to cooperate with the Soviets in space exploration, was rebuffed and then took up the challenge. In May 1961 Kennedy vowed to land a man on the moon before the decade was out. The race to the moon was on, as national pride dictated that this feat be accomplished ahead of the Russians. The cost was put at $20 billion, and many questioned the need when the money could be spent in so many other ways. Why talk of poverty and spend to get to the moon? The New Frontier called for priority in space, and the budget requests went up; in 1961 $0.7 billion was spent on space research and technology; in 1961 $1.3 billion; in 1963 $2.6 billion.

National chauvinism and the desire to exhibit technical superiority can help explain the race to obtain first place in the space race. Of course, national defense cannot be ruled out as another powerful rationale for pursuing space technology. Another confrontation between the superpowers, however, nearly made the race irrelevant. In October 1962 the Cuban missile crisis brought the world to the brink of war that fortunately was averted.

The turbulent 1960s had begun, and the serenity of the Eisenhower years was shattered. These trends would continue throughout the decade and influence the economy in many ways, some observable and some that can only be postulated. Neither the society nor the economy would ever again be the same—the continuity of which gave the characterization of dullness to the Eisenhower era.

Evaluation of the Kennedy Administration's Policies

To evaluate the Kennedy economic program it is first necessary to avoid the myths and legends that have developed around his administration. Kennedy's White House became Camelot to the captivated press corps, and his personal charm, wealth, and appearance, combined with his equally charming family, helped to create the climate out of which myths are born. His tragic death in Dallas magnified him in the eyes of a shocked nation. When his assassin, Lee Harvey Oswald, was himself killed by Jack Ruby on live television, the drama was heightened. Since the controversy over the circumstances of his assassination has never ceased, the mystery serves only to reinforce the legendary aura surrounding him and his presidency.[41]

Turning first to the question of whether or not his economic policies were justified, it is clear that the evidence is mixed and still controversial. In retrospect, we know that the economy had begun to recover before he took office or shortly thereafter. The recovery probably would have continued without the New Frontier and perhaps despite it. It is equally probable that the recovery would have been a weak one, since economic stagnation was evident in the U.S. economy for the latter half of the 1950s and was likely to continue in the early 1960s. No doubt some would have preferred such a recovery to increased government intervention. Indeed, that controversy has continued to the present.

Nevertheless, the New Economics made its real debut in the Kennedy administration. The Keynesian paradigm simply could not be forestalled, once economic advisors were committed to it in both theory and policy. The confluence of economic advisors, a receptive president, and an ideal economic situation in which to experiment with the approaches made the application of Keynesian ideas almost inevitable. Whether or not this coalescence of factors is sufficient to justify a departure from past policymaking thus depends as much on ideological predilection as on objective analysis.

It is possible to look upon the philosophy that sanctions and encourages more government intervention in the economy with horror or to welcome it as long overdue. The point here is that the Keynesian model, so long in developing since it was expounded, finally could not be suppressed any longer. The time had come for its adoption in a practical sense. The turn toward fiscal policy and away from monetary policy was just what was needed for an administration that had promised to get the country moving again and reach new frontiers. The previous orthodoxy simply would not allow such experimentation nor excite the imagination to accept change, and change was needed.

Clearly the political pressures to change course were there, but the social pressures were not. There was no clamoring for new directions in policymaking emanating from a disenchanted public. Indeed, the acceptance of the New Economics came slowly even to the president, and the public was even farther removed. Walter Heller patiently educated both, but was more successful with the former.

In the end the justification for the change in direction of policymaking and the acceptance of the new paradigm came not from pressures for change, not from a pressing economic condition, but from an unstoppable evolution of ideas that now found an ideal outlet for expression and employment. Once the corner was turned, macroeconomic policymaking would never be the same, nor would the role of the public sector in the economy. Walter Heller could write that economics came of age in the 1960s.[42]

If economics came of age in the 1960s, and more particularly the New Economics, much of the credit belongs to the Eisenhower administration. Eisenhower gave the Kennedy administration a stagnating economy that furnished the rallying cry of the New Frontier to get the country moving again. More important, the Eisenhower administration's unwillingness to alter its policies in the face of a recession allowed just enough acceptance for something new that the Kennedy economists had an easier time than might otherwise have been the case. Eisenhower's defense of the balanced-budget philosophy, the reliance on monetary policy, and the protests over government meddling in the economy still did not prevent the occurrence of recessions every few years. Some impatience with the past policies was inevitable.

This is not to suggest that the acceptance of Keynesian economics came easily or was embraced by all. The failure of the Eisenhower policies, however, did help to remove some obstacles to the new ideas;

why would new policies be devised or attempted if the old ones had been successful?

Just as important, if not as readily identifiable, are the changes in the society that accompanied the new administration. Economic policymaking is not made in a vacuum, as we must be reminded continuously, and may be affected by seemingly extraneous events. If the society was being slowly transformed through its concerns for poverty, civil rights, and environmental problems, and if it was being made uneasy by missiles, threats of war, space races, and so on, would changes in economic thinking be out of order? In a period when much commonplace thinking was being challenged, it is not unlikely that some of that spirit would affect economic orthodoxy as well. The institutional changes that were taking place, or about to, could be expected to affect all facets of life in the early 1960s.

Changes in foreign policy were forced on the new administration, as has been pointed out, but also changes in international trade relations were thrust upon it in the form of the Common Market. The threat to U.S. hegemony was hardly welcomed by the administration, and a response had to be made. Thus the Kennedy Round of tariff negotiations that was hailed by everyone was really a defensive move forced upon the administration. Yet the move was accepted as necessary to meet the requirements of a changing world community.

How successful was the Kennedy administration in implementing policies for the new conditions? Looking first at the trade problems, the Kennedy Round, Operation Twist, buy American pleas, the interest-equalization tax, the controls on lending overseas, the reduction in duty-free tourist imports, and the attempt to tie foreign aid to purchases in the United States were all policies designed to reduce the outflow of capital and correct balance-of-payments deficits. They were not very successful and could only slow the deterioration in the short run. These solutions did not address the real problems of U.S. trade or of international world trade in general.

The IMF needed overhauling, and the entire exchange rate mechanisms, the question of adequate reserves, and the role of the dollar in financing world trade needed to be reexamined. The gold exchange standard, with the dollar at its center, was breaking down, and although there was some recognition of this, little was being done officially. Monetary reforms were needed, but the United States was not ready to take the lead in seeking them at this time. The Kennedy administration was caught between conflicting goals. Domestically, it wanted to pursue its growth policies through Keynesian economics, but this conflicted with its desires to promote liberalization of world trade and development. For the former, capital outflows were seen as detrimental for the pressure they would put on interest rates; for the latter, capital outflows represented the spread of U.S. hegemony and the opening up of world markets. The contradiction between domestic and foreign policies led the administration to ad hoc measures designed to forestall the confrontation between them and avoid the resolution of which should take precedence. In the end, little was accomplished in resolving the trade problems either of the United States or of the world.

In domestic matters economic growth became the primary goal, and the elimination of the gap between potential and actual GNP became the indicator of achievement. Other goals of the economy, such as justice in the distribution of the output, would have to wait until the proper rate of growth had been reached. To this end, two basically probusiness policies were instituted: the investment tax credit and accelerated depreciation allowances. After some reluctance on the part of those who stood to benefit, these programs turned out to be somewhat successful. Businessmen had to overcome their distrust of a Democratic president and eventually took advantage of the tax breaks. Still, the failure to confine the tax credit to new net investment instead of gross investment often meant a profit subsidy rather than a stimulus to investment and economic growth.

If the switch to a more active government intervention into the economy should result in pressures on inflation, the administration proposed the guideposts. Used as a guide to the proper noninflationary wage increase, firms could determine their wage policies with the understanding that other firms would be doing likewise. Overt collusion was not necessary, a national standard would do just as well. Labor, meanwhile, would have to settle for a constant real share of the national output, for wage increases would match the productivity change and no more. A constant income share would be acceptable in the long run only if the original distribution of output was regarded as equitable. Since it was not, labor's cooperation would last only as long as the goodwill toward the president was operative and then would gradually erode. This came later, but in the Kennedy years the guidepost policy probably helped to modify some wage demands, and for a while this voluntary program had some minimal success. Being voluntary, however, meant that the government was using up some of its prestige and clout for a program without teeth and possibly preventing the enactment of a stronger program, should the voluntary one fail. Failure would be used to suggest that all government attempts along these lines would be futile, instead of judging only the one that failed. Those who look for evidence that government intervention is to be avoided will find it, regardless of whether such evidence is appropriate; the risk of this voluntary program seemed too great and the rewards too minimal.

For households the tax cut was designed to stimulate consumption. Thus, the administration sought to increase the spending of all sectors of demand—investment, consumption, government, and exports. This is typical Keynesian demand-side policy that follows from the analysis of the cause of economic stagnation. Tax reform was sacrificed early in return for action on tax reduction. That action came in 1964, but the groundwork was laid in the Kennedy administration.

Thus the real success of the Kennedy administration was in education. The Keynesian model and policies that flow from it had to be explained, and fiscal policy, deficit spending, fiscal drag, and the full-employment surplus made familiar before they could be made acceptable. This the Kennedy economists did and did quite well. Fully committed to the vision of Keynes, they were able to communicate their ideas with passion and patience, until many skeptics were willing to try the experiment. Of course, the spending and tax proposals made good political sense as well, and again the timely introduction of the New Economics is evident.

It is difficult and perhaps even unfair to judge the Kennedy administration in terms of success or failure of its economic policies. Just when it appeared to be making some headway in getting its programs adopted, the president was assassinated. With that act the entire picture changed, making all judgments suspect and premature. It is not known what new directions the administration might have taken, so it is prudent to avoid final assessments and settle for the preliminary ones made in the above discussion. It will be necessary and interesting, however, to trace the incomplete policies into the next administration, which would benefit from the progress already made.

Were the policies rational in terms of their desire to reach well-defined goals without ulterior motives or to reach unstated goals? The answer is basically affirmative, for in the process of educating everyone, administration economists were forced to be fairly explicit and open as to what they hoped to achieve and how they hoped to achieve it. The main goal of economic growth was clearly designated, and the closing of the gap between potential and actual GNP clearly spelled out the terms of success or failure. Less successful explanations of the benefits of budget deficits can be traced to years of indoctrination into the reverse conclusions. It would be difficult to reverse previous definitions of sound financial policy in a short time period.

What was misleading was the belief that economists could manipulate the economy with a high degree of accuracy. In their zeal to explain procedures, and later in the euphoria following the tax cut, administration economists oversold their knowledge and ability to prescribe for the economy. In Heller's unhappy phrase, they could "fine tune" the economy. Just find some expression of society's wants in the economy—level of unemployment and what price-level change—and the economists could secure that combination or any other. This trade-off, as understood by the Phillips Curve, just coming into vogue, was available in any number of combinations, and given a goal, macroeconomic policies could be utilized to reach it. While their zeal to gain acceptance of their methodology is certainly understandable, there were insufficient warnings that the adoption of Keynesian economics might lead to other problems for which the model was not well suited—for example, inflation. The political implications of Keynesian economics were not adequately expressed, either. Once the lessons of Keynesian economics were learned by politicians, was there not the risk that the message would be learned too well and perverted for political purposes?

Administration economists stressed the positive aspects of the model without considering how the model would be treated, once it fell into less responsible hands. Understandable as this bias may be, the end result may have been to defeat the approach in the longer run. Being oversold, the model was bound to fail, for it could not live up to all its promises. This, of course, was not the intent of Keynesian economists, but they did set up an unattainable ideal in order to convince others of their beliefs. If they had wanted the model to fail, it would have been rational to oversell it and, when it did fail, lead the others back to a pre-Keynesian world.

Thus these Keynesian economists did a disservice to their own convictions. Focusing on growth and stabilization as the major concerns of their analysis, they were aware of distribution problems and economic-freedom matters, but just to gain acceptance they had to achieve dramatic quick results, and longer-run problems would have to be sacrificed. For example, tax reform was a quick casualty in the quest for a tax measure. And almost like an afterthought was the recognition that the drive for economic growth would leave some people behind and that poverty should receive more attention. Again, it is not the sincerity of these economists that is at issue here; it is only that the claims made for their model resulted in the attention focused on growth to the exclusion of other targets. Politicians and business-men could accept growth as a target and relaxed their opposition only to that extent. In effect, they accepted only part of the Keynesian message—the part they liked and reasoned would benefit them.

In the end the real Keynesian message became distorted, and the administration economists must bear some responsibility for it. Not many understood the Keynesian analysis of the troubles of capitalism, nor would they have been ready to accept the socialization of investment. If aggregate demand could be assured, however, firms could operate with more certainty and politicians could manipulate the economy to affect election outcomes. Again administration economists must bear some responsibility for the misinterpretation of the Keynesian model and its misapplication.

The dilemma of the Kennedy administration in the area of international trade has already been mentioned. On the one hand, it wanted to pursue Keynesian economics at home, while continuing to press for the liberalization of trade for the world. Its policies in this area were clearly insufficient for the problem, and it tried to retain the old monetary system that was incompatible with domestic monetary conditions. Were its attempts designed to fail and force changes in the international financial arrangements? Or were they simply holding actions, because there were no ready answers? In either case it was less than candid.

Businessmen could respond to the liberalization of trade, since they stood ready to benefit. U.S. firms were searching the globe for investment opportunities and sales outlets, and the world as a great trading place had immediate appeal to them. So, too, were the investment tax credit and accelerated depreciation methods acceptable. Reluctant at first, they came to appreciate the investment tax credit, especially after they received the desired depreciation liberalization as well. These programs make sense if the goal is economic growth, but a side effect is to make it profitable to substitute capital for labor in the production process. If the main goal is full employment of labor, the policy is contradictory. The bias in favor of capital is obvious, and a capital shortage is assumed.

Otherwise a labor investment tax credit could have been proposed. Costs of training the unemployed could have received a tax break. Such a program would have attacked the unemployment problem directly, rather than subsidize firms to buy capital goods that might provide jobs in the short run but eliminate them in the long run.

Some of these criticisms are more clearly visible in hindsight, and no blanket condemnation is warranted or intended. Still, they add up to an indictment of those who oversold a misinterpretated model to an audience that accepted only parts of it. Later, when Keynesian economics was said to have failed, it would be the wrong model that had been tried and found unacceptable. To this end the early exponents must bear some of the blame for the model's misapplication. In the following chapters we will have the opportunity to observe the evolution of the model in use and its later rejection.

chapter 10

Lyndon B. Johnson
and the Great Society

On November 22, 1963, Lyndon Baines Johnson was sworn in as the thirty-sixth president of the United States. The ceremony took place aboard Air Force One, while the recent widow looked on, benumbed, as were the other 26 witnesses aboard the presidential plane. A shocked nation began a period of mourning, not just for the slain man, but for the loss of part of the American Dream and its promise; national shame and hurt replaced self-confidence and idealism.

Probably no one felt more confounded than Johnson. Alienated and often ridiculed by Kennedy's men, he now had to reconstruct the government and make it operational again. He managed to persuade the cabinet to stay on by appealing to their loyalty to Kennedy; if he had needed them, Johnson needed them more.[1] Johnson later revealed that he respected intelligent men and viewed Kennedy's appointments as excellent ones. Lacking their respect, he would earn it by picking up the pieces of Kennedy's unfinished program before putting his stamp on the presidency.

The transition phase of the new administration was cleverly put by Mr. Johnson, when he added to Kennedy's inaugural words, "Let us begin ... ," the phrase, "Let us continue ...". In his stirring speech to Congress on November 27 he made this quite clear by declaring: "First, no memorial oration or eulogy could more eloquently honor President Kennedy's memory than the earliest passage of the civil rights bill for which he fought so long. ... And second, no act of ours could more fittingly continue the work of President Kennedy than the

early passage of the tax bill for which he fought all this long year."
This eloquent apeech, written by J. K. Galbraith, Ted Sorensen, and
Abe Fortas, earned Johnson the respect of the nation, and his devotion
to the programs of President Kennedy led him to seek passage of the
pending business by seeking a consensus among opposing views. The
word "consensus" stuck as a label for this transition administration.

The Johnson administration moved quickly on the tax cut.
Johnson applied his well-known lobbying pressure, carried over from
his former duties as Senate majority leader, to members of Congress
who were already feeling sympathetic to the programs of the slain
president. Johnson was eager to evoke the name of Kennedy in the
hopes that the sympathy and sorrow would be translated into action on
bills that the late president favored. Thus the Senate moved quickly to
enact the tax bill, and on February 26, 1964, the Revenue Act of 1964
was signed into law by the new president, declaring that this was "the
single most important step that we have taken to strengthen our
economy since World War II."

Many agreed with President Johnson. The tax cut of 1964 would
come to represent the triumph of Keynesian economics, and the new
economists hailed the action. The tax reduction would soon show the
benefits of fiscal policy, and the results would provide the standard for
Keynesian economics in practice.

The act reduced taxes for individuals by about 20 percent or by
over $11 billion (at 1964 levels of income) over 1964 and 1965.
Marginal tax rates were reduced in stages to a range of 14–70 percent
from 20–91 percent, but, more important, withholding rates were
immediately cut from 18 percent to 14 percent to encourage consumption spending. In addition, tax rates on corporations were reduced from
52 to 48 percent, or by some $3 billion at 1964 levels of income. This
was the largest single tax reduction in history; it was, of course,
designed to reduce the impact of taxes on the economy, but it also
removed some $1.5 million from the taxpayer rolls by providing a
minimum standard deduction.

Being a truly revolutionary measure, the Revenue Act of 1964
has generated a great deal of controversy. Just how successful was it in
the expansion of demand and consequent economic growth? In the first
place, many things were happening in 1964 and 1965. There was a
presidential election in 1964 and a defense buildup that was in the
initial stages in 1965. In the second place, the economy was already
expanding since 1961, which probably would have continued in the
absence of a tax measure. It is therefore difficult to measure the impact
of the tax cut when the rest of the world does not stand still. Yet that is

a familiar complaint about empiricism in economics and should not dissuade attempts to calculate the best estimates with the tools that are at hand.

More important is the criticism of monetarists who claim that monetary policy is responsible for the observed increase in national income over the period. To those who consider the rate of growth of the money supply to be the main explanatory factor in the determination of the level of national income, the accommodating monetary policy of the Federal Reserve System explains the growth in GNP, not the tax cut. The easy-money policy saw the money supply (M1) grow steadily from about 3 percent in 1963, to 4 percent, to 4.2 percent in the next few years. The monetary base (bank reserves plus currency) grew at similar rates.[2]

The Keynesians countered with their own estimates of the effectiveness of the tax cut, which showed that the initial tax cuts had been multiplied, as people consumed a large fraction (95 percent) of their tax reductions. These expenditures were in turn respent by other consumers, and with the investment stimulated by the increases in consumption, the national income grew by $24 billion (annual rate) by the second quarter of 1965, and eventually by $36 billion in total ($25.9 billion attributed to the individual tax reduction and $10.3 to the corporate tax reduction, giving multipliers of 2.59 and 3.4, respectively).[3] Using the annual change in the full-employment surplus as an indicator of fiscal policy, the tax cut was to prove the largest stimulus in the decade (see Table 10.1).

Not only was the tax cut effective in stimulating economic growth, but it also almost wiped out the full employment surplus of $11 billion that was acting as a drag on the economy.[4] "Thus," wrote Heller, "the rationale of the 1964 tax-cut proposal came straight out of the country's postwar textbooks."[5] The economy performed just as predicted, and the new economists were basking in the glory of their success.

The question of which side is correct in claiming the credit for the expansion in the economy, following the tax cut of 1964, cannot be conclusively settled, and the debate continues still. While it appears that the Keynesians have a stronger argument, the monetarists have not surrendered. In either case, the success came from the demand-side stimulus. In the 1980s the 1964 tax cut would be used as a precedent to justify massive tax cuts designed ostensibly to affect the supply side. While the stimulus to incentives that stem from tax reductions were, and probably always will be, part of the justification for tax reductions, the primary aim of the 1964 cuts was to stimulate spending, both consumption and investment. Nor was there any pretense that the tax

Table 10.1 Government Finances in Kennedy-Johnson Period, 1961-69 (billions of dollars)

Year	1961	1962	1963	1964	1965	1966	1967	1968	1969
Fiscal-year basis									
Receipts	94.4	99.7	106.6	112.7	116.8	130.9	149.6	153.7	187.8
Expenditures	97.8	106.8	111.3	118.6	118.4	134.7	158.3	178.8	184.5
Surplus or deficit (−)	−3.4	−7.1	−4.8	−5.9	−1.6	−3.8	−8.7	−25.2	3.2
Calendar-year basis									
National income and product accounts basis									
Receipts	98.3	106.4	114.5	115.0	124.7	142.5	151.2	175.4	200.6
Expenditures	102.1	110.3	113.9	118.1	123.5	142.8	163.6	181.6	191.3
Surplus or Deficit (−)	−3.8	−3.8	0.7	−3.0	1.2	−0.2	−12.4	−6.2	9.3
High-employment-budget basis									
Receipts	109.2	113.8	121.8	119.2	124.2	139.3	153.1	175.7	203.3
Expenditures	100.4	109.4	112.8	117.5	123.2	142.9	163.6	181.7	191.7
Surplus or deficit (−)	8.8	4.4	9.0	1.8	1.0	−3.6	−10.5	−6.0	11.7
Change in surplus from preceding year	−4.2	−4.4	4.6	−7.2	−0.8	−4.6	−6.9	4.5	17.7
Change as a Percent of full employment GNP	−0.7	−0.7	0.7	−1.1	−0.1	−0.6	−0.9	0.5	1.9

Source: Council of Economic Advisors, *Economic Report of the President*, (Washington, DC: GPO, 1971), pp. 272–75.

309

cut would so greatly increase revenues from the expanding economy that they would more than cover the revenues lost from taxes.[6]

Thus the 1964 tax cut was truly a turning point in the history of macroeconomic policymaking. It became a symbol of success of Keynesian theory, or the New Economics, and the proof of the correctness of the paradigm. Any account of the history of macroeconomic policymaking is thus forced to return again and again to this initial experiment in Keynesian fiscal policy.

The War on Poverty

The second item of unfinished business was quickly transformed into the first Johnson program. On Johnson's first day in office, Walter Heller sought direction from the new president concerning the issue of poverty. The CEA had been directed by Kennedy to study the problem of poverty, but no plans were made to implement any particular program of action. When asked whether the CEA should continue its work, Johnson responded, "I'm interested. I'm sympathetic. Go ahead. Give it the highest priority. Push ahead full tilt."[7] This was the kind of program the populist president could embrace with enthusiasm; there was the opportunity to aid the disadvantaged with whom he identified and to use the presidency to speak out for the unrepresented. With characteristic gusto, Johnson deftly managed to make poverty a national issue and gathered the necessary consensus to move forward on a national program. When he was through, "it was not only bad politics but quite immoral to question the propriety of the government's attack on poverty."[8]

In his first State of the Union speech on January 8, 1964, he announced, "This administration today, here and now, declares unconditional war on poverty in America." The war on poverty faced considerable opposition, but the Economic Opportunity Act was finally passed in August 1964. When he signed the act on August 20, Johnson declared that "today, for the first time in all the history of the human race, a great nation is able to make and is willing to make a commitment to eradicate poverty among its people."[9]

The commitment, however, did not match the rhetoric. The administration took $500 million from a program for manpower training already in the budget and transferred it to the Office of Economic Opportunity (OEO), the agency set up to fight the war. Another $500 million was obtained from a $1.3 billion reduction in defense spending. Thus Sargent Shriver, the head of OEO, was given $1 billion to fight the battle against poverty in the United States.

Although the administration of the Economic Opportunity Act was in Washington, most of the programs were designed to be administered at the local level. They included programs of education, job training, and work experience for the young: for example, Head Start for preschool children; Upward Bound for precollege students in campus programs; Job Opportunities in the Business Section (JOBS); Neighborhood Youth Corps for part-time jobs for teenagers; Volunteers in Service for America (VISTA), a domestic Peace Corps; Community Action Programs (CAP) that planned and operated a variety of programs in health, housing, employment services, and free legal services.

Not since the New Deal had social programs proliferated so rapidly. Some were bound to fail, some to achieve a modest success, and some to prove remarkably successful—Head Start, for instance. There is no doubt that Johnson viewed himself as the successor to FDR, a man he greatly admired, but the resources to do the job of eliminating poverty were to prove woefully insufficient.

Who were the poor and how many were there? Poverty had been and will always be difficult to define, and one could quibble about any definition offered. The CEA, recognizing this, decided to define poverty in terms of food consumption. If one-third of a family's expenditures went for food, then some calculation of the needs of a family of four in terms of food requirements could be obtained. This latter figure, representing a minimum food allowance, could then be multiplied by three to obtain a minimum income level necessary for a family of four to exist. In 1963 that level of income was calculated to be about $3,000. With this definition the CEA found that 33,440,000 persons were living in poverty, about 18 percent of the total population.

The CEA's calculations of the minimum income necessary did not, however, adjust for family size, for type of residential area—rural or urban—for the sex of the head of the household, and so on. The calculations were criticized for these failures, which threatened to divert attention away from the plight of the poor. Mollie Orshansky of the Social Security Administration attempted to make the necessary adjustments and concluded that 34 million persons were living in poverty. This was not far different from the CEA's estimate and neither was the cut-off income level for a family of four, $3,130. (Orshansky's methodology has been used to the present, being adjusted only for inflation.)[10]

Again, any definition of poverty must be somewhat arbitary. Indeed, some would go beyond the bare-necessities definition to include items that would increase the number of poor if some minimum standard of living were considered. In any case, as Michael Harrington told us, we should not allow "statistical quibbling to obscure the huge, enormous, and intolerable fact of poverty in America."[11] After all, in 1963, 44 percent of the poor were children, and one-third of them were living in households where the head was employed!

The success or failure of the war on poverty will be determined as the record unfolds. The real importance of drawing attention to the existence of poverty in the United States, aside from the immediate programs to combat it, goes beyond the initial recognition to the rising expectations of the poor that such attention fostered, and the conscience of the nation that was piqued, as poverty amidst plenty became a moral issue difficult to rationalize. As a result of these and other factors, such as the steady expansion of the national income, transfer payments and social programs were allowed to grow and find a permanent place in the acceptable activities of the public sector. The consequences of these factors will also have to be reviewed in the years ahead.

The Post-Tax-Cut Expansion and the Great Society

In addition to the antipoverty act, Congress also passed other liberal programs in 1964. Among them were a mass transit bill and several natural-resource measures. It also enacted additional regulations on the securities industries by forcing more disclosure information on stock traded over the counter, and passed the interest-equilization tax on foreign securities already mentioned. It failed, however, to act on Medicare for the aged, on aid to public schools, on more funds for depressed areas, and on special programs for the Appalachia region. With a great deal of reluctance, Congress extended the temporary excise taxes again, as it had done since 1954.[12]

Johnson was rather anxious about demonstrating his frugality, lest the Great Society be sacrificed as unaffordable. Accordingly he pared down the budget, including the defense cut of $1.3 billion, to keep expenditures below the $100 billion mark. He estimated expenditures for FY 1964 to be $97.9 billion, with receipts of $93 billion, for a deficit of $4.9 billion. The growth of GNP was supposed to bring in additional revenue, reduce the deficit, and move toward the cherished balanced budget. Actual deficits turned out to be $5.9 billion for FY 1964 and $1.6 billion for FY 1965. Johnson did not mention that the requests for obligational authority totaled over the $100 billion mark, and larger future expenditures were a certainty.

The economy was expanding nicely, however, with GNP growing by 7.1 percent to $632.4 billion in 1964 and 8.3 percent to $684.9 in

1965, both in nominal terms, and by 5.5 percent and 6.3 percent in real terms for the same years. This marked the fourth year in the expansion that had begun in 1961 (see Table 10.2). Prices were fairly stable in 1964, rising by 1.6 percent in the GNP deflator, −0.6 in the WPI, and 1.3 percent in the CPI. In 1965, however, prices were beginning to increase faster; for the first six months, the increases were small, but as the year wore on, prices began to accelerate, and by year's end the average increases for the year were 2.2 percent, 4.2 percent, and 1.7 percent for the GNP deflator, the WPI, and the CPI. Fears of creeping inflation were expressed, but were deemed premature by most economists basking in the success of the fiscal-policy actions.

From 1964 to 1965 sales were growing by over 8 percent, corporate profits by over 21 percent, industrial production by over 9 percent, and manufacturers were using much more of their capacity, up to about 89 percent. Clearly the economy was taking off in a healthy expansion, and early signs of trouble were discounted.

Only the unemployment rate was disturbing. In 1964 the rate slowly declined from 6.2 percent in January to 5.4 percent in December, a rate regarded as too high, given the administration's goal of 4 percent. In December 1965 the rate declined to 4.4 percent, much closer to the targeted rate. The slow decline in the unemployment rate was attributed to the number of new entrants into the labor force and the growth in the productivity of labor; from 1964 to 1965 the increases were approximately 2 percent in the labor force and 3 percent in the productivity of labor in manufacturing. The slow decline in the unemployment rate probably enabled the passage of the cuts in excise taxes that were enacted in 1965. The reductions in excise taxes had long been promised, ever since they were imposed as temporary during World War II. The cuts were spread out until 1969, a total of $4.7 billion. The immediate effect was a reduction of $1.8 billion in June 1965, with another reduction scheduled for January 1, 1966, of $1.6 billion.

Economists within and outside the administration were pleased with the economic expansion and were wary of anything that might halt the upswing. Indeed, many applauded when Wright Patman, chairman of the House Banking and Currency Committee, a long-time foe of the Federal Reserve, began in 1964 to attack it, lest it follow the monetary policy of the Eisenhower administration and slow the recovery. He proposed to revamp the Federal Reserve System in order to give the executive branch more control over the conduct of monetary policy. To illustrate the essence of the proposal, he would have replaced the board of governors and the Open-Market Committee with a 12-member board headed by the secretary of the Treasury and the

TABLE 10.2 Selected Economic Series, 1965–68

Item	1964 Amount	1964 Percent Change from 1963	1965 Amount	1965 Percent Change from 1964	1966 Amount	1966 Percent Change from 1965	1967 Amount	1967 Percent Change from 1966	1968 Amount	1968 Percent Change from 1967
GNP*	632.4	7.1	684.9	8.3	749.9	9.5	793.5	5.8	865.7	9.1
GNP (in 1958 dollars*	581.1	5.5	617.8	6.3	658.1	6.5	674.6	2.5	707.6	4.9
Consumption	373.7	5.8	397.7	6.4	418.1	5.1	430.3	2.9	452.6	5.2
Investment	87.8	6.4	99.2	13.0	109.3	10.2	100.8	−7.8	105.7	4.9
Net exports	8.3	48.2	6.2	−25.3	4.2	−32.3	3.6	−14.3	0.9	−75.0
Government	111.2	1.4	114.7	3.1	126.5	10.3	140.0	10.6	148.4	6.0
Federal	58.1	−2.4	57.9	−0.3	65.4	13.0	74.8	14.4	78.9	5.5
State and local	53.2	6.2	56.8	6.8	61.1	7.6	65.2	6.7	69.5	6.6

Unemployment rate (percent)	5.2	-8.8	4.5	-13.5	3.8	-15.6	3.8	0	3.6	-5.3
Manufacturing capacity-utilization rate (percent)	85.7	2.9	88.5	3.3	90.5	2.3	85.3	-5.7	84.6	-0.8
Output per hour of all persons (percent change)		3.7		3.3		2.5		1.9		3.2
Unit labor costs (percent change)		1.0		0.1		3.4		3.4		3.8
Prices: Percent change in										
GNP Index		1.6		2.2		3.3		2.9		4.5
WPI		-0.6		4.2		6.6		-3.4		2.4
CPI		1.3		1.7		2.9		2.9		4.2

*GNP figures in billions of dollars.

Source: Council of Economic Advisors, *Economic Report of the President* (Washington, DC: GPO, 1970, 1978).

others appointed by the president for four-year terms. In addition, he would have required the Federal Reserve to prevent the yields of government securities from rising above 4.25 percent.

These provisions and others surely would have transformed monetary policy in the United States, but of course they were never enacted, as opposition to them was immediate and widespread. The Federal Reserve was put on notice, however, that the administration would not tolerate any interference with the economic recovery. Thus the administration was appalled when Federal Reserve Board Chairman Martin made a speech in June 1965 in which he stated that he saw some "disquieting similarities" between the present state of the economy and that of the 1920s prior to the depression. Administration denials were swift, but could not prevent the shiver that swept through the economy.

Then, in December 1965 this plucky chairman maneuvered the Federal Reserve Board into increasing the discount rate from 4.0 percent to 4.5 percent.[13] (An earlier increase in the discount rate to 4.0 percent was made in November 1964 in response to an increase in the bank rate of Britain to prevent capital outflows.) The move toward monetary restraint angered the administration, which argued that the Federal Reserve should not have acted prior to the release of the budget. Later the administration economists were to admit that the move toward monetary restraint was a proper one.[14] Previously the monetary policy could be described as accommodating, with the money supply growing by over 4 percent in both 1964 and 1965, up from the 2–3 percent range in the previous three years.

Meanwhile, the Great Society programs were being enacted. In March federal aid to Appalachia was approved; in April federal grants to education were authorized and manpower programs were extended and expanded; in July Medicare was passed, providing medical-care insurance to the aged, and at the same time Social Security benefits were increased, retroactive to January 1, 1965—while Social Security taxes were raised, effective January 1966; in August health-center grants to states were enacted, community health services were extended, a housing program for low-income families was passed (providing for rent subsidies), grants were made available for water and sewage facilities, as were grants and loans to depressed areas of $3.25 billion for public works; in October water- and air-pollution programs were established, vocational school student loans were granted, and federal grants for medical school construction, scholarships, and libraries were authorized; and in December federal scholarships for needy students and loan guarantees for others were established. These and other programs were enacted, largely through the famous Johnson techniques of pleading, bullying, bargaining, and dealing, which were successful in getting these controversial programs passed by a bewildered Congress.

As the Great Society was flowering, the reason for its eventual demise was also. In August 1964 U.S. destroyers were provoking the North Vietnamese and the Chinese into revealing radar installations. As they moved close to the North Vietnamese coast, they were fired upon (there is still some doubt about this), and shortly thereafter the U.S. Senate passed the Tonkin Gulf Resolution, giving the president broad powers to retaliate and respond. The secret involvement became public in 1964 and in 1965 became obvious, as the controversial Vietnam War began in earnest.

The economic costs in 1965 were minimal, about $103 million, and Johnson estimated that another $2 billion would be required to cover the cost of U.S. troops. From this date on, there would be a series of underestimations of the cost of the war, misleading reports of when it would end, budgetary miscalculations, and so on. The consequences for the society and the economy would be immense and staggering. Students demonstrated on the Berkeley campus in the first evidence of the revolt of the young, and blacks rioted in the ghettos of Watts in Los Angeles in August—the first responses to the failure of reality to live up to the rising expectations. As 1965 came to a close, however, there was still confusion over the war—particularly as to how long it would last. Thus the main concern was how the added defense expenditures would affect the economy. The CEA was reassuring in its annual report,[15] but a note of caution crept into its analysis. There was more talk of inflation, now that the output gap had shrunk to only $10 billion and the economy showed signs of heating up. Could we have both guns and butter? Mr. Johnson answered yes, and in 1965 it was possible to believe him, but the New Economics was about to be tested for the first time, even before its lessons had become fully acceptable.

The Vietnam Conflict and the Transformation of the Economy

With the Vietnam War now out into the open, the country was becoming more and more divided over its justification and its conduct. Amazingly, during the campaign for the presidency in 1964, both Johnson and the Republican nominee, Barry Goldwater, agreed not to debate the Vietnam War, lest it divide the country. (A similar agreement was made over civil rights.[16]) But the country was being divided anyway. Goldwater was defeated badly in his bid for the presidency, winning only six states with 52 electoral votes. Goldwater was pictured as a warmonger and a destroyer of the Social Security System. He advocated either winning the war (by using air power) or getting out. Now the United States was increasing the bombing effort, but also committing ground forces in Asia, a move considered foolhardy by many, including Goldwater.

Economists, of course, were concerned, not over the conduct of the war but its effect on the economy. Recall that, in its 1966 *Economic Report*, the CEA was confident that the economy could handle the extra burden of war expenditure without upsetting the record of steady growth without inflation. Stability, however, was not to be, for in 1966 a serious underestimate of the costs of the Vietnam War was to cause havoc with the forecasts of economic programs; 1966 would prove to be a turning point for the economy, and it can even be justly concluded that the U.S. economy was permanently transformed and would never be quite the same again.

The trouble began when Robert McNamara, secretary of defense, put the war costs at $10 billion for FY 1967, with the secret and arbitrary assumption that the war would be over by June 30, 1967. The costs of the war were deliberately underestimated, for the full costs would have been too upsetting if made public, particularly for the continuation of Great Society programs. McNamara was allegedly trying to avoid the unnecessary accumulation of war materials, a situation that had occurred in the Korean war.[17]

Administration economists were not aware of the underestimation of defense costs, but to their credit the CEA, now chaired by Gardner Ackley, did inform the president in December 1965 that a tax increase would be necessary if he were to have the Great Society programs, increased war expenditures, and no inflation. A quick across-the-board levy was suggested, but ignored by the president; he had not given up on the guns-and-butter dream.[18]

This was not the first instance of concealing information from Congress and the public. Earlier estimates of troop requirements were also understated, and the famous "credibility gap," the euphemism for deceit, was born. Yet the attempt to influence public opinion is different from manipulation of economic estimates. The deceit of the former may never be uncovered or, if so, only after some time has elapsed and the damage is minimized. The deceit of the latter cannot be contained so readily.

To illustrate the difference and to justify calling 1966 a pivotal year, let us record what happened to the U.S. economy. Since it is important to use data that were available at the time, the *Economic Report of the President* for 1967 will be utilized. (See Table 10.2 for the revised data.) First, GNP spurted to $739.5 billion, an 8.6 percent increase over 1965. In real terms the increase was 5.4 percent. More important, the economy closed the gap between potential and actual GNP. Making full use of the economy's potential was hailed, of course, but there were warnings that this performance could not be maintained.[19] Potential GNP was growing at a 4 percent rate as labor productivity was increasing at a rate of over 2.5 percent and labor hours at about 1.5 percent. While there was some hope that productivity could continue to increase, due primarily to the investment boom, the increase in the labor force could not continue, since the economy was approaching full employment. As long as there was slack in the economy, such growth rates were feasible, but now that the economy was approaching the full use of its productive capacity, future growth would be more difficult. As with labor, manufacturers were utilizing much more of their capacity, up to 91 percent.

As might be expected, the unemployment rate fell to an average 3.9 percent in 1966 and in December was down to 3.8 percent. Since full employment was still being defined as 4 percent, there was a situation of overfull employment. Average weekly earnings rose 3.4 percent in current prices and 1.4 percent in real terms. Prices began to rise as the slack in the economy was removed: The CPI rose by 2.9 percent, the WPI by 3.2 percent, and the implicit price index by 3 percent.

Clearly, the economy began to overheat, and excess demand was putting pressure on prices and productive capacity. All sectors of demand increased, as federal government expenditures rose by nearly 11 percent, business fixed investment by over 11 percent, and consumption by 5.4 percent. With all these danger signs flashing, what economic policies were contemplated and which taken?

In the fiscal area, Johnson refused to consider wage and price controls, preferring voluntary restraint. Excise taxes on transportation and telephone services were restored to the rates before January 1966 by the Tax Adjustment Act of 1966. Also, graduated withholding rates were introduced to put the personal tax on a "pay-as-you-go" basis. In September the administration asked for a suspension of the investment tax credit, which was granted in October. Apparently the administration considered the stimulus to investment unnecessary, now that investment was booming; perhaps the credit had been too successful. Rising sales, profits, and government expenditures were stimulating investment, and expectations of a continual boom were reinforcing the current good results.

Nondefense expenditures were held down by the administration to increases of only $300 million. Still, the administration budget showed another deficit of $2.3 billion for FY 1966 and an estimated deficit of \$9.7 billion for FY 1967. The federal budget, however, on a national income accounts basis that included trust funds and is calculated on an accrual basis, began to shift into a surplus in early 1966 and was nearly in balance by year's end. Payroll taxes were increased in January and, together with fiscal restraint elsewhere helped to produce this result. Thus there was some restraining influence on the fiscal side, but not enough to prevent or even seriously limit the overheating in the economy caused by the increase in defense expenditures.

The failure of the administration to increase taxes and meet the challenge of a full-employment economy, with defense expenditures creeping up, meant problems for both the economy and the New Economics. In the words of two important practitioners,

> From these figures one wistfully concludes that were it not for Vietnam, early 1966 would have found us comfortably contemplating the form and size of the fiscal dividends needed to keep us on the road to full employment, rather than considering what further actions might be needed to ease the strain on our productive capacity and deal with the vexing and perplexing problem of inflation.[20]

And even more directly:

> The economists in the administration watched with pain and frustration as fiscal policy veered off course. The new developments meant they were no longer calling the shots in fiscal policy. The January 1966 budget marked the first defeat of the New Economics by the old politics since Kennedy's decision in August 1962 to delay a tax-cut recommendation. Even more important, the New Economics could not pass its critical test because of the defense upsurge and the political paralysis of tax rates. The new economists had insisted repeatedly to their critics that the policy of fiscal stimulus would be turned off in time and would be amended to head off inflation when the economy did reach full employment. For political—not economic—reasons, the skeptics won the debate.[21]

Thus the decline of the New Economics can be dated rather precisely. Notions of fiscal dividends would soon appear rather quaint. Also it would become apparent, as Okun infers, that the New Economics was better suited to situations where slack was evident in the economy than to situations where inflation was the problem. It is easier to fight recessions than to curb demand to fight inflation.

Another casualty of 1966 was the guidepost program. As prices began to rise, organized labor joined with employers in declaring the guideposts unworkable. A midsummer strike of airline machinists was settled by wage increases far in excess of guideposts. From this episode the guideposts gradually fell into disuse, as other major wage settlements violated the standards. The administration continued to jawbone for restraint from both sides, but moral suasion has its limits, and the pleas were to no avail. As if to underscore the demise of restraint, Congress passed a bill broadening federal minimum-wage coverage and increasing the minimum wage from $1.25 to $1.60 in stages, becoming fully effective on February 1, 1967.

Lacking any real fiscal restraint, the burden of stabilization fell to monetary policy. As the economy heated up, the demand for credit grew rapidly. Businesses needed credit to finance their booming demand for investment goods, since profits did not cover their requirements. Corporations did sell more stock, but still there was excess demand for funds. Governments were also borrowing in large amounts during this period. The Federal Reserve was forced to choose between supplying the needed credit and risking inflation or holding the line on additional credit and providing restraint. It chose the latter, and a "credit crunch" ensued.

The basic money supply, M1, was allowed to grow at a rate of just under 2 percent for the first six months of 1966, and then the rate fell to zero. Time deposits grew faster, as M2 grew by 3.4 percent over the year, reflecting the competition of banks for funds and the development of new savings accounts for households (the nonnegotiable certificates of deposit). With the demand for funds high and the supply stable, something had to give.

Banks began to compete for funds in a serious way. Commercial banks made more use of negotiable CDs to attract corporate funds, increased interest rates where they could to attract more funds, brought funds back from abroad, borrowed from the Federal Reserve, and so on, in the attempt to accommodate borrowers. Still, funds flowed into securities markets and out of banks. The big losers were the thrift banks that normally finance mortgages. As the funds poured out of these institutions, the housing markets collapsed. New housing starts fell from over 1.4 million to 0.9 million at year's end.

Investment houses with large stocks of securities found insufficient buyers and were on the brink of insolvency, and many states and localities could not sell their bonds and were fiscally restrained. The drive for liquidity was immense, and the credit squeeze brought the economy to the point of disaster. Of course, interest rates rose dramatically. Three-month treasury bills rose from 4.596 in January to 5.387 in October, before falling to 5.007 in December. The prime rate rose steadily to a high of 6 percent in the last quarter, and mortgage rates were approaching 7 percent. The Federal Reserve's discount rate remained through all this at a constant 4.5.

High interest rates did not discourage investment spending, but they wrecked the housing industry. By this time expectations of future economic conditions only heightened the desire of firms to invest in capital goods now to take advantage of the boom; the high interest rates did not deter the investment plans. There were many complaints against the tight-money policy of the Federal Reserve, but they were ignored, as inflation became the major problem. As Arthur Okun observed, "In this episode, the Federal Reserve's independence proved to be a valuable national asset. It permitted the President and his administration to assume a passive role, tolerating an unpopular tight money policy silently without explicitly approving or endorsing it."[22]

Just as fiscal policy and the New Economics were failing, monetary policy was demonstrating its strength and usefulness. Soon the worry was that monetary stringency, together with whatever fiscal restraint was available, would not only halt the boom but turn it around. Indeed, in the last quarter of 1966, demand pressures for funds began to ease somewhat, interest rates fell, and some of the competition among banks was slowed by Federal Reserve actions to lower the interest rates on time deposits from 5.5 to 5 percent. Moreover, the housing market was aided by the addition of $4.8 billion in funds available through the Federal National Mortgage Association.

The end result was that monetary policy had proved it could bring the economy to its knees, but in the absence of a coordinated fiscal policy, the effects could prove disastrous. The uneven impact of monetary policy on various sectors raised questions of equity: the effects on the housing market, small businesses, and the redistributional effects of high interest rates. Yet the efficacy of monetary policy and the irresolution of fiscal policy was not lost on many observers.

Macroeconomic Policymaking
for a Confusing, Overheating Economy

The outlook for 1967 was confusing for everyone, and a recession or inflation and sometimes both were forecast. The CEA saw a slowdown in the first half of the year, followed by a resumption of the expansion. It advocated a stimulative policy for the first half of the year and some restraint for the latter half.

It turns out that they were correct. GNP increased by only 1.7 percent from the last quarter of 1966 to the second quarter of 1967 (0.6 percent in real terms) and by 4.2 percent in the latter half of the year (4.9 percent in real terms). Prices, however, continued their steady rise, as the CPI rose by 1.1 percent and 1.9 percent over the two halves of the year, matching the increases in the GNP deflator. Only wholesale prices remained stable. Unemployment rates fluctuated very little, remaining below the targeted 4 percent rate for most of the year, and the average for the year was 3.8 percent.

Other signs in the economy were confusing, unclear, and, for some, unexplainable. Gross investment fell for the year by about $6 billion. In 1966, inventories piled up to a record high of over $18 billion and then were worked off until the second quarter of 1967, when the change was virtually zero. Fixed investment also fell until late in the year, when it regained its 1966 level. Housing started up following the monetary ease at the end of 1966 and increased throughout the year. Some of these trends in investment can be attributed to the fluctuations in monetary policy, but long-run interest rates did not change by very much from 1966, a time when investment was booming. Perhaps there was overextension in 1966, since the capacity-utilization rate fell in 1967, from 90 to 85 percent.

Yet unemployment did not rise, but the average workweek fell. Firms apparently wanted to retain (hoard) their work force in a tight labor market and so reduced weekly hours, rather than lay off workers and risk their permanent loss. The tight labor market found females entering the work force in large numbers, accounting for most of the increase in employment (80 percent).[23] The rate of growth of productivity fell, as output slowed and employment remained stable.

Added to these developments, the savings rate jumped from 5.9 percent to 7.1 percent in 1967. The CEA had no ready explanation for the change, but it seemed to overlook the possibility that households tend to save more in the face of uncertainty. As we shall see, 1967 was a year that could well have provoked a large number of fears for households, tending to make them rather conservative in their spending plans.

Other events of 1967 only added to the policymaker's normal woes. The Vietnam War was draining the nation of its resources, its strength, its pride, and its unity. Demonstrations against the war were held in Washington, in New York—led by Martin Luther King—and in San Francisco. Many more would follows. Blacks rioted in Cleveland, Newark, and Detroit. In the spring of 1967 the Six-Day War between Israel and the Arab nations erupted, increasing still further the problems in the Middle East. Households, many already divided over the Vietnam War, now had new apprehensions to contend with. Uncertainty, the enemy of investment, began to threaten household behavior as well.

Faced with these and other developments, how did the administration and the monetary authorities react? In March, when the decline in investment spending became apparent, the administration requested that the investment tax credit be restored. The request was granted by Congress in June 1967. With excess capacity developing, the administration wanted to head off a real collapse in investment spending; however, with excess capacity developing, why would firms invest?

In January Johnson submitted his budget for FY 1968, which included a 6 percent surcharge on personal and corporate income taxes. The tax would go into effect on July 1, 1967 (chosen to coincide with the CEA's estimate of when the economy would begin to heat up again) and would remain in effect for two years or for as long as the Vietnam War required it. The optimistic assessment that the war would soon be over was now quietly forgotten. Indeed, Johnson asked for supplemental funds for FY 1967 of some $14 billion, $12 of which was for defense. Even with this tax increase and an increase in Social Security taxes to cover the 20 percent increase in benefits, the federal budget deficits continued to rise. In the national income accounts budget, which the administration favored, the estimated deficit for 1967 was $ −3.8 billion and for 1968, $ −2.1; in the administrative budget the deficits were estimated at $ −9.7 and $ −8.1 billion for the same years.

The administration's case for a tax increase was not well received on Capitol Hill. The House Ways and Means Committee, headed by the powerful Wilbur Mills, was not convinced that the economy would require restraint in the second half of the year. In the midst of an economic slowdown, members were not swayed by the CEA's forecasts of further demand pressures. In congressional testimony, Mills badgered the administration's representatives, as he led them, sector by sector, recounting declines in demand; what need was there for a tax increase to fight demand inflation when demand was falling? Mills apparently felt that any inflationary pressures would come from the cost side—cost-push inflation—and a tax increase to curb demand would be ineffective in such circumstances.[24]

Johnson's reluctance to impose a war tax a year earlier to pay for an unpopular war was still a valid concern in 1967. The general public was not enthusiastic about paying higher taxes, and popular sentiment for the war would be difficult to harness. Thus no tax measure was passed in 1967, and another year of economic momentum would go uncontrolled.

Monetary policy began to change in 1966, moving toward ease late in the year. Given the forecasts for 1967, the effects on housing of monetary policy in 1966, and the uncertainty over the length of the war, the proper monetary policy was difficult to devise. A policy of monetary ease was decided on, based on the assumption that the tax increases would be enacted in 1967. The Federal Reserve and the administration agreed to this course of action, but since no tax increase was enacted, the decision turned out to be an unfortunate one.

The money supply increased by 6.6 percent over the year and, including time deposits, rose 10.3 percent. In April the Federal Reserve reduced the discount rate to 4 percent; deposits flowed into thrift institutions; bank reserves grew; and, in general, monetary policy was quite accommodating. Still, interest rates continued to rise, which caused some confusion, but the demand for funds was very strong. Many feared a return to the credit-crunch conditions of 1966 and borrowed while the funds were available; all levels of government were borrowing heavily, and corporations were also. Expectations of even higher interest rates in the future made borrowing now a sound move. By the year's end the three-month treasury bill was yielding 5.012; long-term bonds, 5.36; high-grade corporate bonds, 6.19; and the prime rate stood at 5.56.

In November, in response to pressure from the international trading community, Great Britain devalued the pound from $2.80 to $2.40. The Federal Reserve responded by increasing the discount rate to 4.5 percent to signal that the United States would protect the exchange rates vis-à-vis the dollar. The United States, too, was under attack for its balance-of-payments problem, and international bankers were demanding that corrective action be taken. Since 1958 government grants and loans and private capital outflows had exceeded the positive trade balance, so that deficits were piling up and dollars were accumulating in foreign hands. The shaky dollar made both the United States and foreign central bankers rather nervous, and there were calls to reform the International Monetary Fund's (IMF) rules. In September 1967 the IMF met in Rio de Janeiro to consider the problems of diminishing international reserves and other trading practices.

In 1968 the economy expanded for the eighth straight year, continuing the expansion that had begun in 1961. For the year, GNP increased to $865.7 billion, a 9 percent increase over 1967; real GNP rose by 5 percent. Real GNP increased by nearly 6.5 percent in the first half of the year and by 4.5 percent in the second half. National defense expenditures led the growth in the first half, while investment and housing expenditures led the way in the second half. Consumption remained high throughout most of the year, but saving continued high by historical standards and was still unexplainable.

The unemployment rate remained below 4 percent for the year and in November dropped to a low of 3.3 percent. The capacity-utilization rate remained stable, but the industrial production index rose by 4.6 percent. Average gross hourly earnings increased sharply, by 6.3 percent, but real spendable earnings did not rise at all, reflecting inflation and high Social Security and income taxes. Prices continued their relentless rise, as the GNP price deflator rose by 4.5 percent, the CPI by 4.2 percent, and the WPI by 2.4 percent. Some restraint was clearly called for, but was just as clearly politically impossible. The credit crunch of 1966 frightened everyone, as the monetary system was brought to the brink of disaster. Even this move was quickly reversed. A war tax was considered unattainable by Johnson, and so the economy expanded too rapidly. Unwilling or unable to give up the Great Society programs, Johnson watched as blacks, their expectations lifted, began to riot when those expectations were unfulfilled. Restraint would be difficult to achieve if it had to come at the expense of the groups who were promised a Great Society.

Johnson, however, was soon forced to make a choice in his priorities. In August 1967 he sent a budget message to Congress, again requesting a tax surcharge, increased now to 10 percent, on personal and corporate income taxes. In January he repeated the plea, yet Congress was not overly receptive to a tax increase, and many members were demanding expenditure cuts as well. After much lobbying, the administration finally won its tax surcharge, but Congress tacked on a $6 billion expenditure reduction for FY 1969, exempting Vietnam spending, Social Security benefits, and veteran's benefits. Johnson reluctantly agreed to the spending limitations in order to secure the tax surcharge, but what it meant was the beginning of the slow demise of the Great Society. Leaving to Johnson the decision as to where to cut spending absolved Congress from the painful exercise, but was still a peculiar move for the legislative branch to take, since it has the ultimate responsibility to appropriate funds anyway.

The Revenue and Expenditure Control Act was passed in June 1968 and included the temporary tax surcharge that was to be effective April 1, 1968 for individuals and January 1, 1968, for corporations; the tax was to expire on June 30, 1969. In addition to the tax surcharge, excise taxes on telephones and automobiles, scheduled to be reduced, were kept unchanged until January 1970.

The question was and is whether the tax surcharge worked or not, or was too little or too late. It would be too little if the demand was too great to be deterred by the tax increase; it would be too late if the long period of debate over the tax led many to discount it and adjust their spending plans long before the tax was enacted.

Also, the fact that it was temporary could have made it less effective than if it were considered permanent. In such a case consumption would not be greatly affected, and the tax would be paid for out of a reduction in saving. This is apparently what happened, as consumption spending continued while the saving rate dropped. It is impossible, however, to factor out the effects of the surcharge in a period when many events were affecting consumer behavior. Thus Arthur Okun, chairman of the CEA at the time, maintained that the tax surcharge was effective, but others arrived at the opposite conclusion.[25] Critics hold that consumers base their spending plans on their notion of their long-run income expectations, and temporary changes in that estimate will not affect current consumption. Okun and others maintained that consumers would be more sensitive to changes in their current, actual incomes and would adjust rather quickly to reductions. The conflicts in economic theory cannot be addressed here, but it is true that spending was not curtailed significantly following the surcharge.

The same is true for investment spending. Despite high interest rates and the tax surcharge, investment spending rebounded in the second half of 1968. Expectations of higher profits may have caused businesses to borrow now with the expectation that interest rates might rise even higher. Residential housing also rebounded, due partly to the actions of the Federal National Mortgage Association (FNMA), now a private corporation, in purchasing more mortgages and making more funds available.

In short, aggregate demand was not reduced to the extent necessary to curb the boom. Of course, without the tax surcharge the expansion could have been greater and the demand pressures even worse. History cannot be replayed, but Lawrence Klein did perform some simulations that essentially absolved Johnson from blame for the inflation, even if taxes had been raised in 1966.[26] This controversial conclusion has never been accepted by most economists, and their collective judgment is that macroeconomic policy failed both because it was not used and because when it was, it was improperly applied. Perhaps Okun said it best: "The difficulties of explaining the movements of private demand and the responses to public policy during 1968–69 remind us of how much economists have to learn. They also remind us that changes in attitudes in the private economy can at times swamp decisions of public policy. They argue for humility in our discussions of the economic outlook and for flexibility in the making of policy."[27]

By the time the tax surcharge was enacted, some startling events had shaken the public. In January the Communists in Vietnam had launched a surprise and powerful attack at the time of the celebration of the lunar New Year—hence, the name the Tet Offensive; they attacked 100 cities, including Saigon, and demonstrated their resolve to continue the fighting in the face of enormous odds. It became clear to all that the war in Vietnam was far from over and would not be won in the near future; the light at the end of the tunnel went out. In March, following the primaries in New Hampshire, which he won, President Johnson shocked everyone by announcing that he would not be a candidate for reelection. Eugene McCarthy had indeed made a strong showing in New Hampshire on an antiwar platform, but Johnson wanted to delay his announcement until he had offered the Communists a bombing halt and peace talks, which he did on March 31. Consider also that the U.S.S. *Pueblo* was seized by the North Koreans in January; Robert Kennedy announced his candidacy in March and was assassinated in Los Angeles in June; Martin Luther King was assassinated in Memphis in April; Richard Nixon won the Republican nomination in August; and Vice-President Hubert Humphrey won the Democratic Nomination in Chicago amid riots in the streets over the war in Vietnam.

The economic side of life must have seemed trivial at times, as matters of much more importance were commanding attention. Economists who attempted to determine the success or failure of their policies often failed to consider the noneconomic motives for actions. Yet economic policies must be undertaken even in the face of uncertainty over their efficacy. For the monetary authorities the situation was even worse, for they were also uncertain over the course of fiscal policy. When the surcharge failed to gain immediate acceptance, the need for monetary restraint was recognized and accepted. Accordingly, the Federal Reserve raised the discount rate twice to a high of 5.5 percent in April and allowed the highest rate to be paid on large deposits under Regulation Q. The growth in the money supply slowed and in the first half of the year rose by only 3.4 percent and in the second half by 3 percent; open-market operations slowed the growth of bank reserves and free reserves turned negative early in the year.

Interest rates shot up to highs that surpassed those in the credit crunch of 1966. By May treasury bills were 5.621 percent, long-term bonds were 5.4 percent, and the prime rate stood at 6.18 percent. After the tax surcharge was enacted, the Federal Reserve backed off somewhat, reduced the discount rate to 5.25, and began accommodating the demands for credit coming from government and private investors who apparently felt that interest rates were going to fall still further and wanted securities. The demand for credit still exceeded the supply, and interest rates, after a slight fall, began to rise again to new highs at year's end. Treasury bills were 5.916 percent in December, the long-term bonds were 5.66 percent, the prime rate was 6.17 percent, and mortgage rates that had climbed all year now stood at 7.36 percent.

Faced with an erratic and uncertain fiscal policy, the monetary authorities responded with actions that won them few friends. They came under increasing attacks for their policies, not just for the year but for the past several years. The Joint Economic Committee (JEC) began calling for greater accountability to Congress and some restraints on Federal Reserve actions. Some targets or ranges of monetary growth were suggested, along with regular reports to Congress by the Federal Reserve to reveal what monetary policies were necessary and what problems were foreseen.[28] Now that monetary policy was showing its might, concern for how that power was to be used was growing and would continue to grow for some time.

Costs of the Vietnam War

As the Vietnam War escalated, so did the level of dissent. The hawks and the doves polarized the society, and the old and the young were pitted against each other; family quarrels were commonplace, and former friends became enemies in the course of discussions over the conduct of U.S. foreign policy. There were disruptions on college campuses, demonstrations were everywhere, draft cards were burned, and all of these events as well as the daily news of the war in Vietnam were watched by millions on the nightly television news. Some blacks opted for more violent means of protest—for example, Stokey Carmichael led the Student Nonviolent Coordinating Committee (SNCC) with the cry for "Black Power"—and many blacks turned away from the example of Martin Luther King to follow the new spokesmen, such as leaders of the Black Muslims. Many whites were shocked at such militance, but were bewildered by the Chicago riots at the Democratic Convention, where the police rioted against the demonstrators,

Table 10.3   Estimated Costs of the Vietnam War

Year	Incremental Vietnam Costs (millions of dollars)	Defense Costs without Vietnam (millions of dollars)
1965	103	46,070
1966	5,812	48,579
1967	19,419	47,531
1968	21,900	50,400

Source: U.S. Budget, FY 1968 (Washington, DC: GPO, 1967).

turning the TV viewers first to disbelief and then to disgust. Led by the Chicago Seven, the demonstration became a focal point for all the dissents against the war that were to follow.

There was also growing dissent in Congress, but it was not sufficient to deny the president the funds he requested to continue this undeclared war. In his budget for FY 1968 was an estimate of the costs of the war. These are given in Table 10.3. The total incremental costs of the Vietnam War were estimated at over $47 billion. Incremental costs refer to the extra military funds required over and above those needed to maintain the normal military requirements, that is, the extra costs of defense due to the war. Note that the estimates in Table 10.3 were made at the time of the budget's preparation. The true and final costs of the Vietnam War will be presented in the next chapter.

Of course, as the costs of the war mounted, the amounts granted to the Great Society programs began to fall. The poor were doing most of the fighting in Vietnam; many of the nonpoor were in college, for example, but the poor at home were to be denied those means of improvement. Actual expenditures of the OEO rose from $211 million in FY 1965 to $1,018 million in FY 1966, $1,483 million in FY 1967, and to an estimated $1,114 million in FY 1968. Although Shriver got the OEO in operation and the number of programs was growing, the funds for them were constantly cut back and spread over more and more programs. The result was destined to be failure; how could it have been otherwise?

Ironically, Johnson appointed his Cabinet Coordinating Committee in March 1967 to develop the economic planning for the end of the war in Vietnam. In the 1969 *Economic Report of the President*, the committee presented its report to suggest how the fiscal dividend could be utilized when the war costs ceased. They listed some $40 billion of projects in which the funds could be employed, either on new programs or on extensions of some existing ones. Unfortunately, the fiscal dividends disappeared.

Poverty in the Great Society

If the distribution of money income can be used as a guide, then all the ferment of the 1960s did little to alter the allocation of income in the United States. Indeed, the distribution of income shows remarkable stability. There are many problems with the income concept used in the data, and problems of interpreting the stability of the distribution of income over time. Some problems can be illustrated by reference to the number of persons classified as poor in the period. From the aggregate distribution of incomes, it would appear that all income groups increased their incomes in relatively the same proportion; hence, the shares of incomes going to each fifth remained constant in this period. (See Table 1.3.) Still, it might be possible to observe that the poor increased their living standards more than did upper-income groups and thus benefited more from the expanding economy. The number of persons classified as poor over the period is given in Table 10.4.

The data in Table 10.4 clearly show a remarkable drop in the numbers living below the poverty line. From 1961 to 1968 the number fell by 14.2 million or 36 percent, and from 1965 (when the war on poverty began) the decline is 7.8 million or 23 percent. Both whites and nonwhites benefited about equally, so that the gains were widespread. Since the poverty numbers do not include such in-kind benefits as Medicaid, free food stamps, or subsidized housing, the numbers of poor may be overstated and the gains made by low-income groups understated in the distribution-of-income data. The levels of living of the lower-income groups could have increased substantially vis-à-vis other groups, but the published data would not reveal such gains.

In other words, the numbers of poor could have been half the published number if income in kind were included; if some absolute income level were used to determine the poverty line, more people would have risen above it. Thus the war on poverty really had some effect on the reduction of the number of people living below the poverty line (however arbitrarily established). On the other hand, the reduction in unemployment caused by the long boom could also have

Table 10.4   Persons below the Low-Income Level, by Race, 1961–68

	Number (millions)			Percent	
Year	Total	White	Nonwhite	White	Nonwhite
1961	39.6	27.9	11.7	17.4	56.1
1962	38.6	26.7	12.0	16.4	55.8
1963	36.4	25.2	11.2	15.3	51.0
1964	36.1	25.0	11.1	14.9	49.6
1965	33.2	22.5	10.7	13.3	47.1
1966	30.4	20.8	9,7	12.2	41.7
1966*	28.5	19.3	9.2	11.3	39.8
1967	27.8	19.0	8.8	11.0	37.2
1968	25.4	17.4	8.0	10.0	33.5

*Beginning in 1967, data based on revised methodology for processing income data.
Source: U.S. Department of Commerce, Bureau of the Census, Current Population Reports, Series P-60, Nos. 81 and 86.

been responsible for the decline in poverty, with more jobs for the previously unemployed. In this case, increases in aggregate demand should be given the credit for reducing poverty—a decidedly Keynesian notion.

Perhaps both factors were at work: the war on poverty helping the poor with in-kind programs, which if counted would have lifted many above the poverty line, and the increases in aggregate demand lifting many above the line by giving them incomes. Many of these people are accounted for in Table 10.4, which clearly shows the reduction in poverty numbers following the Vietnam buildup in early 1966.

Changes in the Economic and Social Systems

Before attempting to assess the justification, success, and rationality of the Johnson administrations, it might be well to pause and suggest some of the fundamental changes that were occurring, changes that would transform the U.S. economic, political, and social systems, but which at the time were certainly not recognized. The power of hindsight permits us to view the changes that, as so often happens, escaped the notice of those who at the time were functioning on the basis of the old systems. As mentioned earlier, the pivotal year for the reversals was 1966, but the effects would be felt over the next two decades.[29] For the present, only an abbreviated list of the factors that account for the shifts need be included; in the coming chapters the repercussions and consequences will be examined more thoroughly.

1. *Cynicism and distrust of government and politicians.* Thanks to the actions and behavior of Mr. Johnson, the distrust of politicians and the questioning of government's ability to solve problems was growing. For the youth, it would be manifested in the distrust of authority of all kinds; for others, it would eventually be registered in the form of tax rebellions and in the emergence of a larger underground economy.

2. *The decline of Keynesian economics.* The failure of Keynesian economics to meet the challenge of inflation and an overheating economy led to the questioning of the model itself. Of course, with the decline of the New Economics, fiscal policy also came under dispute. Politicians could not be trusted to curb spending or increase taxes when required. It follows that liberalism suffered a heavy blow. With the cynicism and distrust, the belief that government had to play a larger role in the economic and social life of the nation was undermined. Conservatism in all forms, and certainly in economics, was given a boost, and attacks on the tenets of the New Economics increased and would prove effective in just a few years.

3. *Distrust of the military and military solutions.* As the war dragged on and even in the early stages, there was a growing suspicion that the military answer was inappropriate, not only in Vietnam but anywhere. Isolationism returned, along with doubts over the usefulness of all that military power. As military expenditures rose, the effects on the economy and society were reexamined.[30]

4. *Radical social changes.* Not only was the making of a counterculture of significance in this period, but also, as the students were radicalized, so was the education curriculum and the choices of careers. Relevance was the password. In addition, the consumer movement was started, giving the consumer a voice in economic affairs. In particular, pollution and environmental concerns grew in importance. So, too, did the movement for zero economic growth and zero population growth. More apparent was the revolution in sexual mores, dress, music, clothing, and so on, but these were only the outward manifestations of deeper concerns that would outlast the fads of one kind or another.

5. *Structural changes in the economy.* Persistent inflation gave rise to an inflationary psychology that imparted an inflationary bias to many transactions. Inflationary expectations became routine. The overvalued dollar not only caused problems with the balance of payments but also gave rise to a new market in dollars—the Eurodollar market. Funds available in this market would be available to thwart monetary policies. Imports grew, as did competition from foreign firms. Even as Europe worried over U.S. domination, many U.S. industries were about to be challenged. Third World countries were

clamoring for a chance at economic development and were no longer willing to be subservient to developed nations' interests. The productivity of labor began to decline. Unions began to demand more wages; minorities began to demand more jobs; females began to enter the work force; and discrimination practices began to be questioned. Expectations of the poor, blacks, minorities, and others were raised, and social programs were introduced to mollify various interests. Costs, however, were mounting. Transfer payments grew along with the expectations, until one or the other had to be curtailed. The welfare state was proving costly.[31]

Even this brief list of changes is sufficient to suggest that the transitional period that is centered on the year 1966 would have profound effects on the economy and the society. In the chapters that follow, it will be interesting and challenging to trace their influence on the evolution of economic theory and policy.

Evaluation of the Johnson Administration's Policies

It would be easy to start an argument by asking a group of economists whether the Kennedy–Johnson administrations' economic policies were justified. Keynesian economists clearly would argue that the tax cut, the investment tax credit policies, and so on were justified, given the stagnating economy from the late 1950s. Something had to be done to get the economy moving again. In addition, it was also a great time to test the Keynesian fiscal-policy prescription.

Others would rue the day that we decided to intervene in this way into the workings of the economy. This decisive turn to the public sector to rescue the floundering economy, even if it worked, resulted in the surrender of more power, more control, and more freedom; people became even more eager to transfer power to government, trusting it to ensure progress and lead us to the promised land. Once the siren's call is heeded, there is no turning back; winning back freedom and control become more difficult with each transfer of power, with each government policy attempted.

Conservative economists saw the danger of these early attempts at a Keynesian fiscal policy and were aware that the effects of repeated attempts would be increased reliance on government and worse— increased acceptance. Yet proponents of the New Economics saw the same sequence of events as a method to gain acceptance for an active government via the Keynesian paradigm. Indeed, they hoped that by demonstrating the operation of the countercyclical policy, more and more social experimentation would be possible.

So the early 1960s became a test period in the movement to a new economic paradigm and was justified in that way by its advocates. The country was ready for new directions, and at hand was the very model to answer the call. Keynesians were eager to explain their views, and they did not shrink from the larger role they had assigned to government. Yet while the public wanted something to be done about the economy, there was no great social pressure to embrace the Keynesian analysis of proper policy. Indeed, as pointed out earlier, much persuasion was necessary to convince many people to abandon the old ideology and accept the new. Many were never persuaded.

If early fiscal policy measures inspired controversy, what of the second leap into the welfare state? The war on poverty, Medicare, and so many other social programs initiated in the Johnson administration were well calculated to arouse heated debates. Conservatives would find such movements predictable, as first one group and then another would look to government to solve their problems. Government, no matter how well-intentioned, could not and should not do the job; it is not equipped nor does it have the knowledge to remedy the ills of each segment of the economy.

Keynesian macroeconomic policies do not require that redistribution of income or wealth be considered directly: Many Keynesians, being liberal, did however advocate that programs for those who get left behind be devised and implemented. To be sure, early Keynesians did talk of redistributing income in order to increase consumption, but these arguments became muted, as consumption functions became more elaborate with their predictions that redistribution schemes would not work to produce the hoped-for increase in aggregate demand.

Unlike macroeconomic policies, there were social pressures for the welfare programs that were instituted. The existence of poverty in the United States was rediscovered in the early 1960s and became a political issue. Political promises to combat it followed, and soon rising expectations were generated among the poor. The Great Society programs responded to the problems of various groups, and with each program's passage, there were calls for more. Where there was acquiescence before, now there was aggression and belligerence; groups previously ignored or dismissed now were demanding their share of the American Dream. And they were vocal. Blacks, minorities, women, the aged, and so on, now were no longer willing to play the roles assigned to them in previous eras. Their demands and objections shattered the complacency made acceptable in the notion that with progress all would share—they simply had to wait their turn. The demands grew louder, the responses inadequate, and, in the end, the frustrations often ended in violence as streets became the political arena.

Surely all the talk of a Great Society stimulated the discontent among the disadvantaged and elevated their expectations of what was possible. The problems would have surfaced sooner or later, of course, but the forms of the demands could have been different. Therefore, how much of the social unrest can be blamed on Johnson and the Great Society cannot be determined. In any case, the point is that the Keynesian economic policies were not dependent on the outcome of these societal conflicts and were not the direct cause of them.

Once the United States was committed to the war in Vietnam, justification for government intervention into the economy became less necessary. In wartime conditions more latitude is granted governments in controlling the economy. Ironically, when the justification for government involvement in the economy was apparent, Johnson chose not to intervene. Despite the economic consensus, noneconomic motives prevented him from utilizing the appropriate economic policies. The unpopular war, the threat to the Great Society programs, and his own political future made him reluctant to expose his programs to the scrutiny of Congress. As indicated earlier, this was the first blow to Keynesian policies, and his failure to follow the proper Keynesian policies now began the erosion for the barely accepted model.

Noneconomic factors, always present to some degree, were especially important in this period. The Vietnam conflict did not receive the support necessary to apply more stringent wartime measures, and even less objectionable ones, necessary to curb inflation, were not attempted for fear of political consequences. Thus, to judge the success or failure of macroeconomic policies in this period requires extraordinary caution.

The success of the tax cut was acknowledged by nearly everyone and became the basis for the belief that economists know how to manage the economy. Keynesians did nothing to discourage such tributes. In fact, the danger became how to avoid intervention into the economy too frequently, rather than not at all. Nothing succeeds like success in the old saying, and congressmen were perhaps unduly impressed with the success of the much-heralded tax-cut measure. What added to the luster of the success of the tax cut was that the results were predicted with a high degree of accuracy. The war, however, put an end to the expansion and to the luster of economic forecasting.

The first casualty was the wage–price guideposts, and soon voluntary restraints in the national interest were sneered at as being naive. More was lost here than was and is apparent. Voluntary cooperation among labor, management, and government might have contributed to the overall economic progress in many ways. In the 1980s, talk of an industrial policy would revive the idea of cooperation, but this time with formal agreements, sanctions, institutions, and so on. Most economists, and particularly the more conservative ones, would be more likely to favor voluntary rather than mandatory restraints and controls. Voluntary actions would be tried again, of course, but they suffered a real defeat in the mid-1960s.

As a countercyclical tool, the investment tax credit might have been able to make a genuine contribution. Allowed in a recession, the tax break might have stimulated a recovery; removed in a boom, it might have curbed spending. Much, of course, depends on the timing of the provision and its removal. Its use in this period, however, was uncertain; the firms were unsure of how it would be applied, when it would be removed. It was to be expected, therefore, that they would press for a permanent investment tax credit. Their objections, understandable as they were, led to the abandonment of what might have been a good countercyclical tool. The investment tax credit became just another tax provision, and its use to influence investment behavior was sacrificed.

Macroeconomic policymaking and Keynesianism were dealt another blow by the failure to pass a tax increase in the face of mounting price pressures. Delays of all kinds made the eventual tax increase in 1968 too little and too late. The first delay was in the determination of what type of inflation was causing the problem—demand- or supply-side? Economists were prepared to fight demand inflation, but there was some concern that this was not the cause. How can one devise policies in the face of such uncertainty?

The subsequent debate in Congress, in which the war was as much an issue as was inflation, was prolonged, and, in the long delay, counterproductive. If Congress could not act decisively when the issue of a tax increase or a reduction in government spending was not questioned, when there was agreement among economists, when forecasts warned of the dangers of not acting, and so on, then how could it be expected to prescribe policy in times when the situation was less clear? This is not to deny that political factors were involved and that spending cuts were controversial, but still the time involved in the consideration of the tax bill was excessive. The timeliness of fiscal policy surely came into question in this episode. The delay in the tax cut of 1964 is more understandable, since the whole idea of fiscal policy had to be sold to skeptical observers. The failure to build on that success weakened fiscal policy as a countercyclical weapon from that time on.

Furthermore, if tax changes engendered such controversy, what would happen when the time arrived to consider expenditure changes? Changes in government spending, involving special-interest groups, would probably face even more difficulty and more delays. Only a strong leadership, willing to overrule special interests and incur their hostility, would be able to accomplish significant changes in spending. Thus fiscal policy, as a practical matter, became questionable. This pragmatic assessment preceded or coincided with the theoretical assessment that was also challenging the Keynesian vision and, with it, macroeconomic policy.

On balance, then, macroeconomic policy in this period must be judged unfavorably, with little in the way of success. Even when justified, too many noneconomic factors were allowed to interfere with proper economic policy. The difficulty was that the failures did not affect that period alone, in which case the next time policy was devised, improvements would be made; the failures in this period were so blatant that rejection of policymaking in general was the result. No chance for improvement would be permitted, no mechanisms to learn from past mistakes tolerated. The rejection of Keynesianism would take some time, of course, but in the end the failures of the 1960s must be the source of the eventual decline.

We are thus forced to question the rationality of the policies followed for an understanding of these failures and contradictions. The 1964 tax cut could be viewed, in Galbraith's words, as "reactionary Keynesianism," concentrating as it did on trying to increase consumption expenditures. For Galbraith, who was concerned for a society that exhibited "private opulence and public squalor," such a judgment is consistent. For others, such as Mrs. Joan Robinson, the term "bastard Keynesianism" would be more appropriate. For Mrs. Robinson, the socialization of investment should have been proper concerns of policy, along with the distribution of income. Thus, a number of economists were not impressed either with the interpretation of Keynes or with the policies adopted in his name. Such tinkering with stability of the economic system was not the message of Keynes, and along with the failures of fiscal policy in the 1960s went the hope of ever achieving the restructuring of the economic system that Keynes actually had in mind.

Thus the policies followed by U.S. Keynesians protected the existing structure of the economy, the existing distribution of rewards, the existing distributions of power, and so on. For instance, the 1964 tax cut, the only real success story in this period, was regressive in nature, giving a larger tax break to upper-income groups than to lower-income groups. A tax measure without regard for the distributional effects is, according to many, not a Keynesian policy. Similarly, the movement to make the investment tax credit permanent can be seen as a method to protect firms from countercyclical policies and throw the burden of such policies onto other, less powerful groups.

Perhaps the war on poverty was instituted partly to counter the regressive tax cuts of 1964. If so, then the program was a sham to begin with, and the lack of funds testifies to it. Was the whole idea one of tokenism, a way to mollify the poor but give them some hope for the longer term? Seen in this light, the war on poverty was bound to fail, and, having failed, it would always be possible to take refuge in the attempt—We tried, but failed—and then on to business as usual.

Poverty became a moral issue, however, and the failure could not be dismissed so lightly. Fearful of the costs of continuing the war, better explanations had to be found to justify the abandonment of the battle. Cheating and fraud were exposed and abuses of all kinds publicized. Soon the victims were blamed for their plight; being lazy, shiftless, lacking in ambition, and so on, not much could be done for them. Besides, poverty could never be eliminated anyway.

In the end a very long-lived problem, poverty, which has plagued societies for centuries, was discarded as a public concern. Policies to help combat it were dropped after a short trial period, as if the problem could be resolved in just a few years with trial-and-error programs. True, any results would be slow to accrue and often unquantifiable in effect, but that should not stop the drive to eliminate it, even if there are early failures or undramatic results.

Opponents could and did argue that poverty programs would not work, either because poverty could not ever be eliminated or because the poor would just take advantage of the handouts and resist upward mobility. If the poor would not be helped, perhaps they should not be helped.

Again, the erosion of poverty programs was gradual, and in the coming chapters we can trace their decline, as well. Meanwhile, a better solution was gaining favor—the trickle-down theory; it is better to reward those who have in the hopes that they will use their wealth to benefit those who have not. This attitude was the very target of Keynes's attack on the distribution of income and wealth, but, as we have seen, that argument was lost in the effort simply to stabilize the economy.

It should be recalled that none of these transformations of the society and the economy were recognized by the majority of those alive at the time. Thus, for many, it would take some time for the realizations to set in, and for others they never did. In the year 1968 many other events were overshadowing these subtle transitions into another economic era. The changing economic structure would take some time before it became observable. In the meantime, the possibility (and for many the likelihood) of biased policies designed to fail cannot be dismissed. Whether consciously designed to fail or not, there are those who desire failure and who seize on any evidence in order to justify discarding a program or modifying it to suit other motives. For example, even if the war on poverty began as an earnest attempt to confront the problems of poverty, the small-scale effort involved and the overly optimistic and unrealistic forecasts of success could cause disillusionment in some, but in others, any failure is a signal to rid the society of such attempts forever. It is then a simple task to mold prior prejudices into all kinds of rationalizations and subtle arguments to demonstrate the folly of the attempt in the first place.

Similarly, deliberate footdragging on the 1968 tax surcharge would not only ensure its ineffectiveness but also would contribute to the rejection of fiscal policy in general. Those who delayed as a protest against the "war tax" inadvertently helped in the repudiation of Keynesian economics. The resulting failure or relative ineffectiveness of the tax measure was as much a creature of politics as of timing. In any case, it would be possible to argue that fiscal policy does not work and should be abandoned, even if a more timely passage would have made it more effective. Those who were predisposed to see failure anyway could easily overgeneralize from a specific example and help ruin any second chance for success.

part IV

Economic Policy in a Changing World

chapter 11

Richard M. Nixon
and the Imperial Presidency

After narrowly defeating Eugene McCarthy in the New Hampshire primary, Lyndon Johnson announced that he would not be a candidate for reelection. McCarthy had succeeded in mobilizing the young and the antiwar sentiment found in all ages. Robert Kennedy also entered the race for the presidency after the results in New Hampshire. Clearly the morality of the war in Southeast Asia would be a campaign issue; that was to be expected, given its unpopularity and divisive nature. What was not expected perhaps was the depth of the peace movement, not just among the college kids who shouted, "Hey, Hey, LBJ, how many kids did you kill today," but extending to all groups and all ages.

Yet the group that attended the Democratic Convention in August 1968 seemed relatively untouched by the virulent controversy that permeated the society and by the uprisings outside their hotels. These delegates had been elected as much as two years earlier, when the controversy was not as heated or widespread. They seemed happy to be in Chicago to affirm their allegiance to the Democratic party and to the president. They were there to nominate Hubert Humphrey to carry on the policies of the Democratic party; they were loyalists.[1]

Outside thousands of concerned people, mostly young, demonstrated against the war and the very policies that those inside were prepared to confirm. The convention, however, plodded dully on to its inevitable conclusion, nominating Vice-President Humphrey and Senator Edmund S. Muskie of Maine to head the national ticket. The shadow of the absent president (he considered himself too divisive to

343

appear) loomed over the convention and, later, the campaign of his exuberant vice-president.

The New Hampshire primary was significant for the Republicans as well. Nixon emerged the frontrunner after George Romney and Nelson Rockefeller had bowed out of the contest. Rockefeller reentered the race in April, but long before the dull convention in Miami, the Republicans had learned to overcome their fear that Richard Nixon was a loser and began to accept his candidacy more willingly. Nixon actually considered running in 1965 and made countless speeches and traveled thousands of miles on behalf of the Republicans; now the sacrifice was being rewarded. Despite some vacillations and periods of indecision, he could not stay out of political life and remain a private lawyer.[2]

Humphrey campaigned with the Vietnam War around his neck like an albatross and also with the defense of the Democratic-inspired social programs for which the public was growing weary of paying. Nixon promised peace with honor (in "the speech," which varied little) and spoke of the wishes of the silent majority, who presumably wanted a return of law and order, of U.S. prestige once again, and of new leadership. Following the Chicago fiasco, the Democrats were far behind, and while the gap was closed late in the campaign, they lost the race by 510,000 votes out of almost 72 million, receiving 42.9 percent of the popular vote (191 electoral votes) to 43.6 percent (301 electoral votes) for the Republicans and 13.6 percent (46 electoral votes) for George Wallace, the candidate of the American Independent Party.[3]

Nixon's narrow victory did not give him a mandate for radical change, although if he had received the vote that went to Wallace, some semblance of a mandate might have been discerned. To compound his difficulties, both houses of Congress were controlled by the Democrats, the first time in over a century that a president took office with both houses controlled by the opposition. Nixon would undoubtedly face obstacles if drastic actions were proposed.

As far as economics was concerned, the danger was minimal, since no great changes were proposed and none contemplated. Aside from the usual conservative antagonism toward big and centralized government, excessive social programs that promised too much, and unnecessary interference with the free economy, Nixon said little about the economy. Indeed, the perceived prosperity of the 1960s prevented too much criticism of the state of the economy. Besides, the Vietnam War pushed the economy into the background, and middle America was more frightened of being robbed than of inflation. Nixon's interest in economic policymaking was minimal anyway, and he soon delegated much of the responsibility for it to others.[4]

The Conservative Trend in Politics and Economics

According to Herbert Stein, who served on the Council of Economic Advisors and later became its chairman, Richard Nixon was no great admirer of big business, feeling that it was willing to use government for its own ends, while espousing the virtues of the free market.[5] Apparently, however, he favored the free market, as demonstrated by his distaste for wage and price controls, learned from his experience with the OPA in World War II.

Yet it was not primarily his brand of conservative economics that got him elected; he managed to reach other, more vital concerns of the population. There was a general mood that favored the turn toward the conservative philosophy. Thus, despite the long period of economic prosperity of the Kennedy–Johnson years, there was still a growing distrust of the liberalism that produced it. This was partly due, first, to the distrust of government and politicians that emanated from Johnson's personal style and the "credibility gap" that developed over the conduct, meaning, and rationale of the Vietnam War.

Second, the inability of Keynesianism-type fiscal policy to halt inflation led to the questioning of fiscal policy and accordingly to more attention to monetary policy. The general public was not concerned with the proper application of Keynesian fiscal-policy principles or with political considerations that prevented their timely use. They saw the difficulty in making choices between guns and butter and concluded that special interests would always succeed in the political arena and proper policies would always be sacrificed.

Third, the Great Society programs were being questioned, not only in terms of their success or failure but also as to their affordability. In time the programs would be attacked for their lack of success, anyway, despite evidence to the contrary.[6] This step was necessary to comply with conservative value judgments that the poor would become dependent on government, would have their incentives impaired, and would experience family breakups, and so on, through the whole litany of arguments that are always used to justify the rejection of government actions as solutions to social problems.

These and other factors enumerated in the previous chapter help explain the more widespread acceptance of conservative economics, even as the economy was booming through Keynesian demand-side stimuli. Of course not everyone admired the source of the prosperity (call it military Keynesianism) or the arrogance of the liberal economists with their talk of fine tuning the economy.

Among those who objected to the government-led prosperity were conservative economists who were busy constructing theoretical models to demonstrate the folly of the transfer of power and responsibility to the federal government for economic wellbeing. Without the theoretical justifications for a free market, it is doubtful whether the questioning of the liberal vision would have gone beyond grumblings, confined to small enclaves of conservative thinkers. It is the power of ideas, whether they are right or wrong, that eventually converts men of action, to paraphrase Keynes, and in times of doubt people will reach for new ideas, or old ones dressed up, for solutions to problems.

Thus it is imperative to introduce the theoretical developments that were beginning to affect and infiltrate the discussion of economic questions. The pendulum of economic orthodoxy would gain adherents, first among young economists seeking ways to make contributions different from the well-defined Keynesian model and then among those who sought justification to confirm their prejudices, and so on, to more widespread public acceptance or perhaps tolerance.[7]

For years Milton Friedman had been expressing his belief that the effects of fiscal policy were only temporary. Attempts to manipulate an economic system through altering the levels of government spending and taxing would, at best, affect the economy only in the short run; in the long run, which is the appropriate time span to gauge the effects of economic policy, the public sector would only drive up the interest rate and the private sector would be discouraged from borrowing—it would be "crowded out" of the money market. Thus, substituting public spending for private investment spending would not only fail to stimulate the economy but would also damage the prospects for long-term growth. In addition, the transfer of power from the private to the public sectors should be avoided in any case and certainly when no purpose is served.

If there was a contribution to be made through public spending, it would have to come from areas that affected growth only over the long run—such items as funds spent on education, research and development, and statistical information on product and labor markets. These long-run factors, among the real variables that determine growth, would be supplemented by technological changes, productivity growth, and other qualitative changes on all kinds of inputs into the production process.

These variables, however, are not easily manipulated by the public sector, which can affect only nominal or money variables. Even so, the attempt to alter an economic system requires adequate forecasting tools, a knowledge of where the economy is at any given time, and proper institutional mechanisms to deal with policy formation in a timely manner. These attributes certainly do not describe the fiscal policy efforts of the past.

It would be better, said conservative economists, to turn to monetary policy where the relation between money and GNP was more reliable: Control the money markets and you control output and employment; monetary impulses are the most important ones in an economic system, and these are controllable, impersonal, and predictable.

Yet even the effects of monetary policy were unclear. Just precisely how the changes in, say, the supply of money were supposed to affect the economy was not spelled out. Moreover, there were lags in its implementation, recognition lags, operational lags, and lags that resulted before the policy change actually affected economic behavior. If these lags were both long and variable, the effectiveness of monetary policy would be seriously limited.

In the end, perhaps both monetary and fiscal policy would be destabilizing, all the more so if the system were basically stable and self-correcting anyway. At least in the long run, this was held to be the case. It follows that it might be preferable to leave the economy alone, instead of even trying to react to every disruption, every fluctuation. No matter how well meaning, the attempt would be worse than not acting at all, or, in other words, laissez-faire, laissez-passer.

The result is the rejection of the short-run concerns of J. M. Keynes with all of his impatience with the long run, and of attempts to fine tune the economy by either fiscal or monetary means. Distrust of the actions of people led inevitably to the search for rules to follow that would be preferable to the discretionary acts of policymakers trying to do the impossible to the unnecessary.

Friedman formulated an easy rule to understand (if not follow): Let the money supply grow at the rate of growth of real GNP and forget about all other monetary targets. If estimating the real rate of growth of GNP is a problem, pick any rate of growth of the money supply, and the economy will adjust to it over time.[8]

Conservatives generally tend to favor rules for policymakers, so in addition to the monetary rule, the fiscal rule was equally simple to understand: Balance the budget annually. Moreover, reduce the role of government in the economy by reducing spending and taxes, and thus return economic power to the private sector.

The monetarism of Friedman was accepted by many and elaborated, refined, and explained by many others. (There were always many variants of the basic model, and hence many shades of monetarism.) Still, the movement billed as counterrevolutionary (to the Keynesian one) may never have attracted the following that it did without the blow inflicted by the attack on the notion of a trade-off between unemployment and inflation—that is, the Phillips Curve. If the trade-off does not exist, it is impossible to speak of fine tuning an economic system.

In a technical sense, the Keynesian model had one serious omission—the price level was not really explained. With the introduction of the Phillips Curve, the theoretical problem was solved. Briefly, fiscal policy affected the level of output and, by extension, employment; once the rate of unemployment was known, the price level could be determined from the Phillips Curve relation. Friedman attacked the very notion of a trade-off and with it the use of fiscal policy to reach socially acceptable rates of inflation and unemployment.

Recall that the Phillips-Curve analysis concluded that macroeconomic policies could be used to affect the economy, but that unemployment and the price level would have to vary in opposite directions. If the policy were one of stimulation, unemployment would fall, but the demand pressures would also insure that the price level would rise; if inflation were attacked by depressing demand, any reduction in the price level would be obtained at the expense of economic activity, and unemployment would rise. The trade-off seemed inevitable.

Friedman explained that any short-run gains that were achieved were obtained on the basis that the changes in the inflation rate were unexpected. For instance, if demand were stimulated, prices would rise relative to wages and employers would be willing to hire more workers. Real wages, however, fell behind, and workers would eventually learn to anticipate rising prices and increase their wage demands. Once they learned how to adjust to changes in fiscal policy, the trade-off would disappear; anticipated inflation would equal actual inflation, and the economy would reach and maintain its "natural rate of unemployment."

Thus fiscal policy would work, if at all, in the short run, where the actual inflation rate exceeded the expected rate and price changes exceeded wage demands. When labor could no longer be fooled and began to anticipate the inflation rate correctly, the short-run employment gains would vanish. In the long run inflation would no longer be able to secure temporary employment increases, and fiscal policy would become ineffective in affecting the unemployment rate.

To reduce the unemployment rate, it would be necessary to match workers with the available jobs, or train them for the jobs, improve labor-market information, increase the mobility of labor, and so on. These programs, however, are not achieved through macroeconomic policies entailing the usual fiscal-policy tools. Still, even with these more appropriate policies, there would be problems. How long would it take for workers to anticipate the inflation rate correctly? Again, time would be an important factor, and the long run becomes vital to this analysis.

Moreover, what is the natural rate of unemployment? If some number is attached to it for one time period, how does it change? The natural rate of unemployment need not be a constant and can change as the composition of the labor force changes. As will become evident later, more women and teens were entering the labor force, and with their historically higher unemployment rates, the natural rate of unemployment could be expected to rise. Add to this the new explanation of how people behave in their quest for jobs, the search theory of unemployment that spelled out Friedman's model, and the situation is even more uncertain.

Often workers think that better jobs are available but lack information on them. They may quit their jobs to search for these jobs (or search longer if they are unemployed and receiving benefits under unemployment compensation). In a period of rising demand and prices, employers may grant higher wages. If workers accept these jobs, interpreting the money wage gains as a better job, they will be disappointed later when they realize that price increases have eroded their money-wage gains. They react by quitting again (or demanding higher wages) and so on.

In this search theory of unemployment, each time they are disappointed they begin to adjust their concept of a good wage by adding the inflation rate of the past period. Therefore, the only way to reduce unemployment is to accelerate the rate of inflation and fool workers into taking the jobs. Eventually they cannot be fooled and they build into wage demands the correct rate of inflation, and when they do, and the expected and actual inflation rates are equal, the economy has reached the natural rate of unemployment. The short-run gains in employment once again vanish.

Later, when this explanation is carried to extremes, workers will view increases in demand as inflation creating and immediately adjust their wage demands so that the trade-off will disappear even in the short run. Workers' expectations would be "rational" instead of merely adapting with a lag to past inflation rates.[9] Obviously, increasing aggregate demand to reduce unemployment is utterly useless now, and not even accelerating inflation can help. Better not even to try; laissez-faire, laissez-passer.

Conservative Macroeconomic Policy

For advisors, Nixon chose basically conservative economists and politicians. While he can also be classified as basically conservative, he was much more pragmatic in his approach to economics. Apparently the memory of the 1960 loss, which he blamed on economic conditions, helped frame his attitude. For the CEA he selected Paul McCracken as chairman and Hendrick Houthakker and Herbert Stein as members; for secretary of labor, George Shultz, who later became secretary of the treasury and special assistant to the president for economic affairs (or economic czar for economic policy, as he came to be called); David Kennedy for secretary of the treasury, soon succeeded by another important economic advisor, John B. Connally; Maurice H. Stans for secretary of commerce; and his friend, Robert H. Finch, for secretary of HEW. Other important advisors included Arthur Burns, Milton Friedman, and Daniel Moynihan.

As is true with most conservatives, they tended to regard government as a large part of economic problems; they were not, however, rigid or fundamentalist in this matter and saw some legitimate functions for the public sector that went beyond the more simplistic conservative doctrines.[10] The CEA characterized itself as "Friedmanesque," meaning that it subscribed to the view that money matters a lot, but not to the view that only money matters. It would also go beyond Friedman in supporting a role for government in the elimination of poverty, for more protection of the environment, and so on, but on other issues it tended to favor the free-market approach of most conservatives.

It is not surprising, then, to record that the economic problem that was elevated to preeminence was that of inflation. When Nixon took office, the unemployment rate was 3.6 percent, while the CPI was increasing at approximately 4.6 percent. The problem was how to reduce the rate of inflation without creating a recession. For believers in the natural-rate-of-unemployment theory, in order to reduce inflation it might be necessary to accept above-natural rates of unemployment for a while until the economy adjusted to the new conditions. How high would unemployment have to rise and for how long?

President Nixon was politically sensitive to high unemployment rates, and policymakers would have to consider this limitation in devising economic policy. Accordingly, the CEA recommended a policy of "gradualism," whereby the rate of inflation would be brought down over time, with unemployment rates not rising significantly above the socially acceptable rate of 4 percent.

For this administration the disinflation would be accomplished primarily through monetary policy. Paying more attention to monetary aggregates, the administration wanted to see a reduction in the growth of the money supply, which was 7.2 percent for 1968. The Federal Reserve Board, chaired by William M. Martin, was eager to comply, and the basic money supply increased by only 2.5 percent for the year as a whole, but in the latter half of 1969, the annualized rate was only 0.7 percent.

In April the Federal Reserve increased the reserve requirement slightly by 0.5 percent and raised the discount rate from 5.5 to 6 percent, and, as might be expected from the slow growth of the money supply, interest rates rose quickly. Three-month treasury bills rose to 7.72 percent in December; long-term bonds rose to 6.81; the prime rate rose to 8.84, and the FHA mortgage rate rose to 8.48. These rates were all record highs, and fears of another credit crunch were widespread. The demand for funds was still strong and showed no signs of a dramatic reversal.

Equally predictable was the fall in time deposits at commercial banks, 5.2 percent for the year, and the process of disintermediation began, as funds flowed to other areas where the yield exceeded the statutory ceilings of the commercial banks. To offset the loss of deposits, the banks turned to new types of commercial paper and to the Eurodollar market, where they raised $7.2 billion in the first half of the year, before the Federal Reserve imposed reserve requirements on new borrowings.[11]

New housing starts declined by nearly 3 percent, a decline that would have been worse had not the federal agencies stepped in to support the mortgage markets. States and localities were also having trouble borrowing at rates that were deemed too high or actually prohibited by legal ceilings.

Fiscal policy, too, would have to show restraint, and the administration tried to retain a surplus in the national income accounts budget. It began by reducing expenditures from the last Johnson budget by $4 billion and later cut another $3.5 billion in the effort to adhere to a budget ceiling for expenditures of $192.9 billion. Of the $7.5 billion in cuts, $4.1 billion came out of the national defense budget, $1 billion from Social Security, and the remainder was spread out over various programs. Eventually the ceiling was broken for FY 1960, but fiscal policy for 1969 was still restrictive on the expenditures side.

On the taxation side the temporary tax surcharge was still in effect in Johnson's last budget, and the Nixon economists pondered what to do about it. The CEA saw no particular reason to retain it, since it was of little or no help in combating inflation (monetary policy would be responsible) and of little use in trying to balance the budget (which was not a high priority anyway). Aware of possible misunderstandings, however, it was decided that it would be best to retain it.[12] Accordingly, in March Nixon recommended its retention until June 30, 1970, but later, in April, he requested that the rate be reduced to 5 percent on January 1, 1970, and that it be allowed to expire on June 30, 1970. In that same budget message to Congress, Nixon also asked for the repeal of the investment tax credit (after being assured that conservative Republicans had no objection), and in response to demands of liberal Democrats, he asked for some limitations on tax shelters and the removal of 2 million lower-income people from any tax liability. These changes would have negligible revenue effects, but Congress added some provisions of its own that would affect future years. It increased the personal exemption to $750 from $600 and increased Social Security benefits, and these changes would result in substantial revenue losses. (Social Security taxes did rise on January 1, 1969, adding $3 billion to the fund for 1969).

The Tax Reform Act of 1969 was reluctantly signed into law by President Nixon on December 30. It went far beyond the administration's wishes, and Nixon was asked to veto it. The administration considered it antibusiness and discouraging to investment, for aside from the repeal of the investment tax credit, the act reduced depletion allowances, restricted the use of accelerated depreciation allowances, provided for a minimum tax on tax preferences, imposed a tax on private foundations' investment income, increased capital gains taxation, and reduced taxes on single people, heads of households, and low-income people. In view of these reform measures and the possible long-term revenue loss of approximately $5 billion, it is surprising that Nixon did not resist more diligently.

The final result of the expenditure and taxation decisions on the budget revealed a surplus of $4.6 billion on a national income accounts basis and $3.2 billion surplus in the regular budget. On a calendar year basis the national income accounts surplus was $9.3 billion, and the full employment surplus was $11.7 billion. (See Table 11.1.)

The administration's "game plan" (it tended to use terms applicable to football) for macroeconomic policy has to be set against the growing unease with the economy and the war in Vietnam. The unease with the state of the economy stemmed from the fear that the administration's policies would lead to a recession. In fact, we know now that the peak of the longest boom in U.S. history occurred in December 1969. At the time there was great uncertainty about the future of the economy.

To see why, consider the results of the policy of gradualism: The rate of growth of GNP fell from 9 percent in 1968 to 7.7 percent in 1969 (4.7 percent to 2.8 percent in real terms); unemployment fell slightly to a very low 3.5 percent; the CPI was rising by 5.4 percent (from 4.2 percent); the WPI was rising by 3.9 percent (from 2.5 percent); and the GNP deflator was rising by 4.7 percent (from 4 percent).

The reduction in the rate of growth of GNP was still accompanied by price increases. In fact, the inflationary psychology was still strong, and neither high interest rates nor rising prices deterred spending; higher future prices, it was thought, would cover the higher costs now. Thus investment and consumption spending continued strong in 1969. Toward the very end of the year, some caution set in and the saving rate increased. Capacity utilization also fell to around 84 percent from 86 percent. The signs were indeed confusing.

Finally, consider some interesting labor-market data. The economy added 2 million people, mostly (75 percent) women and teens, to the number of employed, but many were in part-time jobs. The growth in the productivity of labor was virtually zero, which was attributed to labor stockpiling by firms and to the inexperience of the new entrants; yet, the average weekly hours of work were still high, and wage and fringe-benefit increases were substantial, in the 7–8 percent range. The stage was set for trouble in the years ahead.

For an administration that had been determined to decrease the inflation rate by restricting demand, largely through monetary policy, the results for 1969 were clearly disappointing. Others were concerned that putting on the brakes would only cause a recession without reducing prices. Nixon's economists had already rejected the route of an incomes policy as possibly a less disrupting method of bringing down inflation.

With his penchant for surprises, Nixon disarmed his critics—who inferred that he had no domestic program—by announcing on August 8, 1969, his plans for a "New Federalism." In the first part of the New Federalism, he surprised everyone with a plan for a guaranteed family income or family assistance plan (FAP) that would clean up much of the welfare mess. Born out of the concept of a negative income tax, formulated by Milton Friedman and acceptable to conservatives, the idea was to remove the welfare bureaucracy by simply using the tax code to determine a direct cash payment to those whose income was too low to pay the federal income tax. Conservatives favored doing away with all other welfare programs, such as food stamps, subsidized lunches, housing, and so on. The only problem was to determine the basic amount of income to guarantee and the rate of taxation on amounts earned above the minimum. Thus the basic guarantee had to be low enough so that welfare recipients would still have to work, and the tax rate would have to be set so as not to discourage them from working.

The original Nixon plan called for an income floor of $1,600 and allowed the first $720 of income earned to be exempt from taxation, but amounts over that amount were to be taxed at a rate of 50 percent. Many variants of this plan were considered, and a competing one that would have set national minimum standards for the Aid to Families with Dependent Children (AFDC) program, with the federal government picking up a large share of the bill, was rejected in the infighting within the administration.[13] Hearings were held in 1969 on FAP, but no action was taken.

Nixon's New Federalism also included a program for revenue sharing, which involved the distribution of federal funds to states and localities with no strings attached as to how the funds were to be spent. The sharing of income tax revenues with other units of governments was not a new idea, having been embraced by Walter Heller and Joseph Pechman of The Brookings Institution and proposed to Johnson in 1964. President Nixon proposed the policy and FAP in the same speech and on August 13 sent a message to Congress with the details. The plan would set aside one-third of 1 percent of federal income tax revenues in the first year, rising to 1 percent in FY 1976, to be distributed to states and localities according to a formula that included the states' population and own tax efforts with a mandatory pass-through to the localities.

Again no action was taken in 1969 on revenue sharing. Both of these initiatives in social policy are interesting in themselves, since they appear contradictory—FAP centering more control in Washington and revenue sharing returning control to the states and localities. The inconsistencies did not seem to bother the Nixon administration as it prepared to confront Congress.

Stagflation and the Recession of 1969-70

The economic outlook for 1970 was unclear to all, including the administration's economists. They cautiously urged that demand management could still accomplish the administration's goals of reducing inflation without severely depressing the economy. The plan called for an easing of monetary conditions without stimulating fiscal policy.

In early 1970 the CEA recognized that the decline in economic activity was more severe than they had anticipated, without the beneficial effects of reducing inflation significantly. They would soon be facing the worst of both worlds, stagflation—high unemployment, depressed economic activity combined with inflation. Gradualism was failing as the economy drifted into a recession, one that was not acknowledged by the administration.

The Federal Reserve acted in the early part of 1970 to reverse its policy of restraint. As a result the money supply, now the Federal Reserve's main operating target, grew by 5.4 percent for the year. This sharp turnaround, from a 1.2 percent increase in the last half of 1969, ended the latest credit crunch and the fears of another 1966 episode. Short-term interest rates fell quickly and by year's end had dropped about 3 percentage points; long-term rates did not fall as quickly or as far and ended up 1 percentage point lower than rates at the beginning of the year.

Ominously, the rates on corporate bonds remained stable, but mortgage rates rose during the year and fell back to opening rates only in late 1970. The money markets were shaken by several events in mid-1970. In May the stock market collapsed, following the news that U.S. troops had invaded Cambodia to clean out the Communist sanctuaries. (On May 4 four protesting students were killed on the campus of Kent State.) Standard & Poor's common stock price index of 500 stocks fell from 90.31 in January (1941–43 = 100) to 76.06 in May, a decline of 15 percent; the sluggish stock market did not recover until the end of the year.

Another major event was the collapse of the Penn Central Railroad, which nearly caused a panic in money markets. Since the earlier credit crunch of 1966, many firms had decided to raise funds by selling commercial paper. These issues were short-term notes that were simply rolled over or refunded when they became due and were based on little evidence of financial soundness. To illustrate their growth, in 1965 only $9 billion was raised in this manner; in May 1970 the total had risen to about $38 billion. When Penn Central could not repay its short-term paper, concern for other firms' ability to repay quickly spread. Firms now about to roll over their paper would have difficulty, and, of course, new issues were impossible. Fears of a liquidity crisis were widespread. Adding to these fears of a known major corporation failure, there were rumors of troubles in other major corporations—Lockheeed, Chrysler (both later bailed out by the U.S.

government guaranteeing their loans), TWA, Pan American, and LTV. The liquidity crisis was real, for where would the funds come from for corporations? The banks were loaned out, and the stock market was depressed. A near panic developed.[14]

The Federal Reserve stepped in and opened the discount window so that banks could make loans and then discount them to the Federal Reserve. The move worked, and the crisis was avoided; the lender of last resort had used its powers to avert a monetary panic. Of course, concern for inflation quickly became secondary.

Later in September of 1970 another crisis occurred, as many brokerage houses were facing bankruptcy. Mismanagement of the operations of these houses resulted in billions of dollars of securities that were essentially lost. Record keeping of an increasing volume of shares traded was so poor that even the computerization of the process failed to improve matters. The New York Stock Exchange arranged mergers for the more troubled larger firms (the smaller ones were allowed to fail), and again the crisis was avoided. So serious was the problem that Congress passed a law, the Securities Investor Protection Act of 1970, to protect customers against losses in cases in which houses failed; up to $1 billion in funds were available from the Treasury to satisfy such claims through the Securities Investor Protection Corporation set up to administer the act.

Fiscal policy also became expansionary in 1970. The surplus in the budget on a national income accounts basis changed from $9.3 billion to a deficit of $ −10.8 billion, a turnaround of over $20 billion. In terms of the full-employment surplus, there was a reduction of some $5 billion (see Table 11.1).

The expansionary fiscal policy was the result of an increase in expenditures of $15 billion, due in large part to the increase in transfer payments in the recession ($10 billion) and to an increase in grants to states and localities ($4 billion). The decrease in defense expenditures of $2 billion did not offset the increases. Receipts also decreased by $5 billion, as the surcharge was removed. With expenditures rising and receipts falling, the stimulating effects of the public sector helped turn the economy around.

The recession turned out to be a brief one, lasting from December 1969 to November 1970. For the year 1970 GNP increased by 4.9 percent, but GNP in 1958 prices decreased by 3.9 percent. The unemployment rate rose steadily through the year and in December stood at 6 percent, the highest rate since 1961. Despite the recession, prices did not fall, with the GNP index rising about 5.3 percent, the CPI by 5.7 percent, and the WPI by 3.7 percent. Industrial production fell by 2.8 percent, and capacity utilization fell to 76 percent in the last

Table 11.1   Federal Government Receipts and Expenditures, National Accounts Basis, 1969–70 (billions of dollars, seasonally adjusted annual rates)

	Actual			Full-Employment Estimates		
Period	Receipts	Expendi-tures	Surplus or Deficit (−)	Receipts	Expendi-tures	Surplus
1969	200.6	191.3	9.3	203.3	191.7	11.7
1970	195.4	206.2	−10.8	212.0	205.3	6.7
1969						
I	197.2	187.7	9.5	197.2	188.1	9.1
II	202.5	189.1	13.4	203.4	189.5	13.9
III	200.8	192.5	8.3	204.3	192.8	11.5
IV	202.0	195.9	6.1	208.3	196.2	12.1
1970						
I	195.9	197.7	−1.7	208.0	197.6	10.4
II	196.7	210.9	−14.2	211.9	209.9	2.0
III	194.9	206.7	−11.8	211.9	205.5	6.4
IV	194.1	209.5	−15.4	216.2	208.3	7.9

Note: Detail will not necessarily add to totals because of rounding.
Source: Council of Economic Advisors, *Economic Report of the President* (Washington, DC: GPO, 1971), p. 24.

quarter. Productivity in manufacturing increased by 1.1 percent, but compensation per man-hour increased by nearly 7 percent.

Thus, wages were rising faster than productivity, and firms were maintaining past rates of changes in prices and reducing output. The result is stagflation. The cause of inflation seemed to shift from demand created to supply created—cost-push inflation. This was sufficient to cause Murray Weidenbaum of the Treasury to suggest to his superior, Paul Volcker, and afterward to Congress (JEC), that some form of incomes policy was necessary, now that demand pressure had been wrung out of the economy. Later, in May, Arthur Burns, now chairman of the Federal Reserve Board, also began to advocate an incomes policy of some type.

The administration was being criticized in many quarters, including business groups, for not doing more about inflation. In a June speech, Nixon reported that he had requested the CEA to sound "inflation alerts" that would spotlight major areas of large price and wage increases. The president, who had earlier pledged not to jawbone or suggest guidelines for private actions, was now doing both; in July the annually balanced budget was disowned in favor of the full-employment surplus budget, a reversal that would lead to Nixon's declaration, "I am now a Keynesian." In August he signed a bill extending the Defense Production Act of 1950 that included the Democratic-inspired power to freeze wages, salaries, prices, and rents; he said, "I have previously indicated that I did not intend to exercise such authority if it were given to me."

Arthur Burns continued to annoy the president with his advocacy of an incomes policy that went beyond jawboning; "It would be desirable to supplement our monetary and fiscal policies with an incomes policy—we are dealing, practically speaking, with a new problem—namely, persistent inflation in the face of substantial unemployment—and ... the classical remedies may not work well enough or fast enough in this case."[15] The new chairman of the Federal Reserve was clearly not a believer in strict monetarism, nor was he willing to deny any usefulness to fiscal policy and embrace rules for either fiscal or monetary policy. For his independence of thought Burns was later smeared by President Nixon, through Charles Colson, when a news story was planted that while Burns favored wage restraints for others he was seeking an increase in his own salary. The story was obviously false—Burns was seeking an increase in the chairman's salary for his successors.[16]

Wage and Price Controls

The outlook for 1971 was basically hopeful. The CEA recognized the difficulties in the unemployment-inflation dilemma but felt that with judicious macroeconomic policies the situation could be managed. Monetary and fiscal policies would continue to play the major roles in bringing about a solution to the problem (the phrase "trade-off" was not used), although other policies—reducing protectionism, for example—could play a part as well. In addition, the president had established the Regulations and Purchasing Review Board to deal with government's contribution to inflation, and in January 1971 he established the Cabinet Committee on Economic Policy to investigate the case of the steel industry.

With appropriate, flexible macroeconomic policies, the CEA thought that the unemployment rates could be brought down to 4.5 percent by mid-1972 and the inflation rate to the 3 percent range.[17] Wage and price controls, however, would be shunned as "undesirable, unnecessary, and probably unworkable."[18] Instead, the anticipated increase in spending of $17 billion, mainly on transfer payments and grants-in-aid, together with the liberalization of depreciation allowances and appropriate monetary policy, would do the job.

During 1970 not much progress was made in either of Nixon's innovations in social policy. His family-assistance plan (FAP) did manage to pass the House but got bogged down in the Senate Finance Committee. Liberals suggested that the income guarantee was too low, and conservatives argued that the disincentives were too high—people would lose too many benefits if they took a job and thus would elect to stay on welfare. In his State of the Union message, Nixon took the advice of Wilbur Mills and increased the income guarantee for a family of four from $1,600 to $2,400, while taking away the family's eligibility for food stamps. In the same message Nixon revised his languishing revenue-sharing scheme, raising the amounts to $5 billion to be divided evenly among the states and localities and an additional $11 billion in special revenue-sharing block grants for education, law enforcement, urban development, transportation, job training, and rural development. It was billed as the "New American Revolution."[19]

Apparently it became clear to the administration after the first two quarters of 1971 that the goals it had set were not going to be achieved in that year. GNP increased at an annual rate of about 13.8 percent in the first quarter and about 7.7 percent in the second quarter; in real terms the increases were 7.9 percent and 3.4 percent, respectively. The first-quarter results were attributed to the rebound following the ten-week strike at General Motors in the final quarter of 1970. When these rates of growth fell back to more sustainable rates, it was clear that they were not sufficient to reduce the unemployment rate; that is confirmed by a look at Table 11.2, where it is evident that the unemployment rate continued to hover around 6 percent.

Looking at the behavior of prices, the CPI rose by a 2.4 percent annual rate in the first quarter and by 5.8 percent in the second; from June to August the rate of increase declined to 3 percent. Wholesale prices rose in the first quarter by 7.4 percent and in the second quarter by 4.7 percent; the GNP implicit price index rose by 5.3 percent, 4.2 percent, and 2.5 percent over the first three quarters of 1971 (see Table 11.2).

After looking over the data for 1971, it is difficult to imagine a conservative administration reacting the way it did. While it is true that the economic growth was not sufficient to reduce the unemployment rate, at least according to the administration's economists, no drastic action seemed to be required, especially since the target rates of 4.5 percent unemployment and 3 percent inflation were expected to be

Table 11.2   Selected Rates of Change of Important Economic Magnitudes, 1969 to 1971 (percent)

	Yearly			1971 at Annual Rates, by Quarters			
	1969	1970	1971	I	II	III	IV
GNP: Money	7.5	4.8	7.4	13.8	7.7	5.3	7.6
In 1958 dollars	2.6	−0.6	2.7	7.9	3.4	2.7	6.1
CPI	5.4	5.9	4.3	2.4	5.8	2.3	3.0
WPI	3.9	3.7	3.2	7.4	4.7	0.7	3.2
GNP index	4.8	5.5	4.6	5.3	4.2	2.5	1.1
Unemployment rate	3.5	4.9	5.9	5.9	6.0	6.0	5.9

Source: Compiled by the author from Council of Economic Advisors, *Economic Report of the President,* 1972.

reached by mid-1972, one year later. Whether or not a faster rate of growth would have reduced unemployment and moderated prices is debatable anyway, since these forecasts were based on assumptions that were not shared by many outside the administration.

Despite the lack of any extraordinary condition in the economy, President Nixon surprised nearly everyone on August 15, 1971, by announcing a 90-day freeze on wages, salaries, rents, and prices and establishing a Cost of Living Council to administer the action and advise on the next steps to be taken. Only a handful of advisors were invited to Camp David, where these actions were discussed and agreed upon. Mr. Nixon was always fond of surprises and this one caught many off balance. What made this New Economic Policy, as it came to be called, necessary—why this drastic anticapitalist move now? When he signed the Economic Stabilization Act of 1970, Nixon disavowed the use of the powers given to him by Congress; most of his advisors were firmly against controls of any kind, and conservative ideological purity rejected such transfers of power and control.

Herbert Stein, who was present in the planning stage, related that there was enormous pressure for an incomes policy of some kind coming from many quarters, caused by the perpetuation of some unrealistic expectations of how the economy should function, based on the Eisenhower, Kennedy–Johnson years.[20] Businesses wanted an incomes policy to curb the demands of labor, while consumers and labor wanted to control prices. Even conservative economists like Arthur Burns were advocating an incomes policy. Yet there had been pressures before and unrealistic expectations that Nixon's promises did little to discourage.

It is difficult to escape the judgment that the actual state of the domestic U.S. economy had little to do with the New Economic Policy. Economic conditions were simply not far enough removed from past performance to warrant this strategy. In fact, prices were stable or declining and the employment rate was stable.

More probably the dramatic reversal of policy was the result of political considerations and the state of international affairs, not pressing domestic ones. Nixon could not afford to wait for the longer-term results of gradualism. He and other Republicans needed something bold and exciting to bolster their images as decisive policymakers. They needed, in Stein's words, "the big political gesture."[21] Earlier, Nixon had appointed John Connally as secretary of the treasury, and his counsel probably persuaded the president to act; Connally had probably been converted to the view by other Treasury economists, and since he had no previous predispositions against controls, he could view the policy change in a pragmatic vein. Without Connally, says Herbert Stein, it is doubtful that the policy of wage and price controls would ever have been adopted.[22] Nixon faced reelection in 1972, and he needed a policy that promised less unemployment and less inflation by the summer of 1972. Whatever ideological beliefs he held would have to be sacrificed for the immediate goal of attaining a second term.

The New Economic Policy

Prior to the New Economic Policy of August 15, the Nixon administration had already begun to move toward more controls. In August 1970 Arthur Burns warned the administration that high wage settlements in the construction industry were worrisome, for they were becoming the pattern for bargaining for other labor groups. He urged the suspension of the Davis–Bacon Act, which required the payment of the prevailing wage (usually union) on government-sponsored construction projects. Fearful of alienating labor, Secretary of Labor Shultz advised against the action.[23] In February 1971 the president did suspend the Davis–Bacon Act in the hope of working out some agreement between labor and management in the industry.

On March 29 such an agreement was reached, and the president reinstituted the Davis–Bacon Act, and by executive order (under powers granted to him by the Economic Stabilization Act of 1970), he established the Construction Industry Stabilization Committee. This 12-member board of labor and management representatives was given the power to review and pass judgment on all collective-bargaining agreements in the construction industry. (This agency continued to operate as a section of the Pay Board during the period of wage and price controls.)

Other concessions to the idea of an incomes policy included the National Commission of Productivity, another multirepresentative body, to confer on a vital national issue; the Government Procurement and Regulations Review Board, designed to investigate cases in which government itself was contributing to inflation; and the inflation alerts, a form of jawboning. These halting steps paved the way to a more formal incomes policy.

The incomes policy actually adopted consisted of the following features:

1. A 90-day freeze on prices, wages, and rents, with the likelihood of continuing mandatory controls after the freeze period.
2. A tax package to stimulate the economy, and, it was hoped, employment.
    a. A job development credit—a tax credit of 10 percent in the first year and 5 percent thereafter for new investment. (This was essentially the renewal of the investment tax credit, now euphemistically called a job development credit. Congress passed a flat 7 percent investment tax credit and other provisions listed below in the Revenue Act of 1971, signed into law on December 10, 1971.)
    b. Repeal of the 7 percent excise tax on automobiles. (This bone to the automobile companies was approved by Congress, which went even further and also repealed the 10 percent excise tax on light trucks.)
    c. A temporary surcharge of 10 percent on dutiable imports. (No congressional action was sought.)
    d. Scheduled changes in personal exemptions (to $750) were advanced to January 1, 1972, and the standard deduction was increased to 15 percent from the same date. (Congress slightly altered the amounts.)
    e. Establishment of the Domestic International Sales Corporation (DISC) to permit exporters to defer taxes payable on exports to match the tax system on exports used abroad. (Congress modified the proposal.)
3. Cancellation of contemplated expenditure programs for revenue sharing and welfare reforms and reductions in planned expenditures for federal pay raises and foreign aid. (Congress restored the federal pay raise.)
4. Suspension of the convertibility of the dollar into gold and other reserve assets. (No congressional action was sought.)

Despite denials to the contrary, it is clear from the foregoing that international concerns dominated the New Economic Policy and that domestic political considerations favored the move at this time.[24]

By closing the gold window, President Nixon unilaterally ended the international trading agreements reached at Bretton Woods some 25 years earlier. Recall that it was U.S. insistence that gold play a role in international finance that led to the dollar attaining its peculiar place in the International Monetary Fund's (IMF's) operations. The dollar was valued in terms of gold, and other currencies were valued in terms of the dollar—the gold exchange standard. The dollar was as good as gold, and other currencies could be freely exchanged for it. Of course, the established exchange rates were to be maintained and allowed to vary only in the narrow range of ±1 percent.

The system worked (not perfectly) as long as the world needed liquidity to finance trade and as long as the rest of the world was willing to accept and utilize dollars as an international currency. U.S. trade deficits began to grow significantly, however, and dollars began to accumulate in the rest of the world. The excess dollars threatened inflation in these nations, as they struggled to maintain their exchange rates, and began also to trigger the fear that the new overvalued dollar would have to be devalued. In either case they would lose. In the late 1960s France claimed gold with its excess dollars. Others realized that their excess dollars amounted to three times more than the U.S. stockpile of gold, and all could not pursue this route.

Just a look at the U.S. balance of payments is sufficient to indicate the growing struggle to maintain the gold exchange standard and the IMF rules. Table 11.3 gives the data for the period of the 1960s and early 1970s.

While no one balance is recognized as the most meaningful measure of a nation's position, just a look at any one of them will reveal the deterioration clearly; whether reference is to the balance on goods and services, on current account, or on the official reserve transactions balance, the trend is unmistakable.

Despite efforts by the United States to restrain foreign lending (interest equalization tax) or foreign travel (limiting duty-free purchases, and so on), and despite the establishment of Special Drawing Rights (SDRs or paper gold), to help provide liquidity to the system, the United States was unable to reverse the balance-of-payments deficits, and the IMF's operating rules were in jeopardy. No one expected the United States to get its house in order—that is, solve its inflation problem, improve its productivity, increase its exports, or alter its monetary policy to reflect international concerns. In fact the expectation was the opposite—further deterioration and capital outflows out of the United States.[25]

Table 11.3 U.S. Balance of Payments, 1961–70 (billions of dollars)

Type of Transaction	1961–65 Average	1966	1967	1968	1969	1970, First Three Quarters[1]
Merchandise trade balance	5.4	3.9	3.9	0.6	0.6	2.7
Exports	23.0	29.4	30.7	33.6	36.5	42.1
Imports	−17.6	−25.5	−26.8	−33.0	−35.8	−39.4
Balance on investment income	3.5	4.1	4.5	4.8	4.4	4.3
U.S. investments abroad	4.9	6.3	6.9	7.7	8.8	9.6
Foreign investments in the United States	−1.3	−2.1	−2.4	−2.9	−4.5	−5.3
Balance on other services	−2.5	−2.7	−3.2	−2.9	−3.1	−3.1
BALANCE ON GOODS AND SERVICES[2]	6.5	5.3	5.2	2.5	1.9	3.9
Unilateral transfers, net; transfers (−)[3]	−2.7	−2.8	−3.0	−2.8	−2.8	−2.9
BALANCE ON CURRENT ACCOUNT	3.8	2.5	2.2	−.3	−.9	1.0
Balance on direct private investments	−2.2	−3.6	−2.9	−2.9	−2.2	−3.8
U.S. direct investments abroad	−2.2	−3.7	−3.1	−3.2	−3.1	−4.8
Foreign direct investments in the United States	.1	.1	.3	.3	.8	1.0
Transactions in securities	−.8	.4	.3	3.1	1.6	1.0
Transactions in U.S. long-term assets	−.6	.2	−.4[4]	.1	−.1	−.6
Transactions in U.S. long-term bank liabilities to other than official foreign agencies, and all long-term nonbank liabilities	.1	.4	.2	.8	.8	.9
Certain transactions in U.S. Governments assets[5]	−1.8	−2.0	−2.4	−2.5	−2.1	−1.8
BALANCE ON CURRENT AND LONG-TERM CAPITAL ACCOUNTS[6]	−1.4	−2.0	−3.1	−1.7	−2.8	−3.3

Transactions in U.S. short-term assets	-.9	-.4	-1.2	-1.1	-.6	-.3
Nonscheduled repayments on U.S. Government credits	.4	.4	-[4]	.2	-.1	.3
Long-term bank liabilities to foreign official agencies	-[4]	.8	.9	.5	-.8	-.8
Transactions in U.S. short-term nonbank private liabilities, and nonmarketable liabilities of U.S. Government	.5	.4	.9	2.7	.2	.9
Errors and unrecorded transactions	-.9	-.5	-1.1	-.5	-2.8	-2.0
Allocations of special drawing rights						.9
BALANCE ON LIQUIDITY BASIS	-2.3	-1.4	-3.5	.2	-7.0	-4.4
Less: Certain nonliquid liabilities to foreign official agencies	.1	.8	1.3	2.3	-1.0	-.2
Plus: Foreign private liquid capital, net	.7	2.4	1.5	3.8	8.7	-4.5
BALANCE ON OFFICIAL RESERVE TRANSACTIONS BASIS	-1.8	.3	-3.4	1.6	2.7	-8.7
Addendum: Special financial tranactions	.6	1.6	1.3	2.7	-.6	.5
BALANCE ON LIQUIDITY BASIS EXCLUDING SPECIAL FINANCIAL TRANSACTIONS AND SDR ALLOCATIONS	-2.9	-2.9	-4.8	-2.6	-6.4	-5.8

[1] Average of the first three quarters at seasonally adjusted annual rates.
[2] Excludes transfers under military grants.
[3] Excludes military grants of goods and services.
[4] Less than $0.05 billion.
[5] Transactions in U.S. Government assets, excluding official reserve assets, net, less nonscheduled repayments on credits (including sales of foreign obligations to foreigners).
[6] One version of the "basic balance" under consideration. Another variant is the "nonmonetary balance" used by the International Monetary Fund.
Note: Detail will not necessarily add to totals because of rounding.
Source: Council of Economic Advisors, *Economic Report of the President* (Washington, DC: GPO, 1971), p. 148.

European nations were more than a little miffed to hear themselves blamed for U.S. problems by Secretary of the Treasury John Connally. He lectured them on the need for surplus countries to begin to revalue their currencies, rather than leave the adjustments solely to deficit countries. Moreover, he reminded them that the United States was bearing the brunt of defending the West, and they should begin to shoulder a greater share of the burden. The United States was again signaling that it was unwilling to let balance-of-payments problems govern its domestic monetary policies or control its handling of the domestic economy. Indeed, there were growing feelings of protectionism in the United States and a push for import quotas on many goods in the Burke–Harte bill before Congress. Japanese cars were inundating California, and foreign steel was threatening the international position of U.S. firms.

This brief sketch of international developments indicated how matters stood on August 15, 1971. Just one week before (August 9), Britain was prepared to convert $3 billion of its dollar holdings into gold.[26] A massive run on U.S. banks appeared imminent, as each nation contemplated converting its dollars for gold before it was too late. Since there were $40 billion of foreign-held dollars and only about $12 billion in gold, the gravity of such a run on world trade and finance is obvious.

On August 15, 1971, the administration averted the crisis by simply suspending the right of conversion: The United States would no longer honor its commitment to exchange dollars for gold or other reserve assets. With this action the future of the IMF was clearly in doubt. Furthermore, the New Economic Policy (NEP) imposed a 10 percent surcharge on dutiable imports to protect the nation's trade balance; it reduced foreign aid by 10 percent to force other nations to increase their defense spending; it repealed the excise taxes on automobiles (remember those Japanese imports); and it limited the job development tax credit to domestically produced machinery and equipment.

The importance of international conditions on the formation of the NEP really needs no additional evidence. The United States wanted to bring about an exchange-rate realignment or a devaluation of the dollar. Since other nations were not willing to agree to these changes, the United States acted on its own.[27] The 10 percent import surcharge and other administration threats were to be used as bargaining chips and to demonstrate the resolve of the U.S. position.

Before looking at other aspects of the New Economic Policy, it might be appropriate to see how successful the administration was in its attempt to force changes in the international trade and finance area. First, it should be noted that the administration had no plan of action to follow after its dramatic moves and no clear idea of what would follow if it did not act at all. The dollar could have depreciated, which would have suited the administration, or it could have floated. The market would have to decide, but there was little discussion at Camp David that August weekend.[28]

Indeed, exchange rates were altered in the marketplace once it was clear that the United States was determined to force changes on the system. In particular, the surplus countries, such as West Germany and Japan, found their currencies appreciating as dollars were exchanged for them. Then confusion caused by a badly damaged IMF and by ambiguities in the U.S. position (refusing devaluation, for instance) led to a meeting of the IMF in Washington, DC, in December 1971. The discussions produced the so-called Smithsonian agreement, which contained the following provisions:

1. The United States agreed to devalue the dollar, and the price of gold in terms of the dollar was to rise by 8 percent to $38 per ounce.
2. A temporary amendment was made to the IMF rules, allowing exchange rates to vary by ±2.25 percent rather than ±1 percent. The provision was considered temporary until more extensive discussions could be held on international monetary reform.
3. The United States removed the 10 percent surcharge after receiving assurances that other nations would end discrimination against U.S. goods and reduce trade barriers.

The reprieve for the system of fixed exchange rates clearly helped calm the more exaggerated fears of a monetary collapse and permitted discussions of the future to take place in a less hectic and confusing atmosphere. It also gave the United States more time to consider its own plans without sacrificing its basic aims of adjusting exchange rates more in its favor. The 10 percent surcharge was easily relinquished, as long as the promise of change was realistic. Indeed the United States had been willing to remove the surcharge if trade barriers had been reduced and a trial period of floating exchange rates was instituted. This position was expressed by Secretary Connally in September 1971 in a speech to the IMF, and while the proposal went unheeded, it did suggest the route of future U.S. plans for reform.

Little progress in instituting reforms was made for a year, as Europeans attempted to cling to fixed exchange rates while the United States was moving in the other direction. Once again the United States took the initiative when the new secretary of the treasury, George Shultz, spoke to the IMF in September 1972, advocating a system of freely floating exchange rates. This firm proposal set the stage for negotiations among the world's leading nations—the so-called Committee of Twenty.

In view of the conflicting positions held by major countries in the world's trading structure, negotiations were likely to be prolonged and delicate. Exogenous events, however, made them almost unnecessary. Inflation became a major worldwide problem in 1973, and as nations sought to maintain their exchange rates according to the Smithsonian rules, they made the inflation worse. The market switch from weak to strong currencies saw central banks intervening in the marketplace to prop up their exchange rates. The efforts proved futile, as they only ensured more inflation. Thus one by one countries began to let their currencies float.

Meanwhile, the United States devalued the dollar once again in February 1973. The dollar price of gold was increased by about 10 percent. Still, inflation continued in 1973, now exacerbated by oil-price increases affecting most of the world. There were also attempts to legitimize the intervention of countries to maintain "orderly markets," without defining what that meant.

In the trade Act of 1974 and in meetings at Rambouillet in 1975, the system of floating exchange rates became more and more acceptable in principle, as it was already in practice. Finally, the IMF Articles of Agreement were amended at the annual meeting in Jamaica in 1976, accepting the system of floating rates. Countries could still intervene in the exchange market whenever events forced severe disturbances, but it was recognized that stable domestic economies were necessary to ensure stable exchange rates. Still, floating exchange rates were adopted, and the agreement was so worded that the United States could veto any move to return to fixed rates (still favored by some European governments).

In addition, gold was ousted as the common denominator for currency values; Special Drawing Rights (SDRs) took its place. There would no longer be any official price for gold, and the private market would perform the necessary price determination. At least officially, gold would no longer play an important role in international finance. Bretton Woods was finally put to rest.

The United States won its power play and succeeded in forcing changes on the international community. The realignment of exchange rates, the trade concessions wrought out of threats and negotiations, and so on, should have helped the U.S. balance-of-payments problem. On this score the United States was much less successful, as the record will soon reveal. But we are getting too far ahead of events, and it is now necessary to review the other parts of the

NEP of 1971 and look at other factors that may have influenced international trade and finance.

The NEP in Action: The Freeze and Phase II

The other apparent rationale for the sweeping economic program was for domestic purposes. Nixon's hopes for reelection in 1972 were, as always, somewhat dependent on the state of the economy. Since the elections were only a year away, and given the lags before any actions would affect the economy, it was time to act. Moreover, it would be unseemly if actions were taken very much later, since they would appear to have been adopted simply for opportunistic reasons—to win the election.

In any case, international actions were pressing, and this represented an opportune time to include domestic policies as well. The administration was aided in its desires by a public that seemed amenable to some type of controls in order to break the inflationary psychology. Arthur Burns and some business leaders had been calling for some demonstration of resolve in fighting inflation and were willing to accept an incomes policy as necessary.

In addition, the general public always appears more willing than its leaders to accept restraints on free markets. Joined now by more professional opinion, some action was almost assured—almost, since the administration was essentially economically conservative, and controls of any kind would be strongly resisted. The irony is that they were not, and political considerations were allowed to triumph over ideological ones.[29]

Thus the Nixon administration was not particularly innovative nor was it faced with strong opposition when it finally determined that something had to be done. What it wanted was a policy to stimulate the economy without aggravating inflation—good politically but economically difficult to achieve. Some sort of control system was required to accompany the stimulative fiscal and monetary actions. For conservative economists to devise one at all woud be traumatic; to devise one in haste would be inconceivable. Ideological purity rather quickly gave way to pragmatism, however, and afterwards restraints on free markets became possible, even reasonable. The first step toward controls was the 90-day freeze on prices, wages, and rents. The freeze was designed as a prelude to more sophisticated controls and purposely devised to hold the economy in a state of suspension, during which time further administrative actions could be contemplated while people could not adjust their economic behavior. The freeze was attractive, since it represented a direct, easily understood and administered method to mark time until further plans could be devised, and at the same time signal the resolve of the administration in confronting inflationary psychology head-on. Of course, the freeze had to be a complete surprise to prevent anyone from adjusting his reward prior to its imposition. The Nixon administration was completely successful in keeping its deliberations secret, which unquestionably helped forestall anticipatory strategies. Its constant disavowal of any interest in direct controls no doubt aided immensely as well.

During the freeze period from August 15 to November 13, 1971, the payments for rents, wages, and prices could not exceed the rate in effect during the base period, July 16 to August 14. While this type of blanket rule is simple to comprehend, and perhaps necessary, there were some inevitable problems. Contracts made for wage increases or price changes that were to take effect during the freeze period presented a major difficulty. These contracts were set aside by the administration, despite the obvious legal questions that could be raised. Other problems came from seasonal price adjustments, the introduction of new products, and import and export prices. These were resolved in the rulings of the Cost of Living Council, and the initial confusion settled down as everyone awaited the next step in the controls process.

Some important exemptions were allowed in the original executive order. Raw agricultural and seafood products were exempt from price controls. Processors, however, were not, and the possibility of their profits being squeezed became a real one as their raw produce costs rose, but they were not allowed to pass them through in the form of higher prices.

Imported goods could register price increases if they reflected higher tariff charges, changing exchange rates, or higher world prices. Dividends and interest rates were not controlled directly, but were expected to conform to voluntary restraints. In addition, price and wage ceilings were not applied to exports, welfare payments, workmen's compensation, some fringe benefits, job promotions, minimum wages, or increases designed to eliminate discriminatory employment practices.[30]

Of course, one of the aims of the freeze was to halt inflation and help break inflationary psychology. By all accounts the freeze worked. During the freeze period, the CPI fell to 1.9 percent at annual rates (from 3.8 percent from December 1970 to August 1971); the WPI fell to

−0.2 percent (from 5.2 percent); and the GNP index fell to 2.2 percent (from 5.1 percent). The Office of Economic Preparedness, which administered the freeze, found a very high degree of compliance with the rules, as many groups—labor, business, consumers—welcomed the action, feeling that something was being done at last about inflation.

The freeze was scheduled to end on November 13, 1971, but the president announced his plans for Phase II, as it was called, long before that, on October 7, 1971. There had been much speculation and discussion on what was to follow the freeze, but it is clear that announcing Phase II at this early date caused many plans to be altered, postponed, shelved, and so on, which may have restricted the effectiveness of the freeze, which still had a month to run. The overlapping of the freeze and Phase II may preclude a proper judgment of the freeze period for effectiveness and compliance.

Lacking a plan for control at the start of the NEP, the administration had to develop one in a rather short time. After much debate over many options, including the idea of a semifreeze that would retain much of the character of the freeze, the administration finally settled on a mandatory system of price and wage controls that would be as comprehensive as administratively feasible, but be self-administered, simple, and direct, to avoid a large bureaucracy and preserve as much of market forces as possible. Accordingly, three main agencies were established to administer the program: the Cost of Living Council (CLC), chaired by John Connally, which was the final authority and coordinator of all programs; the Price Commission, composed of seven public members, which was given the power to rule on price and rent cases; and the Pay Board, composed initially of fifteen members from labor, business, and the public, which was to rule on matters of wages, salaries, and fringe benefits. In addition, there were several advisory commissions to promote compliance in sectors not directly controlled by the CLC: the Rent Advisory Commission, the Construction Industry Stabilization Committee, and the National Commission on Productivity.

In order to limit the bureaucracy that usually accompanies a system of price and wage controls, the program called for self-administration by smaller firms (sales of less than $50 million, affecting less than 1,000 workers); for notification of price and wage decisions by somewhat larger firms (sales of $50–100 million and affecting 1,000–5,000 workers—Tier II firms); and prenotification for the Tier I firms of any contemplated price or wage actions (sales of over $100 million or affecting 5,000 or more workers). Thus many small firms, thought to have little influence or control in the market and little responsibility for causing inflation, were exempt from the full reporting requirements, but they still had to maintain records to prove compliance, should that be necessary.

The Cost of Living Council announced its goal of reducing inflation to the range of 2 to 3 percent by the end of 1972. With this goal in mind, the Price Commission and Pay Board set about formulating regulations to conform to this target.

Price Commission.   Manufacturing and service firms were permitted to increase their prices when allowable costs increased, but could not increase prices if the effect was to increase the firm's profit margins over the base period (highest average of two out of three prior fiscal years). Thus, absolute profits could rise, but profit margins could not: Prices could rise to reflect price increases in raw materials, labor costs (less any gains in productivity), and so on. In some cases the Price Commission worked out arrangements with large firms on the average price increase permissible for the firm's products without the need to apply each time. Many other exceptions were made in the application of the general standard.

Other policies set by the Price Commission included the following: Retailers could choose to maintain their customary markups or be guided by the same rules as manufacturing firms; rents were allowed to increase by 2.5 percent annually, as long as 30 days' notice was given, and further increases were allowed if capital improvements were made; special provisions were included for insurance firms, public utilities, and the health-care industry, but control over prices and rates was left in the hands of other regulatory bodies. Prices, fees, and charges of other levels of government were not controlled, nor were interest rates or dividend income, although firms were asked to limit their dividends to an increase of 4 percent per share in 1972, based on previous years' payouts.

Pay Board.   The Pay Board reached its standard wage increase by considering both productivity and cost-of-living factors. Thus, it proposed to limit wage increases to 5.5 percent. With an estimated increase in productivity of approximately 3 percent, this left the remainder at 2.5 percent, which was entirely consistent with the CLC's goal of a 2–3 percent inflation rate. In addition, existing pay practices operating before November 14 could be challenged, if five board members agreed. Contracts for pay increases completed before the freeze could be honored and paid retroactively, if the board approved. Organized labor insisted on this latter provision and heavily lobbied Congress, which responded when the Economic Stabilization Act (due to expire on April 1972) was extended to April 1973. In the extension bill, Congress ordered such payments retroactively unless "unreasonably inconsistent" with the board's standards. Congress went even further, exempting many fringe benefits from the definition of wages and salaries and removing the ceilings from any individual whose earnings were substandard. As a result, wage increases beyond the 5.5 percent standard were made possible.

While the rules and regulations appear straightforward enough, there was still much confusion over how to apply them in practice. In such a complex economy, it would be impossible to devise rules that would fit all firms and all situations; there are just too many cases that do not easily fit into general rules. Thus the number of inquiries averaged over 24,000 per day from the beginning of Phase II to mid-January, with half of the questions about recent regulations.[31] The confusion was compounded by the first decisions of the two agencies. The Pay Board awarded the coal miners a wage increase of 15 percent, and although some special circumstances surrounded this case, in the minds of the public there was something amiss. The Price Commission granted a price increase of 7 percent on tin plate to two steel companies. If the standards were regarded as loose, it would be difficult to get widespread compliance.

As might be expected, both firms and labor objected to the regulations set. Labor, in fact, was belligerent and threatened to withdraw from the Pay Board unless its demands were met. Organized labor felt it was being singled out for controls, while profits, rents, interest payments, and dividends were free of them. It fought hard for payment of wages negotiated during the freeze and for their retroactive payment. As shown above, labor won this battle. Still smarting from the exclusion of other types of rewards from controls, organized labor was ready to boycott the regulations. George Meany, at the AFL–CIO meetings in Miami in November, put it bluntly: "If the President doesn't want our membership on the Pay Board, he knows what he can do." Nixon flew to Miami and told the delegates that his program would succeed with or without them. "I know exactly what I can do. And I am going to do it."[32] Several months later four of the five labor representatives withdrew from the Pay Board.

Phase III and Phase IV of the NEP. At the end of 1972 the economy seemed to be progressing nicely and according to plan. Here are the relevant data to support that contention: GNP increased by 9.8 percent in nominal terms, 6.2 percent in real terms; real consumption and investment increased by 6.2 percent and 12.5 percent, respectively, as the private sector was responding; the unemployment rate had fallen to 5.2 percent in December, while average hourly earnings fell to a 6.2 percent rate of increase; productivity increased, and unit labor costs fell; industrial production rose by 7.9 percent, and capacity utilization rose to over 81 percent; finally, consumer prices rose by 3.4 percent over the year, wholesale prices rose 6.5 percent, and the implicit price index rose by 3.4 percent.

Under these circumstances, Nixon's announcement in mid-January that Phase II would be replaced by Phase III came as a surprise. What made the decision so puzzling was the movement toward voluntary controls that was described. Most of the rules were carried over from Phase II, but the program was now to be self-administered. Gone was the prenotification requirement of price and wage changes, except for the very large firms. The Price Commission and Pay Board were abolished and their duties taken over by the Cost of Living Council. A new price standard was initiated as well: The profit-margin limit was eliminated if the firm's average price increase did not exceed 1.5 percent per year. Furthermore, price increases were allowed where "necessary for efficient allocation of resources or to maintain adequate levels of supply." Firms were also given the choice of a larger number of years to calculate their profit-margin average.

The question is, Why the changes now and why the liberalization? One answer, frequently given by the administation, was its distaste for controls and its desire to remove them as quickly as possible. That the administration viewed controls as temporary came to be widely known and accepted.[33] This would be a step toward their eventual elimination. There was also the contention that the controls imposed heavy burdens, particularly in their inflexibility. The strains on some markets could not be relieved within the framework of fixed standards and rules. Yet the administration itself found a remarkable degree of flexibility during 1972.[34] It is likely that the strains were indeed growing and the movement toward voluntary controls would help relieve them, but it is not clear how. The only burden that was really lessened was the cost of administering the controls program; both the paperwork and the bureaucracy were reduced.

Thus the only real justification appears to be a worry that future private decisions would be adversely affected by the controls system. The fear was that a growing economy would soon begin to feel the shackles of controls, and a barrier to further growth would develop. Whether legitimate or not, this concern (and the desire to be rid of controls) was supplied as the rationale for scrapping Phase II, even as the economy showed progress.

In any case, Phase III did not last very long. Despite some tightening of controls on producers of crude oil and petroleum products and on meat processors, prices began to rise. In the five-month period of January through May, the CPI rose by 3 percent (over 7 percent at annual rates), as food prices alone jumped by 8.7 percent (or over 22 percent at annual rates); wholesale prices rose by 7.2 percent in the same period (or over 18 percent at annual rates), and again the increases in farm products led the way with a 13 percent rise (or over 34 percent at annual rates).

With food prices (not wholly controlled) and fuel prices rising at rapid rates, the pressure on the administration to do something became intense. What response to make was evidently less clear. A large part of the pressure on price levels was coming from commodities like leather, petroleum, agricultural products, and the like. Some of these were imported, and those that were not were flowing out of the country; export prices were not controlled, and better prices could be obtained abroad. The second devaluation of the dollar in January 1973 exacerbated the problem.

Some commodities, like lumber, were exported and reimported at inflated prices, since import prices were also not controlled. Thus lumber was exported to Canada and then illegally reshipped to the Unites States as Canadian lumber at uncontrolled prices. Controlling prices under these circumstances would be difficult indeed.[35]

The administration chose to employ the freeze tactic again, this time for a maximum of 60 days. Phase IV would follow as soon as the plans were developed. The second freeze was not nearly as successful as the first one. Herbert Stein, chairman of the Council of Economic Advisors, warned the president, "You can't step in the same river twice," to which the president replied, "You could, if it was frozen."[36]

This time the freeze did not generate the same favorable public attitude as did the first one. After all, the controls had been in place for some time now, and consumers were not shocked or surprised by the New Economic Program, and, besides, prices were rising and soon shortages of foodstuffs would appear; hence the suspicion of this latest attempt to manage prices. Food prices continued their upward rise, as heavy demands for farm products, coupled with poor harvests in 1972, put additional pressures on prices over and above the effects of devaluation and the lack of controls on raw farm goods. Food processors and distributors, however, got caught in the middle, as their costs went up but their ability to pass them on in higher prices was constrained. They began to cut back production, and shortages of poultry, meats, canned foods, vegetables, and so on developed, further annoying the consumer.

The administration feared that additional controls would only have reduced production further or resulted in even greater shortages.[37] Phase IV would have to respond to the dilemma anyway.

The first part of Phase IV was designed to relieve pressures on food processors, as they were now allowed (July 18) to pass through all farm price increases. The second step of Phase IV was to return the health industry to Phase II standards. Finally, in August, the other sectors of the economy were brought under new regulations. As before, interest rates and dividends were not controlled.

The new controls were in some ways stricter than the previous ones. Price increases were limited to actual cost increases incurred since the last fiscal quarter of 1972, and additional markups or increases in profits margins were denied. Prenotification for large firms (sales over $100 million) were again required, and other, smaller firms had to file quarterly reports.

The pay standard remained as used in Phase II: 5.5 percent for wages and 0.7 percent for approved fringe benefits. In an apparent move to return to free markets, however, certain key wage bargains received increased attention to prevent "ripple effects" and to hasten the retreat from the application of fixed and rigid standards.

The move toward free markets can also be found in the list of industries that were decontrolled in Phase IV. The decontrol program was devised to dismantle the controls gradually, on a sector-by-sector basis, to prevent a bulge in prices after the controls were removed. Supply considerations and the informal agreements with industries were major factors in deciding which industries to decontrol first. The fertilizer, nonferrous metals, lumber, automobile, and cement industries topped the list. The list grew in January, February, and March, until finally the controls were terminated on April 30, 1974.

Evaluation of the Controls Program

Now that the entire controls program has been outlined, it is time to ask how successful it was in achieving its desired ends. Table 11.4 reveals the necessary data for a preliminary evaluation of its success in reducing the rate of inflation. The record of controls during the first freeze and Phase II is good; the controls worked, and the rate of inflation is close to the goals set by the administration. The considerable slack in the economy may have helped in the attainment of the target set.

During Phase III, price and wage increases had begun to exceed the goals of the program. The change in the CPI from 3.4 percent in Phase II to 8.3 percent in Phase III represents a 144 percent increase, while wages rose about 49 percent over the same period. Note, however, the increase in food prices—over 242 percent over Phase II. The uncontrolled food and farm products price increase is seen even better in the wholesale price index. In total the WPI rose by over 276 percent, with farm products rising by 265 percent and crude materials by 319 percent. It would appear that the uncontrolled items in the economy were wrecking the price-control program.

Prices continued to rise during Phase III, with food and farm-products prices moderating somewhat. Now, in fact, crude materials began to increase still further, led by the high price increases for crude oil. While these price changes were occurring, the rate of increase in wages was falling during Phase III and holding steady during Phase IV.

During Phase IV prices continued to rise, increasing by 12 percent in the CPI and 22 percent in the WPI. The rate of increase in food and farm output continued to fall, but now oil prices forced up prices of industrial commodities and crude materials whose prices had increased by over 986 percent from Phase II. Finally, the postcontrols bulge in prices can be seen in the last two columns.

The CEA had a difficult time evaluating the controls. On the one hand, it was an administration program and could hardly be dismissed. On the other hand, its distaste for controls forced it to equivocate. The CEA was reluctant to make any judgments about the controls system, which would be difficult to evaluate since there is no way to calculate what would have happened to the economy in the absence of controls. It did conclude, however, that "whatever contribution it may have made was probably concentrated in its first 16 months, when the economy was operating well below its potential. ... The sharply rising costs of basic material, often reflecting world market influences and dollar devaluation, were largely uncontrolled; when passed through to consumers, they resulted in accelerating inflation."[38]

Admittedly, trying to evaluate the controls program is and would always be a difficult, not to mention controversial, undertaking. Universal agreement among economists would be unlikely, but most would subscribe to the conclusions of Robert J. Gordon who tried to simulate what would have happened in the absence of controls. His conclusions are worth quoting at length for this reason.[39]

> Controls worked not by moderating the behavior of wages relative to prices, but rather by squeezing profit margins sufficiently to hold prices below their free market levels. ... If instead profit margins eventually return to their no-controls level, there will be a catch-up period after the controls are lifted, during which the rate

Table 11.4 Measures of Price and Wage Change during and after the Economic Stabilization Program (percent change: seasonally adjusted annual rate)

Price or Wage Measure	Freeze and Phase II Aug. 1971 to Jan. 1973	Phase III Jan. 1973 to June 1973	Second freeze and Phase IV June 1973 to Apr. 1974	Phase IV Dec. 1973 to Apr. 1974	1974 Apr. to Aug.	1974 Aug. to Dec.
PRICES						
Consumer price index:						
All items	3.4	8.3	10.7	12.2	12.7	11.8
Food	5.9	20.2	16.2	12.8	7.0	17.0
All items less food	2.7	5.0	8.7	11.8	15.3	9.7
Commodities less food	2.2	4.8	9.2	14.9	16.4	8.6
Services[1]	3.5	4.3	8.6	8.8	13.3	11.7
Personal consumption expenditures deflator[2]	2.8	6.7	10.8	13.9	11.8	11.4
Wholesale price index*[3]						
All commodities	5.9	22.2	15.2	21.9	31.8	10.2
Farm products and processed foods and feeds	13.4	48.9	6.3	.4	24.5	9.5
Industrial commodities[4]	2.9	12.3	19.6	33.9	35.5	9.4
Finished goods, consumer and produce[5]	1.9	7.2	13.4	23.4	25.8	14.6
Crude and intermediate materials[5]	3.6	15.1	23.3	39.1	40.9	7.1

378

WAGES[6]

	(col. 1)	(col. 2)	(col. 3)	(col. 4)	(col. 5)	(col. 6)
Average hourly earnings, private nonfarm economy:[7]						
Monthly series	6.2	6.3	6.9	6.5	11.9	9.3
Quarterly series[2]	6.4	5.9	7.0	6.3	10.3	9.7
Average hourly compensation:						
Total private economy[2]	5.8	8.9	7.0	7.0	11.2	9.0
Nonfarm[2]	5.9	8.8	7.5	7.9	10.7	9.3

[1]Not seasonally adjusted.

[2]Percent changes based on quarterly date: 1971–III to 1972–IV (col. 1), 1972–IV to 1973–II (col. 2), 1973–II to 1974–I (col. 3), 1973–IV to 1974–I (col. 4), 1974–I to 1974–III (col. 5), 1974–III to 1974–IV (col.6).

[3]Seasonally adjusted percentage changes in components of the WPI do not necessarily average to the seasonally adjusted percentage change in the total index because adjustment of the components and the total are calculated separately.

[4]Includes a small number of items not shown separately.

[5]Excludes foods but includes a small number of items not in the industrial commodity index.

[6]Average hourly earnings are for production workers or nonsupervisory employees and average hourly compensation for all employees.

[7]Adjusted for overtime (in manufacturing only) and interindustry shifts.

Source: Council of Economic Advisors, *Economic Report of the President* (Washington, DC: GPO, 1975), p. 227.

of inflation will be substantially faster than it would have been had the controls not been imposed. On the assumption that profit margins will eventually be reestablished, one can cite at least four reasons for concluding that the controls were a failure:

1. Controls will have had no long-run effect on inflation.
2. The removal of controls will cause an extra, "catch-up," inflation at some point; the timing of this catch-up may be awkward, if, for example, nonfarm prices are simultaneously escalating because of the energy shortage.
3. Controls have caused shortages and misallocations of re-sources in several sectors.
4. The administration of controls has consumed real resources.

In an earlier article he showed that the controls worked during the first year, but were costly, and any reductions in inflation were temporary. Others reached similar conclusions.[40] Both Herbert Stein, who was chairman of the CEA, and C. Jackson Grayson, who was chairman of the Price Commission, have written of the failures of controls.[41] It would be fair to assume that the majority of economists would concur with these judgments.

For others, more liberal in outlook, wage and price controls are and will be inevitable. John K. Galbraith, wage and price controls' most consistent and vocal advocate, commended the president for his contribution to economic understanding, while castigating his econom-ists for abandoning the policy of controls just when it was working. He and others noted that it was a curious approach to public policy to abandon one that is working. He echoed the criticism of many when he wrote, "Since the policy has had no standing among reputable economists, virtually no thought has been given to the problems of administration."[42] Clearly the controls system was rushed through without adequate attention being paid to details; accordingly, they were ill conceived. There were constant reminders from the adminis-tration that a return to the free market was imminent, setting up expectations that no controls system could overcome; accordingly, it was ill administered.

Political considerations also got in the way of proper administra-tion, giving the controls an element of unfairness and inequity. The controls were changed too often, making for confusion and uncertainty, and some decisions must have been altered or delayed in anticipation of later changes.[43] These were the criticisms that were voiced by advocates of wage and price controls in the hope that the policy would not be discarded due to this unfortunate experience with them. Galbraith, for instance, had always maintained that controls would have to be permanent in order to work; they would have to be administered properly, but would still be messy. The alternative is to let prices be controlled by private large firms in their own interest.[44]

The Nixon version of controls was crippled by poor administration, according to the critics. They point to the lack of controls on food and food products, imports and exports, and property incomes as examples of why the controls had difficulties. Many question whether the second devaluation was really necessary, since it drove up the price of imports with the now undervalued dollar. Finally, as will be discussed, the stimulative monetary and fiscal policy made the job of controls unnecessarily arduous, but of course one of the reasons for imposing controls in the first place was to allow such stimulation from macroeconomic policies.

The debate over whether or not the controls worked has long since passed from consideration. Both sides can claim victory, since the final answer can never be known. What remains, however, is the question of whether or not controls could ever work, even under the right conditions. Here the judgment is clearer: Nixon's control system dealt a severe blow to any future controls program. When it finally died, the policy of wage and price controls as a public policy nearly went with it. The general public still considers controls an option and favors them whenever inflation threatens. Most economists, however, have given up on controls as an answer to inflation and have ammunition to support their conclusions by referring to the Nixon experience. Those who favored controls still do so and later devised alternative systems, such as Taxed-Based Incomes Policies (TIP).

Political Content of Controls and Their Demise in the Oil Crisis

The debate over whether or not the controls worked becomes quite esoteric, centering as it does on the structure of the econometric models used to simulate history. Many have dismissed such models as deficient, while others defend them as serviceable. Few minds were changed by the evidence of these models, and defenders of controls insist that they have a role in macroeconomic policy; the model builders have concluded otherwise. The fact is that if they are basing their conclusions on the Nixon version of controls, they may well be missing the point.

Wage and price controls under Nixon must be viewed as a political, not an economic, policy. The controls were instituted to demonstrate the administration's resolve in fighting inflation, to be sure, but the rationale behind them was to allow the administration to pursue expansionary monetary and fiscal policies, and with a stimulated economy, win an election. Judging controls in isolation, as an economic policy, is to misinterpret the whole experience.

As 1972 came to a close, the administration was concerned that the economic data were not looking better. While real GNP was increasing at an annual rate of 6.7 percent in the last quarter, the unemployment rate remained stable at a high 6 percent, and capacity usage remained low, at about 75 percent; industrial production was not increasing significantly, and the economy seemed stalled.

It was now time to pursue the expansionary policies that would address these problems directly. The administration began to urge federal departments to spend, spend, and spend. Since the federal budget would show a large deficit anyway, a larger one would not be shocking, and later, presumably after the election, reductions in government spending could be carried out. Recall that Roosevelt used the same tactic in incurring large deficits at one point, so that future deficits would appear small by comparison.[45] The deficit for FY 1972 was large—$ −23.2 billion—but not significantly larger than for FY 1971, which was $ −23.0 billion; the increase in government spending of $20 billion was matched by a corresponding increase in revenues. This fiscal ploy became obvious when the Nixon administration asked Congress for a spending ceiling for FY 1973 of $246 billion. The increase in the spending totals over FY 1972 reflected the delayed increases due to Nixon's spending splurge.

The increases consisted of $9 billion in national defense, $5.2 billion in revenue sharing, and $3.5 billion in Social Security benefits, which Congress upped to $8 billion, starting in the fourth quarter of 1972! Members of Congress, too, had to run for reelection. These expenditures, combined with the temporary overwithholding of taxes on individuals, swung the full-employment surplus of $1 billion to a deficit of $4 billion—or to $13 billion, if the overwithholding tax receipts are excluded. Certainly fiscal policy was expansionary.

In the fall of 1969 Nixon appointed Arthur Burns, an old friend, as chairman of the Federal Reserve Board, replacing William M. Martin. Feeling the key to the economy was the Federal Reserve, Nixon wanted to replace the independent-minded Martin with a man of his own. The money supply was growing too slowly to suit the administration. Burns soon asserted his own independence, frequently irritating the president, as he continued to call for an incomes policy of some kind to build confidence in the economy. Even after the controls were instituted, Burns was often critical of them, prompting the administration to malign him by declaring that his opposition was only in self-interest.[46]

The appointment of Burns was not immediately satisfactory to the administration, since the money supply grew by "only" 5.4 percent from December 1969 to December 1970 and by 6.2 percent from December 1970 to December 1971. Continued pressure on Burns and the Federal Reserve finally worked, and the money supply increased by 9.2 percent in the first quarter of 1972 and for the year rose by 8.2 percent. This growth rate of the money supply proved more satisfactory, as short-term interest rates fell slightly in the first quarter of 1972 and then rose slowly throughout the year; long-term interest rates remained stable, even in the face of growing demands caused by an expanding economy.

The economy responded to the plans of the Nixon administration, and reelection seemed assured. Real GNP was growing at a respectable 6.5 percent, unemployment was declining and at year's end stood at 5.1 percent. Prices were behaving, thanks to controls; real wages were rising; Social Security recipients were pleased with their increase; industrial production was increasing over that in 1971 by 7 percent; capacity-utilization rates climbed to 80 percent; corporate profits were up 12 percent; and only the balance of payments was moving in the unfavorable direction, climbing to a deficit of $9.8 billion on current account alone and over $10 billion on the official reserve balance. Devaluation had not yet had its full impact, and meanwhile imports were temporarily more expensive in dollar terms. Nevertheless, 1972 turned out to be quite satisfactory to the administration, as it saw its domestic plans carried out.

The economic maneuvers of the Nixon administration clearly worked. The economy was surely stimulated by macroeconomic policies, as previously discussed, and Social Security increases clearly helped the pocketbook issue; but such is the power of incumbency that even the timing of other payments could be made to suit political ends. Transfer payments, such as for veterans' payments and grant-in-aid to states and localities, were increased; in the fourth quarter of 1972, they jumped over 33 percent over the previous quarter.[47]

The antiwar, antidraft, anti-imperial-presidency, antibusiness movements all paled by comparison. Nixon's opponent was Senator George S. McGovern of South Dakota who was a ranking liberal (some would have said progressive) in the Democratic party. The liberals gleefully endorsed him, but on the whole his proposals seemed too radical for most people. His promises to cut defense spending by 50 percent, while providing a guaranteed income for every family, illustrate only two of the programs he advocated. The promise of peace was not as pressing an issue, now that the end of the war seemed in sight. Henry Kissinger, the national security advisor, had been negotiating with the North Vietnamese and had engineered a visit to China, which Nixon undertook in February 1972.

On June 17, 1972, five men were arrested for breaking into the Democratic National Committee offices at the Watergate complex in Washington. In November, however, the incident was considered a minor, third-rate burglary attempt. There seemed to be nothing standing in the way of Nixon's reelection, and that was confirmed in November when he won by a landslide, receiving over 60 percent of the popular vote and 520 electoral votes; McGovern carried only Massachusetts and the District of Columbia for 17 electoral votes. The Democrats, however, continued to control both houses of Congress by wide margins.

Nixon's second term began brightly enough, as a peace treaty with North Vietnam was signed in Paris on January 27, 1973, and the POWs began returning in February. In that same month, however, Judge John J. Sirica charged that the prosecutor of the Watergate burglary, while obtaining convictions for all involved, failed to investigate the whole affair fully and ordered the government to continue its investigations. Slowly, month after month, the Nixon administration began to unravel, until it could scarcely govern. In response to allegations of additional political espionage, the Senate voted to form a seven-member special committee to investigate. The Watergate affair was launched.

In October the House Judiciary Committee voted to proceed with impeachment proceedings, and Spiro Agnew, the vice-president, resigned over charges that he had accepted bribes while governor of Maryland. Nixon had wanted to rid himself of Agnew for some time, but now on top of his other troubles, it was unfortunate timing. Representative Gerald Ford was named as his replacement.

The House Judiciary Committee began impeachment proceedings in May and later was prepared to recommend impeachment on three grounds. Nixon resigned on August 9, 1974, and was replaced by Gerald Ford, who pardoned him on September 8. This controversial act sealed the case and prevented the conviction of President Nixon for federal crimes that he "committed or may have committed."

As the affair dragged on in the courts, in the press, and in the general public conscience, the mood of the nation changed. Congress became antagonistic and began opposing Nixon's programs and actions. As might be expected, the Nixon administration itself began to pay less and less attention to running the nation and turned to self-defense. Nixon, never deeply interested in economic matters, turned even farther away and left them to George Shultz and other economic advisors. Therefore, the economic policies of the period must be judged in the light of this background. Economic concerns began to recede in importance, in comparison to more immediate concerns, and those policies undertaken must be examined more for their political content than would ordinarily be the case. Economic problems, however, did not recognize these other concerns and kept coming to the foreground; the administration's response to them has to be viewed in the wider context of its own survival problems and the probably increasing distrust of politicians and government that its own actions helped to perpetuate.

Some of the problems were new, while others were old ones finally being seriously considered. The growing concern over the environment in the 1960s led to the Clean Air Act and other laws to protect and preserve the environment; concern for safety led to the Occupational Health and Safety Act and consumer-protection laws, and most important were the many regulatory acts concerning the pressing problem of energy. Herbert Stein was not exaggerating when he wrote, "Probably more new regulation was imposed on the economy during the Nixon administration than in any other presidency since the New Deal."[48]

Important as these responses were to national concerns, the most attention was given to the problem of energy. Despite warnings that dated back 20 years, the United States continued to increase its demand for energy, which was fostered by stable or falling energy prices. Prior to 1973 prices were either stable or falling in relation to other prices. Sometimes public policy was responsible for the low energy prices through such policies as depletion allowances and controlled prices. Of course, low energy prices caused the United States to become more dependent on energy as the economy reacted to the situation. It responded by substituting energy capital for labor as wages rose; by transforming the society through suburban growth for both families and business, while at the same time spurning mass-transit possibilities; and finally, by encouraging inefficient energy-using facilities in the home and in the workplace. With the increased demand for energy, the United States, once self-sufficient in energy, now had to import more and more to satisfy its appetite.

There were sufficient warnings, of "brown-outs" and actual power failures, but genuine concern was only beginning; there was always the hope that technical change would bail the nation out. Nuclear, solar, and geothermal sources of power received more attention as possible answers; conservation of energy was an idea for only a small number of people, as most clung to their old consumption habits. This complacency was shattered by the five-month oil embargo imposed by several Arab countries in October 1973. Only about 17 percent of domestic demand was satisfied by imported oil, but this was enough to cause severe disruptions to the nation's economy. Consumers were forced to wait in long lines to buy gasoline; firms were forced to cut back production, sometimes for lack of energy, sometimes because higher energy prices forced prices up and consumption fell; inflation was once again heated up, and consumers were forced to spend more on energy and less on other commodities, causing some unemployment and output loss.

The effect on energy prices was dramatic. In January 1973 the price of crude oil per barrel was $1.62; by the time Mr. Nixon left office in August, the imported price had risen to $12.68 per barrel, a 683 percent increase! Of course, the price of other energy sources rose as well, and substitution was of little avail to consumers. The domestic price of crude oil was still controlled at just over $5 per barrel, giving a two-tier pricing system. The controlled price referred to "old oil," equal to what was produced in the same month in 1972; the price of "new" oil, (the excess) was not controlled. Since prices at the pump had to be uniform, this led to a composite price made up of old, new, and imported oil. The controls on domestic oil prices discouraged production and helped to encourage imports and therefore dependency. The OPEC countries quickly took advantage of our vulnerability and further increased prices, until by the 1980s the price per barrel had risen to over $35.

The administration did respond by creating the Federal Energy Administration, which was given the power to regulate oil supplies and prices, even after wage and price controls had been abandoned. The FEA found that shortages of oil had arisen in various parts of the country, due to the refiners and distributors having different access to combinations of new and old oil and, of course, different profits from operations. It responded by allocating the scarce supplies of oil and by recommending a "windfall profits" tax to prevent undue profits being made on old oil being sold at the market price, which was always higher than the controlled price.

There followed many more schemes for allocating and pricing oil products and other approaches to foster conservation, including the 55-mile-per-hour speed limit, tax credits for home improvements that conserved energy, and the requirement on automobile producers to make cars that met a specified gas mileage per gallon. In addition to its disruption of economic activity, the energy crisis removed all hopes of controlling inflation. Already witnessed was the effect of commodity prices on the wage-and-price controls program. The controls program would have been wrecked by the price of crude oil alone—recall that import prices were not controlled.

Still, the Nixon administration was reluctant to let the price of energy sources rise to force conservation of them and remove the endless controls and allocation schemes designed to accomplish what the marketplace was not allowed to do. Equity concerns overruled the free market. Consumers were not only faced with shortages, but the shortages were not evenly felt across the nation, and rising prices meant less left over for consumption of other goods, sometimes forcing the reduction of food purchases as the only item in the budget that was discretionary. To show the effects of price increases, Table 11.5 gives the rates of change of the major fuel-source prices.

In the postcontrol period, however, all prices began to increase, as anticipated by everyone in the "bulge period." Wholesale prices rose by 13.1 percent in 1973 and by 18.9 percent in 1974. Farm products rose by 3.0 and 11.5 percent in 1973 and 1974, while fuel prices rose by 10.6 and 33.4 percent in the same periods. These wholesale prices soon found their way into consumer prices, with the CPI rising by 6.2 and 11.0 percent in 1973 and 1974; food prices were rising by over 14 percent in both years, and fuel and utility prices were rising by over 11 and 16 percent, respectively. The price increases were the highest since the end of World War II, and there were no signs of significant improvement in the near future.

Wage and price controls were useless under these conditions, and the era of even modest price stability appeared to be over. Double-digit inflation seemed to be inevitable, as the implicit price index, and the most inclusive index, rose from 5.6 percent in 1973 to 10.2 percent in 1974. The price increases were widespread, with just over half the rise in the CPI from 1973 to 1974 being accounted for by items other than food and directly purchased energy.[49]

The economy entered into a period of stagflation, with prices rising while output and employment were falling. The unemployment rate held steady during 1973, averaging 4.9 percent, and then slowly crept up to 7.2 percent in December 1974. Meanwhile, real wages were falling by 5 percent in 1974, industrial production by 0.7 percent with only a few areas registering increases; capacity utilization fell from 83 to 79 percent, and construction activity fell—private housing by over 22 percent.

Clearly the economy was sinking into a recession, and the NBER settled on the peak of the cycle as November 1973 from the previous trough that began in November 1970. The downturn would last until

Table 11.5   Changes in Wholesale Prices of Selected Fuels, 1964 to 1974 (percent change; quarterly rate)

Period	Coal	Natural Gas	Refined Petroleum Products*	Electric Power
Average quarterly change				
1964 to 1969	0.9	0.3	0.5	0.1
1969 to 1972	4.6	1.4	0.7	1.5
1972 to 1973	3.0	2.3	5.1	1.7
1973 to 1974	11.1	—	—	—
Changes from 3 months earlier				
1973: March	0.9	3.0	9.5	3.1
June	3.7	3.3	6.0	1.1
September	3.5	1.6	3.2	2.4
December	8.1	7.1	24.2	4.1
1974: March	7.7	3.3	29.7	11.6
June	24.0	3.0	10.9	9.3
September	15.6	12.2	2.0	6.4
December	15.2	—	—	—

*Through February 1973 there were no lags in this series. Since March 1973, index numbers of the major products in this series refer to prices of the previous month. The unlagged portion of the series has a very small weight.

Note: The price changes shown in this table have been calculated from the wholesale price index, adjusted for the lags embodied in some fuel price series. For example, changes shown in this table from June to September 1973 would be presented in the wholesale price index as changes in natural gas prices from August to November, in refined petroleum products and electric power prices from July to October, and in coal prices from June to September.

Source: Council of Economic Advisors, Economic Report of the President (Washington, DC: GPO, 1975), p. 77.

March 1975, a period of 16 months. Real GNP fell throughout 1974, and for the year the rate of increase was −2.2, down from the 1973 rate of 5.9 percent. All components showed declines except exports and state and local government purchases. The changes in the last years of the Nixon administration, as well as those in the earlier years, can be seen in Table 11.6. The two recessions of 1970 and 1973–74 are clearly apparent in the real GNP data, and the record of government purchases is of particular interest in the analysis of fiscal policy that follows.

Restrictive Macroeconomic Policies
in the Post-1971-Election Period
and the Recession of 1969–70

The expansionary fiscal policy of 1972 gave way to a restrictive one for 1973 and 1974. The postelection reversal of fiscal policy provides ready evidence for charges that the Nixon administration played politics with the economy. Federal expenditures rose by 8.2 percent in the calendar year from 1972 to 1973, after having risen by 10.9 percent from 1971 to 1972; from 1973 to 1974 the increase was 13.3 percent. The fiscal-year budgets show increases of 9.6 percent and 6.3 percent for the same yearly periods. (See Tables 11.7 and 11.8.)

Just a glance at Table 11.7 reveals the speedup in government spending in 1972, particularly in the fourth quarter. Then in 1973 and 1974 spending becomes more restrictive, as can be seen in the full-employment budget. In 1972 it registered an $8.4 billion deficit, while in 1973 and 1974 the deficits turned to surpluses of $7.5 and $25.4 billion, respectively.

Whatever increases in expenditures there were, were caused by conditions over which the administration had no control. Nixon's own version of federalism saw the promise of from $6 to $6.5 billion being transferred from the federal government to states and localities. This began with $3.5 billion in 1973, after the Revenue Sharing Act was passed in October 1972, and grew to $6 billion in 1974.[50] The 1972 increases in Social Security payments were coming due, and there was no possibility of rescinding them now. In other areas, however, Nixon wanted to reduce spending in 1973 and threatened to veto all bills that increased domestic spending above his budget. The contest between the president and Congress grew heated, the more so as the Watergate affair unfolded.

Congress forced the administration to grant pay increases of 5 percent to civilian and military personnel. The president did veto many bills and impounded rural water and sewer funds, and in so doing angered Congress to such an extent that it later passed the Congressional Budget and Impoundment Control Act of 1974, which limited the president's ability to refuse to spend funds in the future. The same act revised the congressional budget process in the hopes of making the budget procedure more rational. As of fiscal year 1977 (now October 1 to September 30), Congress has to vote on budget totals before it considers appropriations by programs, and these spending requests have to fit into the overall budget totals. Previously, the

Table 11.6   Changes in Gross National Product in Current and Constant Dollars, 1968 to 1974 (percent)

Component	1968 to 1969	1969 to 1970	1970 to 1971	1971 to 1972	1972 to 1973	1973 to 1974
CURRENT DOLLARS						
Percent change						
Total GNP	7.6	5.0	8.0	9.8	11.8	7.9
Personal consumption expenditures	8.1	6.6	8.0	9.3	10.5	8.9
Durable goods	8.1	.6	13.8	14.0	10.1	-1.9
Nondurable goods	6.5	7.3	5.5	7.7	12.8	12.5
Services	9.7	8.2	8.5	9.2	8.4	9.6
Gross private domestic investment	10.3	-1.9	12.8	16.7	16.8	-.2
Business fixed investment	10.9	2.1	4.0	11.7	17.1	9.4
Residential structures	8.3	-4.3	37.2	26.2	5.9	-19.6
Government purchases	5.2	4.5	6.7	9.2	8.1	11.7
Federal purchases	.0	-2.6	1.5	7.5	1.6	9.2
State and local purchases	10.3	10.9	10.8	10.4	12.6	13.3
Addendum:						
Final sales	7.6	5.4	7.8	9.6	11.3	8.1
Domestic final sales	7.7	5.3	8.2	10.2	10.4	8.3
Change in billions of dollars						
Inventory accumulation	.7	-3.3	1.8	2.2	6.9	-2.0
Net exports of goods and services	-.6	1.7	-3.8	-5.8	9.9	-1.9

CONSTANT (1958) DOLLARS

Percent change

Total GNP	2.7	−.4	3.3	6.2	5.9	−2.2
Personal consumption expenditures	3.6	1.8	4.0	6.2	4.7	−2.2
Durable goods	5.3	−2.1	10.4	13.4	8.3	−9.0
Nondurable gods	2.1	2.6	2.3	4.2	3.8	−2.1
Services	4.5	2.7	2.9	5.0	3.8	1.4
Gross private domestic investment	5.0	−6.4	7.4	12.5	10.5	−8.5
Business fixed investment	6.0	−3.6	−.6	9.1	12.8	−.3
Residential structures	2.2	−6.3	31.1	17.9	−4.1	−27.1
Government purchases	−1.2	−4.5	.0	2.7	.9	1.0
Federal purchases	−5.9	−12.5	−5.3	.2	−6.1	−1.7
State and local purchases	4.0	3.6	4.5	4.7	6.0	2.9
Addendum						
Final sales	2.7	−.1	3.1	6.0	5.5	−1.9
Domestic final sales	2.8	−.3	3.5	6.3	4.5	−2.4
Change in billions of dollars						
Inventory accumulation	.3	−2.8	1.4	1.7	3.8	−2.6
Net exports of goods and services	−.8	2.1	−2.8	−2.5	7.6	4.4

Source: Council of Economic Advisors, *Economic Report of the President* (Washington, DC: GPO, 1975), p. 38.

Table 11.7 Actual and Full-Employment Federal Government Receipts and Expenditures, Calendar Years 1969–74 (billions of seasonally adjusted dollars at annual rates)

Year	National Income Accounts Basis		
	Receipts	Expenditures	Surplus or Deficit (−)
Actual			
1969	197.0	188.4	8.5
1970	192.1	204.2	−12.1
1971	198.6	220.6	−22.0
1972	227.5	244.7	−17.3
1973	257.9	264.8	−6.9
1974	288.4	300.1	−11.7
1972 I	222.9	236.6	−13.8
II	225.4	244.4	−19.0
III	229.6	237.0	−7.4
IV	236.9	260.3	−23.4
1973 I	249.1	260.2	−11.2
II	255.0	262.4	−7.4
II	261.8	263.4	−1.7
IV	268.3	270.6	−2.3
1974 I	275.7	281.1	−5.3
II	285.6	293.5	−7.9
III	299.2	307.2	−8.0
IV	293.1	318.6	−25.5
Full employment			
1969	199.7	188.8	10.9
1970	208.9	202.9	5.9
1971	218.6	218.2	0.4
1972	234.4	242.7	−8.4
1973	271.2	263.7	7.5
1974	323.2	297.8	25.4
1972 I	230.2	234.3	−4.1
II	232.6	242.3	−9.7
III	236.6	235.0	1.6
IV	240.1	258.7	−18.6
1973 I	253.8	258.9	−5.1
II	261.2	261.2	−0.1
III	270.2	262.5	7.7
IV	278.3	269.7	8.6
1974 I	297.3	279.5	17.8
II	315.6	291.9	23.7
III	337.0	305.0	32.0
IV	342.7	314.7	28.0

Source: Council of Economic Advisors, *Economic Report of the President* (Washington, DC: GPO, various years).

**Table 11.8   Federal Budget Receipts and Outlays, Fiscal Year 1969–74
(billions of dollars)**

Receipt or Expenditure Category	1969	1971	1972	1973	1974
Budget receipts	187.8	188.4	208.6	232.2	264.9
Individual income taxes	87.2	86.2	94.7	107.2	119.0
Corporation income taxes	36.7	26.8	32.2	36.2	38.6
Social insurance taxes	39.9	48.6	53.9	64.5	76.8
Other	24.0	26.8	27.8	28.3	30.8
Budget outlays	184.5	211.4	231.9	246.5	268.4
National defense	80.2	76.8	77.4	75.1	78.6
Education, training, social services and health	18.6	23.8	29.2	30.7	33.7
Income security	37.3	55.4	63.9	73.0	84.4
Interest	15.8	19.6	20.6	22.8	28.1
Other	32.6	35.6	40.8	44.9	43.6
Surplus or deficit (−)	3.2	−23.0	−23.2	−14.3	−3.5

Source: Council of Economic Advisors, *Economic Report of the President* (Washington, DC: GPO, 1976), pp. 245–47.

opposite was the case—congressional committees would pass appropriation bills without reference to any total budget, and thus spending was encouraged, as no one committee knew what impact its decisions had on the total spending plans. Now that Congress was given more responsibility for formulating the budget, the act also created the Congressional Budget Office to advise and help implement the new, rather tight budget process.

In 1973 the president was largely successful in limiting spending by vetoing bills considered too costly. Some compromises, however, were forced on him—for example, in old-age benefits and health and medical programs. In 1974 the spending increases came in transfer payments, which rose by 23 percent, as Social Security again increased along with Medicare, food stamps, and unemployment compensation. By this time the whole nation was preoccupied with Watergate, and many increases in economic programs that were already in operation were affecting the budget. To emphasize the point, real purchases by the federal government actually declined in 1973 and 1974, continuing the trend that had begun in 1969.

Meanwhile, federal receipts were rising, by 13.3 percent from 1972 to 1973 and by 11.8 percent from 1973 and 1974. Social Security taxes were increasing, due to increases in rates and in the base subject to taxation: Rates were increased from 10.4 percent to 11.7 percent (combined rate for employer and employee), and the base rose from $9,000 to $10,800 in 1973 to $13,200 in 1974. For 1975 the base was scheduled to rise to $14,100.

These regressive tax increases were made more onerous by the increases in income taxes caused by inflation. Federal tax receipts grew, and with expenditures held in check, the deficits fell to $6.9 billion in 1973 and rose to 11.7 billion in 1974 as transfer payments rose; fiscal-year budgets showed an equally dramatic reduction in the deficits, falling over 85 percent from FY 1972 to FY 1974.

Clearly, since the spending binge of 1972, fiscal policy had become relatively passive and restrictive. Federal expenditures grew from causes largely beyond the administration's control, such as with the growth in Social Security benefits and other entitlement programs that raised transfer payments. Federal tax receipts increased through inflation, not through legislated changes in the tax laws. Discretionary fiscal policy took a back seat in the later years of the Nixon administration. It was now time to turn conservative again, abandon all controls on the economy, and pursue what has been called the "old-time religion"; that is, forsake attempts to manage the economy and fight inflation in a painless way and recognize that only the bitter pill of contractionary fiscal and monetary policy would do the job. Some suffering was inevitable until the economy righted itself; with the election over, such considerations were acceptable. To change the metaphor, it was time to bite the bullet.

Monetary policy also moved to more restraint in 1973. Since 1970 the Federal Reserve had been experimenting with controlling monetary aggregates, mostly M1, as its principal policy to influence money and credit conditions. It was seeking target growth rates for M1 and M2, but was finding it difficult to keep within the ranges set in the short run and would soon begin to lengthen the time horizon for achieving its aims. To control the money aggregates, the Federal Reserve was relying on maintaining reserves against private deposits (RPDs) in ranges that would ensure the desired growth of M1.[51]

Monetary policy, then, as reflected in the growth of M1, must be considered restrictive, since M1 grew by 6.2 percent in 1973, compared to 7.7 percent in 1972. (M2 growth rates also fell to 8.8 percent from

10.9 percent.) In 1974 the declining growth rates continued, as M1 grew by only about 5 percent, while M2 grew by 7.7 percent.

Interacting with the decline in the growth of the money supply was a rapid increase in the demand for credit in 1973. Under these circumstances, interest rates could be expected to rise, and they did; three-month treasury bills rose in December to 6.80 from 6.07; long-term bonds rose from 5.65 to 6.35; the prime rate rose from 5.45 to 9.08, and the mortgage rate rose to 8.86 from 7.57. The Federal Reserve raised the discount rate in several steps, and by year's end the rate stood at 7.5 percent, up from 5 percent at the beginning of the year.

In July the Federal Reserve increased the rate payable on savings accounts to 5 percent (from 4.5 percent) and removed the ceiling on large, long-term CDs to prevent another outflow of funds from commercial banks. In November Congress restored the ceilings on all CDs less than $100,000. By that time the economy was in a recession, but the Federal Reserve was successful in its attempt to prevent the outflow of funds from commercial banks.

Also in July 1973 the Federal Reserve raised the reserve requirements on larger banks' demand deposits by 0.5 percent to 10.25, and 18 percent for the largest banks. The Federal Reserve also raised the reserve requirement on large CDs and thus raised the cost of funds to banks.

As the economy sank into the recession in late 1973, the Federal Reserve and the money markets were becoming increasingly concerned over inflation. As price increases approached the double-digit range, the rate of monetary growth was falling, as indicated earlier, at rates of 1 percent below those of the previous year.

As a result, real money balances fell and interest rates rose to their highest levels (up to that time) in U.S. history. Lenders adjusted their rates to reflect an inflation premium, and savers directed their funds to higher-interest-paying deposits. In the summer of 1974, when Nixon left office, interest rates had risen to 8.7 percent on three-month treasury bills, 7.33 on long-term bonds, 11.65 for the prime rate, and 9.85 for mortgage rates. The federal funds rate stood at 12 percent. The stock market fell dramatically, with the Standard & Poor Index at 76.03 (1941–43 = 100), down from 107.43 in 1972, a 29 percent drop, and the New York Stock Exchange Index fell to 39.86 (December 1965 = 100) from 57.42 in 1972, a 31 percent decline.

Thus, in response to rapid inflation, caused primarily by energy prices, both monetary and fiscal policy were restrictive. The overly stimulative macroeconomic policies in 1972 were also taking their toll on the economy in 1973–74. The reversal of both monetary and fiscal policies surely helped to dampen the economy and ease it into a recession; the reversal of macroeconomic policies toward restraint did little to fight inflation, however, since domestic considerations were secondary to the energy problems.

The attempt to pursue contractionary monetary and fiscal policies led only to economic stagflation as unemployment rose, GNP fell, and prices and interest rates soared. Lacking any real energy policy, all that policymakers could think to do was to fight inflation through traditional measures. Clearly monetary and fiscal policies are ineffective or inefficient in combating stagflation. Engineering a recession to fight inflation would not work when the source of the problem was not mainly internal.

The Aftermath of Watergate

Nixon left office with the nation searching for stability and a sense of purpose. The social cohesion had been strained during the long war in ways that have not been totally examined, even now. The effects on the economy were enormous, as indicated in the foregoing analysis, but even here the true costs may never be precisely known. Indeed one analysis of the economic costs of the war puts the total costs at approximately $900 billion. This huge sum includes the costs of inflation, the indirect and direct costs of recession, foreign aid, and the sacrificed earnings of the men who served in it.[52]

The social costs are not as readily calculated, but they are likely to be equally large. Add to these the social costs associated with the Watergate affair, which further rocked the nation, and the total could be staggering. No attempt will be made here to make such a calculation, even if one could be made, but some reminder is necessary, if only to understand the general mood of the nation and to better appreciate subsequent political and economic events. A nation consumed by self-doubt, despairing of politicians and government, is likely to react differently from one full of optimism and confident of the future.

Once again the United States demonstrated its political stability through all this, as first one president was driven from seeking reelection, then a vice-president resigned over financial scandals, followed by another president resigning from office under the threat of impeachment, and his appointee to the vice-presidency assumed the presidency and promptly pardoned him. Such changes at the highest

levels of government could be expected to hamper economic development, but there is scant evidence that it did. Indeed, most fluctuations
in economic activity could be logically traced to the effects of the
recession and the oil embargo.

Two barometers of expectations and confidence in the future are
business investment and stock-market activity. Real investment
actually increased as a proportion of GNP, rising from 10.3 percent in
1971 to 11.5 percent in 1974. Stock prices rose until the fall of 1973 and
then fell dramatically, which may have been more an indicator of the
recession than a reaction to political changes. Without dwelling on the
issue, it seems that the transfer of power over the period did not
impede economic development or seriously affect economic decisions.

The smooth transition between administrations testifies to the
political stability, but does not guarantee economic stability or proper
macroeconomic actions. Before scrutinizing the actual politics the
Nixon administrations pursued and judging them for success and
rationality, it would be better to include the brief administration of
Gerald R. Ford and treat them in tandem.

chapter 12

The Ford Administration

Gerald R. Ford was sworn in on the same day that Nixon departed—August 9, 1974. The former minority leader of the House from Michigan became vice-president when Vice-President Agnew resigned and became the 38th president when Nixon resigned.[1] In his remarks he declared, "Our Constitution works. Our great republic is a government of laws and not of men."

President Ford had been recognized as a conservative in the House, voting against most social legislation, voting for defense expenditures, and generally remaining loyal to conservative doctrines. Nixon considered him a team player, often enlisting him in battles, as he did when he got him to lead the fight for the impeachment of Justice William O. Douglas, following the Senate opposition to Nixon's appointees to the bench. His colleagues considered him a determined, sincere, but modest man; many others would have agreed with the characterization by John Ehrlichman: "I came away from his office with the impression that Jerry Ford might have become a pretty good Grand Rapids insurance agent; he played a good game of golf, but he wasn't excessively bright."[2] Lyndon Johnson's characterization was predictably more vicious: "He couldn't walk and chew gum at the same time."[3]

Still, his reputation as a conservative team player made him a valuable man in the Republican party. Together with Senate Minority Leader Everett Dirksen, with whom he had a radio show, the party message was clearly communicated. Now, through a series of chance events, nearly improbable, he was president of the United States.

Unfortunately for Mr. Ford, it was not an opportune time to assume the responsibility for the economy. The country was in the middle of a recession that had begun in November 1973; worse was the problem of stagflation—GNP was falling, unemployment was rising, and prices were rising at double-digit rates. Oil shortages were real or threatened, and energy problems in general were demanding action.

While the problems were clear enough, the solutions were not. Thus, in September, President Ford initiated a series of conferences on inflation—Summit Conferences on Inflation, as they were called. They were attended by economists, bankers, labor leaders, and business-men, and the opinions on what was causing inflation and how it could be stopped were as many and as varied as the number of participants. The wide array of options indicated clearly that the inflationary problem was more complex than had been imagined, and, of course, no magic solution emerged.

Inflation was perceived as the main economic problem in September 1974—a fact reflected in a Gallup poll, where 81 percent identified it as the most important problem facing the country. The Joint Economic Committee had just released its own program to reduce inflation; Galbraith had just written an article for the *New York Times* on how to control inflation; Milton Friedman had just published an article in *Fortune* on the use of escalators to fight inflation, and so on.[4]

Everyone seemed to be preoccupied with inflation, and while various solutions did recognize that unemployment could develop and must be addressed, not many saw the severe recession at hand. Accordingly, on October 8, 1974, President Ford presented his program to control inflation and encourage growth. Among the many proposals made were the following:

- A 5 percent surcharge on individuals and corporate income taxes
- An increase in the investment tax credit from 7 to 10 percent
- Support for a pending bill giving some tax relief to low-income individuals and a windfall-profits tax on oil
- Programs to conserve energy and encourage the substitution of coal for oil in electricity generation
- Promotion of competition and removal of government regulations to stimulate production
- Employment assistance for those who might suffer temporary income losses, including public-service employment
- Control of federal expenditures by holding outlays to less than $300 billion for FY 1975
- Increase in food production by ensuring farmers ample supplies of fuel and fertilizers
- Monitoring by the Council on Wage and Price Stability of actions of both the public and private sector that raised costs and prices.

Finally, Ford exhorted the nation to "whip inflation now" (WIN), for "I say to you with all sincerity, that our inflation, our public enemy number one, will, unless whipped destroy our country, our homes, our liberties, our property, and finally our national pride, as surely as any well-armed wartime enemy." This hyperbolic language was followed by the disbursement of WIN buttons to enlist all citizens in the anti-inflation army. The WIN buttons were, of course, ridiculed and mercifully disappeared, but it does show the lengths to which it was felt necessary to go to fight public enemy number one.

The program was basically contractionary, as it should have been if fighting inflation were the target. There was nothing innovative in the proposals (the JEC Report was very similar, for instance), and many could subscribe to all or portions of it. The problem, however, was that the economy was on the verge of a severe recession, in which such a program would be largely counterproductive. The slide into recession was not noticed at the time, perhaps because more attention was devoted to the nomination proceedings of Nelson Rockefeller for vice-president. His financial dealings and tax problems caused the investigation to continue until December, when he was confirmed by the Senate and sworn in as the second man to assume the vice-presidency without a public vote.

The recession could not be ignored for long, however, as the unemployment rate shot up to 6.6 percent in November and reached 7.2 percent in December. Industrial production fell at a 2.8 percent rate in December or over 12 percent in the last quarter of 1974. Soon GNP data would reveal a decline in real terms of 9.1 percent at an annual rate in the last quarter of 1974, the sharpest decline in many years.

In late November and early December, the Ford administration gradually shifted to the recognition that a recession was in progress and deserved equal priority with inflation. Ford ruled out, however, any quick solutions, such as wage and price controls and was still calling for budget cuts as late as the end of November.

In January, in a complete reversal, Ford called for tax reductions to fight the now obvious recession. There was no mention of the inappropriate tax-increase policy of October. The administration's proposal called for a reduction or rebate of 1974 taxes, made up of $12 billion for individuals through a temporary reduction in tax rates, with the major cut in the first tax bracket (from 14 to 7 percent) and increases in the minimum standard deduction. For corporations a temporary reduction in tax rates, from 48 to 42 percent, was proposed for a total of $4 billion. In addition, the investment tax credit would be temporarily increased to 12 percent. (Taxes on energy sources will be taken up later.)

The tax reductions were temporary to avoid large budget deficits, which the then secretary of the treasury, William E. Simon, began to identify as the major source of inflation. The administration resisted budget increases, because it believed they tended to become permanent and worked more slowly than tax reductions.[5]

Congress gave the president virtually all he asked for, but went even further for a total tax reduction of $23 billion. In signing the Tax Reduction Act of 1975, the president noted that while it was a reasonable compromise, the act short-changed the middle-income taxpayer in favor of lower-income recipients. He also warned that he would not accept any additional government expenditure programs unless they involved national security or energy problems. As passed, the act gave individuals an $8.1 billion refund of 1974 taxes, an increase in the standard deduction for $2.5 billion, and a one-year $30 exemption tax credit for $5.3 billion; other items including an earned income credit brought the total to $18.1 billion.

To business the act gave an increase in the investment tax credit for $3.3 billion, a reduction in tax rates, and an increase in exemptions for a total of $1.2 billion, or $4.8 billion in total. The act also eliminated depletion allowances for major energy producers.

Other provisions were a one-time payment of $50 to Social Security recipients, at a cost of $1.7 billion; and an extension of the maximum period for unemployment compensation from 52 to 65 weeks, at a cost of $0.2 billion.

The fact that the tax cuts were temporary revived the argument over how much of them would be spent, compared to permanent tax cuts of the same magnitude. If consumers adjust their spending plans only on expected changes in their permanent income, then temporary tax reductions will not affect current spending plans, since they do not affect permanent income. A less stringent interpretation would expect some increase in spending in the short run, but much less than if households considered the increase in disposable income to be permanent. Alan Blinder made some estimates of these tax cuts (and their extensions in 1976) and concluded that very little of the tax rebate and reductions was spent in 1975 and that most of the spending occurred in the year after passage.[6]

Thus, as a short-run stimulus, the temporary tax package was not an efficient weapon, contrary to what Secretary Simon was saying. The tax bill might better have been labeled permanent, even if there were no such intentions, or at least the temporary nature of the reductions should not have been stressed as much as it was. In any case, the tax reductions were enacted in March 1975, when the economy had reached the trough of the cycle that had begun in November 1973. Thus, they had little impact on the subsequent recovery until it had been under way for nearly a year.

With the recession, all hopes of keeping federal spending below the $300 billion mark faded rapidly. Expenditures for FY 1975 rose to $326 billion, largely through increases in defense spending of $8 billion and in transfer payments ($24 billion in income security alone). Even with tax receipts rising by $16 billion, the deficit soared to $45 billion from just $4.6 billion in FY 1974.

Over the course of this recession, GNP fell sharply, from its peak in November 1973, to March 1975. Nominal GNP increased by 6 percent, but real GNP fell by 6.6 percent. From the last quarter of 1974 to the first quarter of 1975, GNP growth fell sharply to 2.1 percent at annual rates for nominal and to −9.2 percent for real GNP. By March the unemployment rate had risen to 8.5 percent and was still rising when the recession bottomed out.

Industrial production fell in the recession by 13.7 percent, and the capacity-utilization rate dropped to 68 percent from 83 percent at the beginning of the period. The evidence indicates an extremely sharp decline in economic activity. Still, consumer prices rose by 14.7 percent over the course of the downturn, while wholesale prices rose by a phenomenal 22.4 percent. The GNP price deflator also rose dramatically—by some 15.2 percent. Of course, energy prices led the way, as the increase in the CPI from the start of the recession to the end of 1974 was 25.5 percent with an additional increase of 6.2 percent for the first quarter of 1975.

Stagflation was painfully evident as the worst of all possible worlds—rising prices combined with decreases in output and employment—making a mockery of past macroeconomic solutions to recessionary and inflationary periods. The administration responded, though against its will, to the problems of recession by reducing taxes and increasing expenditures.

The Federal Reserve, meanwhile, had increased the discount rate in April 1974 and reversed itself only in December. In 1975 it continued to reduce the rate in steps, until by mid-March the rate had fallen to 6.25 percent from the 7.5 percent rate in effect at the start of the recession. Reserve requirements were also reduced slightly in December 1974 and again in February 1975 and now stood at 16.5 percent (from 18 percent) for large banks; reserve requirements for smaller banks were reduced only 0.5 percent.

Monetary conditions, as measured by the growth of monetary aggregates, were tight. In the last quarter of 1973, M1 was growing at an 8.7 percent annual rate and M2 at 10.8 percent. These annual rates of growth by the last quarter of 1974 were 3.9 and 6.2 percent, respectively. In the first quarter of 1975, when the recession was coming to an end, the M1 rate had fallen to 0.6 percent and M2 to 5.6 percent. The slowing of the growth of these monetary aggregates again signaled the Federal Reserve's greater concern about inflation and the international situation than about recessionary problems. Under these conditions, interest rates rose somewhat from November 1973 to March 1975, but the lack of demand for funds exerted downward pressure as well. Thus short-term interest rates declined from 7.866 to 5.544 for three-month treasury bills, rose slightly for long-term bonds from 6.31 to 6.73, but most other rates exhibited an increase in 1974 and then a decrease to the trough of the recession.

Monetary and Fiscal Policy in the Expansion of 1975–76

The economy expanded throughout the remainder of the Ford administration, with GNP growing by 7.3 percent in 1975 and 11.6 percent in 1976. Real GNP, however, fell in 1975 by 1.8 percent before rising sharply by 6.2 percent. Table 12.1 shows the breakdown of the turnaround. Real consumption spending rebounded sharply, especially in consumer durables. Consumer-durables expenditures in this period were dominated by automobile sales, as the latter part of 1974 saw the collapse of this market. In early January automobile manufacturers began giving rebates, and these stimulated sales, and while rebate sales later moderated, they still showed steady increases to early 1976. Thereafter sales fell off again as prices rose, causing used-car and foreign sales to rise.

The recession left firms with a great deal of excess capacity, and utilization was only 77 percent of existing capacity in 1975 and only 81 percent in 1976. The decline in real investment in 1975 reflects the excess capacity, as automobile and textile firms, both suffering from foreign competition, reduced their capital expenditures. In 1976 these trends were reversed, as lower inflation, lower interest rates, rising consumer expenditures, and increases in the investment tax credit all combined to affect expectations of firms favorably. Similar swings took place in residential investment and inventory accumulation.

Note that the government did not contribute as much to the expansion as did the private sector. The growth of federal expenditures was modest, while state and local expenditures were contractionary. Similarly, rising imports and stable exports made net exports negative.

There were other trouble areas as well: Unemployment rates refused to fall and by December 1976 stood at a high 7.8 percent, not far from the trough rate of 8.5 percent. Prices, too, did not decline very much at first, with the CPI falling from an 11 percent rate in 1974 to 9.1 percent in 1975 before falling to 5.8 percent in 1976. Wholesale

Table 12.1   Changes in Gross National Product in Constant (1972) Dollars, 1975–76 (percent changes; quarterly changes at seasonally adjusted annual rates)

Component	1975	1976	1976 I	II	III	IV
Percent change in 1972 dollars:						
Total GNP	−1.8	6.2	9.2	4.5	3.9	3.0
Personal consumption						
Expenditures	1.5	5.5	8.8	4.0	3.6	5.4
Durable goods	−0.4	12.3	23.2	3.0	3.2	2.3
Nondurable goods	0.9	4.3	6.8	3.8	1.7	8.5
Services	2.6	4.5	6.2	4.6	5.3	3.9
Business fixed investment	−13.3	3.8	7.8	8.3	9.6	0.8
Residential investment	−14.7	22.7	22.3	15.1	16.1	37.0
Government purchases	1.8	1.3	−4.9	2.6	2.9	0.4
Federal purchases	0.4	1.0	−7.2	2.5	5.7	3.5
State and local purchases	2.6	1.4	−3.5	2.7	1.4	−1.3
Change in billions of 1972 dollars:						
Inventory accumulation	−20.5	21.1	15.9	0.7	−0.9	−5.5
Net exports of goods and services	6.1	−6.7	−6.5	−0.6	−0.3	−0.4

Source: Council of Economic Advisors, *Economic Report of the President* (Washington, DC: GPO, 1979), p. 59.

**Table 12.2   Federal Government Receipts and Expenditures, 1974–76
(billions of dollars)**

Receipt or Expenditure Category	1974	1975	1976
National income basis: calendar year			
Federal government receipts	288.4	286.5	330.6
Personal tax and nontax receipts	131.4	125.7	145.3
Corporate tax accruals	45.9	42.6	55.9
Indirect business tax and nontax accruals	21.7	23.9	23.5
Contributions for social insurance	89.4	94.3	105.8
Federal government expenditures	300.1	357.8	388.9
Purchases of goods and services	111.7	124.4	133.4
National defense	77.4	84.3	88.2
Nondefense	34.3	40.1	45.2
Transfer payments	117.7	148.9	162.2
To persons	114.5	145.8	159.0
To foreigners	3.2	3.1	3.2
Grants-in-aid to state and local governments	43.9	54.4	60.2
Net interest paid	21.0	23.5	27.5
Subsidies less current surplus of government enterprises	4.7	6.5	5.6
Surplus or deficit (−)	−11.7	−71.2	−58.3
On fiscal year basis			
Receipts	264.9	281.0	300.0
Expenditures	269.6	326.1	366.5
Surplus or deficit (−)	−4.7	−45.1	−66.5

Source: Council of Economic Advisors, *Economic Report of the President* (Washington, DC: GPO, 1976 and 1977).

prices exhibited a similar pattern, falling from a rate of 18.9 percent in 1974 to 9.2 percent in 1975 and then to 4.6 percent in 1976.

Fiscal policy was expansionary in 1975, as the Tax Reduction Act of 1975 took effect. Combined with a sharp increase in expenditures of nearly 20 percent on a calendar year basis, the budget was thrown into a deficit of $71 billion, $45 billion on a fiscal year basis. Looking at the calendar-year totals, the spending increases can be traced to more national defense expenditures, large grants-in-aid to states for education and medicaid programs, and larger transfer payments to individuals as a result of higher unemployment benefits. These increases are easily seen in Table 12.2.

In December 1975 the tax cuts of 1975 were extended for the first six months of 1976. The Revenue Adjustment Act of 1975 and the Tax Reform Act of 1975 gave a tax credit per dependent of $35 through 1977, increased the standard deduction permanently, and extended the earned income credit. Corporate tax reductions were also extended, with the first $25,000 of income taxed at the lower rate through 1977 and the 10 percent investment tax credit extended through 1980. The total tax reduction was estimated at $16 billion for 1976.[7]

Beyond the tax-cut extensions, the Tax Reform Act of 1977, initiated to simplify and reform the tax laws, unified estate and gift taxes, tightened rules for tax shelters and allowable deductions, and increased the minimum tax.

These tax cuts and extensions can be viewed as a form of indexing, since inflation was pushing more people into higher tax brackets. The tax relief measures helped to reduce the impact of these inflation-induced taxes. Meanwhile, the increase in federal expenditures was less than the previous year's by half. President Ford had been preaching fiscal restraint to stop inflation since his State of the Union message. Indeed, he and Congress were at odds during the years, as the president vetoed bills for public works of $6.1 billion, a milk price bill, and a foreign aid bill of $4.4 billion. Congress overrode other Ford vetoes of bills for public-works jobs ($3.95 billion) and funds for HEW.

As can be seen from Table 12.2 the rate of increase of federal expenditures fell to around 9 percent from 1975 to 1976, and the deficit fell to $58 billion ($66 billion for the fiscal year). The slowdown in spending was in transfer payments and grants-in-aid. Indeed, federal spending for the year fell by $3 billion more than had been anticipated by the Ford administration. The slowdown in spending caused much discussion, since part seemed to be deliberate (slowdowns in making new outlays and budget overestimates), and part due to lower inflation rates.

At any rate, the slowdown occurred mainly in the second quarter of 1976 ($10 billion at an annual rate), and the economy began to stall. The tax cuts and tax changes followed in the third quarter. Critics of the administration's anti-inflation stance grew even more concerned at the apparent incorrect fiscal program.[8]

The trend toward fiscal restraint can best be seen by examining the full-employment budget. Table 12.3 shows the full-employment deficit falling from $12.5 billion in 1975 to $10.3 billion in 1976, a change of $ +2.2 billion—a sharp turnaround from the previous year's enormous change of $ −26.5 billion. Thus in the latter half of 1976, the economy was stalling in the midst of the recovery, partly due to the

Table 12.3   Actual and Full-Employment Receipts and Expenditures, National Income and Product Accounts Basis, Calendar Years 1970–76 (billions of dollars; quarterly data at seasonally adjusted annual rates)

			Federal Government	
			Surplus or Deficit (−)	
Calendar Year	Receipts	Expendi-tures	Amount	Change
Actual				
1970	192.1	204.2	−12.1	−20.6
1971	198.6	220.6	−22.0	−9.9
1972	227.5	244.7	−17.3	4.7
1973	258.3	265.0	−6.7	10.6
1974	288.2	299.7	−11.5	−4.8
1975	286.5	357.8	−71.2	−59.7
1976*	330.6	388.9	−58.3	12.9
1976: I	316.5	380.3	−63.8	5.6
II	324.6	378.7	−54.1	9.7
III	333.8	391.1	−57.4	−3.3
Full-employment				
1970	201.0	203.6	−2.6	−6.3
1971	210.0	219.1	−9.2	−6.6
1972	222.1	243.6	−21.5	−12.3
1973	257.5	265.4	−7.9	13.6
1074	311.8	297.7	14.1	22.0
1975	337.6	350.1	−12.5	−26.5
1976*	371.6	381.9	−10.3	2.2
1976: I	358.5	372.6	−14.1	0.6
II	365.3	371.9	−6.7	7.4
III	376.1	384.3	−8.2	−1.5

*Surplus or deficit excluding social insurance funds.
Source: Council of Economic Advisors, *Economic Report of the President* (Washington, DC: GPO, 1977), p. 76.

movement toward fiscal restraint. The rate of growth of real GNP fell sharply in the second quarter of 1976, from 9.2 percent to 4.5 percent, and continued to decline for the remainder of the year. Unemployment rates were still high and stable.

These trends, combined with moderating prices, gave rather confusing signals to the electorate to consider in Ford's reelection bid. In late 1976 less than half of those polled thought that business conditions for the coming year were good, and nearly the same number continued to rate inflation as the number-one problem of the United States.[9]

Where fiscal-policy measures over the period are more predictable, monetary-policy actions appear erratic. In 1972 there was the rather obvious easing of monetary conditions, followed by the postelection stringency in 1973 that many hold helped to bring on the recession of 1974–75. In 1974 the move toward restraint continued, prompting criticism from all shades of economic opinion, from Keynesians to monetarists. The sharp decline in the rate of growth of money in the last half of 1974 is clearly evident in Table 12.4. Milton Friedman blamed the Federal Reserve for this deepening of the recession in late 1974.[10]

As the economy was reaching the trough of the cycle in the first quarter of 1975, the rate of growth of M1 actually turned negative, and M2 growth continued to decline. In May the Federal Reserve acceded to congressional requests to announce its target growth rates for monetary aggregates, and its first target ranges were set for the period of March 1975 to March 1976 (later altered slightly to accommodate larger growth rates). As shown in Table 12.4, the Federal Reserve exceeded the range in the second quarter of 1975, due probably to the tax-cut receipts affecting the supply of money without being offset. For the remainder of 1975, the M1 growth rate fell, and for 1976 the rate was erratic. M2 showed more stability, falling in late 1975 but rebounding in 1976 for rather steady growth.

The inability of the Federal Reserve to control monetary aggregates and its stop-and-go policies have long been criticized by monetarists, and the evidence of variability in this period supports their contention. Yet other factors must be considered—the most important of these being the demand for money, which also varies over the course of a cycle. In a study of the demand for money, Stephen Goldfeld found that his model performed well until 1974, when suddenly it overpredicted the demand for M1 balances by larger amounts for the period of 1974–76. Apparently, the demand-for-money function had shifted downward, and less money was demanded at each income level. This the Federal Reserve could not have known, but it was fortuitously in support of what Chairman Burns wanted to do anyway—that is, finance the recovery with increases in velocity and less monetary growth. Therefore what appears to be a restrictive rate of growth of money would be adequate if the recovery were fueled by velocity increases or a decline in the demand for money. The Federal Reserve hoped for the former, but did not expect the latter.

The erratic growth of M1 and the stable growth of M2 over the course of the recovery may not be very unusual, but the behavior of interest rates was. Interest rates generally rise in a recovery period, but Table 12.4 shows them declining, with short-term rates falling more than long-term rates. What accounts for this reversal of past trends?

Past analysis would suggest an easy-money policy, but monetary growth rates do not appear excessive. Nominal GNP was rising by over 11 percent, and the demand for money, even if declining somewhat, would require close to the observed growth rates of M2, as shown in Table 12.4. Thus, except for the period 1975 IV to 1976 I, monetary growth was in line with the recovery.

The answer may well lie with new behavior caused by rapid and high rates of inflation. Money markets became more concerned with real rates of interest (nominal rates corrected for inflation). With double-digit inflation, lenders quickly found the real rate of interest to be crucial, especially when it turned negative. They began to build an inflation premium into their nominal quotations. Of course, the rate of inflation that figures in the calculations was the expected rate, which is nonobservable directly.

As the actual inflation rates slowed, however, expectations could have been revised downward as well. Thus the observed fall in nominal interest rates in Table 12.4 could be at least partially explained for the short-term rates. For long-term rates, perhaps different price expectations were involved. If the fall in prices was deemed temporary or if there remained a great deal of uncertainty as to long-term inflation prospects, the long-term rates could have remained rather constant.

A more definite answer may not be possible for this period. Traumatic shocks to the economy could have provoked responses that broke with past behavior in ways not readily discernible. It is certainly questionable whether the Federal Reserve was cognizant of the shifts occurring in the demand for money or in the behavior of interest rates. Note, for instance, how the discount-rate reductions (see Table 12.4) followed the lead of the market; not unusual perhaps, but the erratic growth of M1 also signifies that the Federal Reserve may have been surprised by monetary conditions in 1975.[11]

Clouding the picture still further were the increases in the income velocity (GNP/M) of both Ms. Less money growth is required if velocity increases. The velocity of M1 and M2 rose sharply in 1975—up to nearly 10 percent in mid-year—and then they declined to more traditional rates. Despite falling interest rates, the increases in income velocity probably occurred as a result of the new NOW account (an

Table 12.4 The Money Stock and Interest Rates, 1974–76

Period	M1		M2		Interest Rates†			
	Target Range	Actual Growth*	Target Range	Actual Growth*	Three-Month Treasury Bill	Government Taxable Bonds	Prime Commercial Paper	Discount Rate (NY)
1973 IV	—	8.7	—	10.8	7.462	6.31	8.98	7.50
For year	—	4.8	—	7.2	7.041	6.30	8.15	6.44
1974 I	—	5.8	—	9.6	7.600	6.63	8.30	7.50
II	—	7.3	—	8.3	8.268	7.05	10.46	8.00
III	—	3.9	—	6.2	8.287	7.27	11.53	8.00
IV	—	3.7	—	6.6	7.336	6.98	9.05	8.00
For year	—	5.3	—	7.9	7.886	6.99	9.87	7.83

1975 I	—	-0.3	—	5.8	5.873	6.67	6.56	7.00
II	—	8.6	—	11.2	5.401	6.96	5.92	6.00
III	5–7.5	6.9	7.5–10.5	10.4	6.337	7.08	6.67	6.00
IV	5–7.5	2.4	7.5–10.5	6.4	5.684	7.22	6.12	6.00
For year	—	4.4	—	8.3	5.838	6.98	6.33	6.25
1976 I	5–7.5	2.9	7.5–10.5	9.9	4.953	6.91	5.29	5.50
II	5–7.5	8.2	7.5–10.5	10.5	5.169	6.88	5.57	5.50
III	5–7.5	4.2	7.5–10.5	9.2	5.169	6.78	5.53	5.50
IV	4.5–6.5	6.3	7.5–10.0	12.3	4.698	6.55	4.99	5.50
For year	—	5.5	—	10.9	4.989	6.78	5.35	5.50

*Quarterly percent growth at annual rates.

†Quarterly averages.

Notes: The Federal Reserve began in May to announce publically its target growth rates, using March data as the base period. Subsequently the base period was revised several times. The targets were set for one-year periods and should not be confused with frequent revisions for internal purposes. Also, money stock data are frequently revised, and the above data are taken as close to the period covered as possible.

Sources: Federal Reserve Bulletins; and Council of Economic Advisors, *Economic Report of the President* (Washington, DC: GPO); various years for both.

interest-bearing checking account not then included in M1). People were learning how to economize on money for transaction purposes anyway, and the change in behavior appears as a change in velocity of M1.[12]

In sum, this recovery period would appear to have been a problem for the monetary authorities. At the time, however, the foregoing trends were not fully appreciated or were not realized, as is the case with the decline in the demand for money.

Evaluation of the Policies
of the Nixon and Ford Administrations

Looking back over the Nixon–Ford administrations, one finds some curious contradictions, whether the question is one of justification for their macro policies or the success or rationality of them. In the Nixon era there were, in the apt phrase of Herbet Stein, "conservative men with liberal ideas."[13] With Ford, a stronger ideological bias became more evident, but despite the president's desire to pull the nation to the right, the pressure of events prevented his doing so.

Appraising the macro policies followed in terms of their justification, first, the Nixon administration's policies were inconsistent and contrary to expected actions—either considering the ideological bias or the conditions that prompted them. For instance, the justification for an overhaul of the welfare system is readily acknowledged by nearly everyone, but why did this administration adopt the family-assistance plan (FAP), a rather liberal idea, over the negative income tax, a more conservative approach? And why, after so much study and effort, was the whole idea dropped and the same old welfare system continued? Was it simply good politics (given McGovern's problems), or was the appearance that something was being done sufficient to satisfy the administration's friends and critics?

Similarly, another proposal that found widespread acceptance was revenue sharing. Surely the states and localities needed help from the federal government, the best tax collector. At least at the time, the revenue-sharing program was viewed as a boon to the states and localities, and it also conformed to conservative beliefs that power should be returned to levels of government best able to recognize and deal with the problems they are forced to solve.

The new federalism found many supporters, even if they were not sold on the conservative argument of the proper power shifts. Yet the power shifts were the reverse for FAP and wage and price controls, shifting from states and localities to the central government. These contradictory movements demonstrated ideological confusion or, as stated earlier, liberal solutions in a conservative mold. Some inconsistencies could thus be expected, but the blurring of conservative and liberal boundaries was also responsible for the lack of any need to justify the attempts at solutions to long-standing problems. Conservatives might grumble, as they did with Nixon's overtures to China, but Nixon was still regarded as a conservative, and he was in command.

So, too, with the wage-and-price-control program. The attempt at a more conservative approach—gradualism—failed, but the perceived need to combat inflation clearly justified in the minds of many the more radical controls system. This anticapitalist solution required little justification by the administration, for the groundwork had been laid—the exaggerated dangers of inflation. It was not justified by the administration as necessary because of the Vietnam War, although that would have been the logical argument to use. Controls have always been necessary in times of war and could easily have been justified on that score alone.

Here again, a policy that could have been easily justified by past experience was not rationalized on grounds of precedents, but was utilized for political purposes and obviously less justified on those grounds. As already indicated, the system of wage and price controls was instituted more by international pressures and domestic politics than for domestic economic reasons. Thus a justifiable policy was perverted to suit political purposes, and an unsuspecting or trusting public was led to accept it as if it were directed at more legitimate ends. Indeed it came to demand some type of controls.

The energy and environmental problems of the 1970s also presented these administrations with something of a dilemma. The free-market solutions, letting prices rise to allocate scarce supplies, for instance, could not be used for equity reasons, and so these conservative administrations were forced to adopt regulatory programs, tariffs, irrational pricing schemes, allocation formulas, and so on. More regulations occurred under Nixon than under any other president.

No one questioned the need for programs to meet these new and emerging problems—no, they were easily justified. Again, the public demanded programs—equitable ones. So two conservative presidents presided over the enlargement of the federal bureaucracy and encroachment on individual liberties. Quite simply, solutions had to be found, and the social pressures to find them were too great to ignore. The conservative solutions were found wanting and were quickly abandoned, but any administration, regardless of ideological concerns, would have been forced to respond to the mounting pressures to do something.

In the more traditional macro policies to stabilize the economic system, neither administration violated past norms. Fiscal and monetary policies, while not securing universal approval, were within the range of expected actions, given the ideological complexion of these administrations. True, there was an outcry over the impoundment of funds by President Nixon, especially for sewer, water, and other social projects, and questions were raised over the legality of this action. Other presidents, however, had also refused to spend all of the funds authorized by Congress, but hostility toward this one caused an outcry that eventually resulted in an act prohibiting the practice.

Similarly, the politicalization of the Federal Reserve in 1972 was not sanctioned by the electorate, but, again, other presidents had manipulated the economy before an election, and most had received the monetary policy they wanted from the Federal Reserve. Thus, while these actions were not justified by abstract principles or social pressures, there were precedents. This is not to condone the policies, but just to suggest that they were not novel.

Less justified was the return to the old-time religion whereby the economy had to be suppressed in order to combat inflation. Creating recessions to fight inflation may be acceptable to those uninjured by the recession, but to others who are, this represents a cruel method of combating problems for which they have no responsibility. Presented as the only way to right the economy and return to equilibrium, development was and is rejected by many economists and laymen alike. Hence the old-time religion may not have had the justification and the widespread approval necessary to embark on such a drastic policy.

Even more controversial was the unilateral dismantling of the international trade agreements reached at Bretton Woods. Whatever the rationale for the action, and there were good reasons, the Nixon administration was not justified in taking this dramatic step without considering other nations' consent and positions. Perhaps it was necessary to shock them into adopting new ideas, but such a treatment might have been more understandable if the United States had no responsibility for the problems of the international community. Since a good portion of the problems of trade could be attributed to U.S. policies, such arrogance was unwarranted. Even foreigners began to feel the effects of the imperial presidency.

Judging the success or failure of the macro policies followed by the Nixon–Ford administrations is difficult, owing again to the degree of political motivations involved. It is generally admitted that the initial policy of gradualism was a failure. Attempting to apply the brakes to the economy over a long period and reverse the trends of monetary and fiscal policy established by previous administrations simply did not work. The Nixon administration was unable or unwilling to act boldly and apply the necessary restraint to halt inflation, curb spending, or increase taxes, because of the fear of resulting unemployment and recession. Again these conservatives with liberal ideas refused to apply the cold-bath treatment to the economy.

Perhaps more careful management of fiscal policy, combined with an accommodating monetary policy, would have worked over a longer time period. Nixon was impatient, however; he was not particularly concerned with economic matters until they threatened to get in the way of his reelection. Then, when the economy floundered and the outlook was uncertain, his past promises to reduce inflation without creating unemployment began to haunt him.

So while liberals might have faulted his administration for not doing more, and conservatives might have faulted his administration for not reversing the past liberal trends, Nixon's middle-of-the-road economic policies might have worked. They were certainly more in line with centrist ideas; perhaps with more persuasion, more people might have been coaxed into waiting longer for positive results.

Thus, as stressed earlier, without political considerations the very dramatic policy of wage and price controls appears unnecessary at best and contradictory to past beliefs. Was the controls system a success? The empirical evidence suggests that only the freeze was successful, and the postfreeze system was not. Without reviewing the evidence, the conclusions are really not surprising. The system was hastily conceived and poorly administered by nonbelievers. There was too little commitment to any incomes policy, let alone direct controls, so that too many changes were allowed, thus adding to the confusion and uncertainty such a program was bound to elicit.

Instead of the various phases, the system needed flexibility as problems emerged. Much of the "failure" of controls can be traced to noncontrolled items, such as agricultural products, and exogenous shocks, such as energy products. The controls were not altered in the light of these developments and consequently were bound to cause problems, from the increased costs to firms to the reduced real wages of labor. Controls, almost always unpopular after a time in operation, increasingly became the problem rather than the solution.

There are always inherent problems with controls, such as firms reducing quality or eliminating low-priced items, and so on, and these require attention and flexible responses. There was little flexibility in this control system, and thus it eventually came to be considered unfair and unworkable. Yet to condemn all controls on the basis of this experience may be premature. The actual success of the system was essentially immaterial to the administration, which had proposed them for political reasons. Thus there was little effort to make them really workable.

Given these conditions, the control system probably worked better than it had the right to and should be credited with more success than it was afforded. No system could work perfectly anyway, but even this ill-designed one achieved some favorable results. Thus in economic terms, the success of the program should be considered ambiguous and debatable, and final conclusions cannot really be reached to justify or condemn economic controls in general. A better-designed and better-administered program is necessary for that judgment.

The return to the old-time religion, following the demise of controls (and the election), was scarcely innovative. What else was left to this administration? Engineering recessions to cool off the economy does not rate high marks in policymaking. Economists had discovered how to cause a recession long ago, but how to manage prosperity eluded them. Giving the patient a more serious illness, however, because he was not responding to a lesser one, hardly constitutes sound medical practice.

If by success one means that a recession was duly created and the economy restrained, then the old-time religion was a success. Yet the policy of restraint itself represents a failure—the failure to understand the management of the economy so that a recession was unnecesssary.

The Ford administration, perhaps more committed to conservative solutions, continued the policy of restraint in order to combat inflation. Yet it, too, showed confusion, alternatively worrying about recession and then inflation, as the thorny condition of stagflation developed. Basically, inflation concerns were preeminent, and the economy floundered in recession and stagnation. As the energy shocks wore off, the inflation rate did decrease, and this good fortune, together with the recession, helped to furnish some measure of "success" to the administration's efforts. As before, however, the inability to deal with stagflation is really a failure of vision and imagination. Applying old solutions to new problems makes them inefficient and ineffective. This is illustrated by the stop-and-go monetary policy, which, although basically restrictive, could not stabilize the economy alone. Yet heavy reliance on monetary policy seemed to assume only one cause of stagflation, excluding alternative explanations.

Stabilization policy was thus somewhat backward looking and not as effective in the era of stagflation. Again, what else was left to this administration? Other solutions were either too radical (for example, nationalization of the oil companies) or had been abandoned (for example, incomes policies). Only more of the same was left—monetary policy, or the ludicrous appeal to voluntary restraint as in the WIN program.

Although concerned primarily with economic stabilization and growth, some mention of the approach of these administrations to energy problems is necessary to illustrate their groping for solutions to new issues. The conclusions are that their efforts were largely unsuccessful. Torn between questions of equity and efficiency, these administrations vacillated among approaches; refusing to ration scarce supplies either by directly allocating them or through the market mechanism, they resorted to irrational price and crude allocation schemes. Elaboration would take us too far afield, but it should be recorded that these administrations failed to confront successfully the most pressing problems of the times.

When examining whether past policies were justified or were successful, it is implicitly assumed that the policies were overtly designed to achieve some specific economic purpose; that is, they were rational. In the foregoing it is apparent that many of the policies of these administrations cannot be so regarded. The policies appear designed to achieve ends other than those advertised.

Perhaps this is most evident in the wage-and-price-control system, where political ends overshadowed the economic ones. As suggested, to judge the system on economic grounds alone misses the point. While economists pronounce the controls system a failure, it was a success in achieving its purpose—to enable expansionary monetary and fiscal policies to reelect Mr. Nixon. Viewed properly, an otherwise seemingly unnecessary program becomes understandable; an otherwise indifferent design of the controls system becomes comprehensible. If reelection is the goal, then the special treatment of property income (the source of future campaign contributions) under the controls becomes rational.

Of course, political considerations are never absent from policy choices—how could they be? Yet the Nixon administration surpassed all others in its desire to appear concerned with addressing problems while diverting attention from its real intentions. Programs that are easily proposed or even started can be postponed or cancelled just as easily, if there was really no commitment to them in the first place. The appearance of action is just as effective as serious proposals and sincere programs.

Consider the family-assistance plan that was dropped so suddenly, or the creation of the EPA when the need to demonstrate concern was necessary but not really supported afterward, or the hesitant energy approaches when solutions were distasteful, controversial, or potentially damaging to special groups. In these cases, it was necessary to seem concerned and appear to be meeting the problems head-on, but the wavering and irresolution were revealing.

These were not the first administrations to put self-preservation over the national interest, and these were, no doubt, confusing times, with new problems replacing old ones. Experimental responses would be in order, even if failures were more common than successes. Still, these administrations looked backward to past solutions and approaches. Was this reaction caused by the need to satisfy groups that did not want radical, new, or upsetting policies? If these groups were learning to adjust to the new situtions, however imperfectly, then they would not welcome innovative ideas, no matter how much better the chances of solving the problems. Better to suffer with what you know than risk even more with untested policies. Cautious men or those who do not suffer unduly from the current wave of problems do not seek answers to them with the same fervor they exhibit when those problems reach them directly.

Thus solutions such as the old-time religion to attack stagflation; thus the policy of decontrol of oil prices to encourage exploration; thus the reliance on monetary policy over fiscal policy; and thus the avoidance of endorsing new programs, and so on. These approaches are rational only to the extent that they preserved the status quo, the same distribution of economic power and control. To propose new solutions is to risk the loss of some of that power.

Such policies are not rational, however, if one is seeking solutions to new problems, where the alteration of the distribution of economic power may be a necessary part of the solution. For instance, letting the price of energy rise would likely be an efficient method to ration the scarce supplies among competing uses. This market solution, however, could result in a reduction in output and employment. A less efficient system of rationing might have avoided the economic slump and apportioned the burden more equitably. The administrations were aware of these effects and sensitive to them to the extent that they did propose price ceilings, but their programs still permitted large profits to be made by the oil companies and permitted wholesale abuses as well. The profits made by the oil companies were not used to further exploration, but to promote mergers with firms outside and inside the industry. The distribution of economic power was made more unequal by the free-market solution.

In this somewhat imperfect example, the administrations are seen as more interested in preserving the past structure of the economy than in solving problems. At the same time, they wanted to appear to be diligently attempting to find a solution to this or that condition. From their viewpoints that is rational behavior, but from the society's viewpoint the opposite conclusion emerges.[14] In this way these administrations were able to deflect the social pressures for actions while remaining faithful to powerful interests and ideological predispositions. Public acquiescence to such ploys is the result of ignorance, either born out of apathy or fostered by crafty politicians.

chapter 13

The Carter Administration

The presidential elections of 1976 pitted the incumbent, Gerald R. Ford (with Robert J. Dole) against the former governor of Georgia, Jimmy (James Earl) Carter (with Walter F. Mondale). Mr. Ford's path to the nomination was a rocky one; during the primary season, an effective challenge was mounted by Ronald W. Reagan, the conservative former governor of California. Right up to the Republican Convention in August in Kansas City, the two appeared to be in a dead heat. Gerald Ford won a very narrow victory at the convention, but was forced to cede the platform to the conservatives. His choice for running mate, Bob Dole, was also forced on him by Reagan and his wide conservative following.

Jimmy Carter's road to the nomination was considerably easier. An early start in the campaign and the numerous liberal Democrats who competed with him divided the party and helped him to become a serious candidate. Carter's early primary wins and the money problems of his opponents eventually forced them to withdraw, until the bandwagon effect took over, and Carter became unstoppable.

The two platforms reflected the power of the writers of them. The Republican platform was dominated by conservative programs—more defense, tax cuts, antibusing, antiabortion planks, support for Taiwan, caution regarding the Soviet Union, and the retention of the Panama Canal. The Democratic platform contained the usual liberal planks— support for jobs programs, health insurance, tax reform, defense reductions, a Panama Canal treaty, and gay rights.

Clearly, the contrasts between the two platforms were dramatic, and the voters had a real choice. Unfortunately, the presidential campaign was rather dull and uninspiring. Three television debates did little to excite the nation, and the candidates made mistakes that called their competence into question. For example, according to Ford, there was no Soviet domination of Eastern Europe, and Poland was not a member of the Soviet camp; Carter proposed to shift the burden of high taxes to higher-income groups by raising the taxes of those above the median income.

Voter disillusionment resulted in the lowest turnout (53.5 percent) since 1948. Carter won, of course, receiving 51.1 percent of the popular vote and 297 electoral votes. The close victory was reflected in the incoming 95th Congress, which retained virtually the same political divisions as its predecessor. In his nomination acceptance speech, Carter declared the need for moral leadership, pleading for the true expression of love and peace, justice, and preservation of human rights. These goals were later to set the tone for his administration.

If the Nixon administration was characterized by conservatives with liberal ideas, then the Carter administration might be said to reflect the reverse—liberals with conservative ideas. Here, in a little-emphasized section of his brief inaugural address, is the first expression of the caution that was to characterize his administration: "We have learned that 'more' is not necessarily 'better,' that even our great nation has its recognized limits, and that we can neither answer all questions nor solve all problems. We cannot afford to do everything, nor can we afford to lack boldness as we meet the future. So together, in a spirit of individual sacrifice for the common good, we must simply do our best."

Carter was not well known by the public and in fact made being an outsider to Washington a campaign issue, presumably making him better able to recognize and deal with problems. Not so with his running mate, as Mondale was a well-known liberal and a protegé of Hubert Humphrey.

Carter surrounded himself with a cadre of young Georgians who had been with him before, but his choices for the cabinet posts included many well-known people as well. Contrary to Carter's claim to being an outsider, he was a member of the Trilateral Commission, an independent group set up by David Rockefeller to promote the economic and political interests of the United States, Western Europe, and Japan; from this group of "insiders" he appointed 16 to government posts, including Harold Brown as secretary of defense, W. Michael Blumenthal as secretary of the treasury, Zbigniew Brzezinski as national security advisor, Elliot Richardson as U.S. ambassador at large, Andrew Young as U.S. ambassador to the UN, and Paul C. Warnke as director of arms control and disarmament; even Walter Mondale was a member of this organization.[1]

Some of his appointments to economic posts included Joseph A. Califano, Jr., as secretary of health, education, and welfare; Juanita M. Kreps as secretary of commerce; F. Ray Marshall as secretary of labor; Bert Lance to the Office of Management and Budget; and Charles Schultze as chairman of the CEA and William Nordhaus as a member of the CEA. The nominations to these economic posts were easily confirmed and elicited no strong opposition or criticism.[2]

Cautious Monetary and Fiscal Policy for a Sluggish Economy

The pause in the economy in 1976 may have helped Carter win the presidential campaign, but it is time to examine the responses he intended to make. Facing his administration was the slowdown in the growth of GNP from 8.8 percent in the first quarter of 1976 to 1.2 percent in the last quarter. Industrial production was falling, while capacity usage and the unemployment rate were holding steady. Consumer prices were declining, as were wholesale prices, but in December the WPI was increasing.

In brief, the economy was slowing down as it entered the second year of recovery from the trough of March 1975. The administration feared that the slowdown would not eliminate the high unemployment, near 8 percent, or the excess manufacturing capacity of nearly 20 percent. Accordingly, it designed a fiscal policy to stimulate the economy and return it to its former growth path.

A two-year, $31-billion stimulus package was proposed, consisting of these main elements:[3]

1. A one-time rebate on 1976 taxes of $50 per individual and $50 payments to recipients of Social Security, supplemental security income, and railroad retirees. These payments would total $11.4 billion in fiscal year 1977.

2. Instead of the percentage deduction, a permanent increase was proposed in the personal standard deduction to a flat level of $2,400 for individuals and $2,800 for joint returns. Treasury receipts would fall by $1.5 billion in fiscal 1977 and by $4 billion a year when fully effective.

3. A reduction in business taxes of $900 million for fiscal 1977 or $2.5 billion when fully effective. Business firms had two choices: a 2 percent increase in the investment tax credit (to 12 percent) or a 4 percent credit against Social Security taxes. The choice was designed to appeal to both capital- and labor-intensive firms.

4. Several increases in jobs programs, adding up to $1.7 billion in fiscal 1977. Public-service jobs under CETA (Comprehensive Employment and Training Act) would rise by over 750,000 by mid-1978.

5. A $4-billion increase in public-works spending, $2 billion for fiscal 1977.

6. An increase of $500 million in the countercyclical grants to states and localities.

The two-year program was designed to be flexible in that spending increases were expected to be spread out over the period, while tax cuts would be effective quickly. In addition, the two-year period allowed for alterations in the package, should economic conditions change.

And change they did, as the first quarter of 1977 saw a sharp reversal in spending and a rapid spurt in economic activity. GNP increased at an annual rate of 13.2 percent (7.5 percent in real terms), due primarily to the increase in consumption expenditures of 12.2 percent (5.1 percent in real terms) and the $10-billion increase in inventory stocks in just one quarter, a phenomenal 2,000+ percent increase. These increases overshadowed the negative effects of net exports (a 23 percent drop in real terms) and no significant change in public spending.

Since prices were beginning to rise again while unemployment remained stable, a further stimulus was deemed unnecessary, and the administration withdrew the rebates (No. 1 above) and business tax proposals (No. 3). This reduced the stimulus package by $14 billion, and the Tax Reduction and Simplification Act of 1977 was passed in May. The act changed the standard deduction amounts in No. 2 to $2,200 for single individuals and $3,200 for joint returns; instituted an employment tax credit for newly hired employees; extended the tax reductions for individuals and businesses passed in 1975 and 1976; and granted the increases in revenue sharing. Later the jobs programs and public-works increases were passed, so that the total stimulus in the budget for 1977 and 1978 (on a calendar-year basis) was $6.1 and $16.9 billion, respectively.[4]

In the second quarter of 1977 the economic trends again reversed direction. Personal consumption, particularly of durable goods, fell, and personal saving, which had been falling, began to approach historic averages. Also, the inventory buildup ended, and thus the two areas of private demand that furnished the spurt in the first quarter were no longer providing the stimulus. Furthermore, net exports continued to register negative values. Government expenditures, both purchases and defense, rose dramatically in the second quarter, by 5.4

percent over the first quarter or over 23 percent at annual rates, just in time to offset the declines in spending of the other sectors. The increase in purchases, together with the continuing increases in transfer payments, pushed spending totals over 1976 by nearly 10 percent.

The tax cuts were offset somewhat by increases in payroll taxes of $4 billion and a temporary bulge in estate and gift taxes due to changes in the tax laws of 1976. The excise tax on telephones was reduced from 5 to 4 percent as well. Tax receipts due to these changes increased by over 19 percent from 1976 and helped to reduce the deficit for FY 1977 to $45 billion, from $66.4 billion in 1976.

Table 13.1 shows the budgetary totals for both fiscal and calendar years. Of particular interest for fiscal policy evaluations is the high-employment budget. Note the dramatic increase in the high-employment deficit in the latter half of the year. The increase in spending and the lagged effects of the tax reductions began to be felt, and the fiscal stimulus is evident.

The professed aim of monetary policy in 1977 was to reduce the rate of growth of money in order to dampen inflation and reverse inflationary expectations.[5] The target ranges for M1 growth were set at 4.5 to 6.5 percent, and for M2 they began at 7–10 percent in January, changed to 7–9.5 percent in April, and were reduced further to 6.5–9 percent in October.

Not much progress was made in reducing growth rates, as M1 expanded by 7.8 percent for the year and indeed in mid-year exceeded even that rate by several percentage points. M2, too, either exceeded or was at the top of its target range, ending the year with an average growth of 9.8 percent. Managing the growth of monetary aggregates was again complicated by shifts of funds out of M1 into NOW accounts, money-market funds, and so on, while M2 seemed more stable as the year progressed.

Inexplicable changes in the velocity of money also complicated the conduct of monetary policy. In the recovery, increases in velocity were taking place despite declines in interest rates; was this a sign of too little money in the system or too much? Ordinarily velocity rises along with increases in interest rates, as people attempt to economize on funds. In 1977 more normal relationships between M1 and GNP growth appeared to be returning, and the Federal Reserve decided to make fewer adjustments to its M1 target range. Yet the changes in the demand for money made some board members question the use of monetary aggregates as guides to monetary policy.

The rather cautious monetary policy for monetary growth was reflected in the federal-funds rate. When monetary aggregates appeared to be growing too fast, the Federal Reserve fostered or

Table 13.1   Federal Government Budgets, 1976–78 (billions of dollars)

	1976	1977	1978
Fiscal year basis			
Receipts:	300.5	357.8	402.0
Individual taxes	131.6	157.6	181.0
Corporate taxes	41.4	54.9	60.0
Social Security	92.7	108.7	123.4
Other	34.8	36.6	37.6
Expenditures:	366.4	402.7	450.8
National defense	89.4	97.5	105.2
Income security	127.4	137.9	146.2
Other	115.1	160.1	161.4
Surplus or deficit (−)	−66.4	−45.0	−48.8
National income and product accounts basis (calendar year)			
Receipts	331.4	374.5	431.6
Expenditures	385.2	422.6	461.0
Surplus or deficit (−)	−53.8	−48.1	−29.4
High-employment budget basis			
Receipts	356.9	394.5	446.6
Expenditures	380.3	419.0	459.6
Surplus or deficit (−)			
Year	−23.4	−24.6	−12.9
Quarters			
I	0.6	−2.1	−29.5
II	7.4	−9.0	−9.0
III	−1.5	−35.3	−7.9
IV	—	−38.0	−5.4

Sources: Council of Economic Advisors, *Economic Report of the President* (Washington, DC: GPO, appropriate years).

allowed the federal-funds rate to increase; it rose from 4⅝ percent in the early part of the year to over 6.5 percent at the end. Thus, depending on your point of view, monetary policy could be considered "easy" by monetary-growth or "tight" by interest-rate measures.

The Federal Reserve considered its policies generally successful. It allowed the demand for funds to rise as the economy expanded, while at the same time it kept close to its ranges of monetary growth so as not to dampen growth or reignite inflationary expectations. The financial community was less certain, worrying about monetary growth—even weekly growth rates—and concerned about future inflation. Thus despite the ample supply of funds in the market, interest rates rose along with the federal-funds rate. At year-end, three-month treasury bills stood at over 6 percent; long-term bonds, showing more stability, were at 7.2 percent; the prime rate was 6⅔; and the discount rate was 6 percent, up from 5.5 in January.

Monetary policy for the year can be characterized as erratic; The Federal Reserve was trying to adjust to changing monetary relationships by being cautious, and at the same time trying to reduce inflationary expectations without dampening economic growth. Few would have agreed that it succeeded in either attempt in 1977.

The results of the third year of economic expansion and of the macroeconomic policies designed to influence it can be seen in Table 13.2. Real GNP grew by 4.9 percent, less than the 6 percent registered in 1976. It was sufficient, however, to reduce the unemployment rate to 7 percent for the year and to 6.4 percent in December. Total employment continued to rise also, and by year's end 92 million were employed, an increase of 4.7 percent over 1976. The capacity-utilization rate was up slightly, helping to increase corporate profits by 9.5 percent for the year. Home building was strong, and despite nearly 2 million housing starts, housing prices continued their upward spiral.

There were, however, potential trouble spots to blemish the record. Business fixed investment rose by 8.8 percent, greater than the previous year but several percentage points below the proportion of investment to GNP prior to 1974. More investment would be needed to absorb the growing labor force.

Prices also continued to rise as past increases in food and energy costs gradually were incorporated into other prices and wages. The underlying rate of inflation, excluding food and energy, was nearly the same as the yearly CPI average of 6.5 percent. Moreover, while output per hour was increasing at a rate of 2.1 percent, compensation per hour was rising at 7.7 percent, pushing unit labor costs up by about 5.5 percent. Even as the productivity of labor was falling, wage earners were attempting to restore their real earnings that they saw eroded by past food and fuel costs.[6]

Clearly there was cause for concern for 1978 and beyond. Accordingly, the administration proposed further tax reductions to stimulate private-sector spending. It foresaw little help from the private sector without tax cuts, and besides there was the need to remove the fiscal restraint caused by inflation pushing people into higher tax brackets. Federal spending was also scheduled to diminish in 1978, as the previous stimulus would begin to dwindle. States and localities were not adding to the income stream but, like net exports, were subtracting from it.[7]

Table 13.2   Selected Economic Series, 1976–78 (dollar amounts in billions)

Item	1976 (dollars)	1977 Amount (dollars)	1977 Percent Change from 1976	1978 Amount (dollars)	1978 Percent Change from 1977
GNP	1.700.1	1,887.2	11.0	2,106.6	11.6
GNP (in 1972 dollars)	1,271.0	1,332.7	4.9	1,385.1	3.9
Consumption	819.4	857.7	4.7	891.2	3.9
Investment	173.4	196.3	13.2	210.1	7.0
Net exports	15.4	9.5	−38.3	8.6	−9.5
Government	262.8	269.2	2.4	275.2	2.2
Federal	96.6	101.6	5.2	100.5	−1.1
State and local	166.2	167.6	0.8	174.7	4.2
Unemployment rate (percent)	7.7	7.0	−9.1	6.0	−14.3
Manufacturing capacity utilization rate (percent)	80.2	82.4	2.7	84.2	2.2
Output per hour of all persons (percent change)	3.3	2.1	—	−0.2	—
Compensation per hour (percent change)	8.6	7.7	—	8.4	—
Unit labor cost (percent change)	5.1	5.5	—	8.6	—
Prices (percent change)					
GNP index	5.2	5.9	—	7.4	
PPI	4.2	6.0	—	7.8	—
CPI	5.8	6.5	—	7.7	—

Source: Council of Economic Advisors, *Economic Report of the President* (Washington, DC: GPO, appropriate years).

The second tax package of the administration consisted of the following:

1. A reduction in personal individual income tax rates and a substitution of a $240 credit for the existing $750 personal exemption. This $17 billion reduction was scheduled to take effect October 1, 1978.

2. Permanent reductions in the corporate tax rates in steps, until the tax on income over $50,000 would fall to 45 percent from 48 percent. The investment tax credit would be increased permanently to 10 percent. These changes were effective October 1, 1978, and further changes on January 1, 1980, reduced the corporate rate to 44 percent and involved extensions to eligilibity for the investment tax credit. The initial tax reduction was for some $6 billion.

3. Repeal of the excise tax on telephones effective October 1, 1978, and the reduction in the unemployment insurance tax rate to 0.5 percent on January 1, 1979. These changes amounted to $2 billion in tax reductions.

These tax reductions of $25 billion, together with proposed increases in outlays of some $60 billion, were calculated to provide the necessary stimulus to keep the economy moving along toward reducing unemployment by 0.5 percent in 1978 while keeping the inflation rate near 6 percent. Over the slightly longer run, the administration was still aiming for a 4 percent rate of unemployment. The changing composition of the labor force, however, forced an interim goal of 4.9 percent in the calculation of potential GNP. The 4 percent target rate for unemployment had somehow become institutionalized and was even being debated in Congress in connection with the Humphrey–Hawkins Bill; the administration was not disconcerted by the seeming optimism.

Further Restraint
and Voluntary Wage and Price Controls

The economic forecasts for 1978 were remarkably close. The administration was predicting a 4.5–5 percent range for real GNP growth, with an unemployment rate of 6–6.25 percent. Private economists' forecasts averaged closer to the lower rate for real GNP growth, 4.1–4.3 percent, with an unemployment rate of 6.7 percent. The GNP price deflator was expected to rise by about 6 percent for the year.[8] Private economists, like their administration counterparts, were counting on federal fiscal policy to keep the economy going and saw little stimulus coming from the private sector. The disagreements were mainly over monetary policy, with fiscalists worrying that the money-supply growth was not fast enough to achieve the 11+ percent in the forecast nominal income growth, while the monetarists were concerned that the money supply had been growing too fast. With Arthur Burns's term ending in January 1978, there was additional concern on all sides over the future of monetary policy.

The results (shown in Table 13.2) for the year were not encouraging. Nominal GNP rose by over 11 percent, and the unemployment rate did decline to 6 percent, but real GNP rose only 3.9 percent, revealing the increase in inflation. The implicit price index rose by 7.4 percent, and similar increases were found in the CPI and the WPI. Accordingly, the administration postponed the tax reduction scheduled for October 1978 to January 1979 and reduced the tax cut from $25 to $20 billion. (Congress did enact these reductions in November 1978 along with the energy tax credits to reduce energy usage and reduce reliance on foreign sources.)

Fiscal policy moved toward restraint, as federal expenditures were cut by over $12 billion and the high-employment deficit was reduced from $24.6 billion in 1977 to $12.9 billion in 1978. Inflation was receiving more and more attention from the administration and the monetary authorities.

The long-run target growth rate for M1 was set at 4–6.5 percent for most of the year, with frequent modifications of the range for two-month intervals. In the last quarter of 1978, the range was reduced to 2–6 percent. Actual monetary growth of M1 exceeded these ranges for the first three quarters of 1978 and then fell to near zero for the last quarter. The job of managing monetary aggregates was becoming more complicated, now that banks were permitted to issue six-month certificates of deposit with a rate tied to the treasury-bill rate for similar maturity. Designed to protect thrifts from disintermediation, these new accounts would likely shift funds, but just how would have to await experience. Also, the new NOW accounts and automatic transfer accounts (ATS) were affecting the definition of transactions balances and thus the definition of M1. The Federal Reserve was proposing a new monetary aggregate called M1+, which would include these new interest-bearing accounts.

In any case it is clear that monetary policy moved toward restraint as well in 1978. The discount rate was changed several times during the year, starting at 6.25 percent in January and in a series of steps rising to 9.25 percent at year's end. Interest rates on treasury bills followed along, moving from 6.448 to 9.122; ten-year bonds rose from 7.96 to 9.01; mortgage rates moved upward from 9.1 to 10; the prime rate followed, increasing from 8 to 11.75 percent.

The Federal Reserve increased interest rates partly to support the dollar, which was declining in world markets. The balance of payments again showed deficits of over $33 billion for merchandise, and the dollar was declining. The Federal Reserve reluctantly agreed to help, but warned that the United States must decrease its imports.

The problems of the economy were compounded by the fall in real investment spending and the continuing fall in the productivity of labor. Spending on producers' durable goods fell from a rate of 11.4 percent to 6.3 percent. The slowdown in capital growth could affect the number of jobs created, as well as the rate of growth of productivity. Productivity did grow, but at a rate of only 0.6 percent for the year, while compensation per hour was growing at a rate of 9.1 percent. Clearly, wage costs were increasing about 8.8 percent, and the implications for inflation are obvious.

These results produced a sense of unease about the economy and for many the prospect of another recession. With tight monetary and fiscal policies, the slowdown in investment spending, the decline in real wages, and so on, the immediate future did not look promising. Having identified inflation as the nation's number one problem, the administration was now forced to admit that the economy was not responding to monetary and fiscal policies as it had in the past.[9] Prices and wages were relatively inflexible, even in the face of slack demand. Still, monetary and fiscal policies had a role to play, one of slowing down the rate of expansion in order to avoid excess demand, now that the economy was closing the gap between potential and actual growth.

To supplement the restraining forces of monetary and fiscal policies, the administration proposed a voluntary wage-and-price-control system. The administration asked for voluntary slowdowns in wages and prices in the beginning of the year, and in October it made the request explicit and proposed numerical standards. The pay standard was set at 7 percent for wages and fringe benefits, with exceptions for low-income workers, and firms were asked to limit price increases for 1979 to 0.5 percent below the firm's average annual rate of price increase in the period 1976–77. Again there were exceptions for firms that could not fit into the standard. The pay standard contained a sweetener for labor: If workers agreed to the pay standard of 7 percent and the CPI increased by more than 7 percent, they would receive a tax credit for the difference, up to a maximum of 3 percent. Congress never approved of this tax credit, and thus the sweetener to entice labor compliance was never allowed to work.

Policy Proposals for Combating Stagflation

The outlook for 1979 and early 1980 was uncertain at best and gloomy at worst. The administration forecast a very modest improvement in the economy, with real GNP falling to a growth rate of only 2 percent, while the GNP deflator was expected to fall only slightly to 7.5 percent and unemployment was expected to rise to over 6 percent again. If the wage and prices standards were followed, the CPI might fall to 7 percent or below by 1980. These can hardly be considered rosy forecasts, nor can they be accused of inspiring confidence in the economy. The administration appeared to be attempting to acknowledge the institutional changes that had taken place in the U.S. economy, which were making the job of managing it much more difficult. It apparently seemed best to proceed with caution, particularly since there were too many unknowns to contend with—that is, what was causing the decline in the productivity of labor, what was happening to money flows as new types of accounts were coming into being, and so on. Confidence in past policies was shaken.

The administration was not alone in its confusion, for not far beneath the general consensus of economic conditions for the coming few years were deep divisions among economists on the role and effectiveness of macroeconomic policies. At their annual meeting in December, economists listened to various views on the efficacy of stabilization policies. Robert J. Gordon provided a summary of the conflicting view for the panel, "Effectiveness of Monetary, Fiscal and Other Policy Techniques."[10] On one side were those who continued to see a role for monetary and fiscal policy, while on the other side were the monetarists, who saw little role for fiscal policy and a limited role for monetary policy. An extreme view saw the futility of macroeconomic policy, owing to the anticipation of recurring policy that would come to be known and discounted. These rational-expectations adherents argued that people would learn to adjust to government policies and take steps to alter their behavior and in doing so negate the policy. Even a constant rate of growth of the money supply, favored by monetarists over stop-and-go monetary policy, would be ineffective as a policy measure. The rational-expectations hypothesis leads to a kind of policy nihilism, in that public policy appears impotent to alter economic states. This analysis returns us to the classical world, where policy was neither necessary nor effective. Without dwelling on these previously mentioned viewpoints, as well as the many shades of differences that existed, it is clear that sharp theoretical divisions were dividing the economics profession, putting macro theory in a state of flux and preventing a uniform approach to macroeconomic problems and policies.

Yet there was also a contention that government policy was indeed necessary, as never before. Many found the answer to stagflation was more, not less, government. They began to clamor for an incomes policy of some kind. Traditional monetary policy and fiscal policy were inefficient, for they required large decreases in output and employment for modest price responses. If full employment were given priority, some restraint on wages and prices would be necessary to allow monetary and fiscal policy to stabilize the economy and permit the attainment of full employment without severe inflation.

Since the policy of direct controls was discredited by the Nixon administration's experience, another, less intrusive scheme was desired. The Carter voluntary-standards system was one response to the call for an incomes policy. Another that was receiving attention was the tax-based incomes policy or TIP. TIP was proposed to meet the challenge of finding an incomes policy that would not interfere directly with market decisions, that would not distort the market, or create an unwieldy bureaucracy, but would be strong enough to be effective. Proponents of TIP did not reject traditional policies but argued that they must be supplemented in periods of chronic inflation, when expectations of inflation become entrenched and inflationary psychology encourages individuals to protect themselves. From a micro perspective, the individual may be acting rationally, but in the aggregate, such actions are self-defeating and may bring about even more inflation.

There are two general approaches to a TIP program, one based on penalties and one on rewards. The penalty version was first proposed by Sidney Weintraub and Henry Wallich.[11] It would levy a surcharge on the corporate income tax if a firm ignored the government-set wage-increase standard. The firm (only the top 1,000–2,000 corporations would be included) would be free to pay whatever wage increase it chose, but if it paid more than the standard wage increase, it would be faced with an income tax surcharge. For instance, if the wage standard were a 4 percent annual wage-and-fringe-benefits increase and the firm paid an 8 percent increase, its penalty would be equal to the 4 percent excess times some multiple, say 5, to yield a tax surcharge of 20 percent.

The purpose of TIP, however, was not to increase tax revenues; in fact, if it did, it was not succeeding in stopping inflation. Therefore, after TIP was instituted, say the national expected rate of wage increase is 6 percent, then the typical excess over the standard would be 2 percent (6 − 4 percent), and the average surcharge would be 10 percent (2 × 5). The TIP program for that year would require a reduction in the corporate income tax rate of 10 percent.

Now a corporation that granted an average wage increase of 5 percent would pay no penalty. The corporation that granted a 10 percent wage increase, however, would suffer a surcharge of 30 percent

[(10 − 4) × 5]. Of course, a corporation that raised wages by less than 5 percent would receive a tax-rate reduction.

The aim of the penalty form of TIP is to strengthen the will of firms to resist excessive wage demands. Moreover, affecting only large corporations would limit administrative difficulties, but the plan makes two basic assumptions: that wage increases in the rest of the economy will follow those of the top corporations, and that prices will bear a stable relationship (markup) to wages.

The other TIP approach, associated with Arthur Okun, is based on rewards. The plan would be open to every employer in the nation on a voluntary basis, but those who chose to participate would have to agree to limit their annual wage increase to the government-set standard, say 6 percent. If the firm so pledged, its employees would receive a tax credit equal to 1.5 percent of their wage income, up to some specified level, say $20,000. If the employer promised to adhere to the standard in advance, workers would receive the credit immediately as a reduction from taxes withheld (an advantage to get worker support); otherwise, the credit would be entered on the worker's income tax return. Also, firms that pledged in advance to adhere to the standard would receive a tax credit equal to one-fourth the total reduction in withholding taxes given to their employees.

With this voluntary program, employers are again free to pay more than the wage standard by simply not participating. The same assumption about prices is made, however—that they will decelerate as a result of wage moderations. Furthermore, Okun's plan does involve a loss of revenue, and since all employers are eligible, the administrative complexities are likely to be much greater than with the penalty TIP.

There are two criticisms of both these approaches. Both types may seriously underestimate the administrative problems involved, and both may fail to elicit the cooperation of labor. Labor is bound to feel discriminated against (if not blamed for the inflation to begin with) and may ask why other rewards—profits, interest income, rents, and dividends—are not controlled as well. Why should labor be singled out and asked to limit its income in the hope that other rewards will adjust eventually? There are other criticisms of these plans, but their authors do not claim perfection and, in fact, see them as only temporary and supplemental measures.

Another response to inflation, revived by Milton Friedman, is to include in all contracts price escalator clauses that would adjust nominal values according to the change in prices over the length of the contract. The policy, called indexation or monetary correction, is already employed in cost-of-living allowances (COLAS) in some union contracts and in Social Security benefits. Thus some or all rewards—wages, interest, rents, taxes—would be adjusted for price changes; Friedman would start with the government sector and make the remaining participation voluntary.

The aim here is not to affect the rate of inflation but to reduce the effects of inflation on economic decisions. Specifically, indexation would reduce the revenue that flows to government in inflationary periods, as people are pushed into higher tax brackets. Friedman asserts that governments often resort to inflation as a way to gain revenue without tax legislation. The question, however, is whether the public would interpret indexation as a signal of defeat in the fight against inflation, and, if so, might this not encourage inflationary expectations? And might not government step up its actions (that is, speed up the rate of inflation) to recoup the revenue lost under the plan? As we have seen, however, tax cuts were made in the 1970s in periods of inflation. These "perverse" fiscal policies may well have been initiated to adjust taxes for inflation—a form of indexation or monetary correction that would be formally introduced in 1981.

The confusion over the causes of and solutions to stagflation did not appear to bother Congress, which passed the Full Employment and Balanced Growth Act of 1978 (amending the Employment Act of 1946) in October. More commonly known as the Humphrey–Hawkins Act, it added the following phrases to the preamble of the 1946 act: "[to] promote full employment and production, increased real income, balanced growth, a balanced Federal budget, adequate productivity growth, proper attention to national priorities, achievement of an improved trade balance through increased export and improvement in the international competitiveness of agriculture, business, and industry, and reasonable price stability." Congress again demonstrated its pragmatism in striking balances and making compromises, finally producing a bill that declares that it is cognizant of all of our economic problems.[12] The act, however, goes beyond the mere enumeration of economic woes to set specific targets and initiate some institutional changes.

The act requires the president to submit to Congress an annual economic report, to include trends in certain economic variables; one-, three-, and five-year goals for employment, production, and prices; and programs and policies contemplated to achieve these goals. The Federal Reserve is also required to submit data to Congress on trends in and plans for monetary conditions in the coming year. Moreover, the Federal Reserve must demonstrate how its policies fit in with those of the executive branch. Congress thus receives both monetary and fiscal forecasts and goals, which are reviewed by the Joint Economic Committee. The act stipulates that other advisory boards may be set up to review and aid in the whole process.

Specific targets were also set for unemployment and inflation rates. The goal for unemployment five years after passage of the act (that is, in 1983) was set at 4 percent for individuals aged 16 and over (3 percent for those 20 years old and over), and the target rate for inflation was 3 percent per year (based on the CPI). Reducing unemployment was specifically given precedence over slowing the inflation rate. The timetables, however, can be amended by the president with due justification.

The 1978 act acknowledges that traditional monetary and fiscal policies have failed to achieve the desired goals and must be supplemented. And it is often quite specific in suggesting programs: employment and training programs for youth and minorities, ways to fight inflation, and ways to encourage growth and aid various sectors.

The Humphrey–Hawkins Act is an example of a recent attempt to rationalize economic policy and set national priorities. Some hoped it would prepare the ground for more government planning; for others, planning was to be firmly resisted. The result is this compromise, with its loopholes and some new institutional arrangements. Whether or not the act represents a serious commitment or a parting tribute to the late Senator Hubert Humphrey remains to be seen.

Economic Stagnation and the Movement toward Monetarism

The long-awaited and frequently anticipated recession did not occur in 1979, but some of the old problems continued, and some new ones were added. It was not a banner year for the United States.

The Shah of Iran was overthrown in a revolution, and later in the year the U.S. embassy in Teheran was overrun and U.S. citizens were taken and held hostage. In retaliation the United States suspended all oil imports from Iran and froze Iranian assets in the United States. Although the amount of oil imported from Iran was not very large, when combined with the actions of other oil-producing countries, the ban pushed oil prices up to close to $28 per barrel or double the price only a year earlier.

These price shocks were administered in several steps over the year, and the United States was unable to increase production of domestic oil rapidly enough to counter the price increases effectively. Gasoline prices rose $0.35 per gallon over 1979, and supply shortages created long lines of consumers waiting to purchase what was available. Various rationing schemes were instituted by states in an effort to meet the crisis. Energy prices added 2½ points to the CPI in 1979, and energy was a source of constant worry for the entire society (to be discussed in more detail later).

Carter's foreign-policy initiatives concerning human rights, the Panama Canal Treaty, and the mediation of the Mideast peace talks between Israel and Egypt were now forgotten, as the Iranian crisis took center stage for the public. Adding to the administration's woes, the Soviet Union invaded Afghanistan and immediately revived the cold war. An embargo on sales of wheat and corn was instituted, and a reduction in trade of technical equipment. U.S. farmers were ultimately to pay for this embargo, as they lost markets to Canada, Argentina, and other nations.

The nation was also rocked by a near catastrophe at a nuclear power plant at Three Mile Island in Pennsylvania. Questions were revived over the issue of nuclear energy, and antinuclear rallies were held in Washington and New York City, marking the resurgence of a popular cause. The economic sanctions against Iran and the Soviet Union were subjects of much debate. Equally controversial was the $1.5 billion loan guarantee of the federal government to the Chrysler Corporation. This domestic bail-out of a major corporation was regarded as undesirable and precedent setting.

In short, there were enough upsetting events in 1979 to disturb the tranquillity of the most stable nation; unfortunately, the United States in the late 1970s could not be characterized as a serene and stable society. The instability was also evident in the economy, as these events impacted on it. Real GNP did rise by 3.2 percent for the year, but it actually fell in the second quarter, as growth was very uneven. It is easy to see why a forecast of a recession was so popular, since every component of aggregate demand seemed to be falling from 1978 rates of change. Particularly disappointing was the drop in the rate of investment spending, from double-digit rates to 1.3 percent in 1979. While producers' durable equipment rose by 5.5 percent, still low in comparison to other years, inventories collapsed by 27.1 percent. Some of the fall in inventories was involuntary—for example, small, fuel-efficient cars—but other inventory declines probably reflected the uncertain economic conditions. The growth in real government expenditures and consumption matched that of 1978, as little stimulus came from these sectors. Only exports rose, partly as a result of the depreciating dollar and partly due to farm exports. Table 13.3 shows these trends.

In other areas of the economy, unemployment fell to an average rate of 5.8 percent for 1979, and capacity utilizaton rose slightly to 86 percent. Again, however, the productivity of labor fell slightly, but unit labor costs rose even faster, by over 10 percent for the year. Of course, prices rose, as the GNP deflator climbed by 8.5 percent, the producers' price index by 11.1 percent (12.5 percent from December 1978 to December 1979), and the CPI by 11.3 percent (13.3 percent from December to December). The price movements were dominated by energy prices, with the CPI rising over 25 percent from this source alone. Add the rising housing costs of 15 percent due to increasing

Table 13.3   Selected Economic Series, 1979–80 (dollar amounts in billons)

	1979		1980	
Item	Amount (dollars)	Percent Change from 1978	Amount (dollars)	Percent Change from 1979
GNP	2,413.9	12.0	2,626.1	8.8
GNP (in 1972 dollars)	1,483.0	3.2	1,480.7	−0.2
Consumption	930.9	2.9	935.1	0.5
Investment	232.6	1.3	203.6	−12.5
Government	281.8	2.3	290.0	2.9
Federal	101.7	1.9	108.1	6.3
State and local	180.1	1.2	181.9	1.0
Unemployment rate (percent)	5.8	−3.3	7.1	22.4
Manufacturing capacity: utilization rate (percent)	85.7	1.5	79.1	−7.7
Output per hour of all persons (percent change)	—	−0.3	—	−0.2
Compensation per hour (percent change)	—	10.1	—	10.2
Unit Labor Costs (percent change)	—	10.4	—	10.4
Prices (percent change)				
GNP index	—	8.5	—	9.0
PPI	—	11.1	—	13.5
CPI	—	11.3	—	13.5

Source: Council of Economic Advisors, *Economic Report of the President* (Washington, DC: GPO, 1982).

interest rates, and food price increases of over 10 percent, and the major sources of inflation are identified.

The economy bumbled along without creating the heralded recession in 1979, but macroeconomic policy cannot claim credit for having averted the downturn. Federal government deficits occurred in all budgets, but they were smaller than those in 1978 (see Table 13.4). In particular, the high-employment budget fell to an annual deficit of $2.2 billion from $12.9 billion in 1978. The federal budget was

Table 13.4   Federal Government Budgets, 1979–80 (billions of dollars)

	1979	1980
Fiscal year basis		
Receipts	463.3	517.1
Individual taxes	217.8	244.1
Corporate taxes	65.7	64.6
Social security	138.9	157.8
Other	40.9	50.6
Expenditures	491.0	576.7
National defense	117.7	135.9
Income security	160.2	193.1
Interest	42.6	52.6
Other	170.5	195.1
Surplus or deficit (−)	−27.7	−59.6
National income and product accounts basis		
(calendar year)		
Receipts	494.4	540.8
Expenditures	509.2	602.0
Surplus or deficit (−)	−14.8	−61.2
High Employment budget basis		
Receipts	504.2	573.2
Expenditures	506.5	591.6
Surplus or deficit (−)		
Year	−2.2	−18.3
Quarters		
I	−4.8	−17.4
II	5.3	−21.3
III	−2.1	−20.7
IV	−7.2	−14.0

Source: Council of Economic Advisors, *Economic Report of the President* (Washington, DC: GPO, 1981), pp. 315, 319.

continuing the movement to restraint; price stability became the foremost goal of the administration as it reacted to social pressures, indicating that inflation was the nation's most serious problem.[13]

The monetary authorities were certainly conscious of the inflationary pressures in 1979 and were convinced of the need to provide restraint in money markets. Despite the expectation that an economic slowdown appeared assured, the Federal Reserve was more concerned with rising prices and their distorting influence on the economy. Accordingly, the target range for the growth of M1 (demand deposits and currency) was set at 1.5 to 4.5 percent for the year, and the M2 (M1 plus savings deposits) range was set at 5 to 8 percent. A federal funds rate in the 10 percent range was considered appropriate for these targets.

The actual growth rates in the first quarter of 1979 were negative for M1 (−1.3 percent) and low for M2 (2.8 percent). (See Table 13.5 for these and other monetary data.) Then in the second and third quarters, both aggregates easily exceeded their respective ranges. Apparently the slowing down of the economy affected the growth rates early in the year, but more important, there were shifts of funds into interest-bearing checking accounts and later into money-market certificates. These shifts among various kinds of deposits led the Federal Reserve to propose the redefining of monetary aggregates, if control over them was to be effective.[14] Changes in bank regulations and new types of deposits were obscuring the difference between funds used for transactions and savings and blurring the difference among financial institutions.

In any case, it is clear that the Federal Reserve was having difficulty managing the growth of monetary aggregates in the first three quarters of 1979. In an effort to gain more control, the federal-funds rate was increased in the third quarter of 1979, and discount rates were increased to 11 percent in September and to 12 percent in October. Still, excessive monetary growth continued, and restraint was lacking. Interest rates were stable through the first half of the year, but began to increase in the third quarter as the Federal Reserve's actions took effect.

The need to control the monetary aggregates better led the Federal Reserve to change its technique for doing so. On October 6, led by Chairman Paul Volcker, it adopted a more direct policy; instead of trying to control monetary aggregates by manipulating the federal-funds rate, it decided to regulate bank reserves directly. Monetarists had been urging such a policy for some time, and the Federal Reserve was acknowledging their criticisms by moving toward their recommendations for the conduct of monetary policy.

To control monetary aggregates, open-market operations would now target bank reserves instead of a federal-funds rate. Lacking direct controls, interest rates could be expected to vary more widely, but that was deemed preferable to having the monetary aggregates vary widely, with stable interest rates, as under the old technique. In addition, stronger resolve in controlling monetary conditions was needed to gain some respect for the falling dollar on international exchange markets.

Interest rates did rise sharply in the period following the announced change in monetary policy, and while moderating later, remained several percentage points above third-quarter levels. Table 13.5 shows these increases in interest rates but also indicates the immediate success in decreasing the growth of M1 to rates within the targeted range, and of M2 to slower rates, but still above its range.

Rising interest rates in the last quarter confronted usury ceilings in many states, and these ceilings had to be suspended by the federal government to prevent the withdrawal of funds from thrift institutions. Still, high mortgage rates had the predictable result on the housing sector, and new home starts fell quickly, by 32 percent in the last quarter. Small firms were also hard hit by high interest rates, as they scrambled for operating funds or were squeezed by higher carrying costs. Furthermore, domestic automobile sales dipped 10.4 percent, while—ominously—imported car sales rose by 16.5 percent.

The Recession of 1980

As the foregoing monetary and fiscal policies were affecting the economy, the administration's other proposal for combating inflation was also in operation for its first full year. The voluntary price and wage standards had been in effect since October 1978, and the administration reported widespread compliance.[15] Critics were quick to point out, however, that they were not able to stop inflation, as firms faced with rising prices opted to switch from the price standard to the profit-margin-limits standard (the average profit margin for two out of the last three fiscal years). Thus they were able to pass on the higher prices.

Workers, on the other hand, suffered a decline in real wages of approximately 4.5 percent; wages increased by over 8 percent, but prices rose by 12.5 percent. Prices of energy, food, and housing rose rapidly, and increases for these essential commodities are difficult for a wage earner to escape. These same price increases affected firms as well, but their ability to pass them on are much greater.

In terms of the difficulty of controlling internally these areas of rising prices, the administration opted to continue the voluntary program for 1980. This time a two-year price standard was chosen, and firms were asked to limit price increases to 5 percent for the two-year period ending September 30, 1980. The base period was 1976–77 for the price standard; for the profit margin standard, profits could rise by less than 13.5 percent of the same two-year period, and the profit margin should be no higher than the average in the last two out of three years prior to the program.

In November the newly established Pay Advisory Committee recommended new wage standards in the range of 7.5–9.5 percent, hoping for an average wage settlement around the midpoint of 8.5 percent. Many others expected wage increases to exceed even these generous standards, but Alfred E. Kahn, chairman of the Council on Wage and Price Stability that oversaw the entire controls program, expected the average rate of 8.5 percent and required that firms with more than 1,000 employees that granted a higher pay increase report their reasons for doing so.

Earlier two new commissions were created to promote greater compliance and wider acceptance: a price commission and the aforementioned Pay Advisory Committee. Despite these attempts to lend credibility to the guidelines program, the whole idea was subjected to increasing criticism from all quarters. Many questioned whether the voluntary controls program would work, under these conditions or under any conditions; others worried that inflation could be made worse if people came to expect direct controls to follow the voluntary ones, and thus moved to raise their rewards before that happened.

The outlook for 1980 was not promising. The Carter administration, now committed to fiscal conservatism, was predicting a mild recession, with real GNP expected to fall by 1 percent. Despite the recession, prices were expected to continue to rise at double-digit rates. This forecast of economic pain was a first for a president seeking reelection. The administration, of course, promised restraint by the public sector.

The promised recession arrived in the second quarter of 1980, ending the five-year expansion that began in March 1975. The NBER actually selected January 1980, however, as the peak of the business cycle. After rising by 3.1 percent in the first quarter, real GNP plummeted by −9.9 percent in the second quarter, the sharpest decline

Table 13.5　Monetary Aggregates and Interest Rates, 1979–80 (annual rates of change, in percent)

Item	1979					1980				
	Q1	Q2	Q3	Q4	Year	Q1	Q2	Q3	Q4	Year
Money concepts										
M1	−1.3	8.1	9.7	5.0	5.0	4.6	−4.4	11.5	8.1	5.0
M1A*	0.2	7.8	8.8	4.7		5.8	−2.6	14.6	10.8	7.3
M1B*	4.8	10.7	10.1	5.3	7.7					
M2 (old)	2.8	8.8	11.9	8.9						
M2 (new)	6.3	10.2	10.3	7.2	9.0	7.3	5.6	16.0	9.1	9.8
Target ranges (percent), long-term										
M1	1.5–4.5	1.5–4.5	1.5–4.5	3–6		3.5–6	3.5–6	3.5–5	3.5–5	
M1A	—	—	—	—		3.5–6	3.5–6			
M1B	—	—	—	—		4–6.5	4–6.5	3.5–6	3.5–6	
M2 (old)	5–8	5–8	5–8	5–8						
M2 (new)	—	—	—	—		6–9	6–9	5.5–8.5	5.5–8.5	

Interest rates								
Short-term								
Federal funds	10.07	10.18	10.94	13.58	12.69	9.83	15.85	16.57
Target range	10.00	10.00+	11.00+	none	12.45	10.35	11.78	13.00
Federal Reserve discount	9.50	9.50	10.21	11.92				
Treasury bills	9.38	9.38	9.67	11.84	9.62	9.15	13.61	14.39
Long-term								
U.S. Government	9.03	9.08	9.03	10.18	10.58	10.95	12.23	12.74
Mortgages	10.33	10.35	11.13	12.38	12.70	13.12	14.62	15.10

*For 1979, data are for comparison purposes only.
Source: Federal Reserve Bulletins, and St. Louis Federal Reserve Bank, *Review* 1979, 1980.

in the postwar period. The economy quickly recovered in the second half of 1980, and for the year real GNP decreased by only 0.2 percent (nominal GNP rose by 8.8 percent).

Table 13.3 shows the data for the analysis of this brief recessionary year. Note particularly the sharp decline in investment spending: Real fixed investment declined by 7.1 percent, inventories by 7.7 percent, and residential structures by 20 percent. Part of the decline in fixed investment can be attributed to the recession that pushed capacity-utilization rates down to 79 percent, and part to declining sales and rising debt costs, due to rising interest rates. Inventories also declined, as uncertainty continued and debt costs mounted. New housing starts again fell, this time by 28 percent, as mortgage interest rates shot up to the 16 percent range. In the second half of the year, housing starts rebounded somewhat, but still failed to match the volume in 1979.

Personal consumption expenditures likewise declined from 1979 levels. This was partly due to the administration's fear of inflationary expectations becoming excessive, and as a consequence it requested the Federal Reserve to devise a system of credit controls to curb spending. As a result, from March to July the Federal Reserve required all lenders to maintain a deposit at a Federal Reserve bank equal to a percentage of credit-card lending and unsecured consumer credit.[16] Other provisions of the Federal Reserve's program called for increases in reserve requirements for large time deposits, a surcharge of 3 percent on banks that borrowed too frequently from Federal Reserve banks, and a voluntary program for consumer creditors to limit the growth in total loans to 6–9 percent over the year.

Whether out of patriotism or from the decline in credit availability, real consumption did fall sharply in the second quarter (−2.6 percent), especially in consumer durables (−13.2 percent), before rebounding to the levels at the beginning of the year. Only net exports and federal government expenditures showed increases over the year. The volume of exports actually fell from prior years, as the economies of other nations floundered, but imports remained stable, even as the U.S. economy slowed.

Federal expenditures on social programs began to drop, as the administration reacted to the growing inflationary fears. Expenditures on national defense, however, began to rise rapidly—by over 15 percent (nearer 6 percent in real terms). Transfer payments of the federal government rose by 20 percent, led by increases in Social Security payments of 20 percent (following a 14.3 percent cost-of-living increase), increases in unemployment benefits of 67 percent, and a 22 percent rise in interest payments.

Clearly the budget was being slowly reallocated from social to military programs—not fast enough for conservatives and too fast for liberals. The administration was trying to practice fiscal restraint without appearing to be weak in the defense area, following the USSR invasion of Afghanistan and the Iranian situation. Still, the high-employment budget for the year shows a large deficit of $18.3 billion. (See Table 13.4.) Actually, the result is illusory, since it includes the lagged response to tax refunds from 1978 and large interest outlays caused by rising interest rates over which the administration had no control. Eliminating these items, the high-employment budget actually tightened by $10 billion in 1980.[17]

Despite the recession, prices repeated their performance of 1979: The GNP deflator rose by 9.0 percent, the CPI by 13.5 percent (12.4 percent from December 1979 to December 1980), and the PPI rose by 13.5 percent (11.8 percent from December to December). The slowing down of the economy had little effect on price levels, and the administration began to echo the belief of many other observers that prices do not respond to reductions in aggregate demand unless the cutbacks are drastic enough to cause a severe recession.[18]

The recession did push the unemployment rate up to 7.4 percent in December 1980, with an average rate for the year of 7.1 percent. Table 13.3 also reveals, however, that once again labor productivity fell slightly, while labor costs matched their rise in 1979 of over 10 percent. Past price increases were again finding their way into wage demands, tending to increase the underlying rate of inflation, the rate in the absence of special price shocks. The average hourly wage increased by 9.1 percent, within the range set by the controls program but disappointing in that it exceeded the 8.5 percent hoped for, and because the rate was exceeded by wider margins in certain sectors such as manufacturing. Still, real wages declined once again, as the CPI exceeded the average by approximately 3 percent. The administration, which had claimed partial success of its wage standards in 1979 in holding wages down by over 1 percent, did not record a similar claim in 1980. Others gave the controls program even less approval, and it quietly expired, to no one's regret.

Macroeconomic Restraint in the Face of Recession

The recession of 1980 did not elicit the usual expansionary macroeconomic policies; in fact, both monetary and fiscal policies moved toward restraint. The shifts in the high-employment budget have already been noted, as has the reduction in nondefense spending. Carter was honoring his pledge to reduce the government's role in fostering inflation. He could blame the increase in national defense spending on external pressures.

The Federal Reserve's Open Market Committee sought to reduce the rate of growth of monetary aggregates in 1980—"the members agreed that monetary growth should slow further in 1980, following some deceleration over 1979, in line with the continuing objective of curbing inflation and providing the basis for restoration of economic stability."[19] The Federal Reserve was only partially successful in meeting its goals. While M1A (the old M1) was within its target range, M1B (M1 and new demand deposits) and M2 exceeded theirs. The Federal Reserve did not correctly calculate the shifts of funds into the new types of deposits and did not expect the volume that was transferred.

Still, the growth of the aggregates was quite erratic (see Table 13.5). In the first half of 1980, monetary growth rates were behaving as the Federal Reserve had desired, falling within the desired ranges. In the second half of the year, however, growth rates shot up and exceeded the targets set. This pattern of money growth reflects partly the state of economic activity, as the demand for money slowed in the first part of the year and revived in the second half, despite high interest rates; and partly the Federal Reserve's program of credit controls instituted in March and removed in July. The response was greater than expected in both cases, and the demand for money continued to be puzzling.

The demand for credit was strong in the early part of the year, fueled by speculative activity in commodities markets and other financial markets. Thus interest rates rose in the first quarter, with three-month treasury bills rising to over 15 percent in March and the prime rate rising to nearly 20 percent. Interest rates declined in the second quarter, but by fall were rising again rapidly. Three-month treasury bills returned to their March highs; the prime rate was over 20 percent in December; the federal funds rate reached nearly 19 percent at year's end; and, in general, interest rates were at all-time highs. The Federal Reserve did adjust the discount rate, more or less in line with the movements in other rates, increasing it until March, then reducing it several times in the summer, and finally increasing it several times, until by December it stood at 13 pecent.

If all these high interest rates were playing havoc with the economy, they were creating all kinds of problems for banks. Many responded by dropping out of the Federal Reserve System because of their objection to tying up funds in non-interest-bearing reserves and claiming overregulation as well. Banks did attempt to meet the situation head-on by introducing new deposits, six-month and one-and-one-half-year money-market certificates, and by introducing variable-interest-rate mortgages to protect themselves against rising interest rates, which fixed mortgage rates obviously failed to do in the decade of the 1970s. Finally, Regulation Q and state usury laws were clearly in conflict, and despite the federal suspension of usury laws, nothing was done about it.

These and many other problems led to the enactment of the Depository Deregulation and Monetary Control Act of 1980. Under this act, interest-rate ceilings were to be removed over a six-year period, and usury ceilings were repealed on mortgage rates and relaxed on other loans. In addition, all banks were permitted to issue NOW accounts, and thrift institutions were allowed to grant consumer and business loans within limits. In return they became subject to the reserve requirements of the Federal Reserve System, but were allowed to use the discount window. Whether or not these provisions would improve or complicate monetary policy would have to await the act's implementation in 1981.

Energy and Labor Force Problems and the Loss of Confidence

The performance of monetary and fiscal policies of the 1970s cannot really be evaluated until other important developments of the period are recognized. Whatever success macroeconomic policies may have achieved, they must be viewed in the larger context that includes events that may have overshadowed them. Indeed, these events might have forced policies that would not have been followed, had they not occurred. The 1970s witnessed a number of shattering events that left the nation floundering, as it attempted to meet new challenges with hastily conceived and partial solutions. In the end, most people felt worse off, even if objective data did not always confirm their suspicions.

Before judging the policies of the Carter administration, some discussion of these special features of the 1970s must be included, or the attempt risks serious misinterpretations. While this risk is always present, the more so the closer to the present, recognition of special factors at least may help in avoiding the more glaring errors of judgment.

Perhaps the most obvious development was the energy crisis. We have already witnessed how it helped to destroy the wage and price control system of the Nixon administration. Passed on to the Ford administration, the energy problem helped to create the sharp recession and all but eliminated any contribution toward economic progress in the troubled Ford era. Carter, too, fell victim to the energy snare, and the inability to escape helped, no doubt, in retiring him from public office.

The problem is simply stated: How does an economy respond to these types of supply shocks that result in inflation? How can the economy cope with these price shocks before they find their way into demands for increases in wages, profits, interest rates, and any other reward—that is, before the price shocks become incorporated in the underlying inflation rate? A reduction in real incomes caused by rising prices of basic commodities encourages everyone to attempt to recapture a former position by demanding greater nominal incomes.

The solutions are not as obvious. Falling real incomes are quickly felt, and there is the inevitable call for government to do something. Unfortunately in cases like this, if inflation is to be avoided, government must call on the nation to make sacrifices: Someone has to pay for the income redistribution from consumers to producers of energy. Calls for sacrifices are not popular, however, and politicians who demand them are not around for very long.[20]

Among the solutions to energy problems, the one probably most favored by traditional economists was to let prices rise to reflect market realities and ration supplies automatically.[21] This meant removing all controls on energy producers who, thus freed, would respond by augmenting the supply. Afterwards prices would stabilize and might even fall. The exploration for additional energy is a longer-run solution to inadequate supplies; in the meantime, sacrifices would be demanded, but who should make them? A possible efficient solution is never enough in the political arena, where equity concerns are more pressing. Letting the market determine supply allocations and encourage production may be efficient, but if it is conceived as being unfair to certain groups, in this case low-income groups and those living in geographical areas that demand high energy usage, then the economic solution conflicts with political considerations, and the latter will prevail. This is true, even if it would have been better to scrap controls and subsidize those who are most injured by market solutions. Some economists, for instance, wanted market prices to govern, but favored a windfall tax on excess profits to be returned to needy consumers.

Those who found that the burden of real-income loss would fall disproportionately on those least able to protect themselves tended to favor a direct-rationing scheme of available supplies.[22] Prices might rise somewhat, but the sacrifice would be shared more equally if the available supplies were distributed more equitably—by household, by motor vehicle registration, and so on. Indeed, the administration seriously considered a direct-rationing scheme and proceeded to print ration coupons (with George Washington's picture on them) for use in the event such a program became necessary.

Another scheme, favored by many but made popular by John Anderson, a presidential candidate for 1980, proposed a tax of $0.50 a gallon on gasoline. The tax would encourage conservation, and the proceeds could be used to fund research into alternative fuels or rebated to consumers most seriously affected.

Of course, many called for simple conservation to minimize costs and preserve supplies. This approach, favored in general by Carter, also called for a sacrifice, but it would be a voluntary one; the benefits would accrue to both the individual and the nation. Indeed, Carter did warn the nation that people had become spoiled and that some cutback in energy usage was both feasible and in the national interest. Otherwise the crisis would get worse and "our decision about energy will test the character of the American people and the ability of the president and the Congress to govern this nation. This difficult effort will be the 'moral equivalent of war,' except that we will be uniting our efforts to build and not to destroy."[23]

Another approach to reduce the vulnerability of the United States to future boycotts was the establishment of The Strategic Petroleum Reserve Program. Under this proposal, the United States embarked on a program for stockpiling oil for use in a future emergency. When Carter left office, the plan called for stockpiling one billion barrels of oil, although only 108 million barrels had been accumulated to that date.[24]

These and other energy policies still transferred wealth from the consuming to the producing countries (or to the oil firms in the middle). To prevent this redistribution, some economists favored an import tariff that would still raise the price of imported oil, but would encourage domestic oil production, while giving the government tariff revenues to distribute as it pleased. Prices would rise—perhaps more than expected, if foreign producers increased their pretariff prices in response.

Therefore, other schemes were suggested. One from M. A. Adelman of MIT involved auctioning imports, by ticket, to prospective importers.[25] Once the level of desired imports was determined, the United States would simply auction off the rights of those wishing to sell in the United States. Competition among supplies for the right to sell oil would soon bid up the price of the tickets and eventually result in cheating, underselling, and so on, and the power of producers would be broken. Any cartel could be attacked in this way by encouraging disunity among members. Since excess capacity is generally the norm, cartel members would soon be attempting to gain immediate advantage by getting rid of their supplies, even at reduced rates. Meanwhile, the United States would not be making any sacrifices, since it would still be getting the level of imports it desired.

Lacking any policy like Adelman's, the United States was forced to submit to the blackmail of rising prices by the producing countries. At the time the United States was importing approximately one-half of its crude oil needs and thus was vulnerable to cutbacks in supply or arbitrary price increases. Since self-denial or self-sacrifice was never seriously considered by the public or policymakers, the nation paid the price. At the time there was a widespread feeling, since confirmed, that oil supplies were not really scarce, despite the administration's claim that they were running out and that exploration costs were driving up prices. The public was confused by estimates of shrinking reserves (provided by the oil companies, since no other data were available, and repeated by successive administrations in numerous warnings), while other estimates showed no such depletion of reserves.[26] The general public was suspicious but far from knowledgeable; in the end, the more numerous voices proclaiming scarcity were able to "convince" the public of the accuracy of their forecasts.[27]

These were some of the main ideas at the time for dealing with the oil and energy problems. It is time to examine the public policies actually followed in the atmosphere of incomplete information, conflicting advice, and the existence of the inevitable efficiency–equity trade-off.

The Ford administration's response was predictably on the conservative side. Aside from encouraging conservation, with which everyone agreed, and the promotion of coal and nuclear substitutes, which many had qualms about, the administration favored raising prices to ration the scarce supplies and encourage domestic production. Its plans called for price controls on crude oil and gas to be lifted and an import fee of $2 per barrel on imported oil to be imposed, along with an excise tax on domestic oil. The tax was to be returned by a scheme of tax credits for individuals and a tax reduction for corporations.

In February 1975 a $1-per-barrel import fee was initiated, which later rose to $2 per barrel in March. In December 1975 Congress passed the Energy Policy and Conservation Act, which featured the phase-out of oil price controls by 1979. The act also included fuel-efficiency standards for automobiles and trucks, effective with the 1978 models. The import fees were removed.

Carter's approach to energy problems stressed conservation, and to encourage it and foster the shift to other energy sources, he proposed a series of measures in his National Energy Plan (NEP) of April 1977. The central feature of this plan was a tax on domestic oil to bring the price up to the imported price. The receipts from the tax would be rebated to consumers on a per capita basis. Oil discovered after April 20, 1977, would be priced at the world market price.

In addition, a user tax on industrial users and utilities was included to bring their costs up (and equal to the social costs) and encourage conservation or conversion to other fuels. Other features of the bill included an additional investment tax credit of 10 percent for conversions to coal usage by firms; greater reliance on nuclear power; provision for utility-rate reform to reflect the costs of generating electricity more accurately; and conservation measures such as a "gas guzzler" tax on fuel-inefficient new automobiles and tax credits for home insulation and solar devices.[28]

Congress balked; "the influence of the special-interest lobbies is almost unbelievable, particularly from the automobile and oil interests," as Carter wrote in his diary.[29] The debates over the NEP were prolonged and heated, and finally in October 1978 a bill was passed, but it included only the "gas guzzler" provision, utility-rate reform measures, and tax credits for conservation. Other provisions encouraged conservation and a shift to other fuel sources.

The act was guided by James Schlesinger, the first secretary of the newly created Department of Energy. Carter's sincerity over the energy issue was never in question, but its importance to the nation required, in his view, more attention than the existing bureaucracy could furnish. Yet by his own admission, "My repeated calls for action on energy had become aggravating, and were increasingly falling on deaf ears among American citizens. In spite of the subject's crucial importance, the public lacked interest in energy except when long gas lines formed or a sudden price increase made people angry."[30]

By this time the Carter administration seemed to be floundering and losing the confidence of the public. In the energy area Carter was pushing for a windfall profits tax and a gradual decontrol of oil prices. Following meetings at Camp David with many invited advisors, Carter made another concerted effort at getting another energy bill through Congress. After much debate, Congress in March 1980 did enact a windfall profits tax and accepted the time period for decontrol of oil prices. The tax proceeds would be used to establish the Energy Security Corporation, which would direct funds to the development of synthetic fuels. Also, the Energy Mobilization Board was established to cut through the inevitable red tape when delays threatened.

For the moral equivalent of war, there was not much to show to match the rhetoric. The combination of the lobbying of special-interest groups, the lack of information on energy supplies, public apathy except in emergencies, and the unwillingness of Congress to act, made a coherent energy policy all but impossible. Also, there was the suspicion on the part of many, since verified, that the energy crisis was manufactured. It is difficult enough to ask for sacrifices and higher taxes when the conditions are evident; how much more difficult is it if the conditions are suspect? (Events such as the completion of the trans-Alaskan pipeline and the subsequent flow of oil in June 1977 may have contributed to creating a feeling that the crisis was over.) Mr. Carter's characterization of the American people as spoiled and selfish began to anger, not provoke.

Less noticeable to the general public were the trends and shifts in the labor market. The changes in labor markets would transform the society in unanticipated ways—from the nature of work itself, what kinds of work were being done, to who was doing it, the composition of the labor force.

Some summary data quickly reveal the startling changes. (Table 13.6 gives the information.) Note that the population increased over the period 1970–80 by 10.8 percent, but within that period the demographic shifts that were occurring had repercussions on the labor market. In the first place, the rate of population increase was slowing down from an annual rate of 1.71 in 1960 to 1.26 in 1970 and 1.25 in 1980.[31] Second, the population was aging, with the median age increasing from 28 to 30 years, while the younger age group actually registered a decline over the period.

Given these trends, note the growth in the civilian labor force of over 29 percent in this decade. The civilian labor force was growing at an average annual rate of 2.5 percent in this period, up from 1.7 percent in the 1960s. The post-World War II baby boom was now accounting for increased entrants into the labor force, continuing a trend that began in the late 1960s. The percentage of the population in the civilian age group 16–24 rose from 15 to 17 percent.

Clearly the economy would be forced to create more jobs for these young people, even if some of this requirement was offset by the increase in early retirement at the other end of the age distribution. Perhaps the economy might have been able to cope with this shift, but it was not prepared for another one—the influx of women into the labor

Table 13.6   Labor-Market Trends, 1970–80

	1970	1980	1970–1980 (percent change)
Population (millions)	204.9	227.0	10.8
Age 0–15	61.9	55.3	−10.7
16–19	15.3	17.2	12.4
20–24	17.2	21.5	25.0
25–44	48.4	62.9	30.0
45–64	42.0	44.5	6.0
65 and over	20.1	25.5	26.9
Civilian labor force (16 and over)	82.8	106.9	29.1
Participation rates			
All workers	60.4	63.8	5.6
White males	80.0	78.3	−2.1
16–19	57.5	63.8	11.0
20 and over	82.8	79.9	−3.5
White females	42.6	51.3	20.4
16–19	45.6	56.4	23.7
20 and over	42.2	50.8	20.4
Black and other minority males	76.5	70.8	−7.5
16–19	47.3	43.3	−8.5
20 and over	81.4	75.1	−7.7
Black and other minority females	40.5	53.4	7.8
16–19	34.0	35.9	5.6
20 and over	51.7	55.8	7.9
Unemployment rates			
All workers	4.9	7.1	
White males	4.0	6.1	
16–19	13.7	16.2	
20 and over	3.2	5.2	
White females	5.4	6.5	
16–19	13.4	14.8	
20 and over	4.4	5.6	
Black and other minority males	7.3	13.3	
16–19	25.0	34.9	
20 and over	5.6	11.4	
Black and other minority females	9.3	13.1	
16–19	34.4	36.9	
20 and over	6.9	11.1	

Source: Council of Economic Advisors, *Economic Report of the President* (Washington, DC: GPO, 1981), pp. 268–69.

453

force. The 1970s witnessed a dramatic increase in the labor market participation rates for females. Table 13.6 reveals that for both white and nonwhite females, the rate climbed to over 50 percent, with the nonwhite rates exceeding those of whites.

Indeed the Department of Labor recorded increases in the participation rates of women in all family situations except widowed. Divorced women, women who never married, and married women with no husband present can be expected to have higher participation rates than others, and they did in this period. The dramatic increases occurred in the category of married, husband present—which rose from a rate of 40.9 percent in 1970 to 50.1 percent in 1980. With children (under 18) the increase was even more dramatic and surprising, from 39.9 to 54.1 percent.[32]

The reasons for the influx are not difficult to find, although they would be difficult to estimate by factor. The baby boomers who entered the labor force in the 1970s chose to have fewer children and at a later age. They were also better educated, more independent, and were encouraged by the feminist movement to seek careers and cease being "just" housewives. In addition, many sought to augment family incomes, in order to make possible a more comfortable existence in some cases, or to supplement the declining real incomes of males in other cases. (Not all females who entered the work force were seeking fulfillment.) Regardless of the cause, more jobs were needed, both full- and part-time. Even more jobs would have been required had not the participation rates of males declined in this period. Table 13.6 shows the declines for white males 20 years of age and over and for black males of all ages. Were these discouraged workers who gave up looking for nonexistent jobs? Were these the jobs that were exported to other nations by investment abroad? Were they the victims of the decline in United States manufacturing output? It is easier to suggest these causes than to prove them.[33]

Was the economy flexible enough to respond to the demand for more jobs? Yes, the system did respond, as the increase in employment was over 18,600 or 24 percent over the period 1970–80. The steady increase in job creation was interrupted only by the recession in 1974. Unfortunately, it did not respond for everyone, as the gains were not evenly distributed among population groups. Table 13.6 shows first that the total unemployment rate rose to over 7 percent in 1980, from 4.7 percent in 1970. Job creation was falling behind the demand.

Moreover, unemployment seemed to be concentrated among teenagers of all races and among blacks and other minorities in general. The unemployment rate for minority groups is double that for whites. This concentration is not just for the years selected, but occurs both before, during, and after the period covered in the table. Government programs to aid minorities in education, training programs, and the like were of no avail in reversing this relation.

Unemployment rates drifted upward in the 1970s, and much interest was centered on just why. To proponents of the natural-rate-of-unemployment hypothesis, there was no mystery at all. They claimed that the rapid influx of new workers demanding jobs combined with relative fiscal restraint, and the resulting failure to create jobs fast enough pushed the unemployment rate up. The demand for labor was simply not matching the augmented supply: The result was a secular upward shift in the unemployment rate. The imbalance of these flows could not easily be corrected without risking greater inflation.

It could also be argued (as by the search theory of unemployment) that improving economic conditions after 1975 meant that the quit rate rose, indicating a desire by the unemployed to search for better jobs. While the layoff rate was declining, these searches added to the problem of the unavailability of jobs for all groups. Those who were engaged in measuring these flows in and out of unemployment maintained that the duration of unemployment was also being lengthened. The availability of unemployment compensation allowed workers to search longer for jobs than they might have without this financial support.[34]

Under these conditions the adequacy of the unemployment rate as an economic indicator became questionable. On one side were those who saw these flows in and out of unemployment as more voluntary than had been previously imagined. On the other side were those who viewed the official unemployment rate as understating the real unemployment. They found the definition of unemployment wanting, since it excluded discouraged workers (those who stopped seeking employment, concluding that no jobs were available), part-time workers who wanted full-time jobs, and so on. To this group the actual unemployment rate was at least double the official rate.[35]

Nearly everyone agreed that the changing composition of the labor force was causing problems. Apparently women and teenagers were regarded as inexperienced workers with little commitment to the labor force (women), who changed jobs too frequently (teens), and thus employers shunned the risks and costs of training them. If they were employable at all, it would be in jobs at the entry level, where training costs were minimal; the turnover rate would be immaterial, since there were always others to fill the vacancy.

With this attitude, women and teenagers could easily be exploited, having to work at low-paying, dead-end jobs in the secondary labor market if they were to work at all.[36] Even here, the minimum wage was often viewed as a barrier to employment, particularly of teens, since they were not productive enough to warrant that wage![37]

Plausibility aside, the arguments still failed to account for the concentration of unemployment among blacks and women. Clearly other factors were at work, unexplained by the age distribution or by search theories of unemployment. Discrimination on the basis of sex and color obviously played as important a role as did the productivity arguments and the voluntary-searching-for-better-job hypotheses.

In a period of stagnation it is not surprising that justifications for the simultaneous existence of high unemployment and high inflation rates would be attempted. The rational-expectation theorists maintained that once workers learned to anticipate price changes correctly, they could not be fooled into taking jobs, and the economy would return to the natural rate of unemployment, and even changes in aggregate demand through macro policy would not be able to reduce the natural rate—the long-run Phillips Curve is a vertical line and the trade-off disappears.[38] Others tried to explain stagflation by suggesting that the Phillips Curve had shifted upward, making the trade-off worse. The reason given was that the new entrants into the labor force, women and teens, did not compete with employed males for the same jobs and hence exerted no downward pressure on wages, regardless of the unemployment rate. Combine this with their relative unemployability, and the result is high rates of unemployment and high rates of inflation, as the employed bargain for higher wages to recoup real earnings losses. Clearly, the changing composition of the labor force and the high unemployment rates were challenging the economic theorists for explanations. Aside from pushing up the unemployment rate, the new entrants were also affecting other labor-market conditions, further aggravating other theoretical explanations.

One of the most startling labor-market developments in the 1970s was the decline in the rate of growth of labor productivity. Table 13.7 supplies the data for one common measurement of productivity: output per hour of all persons in the nonfarm sector. Only a glance at Table 13.7 is needed to see the wide variations in the rate of productivity growth over the decade. The recessionary year of 1970 shows the expected low rate of growth (productivity is procyclical, for as output falls, firms retain many skilled employees, and, in the recovery, output rises without additional labor input), and the recovery period also exhibits the expected rebound of productivity growth. Beginning in 1973, however, productivity shows almost steady deterioration. Indeed, productivity growth turned out to be a meager

Table 13.7 Labor Productivity and Compensation, 1970–80 (percent change from preceding period)

	1970	1971	1972	1973	1974	1975	1976	1977	1978	1979	1980	Rate of Change 1970–1980
Productivity: output/hour—all persons, nonfarm business	0.3	3.3	3.7	2.5	−2.4	2.1	3.2	2.0	−0.2	−0.7	−0.3	1.3
Compensation per hour	7.0	6.6	6.7	7.6	9.4	9.6	8.1	7.6	8.5	9.7	9.9	8.4
Unit labor costs	6.6	3.1	2.8	4.9	12.1	7.4	4.7	5.5	8.7	10.4	10.3	7.0
Hourly earnings												
Current dollars	6.6	7.2	6.2	6.2	8.0	8.4	7.2	7.6	8.1	8.0	9.0	7.4
1977 dollars	0.7	2.7	3.0	−0.1	−2.8	−0.7	1.4	1.0	0.5	−3.1	−4.0	0.2*

*1970–1979.

Source: Council of Economic Advisors, *Economic Report of the President* (Washington, DC: GPO, 1981), pp. 276–77.

1.3 percent. This rate compares with 2.0 percent for 1950–60, 2.5 percent for the period 1960–70, and a similar rate for the entire period 1948–73. From 1973 to 1980, however, the rate declined to only 0.5 percent and was this high only because of the recovery period of 1975–76.

Why the sudden reversal of productivity behavior? Even now the question has not been answered to the satisfaction of all who have endeavored to find reasons—first, because labor productivity is notoriously difficult to measure. Measuring output per worker in manufacturing is difficult enough but is at least plausible, but how can the productivity of workers in the service sectors, of government employees, of construction workers, and so on, be measured with any accuracy?

Accordingly, many dismissed the decline as a statistical artifact, as the economy was moving into a new industrial structure, where service industries were expanding at the expense of manufacturing firms. Some claim the shift was from high-productivity sectors to low-productivity sectors, while others stressed that the sectors responsible for the decline were those in which productivity is simply most difficult to measure—for example, construction.[39]

By the end of the period, however, most economists had become convinced that the slowdown in productivity was real and not a statistical aberration. While they acknowledged the measurement problem, they were not willing to dismiss the evidence on that score alone. The problem was too intriguing to set aside anyway.

The second reason no agreement has been possible on the explanation of the changes in labor productivity is that no single cause appears to dominate and rule out other explanations. For example, Edward Denison examined 17 factors that might have caused the productivity decline and found that none of them could adequately explain the deterioration.[40] It might be instructive to list the possible causes without examining in detail the reasons they turn out to be insufficient explanations.

Suggestions Affecting Advances in Knowledge

1. Curtailment of expenditures on research and development
2. Decline in opportunity for major new technical advances
3. Decline of Yankee ingenuity and deterioration of U.S. technology
4. Increased lag in the application of knowledge, due to the aging of capital

Suggested Effects of Government Regulation and Taxation

5. Diversion of inputs to comply with government regulations, except pollution and safety

6. Government-imposed paperwork
7. Regulation and taxation: diversion of executive attention
8. Government regulation: delay of new projects
9. Regulation and taxation: misallocation of resources
10. Effects of high tax rates on invention and efficiency
11. Capital gains provisions of the Revenue Act of 1969

Other Suggestions Affecting Miscellaneous Determinants

12. "People don't want to work any more."
13. Impairment of efficiency by inflation
14. Lessening of competitive pressure and change in the quality of management
15. Rise in energy prices
16. The "shift to the services" and other structural changes
17. Possible errors in the data

Denison admitted that he was unable to explain the productivity slowdown by any outstanding factor, and this situation was made worse if one looked only at the period after 1973. Others found alternative ways to approach the problem or added variables to the list. The CEA added the age–sex shift in the composition of the labor force as a possible cause. Inexperienced, less productive females and teenagers were being employed, replacing the older, more productive workers.[41]

Others contended that Denison dismissed some factors too quickly. They found some explanations to be more important than others: the slowdown in capital formation and the prices of energy, forcing the substitution of labor for capital in the production process.[42] Bowles, Gordon, and Weisskopf find the answer to the productivity riddle in the social determinants—that is, in the worker–management conflict that results in the lack of motivation of workers who become dissatisfied and rebel against corporation domination by demanding safety measures, and the like. Poor management is also mentioned as a cause, and this finds support in other studies of the decline in U.S. industry.[43]

Obviously, an embarrassing number of factors explain the decline in productivity in the 1970s. Since no one factor emerged as the predominant influence, substantial disagreement was inevitable among investigators, and substantial confusion was unavoidable for everyone else. In the end there may never be a satisfactory explanation for the observed productivity reversals.

One of the effects, however, is clear. Table 13.7 shows the percent change over the period in the compensation per hour of workers. Note that when productivity was increasing, unit labor costs were kept within a reasonable range. Beyond 1973, however, when productivity began falling off, unit labor costs began rising dramatically. These rising unit labor costs then made their way into rising prices, as discussed earlier. Hence, it should be clear why labor productivity is so important in the U.S. economy; as long as productivity is rising, real wages can rise along with it. When productivity falls, however, prices rise and real wages can and often do fall. In the 1970s real wages remained unchanged, as the gains were balanced by losses. Table 13.7 shows these labor-market relations.

What the table data do not reveal is the belief on the part of the workers that they were worse off than they were in the early years of the period. Some no doubt were, but many were holding their own in terms of real incomes. Much depends upon what price index is used to deflate money wages. The CEA in its *Economic Report of the President* was suggesting that wide variations of real wages loss could be obtained, depending on the price deflator used.[44] Such exercises fell on deaf ears, for the most part, and workers were concerned for their real income losses, using rule-of-thumb measurements.

The final development of the 1970s to be discussed was the continuing shift of employment away from manufacturing to the service sectors. Table 13.8 shows the unmistakable trend. As a percent of total employment, manufacturing declined from 27.3 to 23.4, while wholesale and retail trade, finance, insurance, and real estate and all other services showed gains, with the latter registering almost a 3 percent gain.

The shift was blamed on a change in demand, on foreign competition, on deindustrialization, on energy problems, and on the sluggish economy. Analyses of these concerns came later (in the 1980s), but even in the late 1970s there was growing concern that the United States was losing ground to other nations and that our industrial base was shrinking. Some were advocating an active government policy to help our ailing manufacturing firms—that is, an industrial policy of some sort. The steel, automobile, and textile industries all faced serious problems that could have been partially solved by government policies for the provision of capital, for changing regulations, or for relief from foreign competition.

The Carter administration's response to the proposal of an industrial policy was cool. In its last *Economic Report of the President* of 1981, it outlined its reasons against government intervention of this kind. The administration was loath to have the government "pick winners" among industries in difficulty, and if they were somehow selected, there would be the inevitable reluctance to abandon them if that proved necessary. Allocating capital to these industries would

Table 13.8 Employment in Nonagricultural Establishments, 1970–79 (percent distribution)

Year	Mining	Construction	Manufacturing	Transportation and Public Utilities	Wholesale and Retail Trade	Finance, Insurance Real Estate	Services	Government
1970	0.9	5.1	27.3	6.4	21.2	5.1	16.3	17.7
1971	0.9	5.2	26.2	6.3	21.6	5.3	16.6	18.1
1972	0.9	5.3	26.0	6.2	21.6	5.3	16.7	18.1
1973	0.8	5.3	26.2	6.1	21.6	5.3	16.7	17.9
1974	0.9	5.1	25.7	6.0	21.7	5.3	17.2	18.1
1975	1.0	4.6	23.8	5.9	22.2	5.4	18.1	19.1
1976	1.0	4.5	23.9	5.8	22.4	5.4	18.3	18.7
1977	1.0	4.7	23.9	5.7	22.5	5.4	18.6	18.3
1978	1.0	4.9	23.7	5.7	22.6	5.5	18.8	17.9
1979	1.1	5.2	23.4	5.8	22.5	5.5	19.0	17.4

Source: U.S. Department of Labor, Employment and Training Report of the President (Washington, DC: GPO, 1980), p 305.

461

face similar problems, and basically government should not and could not be expected to supplement the allocation of capital by the private market. Instead, the administration preferred more traditional fiscal policies to help U.S. industries, or appropriate trade policies for those adversely affected by foreign trade.[45]

The debate over industrial policy did not become heated for a few years, but the obvious difficulty faced by domestic firms in steel and automobiles was difficult to avoid. Again there was a general feeling of unease in the society that contributed to the more widespread perception that the United States was in trouble and that we were becoming worse off.

Still, the employment shifts of Table 13.8 are revealing for what they show and do not show. Clearly many of these service-related jobs were filled by the women and teenagers entering the labor force. These were generally lower-paying, nonunionized, and lower-skilled jobs than were the manufacturing jobs being lost. Thus females continued to receive somewhere between 50 and 60 percent of what male workers were earning. Of course, not all women were entering at the bottom, but those who were not were participating in the trend toward high-tech industries and in the general societal movement toward an information society. The gains in other professions were increasing, but the gap between males and females as to occupation and earnings was still very wide.

These conditons were well recognized at the time.[46] (Moreover, blacks and teenagers fared even worse than did females.) The point here is that these groups also felt worse off in this period, as their plight became more public. Women at least had some organizations to protest on their behalf and make vocal the substance of their objections to being exploited. As is usually the case, the voices of protest got louder just as some progress was being made in breaking down the barriers of sex, color, and age.

Finally the structure of work was being transformed. The trend of employment into high-tech and service industries did not bode well for unions, which stagnated during this period. Unions found that their inability to cope with the new trends reduced their membership from 28 percent in 1970 to 24 percent in 1978. Nor did the trend toward the use of computers and robots bode well for the less educated. In the growing information society, there was less need for the unskilled workers, as automation began replacing them. In the past, automation created some jobs, even as it destroyed others. This time, however, the new types of automation may not be so beneficial; the artificial intelligence of computers and robots may not require the former human servicing and maintenance. Not many were concerned with the structure of industry and employment in the period, and these technical innovations were employed to maximum efficiency.[47]

Labor, however, had cause to fear the introduction of the technical gadgets that displaced them. Again the general sense of diminishing wellbeing found a new ally in the fear caused by technical advances; another group felt worse off and threatened.

International Trade Problems

As if the problems in the domestic economy were not sufficient for the Carter administration, international trade difficulties continued as well. The problems were not new, of course, but they were added to the other economic problems at a time when solutions were scarce. Indeed, just a glance at Table 13.9 is enough to reveal the deterioration in nearly every area of trade relations.

As indicated in a previous chapter, no one statistic or balance can reveal the foreign trade situation satisfactorily. Yet the balance of merchandise trade is a striking figure and was so regarded at the time; the deficit rose dramatically from $ -9.3 in 1976 to $ -25.3 billion in 1980. Investment income continued to grow, making the deficit balance on current account much less in 1977 and 1978 and thereafter turning positive.

To complete the sketch of foreign trade balances, note the dramatic increase in capital flows in this period. U.S. private-capital outflows nearly doubled from 1975, sending the total to over $84 billion in 1980; yet foreign inflows of capital soared to triple the 1975 amounts. One obvious reason for the capital inflow is shown in the table as coming from OPEC countries, as they began to recycle their "petrodollars" earned from the sale of oil.

Interestingly, these petrodollars were reminiscent of the recycling that occurred after World War I. Recall that the United States loaned money to Germany, and these funds were used to pay reparations to Great Britain and France; the allies then took these funds and repaid their loans to the United States. It all worked for a while, until the United States refused to loan any more to Germany, and then the triangle broke apart. In the 1970s the oil-producing countries took their oil sale proceeds (denominated in the dollar) and made deposits in U.S. banks, which then reloaned them to Third World countries that needed them to purchase oil and to pursue plans for economic development. Again, as we shall see, the system worked as long as the Third World countries were not required to repay the loans

Table 13.9   U.S. International Transactions, 1970–80 (billions of dollars)

Item*	1970	1971	1972	1973	1974	1975	1976	1977	1978	1979	1980
Merchandise trade balance	2.6	−2.3	−6.4	0.9	−5.3	9.0	−9.3	−30.9	−33.8	−27.3	−25.3
Exports	42.5	43.3	49.4	71.4	98.3	107.1	114.7	120.8	142.1	184.5	224.0
Imports	−39.9	−45.6	−55.8	−70.5	−103.6	−98.0	−124.1	−151.7	−175.8	−211.8	−249.3
Investment income (net)	6.2	7.3	6.8	12.2	15.5	12.8	16.0	18.0	21.4	33.5	32.8
Other services (net)	−3.2	−2.7	−3.7	−2.0	−0.9	1.1	2.7	3.4	3.4	0.9	3.4
Balance on goods and services	5.6	2.3	−1.9	11.0	9.3	22.9	9.4	−9.5	−9.0	7.0	10.8
Unilateral transfers, net	−3.3	−3.7	−3.9	−3.9	−7.2	−4.6	−5.0	−4.6	−5.1	−5.6	−7.1
Balance on current account	2.3	−1.4	−5.8	7.1	2.1	18.3	4.4	−14.1	−14.1	1.4	3.7

U.S. assets abroad [capital outflow (−)]	−9.3	−12.5	−14.5	−22.9	−34.7	−39.7	−51.3	−34.8	−61.1	−62.6	−84.8
U.S. Government	0.9	0.5	−1.5	−2.4	−1.1	−4.3	−6.8	−4.1	−3.9	−4.9	−13.3
Private	−10.2	−12.9	−12.9	−20.4	−33.6	−35.4	−44.5	−30.7	−57.2	−57.7	−71.5
Foreign assets in the United States [capital outflow (+)]	6.3	23.0	21.5	18.4	34.2	15.7	36.5	51.2	63.7	38.9	50.3
Foreign official	6.9	26.9	10.5	6.0	10.5	7.0	17.7	36.8	33.6	−13.8	15.5
Other	−0.6	−3.9	11.0	12.4	23.7	8.6	18.8	14.4	30.2	52.7	34.8
Change in OPEC official assets in the United States	—	—	—	—	10.8	7.1	9.6	6.4	−0.7	5.5	12.7

*Credits, +; debits, −.

Source: U.S. Department of Commerce, *Survey of Current Business*, 61, No. 6 (June 1981); and *Federal Reserve Bulletins*, various years.

and as long as the oil-producing countries were accumulating excess funds and had surpluses. When these conditions changed and the Third World countries were unable to repay their debts, the international world would be shaken. We shall return to this topic later when the problem becomes acute.

Returning to the trade situation of the United States, it is time to inquire how the system of floating exchange rates was working in this rather trying period of oil-price shocks, of the grain embargo imposed by Carter following the USSR invasion of Afghanistan, and of other commodity price increases. Recall the alleged advantages of floating exchange rates: The flexibility of exchange rates allows for a market-determined automatic adjustment process without the need for maintaining large reserves—the exchange rate moves to equilibrate trade flows, and therefore there is no requirement that economies adjust their domestic macro policies to the conditions of the trade balance. Nations can act more independently and can fashion their domestic policies to meet internal conditions.

It is easy to criticize floating rates in this period: They did not eliminate balance-of-payments problems, did not allow for the independence claimed, but did contribute to inflation and may have caused new problems in the old areas of uncertainty and instability.[48] The floating exchange rates did not bring about the equilibrating mechanism, but functioned only because surplus countries were willing to finance the trade deficits of the United States and other debtor nations. In fact, nations have deemed it necessary to intervene in the market to influence the exchange value of their currencies. The United States did so in 1978, feeling that the dollar had depreciated unnecessarily, and moved to strengthen it. It is clear that nations are not willing to accept the dictates of the market and will intervene to improve upon market determinations.

Nor did floating exchange rates allow for independence in policymaking. Nations are not and cannot be insulated from the actions of others. Policies followed by one country affect all of its trading partners to various degrees, and the responses they make reduce their independence.

Floating exchange rates contribute to inflation whenever conditions that lead to inflation in one country and hence to the depreciation of its currency do not lead to price decreases in countries whose currencies are appreciating. Thus price rigidities lead to worldwide inflationary pressures. In this connection we can ask why the dollar did not gain in strength, following the extremely high interest rates experienced in the late 1970s and in 1980; inflationary expectations have been given as one answer to this seeming contradiction.[49]

Finally, the record indicates a high degree of exchange-rate volatility and unpredictability, hardly the conditions leading to stability in world trade. Nor are such conditions likely to lead to increased trade, since they create uncertainty, the bane of international exchanges. Perhaps inflation in the United States helped to create and encourage the instability in exchange rates, since U.S. economic policy was neither consistent nor coherent.[50]

These problems with floating exchange rates are controversial and still under intense investigation. Perhaps the problems will be found elsewhere and the system of floating rates exonerated from blame; perhaps they were instituted at a time when nothing would have solved the trading problems. In any case, more than just exchange-rate problems were besetting U.S. trade conditions. Only some of them can be enumerated here.

The deficit in the merchandise balance reveals one source of difficulty for the United States in this period. Imports soared, while exports grew at a modest pace. Imports of steel, appliances, television sets, cameras, radial tires, textiles, automobiles, and so on led the way, but the developments in steel and automobiles really shocked the nation.[51] The steel firms reacted to competition by charging that other nations were dumping their steel in the United States at below-cost prices and demanding protection instead of remodeling their plants. The Carter administration responded in 1978 by imposing a trigger-price mechanism that effectively barred imports from all but the most efficient producers.

Competition was coming from many countries—West Germany, Sweden, France, Italy, Brazil, Korea, Taiwan, and so on—but the most irksome was undoubtedly Japan. Japanese firms were flooding the U.S. market with steel, TV sets, stereo equipment, and so on; the inroad into the U.S. market by Japanese automakers was the most shocking. In 1970, 381,000 cars were imported from Japan; by 1980 the number had grown to 1,992,000, an increase of 423 percent. (The increase from all countries, excluding Japan, was −23 percent.) Still, the import share of the domestic automobile market rose from 14.7 percent in 1970 to 28.2 percent in 1980.

The response to foreign competition was predictable, if not enlightened. Our trading partners were using all kinds of unfair trade practices—dumping their surplus output, erecting trade barriers to U.S. goods, and so on. Other nations employed cheap labor, taxed their firms less, regulated them less, imposed fewer restrictions—pollution controls, safety regulations, and the like. It was also easy to blame government for economic policies that crowded out the private sector from borrowing at reasonable interest rates. Few of these charges withstood serious investigation, and the alarming fact was that the United States had allowed itself to fall behind in technology, or rather, that it failed to use the technology it had developed and let other nations take the lead in innovation and product development.[52]

As competition from abroad increased over the years, so did the cries for protection, special subsidies, tax concessions, loan guarantees, and so on, all designed to enable U.S. firms to recover and then to be able to compete. All too often, whatever special considerations were extended resulted not in a more competitive industry but in a dependent one. Sometimes the protected industries used the time and funds to branch out into another industry, as in the case of U.S. Steel, which purchased Marathon Oil Company instead of investing in steel assets. This case was not unique, as other firms sought diversification instead of capital investment.[53]

Thus the serious deterioration in international trade, with all the chauvinism that accompanied it, presented the Carter administration with another problem that it was not responsible for but was unprepared to meet. The solutions, if there were any, were long-run; the problem was that political horizons are short-run.

Conservative Trends toward Deregulation, Tax Limitations, Balanced Budgets, and Militarism

Before turning to an evaluation of the main macroeconomic policies of the Carter administration, some other important economic movements should be observed. Foremost was the movement toward deregulation of industry. The conservative side of the Carter administration is clearly demonstrated by the acceptance of the long-held view that some industries should not be controlled but left to market forces. For some time the business sector had complained of overregulation, and even the public occasionally questioned some unnecessary regulations. At times the costs of compliance seemed to be the main consideration, while at other times, red tape or irrational rules caused the complaints. Economists seemed to stress the diversion of capital into unproductive uses and the consequent loss in productivity.

Whatever the impetus, the Carter administration took action in a few major industries, including airlines, banking, and natural gas, and was considering action in others such as the railroad, trucking, and telecommunications industries. In 1978 both the airline and natural gas industries were deregulated. In the airline case, the administration rejected the view that competition would be destructive or that service would be curtailed in favor of letting market forces determine prices and routes. The CAB would also be eventually eliminated under the plan. In the case of natural gas deregulation, the aim was to bring up the price of new natural gas to market levels more quickly and thus encourage exploration. Recall that energy prices and supplies were a major concern of this administration and the public as well.

Banking reform came with the Depository Institutions Deregulation and Monetary Control Act of 1980. Bankers and economists had complained of interest-rate regulations that hampered lending in periods of inflation. They also were concerned with state usury laws that put ceilings on the rate of interest, often crippling the housing market. Some attempts at relaxation of regulations were tried over the years, of course, but the extent of the reforms was not sufficient. Many banks decided to leave the Federal Reserve System, making less restrictive states the regulatory bodies.[54] As banks deserted the system, the efficacy of monetary policy was questionable. Finally, the structure of the banking industry had become cumbersome and confusing, with artificial separation of accounts by institutions, with some banks able to loan to businesses and others not, with some banks able to pay interest on demand deposits and others not, and so on.

Thus the loss of control of the Federal Reserve System and the power of bankers finally resulted in deregulation. The act removed interest-rate ceilings on time deposits in six years, allowed all banks to issue NOW accounts, repealed state usury laws on mortgage rates and relaxed other usury laws on other loans, allowed savings and loan associations to loan to consumers up to 20 percent of their assets, and mutual savings institutions to loan to business (up to 5 percent of their assets). More critical for monetary policy, the Federal Reserve was able to apply uniform reserve requirements to all depository institutions by the end of an eight-year period.

The Federal Reserve had become quite concerned over the loss of control as a result of bank desertions of the system. The proposal for changing the definition of monetary aggregates in 1979 became even more imperative now with the breakdown in the distinction between commercial banks and thrifts. Accordingly the Federal Reserve did redefine monetary aggregates, breaking transactions balances into M1A which was essentially the old M1, and M1B which added to M1A the checking deposits of other depository institutions. M2 now included time deposits at all institutions, as well as money-market funds. Finally, M3 added to M2 large time deposits plus repurchase agreements. These new definitions were supposed to aid in the control of monetary aggregates. (As a testimony to rapidly changing monetary conditions and instruments, it is revealing to note that these definitions did not last very long.)

The movement to deregulate other industries stalled in the process of development. In general, the Carter administration was attempting to apply "smart regulation" more in line with economic thinking. The use of marketing permits for pollution control, the tailoring of regulations to fit the type of organization being regulated, or the application of the limitation of pollutants to an area rather than target levels of each source of pollution separately are a few illustrations of the smart regulatory procedures. The aim was not zero regulation but sensible regulation where needed. Indeed a Regulatory Council composed of 36 federal departments and agencies was established in the hope of improving the regulatory process by publishing regulations and rooting out overlapping ones.[55]

Another interesting movement in the period has come to be known as the tax revolt. The first real manifestation of it occurred in California, where a tax limitation was placed on the ballot— Proposition 13. The proposition called for the restriction of property taxes to no more than 1 percent of the 1975 market values. It passed and was subsequently copied by many other states, until by the mid-1980s nearly half of the states had imposed such tax limitations. Frustration over the property tax has a long history, and it has always been the cause of considerable controversy, not to mention public complaints. The voting public, given the chance to voice its discontent, clearly indicated its unhappiness over this particular tax.

Of course, other taxes went up as a result, since the functions of local governments were not curtailed sufficiently. Still, tax limitations are one way to attempt to restrain government spending or at least pose constraints on its growth. The concept has its origin in conservative doctrine that wants to limit government involvement in the economy and sees limiting tax revenue as one way to achieve it. This may not be what the voters of California had in mind when they passed Proposition 13, and there is evidence that other factors were responsible, but they did start a movement that conformed with conservative thought.

Conservatives wasted no time in capitalizing on the general mood and sympathy for tax-limitation schemes. They launched a drive to force the federal government to balance its budget annually. If enough states could pass a resolution calling for a constitutional convention to consider a balanced-budget amendment, Congress would be forced to convene one for that purpose. Many states quickly passed such a resolution (with considerable variations), and by the end of the decade 30 states out of the needed 34 had reacted favorably to the call. Of the many variants of the resolution, here is the one proposed by Milton Friedman and the Committee on National Tax Limitation:

> Total outlays in any fiscal year shall increase by a percentage no greater than the percentage increase in nominal gross national product in the last calendar year ending prior to the beginning of said fiscal year. If inflation for that year is more than three percent, the permissible percentage increase in total outlays shall be reduced by one-fourth of the excess of inflation over three percent. Inflation shall be measured by the difference between the percentage increase in nominal gross national product and the percentage increase in real gross national product.

Not the most eloquent language compared to the first ten amendments, said the *Washington Post* when it published the foregoing proposal.[56] In addition to this language, which contains many concepts that require explicit definition and thus leave plenty of room for interpretation and exercises in creative accounting, there are often other escape clauses as well. For instance, Congress could vote to override the prohibition if a certain number, three-fifths, deemed it necessary; or, in times of war, the restrictions could be set aside.

The rationale for a balanced-budget amendment scarcely needs elaboration: To force the federal government to balance its budget annually is to provide a constraint on spending that Congress is unable or unwilling to fashion;[57] to constrain government spending is to reduce government involvement in the economy.

Leaving aside the economic arguments in opposition for the moment, how could such a law be enforced? Who would be punished if the budget were not balanced—Congress? The president? At the other extreme, it would be easy to start a war or a semblance of one in order to achieve the level of spending desired. Among the economic arguments, the matter of definitions is crucial: what is meant by national income, how outlays and revenues are to be defined, and so on. Also, to prepare budgets, forecasts of expenditures and revenues are required. Whose forecasts will be used? The administration's? Private ones? The Congressional Budget Office's? The alleged simplicity of the balanced-budget concept quickly vanishes, and no constitutional amendment could possibly be explicit enough to be workable.

Keynesians like Walter Heller were quick to point out all the fallacies in balanced-budget reasoning. Chief among them, however, is the procyclical fiscal policy. If national income falls, incomes, profits, and employment decline as well, and, of course, tax receipts fall too. To balance the budget, it would be necessary to cut government spending or raise taxes; in either case, the economic situation is made worse, creating more unemployment, less income, and reducing tax revenues even further, and so on. The reverse condition holds as well; in the upturn, incomes rise, as do tax collections. To balance the budget, government spending must rise or taxes must be reduced. In either case, the situation is once again made worse.[58]

Not only Keynesians were skeptical of the balanced-budget philosophy. Herbert Stein expressed his doubts in a simple version of an annually balanced budget and argued for reasonable debate to find a better formula.[59] Many others argued the merits of an annually balanced budget, and, often as not, ideological concerns took priority over sound economics. Still others, familiar with traditional accounting practices, asked, Is the federal budget balanced already? If the federal budget were divided into capital and operating budgets, much of the deficit would disappear. The federal budget does not distinguish between expenditures for buildings, tanks, and equipment and for wages and paper clips. An account for capital items, it is held, could provide a more realistic analysis of deficits or surpluses. On the other hand, a capital budget could make things worse, depending on how it is used and what is expected of it. It could be used to escape from constraints, such as the balanced-budget requirement, to provide information, to justify the way various programs are financed (capital items would support borrowing), or to control spending of government agencies.[60]

The controversy over the balanced budget, which began decades ago, continues to the present. The budget, however, is as much a political as an economic document, and therefore ideological positions are an intricate part of the budget process. Conservatives may simply want to reduce government spending; liberals may simply want to solve many of society's problems through government programs. Neither side is likely to be able to view the budget process in the abstract and search for alternative solutions to the problems they envision.

Finally, a brief look at the return of the cold war and the remilitarization of the economy is necessary here to avoid misperceptions of this administration. A more complete analysis is given in the next chapter.

Mr. Carter's brand of foreign policy, with its emphasis on human rights, peace, and love, may receive more approval from future historians than from contemporary ones. Perhaps more time was needed in which to demonstrate sincerity and commitment. As his administration progressed, however, more emphasis was placed on military preparedness and national security.

In his final budget message he wrote:

> The long decline in real spending for defense that began in 1969 has been reversed. The uncertain and sometimes hostile world we live in requires that we continue to rebuild our defense forces. The United States will continue to seek peaceful means to settle international disputes. But I cannot ignore the major increases in Soviet military spending that have taken place inexorably over the past twenty years. I cannot ignore our commitment to our NATO allies. ... I cannot ignore the implications of terrorism in Iran, or Soviet aggression in Afghanistan.

Yet the military buildup began before these events. The MX missile, which was supposed to move about to escape detection, was approved prior to the Iranian hostage episode. These events instantly revived the cold war, however, emotions were stirred up, and foreign policy returned to more simplistic responses. Carter, who had opposed the B-1 bomber and the neutron bomb, now seemed to reverse himself, having been stung by political criticism and world events over which he had no control. In U.S. politics, being perceived as soft on communism is akin to political suicide, and to allow even a doubt as to our military preparedness is to court disaster at the polls.

Accordingly, the budget for national defense spending, which had shown no increase in real terms from FY 1976 to FY 1978, began to increase. In real terms, the defense budget rose by 4.1 percent in 1979, 2 percent in 1980, and was scheduled to rise by 3.5 percent in 1981, 4.6 percent in 1982, and 4.4 percent in 1983. The increase in defense spending under the Carter administration totaled 10 percent in real terms, but projections to 1983 would have increased the total to 22 percent, with even greater increases promised through 1985. Looked at another way, the proportion of national defense to total outlays would have risen from 24.4 percent in 1977 to 25.6 percent in 1983.

Since the budget for FY 1981 proposed a deficit of $15.8 billion, followed by a surplus of $5 billion in 1982 and thereafter, the increase in national defense spending without reducing other programs would be paid for by a strong economic recovery and proceeds from the windfall profits tax. By the time the administration issued its final *Economic Report of the President* in January 1981, it was clear that the budget prepared a year earlier was too optimistic, that the recovery was a good deal more modest, and that nondefense spending had to be reduced. The move toward fiscal conservatism, already alluded to, is nowhere more obvious than in these general trends.

Evaluation of the Carter Administration's Macroeconomic Policies

Unfortunately for Carter, the latter half of the 1970s was not a good time to be responsible for the nation's present or future wellbeing. Challenging world developments, vital-resource shortages, the resurrection of the cold war, and the revolutions in Third World countries, combined with the ongoing problems of Latin America, encompassed more than any one administration could handle. Toward the end, many had come to believe that this populist, symbolic president was not able to cope with these sizable problems.

Carter was unlucky in domestic areas as well. In particular, the late 1970s was a time for humility for economists, as past analyses and solutions no longer seemed applicable. The structure of the economy was changing rapidly, and no one seemed capable of comprehending the results. Thus, as economists floundered in the explanation of stagflation, the decline in labor productivity, the changing structure of industry, and the revolution in the composition of the labor force, both the economics profession and those who rely upon its knowledge—that is, politicians as policymakers—suffered when they appeared inept and confused. It was not a happy time, if there is ever one, for macroeconomic policymakers.

The disarray of mainstream economists was even more irksome, since there were groups of economists, with their specialized and individualistic models, who were loudly proclaiming that they, indeed, knew the answers to our problems and that they could be simply explained and treated. Monetarists, rational-expectation practitioners, supply-siders, and government blamers all seemed to offer simple solutions, while more traditional economists were complaining of the complexity of our problems, which required patience and a willingness to experiment with different solutions.

The simple view that government itself was the problem and that a return to market solutions was necessary contrasted sharply with the view that more government was necessary to control and rationalize the working of the system. The public was understandably confused (as was a significant proportion of the economics profession), but the general perception was that Carter's brand of economics was somehow wanting, even though no one could agree on a replacement.

The public grew impatient with Mr. Carter on economic matters, just as it had on energy matters or relations with Iran and the Soviet Union. There was the latent belief, more openly expressed as the presidential campaign approached, that there must be a better way to confront all of the problems facing the United States, including the economic ones. Carter, however, did not appear to be the leader to propose the exciting new initiatives; here, as in other matters, hesitation and deliberation appeared as timidity and indecisiveness.

So President Carter fell victim to events he could not control, including the clashes of economic theorists who were becoming acrimonious in their public debate. The more certain opponents of his economic policies became convinced of the supremacy of their analysis and solutions, the more defensive became the standard bearers of the traditional approaches—even when they tried to suggest (what were for them) more radical solutions.

Given this cacophony of advice and criticisms, let us examine the Carter administration's policy prescriptions for the seemingly intractable economic problems. Looking first at whether the policies followed were justified or not reveals mixed results. Certainly the public wanted a solution to the energy problem, and a majority probably thought government should attempt to find one. In times of national problems or emergencies, the U.S. public, rightly or wrongly, tends to turn to the federal government for help. The energy problem was considered to be serious enough that federal relief was sought to ration supplies, to encourage production, to stockpile supplies, and, most important, to negotiate with foreign governments to avoid embargoes and the cutoff of supplies.

There were sufficient reports of U.S. oil companies manipulating the data on oil supplies, enough reports that there was plenty of oil, some located offshore in boats, that the public was suspicious of the entire episode of the energy shortage. Only the federal government could cope with the power of the oil companies or negotiate with foreign nations; only the federal government could guarantee that the available supplies were apportioned in a reasonably fair manner.

Despite the public pressure on the federal government to act in the national interest, there were many economists who were calling for market solutions—that is, to let the market price rise to ration supplies and encourage production. This is an illustration of the conflict among economic theorists, for many other economists were advocating direct controls on oil and gas prices, tariffs on imports, and so on. Clearly, this put the Carter administration on the spot, not only to devise a solution to an entirely new situation but to reconcile the conflicts among contending groups with opposite solutions.

The administration's responses have already been discussed. The point here is that lacking a unified public, the administration was unable to secure support for any policy; lacking the support of the public, Congress was unwilling to get out front on this issue. As a result, the U.S. response to the energy crisis was far less cohesive and effective than those of other nations.

Similarly, there was considerable public pressure to reduce the rate of inflation. Again, since many of the price increases could be traced to energy sources, there was the same division about how to accomplish reductions in inflation. Commodity-price shocks were new to the U.S. economy, and no one knew how to prevent them from being incorporated into wage demands and price adjustments to protect previous living standards or profit margins.

Responding to what it perceived as the public's desires, the administration's monetary and fiscal policies attempted to fight inflation without increasing unemployment. Yet its policy of voluntary wage and price controls won little support from the public or from economists. The program seemed little more than face saving in order to show that the administration was doing something. Indeed, to ask wage earners to forego wage increases when their real incomes were diminishing, or firms to forego price increases when their profits were threatened, or, in other words, to ask for actions consistent with the national interest, rather than self-interest, is to court disobedience. For such a voluntary program to work, the administration would have had to marshal considerable public enthusiasm. This it failed to do, and calls for sacrifices fell on deaf ears.

High interest rates and the rising prices of necessities were upsetting to the general public, and inflation was certainly a major concern. Action was demanded, but not at the cost of a recession or rising unemployment. Since the Carter administration was unable to promise that it could reduce inflation without increasing unemployment, its policies vacillated between the goals; it simply was unwilling to take whatever steps were necessary, including creating a recession, to drive down the rate of inflation.

Similarly, while some increases in national defense spending might have been acceptable to the general public, reductions in social programs were not sanctioned. Reduction in government spending to fight inflation might have been justified, but the priorities were not. Thus the move toward fiscal conservatism by Carter, while made in the name of avoiding more inflation, could also be viewed as a political ploy to avoid the stigma of weakness in international affairs.

In the latter vein, the grain embargo on sales to the Soviet Union was not welcomed by many, since the fear was that it would backfire. It did, as U.S. farmers lost markets to other nations who were not as morally outraged as the United States. The initial chauvinism soon gave way and exposed the futility of embargoes when the international community did not sanction them and found no justification for them.

Deregulation, too, found mixed reactions. Certainly, special-interest groups could be expected to feel strongly about the policies that concerned them. Thus the bankers were favorably inclined to banking deregulation, since the provisions discussed allowed them to do what they wanted to do anyway. The general public was not as aware of banking problems and not convinced that the solutions lay in higher interest rates, higher service charges, and the like. The banking industry is too esoteric to elicit much public concern for regulations; it cares only for safety, and in this, deregulation was not reassuring.

In other areas of deregulation, the administration met with considerable opposition. In the airline industry there was no great consensus that deregulation was called for and that this was the time. Both within and outside the industry there was a wide variety of opinion, and the move was controversial. The trucking industry actively fought deregulation and continues to do so.

The point here is not to argue the merits of the cases for or against deregulation, but to demonstrate the lack of public pressure. With deregulation, as with the other policies mentioned above, there seemed to be no consensus for the programs. The Carter administration did not or could not take the time to build the case for its actions and thus won little public support. As a result, it was almost as if the public were wary of Carter, unwilling to trust him with new programs and unwilling to go along with just the old ones. The sense was that things may have been slightly out of control.

From the foregoing it would appear that the administration's programs had little chance for success, and that verdict seems justified. Few problems were solved by deliberate actions. Energy problems were not solved by the types of programs initiated and finally passed in some form by a reluctant Congress. In fact, the immediate energy problems disappeared only as a result of conflicts among the oil-producing countries and not as a result of conscious U.S. policy. Conservation worked because it was in the interests of consumers, as they reduced consumption and demanded small cars, efficient appliances, and so on. Self-interest, not the national interest, prompted the movement toward conservation. As we shall see, when the scarcity and rising-prices factors were removed, the drive to conserve was also.[61]

Indeed two-tiered (or more) pricing systems for oil and gas, instituted to protect consumers, were confusing and easily evaded and did not work to increase production.[62] The halfway measures between market forces and controls just could not do the job.

The more traditional macroeconomic monetary and fiscal policies also were not effective in this period. Neither the rate of inflation nor the unemployment rate were reduced to previous rates. With stop-and-go monetary and fiscal policies, switching from stimulation to restraint, not much was achieved. Perhaps traditional policies would not have worked in any case, since the sources of many of our problems were external to the economy. Commodity-price shocks cannot be controlled by manipulating the domestic economy. At least, we did not know how to limit the effects of these price shocks.[63] The fear was that a slowdown to control inflation would deepen into a severe recession, and, as noted above, there was no sentiment for that. Therefore the traditional policies were used more as a holding action than as aggressive means to affect the economy drastically.

The administration seriously considered supplementing monetary and fiscal policies with controls, as it touted the TIP proposal in its last *Economic Report of the President*. Perhaps had the administration had another term, some such scheme would have been suggested. What is clear is that the effectiveness of monetary and fiscal policies was questioned, and the need to supplement them was accepted.

The voluntary wage-and-price-controls system was acknowledged to have failed in its purpose to halt the spread of energy prices from being built into wage demands and from being incorporated into the underlying rate of inflation. The controls were simply asked to do too much in modifying behavior learned over a generation. Again the calls for sacrifice, at a time when the expectations were that living standards would continue to increase without limit and in an era of the "me" generation, were hopelessly naive.

Similarly, the grain embargo showed a naiveté in international matters. Other countries eagerly assumed the markets we so willingly surrendered in the name of international morality.[64] Farm exports fell and have not recovered, not all due to the embargo, but the episode came at the wrong time. Farmers who had been encouraged to plant for exports began to enlarge their farms, expand their capital, and in general gear up for a new age for agriculture. Instead, despite the assurances of the federal government's program to purchase the grain, farmers found themselves with excess productive capacity. Further limitations on grain sales to the Soviet Union further aggravated the situation.

The success or failure of the movement toward deregulation cannot be determined from the Carter administration's term; the adjustment process from controls to market forces would naturally take some time, and so, for the present, any judgments must be delayed. So, too, with the switch to monetarism as the explicit form of direction for monetary policy. Both of these initiatives will be explored further in the next chapter.

As observed earlier, moral considerations frequently came to the forefront in the Carter administration. Given the opportunity, that is, Carter would have preferred to follow policies that conformed with his view of morality. Yet public office may not be the most desirable position in which to practice moral leadership, or so it seemed in the Carter years. The public was in general suspicious, and probably would not have permitted too much experimentation, had Mr. Carter chosen to depart too radically from traditional forms.

Some of his suggestions—for instance, calling for personal sacrifices in energy matters—caused him to be regarded as heretical; when he made human rights an issue in foreign affairs, he was regarded as naive. Perhaps these early rebuffs made him retreat, because the actions of his administration did not stray far beyond the normal, whatever the rhetoric or whatever the characterization of him by the press.

Consider the energy crisis that he himself compared to a war effort. What emerged out of all the rhetoric were tax provisions that would aid the middle and upper classes in taking the steps to conserve energy that they would have taken anyway. Where were the provisions for the poor who could not afford the energy-saving measures, but who were forced to spend more of their incomes on energy and less on other items in their budgets? There were programs to aid some of the less fortunate, to be sure, but the point is that morality would have required more attention to be paid to the distribution, along both income and geographical lines, of the pain involved in energy programs. Letting market prices rise to ration supplies may be an efficient solution to the energy type of problem, but it is not an equitable one.

Similarly, the concern about inflation as the primary economic problem no doubt found many supporters, but not from the ranks of the disadvantaged. Again the use of traditional monetary and fiscal policies to restrain inflation belies the moral basis for economic policy. The reduction of social programs as the military budget grew is or has become business as usual. Thus, whenever difficult choices had to be made, this administration, like its predecessors, opted to preserve the existing distribution of income and power by employing the types of policies that were acceptable.

The point is that this administration's actions were inconsistent with its underlying philosophy. Not only did it masquerade as liberal but followed conservative policies, it also failed to live up to its proclaimed desire to help those who were most in need. "The Southern brand of populism was to help the poor and the aged, to improve education, and to provide jobs. At the same time the populists tried not to waste money, having almost an obsession about the burden of the excessive debt. These same political beliefs—some of them creating inherent conflicts—were to guide me in the Oval Office."[65] Mr. Carter was never able to overcome the "inherent conflicts," and his policies irrationally tried to reconcile them, earning him nothing but the labels of indecisive and weak.

Examples are easy to find—the on-and-off-again tax cuts, the voluntary wage-and-price-controls system, the symbolic grain embargo, and so on. These programs cannot be blamed on a hostile Congress, as some of the other compromises he was forced to make could be, but are the administration's own doing.

Ironically, one of the administration's "successes," banking deregulation, is also a good example of results contrary to the basic thrust of Carter's philosophy. Banking deregulation played right into the hands of the bankers, who got most of what they wanted. Now interest rates were free to rise to whatever heights were necessary, and bankers were free to initiate all kinds of special charges, negotiable instruments, and institutions, in order to make additional profits. Again the appeal to market forces was apparently irresistible.

High interest rates could now be blamed on inflation, world markets, or, most important, on the deficit. Financing the deficit would result in crowding out private investment, raising interest rates, and thus creating a strong dollar, making it difficult to export, and so on and so on. Yet the deficit in World War II was a greater proportion of the national output than current deficits are, and those deficits were financed at very low interest rates. What was different was the cooperation of the nation, which tolerated wage and price controls, rationing, restraints of all kinds—in brief, some sacrifices and cooperation for the common good.[66] This is what Carter probably would have liked to harness, but what he, like Hoover before him, was unable to achieve.

Thus in the end, unable to overcome the established tradition and the ultimate sources of power, he failed to achieve anything of lasting value in the way of policy initiatives. Instead, the inherent conflicts got in the way, and losing power and facing another election, he simply retreated into the more familiar and acceptable patterns of behavior. His administration became more outwardly conservative, but the retreat was too late for the generation that was unable to subscribe to the notions of self-denial and cooperation.

chapter 14

The Reagan Administration and the Economics of Joy

The 1980 presidential election saw Jimmy Carter (and Walter Mondale) running against Ronald Reagan (and George Bush). For Mr. Carter the road to renomination was not a smooth one, for he was severely challenged by Senator Ted Kennedy. A challenge to an incumbent president is likely to be damaging to the party in power, and this case was no exception. Carter felt that the bruising primary campaign had seriously hurt him personally and the Democratic party in general.[1]

In addition, all the Carter initiatives—the Camp David Accords, the opening up of Africa, the Cuban refugees episode, the Panama Canal Treaty, the normalization of relations with China, the energy legislation, plus the extremely damaging hostage crisis and the Soviet invasion of Afghanistan—were now costing him votes.[2] Moreover, inflation continued to be identified by the public as the number one economic problem, and the blame for it was attributed to the Carter administration and its policies.

The fact that the causes of inflation were largely beyond the administration's immediate control and that economists were deeply divided over the treatment of stagflation did not concern the voting public. It saw only the erosion of its monetary gains and felt cheated. In periods of inflation individuals very often regard their own monetary gains, salary increases, and so on, as well deserved and merited by productive efforts, while the price increases that offset their earned rewards are due to the selfish acts of others.[3] No doubt some of this attitude is reflected in their dissatisfaction with the state of the economy.

Yet the distribution of the burden of inflation is not well understood—some lose and some gain in periods of inflation. Much depends on the asset portfolios held by groups. Just which groups or income classes win or lose cannot easily be determined by empirical evidence; the economic evidence is inconclusive.[4]

The long-term effects of inflation, however, are not important to voters who must act in the short run. Just a glance at some of the data is revealing: For manufacturing workers, real spendable weekly earnings (average gross earnings less Social Security and taxes) were $165 in 1980 for a worker with no dependents and $181 for a worker with three dependents; these totals match those for 1970, meaning that all gains in the 1970s had been eroded by inflation. Similarly, for all nonagricultural workers the 1980 totals of $138 and $151 require that one go back to 1960 for similar weekly real earnings. To underscore the point, much of the decline in hourly or spendable earnings occurred in the period from 1978–80.

These data are inadequate for determining real income changes, and some care must be exercised in their use, but a high degree of accuracy is not necessary to make some judgments. At least some people had some justification for making inflation the number-one problem, and if these people normally would have voted Democratic, Carter was in trouble. Even if the public knew that Carter was basically not to blame for the inflationary problem, it may still have been receptive to a change, any change, that promised relief. Even if the public did not fully comprehend what inflation was doing to their incomes, it was certain to recognize that living standards were obviously not rising. Again, the expectations that real living standards ought to improve steadily, as they had in the past, were thwarted in this period, making people feel worse off.

Under these conditions many could be expected to desert their political loyalities in favor of self-interest and to turn from national concerns to private ones. Some were tired of paying taxes, others were disillusioned with social programs, some feared foreign inroads into the economy, and all feared further inflation. Perhaps had Carter proposed bold new programs to reverse directions, he might have been able to retain the faithful in the Democratic party, but this he did not do, preferring his steady-as-you-go approach that seemed to the public to promise more of the same. What Carter missed was the mood of the nation for change and some hope for reversal of recent trends in both the economy and foreign affairs. What he offered instead (in his last

Economic Report) was a prediction that the economy would soon enter into a recessionary period.

His opponent, Ronald W. Reagan, ex-governor of California and long-time Goldwater-type Republican, seemed to offer more hope of improvement. Mr. Reagan, who lost the nomination to Gerald Ford in 1976, was challenged by several other Republicans, notably George Bush, Howard Baker, Robert Dole, and John Connally. In addition, a serious challenge to both parties was mounted by the newly declared independent, John Anderson. Surviving some early setbacks (discussed below) Ronald Reagan rather handily won the nomination at the July convention in Detroit. Since this election has been interpreted as representing a turning point in economic policymaking, it is important to spend more than the usual time on the formation of this candidate's economic philosophy and the evolution of economic ideas that formed the basis for the Republican platform.

Reagan began his political awareness as a loyal Democrat, supporting Truman and Humphrey in 1948 and 1950 and in general approving of the New Deal of FDR.[5] After a controversial turn as president of the Screen Actors Guild during the early 1950s, when Congress was investigating Communists in Hollwood, Reagan found his movie career floundering and in 1954 eagerly accepted an offer by General Electric to host a TV Program, "Death Valley Days." As part of his duties he was expected to make speeches to GE employees around the country. Perhaps, as he became exposed to the world of business and learned firsthand of the free-enterprise system, at least through the eyes of conservative managers of GE, he turned conservative as well. Or perhaps he simply went along with the views of his employers and his new wife, Nancy.

The nation became aware of Ronald Reagan, the politician, in a speech that he made on behalf of Goldwater in October 1964, when all seemed hopeless for the GOP cause. Suddenly he was elevated to the ranks of potential leaders, and in California a group of wealthy businessmen saw him as the next governor and then beyond. Led by Holmes P. Tuttle, A. C. Rubel, and Henry Salvatori, this group found in Mr. Reagan the communicating skills to put across their conservative philosophy. He thus became a candidate for governor in 1966, stressing high taxes, the costs of welfare, and the turmoil on university campuses, caused by protests over free-speech issues and the Vietnam War. He touched on the correct issues to win public support, although reporters found him ignorant of state issues and repetitious in his pat answers to questions. He won easily over the hapless Democrats, and his campaign skills were clearly revealed.

Even before his first term as governor was over and his second term begun, Reagan was eyeing the White House. In 1968 he was a late candidate for the office and lost badly, but was clearly being groomed for the presidency and learning how to achieve it. The loss in 1976 only served to prepare him for the next attempt.

What did he learn about economic issues over this time period to prepare him for 1980?

Supply-Side Economics and Reagan's Campaign Program

Reagan began his political career as a follower of Goldwater, whose economic plans called for a reduction in government involvement in the economy. This meant that he favored cutting government spending and reducing the role of the federal government in redistributing income through social programs. After government spending was reduced (and programs transferred to the states and localities), taxes could be reduced. To cut taxes before government spending was cut would, of course, mean an increase in the budget deficit—a result that must be avoided if future generations were not to be burdened.

Unfortunately, there were costs connected with this approach— variously called "the old-time religion," "castor oil," or "deep-root-canal" economics.[6] In order to reach the better economy in the long run, a recession had to be endured in the short run. Thus the economics of austerity called for increasing unemployment, bankruptcies, and so on, all of which are not likely to be popular. Whenever the Republicans were in power, they began their policy of austerity and soon found themselves out of power.

There seemed to be no alternative to "biting the bullet" (another phrase to describe the action), which meant economic hardship for some. Understandably, politicians running for office do not like to espouse policies that lead to hardships. In the past they simply resorted to downplaying the adverse effects of the policies they advocated.

In the late 1970s a group of Republican legislators began to reject this party label of doomsday economics and sought to shed the image of Republicans as recession makers and naysayers. Led by Congressman Jack Kemp (R., NY) they sought to achieve long-run goals without incurring the short-run pain. They found the answer in a "new" economic analysis of the economy by Arthur Laffer, later called "supply-side" economics.[7] Laffer explained the concept to journalist

Jude Wanniski of the *Wall Street Journal* (allegedly on a restaurant napkin), who later popularized it. Supply-siders contended that the difficulty in the U.S. economy lay in the punitive tax system that robbed people of the incentive to produce. Cut taxes and incentives would increase, savings would rise, fostering greater investment, which would increase productivity, economic growth, and employment. Best of all, the deficit need not grow; the tax revenues that flowed from the increased economic activity would offset the loss of revenue due to the tax cut. There was no need to worry about government spending at all—that could come later.

This was, of course, the same message that Andrew Mellon conveyed to Calvin Coolidge in the 1920s.[8] Such a policy had been branded "trickle-down" economics in the past, since the tax cuts favored the wealthy and had been accordingly derided by many economists, including Keynes. The tax-cutting episodes in the 1920s were not cited as a precedent for the new supply-side approach, but the Kennedy–Johnson tax reduction was. The Kennedy–Johnson tax cut was not a good example to choose as a precedent, for that program was clearly a Keynesian move designed to stimulate economic activity on the demand side in a period of economic slack. This was not the situation in the late 1970s.[9]

Still, the Kennedy–Johnson tax cut was used as a justification for supply-side tax reductions. Another, more important rationale for tax policies was the proposed relationship between tax rates and tax revenues, apparently first outlined for Jude Wanniski and later formalized as the Laffer Curve. Arthur Laffer's explanation of the relationship between tax rates and tax revenues, shown in Figure 14.1, convinced Mr. Wanniski, who then promoted and proselytized for it.[10]

The rather straightforward relationship between tax rates and tax revenues is shown in Figure 14.1.[11] The parabola shows how tax revenues vary with tax rates—that is, tax rates t_1 and t_2 yield the same revenue (R_1) as do tax rates t_3, and t_4 (R_2). Clearly there is some tax rate, t_0, not necessarily 50 percent, that yields the maximum revenue; increasing tax rates to the left of t_0 yields increasing tax revenues, while increasing tax rates to the right of t_0, in the shaded area, yields declining tax revenues.

Had the analysis stopped there, nothing much would have been added to economic knowledge by the Laffer Curve. In fact, Andrew Mellon wrote of the same relationship in 1924.[12] Carried to extremes, the Laffer Curve represents an example of devotion to the obvious.

The analysis did not stop with the construction of the curve, however, for it was the contention of the supply-siders that the tax rate for the United States was to the right of t_0, and thus reducing tax

Figure 14.1   The Laffer Curve

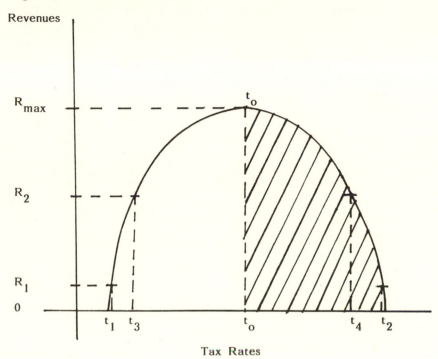

Source: Based on curve in Jude Wanniski, *The Way the World Works* (New York: Simon and Schuster, 1978), p. 97.

rates would increase tax revenues. Here was the closest thing to a free lunch that the Republicans had been at pains to insist did not exist. The route by which revenues would rise follows the path from an increase in saving, and thus investment, which would increase economic activity, to an increase in economic growth, which would bring in greater tax revenues. Along the way private incentives would be restored, since high tax rates discourage risk taking and investment and divert investment into unproductive investment in the attempt to minimize taxation; productivity would rise, as people would feel they could retain more of their hard-earned income, and, of course, more jobs would be created by the economic growth bringing in more revenue, and so on.

Most economists did not subscribe to the supply-side diagnosis. First, what is meant by "the" tax rate in a system of many rates, and how was the shape of the curve determined? No empirical analysis preceded the assertions made. Second, it seemed to stand Keynesian analysis on its head, maintaining that an increase in saving would produce an increase in investment—Keynes held the opposite view. Third, and perhaps more devastating, there was no empirical support for the contention that tax rates in the United States were too high and stifled incentives. Nor was there any evidence to suggest that reducing tax rates would increase work effort and increase productivity. As a result of tax cuts, some people might choose to work more, and some would choose to work less, and many would be unaffected, either by choice or because they simply could not alter their work hours. On balance, it was and is impossible to predict the effect on work effort in advance.[13]

In short, there were a number of implicit and explicit assumptions in the Laffer Curve analysis and the policy of cutting taxes that followed. The conclusions were a matter of faith, rather than serious economic analysis. Not many economists, on the basis of such intuitive reasoning, were willing to subscribe to the conclusions that supply-siders were willing to reach.

Although economists were not willing to endorse the supply-side hypothesis, politicians were. Here was a chance to cut taxes (always popular) without having to pay any price: The deficit would not increase, no difficult choices had to be made in reducing government spending (unpopular), and the economy would boom, with greater economic growth and employment.

The Sirens could not have surpassed this irresistible message, and soon Congressman Jack Kemp (R., NY) and Senator William Roth (R., DE) sponsored a bill that would reduce personal taxes by 30 percent over three years. Jack Kemp in particular began to champion the cause of supply-side economics and soon found a convert in Ronald Reagan. The old-time religion was no longer needed—forget about cutting government spending first and risking a recession, just cut taxes and worry about spending later. With no effect on the deficit, what better program for winning public approval could there be? Reagan thus began to campaign on the basis of Kemp–Roth as a major plank in his economic platform.

While not always articulated coherently or consistently, the other planks that emerged in the campaign included the following:

- A planned increase in national defense expenditures
- A reduction in inflation, to be achieved largely through a slower growth in the money supply
- A reduction in government regulations to get government off our backs

- A promise to balance the budget in 1983 or 1984
- A plan to reduce the "waste" in government programs (No specific programs were mentioned, although references to welfare cheats were frequent.)
- A large reduction in taxes.

Thus was born the economics of joy—the painless solutions to our economic woes. We could reduce taxes, increase spending on national defense, remove waste from government, reduce regulations, fight inflation, and balance the budget, and we could do these things simultaneously! While some economists would agree with parts of this program, few would have been willing to agree that all of these things could be accomplished at all, not to speak of their being done all at once; neither did George Bush, who labeled it "Voodoo Economics."

The program did fit in beautifully, however, with the prevailing mood of many in the country. The "me" generation wanted their taxes reduced and government spending (read welfare programs) cut, and they were delighted to be told that no self-denial was involved and no need for Carter-like sacrifices. Moreover it was OK to make money and enjoy its fruits without guilt—greed was in.

Was Mr. Reagan playing the role of Pollyanna, or did he believe this unrealistic package? Probably he came to believe in it because he wanted to believe in it. An optimistic man to begin with, and one who never troubled himself with details, he must have found it quite natural to grasp such pleasant outcomes from the complexities of economics without confronting the obvious contradictions in his program. Even his economic advisors, who included George Shultz, Milton Friedman, Arthur Burns, Alan Greenspan, Paul McCracken, and Arthur Laffer, had some doubts about the supply-side prescription, and some had doubts about other features of the program. Others, including many critics, saw the inherent contradictions in the program and had some qualms about them. The economic program was propelled forward, however, even if, in Stein's words, "whatever may have been true of any one of his various advisors, he [Reagan] did not have a precise, comprehensive, internally consistent, durable model of the economy and of economic policy in his mind."[14]

The Program for Economic Recovery

The constrast between the economic programs of the candidates was clearly a major factor in this campaign. Another was the sharp contrast between the men themselves: Reagan became the master campaigner, while Carter was preoccupied with the Iranian crisis and stayed close to the White House; the affable Mr. Reagan appeared as a charming person with a pleasing personality, a ready wit, a disarming smile, and as a friendly fellow; Mr. Carter seemed reserved, even cool, compared to Reagan, as if the fire had gone out. The stark contrast between the two was most evident in the televised debates.

The public-relations approach to U.S. politics that began with the Wilson administration really was brought to a science with the Reagan campaign. Armed with simple, easily understood answers, Mr. Reagan smoothly outperformed the president, and in his gentle prodding of Carter—"there you go again"—he remonstrated with Carter, implying exaggerations or falsehoods.

Finally, Reagan appealed to those who had felt left out of the political process for many years: fundamentalist religious groups, protectors of the family values seen as eroding in an age of secularism, rabid anti-Communists, states righters, complainers of leniency of criminals, and so on. These groups rallied behind the candidate and worked diligently on his behalf.

For all these reasons—an attractive economic program with its appeal to self-interest, a hard-line approach to communism, a recognition of the need to return to family values and religious principles, and his own personality—Mr. Reagan was victorious in November. He won 489 electoral votes to Carter's 49, and this has been responsible for the impression that he won some sort of mandate for his programs and philosophy. The evidence shows, however, that the election was more a rejection of Carter than a swing in philosophy. He won about 51 percent of the popular vote, about 10 points more than Carter, but since only about 54 percent of the eligible voters turned out to vote (the lowest turnout in 32 years), Reagan was elected by only 27 percent of the registered voters.

Moreover, the margin of victory was not as large as in previous elections, and hence a mandate is difficult to claim. According to the polls, dissatisfaction with the economy was the major factor in the switch of Democrats to the Republican party. They really did feel worse off under Carter and made their protest known by defecting to Reagan. Neither was this a switch to conservative philosophy, since there was no increase in the number of people who identified themselves as conservatives, from 1976 to 1980.[15] There was no mistaking in the voting outcome, however, the desire for something new, for a change from business as usual. The Republicans were happy, too, with winning control of the Senate for the first time since 1954 and making gains in the House as well. These results and the ambiguities associated with the interpretation of why people voted as they did made the true meaning of the Reagan victory obscure.

The diverse group of economists giving advice to the administration attests to the eclectic, something-for-everyone economic program. There was recognition of the possibility of inconsistencies among the various parts, but in the euphoric atmosphere of victory the contradictions were downgraded. Consider only the three main groups, out of the many that were enticed to Washington with the hope of guiding economic policy: supply-siders, budget balancers, and monetarists.

The supply-siders wanted to cut taxes to stimulate investment spending without worrying about government spending; the budget balancers wanted to balance the budget, which means that if taxes were cut, government spending would have to be reduced as well; the monetarists wanted to reduce inflation by slowing the rate of growth of the money supply, which would entail an increase in the rate of interest and deter investment spending. Only a casual glance at these elements in the total program is sufficient to reveal the basic inconsistencies and contradictions inherent in the package.

The response to critics accused them of reasoning on the basis of past economic (Keynesian) models rather than the new approach. The critics, it was said, were not considering the change in expectations that would occur, once the public saw that taxes were being reduced and inflation conquered. The firm resolve of the administration to fight inflation and get government off the backs of business, reduce regulations, eliminate waste in government, and so on would reassure the business community and it would respond by investing. Remove the uncertainty created by inflation and by Carter-type policies, and faith in the future would be restored.

It follows that to reverse expectations, actions would have to be swift and delays would have to be avoided. All parts of the program would have to be enacted simultaneously. Thus full advantage would have to be taken of the honeymoon period with Congress: The administration was determined to "hit the ground running." To assure the success of this strategy, the centralization of power in the White House was a must. Power would be shared by the three presidential aides, James Baker, Michael Deaver, and Edwin Meese, with the president involved in only a few issues of importance.[16] In addition, the Office of Budget and Management (OMB) was virtually taken over by one man, David Stockman, who ran roughshod over career employees and ignored the usual inputs of department and agency heads.

Even the budgetary process was revised to suit the plans of the administration: Instead of the usual budget reconciliation process that Congress approves toward the end of the budget process, the administration moved the reconciliation process to the beginning of the budget process, and thus the budget had to be considered as a whole and could not be picked apart by the consideration of this or that program. The process required such speed that proposed cuts in government spending were indicated by asterisks, with the statement that they would be spelled out later. This incredible maneuver can be explained only by the popularity of the president, the energy of David Stockman, and the collapse of the Democratic party.

To some extent the acquiescence could also be explained by the political appointment process: Only true believers were appointed to office; nonbelievers were eased out of government. Team play and loyalty were demanded and largely received by the administration, which was determined to keep a tight rein on governing institutions. The political appointees quickly began to implement the Reagan philosophy in administering the laws and regulations that did not require congressional approval, while the focus of attention was diverted to the larger issues—tax cuts, for example. Add to these elements a remarkable public-relations job, and the stage is set for the great push for the economic package.

The grand design was certainly successful, as the Reagan administration quickly compiled an impressive list of victories in achieving its goals. The economic program was given to Congress in February 1981, with a document called *A Program For Economic Recovery* that outlined the administration's goals, as well as the means to achieve them. The overall plan was now reduced to four parts: a substantial cut in government spending, a reduction in taxes, a reduction in government regulations, and a monetary policy consistent with these goals.[17]

Gone was the possibility of reducing government spending by merely cutting waste, extravagances, and the bureaucracies. The campaign rhetoric had now given way to reality: To cut government spending would mean the elimination of government programs, and choices would have to be made among them, some that might affect benefits that flowed to the middle class. Gone too was the belief that all pieces of the program fit together neatly. Critics had argued convincingly that the contradictions were real. Still, the Reagan administration refused to set priorities and kept insisting that the parts would all mesh. It was far too late now to admit that the campaign promises were just that, without upsetting the expectations such a program was supposed to generate.

Skepticism was not a ghost the administration wanted to summon. As long as individuals were willing to look at only the parts of the program that benefited them and ignore the parts they disagreed with or deemed questionable, the administration could proceed with its contradictory program.

The administration proposed to cut government spending by $49 billion in FY 1982, and it used a set of nine specific guidelines to determine where the reductions should be made. They are worth reproducing in some detail:[18]

1. *Preserve the "social safety net."* The social safety net was supposed to protect the elderly, the poor, the veterans, and the unemployed from major budget cuts. The programs affecting these groups were Medicare, unemployment benefits, Social Security, AFDC, SSI, and veterans' payments and health care.

2. *Revise entitlements to eliminate unintended benefits.* Since the administration regarded the growth of entitlement programs in the 1970s as a major contributor to excessive government spending, it sought in its first budget to reverse the trend. Budget reductions in this area included Medicaid, food and nutrition, extended unemployment aid, housing assistance, and other non-safety-net programs. Reductions in these programs would permit more aid to be focused on the "truly needy."

3. *Reduce subsidies to middle- and upper-income groups.* Programs such as school lunches, student aid, and housing finance, which benefited groups that do not require government aid, should be reduced or eliminated.

4. *Impose fiscal restraint on other national-interest programs.* Programs considered of low priority or of low merit fell under this general category. Examples are arts and humanities and science and technology programs.

5. *Recover costs that can be clearly allocated to users.* User fees were to be imposed on those who benefited from federal programs. Among those identified as receiving direct economic benefits included users of inland waterways, airports, and Coast Guard services.

6. *Stretch out and retarget public-sector capital-investment programs.* These programs for water-resource projects, waste-treatment plants, highways, mass transit, and airport projects would face restraints or reductions.

7. *Reduce overhead and personnel costs of the federal government.* The administration hoped to reduce inefficiencies in the management of the federal government. Cost savings were to be made in such areas as surplus property disposal, employee travel, and federal employment practices.

8. *Apply sound economic criteria to subsidy programs.* Free-market principles dictated that subsidies were harmful to the economy and thus should be eliminated. Programs for mass transit, public service, employment (CETA), community development, and subsidies for new energy development were identified as the type of program under review.

9. *Consolidate categorical grant programs into block grants.* Under this guideline, 77 categorical grants in the social, educational, and health areas were combined into five block grants (unrestricted). The move was designed to return greater control over federal funds to the states and

localities. Later Mr. Reagan would introduce his New Federalism, which would continue this movement and transfer specific programs to the states and localities to fund and administer.

The tax-reduction proposal clearly adopted the Kemp-Roth bill that called for a three-year, across-the-board reduction in individual income tax rates. For business a new depreciation schedule for plant and equipment was introduced to promote investment spending, job creation, and industrial revitalization.

After the cutbacks in government spending and the reductions in tax rates were in force, the budget totals should have resembled those shown in Table 14.1.

From Table 14.1 it is clear that the rate of change of government spending was expected to slow to 6 percent from 1981 to 1986, down from 12 percent in 1976–79. Revenues would grow by 10 percent annually, instead of the 14 percent rate of the recent past. The result would be a balanced budget by 1984, with surpluses thereafter. Moreover, the share of the federal budget as a percent of GNP would drop to 19 percent in 1986, from 23 percent in 1981.

The totals, however, mask the shift in spending priorities. By 1984 the Department of Defense would see its budget increased to account for 32.4 percent of the total budget (from 24.1 percent in 1981), while the growth in social programs would fall. The administration insisted that the "truly needy" would still be provided for, but others, apparently not needy, would find their benefits reduced. The social safety net was to grow to account for 40.6 percent of the budget in 1984, from 36.6 percent in 1981, and this growth was deemed sufficient to catch the truly needy, while letting the others fall through the net.

These budget forecasts rested on economic assumptions, of course, and not everyone agreed with the rosy forecasts of the real rate of growth of GNP of 5.2 percent for 1981 and over 4 percent per year to 1986. Interest rates (treasury bills) were expected to fall to 8.9 percent in 1981 and eventually to 5.6 percent in 1986, and unemployment rates would decline to 5.6 percent in 1986 and the CPI to 4.2 percent.

The critics who presented more "realistic" assumptions consistently came up with much different estimates for receipts, outlays, deficits, and so on. At first Congress was in no position to challenge the popular president and reserved judgment on this economic package. Doubts continued to grow, but voting for tax cuts is nearly irresistible for politicians, especially if they have no effect on the deficit. Defenders of social programs were bucking the tide, as their constituents, the poor or disadvantaged, had little voice, little power, and did not vote anyway.

Table 14.1   Estimated Budget Outlook, 1981–86 (billions of dollars)

	1981	*1982*	*1983*	*1984*	*1985*	*1986*
Outlays	654.7	695.5	733.1	771.6	844.0	912.1
Receipts	600.2	650.5	710.2	772.1	840.9	942.0
Deficit (−) or surplus	−54.5	−45.0	−22.9	+0.5	+6.9	+29.9
Share of GNP						
Outlays	23.0	21.8	20.4	19.3	19.2	19.0
Receipts	21.1	20.4	19.7	19.3	19.3	19.6

Source: A Program For Economic Recovery, a White House Report, p.9.

Whatever opposition there was to the economic program melted away after the president was wounded in an assassination attempt on March 30, 1981, in Washington. Sympathy for the president and a desire to let him try his new economic policies led the Congress to acquiesce in matters that it would probably have resisted in other times.

Tax Cuts and Restrictive Monetary Policy

By any criterion the president was extremely successful in getting his program through Congress. The omnibus Budget Reconciliation Act was passed by Congress in June 1981, and the Economic Recovery Tax Act (ERTA) sailed through Congress and was signed into law in August 1981.

Looking at the budget outlays first, Congress gave the president much of what he wanted. Nondefense outlays were cut by $43 billion on paper but more like $31 billion in true cuts. Congress fell all over itself to overestimate the nondefense cuts and thus indulged in some creative accounting practices, such as moving the strategic petroleum reserve out of the budget and "saving" $3.7 billion and shifting Medicare payments from FY 1982 to FY 1981 and "saving" millions. Increases in national defense, on the other hand, rose by $7.3 billion in FY 1982, and approval was granted for increases totaling $33 billion by 1986. Thus both the shifts in the budget and the approximate amounts requested were granted by a compliant Congress.

The 1981 tax act also gave the president much of what he asked for and, in some respects, more. Individual income tax rates were reduced 25 percent, 5 percent in the first year and 10 percent in the next two years. The administration expressed displeasure at the reduction in rates and the postponement, but essentially it had already reached the decision that delay over the effective date of the reductions was inevitable.[19]

Other provisions, consistent with supply-side views, were also enacted. The top marginal tax rate was reduced from 70 percent to 50 percent as of January 1, 1982, and as a result the maximum capital gains tax was reduced to 20 percent from 28 percent. Starting in 1985, the income tax would be indexed for inflation by increasing the income tax brackets, the standard deduction (the zero bracket amount), and the personal exemption by the rate of change in the CPI.

Other provisions included a marriage deduction for two-earner couples, more liberal child-care credit, and the extension of eligibility for individual retirement accounts (IRAs) to employees who were already covered by employer plans. The amount for IRAs was established at $2,000 per worker with some allowance for nonworking spouses. In addition, Keogh retirement plans were raised to $15,000 from $7,500, and a one-year exclusion of interest in a special "all savers" deposit was granted.

Obviously these provisions were aimed at increasing saving, which is what the supply-siders were seeking. To augment the reductions in the taxation of income, wealth taxes were also decreased. Estate and gift tax rates were cut, exemptions were increased, and the inheritance tax for surviving spouses was eliminated. Clearly, the tax revisions were tilted toward the upper-income groups and were promptly labeled unfair and unjust. (The equity question will be considered later.)

For businesses, the Economic Recovery Tax Act of 1981 made four major changes in the taxation of business income. The most important was the generous treatment of depreciation—the writing off of plant and equipment against income. In general, the act shortened the period over which assets can be depreciated: For certain types of equipment—for example, trucks—the period was reduced to three years; for other types of equipment the period was reduced to five years, and for plant the period was shortened to fifteen years. The new system, known as accelerated cost recovery system (ACRS), with its 3–5–15-year schedules, drastically reduced the accounting period for depreciation. The aim was to increase the rate of return on investment in order to stimulate investment spending. It is important to note that the ACRS system is more important for firms that invest in equipment than for those that employ more labor in their products: That is, capital-intensive firms would receive more benefit than labor-intensive or service industries. Despite claims to the contrary, this constitutes an industrial policy and encourages investment in some areas and not in others.

The same aims prompted an increase in the investment tax credit for some types of equipment. Designed to stimulate an increase in investment spending by raising the rate of return on investment, the investment tax credit also favors capital-using industries and ignores the labor-intensive or service industries. Together with the ACRS, the rate of taxation in some industries could be negative for new investment. Here is the capital-shortage argument carried to extremes.

Unfortunately, firms with no taxable income could not take advantage of these generous provisions, and therefore a special provision was inserted for them. They could "sell" their equipment to firms that had taxable income, and then these firms could use the credits and depreciation to reduce their taxable income. In return the acquiring firm would lease the equipment back to the original firm. Both firms benefited, since the profitable firm had additional tax deductions and the unprofitable firm had cash: The loser was the U.S. Treasury. This incredible provision, ostensibly designed to increase investment in unprofitable industries, created such a controversy over its obvious raid on the Treasury that it was severely limited a year later.

The final provision allowed businesses to expense equipment up to $5,000 on new investment in 1982 and 1983. Thereafter the amounts that could be expensed immediately were to rise to $7,500 to 1984 and 1985 and to $10,000 after that. The aim, as above, was to increase investment by increasing the after-tax rate of return on new investment.

Monetary policy, too, was generally in accord with the administration's wishes. The monetary authorities were committed to reducing inflation and were willing to reduce the rate of growth of monetary aggregates. The difficulty was which monetary aggregate to control. The extension of NOW accounts to the entire nation, the introduction of all-savers accounts, the relaxation of interest rate ceilings on small savings accounts, and the continued growth of money-market funds made the definition of monetary aggregates arbitrary and of course, made control difficult. Just how the innovations in money markets would affect the shifts of funds was unclear to the Federal Reserve, so that the targets it set for monetary aggregates were tentative and changed frequently over the course of the year.[20]

Due to the likely shifts of funds, M1A was abandoned as a target aggregate, and an adjusted M1B took its place. Along with M2, now increasing in importance, the new M1B became the focus for control. The long-run operating ranges for these aggregates were 3–5.5 percent for M1B and 6–9 percent for M2. During the year M1B grew at rates that exceeded the target range. Considerable variations within the year, especially in mid-year when the growth rates plummeted, had the Federal Reserve concerned over how best to achieve monetary control.

The end result was that M1B grew at a rate of 4.7 percent and M2 at 9.7 percent. The move toward monetary restraint can probably be seen better in the growth of M1, which includes M1A, as the growth of this aggregate fell from 7.3 percent in 1980 to 4.9 percent in 1981, a substantial reduction. Thus, the Federal Reserve made a reasonable first step toward reducing the rate of growth of monetary aggregates to reach its goal of reducing the rate of inflation.[21]

For 1982 the Federal Reserve reduced its target ranges for monetary aggregates, in keeping with the goal of reducing inflation. The long-run range for M1 was set at 2.5–5.5 percent, and for M2, 6–9 percent. Both M1 and M2 exceeded their ranges throughout the year—M1 growth for the year was 8.5 percent and that of M2 was 9.9 percent.

In October the Federal Reserve decided to concentrate on M2, since the maturation of all-savers accounts and the introduction of money-market accounts would have depressed M1 as funds were transferred out, and thus movements in M1 would be difficult to interpret. In view of the uncertainty of what would happen to M1, the Federal Reserve set no short-run objectives for M1 in the fourth quarter of 1982.

Throughout 1982 the Federal Reserve was concerned with the deterioration in the economy and let the money-supply growth exceed target rates, particularly for M1. In October the Federal Reserve announced that it would pay more attention to a variety of indicators, including interest rates, in determining monetary policy. This was due partly to the international debt crisis and partly to the sharp decline in the velocity of money. The income velocity of money (GNP/M) for M1 fell 4.75 percent and for M2, 5.5 percent. If the Federal Reserve had kept to its targets, monetary policy would have been much more restrictive than desired.[22]

The decline in velocity probably reflected the increased desire for liquidity, brought about by uncertainty over the future of the economy: the precautionary demand for liquidity. Declining interest rates and the recession would also have worked to reduce velocity, but the sharp declines in this period were abnormal.

Thus the Federal Reseve became increasingly concerned with the slow rate of growth of the economy and began to acquiesce to the above-targeted rates of monetary growth. It also moved away from the strict monetarist prescription in favor of a more eclectic view toward monetary policy.

The Depression of 1981–82

The Reagan economic program and philosophy have been described in some detail, since they were billed as revolutionary and visionary. Presumably the conservative tide had swept away the ill-conceived liberal tradition and along with it the outdated theories of J. M. Keynes. The United States was ready for new ideas, new challenges, and a new beginning.

It is now time to examine the program in operation. We have seen that the administration received from Congress most of what was wanted—indeed, probably more than most presidents had been able to secure. What, then, did "The Program for Economic Recovery" accomplish?

In the first quarter the economy continued in the expansionary phase following the 1980 recession. Thereafter, the trouble began, and real GNP fell by −1.6 percent in the second quarter, and in July 1981 the economy slid into a recession. In the fourth quarter GNP fell by 5.2 percent and for the year rose by only 1.9 percent. To give some idea of the severe fluctuations, current-dollar GNP rose by 19.2 percent in the first quarter and by only 2.7 percent in the last quarter. Thus began the deepest recession (or depression, depending on one's definition) since the 1930s. This very sharp decline continued until December 1982 when the economy began to recover. Table 14.2 contains some of the economic data that are pertinent in judging the severity of the downturn, but as will be shown, the numbers do not reveal the economic impact of the president's program.

The decline in the rate of growth of GNP is clearly evident, but one item in particular stands out in 1981—the turnaround in net exports—and the trend continued in 1982. This development will require more discussion later. The unemployment rate rose to 7.6 percent in 1981 and to 9.7 percent in 1982. The rate rose again, however, to 10.8 percent in December 1982, the highest rate in the post-World War II period. If one defines a depression as any period when the unemployment rate exceeds 10 percent, then this is the first depression since the 1930s. As the depression evolved, manufacturers used less of their capacity, and the utilization rate fell below 70 percent

Table 14.2   Selected Economic Series, 1981–82 (dollar amounts in billions)

	1981		1982	
	Amount (dollars)	Percent Change from 1980	Amount (dollars)	Percent Change from 1981
GNP	2,937.7	11.6	3,057.5	4.1
GNP (in 1972 dollars)	1,502.6	1.9	1,475.5	−1.8
Consumption	947.6	1.8	957.1	1.0
Investment	225.8	8.3	196.9	−12.8
Net exports	42.0	−17.0	30.3	−27.9
Government	287.1	0.9	291.2	1.4
Federal	110.4	3.7	116.1	5.2
State and local	176.7	−0.8	175.0	1.0
Unemployment rate (percent)	7.6	7.0	9.7	27.6
Manufacturing capacity-utilization rate (percent)	78.5	−0.8	69.8	−11.1
Output per hour of all persons (percent change)	—	1.8	—	0.4
Compensation per hour (percent change)	—	9.6	—	7.3
In real terms	—	−0.7	—	1.1
Unit labor costs (percent change)	—	7.7	—	6.9
Prices: Percent Change in				
GNP index (year to year)	—	9.4	—	6.0
PPI (year to year)	—	9.2	—	4.0
(year to year)	—	10.4	—	6.1
CPI (December to December)	—	8.9	—	3.9

Source: Council of Economic Advisors, *Economic Report of the President* (Washington, DC: GPO, 1983).

in 1982, reaching 67 percent in December, and industrial production fell by nearly 12 percent from 1980 to 1982.

As expected in recessions, labor productivity fell sharply to negligible amounts in 1982, while compensation per hour and unit labor costs also began to decline; developments that also require additional discussion after the downturn have been described. Prices started down in 1981 and that trend continued to 1982, when the CPI fell to 3.9 percent on a December-to-December basis. All other price indexes showed similar declines. Inflation seemed to be beaten, but fears for its return lingered.

Despite the recession and the rapid decline in prices, interest rates remained relatively high for most of the period. Only in the last part of 1982 did they drop significantly. For instance, three-month treasury bills were yielding 14.7 percent in July 1981, and a year later were yielding 11.9 percent, declining to 8 percent in December 1982; the prime commercial rate was 16 percent in July 1982 and a year later was over 12 percent. Mortgage rates were nearly 15 percent at the start of the recession and at the end were about 14 percent; the prime rate fell very gradually from over 20 percent at the start to nearly 12 percent at the end. The Federal Reserve did little with respect to the discount rate, decreasing it only after a year into the recession and then very gradually—to around 11 percent, and then in steps to 8.5 percent in December 1982.

Worst of all for conservative Republicans, the budget deficit mushroomed, growing from $57.9 billion in 1981 to $110.6 billion in 1982. A glance at Table 14.3 is sufficient to note that the increase in deficits is the same when the budget is measured on a fiscal-year basis as it is on the national-income accounts basis. In passing for now,

Table 14.3   Federal Government Budgets, 1980–82 (billions of dollars)

	1980	*1981*	*1982*
Fiscal year basis			
Receipts	517.1	599.3	617.8
Individual taxes	244.1	285.9	297.7
Corporate taxes	64.6	61.1	49.2
Social Security	157.8	182.7	201.5
Other	50.6	70.6	69.4
Expenditures	576.7	657.2	728.3
National defense	135.9	159.8	187.4
Income security	193.1	225.1	248.3
Interest	52.5	68.7	84.7
Other	195.2	203.6	207.9
Surplus or deficit (−)	−59.6	−57.9	−110.6
National income and product account basis (calendar year)			
Receipts	540.7	628.2	614.7
Expenditures	602.1	688.2	762.6
Surplus o Deficit (−)	−61.4	−60.0	−147.9

Source: Council of Economic Advisors, *Economic Report of the President* (Washington, DC: GPO, 1983), pp. 217, 251.

note the decline in corporate income taxes and the increase in interest payments; both need further elaboration.

Failures and Achievements
of the Program for Economic Recovery

What went wrong? Quite simply, the Reagan program ran into reality, and the promised free lunch did not materialize. The contradictions and inconsistencies embodied in the economics of joy were finally revealed, and the delusions that were so readily accepted became apparent. In the words of David Stockman, the influential head of OMB:

> None of us really understands what's going on with all these numbers. ... The defense numbers got out of control and we were doing that whole budget-cutting exercise so frenetically. In other words, you were juggling details, ... but the pieces were moving on independent tracks. ... And it didn't quite mesh. ... But, you see, for about a month and a half we got away with that because of the novelty of all these budget reductions.[23]

At the same time, Mr. Stockman was testifying before Congress that the administration was carefully reviewing each program for its cost effectiveness and painstakingly weighing the costs and benefits of each program. He survived these revelations (and others later) and continued as OMB chief until he resigned in the summer of 1985.

The critics were correct—the economic program based on hopelessly optimistic forecasts promised too much, too quickly; the mutually exclusive goals could not be achieved simultaneously, if at all. Let us review the major pieces of the economic program—first, the tax cuts.

Whatever short-run effects the tax cuts might have had were dissipated by their structure, the spreading out of the effective dates, and by an increase in taxes when Reagan bowed to pressure and remembered that he was opposed to large deficits.

The across-the-board tax cut rewarded higher-income groups more than lower-income groups. That is the nature of a progressive rate structure—an equal percentage cut in taxes will leave higher-income groups with a larger after-tax income than lower-income groups. In addition, the personal exemption and standard deduction were not changed, and this meant that these elements would be eroded by inflation (until 1985). Together with the across-the-board dichotomy between income groups, the tax cuts were viewed as unfair. Questions of equity inevitably involve value judgments that cannot be resolved. Yet the conclusions of many, fueled by numerous illustrations in the media, were that the tax cuts were inequitable.

Again Mr. Stockman did little to assuage the discontent:

> The hard part of the supply-side tax cut is dropping the top rate from 70 to 50 percent—the rest of it is a secondary matter. ... The original argument was that the top bracket was too high, and that's having the most devastating effect on the economy. Then, the general argument was that, in order to make this palatable as a political matter, you had to bring down all the brackets. But, I mean, Kemp-Roth was always a Trojan Horse to bring down the top rate.[24]

And in regard to supply-side economics, "I've never believed that just cutting taxes alone will cause output and employment to expand. ... It's kind of hard to sell 'trickle down,' so the supply-side formula was the only way to get a tax policy that was really 'trickle down.' Supply-side is 'trickle-down' theory."[25]

To be effective the tax cuts had to stimulate saving and investment and hence economic growth and employment. Moreover, the ERTA was supposed to encourage saving by liberalizing IRA eligibility, by introducing all-savers accounts, and so on. Of course the latter did not work, as people simply shifted funds in these accounts without increasing their saving. It was predictable perhaps, but the administration may not have been primarily interested in increasing saving from these sources, but in rewarding certain income groups (the poor did not have IRAs, nor could they afford the minimum balances of all-savers accounts) and providing a temporary pool of savings for the short run; or, as some have suggested, providing a substitute for Social Security to demonstrate the dispensability of the program.

Recall that the Reagan diagnosis of the economy's ills included the lack of saving to finance investment and the assumption, not often stated or stated correctly, that the United States had a capital shortage, caused in some part by the heavy taxation of investment income, and in part by overconsumption, which leads to the lack of saving. Government also crowds out private investment by competing for funds to finance the deficit. Supply-siders, turning Keynes on his head, wanted to increase saving to stimulate investment.

What happened to saving? The percent of disposable income devoted to saving fell to 5.8 percent in 1982 from 6.6 percent in 1981; the rate of 5.8 percent is not significantly different from the rates in the past, showing that the saving rate in the United States exhibits a great deal of stability and does not immediately respond to tax changes. Furthermore, the recession was so severe that many had to stop saving or reduce past savings. So, despite the tilting of the tax reductions to higher-income groups who do most of the saving, the volume of savings available did not increase. In the longer run, the increasing federal deficit will compete even more for the available savings, thus making the situation even worse.

The assumption of a capital shortage was always a questionable one, given the large amount of unused capacity. The proportion of real gross nonresidential investment to real GNP was 14.4 percent in 1980, 14.5 percent in 1981, and 13.7 percent in 1982. The average for the decade of the 1970s was 14.9 percent. Thus there was no capital shortage as such.[26] What was implied but not correctly stated was that the past proportion of GNP going to investment was not sufficient, whatever the reason expressed.

Despite the business tax cuts, investment declined. The tax provisions for business virtually eliminated the corporation income tax and should have increased the return to investment, as the effective tax rate on income from capital fell by 14 percent and the tax on new investment fell by 52 percent.[27] Businessmen simply are not likely to invest when sales are tumbling and the future uncertain. Particularly when there is excess capacity to begin with, reductions in taxes are not likely to stimulate the need to acquire more capital stock. More probably, firms will take advantage of the increase in after-tax profits to strengthen their economic position by merging, diversifying into other industries, increasing dividends, or even going abroad to invest in more profitable areas. In fact, this is what really happened to the business tax cuts. One study found that those firms that received the largest tax cuts did less investing than those that did not receive similar tax breaks.[28]

High interest rates also contributed to the lack of response of investment spending. The move toward monetary restraint helped keep interest rates high, and to the extent that investment is sensitive to interest rates, investment spending was discouraged. Of course, these relationships were pointed out to supply-siders and to the administration, but the criticisms were dismissed. The failure of investment to respond to the tax cuts meant that economic growth was stymied, but in the short run this meant trouble. The supply-side program was a long-term solution at best, but now in the short run, aggregate supply was not growing and neither was the demand for labor.

The supply-siders could not be blamed for the increase in interest rates, and in fact they deplored them and the monetary policy that brought them about. They began to turn to alternative means to fight inflation and to advocate a commodity standard for the money supply, particularly gold. A return to the gold standard, it was held, could control prices automatically without having to suffer the consequences of high interest rates. Again, not many economists subscribed to the return to the gold (or any other commodity) standard, as just a glance at the record would reveal that prices were not controlled very well by the gold standard of the past.

Nor could the supply-siders be blamed for the political compromises that forced the tax cuts to be spread out over three years. Most supply-siders would have preferred to have the tax reductions all at once to forestall the postponement of plans until the whole program was in place. Still, as indicated earlier, they got most of what they wanted, which is more than policymakers of the past could boast.

Finally, there was a large tax increase in 1982, which supply-siders fought as counterproductive. In the face of looming large budget deficits, however, Mr. Reagan retreated into standard orthodoxy and backed a large tax increase to raise revenue, apparently rejecting temporarily the Laffer supply-side nostrums that a tax decrease would bring in more revenue. In late 1982 he favored a five-cent-per-gallon tax on gasoline, for highways, bridges, and mass transit, which was passed in January 1983, and an increase in Social Security taxes to rescue the system—at least according to the commission appointed to study the finances of the Social Security System.

Reagan, however, was always primarily in favor of lower taxes, even when he was governor of California.[29] Thus, to advocate tax increases must have been due to pleas from old-time Republicans to do something about the deficit. An easy and costless thing to do was to advocate a balanced-budget amendment to the Constitution, so that he could show support for the principle without having to abide by the restraint. So while running up the largest deficits in U.S. history, Reagan enthusiastically endorsed the balanced-budget amendment, as did fellow conservatives in Congress and elsewhere.

The Tax Equity and Fiscal Responsibility Act of 1982 was signed into law in August by Mr. Reagan, who uncharacteristically prohibited cameras from recording the event. It was billed as the largest tax increase in history, amounting to nearly $99 billion in total over FY 1983–85. Its major provisions can be summarized briefly: For individuals, modified minimum tax provisions reduced the medical-expense and casualty deductions by limiting the deduction to losses in excess of 5 percent of adjusted gross income and to 10 percent, respectively. For business, the act scaled back some tax preferences and amounts subject to the investment tax credit; repealed the more generous accelerated depreciation schedules due to go into effect in 1985 and 1986; and repealed the safe-harbor leasing provision of the 1981 Tax Act after 1982 (which permitted owners of assets to "sell" them to another firm, which would take depreciation and an investment tax credit and then "lease" the assets back to the original firm, which would use them in its operations). On compliance, the act imposed a 10 percent withholding on dividends and interest payments, similar to the withholding on wages, to improve tax compliance—they were always taxable. This provision of the act was repealed after an overwhelming campaign by banks and businesses complaining about the cost of administering the provision. As to other taxes, the act raised the federal unemployment tax to $7,000 and the rate to 3.5 percent; increased the excise tax on aviation; doubled the cigarette excise tax to 16 cents per pack for the period January 1, 1983, through September 30, 1985; and increased the excise tax on telephone services from 1 to 3 percent for 1983 through 1985.

Some of the stimulus of the tax cuts was undoubtedly removed by the increase in taxes in 1982. Supply-siders complained that their efforts were undermined, and to some extent they have some basis for that claim. Monetarists, too, claimed that their advice was not taken in total by the Federal Reserve System. They disclaim the Federal Reserve's action as monetarist, but then they have seldom been happy with the monetary policy of the System.

The avowed aim of the Federal Reserve over this period was to reduce the rate of inflation. As a consequence, its policies helped to bring about the recession of 1981–82 and with it a decline in the rate of inflation. Prices, however, dropped more sharply than anyone had anticipated. This was due partly to the severity of the recession and partly to the decline in oil and food prices, which were unrelated to the administration's economic policies. In any case, the administration took credit for the reduction in inflation without claiming credit for the recession.[30]

Yet even after the Federal Reserve saw the signs of recovery, it was still concerned over the possible recrudescence of inflation and it remained "committed to a course of monetary discipline that is essential to avoid a resurgence of inflationary pressures as economic expansion proceeds."[31]

How much did monetary policy reduce inflation? One estimate attributes nearly 50 percent of the decline in prices to the recession, 33 percent to the autonomous decline in food and energy prices, and the

rest to the change in the computation of the homeownership component of the CPI. Accordingly, "perhaps ⅓ to ½ of the decline in
inflation since 1980 would have occurred without a severe recession."[32]
The share of the reduction in inflation attributed to monetary policy
depends upon one's views as to the cause of the recession; the more
tight money is blamed for the recession, the more monetary policy can
be given credit for the decline in prices.

Monetary policy certainly helped to keep interest rates high, and
the consequences for investment spending have already been indicated. The effects on the housing sector and small businesses were
particularly devastating. New housing starts, for instance, which had
just recovered from the recession of 1980, now plunged—17 percent
from 1981 to 1982. Small businesses were severely hampered, and
many were either stymied in their growth or went bankrupt.

Large firms, meanwhile, benefited from the tax cuts and took the
opportunity to venture into other industries to diversify or take over
other firms. Du Pont paid $7.5 billion (borrowing over $3 billion from a
group of banks) for Conoco; Flur, $2.7 billion for St. Joe Minerals; Gulf
Oil, $325 million for Kemmerer Coal; and U.S. Steel, $5.9 billion for a
controlling interest in Marathon, and so forth and so on. Lack of funds
did not stop the larger firms from playing "paper entrepreneurialism";
for if profits were not at hand, banks were ready to lend for these
purposes. "Despite widely advertised concern over a capital shortage
and calls for corporate tax breaks to spur new investment, firms bent
on acquisition have seldom been deterred by price."[33]

The wave of mergers and takeovers did not bother the Reagan
administration nor its chief of the Justice Department's Antitrust
Division, William Baxter, who expressed no concern for the concentration of wealth and power in fewer conglomerates.[34] Thus very early in
the Reagan administration the word went out that this would be an
extremely probusiness administration, surpassing even the dreams of
business. Later the antitrust cases against AT&T and IBM were
dropped, and that early trend continued all through the first term of
the Reagan years.

Again this is another example of an industrial policy without
acknowledging it. The refusal to apply antitrust statutes or pursue
antitrust cases was often justified on the grounds that these laws were
obsolete in the era of global capitalism, where foreign competition was
challenging U.S. industries. While many economists would agree with
the diagnosis, some would question the beneficiaries of the relaxation;
still more would question the tax breaks that favored the "wrong"
industries. The tax breaks favored many industries that had plenty of
cash and did not require additional funds for investment, like oil

companies, so that additional incentives for investment were simply superfluous. And if cash were not available, banks were somehow able to lend funds in a period of monetary restraint.

Interestingly, the real rate of interest (monetary interest rates minus the inflation rate) remained abnormally high compared to past relationships. While prices fell dramatically, nominal interest rates remained sticky. Banks, which were squeezed in the 1970s when real rates of interest were often negative, either were fearful of the return of inflation and kept their interest rates high, or took the opportunity to recoup profits lost in the recent past. This boon to lenders and savers came at the expense of borrowers, of course, and many painful losses were incurred in businesses, construction, and farming.

What was achieved, then, in the first two years of the Reagan administration's "Program for Economic Recovery"? A brief look at the goals and results is revealing.

As to the budget, the rate of spending by government was not slowed, but actually increased from 22.4 percent of GNP in 1980 to 23.8 percent in 1982 (and to 24.7 percent in 1983). (See Table 14.4.) National defense spending was increased as promised from 5.2 percent in 1980 to 6.1 percent of GNP in 1982; non-Social-Security domestic spending was reduced to 8.4 percent, from 9.3 percent. The cuts in

Table 14.4   Budget Outlays and Receipts as Percent of GNP, 1980–83

Item	1980	1981	1982	1983
Total outlays	22.4	22.8	23.8	24.7
National defense	5.2	5.5	6.1	6.5
Net interest	2.0	2.4	2.8	2.8
Other	15.1	15.0	15.0	15.4
Non-OASDHI*	9.3	8.8	8.4	8.4
OASDI	5.8	6.2	6.6	6.9
Social Security	4.6	4.8	5.1	5.3
Medicare	1.2	1.4	1.5	1.6
Total receipts	20.1	20.8	20.2	18.6
OASDHI	5.3	5.6	5.8	5.7
Other	14.8	15.2	14.4	12.9
Deficit	2.3	2.0	3.6	6.1

*Old age, survivors, disability, and health insurance.
Source: Council of Economic Advisors, *Economic Report of the President* (Washington, DC: GPO, 1984), p. 29.

social programs would have been even larger, but Congress restored many of the programs scheduled for elimination and funded others scheduled for more severe cuts. Any progress made in reducing government spending, however, was reversed by the rising costs of interest payments—in fact, interest costs on the rising deficit exceeded the cuts in social programs!

Taxes were reduced as planned, but the economy plunged into a deep recession and (together with the reductions in social programs that reduced consumption spending immediately, and the increases in national defense spending that would be spread out over several years) the budget deficit soared.

Hopes for a balanced budget faded, and despite the president's homilies on the virtues of a balanced budget and the administration's changing identifications of it—all sorts of evils, from inflation to high interest rates, to the trade collapse, and to higher taxes in the future of our grandchildren—the goal was virtually abandoned. Neither support for the balanced-budget amendment nor the president's call (in the State of the Union speech in January 1983) for "standby" tax increases of up to $50 billion annually if the deficit was not cut to 2.5 percent of GNP, were convincing. Instead, the deficits were now hailed as a means to reduce government spending, since in the face of such large deficits, no new programs would be introduced and many of the old ones could be cut back. Large deficits would focus attention on government spending and refocus the issues for debate as well.

As for inflation, clearly prices were reduced and reduced even more than anticipated in a shorter time period. Yet as already noted, much of the decline was due to declines in food and energy prices and the rest to monetary policy and the recession. Reaganomics could not (but did) claim much of the credit for the fall in prices, at least without accepting the blame for the sharp recession.

With regard to regulation, while many regulatory rules were indeed rewritten, the trend toward deregulation, begun under Carter, was not followed through. Neither was the threat to eliminate the Department of Education, the EPA, and the Department of Energy carried out. In fact, the EPA was wracked with scandals, and in its zeal to carry out the apparent wishes of the president, its rulings were frequently overturned or modified until Secretary James Watt was forced to resign in what would otherwise have been an insignificant incident.

In summary, Reaganomics must be judged a failure in the short run, since it did not achieve its goals but produced a horrendous recession. Even the period's major achievement, the reduction in the inflation rate, cannot be attributed to the administration's plans.

Costs and Benefits of Reduced Inflation

Were the reduction of a few percentage points in the inflation rate (the remainder would have occurred anyway) and the redistribution of government spending toward militarization of the economy worth the costs? The benefits of a lower rate of inflation are not easily summarized, since the evidence on the effects of inflation has been surprisingly scarce. Some of the adverse effects of uncertainty on investment, saving, and planning in general are certainly reduced, as are the disrupting effects of the dead-weight loss of people spending time trying to adjust their behavior to anticipated future price changes. Who wins and loses in periods of inflation is more difficult to determine and hence more controversial, and the conflicting evidence cannot easily be digested.[35]

The acceptance of the redistribution of government spending, an avowed aim of the Reagan administration, depends upon value judgments. Whether or not the United States had fallen behind the Soviet Union in military preparedness (as claimed by Reagan) cannot be determined by the public, but subsequent analysis revealed this claim to be unfounded.[36] Nor is there persuasive evidence that the public really wanted the wholesale elimination of social programs, at least those that benefited the middle class, such as Social Security and Medicare, but the Reagan administration used the frustration over the lack of sufficient results of the programs to slash them in the name of economy.

Putting these issues aside for the present, the question remains, Were the changes worth the drastic costs? Only a partial answer will be addressed in this section, reserving for later a more complete assessment of the Reagan experiment. One study that assumes that the unemployment rate had remained at 6 percent concludes that the economy would have produced $654 billion more from 1980 to 1983 and that the loss fell primarily on workers (58 percent), as against corporate profits (25 percent) and farmers (13 percent).[37] Sawhill and Stone put the matter succinctly: "The odds of being drafted into the fight against inflation increase steadily the lower the individual's earnings and family income to begin with. The relative income losses suffered by the working heads of poor families, for example, are four to five times as great as the losses for those heading high-income families ... and the 1981–1982 recession drove 4.3 million people into poverty."[38]

Mr. Reagan and to some extent the Federal Reserve were determined to apply and continue the cold-bath approach to the economy to fight inflation. Unlike past administrations, this one was willing to stay the course, even after the recession had developed, regardless of the costs. What if the administration had been more willing to reduce inflation gradually instead of cold turkey? A recession might still have ensued, but it would have been much less severe and devastating.[39] History cannot be replayed, however, nor can adverse economic effects on individuals or the society be mitigated. These costs will be assessed after the remainder of the Reagan administration has been recorded.

A Keynesian Economic Recovery Produces Deficits

The recovery began in 1983 and continued slowly throughout 1984 and 1985. While the Reagan administration claimed vindication for its policies, little of the recovery can be attributed to Reaganomics. As will become evident, this was a typical Keynesian recovery, owing scarcely anything to supply-side economics. Tables 14.5 and 14.6 provide the summary data for this period.

Real GNP increased 3.7 percent in 1983, 6.8 percent in 1984, and an estimated 2.4 percent for 1985. As a consequence, the unemployment rate declined to 7.4 percent in 1984, but remained at that level until the summer of 1985, when it declined to approximately 7 percent, where it remained at year's end. The administration, continuing its optimistic forecasts, maintained that real GNP would grow by 4 percent each year until 1989, when it would taper off gradually to 3.6 percent in 1990. Such growth rates could be expected to drive down the unemployment rate by 0.2 or 0.3 percentage points a year until 1991, when the unemployment rate would be 5.6 percent. Again, not many private economists were willing to forecast such growth in the economy, especially in view of the 1 percent decline in capital outlays for 1986 that was revealed in a Department of Commerce survey taken the last quarter of 1985.

Inflation, however, seemed under control, as prices continued their moderate increases. For 1985 the preliminary estimates promise more of the same, as the GNP deflator shows a 3.3 percent increase, the CPI a 3.6 percent increase, and no increase in the PPI. The administration, pleased with the results, forecast a 4 percent increase in the GNP deflator for 1986, 4.1 percent for 1987, gradually falling to 2.0 percent in 1991.[40]

The reasons for the economy's failure to grow as forecast and to reduce the unemployment rate are numerous, but among the more important is the failure of investment spending to create new jobs.

Real investment spending increased by 13.7 percent in 1983 and 31 percent in 1984, but a large portion of that was in rebuilding inventories (see Table 14.5). Barry Bosworth took a closer look at the growth in investment spending and found that little could be attributed to the tax cuts that were supposed to stimulate investment incentives. He found that office equipment and business automobiles accounted for 93 percent of the growth in equipment spending since

Table 14.5 Selected Economic Series, 1983–84 (dollar amounts in billions)

	1983		1984	
	Amount (dollars)	Percent Change from 1982	Amount (dollars)	Percent Change from 1983
GNP	3,304.8	7.7	3,661.3	10.8
GNP (in 1972 dollars)	1,534.7	3.7	1,639.0	6.8
Consumption	1,009.2	4.8	1,062.6	5.3
Investment	221.0	13.7	289.7	31.1
Change in inventory	6.8	65.4	27.8	772.2
Net exports	12.6	−57.6	−15.5	−223.0
Government	291.9	−0.3	302.2	3.5
Federal	116.2	−0.7	122.4	5.3
State and Local	175.7	0	179.8	2.3
Unemployment rate (percent)	9.5	—	7.4	
Manufacturing capacity-utilization rate (percent)	75.2	—	81.7	
Output per hour of all persons (percent change)	—	2.7	—	3.6
Compensation per hour (percent change)	—	4.3	—	4.7
In real terms	—	1.1	—	0.4
Unit labor costs (percent change)	—	1.6	—	1.1
Prices: percent change				
GNP index (year to year)	—	3.8	—	3.7
PPI (year to year)	—	1.6	—	2.1
CPI (year to year)	—	3.2	—	4.3
CPI (December to December)	—	3.8	—	4.0

Source: Council of Economic Advisors, *Economic Report of the President* (Washington, DC: GPO, 1985).

1979, and these areas were either unaided by the tax cuts or actually had tax increases (computers) in 1981–82. Investment spending undeniably increased, of course, but much of it was being produced outside the United States. According to Bosworth, "Thus, for the American capital-goods producers the 1980–1982 recession was very severe; the recovery, incomplete. Not only is American investment being financed by well-publicized foreign borrowing; much of it is being built overseas."[41]

If the recovery could not be attributed to domestic investment spending, neither could it be attributed to foreign trade. Exports (in real terms) fell steadily until mid-1983 and then began to climb back to prerecession levels. Imports, however, rose steadily throughout the period, increasing by over 27 percent from 1983 to 1984. The U.S. merchandise trade balance soared from $ −27 billion in 1981 to over $ −107 billion in 1984. Preliminary data for 1985 show no improvement in trade balances.

Government spending also cannot be given much credit for the recovery, since federal spending actually declined in 1983 and rose slightly in 1984 and 1985. The increases in spending were mainly in national defense and interest payments on the debt.

We are left with the increases in personal consumption expenditures as the major explanatory variable in accounting for the recovery. Keynesians would have predicted that reductions in taxes would stimulate consumption, which would increase national income, which would increase investment spending, create jobs, reduce unemployment, and increase output, and so on. This scenario is straight out of the textbook for a Keynesian solution to a slumping economy; it is in direct contrast to the scenario of supply-siders.

Creating deficits to cure recessions is no problem for Keynesians, but for conservative Republicans it is close to treason. Having railed against budget deficits for many years and having blamed them for everything from inflation to the destruction of the American way, they had to stand by and watch a recovery that was largely due to federal budget excesses. The tax cuts brought the deficits about, of course, but this could not be admitted, either. The solution to their dilemma was easy—forget about the deficit except in speeches and homilies; the fight over the balanced budget appeared to be over. It was not an easy trick to accomplish, with budget deficits of $207 billion in 1983 and even larger ones looming in the future (see Table 14.6), especially since they were approaching a quadrupling of Carter's last budget deficit.

Then in October 1985, a rider was attached to the Senate bill to raise the debt ceiling, which would force the federal government to balance its budget by FY 1991. Promoted by Senators Phil Gramm (R., Texas) and Warren Rudman (R., New Hampshire), the rider proposed to cut the budget deficit in stages by setting target deficits for each year, which, if not met, would require across-the-board spending reductions in all federal programs. This shock-treatment effect was held to be necessary in order to spur the president and Congress to act responsibly with regard to government spending and budget deficits.

House Democratic leaders, taken by surprise, managed to delay action on the debt-ceiling bill and its rider until they could formulate some plan of their own. Clearly, this was a sensitive issue for politicians, since it forced them to admit either that they had not acted responsibly in the past or that they did not really favor a balanced budget and thus planned to act irresponsibly in the future.

The president, too, was put on the spot, since he was on record as favoring a balanced budget and reduced government spending, but

Table 14.6   Federal Government Budgets, 1983–85 (billions of dollars)

	1983	1984	1985 (estimated)
Fiscal Year Basis			
Receipts	600.6	666.5	734.1
Individual taxes	288.9	298.4	334.5
Corporate taxes	37.0	56.9	61.3
Social Security	209.0	239.4	265.2
Other	65.7	71.8	73.1
Expenditures	808.3	851.8	946.3
National defense	209.9	227.4	252.7
Income security	122.6	112.7	128.2
Social Security	223.3	235.8	254.4
Interest	90.0	111.1	129.4
Other	162.5	164.8	181.6
Surplus or Deficit (−)	−207.8	−185.3	−212.3
National income and product account basis (calendar year)			
Receipts	658.1	725.1	785.7
Expenditures	837.5	898.0	983.0
Surplus or Deficit (−)	−179.4	−172.9	−197.3

Source: Council of Economic Advisors, *Economic Report of the President* (Washington, DC: GPO, 1986), pp. 341, 343.

across-the-board cuts would reduce national defense spending and might affect his ability to control the allocation of the spending reductions. In the end he endorsed the bill over the objections of Casper Weinberger, the secretary of defense.

After prolonged debate the Senate–House Conference Committee emerged with a bill that indeed did require a balanced budget by FY 1991. The House leaders did manage to exempt veterans' programs, six antipoverty programs, and limit the cuts in Medicare, to add to the other exempt areas—Social Security and interest on the national debt. Thus a sizable chunk of the budget was eliminated—approximately 40 percent. The bill set target deficits for the next few years—$144 billion for FY 1987, $108 billion for FY 1988, and so on, until the deficit disappeared in FY 1991. In addition, $11.7 billion in spending cuts was required for FY 1986 to make the Republicans feel some pain in the 1986 elections.

This bizarre plan would work as follows: Early in January, the Office of Management and Budget (OMB) and the Congressional Budget Office (CBO) are required to determine whether the target deficit for the year will be reached and if not, how much spending reduction is necessary. These agencies then submit their findings to the General Accounting Office, which then informs the president on January 20. If the president and Congress cannot agree on the spending cuts necessary, across-the-board spending cuts will be made by the president. The only stipulation, inserted by the House, is that half the cuts must come from national defense.

In December the Gramm–Rudman Act was signed into law by the president, understandably without fanfare and TV cameras. Opposed to any tax increases, he was facing drastic cuts in national defense spending and no way out of the target restraints. Besides, the act gives both Congress and the president ample time for posturing and a real potential for a stalemate in the confrontation. The budget process had already broken down in the fall of 1985, and prospects for cooperation in the future seemed remote, regardless of artificial restraints.

Most economists labeled the act nonsensical and silly, for it imposes restraints regardless of the state of the economy, cuts programs without regard to merit, and in general makes a shambles of sound fiscal policy in favor of the panacea of a balanced budget. Legal scholars question the constitutionality of the act, since it makes unelected officials determine spending and transfers spending decisions to the president.

Thus not many were in favor of this meat-ax approach to government, not even some who voted for it, but the political costs of opposing it appeared too great. The test would have come in FY 1987 when it would have been first applied, but it was declared unconstitutional by the Supreme Court in July 1986.

What, then, did Reaganomics contribute to the recovery and to the improved state of the economy? Perhaps the only real factor that can be identified is the spirit of optimism that the president exuded. He seemed to inspire a confidence in the future that surely contributed to favorable expectations on the part of many. While often berated and labeled insensitive by critics, his cheery outlook probably helped to prevent, or moderate, the pessimism about the U.S. economy that is often recognized, if not always articulated. For the remainder, the reduction in inflation and the recovery of economic activity, and so on, Reaganomics was not responsible. That does not mean that the experiment did not have repercussions on the economy and on the society; indeed, there are many alterations in both, and it is to these that we must look for the real impact of the Reagan administration.

Short-Run Legacy of Reagan Economics: Polarization and Poverty

The expanding economy played a major role in the reelection of Ronald Reagan in 1984. So did the invasion of Grenada, as the theme "America is back" struck a responsive chord. Of particular interest in this campaign was the personal charm of the president, since he avoided most of the issues and made his customary pitches to his loyal following. He refused to talk about the deficit, blaming it on Congress, and refused to consider any tax increase, referring questions about taxes to a Treasury study under way that would examine tax issues. In short, except for one poor showing in a televised debate, Reagan proved once again to be a master campaigner and the great communicator.

His opponent was Walter Mondale, vice-president under Carter, along with Congresswoman Geraldine Ferraro (NY) as his running mate. Mondale mistakenly identified the deficit as a major concern of the U.S. public and hence harped on the huge deficits created by the Reagan administration; to cure the problem, Mondale proposed a tax increase and claimed the moral high ground, since he believed Reagan would also increase taxes if reelected. Contrary to Mondale's beliefs, the public was not at all that bothered by the deficit and certainly did not support a tax increase to resolve the problem. His campaign was doomed after these positions were made public, and no other positions he took would have had any impact; nor would his selection of the first woman to run for the national ticket in a major political party make that much difference.

So while the Republicans were burying the issues of deficits and taxes and should have been on the defensive, the Democrats found themselves saddled with potential offensive issues that ended up putting them on the defensive. It was that kind of campaign—confusing, ineptly conducted, with the issues fading into the background and personalities allowed once again to determine the outcome.

The election was anticlimatic, as Reagan won 59 percent of the popular vote and 525 electoral votes. This was certainly a convincing win; the trouble was how to interpret it. Was it a personal victory for a popular president or a shift toward more conservative ideology? With time the answer will become clear; some thoughts on the subject are given later. One indicator would be the congressional makeup after the election. The Republicans lost two Senate seats but still retained control; the Democrats lost thirteen House seats but still retained control of that body. These results are scarcely indicators of any major shift in political alignment, but of course it is necessary to go beyond the voting patterns for Congress, since so many local issues are involved.

A contrary piece of evidence is the fact that most of Reagan's policy moves were anticipated by Carter—the increases in national defense, deregulation, tax reductions, more restrictive monetary policy, and, in general, fiscal conservatism as spending was reduced. The only difference was that Reagan was willing to push his program through quickly and stick with it, regardless of short-run results. Had Carter won reelection, the movement would have been much slower and would likely have been reversed at the first sign of serious economic problems. Mr. Reagan was willing to stick with the cold-bath technique, while past presidents had retreated when faced with severe economic conditions. The point remains, however, that the trend toward fiscal conservatism predated Reagan's "new beginnings" and does indicate a disenchantment with government and its attempts to solve social problems—a disenchantment that Reagan was able to capitalize on.

The leaders were responding, of course, to perceived public opinions about government spending. Indeed, polls always indicate that government is spending too much and taxing too heavily. Yet the public wants to spend more—more for national health—more for protecting the environment—more for education—more for aid to cities—more to aid minorities. Poll after poll reveals that people are against spending for others' programs but are for more spending on programs that benefit them. The public overwhelmingly supports wage and price controls (61/39 percent), national health insurance (67/33 percent), government-guaranteed jobs (77/23 percent), and opposes only "welfare" with its image of undeserved handouts to people who do not want to work.[42]

Thus, the apparent movement toward conservative ideology must be reexamined and questioned. The seeming contradiction between what political leaders interpret as the mood of the public and what the public really feels permits a great deal of confusion and admits the possibility of clever exploitation of the many by the few. It is possible to play off one group against another, to play the broker in a game that promises one group this and another group that, and in the end this catering to special interests separates the nation into blocs. The polarization of the nation into groups who win in the game and those who do not, or who do not win as much as promised, sets up a possible confrontation and represents a dangerous and cynical ploy.

As one critic put it, "The President and co-conspirators have been conducting undeclared war against blacks and Hispanics, welfare clients, women, children, and blue-collar workers. Under way is still another episode of class conflict between rich and poor. Americans are uncomfortable with the idea of social and economic class. No major politician, least of all virtuosos of sweet talk like the Republican leaders in Congress and the head man himself, entertains the notion of politics as class conflict."[43]

The Short-Run Legacy of Reaganomics

The first short-run legacy of Reaganomics is thus the polarization of the nation. Perhaps the most divisive partition pitted the haves against the have-nots. The large redistribution of income, wealth, and economic power from lower- to higher-income groups was accomplished in the name of economic progress; both the tax and expenditure cuts came at the expense of lower-income groups.

The increase in unemployment has already been discussed, but the distribution of it is the pertinent issue here. The inflation fighters were largely drawn from those who could least afford to fight. For instance, when the unemployment rate was hovering between 10 and 11 percent in late 1982 and early 1983, the official rate for whites was 9.6 percent and for blacks, 18.9 percent. For black teenagers the rate was nearly 50 percent for males and almost as high for females. The unemployment rate for white teens was only half these rates.

As a result of the recession, blue-collar workers suffered more than salaried and white-collar ones. For those who remained employed, real wages in terms of average weekly earnings fell in 1981–82 by −1.5 percent and −1.3 percent. For those who lost their jobs in that same period, unemployment insurance ran out for over 137,000 of them, leaving many without a source of income.

These patterns are familiar, of course, but what makes the situation different this time is that this very deep recession rendered labor powerless and unions ineffectual (this legacy is discussed separately), and more and more people ended up in the poverty status. Those who did not were forced in many cases to accept lower-paying jobs or forced to become part-time workers.

The unequal impact of unemployment was only the most obvious outcome that divided the nation into those affected and those who were not. Even in the recovery period, unemployment remained at the high rate of 7 percent. Let us look briefly at other measures that lend support to the polarization hypothesis.

The tax and expenditure actions of 1981–82 were regarded by many as inequitable and widely publicized as such at the time of enactment. Congress must therefore also share the responsibility for the redistribution of the tax burden from higher- to lower-income groups, as well as for the expenditure cuts. Analyses of the effects of the tax and expenditure cuts vary, but one reliable source, the Congressional Budget Office, estimated them as shown in Table 14.7.

Table 14.7 needs no elaboration, with the wealthiest 1.5 percent of the population scheduled to receive $35 billion in gains, as against the loss of $20 billion for those households with incomes under

Table 14.7   Impacts of Budget and Tax Cuts Enacted 1981–83 (billions of dollars)

	Households under $20,000	Households over $80,000
1983	−4.2	+9.9
1984	−7.5	+11.9
1985	−8.0	+13.1
Three-year total	−19.7	+34.9

Source: Congressional Budget Office, *The Combined Effects of Major Changes in Federal Taxes and Spending Programs since 1981,* (Washington, DC, April 1984).

$20,000. For individual taxpayers with incomes over $80,000, the gain would be $24,000, and for those with incomes below $10,000, the loss would be $1,100 for 1983–85.

The Congressional Budget Office report also indicated that nearly one-third of the budget cuts in the administration's first three years came from low-income programs; nearly one-half of total reductions in benefits fell on households with incomes below $10,000 per year; households over $80,000 bore only 1 percent of the budget cuts enacted in the first three years.[44] Indeed, the percentage reductions (in real terms) for programs targeted for low-income families (the means-tested programs such as food stamps, AFDC, housing subsidies, legal services, education and training, Medicaid, and the like) were reduced 40 percent from 1981 to 1984.

Many other studies documented the inequities of the tax and budget cuts, but little would be served by summarizing them, for even the supporters of the administration's policies acknowledge the unequal burden.[45] The aim of the administration was quite simply to dismantle the New Deal and the Great Society programs and policies; it made some advances in that direction and was forced to retreat in others, especially Social Security.[46]

The result of this subterfuge was that many people fell through the net, either entering the poverty ranks for the first time or ensuring their stay in poverty. Table 14.8 shows the rise in the poverty rate from

Table 14.8   Poverty Rate in the United States, 1980 and 1982 (percent of population)

	Poverty Rate	
Characteristic	1980	1982
Total	13.2	15.0
White	10.4	12.0
Black	32.4	35.6
Hispanic	26.2	29.9
Children under 6	20.3	23.8
Elderly	15.9	14.6
Married couples	6.3	7.6
Families headed by women	33.3	36.3

Source: U.S. Department of Commerce, Bureau of the Census, Current Population Reports, Series p. 60, 1983.

1980 to 1982. The data do not include income in kind; if such benefits were included, the numbers would be reduced, but the relative percentage changes would remain. The increase in poverty rates is dramatic, as all groups but the elderly were affected adversely. Of particular interest to the hypothesis is the increase in black and Hispanic poverty rates and in the "feminization of poverty," evidenced by the phenomenal number of families headed by females. Indeed, the poverty rate for black and Hispanic female-headed families is well over one-half.

Furthermore, many of the budget cuts made by the administration affected predominantly women (and even more tragically, children)—cuts in AFDC, housing subsidies, food stamps, training programs, day-care services, and so on, making the cuts that much more severe. Black families in general fared badly with the budget cuts, since they were more likely to fall into the income groups that used the government programs the most. One study found that the 1981 budget cuts affected black families three times as much as white families.[47]

The Reagan administration was accused of racist policies, which became another item in the polarization argument. Its policies severely affected the black community, wich was already smarting over the administration's opposition to the civil rights bill extension, its antibusing stance, its policy toward apartheid in South Africa, its Latin American policies, and its opposition to affirmative action programs.

Finally, a look at the distribution of income lends support to the unfairness charge and to the concern for the redistribution of economic power. Table 14.9 provides the summary data.

The income shares, by quintiles, again shows the trend toward greater inequality. The distribution is but one more piece of evidence supporting the belief that the nation was being divided by the Reagan administration's policies. Indeed, Lester Thurow could write of the decline of the middle class (defined as a household falling between 75 and 125 percent of the median household income).[48] He attributed the decline to the changing structure of U.S. industry, which was losing middle-income-type jobs in international trade competition, and to the newer growth industries offering either high- or low-paying jobs. Social factors also play a role, as the number of two-earner families is growing, while at the other end, female-headed families are nearly always low-income ones, and the number of this type of family is growing also. Unemployment, too, accounts in some measure for the fall-out of the middle class, as suggested above.

Whatever the cause, here again is another way to view the polarization of the nation. Both ends of the spectrum of income classes were growing, while the middle was disappearing. Thurow was concerned for democracy, as the middle class acted as a buffer to lower-class rebellion, as predicted by Marx. He viewed the middle class as the preserver of capitalism and as a moderator to its excesses, largely through its support of social programs to help the poor. For capitalists this should be a rather dire warning.

The Reagan administration's policies were certainly divisive, pitting race against race, the haves against the have-nots, males against females, cities against states, and region against region. Cities were pitted against states in competition for block grants that replaced the categorical grants with their specific formulas of how the money was to be distributed. Now, in the latest version of a new federalism, Reagan turned to block grants (no strings attached) in the hope of eventually turning over many federal programs to the states and localities. While his New Federalism did not get very far, the block grants did create a scramble for the reduced funds available.

Taxes at the state and local level would have to be increased, if previous programs were to be continued or enlarged, or new ways to share state revenues with the towns and cities would have to be devised. In the rust belt or snow belt of the North and Northeast, already hit by unemployment, the reductions in federal grants for housing and welfare programs hurt the most, since a large proportion of the population in these areas was affected. For these areas to raise taxes was tantamount to inviting industry to move to the sun belt,

Table 14.9   Income Distribution in the United States

U.S. Population in Quintiles	Total Percent of Income Received			Comparison of 1983 to Past Percentages
	1978	1981	1983	
Top 5 percent	15.6	15.4	15.8	
Highest fifth	41.5	41.9	42.7	Highest percent since 1950
Fourth fifth	24.1	24.4	24.4	Highest percent since 1950
Middle fifth	17.5	17.4	17.1	Lowest percent since 1947
Second fifth	11.6	11.3	11.1	Lowest percent on record
Lowest fifth	5.2	5.0	4.7	Lowest percent since 1961

Sources: U.S. Department of Commerce, *Money Income of Households, Families and Persons in the United States,* 1983, p. 49. Bureau of the Census, and *In These Times,* August 22–September 4, 1984.

where conditions were more favorable. Already the unemployed had begun the move to the sun belt in search of jobs. The headline in the *Wall Street Journal* of November 12, 1982, page 1, says it succinctly: "The Dispossessed: Homeless Northerners Unable to Find Work Crowd Sun Belt Cities: They Gather in Tent Towns and 'Cardboard Camps' Scavenging for Survival; Soup Kitchens and Suicides." "Homeless in America" became a headline for a *Newsweek* story.[49]

Thus the North was pitted against the South, and once again the unequal impact of the administration's policies was recognized. While the industries of the North were fading, the South and West were growing and attracting the high-tech firms that became the hope for the future of U.S. enterprise.

There were other sources of divisiveness in the Reagan policies, but enough have been discussed to support the contention that the administration's policies were destructive to the cohesiveness of the nation and to the sense of community. Whatever was hoped to be achieved by such brokerage policies would surely have been dissipated in unnecessary bitterness and competition among groups or factions.

The Reagan Administration and the Decline of Labor Power

Another legacy of the Reagan administration's first term was the decline of labor's power. The severe recession helped to send labor scrambling to keep the existing jobs and obviously reduced its bargaining power. Workers faced with plant shutdowns, or threatened with the loss of jobs if firms moved overseas, gave in to management demands for "give-backs"—reduced wages, two-tier wage systems, COLA scalebacks, changes in work rules. Forced to make concessions, workers in the automobile, steel, meat-packing, airline, and trucking industries gave up previous gains or accepted less for the future. Labor was indeed reeling from this deep recession, and the disorientation soon turned to bitterness when executives failed to make any sacrifice, or in the case of automobile executives, granted themselves large bonuses and promised not to reduce prices but rebuild profit margins.

It was not, however, just the recession that crippled labor. First, the Reagan administration was overtly hostile to labor; Reagan appointed Ray Donovan to be secretary of labor, a relatively unknown vice-president of a construction company, Schiavone Construction, which was accused of violating safety standards and accepting kickbacks from corrupt union officials. Mr. Donovan was not a very active secretary and certainly no spokesman for labor; cleared of charges in the first investigation, he eventually resigned in the face of further charges. Another Reagan appointee, Thorne Auchter, named Occupational Safety and Health Administration (OSHA) director, was vice-president of a Florida construction company that was cited for 48 OSHA violations. OSHA rules were revised and reinterpreted and enforcement cut back. Unions had used the law to attack hazardous conditions in the workplace, particularly in the chemical and oil industries. Now the movement to provide a safe workplace was stalled by officials who did not choose to enforce the law or tolerate extensions. Similarly, Reagan's appointees to the NLRB were decidedly pro-management and proceeded to reinterpret the laws they were called on to administer.

Thus, Mr. Reagan's antiregulation stance severely limited the operation of OSHA, and he also sought to repeal the Davis–Bacon Act that required the payment of union wages on government projects. The message was clear, but in case it was missed, Reagan's firing of all striking members of the Professional Air Traffic Controllers Organization (PATCO) in August 1981 really announced to all the antilabor stance of the administration, and the incident sent a clear message to all public employees of their precarious position. The workers who replaced the PATCO workers were forced to sign a pledge that they would not strike or engage in other job actions. As Frank Ackerman points out, in the 1920s employers fired union activists and replaced them with strikebreakers who were made to sign "yellow-dog" contracts promising not to unionize or strike. The history lesson was not lost on organized labor.[50]

Yet all of labor's woes were not inflicted by the current administration. Union membership, for instance, had been declining steadily for some time. In the early 1950s about one-third of the labor force belonged to unions; in 1975, 25 percent of the labor force was unionized, but in 1983 only about 19 percent. Hence, organized labor could not afford to lose more members or be put on the defensive and appear helpless.

The causes for the decline of the labor movement are easily listed. The decline of manufacturing and the rise of service-industry jobs clearly accounts for some of the decline in membership. Workers in the service sector have always been more difficult to organize, but now with jobs opening up in high-tech areas, the problems have changed along with the shift. The promise of more income is not sufficient for these new entrants, who view themselves as part of management; and being young, they are very mobile and uncommitted. They do not wish to waste time on strikes or drawn-out battles. Besides, many of the jobs moved to the sun belt, where antiunion attitudes are traditional and right-to-work laws have been enacted.[51]

Other factors that help explain the decline in union strength are internal: Unions failed to respond to changing conditions. They missed the opportunity to expand their membership by making equal opportunity a rallying cry. Instead, when women and blacks attempted to enter the jobs formerly denied them, unions frequently reacted by protecting their members from this unsought and unfortunately unwelcome competition. Unions found themselves on the wrong side of fair employment practices—legally or not.

Unions also failed to respond to opportunities to protect public health. Occupational exposure to hazards of all kinds could have been used to demonstrate that the labor movement was not deaf to contemporary concerns and could adapt. Instead, the health and safety laws that were enacted quickly came under pressure by an unsympathetic administration bent on deregulation.[52]

Again, the changing composition of the labor force works against union membership. Many women, glad to have a job, have not insisted on liberal fringe benefits and high salaries. Unions in the past were best when pressing for higher wages or higher fringe benefits, but such actions could lead to the loss of jobs, to automation, or to foreign competition.

Without pursing the matter further, it is clear that the Reagan administration was hostile to labor and took actions that reduced its power. Unions, however, were sometimes victims of circumstances they could not fully control, but were also unresponsive to those they could. The union movement declined partly because it could not or would not respond to changing labor market conditions or to the contemporary concerns of modern workers and society. Whether or not labor can react in the longer run is unclear. Some recognition of their problems has already begun. In the short run, however, labor was decimated and demoralized by the events of the 1980s.

Antitrust and Agricultural Policies

One of the professed aims of the Reagan administration when it took office was "to get government off our backs," meaning to reduce the regulation of business and society. The first of these, economic regulation, is designed to control the conditions of certain markets in regard to entry, prices, and efficiency. Despite the rhetoric and the special task force set up to find areas where government was intrusive, the Reagan administration did not deliver on its promise to continue deregulation. Only two initiatives have been passed to date: the deregulation of buses and some continuation of the deregulation of financial institutions.[53]

The major impact on business has been in the enforcement of the antitrust laws. As mentioned above, the administration clearly announced its views that big was not necessarily bad, that concentration did not ensure either excess profits or market power. Its attitude encouraged mergers, takeovers, and conglomeration; as a result, the further concentration of economic power in the future could become another legacy of the Reagan years. It is too soon to assess the long-term consequences of the new attitudes toward antitrust policy. Perhaps, in an era of intense international competition, the antitrust statutes are obsolete and unworkable, but a decision to ignore them should be debated by Congress and changes made if necessary; they should not be swept aside by administrative actions.

One highly visible example of the effects of the movement toward deregulation occurred in the banking industry. Many banks were stung by the shaky loans in the once highly desirable areas of energy, real estate, agriculture, and basic manufacturing. High real interest rates made the servicing of the debt burdensome for farmers, manufacturers, and construction firms, while the strong dollar encouraged imports and hurt domestic sales and exports. The casualties in the banking industry mounted. Many banks found themselves in trouble and many failed, including some large ones, such as Continental Illinois. To illustrate the extent of the problem, 10 banks failed in 1981, 42 in 1982 (a 320 percent increase), 48 in 1983, and 79 in 1984, nearly eight times the failure rate in 1981! In addition many more banks were on the problems list of the Federal Deposit Insurance Corporation (FDIC).[54]

In the areas of social regulation, the administration failed "to achieve fundamental changes in the legislative framework."[55] No important regulatory legislation was eliminated or fundamentally changed. True, operating procedures and enforcement policies were initiated, as in the case of OSHA, but the savings achieved by business were not nearly the amount anticipated when the assault on regulation was begun.[56] Political opposition to the policies of the administration gradually became so intense that further attempts at deregulation were all but abandoned in 1983. Public outcries over the regulations and policies of the EPA and the Department of the Interior forced the administration to retreat from further efforts of social deregulation.

While not exactly in the same category as other areas of regulation, the case of agriculture represents an interesting case for a laissez-faire administration. The Reagan administration's approach to the farm problem was simple—reduce the payments to farmers by cutting or eliminating price supports for dairy products and grain and cotton crops. Some reductions were made in milk supports, but Congress denied the president the full reductions in other crops.

Unfortunately for the administration, good harvests in 1981–82 and the sharp decline in exports due to the strong dollar helped to fill the storage bins with crops, and farm income stabilization outlays grew to $22 billion in FY 1982, from $9 billion in 1980, and the numbers were still growing.

Accordingly, the administration announced a new program to reduce supply and current stockpiles and raise prices—a payment-in-kind or PIK. Under PIK farmers who agreed to withdraw acreage of 10–30 percent of their land from production would receive up to 80–95 percent of the crops they would have grown on that land. No cash would be paid, and therefore the budgetary costs of farm subsidies would be reduced.

The PIK program, rational on the surface, failed to work as planned, owing to two circumstances.[57] First, the terms of the program were so generous that twice as many farmers signed up as anticipated, making it the largest acreage diversion in history. Second, a drought hit the farm belt, reducing supplies and increasing prices. The administration did not have enough supplies of some commodities to pay farmers for diverting their land and had to buy crops to fulfill the promises to farmers. The result was that agricultural price supports increased sharply (to $19 billion) and income stabilization outlays reached $33 billion in FY 1983.

Embarrassed, the administration abandoned the PIK program in 1984, except for wheat. Consumers paid twice for the failure of the program, once in higher food prices and again as taxpayers. Furthermore, producers of fertilizers and farm machinery were devastated by the decline in orders for their products, and many faced bankruptcy, including such firms as International Harvester. If farmers were not producing as much, they had less need for fertilizer or machinery, and repercussions of the reduced demand for farm supplies were widespread.

With the demise of PIK the farm program has been on hold, waiting for another solution, another program. The Reagan administration was not interested, however, in developing new farm programs, but instead began advocating free markets for agriculture. Congress, on the other hand, was pressured with pleas to rescue the farmer, and once again in December 1985 it responded. It extended the farm subsidies program for several years with the prospect of gradually reducing it afterwards.

The Legacy of Huge Budget and Trade Deficits

Without question the most discussed short-run legacies of the Reagan administration have been the huge twin deficits—the budget deficit and the trade deficit. That is not to say that the other short-run legacies discussed above (and others not covered) have not received attention or are not equally important, but only that the headlines have gone to the deficits. The administration itself is responsible for calling attention to the budget deficit and identifying it as a major problem. The trade deficit, much less understood and hence of much less immediate concern, was of interest to specialists and to those who regarded themselves hurt by international trade and finance.

The two deficits are related, as will become evident, but for purposes of exposition, let us analyze one at a time. Frequent references have already been made to the budget deficit, so that much of the discussion can be abbreviated.

When Mr. Reagan was campaigning for the presidency, he often cited the budget deficit as the symbol of what was wrong with government and identified the deficit as the cause of inflation. His promise to balance the budget by 1983 shows the importance he attached to the issue; later, when that proved impossible, he supported the balanced-budget amendment as a face-saving measure, but he essentially retained his belief in balanced budgets as the epitome of sound finance.

Yet the link between budget deficits and inflation was never strong[58] as Mr. Reagan would learn firsthand, since he produced the largest deficits in history while the price level was falling to the lowest rates of inflation since price controls went into effect in the early 1970s. Soon enough, the government deficit as the cause of inflation vanished as an explanation.

The goal of a balanced budget had a somewhat longer life, as so many conservative hopes rested on the pledges of the most conservative president in decades. In the end, however, Mr. Reagan's tax-cut package and military buildup were more important, and the balanced budget was subordinated to other goals. Conservatives were left with the balanced-budget amendment and finally, in frustration, the Gramm–Rudman Act discussed above.

The question then turned to just what the effects of budget deficits are. In fact, when the deficits began to appear, the administration was forced to downgrade their importance. The ambiguity toward deficits can be seen in the *Economic Report of the President*, 1982, where the possible effects of budget deficits are spelled out. Deficits cause or may cause interest rates to rise; uncertainty to grow about the ability of government to limit spending; crowding out to occur as government soaks up the available saving, bids up the interest rate by its need to fund the debt, and as businesses cannot afford to borrow or are outbid by government; burdens to shift to future generations, and so on. While these results are all bad, balancing the budget too quickly could be worse, and the balanced budget "needs to be seen as a long-run rule."[59]

Perhaps the supply-side forecasts, which proved so wildly optimistic, got in the way of rational analysis of the problems caused by deficits. But when Martin Feldstein replaced Murray Weidenbaum as chairman of the CEA in 1982, the wavering and uncertainty over the effects of the deficit was replaced as well. The *Economic Report of the President*, 1983 stated flatly that "the Federal budget deficit has become a major problem for the American economy. . . . A succession of large budget deficits is likely to reduce substantially the rate of capital formation . . . budget deficits would cause interest rates to rise . . . [and] the potential crowding out of private investment is immense."[60]

Much to the consternation of Mr. Reagan, the CEA continued to warn of the dire consequences of the budget deficit in its report of 1983. To show the "still . . . serious potential problem of a long string of huge budget deficits,"[61] the CEA divided the deficit into two components: a cyclical component that occurs because unemployment exceeds the rate of unemployment that is noninflationary (6.5 percent, according to the CEA), and hence revenues are less and expenditures are greater for unemployment and other social programs; and a structural component, which is that portion of the deficit that would remain even if unemployment were at the noninflationary rate of 6.5 percent. Table 14.10 gives the estimates for both components.

Clearly the information in Table 14.10 presents some alarming forecasts, for even if "full" employment were achieved, budget deficits would grow and be well above past amounts. The CEA did not feel that the economy would grow at sufficient rates to reduce the budget deficit by recovery means alone—either taxes would have to be increased or expenditures reduced further. Otherwise, the current trends of crowding out would continue—crowding out investment and crowding out exports. The recovery could well be affected adversely.

The Reagan administration was not pleased with this type of analysis and did its best to isolate and berate Feldstein for his analysis

Table 14.10   Cyclical and Structural Components of the Deficit, Fiscal Years 1980–83 (billions of dollars)

Fiscal Year	Total	Cyclical	Structural
1980	60	4	55
1981	58	19	39
1982	111	62	48
1983	195	95	101

Source: Council of Economic Advisors, *Economic Report of the President* (Washington, DC: GPO, 1984), p. 36.

and for his independence.[62] Feldstein resigned his post in the summer of 1984, and the following *Economic Report* did not discuss the budget deficit at all! The potentially serious problem had disappeared. In the words of Senator Daniel Patrick Moynihan (D., NY), "The Reagan administration came to office with, at most, a marginal interest in balancing the budget—contrary to rhetoric, there was no great budget problem at the time—but with a real interest in dismantling a fair amount of social legislation of the preceding fifty years. The strategy was to induce a deficit and use that as grounds for the dismantling."[63] Moynihan reminds us that the president himself warned the nation of his strategy in a speech on February 5, 1981, his first address to the nation: "There were always those who told us that taxes couldn't be cut until spending was reduced [Goldwater et al.]. Well, you know, we can lecture our children about extravagance until we run out of voice and breath. Or we can cure their extravagance by simply reducing their allowance."

The other serious short-run legacy that has long-run consequences is the trade deficit. The administration blamed the growing deficit on the strong dollar, the loss in net exports to debt-ridden countries, and the more rapid growth of the U.S. economy as opposed to its trading partners. We will concentrate here on the effects of the strong dollar, but a brief analysis of the other sources of the problem might be helpful.[64]

The loss of exports to Third World countries contributed to the U.S. trade deficit, as our former trading partners simply could not buy from us or were not allowed to import as much as a condition of further IMF help. In either case, the United States could not sell as much to these countries, particularly Latin American nations, and the trade balance with Latin American countries plummeted from a surplus of

$6 billion in 1980 to a deficit of $14 billion in 1983. These were the recipient countries of those recycled petro dollars in the 1970s, which borrowed when real interest rates were low, oil prices high, and inflation rates climbing. The loans seemed easy to repay, and neither the borrowers nor the lenders looked for any changes in economic conditions. Yet in the 1980s all of them did change, leaving these countries with a burdensome real debt they could not repay.[65]

Since most of the loans were short-term or had floating interest rates, the debt burden mounted as interest rates rose. Then the recession hit, their exports prices fell, and soon countries like Mexico, which was counting on its oil exports to furnish the necessary means to repay its debts, now found the value of their exports falling; as a consequence, the loans could not be repaid and not even the interest payments could be covered. The failure of these countries to repay their debts caused consternation among banks that had so cavalierly lent the funds, and many were in trouble because of the volume of loans to these Third World countries. Many loans were rolled over, a policy that merely postponed the problem, and many debtor countries were forced to resort to the IMF for help. The IMF responded by insisting on rather extreme austerity programs that discouraged imports and encouraged exports, among other conditions.

To the extent that the Reagan administration's policies brought about the reversal of conditions that would have permitted the repayment of these loans—for example, the recession or the strong dollar—it must share in the legacy of those actions. The effects on Third World countries have been devasting, of course, and their future development imperiled, but for our purposes, the legacy of a shaky financial structure is paramount. Too many banks, many of them quite large, such as Chase Manhattan, have been carrying these loans as if there were a likelihood of repayment. If they are not repaid, many banks face bankruptcy or severe financial stress. The banking structure, already in difficulties, could not withstand such a blow and would have to be rescued by government—hardly the type of policy favored by free-market advocates. Again the free-market advocacy disappears whenever financial markets are threatened, and it is clear that no large bank will be allowed to fail—this at a time of bank deregulation.[66]

The explanation that attributes the trade deficit to the slower growth of other industrial countries is less convincing. The growth of the economies of Japan and Canada has not lagged behind ours by very much. Our European trading partners, on the other hand, have experienced less rapid growth and could account for reduced U.S. exports. There are so many other explanations, however (quality, design), for the failure of U.S. firms to increase exports to the EEC countries that differential growth rates alone should not be isolated as the main cause. In fact, these countries benefited from the strong dollar, since their exports appeared more attractive as the exchange rate became favorable. If U.S. goods had been competitive, the demand for them would have risen and the exchange rate differences modified; even if exports continue to help pull the ECC countries out of their recession, it does not follow that U.S. exporters will benefit. Some of those markets may be lost or diminished for reasons other than depressed economic conditions, and that is a legacy that no one wants to claim.

Whatever the trade consequences of these explanations, it is the strong dollar that has preempted all other analyses. Not since the 1950s has the dollar dominated the world economy and put the world on virtually a dollar standard.[67] The dollar rose by over 58 percent from 1980 to 1984, as against the average of the ten most important trading partners' currencies, weighted by their shares in world trade. In real terms the increase was 52 percent, so that the dollar appreciated in both nominal and real terms, leaving U.S. firms to compete in world markets with prices that had risen much more than those of their foreign competitors. With this handicap, it is no wonder that U.S. firms lost markets to the lower-priced goods of competitors.

What caused the strong dollar? The administration identified three main causes: reduced expectations of inflation in the United States, increased real interest rates in the United States, and the safe haven in the United States for investors. The first of these, the reduced inflationary expectations of inflation in the United States made dollar assets attractive, and the increased demand for dollar assets drove up their prices and the exchange rate.

The increase in the real rate of interest has been the source of most of the strengthening of the dollar, according to many.[68] The real interest rate differential between U.S. and foreign assets made the United States an attractive place to invest for a higher rate of return. The result has been a heavy demand for U.S. assets, so heavy that the United States has become a net debtor to the rest of the world for the first time since pre-World War I. Not only are foreigners helping to finance our deficit, but many foreign firms have begun to invest in plants in the United States as well. These developments have made Europeans very unhappy with the economic policies of the United States, particularly the Federal Reserve's, in keeping interest rates high, thereby inhibiting their economic recovery, while capital flows out of Europe to the United States.

While the administration blamed the increase in the real interest rate on its tax policies of 1981, which increased the after-tax rate of return on new business investment, most other observers blamed it on the huge budget deficits.[69] But even when interest rates fell, the demand for U.S. assets continued strong. Falling interest rates could signal an even stronger recovery and an even brighter economic future for the United States. Thus the United States is the recipient of capital inflows, even with the rate of return falling. Just when the flow will stop, or how far interest rates have to fall to precipitate it, is anyone's guess for now, but if the dollar should fall, financing the deficit will be troublesome.

Some of the other effects of the strong dollar are not as obvious at first glance. For instance domestic prices were held down by the influx of foreign goods. Domestic firms were afraid to raise prices and risk losing additional market shares. Firms were also able to resist worker demands for wage increases, pleading the case of foreign competition restricting their ability to raise prices. Some firms responded to foreign competition by attempting to compete by modernizing their plants and equipment. Some additional domestic investment would be beneficial in the longer run, if the attempts proved successful. The problem was that the increase in investment did not aid the capital-goods industries in the United States, since the capital stock was imported from abroad.

As the United States was losing market shares of many goods traded internationally, so jobs were lost as well. Many firms moved abroad to produce where labor and other costs were less; other firms became sellers of the output of their competitors, as in the case of the automobile companies, or entered into joint venture projects to produce goods with foreigners who were former competitors. In many of these cases, labor was the loser, as either jobs moved abroad or those that remained were nonunion, lower paying, or in different (service) industries.

Finally, the United States is viewed as a safe haven for investment, both for its political and social climate and for its more rapid economic recovery. Foreign investment jumped from $325 billion in 1980 to $588 billion in 1983; of that increase, direct investment rose by over 60 percent and U.S. Treasury securities rose by over 110 percent. Even corporate securities were purchased by foreigners in amounts that exceeded a 50 percent increase in the period. Just how long the United States will be regarded as safe depends on conditions that cannot be precisely stated. After all, Europe is safe by most investor standards, so that other factors must weigh more heavily in the investor's mind than this often-cited rationale for the strong dollar.

The end result of the trade imbalance and the strong dollar has been the cry for protectionism, from both firms and organized labor. Blaming unfair competition from abroad, in the form of tariffs and trade barriers, subsidized foreign firms, cheap labor, dumping, lower taxes on exports, and so on, the fight has been carried to Washington, where relief is being sought. "Unfair" trade practices, however, account for only 10 percent of the annual trade, and even if protectionism could cure that 10 percent problem, the other 90 percent of the problem would remain.[70] The Reagan administration, ostensibly free traders along with the majority of economists, despite the import controls on steel and automobiles from Japan, has created a politically explosive situation from which there is no easy escape. The cry for protectionism is overwhelming; Congress passed legislation to protect U.S. firms and workers, which the president vetoed.

Paul Samuelson and Richard Gardner, as well as many others, suggest that the trade problem will not disappear until the budget deficits are brought under control—through interventions by the United States into foreign exchange markets to bring down the overvalued dollar; perhaps through some form of industrial policy, such as aid for workers displaced by imports as a serious program; and by dealing with the debt of Third World countries correctly, allowing them to restore their imports.[71] Of the three suggestions, only U.S. intervention, along with its major trading partners, into foreign exchange markets has been followed. The intervention into exchange markets has driven the dollar down by about 20 percent in 1985, helping to slow if not stop the drive toward protectionism. Other administration attempts to open up foreign markets to U.S. goods have proved less successful.

The legacy of large trade deficits, caused in large part by the macroeconomic policies of the Reagan administration, will remain long after the second term ends. Whether or not the trade deficit has added permanently to the deindustrialization of the United States remains to be seen.[72]

Adoption of a Conservative Agenda Questioned and Tax Reform Pushed

The short-run legacies of the Reagan administration are easy to describe, if not to resolve. But what of the longer term? Has there been a conservative revolution in the United States? Has the traditional conservative economic program become the dogma of the 1980s? No definitive answer is possible as this is being written, but in the words of neoconservative, Irving Kristol, "the Reagan Administration has not inaugurated any kind of serious 'conservative revolution.' Indeed it has not, though ... and this is its real significance—it may have laid the groundwork for one."[73] Apparently, when the Republican party puts to rest the old-style conservatism and adopts the populist stance of up-and-coming Jack Kemp or Newt Ginrich, then the revolution will have truly begun. Ronald Reagan still retains too much of the Goldwater-type of conservatism.

Others feel that the Reagan administration has achieved some impressive victories—in the buildup of national defense, in the revenue reductions and program cuts, and the like, but "the administration's unwillingness to substantially compromise its program in order to develop a broader working coalition has left it more dependent on a major political realignment to accomplish its objectives. Thus far, there is little evidence that such a realignment is occurring."[74] Furthermore,

> The Reagan Administration's promotion of the "politics of detachment"—detachment of the government from the problems of the nation and detachment of the presidency, or at least this president, from the problems of the government—may create its own backlash. By taking so strident an antigovernment posture, the administration was clearly taking advantage of a strong antigovernment mood in the nation. The problem, however, is that virtually every public opinion poll taken at the time of the 1980 election and since has demonstrated that the public's antigovernment mood is nicely balanced by a progovernment mood: people register eagerness to reduce government involvement in the abstract but insist on retaining a significant governmental role in programs affecting them.[75]

Thus Mr. Reagan has not been as successful in shifting the nation's agenda as he would have liked, but he must share part of the blame for not taking the time to build a political coalition to help him achieve his ends. Yet if he has not succeeded in dismantling the New Deal, he has managed to prevent new programs from being proposed or the old ones enlarged. The deficit prevents the entertainment of new initiatives, except in the defense area. The nation, however, has not been willing to go along with the assertion that government is all bad and to blame for all the nation's ills; it has seen that "if government is not always the solution, neither is it always the problem."[76] Both investment and consumer spending began falling off, and worries over another downturn surfaced. The economic indicators began to warn of possible difficulties ahead, as they showed very modest positive results. The administration, however—in this case the president himself—seemed unconcerned with the possible slowdown and instead began stumping for tax reform, an idea that seemed popular at first and then languished as the details of the reform package became known.

Tax reform is not a new concept, arising as it does in nearly every tax bill, but it is quickly put aside in favor of changing rates or amending sections of the old code. Critics of the old tax code are as numerous as the taxpaying population; it has always been regarded too unfair, too complex, too riddled with exceptions or loopholes, and too punitive. Few would have disagreed with Carter's assessment of it as a national disgrace, and many longed for an equitable and simple system. Reagan's tax policies, widely viewed as unfair, may have hastened the pace to supplant the old, unworkable system.

During the campaign of 1984, Mr. Reagan responded to all questions on taxation by deferring to a study being conducted by the Treasury Department and turning aside all attempts to uncover the details. Meanwhile, others were busy devising their own versions of a simple tax system with varying degrees of equity provisions: Senator William Bradley and Congressman Richard Gephardt provided one called the "Fair Tax"; Congressman Kemp and Senator Robert Kasten supplied the "Fair and Simple Tax" (FAST); a "Flat Tax" was devised by Robert E. Hall and Alvin Rabushka; and a "Cash Flow Tax System" was introduced by Henry J. Aaron and Harvey Galper; and of course, there were others, variants, extensions, and so on.[77]

Reagan made the "mistake" of delegating the administration's tax proposal to economists in the Treasury Department, who proceeded to develop a system to fit into economists' definition of a good tax system. This system, dubbed Treasury I, was not politically appealing, and it was revised after Reagan finally got around to examining it. The result, Treasury II, was introduced to the public by Mr. Reagan on May 28, 1985, in a televised speech to the nation in which he called for tax "revolution" to transform an "un-American" income tax system into one that is "clear, simple, and fair for all."

A full-scale discussion of all these tax proposals would be impossible, and only the administration's proposal will be outlined. The tax bill (Treasury II) that the administration proposed to Congress contained these major provisions: a reduction in the number of tax rates to just three, 15–25–35 percent, with the first rate applied to incomes up to $29,000, the second rate to incomes between $29,000 and $70,000, and the highest rate, 35 percent, to incomes above $70,000; increases in the zero-bracket amounts and in personal exemptions to

$2,000; deductions for mortgage interest paid would be retained, but state and local taxes would not be permitted; deductions for charitable contributions would be limited to itemizers, and the two-earner deduction eliminated; indexing would be retained, but income averaging would not be allowed.

The maximum capital gains tax would be 17.5 percent under Treasury II, but under Treasury I the inflation-adjusted gains would be taxed at ordinary rates—a major difference between the two plans. Another major difference was in the treatment of depreciation: Under Treasury I only economic depreciation was recognized; under Treasury II depreciation would be indexed for inflation and incentives for investment included. In both, the investment tax credit would be eliminated, but the corporation income tax rate would be reduced to 33 percent.

Other provisions for individuals included the taxation of unemployment compensation and some fringe benefits such as health and life insurance (Treasury I would have taxed workmen's compensation as well), but IRAs and Keogh accounts were extended to nonworking spouses.

Without pausing to discuss the issue, Treasury II was regarded as a retreat from the equity and fairness that Mr. Reagan was championing. (Higher-income groups came out better, and special tax breaks were reinstituted for oil and gas industries, for instance.) The tax plan was not simple, although a step in that direction was discernible.

The president was unable to drum up support for his tax proposal and appeared to be fighting a losing battle, when the House Ways and Means Committee, led by its chairman, Daniel Rostenkowski, decided to adopt the tax-reform issue. In a masterful job against much opposition and indifference, Rostenkowski managed to steer the committee to the completion of a tax bill that committee members could support. It contained provisions that were significantly different from Reagan's tax proposal, and, as a result, Reagan indicated he would veto it if presented to him.

The House bill retained the more popular tax deductions—mortage interest, charitable contributions, and state and local taxes—and also exempted the taxation of fringe benefits and the tax-free appreciation of the cash value of life insurance. The administration basically opposed these features, except for the mortgage-interest deduction.

Meanwhile, tax reform in the Senate was also in trouble. The special interests were busy protecting their favorite tax concessions, and the whole exercise in tax reform appeared to be in jeopardy. As was the case in the House, one man, Senator Robert Packwood of Oregon, steered the Finance Committee to the formation of a tax bill. The bill was regarded as more favorable to business as it included more generous depreciation allowances and special provisions for the oil, gas, timber, and banking sectors.

Aside from the special provisions for business, the House and Senate versions differed in several crucial respects. The House plan had four tax rates: 15 percent on the first $22,500 of income; 25 percent up to $43,000; 35 percent up to $100,000; and 38 percent on incomes over $100,000. The Senate version contained only two tax rates: 15 percent up to $29,300, and 27 percent over $29,300. These tax rates, of course, altered the capital gains tax rate to a maximum of 38 percent in the House and 27 percent in the Senate. Capital gains would be taxed as ordinary income in both versions.

Other areas that would require reconciliation included the treatment of sales taxes (deductible in the House version but not in the Senate's) and the deductibility of the Individual Retirement Account (IRA) which the House wanted to keep while the Senate wanted to limit the deduction to those who did not have a pension plan. Other differences were expected to be resolved in the conference committee. The administration abandoned all attempts to get its version of tax reform passed and endorsed the efforts of Congress to push a bill through. Reagan indicated that while he favored the Senate version, a compromise would probably be acceptable.

The conference committee, after much wrangling, did produce a bill that generally met with the administration's approval. The major features were: the reduction in tax rates to two, 15 percent on taxable incomes up to $29,750, and 28 percent on incomes above that; personal exemptions were raised as was the standard deduction; the IRA deduction was limited and many deductions were eliminated, including the states' sales tax, consumer interest payments, the two-earner feature and many others; less favorable treatment of business as some special provisions were deleted (the investment tax credit and special depreciation allowances), but in turn, tax rates for corporations were reduced from a maximum 46 percent to 34 percent.

Overall, the tax reform measure was supposed to be neutral in its effects on tax receipts (very doubtful) as it shifted more of the tax burden away from individuals to business. Most people would receive some tax reduction, it was claimed, although the clear beneficiaries were in the lower income groups where the standard deduction and personal exemption were raised, and the higher income groups through lower tax rates. Those in the middle faced an uncertain prospect. In the final conference bill, there were some elements of tax reform, some straightforward tax reductions, and some movement toward tax simplification. Yet the bill is not likely to please the advocates of complete tax reform, the proponents of tax simplicity or progressive taxation, or those whose tax payments increase. Neither would it please those who were arguing for a general tax increase to combat the budget deficit. Indeed calls for tax increases, including a new type of taxation—the value added tax (VAT)—were being made even before the tax measure was considered by the full House or Senate.

How these legacies, both short- and long-run, will fare in the recovery period and in Mr. Reagan's final term remains to be seen. Whatever the changes in its basic philosophy that are accepted by the administration or forced on it by economic events that it cannot control, one conclusion stands out—the economic system was and is not as simple to comprehend or manipulate as it was first purported to be by an administration that promised new beginnings.

Evaluation of Reaganomics

An evaluation of the Reagan administration's macroeconomic policies may be premature, since its second term is not completed. Some preliminary remarks are in order, however, especially since this administration's policies have been considered in detail and an evaluation of them made in conjunction with their description.

The most intriguing question is whether or not the policy shifts attempted were justified. Was the professed aim of this administration to reverse the role of government as a problem solver and return to a more laissez-faire economy justified in the sense that the general public appeared favorably inclined to the plan? Previously it was shown that the mandate for such a reversal of public policy did not exist in the election of 1980, nor did it suddenly blossom in the election of 1984. There was no consensus that government was the cause of all of our problems, and, in fact, most people indicated they wanted government programs to continue, especially those that benefited them. Witness the outcry when middle-class programs, such as Social Security, were threatened. The hasty retreat from tampering with such programs clearly indicates that the administration was wrong in its assessment of the desires of the public on government involvement in the economic life of the nation. Only "welfare" programs found a sympathetic audience, and then only because people were tired of paying taxes for programs that did not seem to work. It is not clear whether the nation had turned its back on the poor or had become less generous, but political pronouncements that most of the poor were undeserving of help may have served to convince many people that money was being wasted on well-meaning but ineffective programs. Who could be opposed to eliminating waste, particularly when the end result would mean a reduction in taxes? No doubt appeals to greed were heeded by many.

The promised reduction of government involvement, however, and the elimination of waste, did not develop to any great extent, and the reduction in taxes only brought another problem—the growing budget deficit. No public opinion poll ever revealed the public's desire for a huge deficit and a growing public debt. Whatever marginal benefit was achieved in cutting social programs was overshadowed by escalating interest costs.

Justification for the goal of reducing inflation is easier to sustain. The nation was weary of the double-digit inflation of the 1970s and wanted prices brought under control, even if that meant wage and price controls. The public is not very aware of the monetary actions designed to accomplish that end and thus was not clamoring for restrictions of the money supply; in fact, if presented with sufficient information, it probably would not have chosen that route to inflation reduction, since high interest rates accompany restrictive monetary policy.

In addition, some dissatisfaction with government regulations could easily be found, but not to the extent assumed by the administration. The administration overstated the costs of compliance with government regulations and blamed too many of the woes of U.S. industry on overregulation. It is understandable that industries affected might wish to have regulations reduced and their profits increased, but few analyses of the benefits of regulation were cited by the administration; it was just an expression of prejudices that allowed the regulation of industries to account for the decline in productivity, for the inability to compete with foreign firms, or for the costs of compliance robbing firms of funds needed for investment.

It is a platitude to state that everyone likes lower taxes, but it is not evident that taxes were burdensome in 1980 or were causing the economy to falter. The nation did not list high taxes as one of its principal concerns, except at the local level, until it was told that high taxes were to blame for the observed economic stagnation. Then, with the promise of a free lunch—that lower taxes would be costless—high taxes became a very popular complaint.

The same scenario was followed in the case of spending on national defense. Only when the fear of an inadequate defense was cultivated did part of the public accept the need for additional spending. Chauvinistic appeals, painting the enemy as inherently evil and godless, wanting only world domination, misstating and misleading calculations of comparative strengths, and reviving the cold war with all of its rhetoric, all helped to convince the more gullible that the United States had fallen behind. Under these circumstances, increases in the defense budget were equated with patriotism and demurrals with treason.

Thus, in brief, it appears that the major goals of this administration had to be manufactured and did not spring from the concerns of the nation. To be sure, some people did agree with all of the aims of the administration and many more agreed with one part or another, but it is doubtful that the administration had a mandate for radical change in any area of national concern, with the possible exception of reducing inflation. As indicated earlier, the conservative tide was simply not observable in either election of the 1980s; just a glance at the retreats from conservative causes by this administration should be sufficient to reveal the lack of depth of its following or the commitment to conservative ideology.

The success of the Reagan administration's policies is not so clear. Mr. Reagan did manage to shift priorities from civilian to military spending and did manage to contain the growth of government programs to confront social problems. Yet Reaganomics, or supply-side economics, failed to fulfill its promises. Taxes were indeed cut, as both Congress and the nation were willing to give the new policy a chance. Similarly, the Federal Reserve Board granted the president the monetary policy he needed. In general, the administration received all that it asked for in its attempt to complete its program to get the country moving again.

The result was a massive recession, or depression, as the forecasts proved wildly inaccurate: Saving did not increase, despite lower taxes, special savings accounts, IRAs, and the like; investment did not respond; together with monetary policy, output and employment fell dramatically; and business expectations were not changed. When the recovery did occur, it was due to consumption spending, which is a decidedly Keynesian economic policy. Incurring deficits to stimulate demand is far removed from Laffer's Curve or supply-side scenarios, and no amount of rationalization made by either could mask the unmistakable fiscal policy prescriptions of the Keynesians.

Aided by fuel and food price declines and the restrictive monetary policy that helped bring on the recession, inflation did fall rather faster than anyone had anticipated. Yet to the extent that macroeconomic policy was responsible for the fall in prices, the credit must go to Mr. Volker and not to Reaganomics. Thus the only credit that Mr. Reagan could claim for the recovery was his unflinching optimism, which could have induced some favorable expectations.

In other areas, the administration has retreated from further deregulations, from free-trade doctrines, from tax increases to reduce budget deficits, from the balanced-budget philosophy, from farm subsidies, from the use of economic sanctions, from intervention in money markets to affect the exchange rate of the dollar, and so on, through the conservative agenda.

These developments are clear from previous discussions; what is not clear are the long-run implications of Reaganomics. The promised results have not materialized, and the economy is once again entering into a period of stagnation. Will longer-run actions of economic units, responding somehow to elements of the Reagan administration's policies, reverse previous trends toward stagnation, or is the economy basically immune from macroeconomic policies and the periodic cycle an integral part of advanced capitalism?

Was Reaganomics rational? Did it accomplish unpublicized ends, even if or because it failed to achieve its stated goals? Some people have suggested that the true aim of this administration was to dismantle the New Deal, Fair Deal, Great Society, New Frontier, and any other attempt made to solve social problems by governmental action. Attacking the programs directly did not work in the past, any more than did attacks on government spending in general. Thus conservatives were forced to postpone tax reductions for fear of the budget deficit.

The other way to reduce government spending is to reduce revenues first, deliberately incurring budget deficits in the hope of forcing program cuts and halting the growth of new ones. If this was the purpose of tax reduction, it has proved partially successful as far as social programs are concerned, but has backfired in that national defense spending has also been affected. Still, many of the social programs survived, as Congress refused to end some and only reduced the budget of others. Thus the dismantling did not occur, and the result is a growing budget deficit that finally produced the incredible Gramm-Rudman Act.

Or was the whole exercise of tax cutting, rationalized by supply-siders, just an excuse to reduce the tax burden of upper-income groups, as David Stockman suggested, and the remainder of Reaganomics just thrown in to justify the action? To ensure acceptance, the notion of the free lunch made it all but irresistible, as for U.S. business did the notion that too many regulations were responsible for the decline of U.S. industry, not poor management or irresponsible self-interest on the part of managers. There was something for everyone in the economics of joy, and while everyone knew the promises were excessive and probably cynical, each group was willing to forego its disbelief for the benefits it received.

These issues are not easily settled by the present generation and may have to await the judgments of future historians who will have the benefit of more evidence to go on. It is clear, even now, that this administration, billed as the most ideological in history, was willing to compromise many of its supposedly firm positions when oppositions arose. Mr. Reagan was able to escape the criticisms that would normally follow from such tactics, especially from his very ideological supporters, but the administration cannot so easily evade responsibility. In the end it has proved to be as pragmatic as previous administrations and hence invites the speculation that its grand design for the economy was never taken seriously and that the only true goal was tax reduction. It has retreated from, compromised, or finessed every other position.

This behavior is not new in U.S. politics or economic policymaking, but it does refute the thesis that there was a mandate for change and that this president had the ready answers to provide the leadership for that change. A U.S. revolution it was not; what it was, was business as usual.

part V

Conclusions

chapter 15

Summary and Future Prospects

The record of policymaking over the period since World War I is now complete, and some overview seems appropriate. Rather than attempt a detailed review of the actions taken over the period, the summary is probably better accomplished by organizing it around the evaluating techniques used in each chapter: Were the policies taken (or not taken) justified, successful, and rational? After this summary an overall evaluation of past macroeconomic policies will be undertaken, with a look at the future of policymaking. Finally, some suggestions will be offered as to new tools and institutions that the changing structure of the economy may require, if policymaking is to be improved.

The question of whether policymaking in the past was justified is a crucial one, for if answered in the negative, the task at hand is the historian's, and attempts at manipulation of the economy should be phased out; if answered in the positive, or even with suitable qualifications, the door is open for future modifications and contributions and further attempts should be made. It would be possible to build on the knowledge of what went before, to learn by increments.

One way to refute any claim justifying policymaking in general is to show that the economy would have performed better in the absence of government intervention; that is, that no matter what the public clamored for or politicians responded to and no matter what motives were involved, or what problems were addressed, the economy would have been better off if government had not succumbed to the desire to improve conditions, but left them to market forces to resolve.

History, of course, cannot be replayed and there is no way to know what might have been or what might have happened, had a different course been followed. The only recourse is to examine the theoretical model that suggests that there is no justification for government intervention. If the laissez-faire model is found wanting and unrealistic, then there is some reason for the public sector to adjust market outcomes. Briefly, the laissez-faire-model argument is based on the supposition that large numbers of rational individuals, acting alone and in a self-interested manner, will maximize their own welfare and, in the process, the welfare of the society as well. This is not the place to embark upon a full-scale critique of this model, and it is also not necessary, for many other attempts have already been made.[1]

If any of these main elements of the model are seriously at variance with reality, the model loses its relevance. For our purposes, the main assumption to be questioned is the existence of large numbers of individuals in every market—that is, the competition assumption; if sufficient market power has been allowed to develop, then the self-regulating, self-policing aspects of market capitalism diminish accordingly and the welfare of the society is not maximized. Indeed, market outcomes would be suboptimal, and proper adjustment could improve on market results.

Again, enough studies have documented the existence of market power that to reexamine the issue once more would surely be redundant. In this book the existence of market power is taken as a given, so that there is room for government intervention to affect market outcomes. Just a glance at the *Fortune* 500 or, indeed, just the top 20 or even 10 firms on that list should be enough to question the competitive model, but the analysis is left to others.[2]

Even if a role for government intervention into the economy is admitted, it is still true that in making adjustments, government could make things worse than they might otherwise have been. Attempts to improve market outcomes, however well intentioned, could end up making conditions worse. That is a risk each generation should evaluate, as will be done later in this chapter. The issue, however, is not whether government intervention is justified or not, but about the means by which such intervention is carried out. Government may well be justified in interfering in the marketplace and still not do a very good job of it.

It is often maintained that government programs to solve a market shortcoming would have been recognized by the market eventually, and then market forces would have done a better job. This may or may not be true, but the market solution may not be optimal anyway. For instance, the market could and did develop alternatives to

Social Security, and many insurance companies stand ready to sell annuities to provide for retirement. The point is that such policies would not be available to everyone, and the only way to reach the general public is through a public program. It is simply irrelevant to suggest, as many have, that such a program should be made voluntary, because a better return can be had by individuals acting for themselves. That simply misses the point, for the public demand arose out of frustration with the inability or unwillingness of the market to provide the type of program needed by everyone, not just the financially aware. Other programs were started because of the inability of the market to correct itself. Health and safety programs provide examples.

Perhaps more time is required for the marketplace to react, but society may well view the situation from a perspective different from that of the economic theorist—that time alone will not correct for market failures. After all, many of these failures have been going on for a long time and by now should be considered part of the system instead of temporary aberrations. In fact, without intervention, the conditions could grow even worse, requiring even more drastic actions than those needed at some earlier date.

Hence, the abuses of the 1920s paved the way for the drastic acts of the 1930s. The excesses of the 1920s, the freest market period of this century, might have been modified by incremental policies designed to curb some abuse or other and to serve as a signal or warning to others to temper their behavior. As it was, conditions were allowed to deteriorate without abatement, leading to public actions that had to be taken in a crisis atmosphere, and many programs were hastily conceived and perhaps ill designed to correct the abuses identified. Public demands to do something were justified in this period, and the market system was seen as flawed and vulnerable and its shortcomings apparent.

Of course, in the 1930s public demands went beyond the obvious desire to stabilize the economic system. The desire for security became the justification for many government programs, as the New Deal programs of Social Security and unemployment compensation attest. These were areas that a free-market economy could not or would not handle. Similarly, many of the problems that followed the post-World War II period could be solved largely or only by a public sector. Such public goods as education, highways, water and sewer systems, environmental concerns, and national defense were in demand, and these are normally provided by the public sector.

Gradually government came to be regarded as a problem solver in many areas. Government budgets grew as a result, and this is the relationship to macroeconomic policies that is of importance here. Fiscal policy was acknowledged as a necessity to stabilize the economy and cushion the fluctuations in economic activity. All sectors of the public, business as well as individuals, came to demand action, despite rhetoric to the contrary that condemns government interference. Free markets are desired in stable times, but when economic disruptions threaten, the public wants help.

To continue the discussion of whether or not macroeconomic policymaking is justified is not productive, and perhaps we are kicking at an open door; no administration has been able to revert to an earlier time when presumably government was not necessary. The economic system is not stable and does not always yield equitable results, and as long as these facts are known, there will be a desire to do something about them. What additional evidence is needed?

Even if a democratic society calls for public policy, however, and the justification for it can be established, the type and frequency are not easily articulated. The public has no direct channel by which to influence policy, nor does it always have the necessary information to determine the proper course of action. The nation could demand public policies that are in the end harmful, but are the ones that have the most appeal or are most easily understood. It is the task of an enlightened society to design institutions that can devise public policy and reflect, wherever possible, the desires of the people. To labor under the belief that government intervention is not necessary or warranted in the United States means that such institutions will not be designed and public policy will always suffer from mismanagement and discontinuity.

Success of Past Policies

Questions of justification aside, have past policies been successful? Since the business cycle is still with us, past attempts at economic stabilization are difficult to evaluate properly. Either they have been unsuccessful or, alternatively, they have prevented the fluctuations from being more severe and pronounced, limiting rather than eliminating them. Again it would be possible to find economists holding views all along the spectrum, from the futility of macroeconomic policy to the defense of past attempts that somehow were prevented from working properly. Not many would contend that there were cycles that were anticipated and prevented by appropriate and timely actions.

Given the nature of the problem of economic stabilization, many economists would conclude that the past record is not that bad. Trying to juggle the many variables so as to succeed in economic stabilization—interest rates, unemployment rates, money supplies, exchange rates, spending and taxing policies, price variations, institutional and political realities, and so on—is quite a task, akin to that of the juggler in the circus balancing dishes on poles and having to run back and forth to each in order to keep them spinning. So no one envies the job of a macroeconomic policymaker, and it may be surprising that the job has been done as well as it has.

Without trying to make excuses, it is obvious to even the most casual observer that our forecasting tools are not as accurate or as timely as needed. If we do not know where we are on the business cycle, how is it possible to devise appropriate policies? Only after the cycle has revealed itself is it possible to react to conditions. Thus we see recessions only after they have developed, and recoveries occur before we realize it. The data are just not available for more timely actions, and at times policies begun in a recessionary period take effect during the recovery period—at the wrong time. These lags in both fiscal and monetary policy have been recognized for some time, and some attempts to reduce them have been made, but unfortunately they are still with us and prevent timely actions that would be more effective in combating the business cycle.

Implicit in the conservative critique of policymaking is the assumption that economists actually know how the economy works, else why devise rules? Another view, more widely acknowleged, is that economists may have overstated their knowledge of how the economy works and hence their ability to prescribe for it. Some early successes in the Kennedy–Johnson era may have led to an arrogance that was undesirable and may have earned more respect for policymaking than was deserved. Certainly the claim that we could fine tune the economy was excessive, and the management of the economy can never be that easy or that exact. The outlines of some general macroeconomic policies were eventually achieved, however, and some general principles derived. So the inadequacies of economics have presented serious problems, but are not basically responsible for past failures.[3] This has become more or less the conventional view, as economies differ over which approach to follow or which variable(s) to control—the money supply or fiscal variables.

Surely the record of the period from the late 1960s should have been a large dose of humility for macroeconomic theorists and policymakers. There is clearly a great deal to be learned about the workings of an economy like that of the United States in the latter half of the twentieth century. Appeals to a simpler economy will not help in the analysis of the far more complex one that exists. Further discussion of these points will come later.

One of the difficulties that arises in the determination of success or failure of past policies is that of definition. Before we can really assess the success of macroeconomic policies, it is necessary to ask, In relation to what? Against what yardsticks is success to be measured? If, for instance, in the absence of stabilization policies, the unemployment rate would have risen to 10 percent and the rate with stabilization policies was held to 7 percent, is that a success story? Who would boast of a 7 percent unemployment rate? And was a more active policy restrained for fear of rising prices?

There are no answers to questions of this type and perhaps there never can be. Yet part of the problem arises because the nation has never bothered to consider seriously what it expects from the economic system and has not reached a consensus as to which goals and targets to aim for. Consider the goals most often cited as desirable: full employment, price stability, economic growth, economic freedom, a fair distribution of income, and reasonable trade balances. But these goals are not achievable simultaneously—at least not over the period we have examined. Indeed, some often appear mutually exclusive—for example, full employment and price stability.

Without more specific goals and targets and without a ranking of them in terms of priorities, how is success to be judged? The only exception to the casual preparation for macroeconomic policies was the Humphrey–Hawkins Act of 1978. Now largely ignored, it did set priorities, putting full employment as the number-one goal, followed by price stability; it did set specific targets for both, within a time frame that prepared the way for more active planning by government; and it did try to suggest some new institutions to carry out the aims of the act, one of which, the CBO, has made some valuable contributions to the national debate over macroeconomic issues. An escape clause has, however, allowed everyone to ignore the provisions of the law and conveniently ignore the commitment to national goals.

We are left with no clear ranking of priorities whenever goals conflict and no institutions to determine them or to carry out and oversee the policies, once determined. This gives an ad hoc approach to policymaking, since the choice of goals and the means to achieve them vary with each political administration; the long-term needs of the nation will thus come second to short-run political considerations.

That our economic knowledge has been and remains deficient in many areas and has at times resulted in faulty advice to policymakers is generally acknowledged by most economists who have been involved in the public-policy debate. Yet the ultimate blame for the failures of macroeconomic policies has been attributed to politics.[4] It has become commonplace to suggest that short-run concerns and special interests got in the way of devising and administering proper policies. The political influence is too dominant and the politician's time horizon is too short. One recalls Johnson's guns-and-butter policy and Nixon's wage-and-price-control system; these are but two dramatic examples of common occurrences.

Looking back over the period surveyed, one finds many examples of failures and some examples of successes. The failures can be attributed to economic ignorance, political interference, and chance. Reactions to problems were often delayed and responses often timid, and frequently extraneous events interceded to change the conditions that policies were designed to affect. Consider only a few examples (others were discussed in the relevant chapters): World War II dragged us out of the depression, as policymakers pulled up short of achieving their goals. Captured by obsolete economic theories, as well as political repercussions, they vacillated. The tax cuts of 1948 and 1954 were fortuitous and unrelated to the upcoming recessions. Even the Kennedy–Johnson tax cut came at the right time and the experiment proved successful. Reagan's attempt to repeat the policy yielded much different results. Throughout these examples, the political input was always present and generally visible.

Monetary policy, ostensibly free of direct political considerations, is also replete with instances of delay in action and timidity in execution. The stop-and-go monetary policy is one of the monetarist's chief complaints against the Federal Reserve System, and the record does provide sufficient examples to justify the concern. The failures of the System are less noticeable by the general public, however—first, because the arcane world of money is baffling, and second, because incorrect policies are more quickly reversed than is the case for fiscal policy. There is also the understandable but erroneous view that the Federal Reserve is an independent body free of political contamination. As often stated, however, Federal Reserve officials read the election results too.

Often, in the past, economic knowledge has played a role in the inability or unwillingness to respond to economic problems. Slavish adherence to dogma has prevented appropriate and timely actions. The balanced-budget philosophy has limited actions in the past, just as the Phillips Curve trade-off between inflation and unemployment does in the present. As if these constraints were not sufficient, there are groups of rather vocal and influential economists who are always prepared to demonstrate the futility of macroeconomic policy and thus confuse policymakers who are already trying to reconcile conflicting economic views. Squabbles among economists, perceived as ineptness by many, only add to the confusion and the difficulty of formulating policy.

Under these circumstances, it is surprising that any past policy has been successful and that the record is not even worse than it is. The shotgun approach of the New Deal did a great deal to foster confidence in the economy, for instance, even though more thoughtful programs might have performed better. The Kennedy–Johnson tax cut was successful in demonstrating the feasibility of Keynesian economics and preparing the groundwork for government intervention on a larger scale. Similarly, monetary policy has demonstrated the capacity to react to changing economic conditions, even if its first response was erroneous or belated.

It would be difficult, however, to find the ideal case of policymakers anticipating economic troubles and formulating policies to confront them. Generally the recognition of economic difficulties has come too late, and the policy responses have been irresolute and deficient. Caution has led to partial successes on occasion in preventing things from getting worse, making success difficult to define; chance, too, has occasionally played its part by making policymakers look good. Perfect examples of policymaking, however, are as rare as unanimity among the consulted economic advisors.

Rationality of Past Policies

One final problem in judging the success or failure of past macroeconomic policies leads us into the last of the evaluation criteria— rationality. Were the policies rational? Were they formulated for the immediate economic situation or for some ulterior purpose? Obviously, if some ulterior motive were involved, the policy could be judged a failure and yet to be a success in terms of achieving this hidden goal. For example, the Nixon wage-and-price-control system is generally held to have failed, according to mainstream economists. Yet the controls were not designed primarily as an economic policy for the domestic economy, but as a policy to force trade changes and as a political move for the 1972 elections. So the policy of wage and price controls was a "failure," but they certainly worked to control prices following the stimulus to aggregate demand and helped Mr. Nixon get reelected in a thriving economy. Thus the policy was rational from that perspective.

It was also rational for Mr. Johnson to withhold information on the costs of the Vietnam War so that the budget would not reflect the added costs and he could get Congress to go along with his plans. For the nation the policy of deception was disastrous.

It was also folly to cut taxes in a period of rapid inflation, as Congress did in the post-World War II period, but if the aim was to win back some of the income shares lost in the 1930s, the policy may not appear so contrary to reason. When Mr. Reagan fired the striking air controllers, the action seemed rather excessive and perhaps unwise for the nation, but when looked at as a warning to labor and as a signal of its probusiness bias, the policy was dramatic and was not lost on firms that later carried out the hidden intent of the message.

Similarly, the Reagan tax cuts can be looked upon as a device to reduce the taxes of higher-income groups under the guise of supply-side economics. Or the tax cuts can be viewed as an avenue to reduce government spending on social programs through the resulting budget deficits. Either way, the policy was rational and at least partially successful, but for the nation the consequences were ruinous.

Perhaps these instances should be classified under political considerations, which often are responsible for making policies fail, but they go beyond mere politics as usual and become deceitful conduct. The difficulty for outsiders is to learn when and how frequently such practices occur. Even then, if this is ever learned, it is mainly in retrospect.

Perhaps even more troublesome are the instances when policies are deliberately designed to fail. It is more understandable to suspect that many proposals are initiated to test the waters or to appear in a favorable light, with full knowledge on the part of the proposers that the policy will be unacceptable. Mr. Reagan, for example, may well have satisfied his right-wing following by proposing changes in the Social Security program, with predictable results.

These trial balloons or public-relations ploys are well known and for the most part recognized for what they are. Moreover, the U.S. political system has witnessed and tolerated all kinds of distortions of reality, face-saving techniques, and blame shifting practices, and they have become part of the amusement of politics. But what if policies that are designed to fail are seriously proposed and enacted? Failure, in this case, is courted to demonstrate something that does not yield to straightforward explanations and persuasion by the usual means.

The war on poverty is such a case. Mr. Johnson's well-intentioned desire to aid the disadvantaged was turned into the reverse by failure to provide for sufficient funding for the job. The program was started with such fanfare that unwarranted expectations were raised. Many people remarked at the time that funding was inadequate, but they were silenced by the obvious fact that something was being done and something was better than nothing. True, the Vietnam War got in the way of adequate funding later, but even before then the Great Society was having difficulty in increasing budget amounts for its programs.

So now it was possible for critics to proclaim that the whole idea was flawed, since poverty was not eliminated. It was just one step further for them to claim that the society had really tried to eliminate economic hardships but could not do it, and that led to the conclusion that government should not be involved in further attempts to do so. We have tried and failed. All we succeeded in doing was to make a segment of the population dependent on the government and discourage individual initiative, and so on, through the litany of complaints about welfare chiselers and lazy bums.[5]

The war on poverty was designed to fail and in the end turned out to be more of a skirmish. The lesson was clear, however—government should not get involved in redistributing income but let existing market results stand. Such a position was easy to justify, as conservatives spoke of equality of opportunity and not equality of results.[6] In fact, this whole episode paved the way for Reagan's popularity and eventual success in halting the growth of government policies for the poor. We had tried to help and failed, and now it was time to try something else—how readily acceptable was the undeniable truth.

In the evaluation of economic policies, this hidden agenda is surely the most disturbing. Evaluating actions of the past is always difficult and subject to all manner of misinterpretations and misconceptions. If deception is an integral part of policymaking, the task becomes that much more demanding and perhaps impracticable. It appears, however, that the most concerted use of this ploy is in establishing the case that government cannot and should not be involved in some action or other, or that government is inefficient or ineffective in carrying out some program. The goal is to return to the free market or to the status quo, in other cases. Witness the crusades against government planning, public housing, nationalized health schemes, and incomes policies.

To pursue this matter further would require a much larger and different type of study, but anyone involved in examining the policies of the past should be aware of the possibility of ulterior goals in the formation of policies. To ignore them is to leave unexplained some seemingly irrational acts, but to see only those is to indulge in conspiratorial fantasies.

Other Assessments of Past Policies

After reviewing the history of economic policy, Robert A. Gordon concluded that "our record is a mixed one with respect to achievement of the three goals [growth, full employment, and price stability] of macroeconomic policy. ... The fourth ... maintaining balance-of-payments equilibrium [was] a complete failure."[7] That assessment was made in 1974 and has not been updated. It is therefore unjust to assume that this was his final judgment. Similarly, others have evaluated past economic policies, but have not had the opportunity to reassess their views with more recent experience.

Subject to this caveat, some expression of views on past economic policy may be helpful. Conservatives, as might be expected, tend toward the denigration of macroeconomic policies. Here, for instance, is Hayek:

> The present unemployment is the direct result of the shortsighted "full employment policies" we have been pursuing for the past twenty-five years. This is the sad truth we must grasp if we are not to be led into measures that will only make matters worse. The sooner we can find our way out of the fool's paradise in which we have been living, the shorter will be the period of suffering.[8]

Or consider this conclusion:

> There is simply no evidence at all that a free economy operating with a regime of fiscal-monetary stability is inherently unstable, or that such an economy must suffer excessive unemployment. There is accumulating evidence that an economy subject to Keynesian management will be unstable, and that such management will itself produce unpredictable changes in employment.[9]

Interestingly, the opposite extreme, although equally upset by Keynesian policies, is far more complimentary to the attempts. Here is one grudging approval by Victor Perlo: "Yet, when all is said and done, a definite degree of effectiveness must be attributed to this regulation [contracyclical]. Considering the depth of contradictions within the U.S. economy, in the absence of government regulation, economic crises of catastrophic dimensions would be likely."[10] A more recent assessment by Edward Boorstein is that "for twenty years after World War II, U.S. capitalism enjoyed favorable conditions and the government applied Keynesianism with a certain degree of success. The success was limited. Unemployment and the business cycle were not eliminated. Inflation was not eradicated. But these ills were—for a capitalist country—kept within bounds."[11]

Magdoff and Sweezy, however, are less generous and their indictment of Keynesianism more sweeping:

> Despite the use of Keynesian palliatives, the leading capitalist nation has not been able to reach full employment except in time of war. And in those countries that have engaged in more advanced forms of government intervention—such as planning and operating state-owned enterprises—the result has been to strengthen and preserve monopoly-capitalist interests, not to clip their wings. ... Furthermore, despite the presumption that there exists a science of business-cycle control, there has never been general agreement on the best techniques to use. Each new crop of would-be economic advisors, using the same Keynesian tool-kit but confronted with a new set of political and economic conditions, has come up with different, and often conflicting, recommendations. ... Meanwhile capitalist reality has displayed more than recurrent business cycles—spiraling inflation together with a secular rise in the rate of unemployment, explosion of private and public debt, extreme financial difficulties, [and] the collapse of the international monetary system put in place after the Second World War.[12]

Of course, all shades of opinion can be found in between these extremes. Some, like Walter Heller, who was responsible for promoting and eventually overselling macroeconomic policy, maintain that the policies were used as well as can be expected, that they have limitations and that the warnings were there, but "in a very real sense, economists have been victims of their own success. Macroeconomic policy, capped by the tax cut, was the major force holding the postwar economy on a vastly higher plane than the prewar economy. ... Yet ... success bred great expectations on the part of the public that economics could deliver prosperity without inflation and with ever-growing material gains in the bargain."[13] Others contend that the policies were not used strongly enough and we were too timid. "The trouble with fiscal and monetary policies has not been that excessive reliance has been placed on them or that they have been too stimulative, but rather that they have moved in the wrong direction and been too restrictive."[14]

Many others, like Galbraith, feel that the macroeconomic policies did not go far enough to recognize economic power and the changing economic structure, and hence do not encompass planning as a necessary ingredient in policymaking. It is unfair, of course, to dwell on these evaluations, since many could have changed their minds.

They are included here to demonstrate the obvious—few economists are satisfied with past attempts at policymaking and all have suggestions as to what went wrong and as to possible improvements, including abandoning the whole idea. Yet enough has been included to give some idea of the range of opinion on this controversial subject and to prepare the groundwork for the presentation of more far-reaching proposals, designed to analyze what really caused the observed problems in the past and to suggest the necessary remedies.

Unfortunately, the fact that all reviewers of past policy have recommendations for improving policymaking suggests not only dissatisfaction but disarray. To illustrate, consider the confusion for the policymaker receiving contrary advice from two Nobel Prize winners in economics: Milton Friedman, who advises a return to laissez-faire economics controlled by rules, and Vassily Leontieff, who advocates more government planning. Include the other U.S. Nobel Prize winners, and the array of advice is broadened to fill up the spectrum of opinion.

Accordingly, there have been calls for more consensus thinking among economists to make the voice of professional opinion more meaningful.[15] Merely calling for a consensus is inadequate to ensure one, however, as economists cling to their own views of appropriate policy. Economics is not a value-free discipline.

How then is it possible to reduce the range of opinions to the point where policymakers can weigh only a few options and feel confident that there is some focus of expert opinion? If this narrowing of views is not accomplished, the future of macroeconomic policymaking will resemble the past experience. That record, though not totally ineffectual, is not one that engenders a great deal of pride. Furthermore, without reduction in the range, the cacophony of advice will continue to permit policymakers to do anything they want, for an economist or group of economists can always be found to support any action. Worse, harsh and bitter disagreements can cause economic advice to be dismissed as irrelevant, and if frustration builds sufficiently, sound economic advice can even be ignored in favor of whatever crank theory is in vogue.

Policymaking should not be subject to the same forces that lead economists to quarrel over esoteric theoretical models, which are often generated by the need to publish or to make professional reputations. The pendulum that swings theoretical niceties from extreme to extreme should not swing as far for policymaking, nor should current theoretical contributions be allowed to influence current policy until sufficient evidence has been accumulated to make experimentation legitimate. Otherwise, first one school of thought will influence policy, and then quite another will follow, pushing the society in another direction.

This is not to argue against experimentation, but only to suggest that new efforts be supported by reasoned thinking. How many economists, for example, would have suported the contentions of supply-side theorists? Nixon's wage-and-price-control scheme? On the other hand, the Kennedy–Johnson tax cut of 1964 would have received far more support, since the presentation of Keynesian macroeconomic theory and the refinements made to it prepared the way for this public policy. The tax cut could have been an incorrect policy, but that is not the point; it was justified at the time by a great deal of discussion, empirical work, and criticism, so that it had some credence.

Of course, the call for rationality in policymaking could lead to a type of policy paralysis or overly conservative policies. Too much caution is as bad as not enough, and the appeal of "do nothing" instead of "do something" can become too enticing.

General Guidelines for Future Policymaking

Before the problem of conflicting advice can be addressed, some general principles should be outlined so that the institutional changes needed, if any, can be made to comply with them. In this section some general guidelines for policy are developed, and while they are not necessarily innovative, they do confront the problems of policymaking in the past. This will become clearer once the details are filled in. The general principles are listed below. Taking each of these items in turn will permit the systematic construction of a different method for policymaking.

1. Long-term goals should be differentiated from short-term goals and policies designed for each. A mixture of long- and short-term programs should be developed and changed as the conditions change or goals are reached.
2. Short-term programs should be flexible—easily started and stopped. They should be directed at solving problems in the current economy and thus are more suitable for stabilization purposes.
3. Long-term programs should not vary drastically with the business cycle. Once they are determined, they should not be subject to vagaries of the business cycle. Public-works projects have traditionally been placed in this category, but other types of programs can be included as well, for example, health, transportation, or agriculture programs.
4. Different sets of policymakers should be involved in determining short- and long-run goals and policies. Interaction between groups should be encouraged, of course, but responsibility should be clearly identified.

5. New institutions should be devised to conduct policymaking under the new accountability for different purposes and time periods. The aim here is to clarify and focus economic advice, not to create more bureaucracy and confusion.

Determination of Goals and Programs

In the past, economic events controlled policy, and we reacted to economic problems without much direction. Thus long-term goals, to the extent that they existed, were often sacrificed or shortchanged because of the problems of the moment. Sometimes we returned to them, as we often did in programs to stimulate investment and economic growth, and sometimes they were forgotten, as is the case for a fair distribution of income.

Yet the fact is that long-term goals have never really been the subject of rational discussion. Whether that is because of the short time horizon of politicians or because of the fear of "planning" is not clear, but the lack of a long-term horizon is responsible for the haphazard development of the economy. A laissez-faire economy will not achieve societal goals except by accident, and economists who advocate such an economic system are indulging in an act of faith. The past experience is replete with examples of market failures that are not easily correctible once power is allowed to develop, and the unequal rewards invite the use of political power to retain cherished positions. Advanced capitalism is a system of privilege.

Using the stimulating analysis of Charles Lindblom, we must escape from the market, which is a prison;[16] every policy action is constrained by the reaction of the market. Combating pollution through public policy means that firms object and react by raising prices or reducing investment; workers who demand a larger share of the national income face either inflation or unemployment, as the market punishes them for their actions. Why not, says Lindblom, put it the other way around? Given the understandable desire of workers to increase their income shares, a market system will produce inflation or unemployment. "We have come to think not of human need and aspiration but of the market system as the fixed element in the light of which we think about policy. We find it difficult to think of the market as the variable."[17]

Thus we must decide what we want to achieve, when we want to achieve it, and when conflicts arise, what comes first. We cannot leave it to the marketplace to resolve, for it is ill designed for that purpose, but responds to inducements to act. Either public policy must find the right inducements to get the results it seeks or it must resort to market controls of some kind. The market cannot remain a prison, if public policy is to be rational and respond to human needs.

What the long-term goals of the society should be cannot and should not be determined in advance of serious consideration by the institutions responsible for them; however, some likely and unlikely candidates can be listed for purposes of illustration. Economic growth would appear on everyone's list of long-term goals, but the means to achieve it would probably vary considerably. Additions to capital stock, net investment, are necessary to increase output and employ-ment and are a vital ingredient of economic growth. In the past the investment decisions have been left to the market and hence have varied over the business cycle or in relation to variables like expectations, confidence, or changes in technology. While the market should continue to guide investment in many areas, it is no longer sufficient for the entire job. Public investment, suggested by Keynes in the 1930s, will have to supplement private investment, particularly in areas not well served by the marketplace. Investment in energy sources, public transportation and communication projects, environ-mental programs, health and safety areas, public recreation and natural resources preservation, and so on come readily to mind as examples.

The market can provide for transportation, for instance, and ration automobiles to those who are willing and able to purchase them, but the market does not provide for transportation for human needs—mass transit is required for health and safety reasons and does provide for those who are unable or unwilling to rely on the automobile as the sole means of transportation. Similarly, the market provides for the housing needs of those who are willing and able to purchase what is constructed, but it does not meet the needs of far too many people. Public housing will be required if adequate shelter is to be provided for those left out of the private housing market. These examples of market failures to meet human needs are well recognized, and many solutions have been proposed to confront the problems, but few have been adopted. Again, government intervention in the market has been resisted, although government subsidies to the automobile industry in the form of public highways or subsidies to the housing industry in the form of mortgage rates or tax concessions for home ownership are seldom mentioned.

Social investment is necessary to correct or modify market results and to begin the process of making the distribution of income and wealth more equitable. The ultimate question is really not whether government is too large or too small, as suggested by typical debates by political factions, but whom government serves.[18] In the past the issues have not been framed properly, and hence only the more overt public expenditures on programs like welfare have been publicized, for obvious reasons. Government investment, however, should not be limited only to the social investment areas mentioned above. Indeed, public investment should be considered whenever and wherever the market fails to perform in a manner to ensure the attainment of national goals. If this means public ownership of oil and gas wells, railroads, or airlines to achieve predetermined goals, then it should not be ruled out by devotion to market principles or ideology.

It is time the nation faced the fact that government is not going to disappear in the next century and that it is needed to perform in areas not well served by private institutions. Where market inducements can be devised to bring about the desired results, they can be used; where market inducement fail, more direct intervention, ownership, or controls will be required. This is not the place, however, to spell out what the national goals should be or how to obtain them, and there is no blueprint for those who are entrusted with the job. Public discussion would soon reveal what the most pressing concerns are, and the necessary policies would soon after emerge. They might include better and less costly educational facilities, a more equitable distribution of income and wealth, the preservation of economic freedom, a just tax system, an incomes policy, programs for labor—such as labor exchanges—national pension schemes, moving allowances, tax provisions for training and education programs, programs for business—for example, such an investment fund as found in Sweden—access to patents, programs for exporters particularly for relocation, and perhaps a formal industrial policy that includes a rational agricultural policy.

Ideal solutions are likely to prove elusive, but as long as the community is willing to experiment and settle for less-than-perfect results (as it already does in the marketplace), some progress toward a better society is possible. Along the way it might prove desirable to experiment with which level of government is appropriate to administer the programs and carry out the policies; interest in federalism has vacillated over time, but this might be an opportunity to reopen the discussion in conjunction with the reallocation of responsibility for the achievement of national goals.

Short-term goals are not easy, nor is it always desirable to separate them from long-run goals, but they are more likely to be concentrated in stabilizing the economy and minimizing the extent of fluctuations on the society. Billions of dollars of lost output have been tolerated in past recessions and so many opportunities squandered in periods of prosperity for fear of inflation. The short-term goals of maintaining full employment with reasonable price stability are clearly the chief claimants for attention in stabilization policies (and, of course, for the long run, as well). Determining what is reasonable for these magnitudes is a value judgment, but as will become evident, concerns over inflation should be minimized; first, because the long-term goals may well eliminate or reduce the sources of inflation (housing and energy costs, food prices, health and education expenses, and so on); and second, because an incomes policy of some kind may well be in effect. (These points are covered in the next section.)

Other short-term goals revolve around maintaining some balance in external trade. Questions of commercial policy, tariffs, subsidies, and so on must be confronted in a world grown smaller by global relocation of industry and the changing structure of technology. Principles of comparative advantage may still be appropriate for some products, but in an era when TVs, stereos, computers, and the like, can be produced anywhere in the world, they may no longer be as applicable as when first enunciated for agricultural products. The question arises, then, as to what to do with workers who are harmed by the application of free-trade principles, and in the longer run, what kinds of output an advanced, high-wage economy can produce. Should export subsidies be allowed or special tax concessions developed to meet the short-term goal of striving for balance in world trade? Should exchange rates fluctuate freely or be controlled by intervention is a similar question to be addressed in this connection.

In brief, the short-term goals are mainly concerned with the current state of the economy, and while they are obviously related to the long-term goals of the society, they have more of a sense of immediacy about them. Conditions must be stable and improving in the present if the future is to realize its potential through public policy. Life can be made better in the present, while awaiting even further improvements that may come in time.

The Need for Flexible Short-Term Programs

The second general principle, that short-term programs should be flexible—easily started and stopped—follows from the short-run stabilization goal. Clearly, the fire-fighting-role of stablization policy has to be quickly implemented when trouble arises and quickly reversed once the difficulty has passed. The difficulties of monetary and fiscal policies, however, pointed out earlier, will not vanish unless other institutional changes are made. The lags involved in each will remain, despite the need for more timely responses by both fiscal and monetary authorities.

Part of this problem should disappear if the institutional changes presented below are adopted. The main change suggested is some form of planning to achieve the national goals and, of course, to rationalize policymaking. With some parameters given or stable, part of the stabilization job is made easier; with some programs not allowed to vary with the business cycle, some control over parts of the budget is assured. Planning will remove some of the fluctuations in spending by government, but also should help reduce the fluctuations in private spending as well. To the extent that uncertainty is reduced, private investment will fluctuate less, and this vital cause of instability in the past will be mitigated.

From the fiscal standpoint, then, stabilization should become easier with some fundamental institutional changes. In addition, another solution to the problem of lags is to use more of the trigger-mechanism technique. That is, if key variables reach critical rates or levels, predetermined government programs automatically become operational. For example, if the unemployment rate reaches 1 percent above its long-run goal, government-sponsored employment programs are instituted or unemployment compensation benefits are extended. When the unemployment rate falls back to its long-run target, temporary programs are gradually phased out. Other trigger mechanisms, such as an inflation rate, could also be used in a similar manner. This type of trigger mechanism allows for flexibility in responding to current conditions and can easily be reversed, unlike the rigid rules found in variants for the balanced budget or for monetary growth.

In the case of temporary employment, it may well be that new careers will be found for the unemployed workers who accepted government jobs at some entry-level wage. These workers could be employed permanently in the public sector, if their services are considered valuable. There is nothing wrong with government as an employer of last resort, but few lives will be enhanced by make-work, low-paying jobs that are degrading to everyone, especially since there are many unmet needs of the public sector that could be partially met by employing those who are made superfluous by the private market. Indeed, some of these workers could receive valuable on-the-job training (as in the CETA program), which could lead to better jobs and better lives earned through self-respect.

Another institutional change, given later, involves new policy-making bodies. If they work as outlined, more consensus reactions should be possible, making policymaking easier to achieve, since some of the time normally spent on deciding if a problem exists will be reduced. Similarly, streamlining the Federal Reserve System should make possible a more responsive monetary policy. These institutional changes, which will be discussed later, are partially designed to improve monetary and fiscal policymaking.

Timing was one of the problems with past policy formation, but another problem seemed even more intractable: the trade-off between inflation and employment. The pursuit of full employment, a recognized goal, was thwarted by the rise in prices that appeared as soon as the economy approached its goal and sometimes long before. Powerful special-interest groups in business and finance were able to convince everyone that inflation was the greater evil (not too difficult at double-digit rates), and full employment was subordinated as a goal. Again, human needs were relegated to the market prison, and many already disadvantaged people were enlisted involuntarily in the fight against inflation.

The unequal sacrifice in stabilization will no longer be necessary if several changes in policymaking are made—first, if the long-term programs of ensuring adequate and affordable health care, housing, energy, and food supplies are enacted. These are the major sources of inflation, so that if programs are adopted to stabilize their prices, the rate of change of prices should moderate as well.[19] Second, a flexible incomes policy will ensure that temporary price shocks are not translated into general price increases. For example, an incomes policy such as TIP could be instituted quickly to curb the tendency of prices to rise as price shocks occurred or as the economy approached full employment. Some sort of incomes policy seems to be required in an advanced market economy where unequal power has been allowed to develop. Otherwise, some form of stagnation will result and policy will be constrained; the market does, indeed, carry its own forms of punishment.

Free-market ideologues will object to these intrusions into market economy, but sufficient evidence is available to refute their contentions that the market, if left alone, will achieve the desired results of full employment and price stability. In fact, the theories that suggest these results have been discredited enough and should not be used as a basis for public policy. The search theory of unemployment, with its suggestion that the unemployed are merely searching for a better job, or the rational-expectationist theories, with their unrealistic assumptions, all lead to the inevitable futility of public policy, but they are seriously flawed and appeal mainly to those who seek to justify their free-market bias.

Similarly, dogmatic monetarism should not be the basis for public policy. There is sufficient evidence to suggest that the old relations between inflation and money growth have been broken (if they ever existed) with recent developments in monetary instruments and institutions. Money is not only difficult to define but difficult to control, as well; neither the demand nor the supply side appears stable enough to predict, and the velocity of money varies too much for monetary growth to be used as a forecasting variable. Predictions of monetarists in the 1980s have been consistently wide of the mark, and as a consequence the monetarists' simple appeal of controlling the economy through control of monetary growth has eroded as well. The disappointment with monetarists' analysis also implies the decline in favor of their main policy prescription of constraining money-supply growth to some predetermined rate.

The money-supply growth rule never did gain wide acceptance, and discretionary actions of the monetary authorities were never threatened. The other rule—annually balanced budgets—survives, and calls for a constitutional convention to consider an amendment to that effect are still heard. As indicated earlier, such a rule for fiscal policy or those contained in the Gramm-Rudman Act are not only perverse but probably unworkable in practice. The president and Congress may enjoy playing games with this emotional issue, but they cannot shirk their responsibility for the budget totals or revenues collected; that is one of the things they are paid to do, and if they are unable to do it, why would a rule suddenly permit them to make the hard choices they refused to make before? Similarly, inane exercises to reduce budget deficits by across-the-board cuts in spending programs are also an example of job shirking and represent the easy way out, when what is needed is determining which programs are worth continuing and which are not.

Political cowardice and ineptitude should not be the basis for inefficient and ineffectual public policy. New institutional arrangements are needed if policymaking is to be made rational. Some suggestions that would help Congress perform its duties and avoid the political games over budgets, deficits, and other economic magnitudes are given below.

Thus, both fiscal and monetary policy should be discretionary and free of arbitrary rules. Rules only constrain action, and while conservatives may welcome that result, the economy is not self-regulating nor does it guarantee equitable outcomes. Either the market is allowed to imprison us or we take steps to escape and attempt to control our own destinies.

Autonomous Long-Term Programs

The third general principle is that long-run programs should not be allowed to vary with the business cycle; once a long-term goal is specified, every effort should be made to achieve it, regardless of the current state of the economy. This is more difficult than it sounds and will be honored only if there is a strong consensus on the purposes of the goal. It will require open discussion on the goal and a special method for gathering a wide array of opinion, so that the goal attains legitimacy.

With a rapidly advancing technology, it should soon be possible to conduct national surveys to determine which concerns are most important in the minds of the U.S. public.[20] Preceded by discussion in Congress and by various experts and concerned individuals and groups on public TV, the main concerns can be identified, and "voted" on. This exercise in democracy would result in a list of vital concerns that could be ranked and eventually translated into national goals.[21] The process would be inelegant, but so is democracy if actually practiced, and far better than the haphazard way of setting national goals and priorities that now exists.

Of course, the list of concerns could be extensive, but it is sure to include most of the common complaints of the public. The responses would have to be weighted by the number of times each item appeared on various lists, and, obviously, the respondents would be asked to rank their concerns. Thus the items would be ranked by importance and perhaps even urgency (as crucial, very important, important, and so on).

The tabulated results would then be sent to a general planning board (described below) for deliberation. Some of the concerns would be considered short-run and therefore not directly the responsibility of the planning agency. That is, suppose inflation or unemployment were identified as the number one and two problems. These concerns should be handled by those responsible for economic stabilization, and after a while these short-run concerns would gravitate to that group and be accepted by all as proper.

Other items on the list, however, could be considered long-run problems, requiring solutions that will take time and commitment. For example, suppose that poverty is identified as the most important long-run problem, with the implicit or explicit complaint that the distribution of income and wealth is too unfair and inequitable. Since an equitable distribution of income and wealth has never been seriously considered as a national goal, despite the rhetoric to the contrary, it will take some time to collect data, discuss options, and arrive at a definition of what a fair distribution of income or wealth really is. Indeed, the possibility for endless debate is a genuine problem, and means must be found to limit the time for consideration or else nothing will ever get done.

There are rough guidelines available[22] and many others could be entertained, but eventually (one year? two?) some standard must be chosen. Once the goal is established, the programs designed to attain it should not be sacrificed to the vagaries of the business cycle, but pursued without regard to the current state of the economy.

A fair distribution of income or wealth is a very difficult issue to consider and more controversial than some of the other problems. It was chosen here as an example simply to demonstrate that it is the type of concern that has not received adequate attention in the past and one that may no longer be safely left to the marketplace, if democracy is permitted to register the shortcomings of market economies.

Some of the other concerns might involve social investment of some kind, and these programs would be more acceptable to a public unfamiliar with or ignorant of the inequitable distribution of rewards. In addition, much more has been written on the needs of education, housing, and social overhead capital, such as water and sewer systems and roads, and more information already exists on the types of programs required to rectify the ills. It is for this reason that social-investment concerns probably should be considered first, if they are near the top of the list. It is important that results follow rather quickly, or the whole exercise will be dismissed as just another institution wasting money and accomplishing little. Concrete results will forestall the cynicism that will inevitably accompany any attempt to manage the future.

To answer some of the other concerns, such as the loss of jobs due to foreign trade, the farm problem, or energy costs, an explicit industrial policy is needed. As pointed out in various places, an industrial policy already exists, but it is not rational in the sense that it is the result of deliberate actions designed to fit into some coherent program. For example, the accelerated depreciation scheme of the 1981 tax law favored capital-using techniques at the same time that comparative-advantage hopes were pinned on high-technology firms that were not capital-using. Similar conclusions can be reached about the investment tax credit, or the requirement that the U.S. Merchant Marine be involved in shipping goods, or subsidies to airports, and so on. So, too, the quota system for automobiles is an industrial policy without the name. Many have suggested the components of an industrial policy, some favoring the Japanese model, some favoring simply a development bank resembling the old RFC of Mr. Hoover, and some have suggested greater use of cooperatives. (Hoover may well have approved of the idea of an industrial policy and the use of voluntary cooperatives.[23]) An industrial policy is not the entire solution to industrial woes, but it could be the beginning of the development of a rational plan to cope with changing world conditions and changing technology. At least the hidden industrial policy will be uncovered and exposed for what it is. If an industrial policy is adopted as part of an overall planning scheme, care must be exercised in who controls the policies, for it would be dangerous if special interests gained control and subverted the process for their own benefit.

An agricultural policy should be developed by agencies free of special interests. Past attempts to rationalize agriculture are not encouraging, but in the past political interests dominated the discussion of agricultural policy and that political interest must be removed, if any measure of success is to be achieved. Thus an agricultural policy would become part of the long-term plan, developed with the aid of the Department of Agriculture and farm interests, but independent of them. Otherwise, the farm bloc will organize to defeat attempts to formulate a workable farm policy. One possibility is to subsidize farmers' incomes directly, rather than guarantee them stipulated prices for their output. Guaranteeing farm prices has resulted only in food surpluses and high prices to the consumer. Programs that limited land in production, or parity programs, and so on, proved costly and subsidized the wrong (large) producers. One way out has long been recognized, but rejected by farmers—let supply and demand (estimated by economists) determine prices, and farmers decide how much to produce at those prices; the market will determine actual prices, and if insufficient to provide for a predetermined income, then farmers would be subsidized directly. Such a program would have to be developed for the society by groups outside the farm bloc, but that is the purpose of an outside agency that can look to the national interest instead of satisfying parochial ones.

It is not the purpose here to anticipate the national goals that would emerge or the types of programs needed to reach them. The foregoing are suggestions as to both aspects, but there is no need to continue with additional examples. Only actual experience would determine how and when to proceed. The point of this section is to stress the importance of determining national goals in a rational manner and to suggest that once the goals and programs necessary to achieve them have been determined, the business cycle should not have any influence over them, and they should proceed autonomously, regardless of the current state of the economy.

Institutional Changes

The fourth and fifth general principles should be considered together, although technically they could be separated. The fourth principle is that different sets of policymakers should be involved in determining short- and long-term goals and policies, and the fifth goal recommends that new institutions be considered, if necessary, to conduct the policies decided by the two sets of policymakers. Clearly, it would be possible to divide the policymaking responsibility by using existing institutions or by modifying them, but it is better to begin with the assumption that new institutions will be needed. New institutions create the feeling that the change is significant, while the use of existing ones creates the impression that not much will change and that the same old prolems will emerge.

As indicated earlier, one of the problems in formulating policy is that economic advice is so diverse and experts seem so far apart, and at times the debate is acrimonious, as well; it becomes all too easy for reasoned economic advice to be ignored in favor of whatever crank idea is in vogue. Economists can never be unanimous, of course, since values are involved, but some method for the expression of widely diverse views must be found, or there will be times when economic advice will be deemed irrelevant.

The other danger in seeking uniformity of views is that legitimate views out of the mainstream will not be given a serious hearing. It would be tragic if only the views of the mainstream economists were considered worthy of consideration and the sound ideas of others passed over. Economists out of the mainstream have devoted a great deal of effort, both theoretical and empirical, to the study of alternative institutions and policies and are not to be lumped together with the unsystematic and inchoate ideas of cranks. Again, these views must be aired without making the voices of all incoherent and cacophonous.

Just a cursory look at Table 15.1 is sufficient to reveal that not every institution on the list is equally influential on policymakers, and

Table 15.1 Institutions Offering Economic Advice

Government Agencies	*Private Agencies*
Council of Economic Advisors	Research organizations
Congression Budget Office	Brookings Institution
Federal Reserve System (12 branches)	American Enterprise Institute
Treasury	Committee for Economic Development
Office of Budget and Management	Hoover Institute
Joint Economic Committee	Urban Institute
Congressional committees	Others
Departments and agencies	Special-Interest Groups
	National Association of Manufacturers
	Bankers Associations
	Labor organizations
	Consumer groups
	Wall Street
	Business corporations
	Minority groups
	Independent economists and businessmen
	Journalists
	World organizations
	UN
	IMF or GATT
	World Bank

Source: Compiled by the author.

that a more serious attempt to measure influence would have to include a weighting system, one that might change with the issue. That is not the purpose here; rather, the aim of the chart is to suggest the wide array of sources available to policymakers, each with a point of view, and each with criticisms of the other's views. It would be possible, therefore, to select the point of view that accords with one's own and ignore the rest—or worse, to ignore all of them.

The difficulty with this arrangement is that only experts are familiar with most of the arguments made by the several groups. There is insufficient airing of the views of the various groups, with the consequence that policy may be based on the views of only the group most influential at the time. Still, the other voices are heard and that makes for confusion for everyone involved. What is needed is some focus to the debate, so that what emerges can be viewed as some sort of consensus among advisors. Disagreements would remain, of course, and could never be eliminated, But the advice that emerged and perhaps actually followed would earn more confidence than now exists in economic policymaking.

Short-term goals and policies should be entrusted to a distinct group in order to focus advice. The short-term goals are dominated by stabilization policies, so that the main job of this group is to reduce the number and size of fluctuations of economic activity.

Recall that one of the main deterrents to sound economic policymaking is the intrustion of political considerations that often made economic policy irrational. It is therefore necessary to remove, as much as possible, the political motives for detemining policy, without defeating the intent of democratic control over decisions. Accordingly this group, let us call it the Economic Council, should be appointed by the major parties to ensure its bipartisan composition and to free it from short-run political concerns.

The composition of the Economic Council would be determined by letting each major party (including third parties if they received, say, over 5 percent of the vote in the previous election) select three economists; the president would select one. This plan follows one suggested by Gordon Tullock for a revision of the Council of Economic Advisors, but is extended to a separate agency here.[24] The candidates could be suggested by the American Economic Association, as is done for judicial appointments by the American Bar Association. The Economic Council could be housed in the Department of Commerce or some similar agency, to give it an independent appearance and to make use of the existing staff.

The Economic Council should replace the Council of Economic Advisors, and its staff should be transferred to the new council. The president may wish to retain economists on his own White House staff to help him interpret the advice of the Economic Council, but the CEA would no longer be needed. The CEA quickly became a partisan agency, and its economic advice, forecasts, and pronouncements were so regarded. In this connection, many economists who served on the CEA found themselves advocating policies they did not agree with or refraining from criticisms of policies they advised against. Over time, the CEA lost its credibility, as a result, and its voice was discounted. It does not serve the role of independent policymaking and should be abolished.

The Congressional Budget Office, formulated to help Congress prepare its own economic analyses, may also no longer be needed, although a staff for budgetary purposes may still be required. Perhaps the role of the CBO should be redefined and part of the excess staff transferred to the new Economic Council. With experience and trust in the new agency, more of the functions of the CBO could be taken over by the Economic Council. A small staff may be useful for some time in interpreting the reports of the council or to prepare special reports not involved in the stabilization function. Thus the job of the CBO may be altered or part of its duties surrendered to the new council.

Other departments and agencies of the federal government may wish to reduce their involvement in the stabilization function of macroeconomic policy and reduce their staffs accordingly. They may still wish to retain economists to investigate areas of their primary responsibility and conduct studies for specific purposes. The aim of the new council is to focus policy advice on economic stabilization in a central place and not to usurp the functions of economic studies in other areas.

The Economic Council, then, is composed of from seven to ten members chosen by political parties, located in an office separate from the president and Congress, and charged with the responsibility of advising on stabilization policies. Now, since the economists are appointed to the council by political parties, we can expect different views to be represented and we can also expect these views to be aired, publicly or not, as the members themselves determine.

When they disagree over policy, the nation will know just how deeply they are divided and the nature of the disagreement. As Tullock put it, "the policymaking organs of our government would have presented to them several economically literate points of view on problems which are genuinely controversial among economists. Thus, the ultimate decision would be better than if they receive only one opinion."[25] Politicians would have to decide which advice to follow in such cases, but that is their duty as decision makers. Again, democracy does involve risks, but that is better than letting economists decide policy, as happens when politicians listen only to advice they want to hear.

When the advice from the council is in general agreement, public confidence in their advice will be much greater than is the case when only one view is heard. If diverse economists agree on general policies, they must be representing a consensus among economists in general, and their advice should be more acceptable as a result. Contrary to the popular view, the periods of agreement are likely to be far more numerous than imagined, and public confidence in their work is likely to grow—the more so, the more successful their advice.

Advising policymakers who then make decisions is the nature of the Economic Council. Fiscal-policy advice to congressional committees and to the OMB will initiate the short-run goals of the council. But regardless of the advice, what institutional reforms will help in the budgetary process? First, many economists have found fault with the budgetary process. Alice Rivlin, for instance, has suggested that the budget process takes up too much time and that Congress is forever debating budget items and never completes the job. She suggests that the budget be made a biannual one, that that would rationalize the budgetary process and make it more thorough and time saving for all involved, including the rest of the economy that awaits the decisions of Congress.[26]

This idea has much merit and should be considered, whether or not other suggestions are, but in the proposal given below it is even more cogent. If some sort of planning agency is adopted, Congress will be forced to prepare long-term budgets and tax programs. With the removal of much uncertainty, planning at the micro level, be it a corporation or state or city, will be possible; now planning is limited because of the uncertainty over what Congress is going to do.

Fiscal policy may be made easier with planning, as well, because many items in the budget will be relatively fixed, since they are directed at achieving long-term goals. Another institutional device favored by Rivlin is the elimination of dual congressional committees, one for authorizations and one for appropriations. This suggestion is also worthy of consideration, even if nothing else is adopted. There is no reason to have two committees, when all the work can be accomplished with one; one committee would save time and force everyone to regard the issue as a program, as a whole, not to be modified later, and so on.

The entire budget timetable, first proposed in 1974, has not worked well in practice. Designed to force Congress to consider the macro effects of the budget totals, it has worked in that regard, but the budget process is not completed as mandated and the process has often bogged down in partisan wrangling. Another purpose of the 1974 Budget Act was to give Congress more control over the budget, but in practice the president has used timetables and procedures to gain even greater control over the budget and to determine spending and taxing priorities.[27] Mr. Reagan has proved to be a master at using the budgetary process for his own purposes.

Perhaps congress ought to submit its own budget totals, say the critics, and require OMB and the president to submit a budget consistent with its spending and taxing totals and priorities. This would return more control to the Congress and reduce the power of the presidency and should appeal to those who fear the centralization of power. Alternatively, the Economic Council could propose to the

Congress budgetary totals that are consistent with economic stabilization, Congress could debate the advice, and then require OMB's compliance with their budget totals. This would accomplish both the return of power to Congress and the rationalization of the budget process. Responsibility for budget deficits or surpluses would be recognized and not shifted, as is the case now, to anyone else.

In any case, a separate budget for capital items ought to be a part of the effort to improve the budgetary process. It makes little sense to mix expenditures for current operations with capital expenditures. Office buildings and tanks last for longer periods than the fiscal year in which they are purchased. Capital items should have their own budget, be viewed as private capital goods, and be depreciated or written off over a longer time period. This should be done long before any efforts are made to balance the budget; balancing a budget that includes capital items with current revenues is not sound finance by normal accounting standards, and should not be so regarded when it comes to government finance. Again, these capital items would be an integral part of the planning process and would automatically receive the proper treatment in long-term planning.

The Federal Reserve System has as many critics as there are observers of it. Recommendations include altering the way the Federal Reserve conducts its business, changing the tools with which it works, and reducing its responsibilities. It has been asked to change its accounting procedures used in counting the bank reserves; it has been asked to use the discount rate differently; it has been asked to give up its regulatory functions, except for the management of the money supply, and so forth and so on. Monetarists have a suggestion every week for the Federal Reserve. Milton Friedman wants the Federal Reserve to give up all functions except control over the money supply but then suggests that the rate of growth of high-powered money (currency and bank reserves) be frozen and that any growth in the money supply should come from private sources competing with the government in creating money. His suggestions would radically transform the Federal Reserve System and severely limit its functions.[28]

At the other extreme, Bowles, Gordon, and Weisskopf want to make the Federal Reserve more democratic and propose that the House elect the board of governors to ensure that the special interests of bankers are not put before the needs of the nation.[29] In between, the number of suggestions of how to reform the Federal Reserve System is staggering, and there is no need to catalog them here. Instead, a few suggestions will suffice.

First, the Federal Reserve System should become part of the Treasury and be responsible to the administration for monetary policy. In reality this is done now, although the Federal Reserve was supposed to be independent of the executive branch; in practice, the Federal Reserve has read the election results and acted accordingly. Second, its sole function should be control over the money supply, with its regulatory functions transferred to other agencies, such as the comptroller of the currency. Any questions over jurisdiction ought to be resolved by reference to whether the problem affects monetary conditions sufficiently for the Federal Reserve to be involved.

Again, the Economic Council would advise the Federal Reserve on the monetary conditions necessary to achieve stabilization in the economy. These would include the desirable rates of growth of the money supply (defined by the council), desirable rates of interest, debt financing, and so on. The Federal Reserve would be required to consider these recommendations in its policy formations for the short term as well as for the longer term.

Thus the Economic Council would be feeding its advice to the agencies responsible for policymaking. It would be suggesting budgetary totals and other fiscal matters to Congress and monetary goals to the Federal Reserve System. With the new institutional arrangements in effect, these recommendations would represent the advice of an independent group of economists free of partisan politics. Minority views would reveal the depth and nature of any disagreements, and these voices should be heard. In the end, the policymaking must be done by elected officials; the goal here is to make the advice as rational as possible so that they may act with as much confidence as possible. Politicians would be able to assert that they were taking the best advice possible and to that extent would stop looking for scapegoats; they could rightfully assert to their constituents that they acted in good faith on the advice of an independent agency. This could give them the necessary strength to withstand special-interest-group pressures and to make policy that is in the interest of the nation as a whole.

Long-Term Goals and Programs and Planning

The long-term goals and policies should be considered separately from the short-run goal of stabilization, for a variety of reasons. First, the short-run programs suitable for stabilization purposes can be started and stopped as the situation demands; for long-run programs the commitment is to the attainment of some long-term goal, and that should not vary with the business cycle. Long-run programs should not be regarded as countercyclical, cut in periods of inflation and revived in periods of slack.

Second, the type of long-term program differs considerably from that of short-run programs. Instead of the usual monetary and fiscal policies needed for stabilization purposes, the long-run goals reflect the concerns of the nation for needs unmet by the marketplace. Table 15.2 lists some of the types of programs that should be considered as long-term under this definition.

Most of these long-term programs are self-explanatory, and much has been written about each, so that, except for a few examples, no attempt to spell them out will be made here. That they differ from short-run programs is also evident, and so all that is needed now is the institutional mechanism to carry out the programs.

Long-term goals and programs require planning, if they are ever to be successful. By their very nature these programs cannot be ad hoc, nor can they vary according to the political whims of those who

Table 15.2   Long-Term Goals and Programs

Social Capital or Social Overhead Items	Projects to Aid Private Markets
Water, sewer, lighting systems	Investment fund for private investment
Roads and waterways	Manpower programs for trade-related
Mass transit	unemployment
Urban development	Research into alternative energy sources
Energy projects	Rationing schemes for energy sources
Public housing or subsidized housing	
Recreation development	
Conservation projects	

Other programs	
Redistribution of income and wealth schemes	Agricultural programs, co-ops, market information for trde to ratinalize farm income
Health programs	
Tax reform	Industrial policy
Education programs	
Federalism issues	

Source: Compiled by the author.

temporarily occupy positions of power. Once the long-term goals have been determined, they should be pursued with the necessary commitment; if they are not, they could not have been vital national concerns to begin with, but temporary problems better solved elsewhere.

To determine which goals to pursue and in what order, a planning board is needed, one that will have as wide a representation as possible. The planning board would be composed of representatives of broad community groups, to ensure that the spectrum of views would be heard and to gain the support of the society. As a beginning, the board could be composed of the following groups:

Three members from the business community, chosen by the NAM or some other organization (The CED furnishes an excellent example.)

Three members from the farming sector, chosen by farm organizations

Three members from organized labor, chosen by election

Three members from consumer grops, chosen by consumer advocacy groups

Three members from elected officials to national offices, one appointed by each of the two major political parties, with the highest third party receiving the third appointment

Three members from elected officials to state and local offices, elected by appropriate organizations; one from state offices and two from local offices

Three members from minority groups or radical groups, elected by appropriate organizations

Fifty staff members—social scientists, statisticians, and support members; economists, sociologists, demographers, and other necessary disciplines would be represented; some of the staff members could be transferees from the CBO or the CEA.

Members would serve for, say, a five-year period, with renewal possible, in staggered terms so that continuity would be assured. High salaries and prestige should assure the attraction of highly qualified and motivated people to serve on this board. In any case, the foregoing is just one suggestion for the composition of the board, and other membership and office terms could be arranged.

The planning board would be housed in the Department of Commerce, perhaps in the Bureau of the Census. It would have access to all departments of government and to all information available; it would hold hearings, solicit views of experts, award grants for studies, and in general be an autonomous part of the administration.

Why is planning necessary? Again there is sufficient evidence that the economy is not self-regulating and must be managed to one degree or another. There is also enough evidence that the market is failing to meet human needs, and many social problems cannot be resolved by relying on the marketplace or the political process as it now exists. Just a glance at Table 15.2 should be sufficient to reveal the failures of our socioeconomic systems to solve some rather basic problems. Appeals to grant more time to the market or to the political process are at best ingenuous and at worst deceptive. The problems of concern here have a long history and a dismal response record and are not likely either to go away or be addressed by existing institutions.

Planning will help push the society to the recognition of its problem and toward the solution to them. It can also reduce the uncertainty involved in private planning at the micro level. Consider only the case of private investment. Perhaps the biggest deterrent to investment spending is uncertainty about the future of the economy. Capital goods last a long time, and there is no guarantee that the economy will be prosperous when the goods are produced, and there is no guarantee that the federal government will be committed to stabilizing the economy and to fighting the business cycle. Once such assurances are realized, private investment can take place in an atmosphere of greater confidence, and while the risk of investment cannot be removed, the climate for investment can be made propitious. With private investment spending more stable, the likelihood of a severe business cycle is reduced, and once the likelihood of the business cycle is removed, investment may become more stable, and so forth.

A planning agency can go further than just creating a climate of confidence by actively promoting a program that reinforces the commitment to a stable economy. For example, one item in Table 15.2 is a scheme for funding private investment. This example is borrowed from Sweden, where firms have been permitted to deduct a certain proportion of their profits for tax purposes, it they deposit about half of this deduction in an interest-free fund at the central bank. When a recession hit, the firms could withdraw the funds, tax free, for use in investment purchases. Thus the fund became a countercyclical device that helped stabilize investment spending and the economy as well.[30] This is an example of a program that achieves a specific purpose that the free market could not reach, and by a system that the free market could never inaugurate.

Nevertheless, the idea of planning in any form has not been well received in the United States. Free marketers and special interests have succeeded in convincing most people that planning is not needed and would be harmful if employed. Despite the obvious failures of the marketplace and despite the fact that planning for any other organization, including the household, is regarded as rational and necessary—and despite the success of schemes such as the investment program above—planning is still deemed inappropriate for an advanced capitalistic system and is considered vaguely socialistic.

For this reason and because it will take some time to gain acceptance, it is better to start with social overhead programs and investment schemes before tackling the more controversial goals—a fairer distribution of income and wealth, for instance. With some successes the idea of planning will cease to be as threatening, and greater acceptance with be forthcoming. Eventually, it may come to be seen as a vital ingredient for an economy with the attributes of the U.S. economy, with its private/public composition.

Making Policymaking More Rational

Coordination will be necessary between the two agencies, as in the case of an incomes policy, for example, and in many other cases as well. Perhaps some key staff members could be given joint appointments to allow for increased interaction. The operational details can be worked out over time, and no blueprint should be imposed on either the Economic Council or the Planning Board. They are, after all, advisors and not decision makers, at least in the early stages of their existence. With time, they may play a more active role in policymaking, but initially the actual decisions should remain with elected officials; but these officials will no longer be able to duck responsibility for their acts; no longer will they be able to claim ignorance of professional advice.

In many ways, the advisors resemble the independent commissions that were appointed to investigate some problem or other. When their findings were released, politicians could quote their results, and even if there was disagreement with them, officials could claim that they voted for this legislation because of commission's findings. This has often mollified constituents and got the politician off the hook for unpopular solutions. Consider the use by Mr. Reagan of the special Social Security Commission, when the issue got too controversial for politicans to handle. Imagine how a tax reform proposal by the Planning Board would relieve many congressmen of election concerns.

More information and more coherent advice may make policymaking more rational, but there is no guarantee; institutional changes may permit better policy decisions, but in the end it is people who make them. In the past many unqualified and incompetent people have been elected to public office, and the situation is not likely to be improved unless government service is looked upon as a prestigious occupation worthy of a career choice. Larger salaries and perks might help, but they will not be sufficient by themselves. What is needed is the attraction of a higher-quality person to public service, and this means basically that some basic reforms are required to finance political campaigns so that the compromises and shady deals, and so on can be resisted. It should not be necessary to have to sell one's soul in order to attain political power. Surely some experimentation is in order to find a better way to finance political campaigns; failure to do so will result in the same problems that fill the record of past policymaking.

Clearly, macroeconomic policymaking has evolved in a rather uneven pattern over the period since the end of World War II. The record indicates that macro policy did not evolve in an orderly manner; that is, the initial application of knowledge in one period, followed by learning from mistakes and improving policies in the next period, and so on. Over time, it was felt that new institutions would be developed to deal with the complex and everchanging economic problems that arise in an advanced capitalist system.

Instead, policymaking proceeded like a pendulum, swinging from utilization of available tools to ignoring them, from underutilization of knowledge to the exaggeration of knowledge, and back again. A large part of this vacillation can be traced to the tenacious hold that free markets have on the minds of intellectuals in and out of government. Government is simply not needed, except occasionally, and the marketplace will solve most of the problems that arise. The distrust of government and the fear of intrusion run deep in the country's set of beliefs. On the one hand, we want to help others, want a stable economy, want a fair distribution of income, and so on, but on the other, we resist attempts to reach these ends.

It takes a rather large capacity for self-deception to adhere to the belief that the marketplace will solve all of our emerging problems without intervention by government. If the past is any guide, more—not less—intrusion is required. The traditional view is comforting and obviously beguiling, but a closer look will reveal that it is often fueled by propaganda and self-serving justifications from those who do not suffer from the economic disruptions, who do not lose their livelihoods, and who do not fear the hunger and the cold. Among those who fear the loss of their economic freedom are not those who get left behind and live those lives of quiet desperation.

The foregoing suggestions for institutional reforms to improve policymaking are, of course, rather utopian and idealistic. The probability of the adoption of any of them, or anything like them, is presently remote. Yet the fact that ideas do not result in immediate acceptance or are not quickly implemented should not be allowed to limit their expression; providing alternatives to what exists can not only stimulate discussion but could result in gradual or partial modifications of existing institutions and procedures. It is in this spirit that the policy reforms and suggestions are offered.

Notes

Introduction

1. Gunnar Myrdal, *Against the Stream: Critical Essays on Economics* (New York: Pantheon Books, 1973), p. 147.
2. Richard A. Musgrave, *The Theory of Public Finance* (New York: McGraw-Hill, 1959).
3. See Andrew Hacker, "Up For Grabs," *New York Review of Books* (April 1981), pp. 8–16.

Chapter 1

1. In fact, this is the title of a good survey of the U.S. record; Robert A. Gordon, *Economic Instability & Growth* (New York: Harper & Row, 1974).
2. For a good discussion of the difficulties involved with the marginal productivity theory, see Lester C. Thurow, *Generating Inequality* (New York: Basic Books, 1975).
3. U.S. Department of Commerce, Bureau of the Census, *Income Distribution in the United Stated*, by Herman P. Miller (Washington, DC: GPO, 1966), p. 2. (1960 Census Monograph)
4. Ibid., p. 3.
5. Robert J. Lampman, *The Share of Top Wealth-Holders in National Wealth, 1922–56*, National Bureau of Economic Research (Princeton, NJ: Princeton University Press, 1962), p. 24.
6. Dorothy S. Projector and Gertrude S. Weiss, *Survey of Financial Characteristics of Consumers*, Board of Governors of the Federal Reserve System, Washington, DC, 1966.
7. Board of Governors of the Federal Reserve System, "Survey of Consumer Finances, 1983," *Federal Reserve Bulletin* (September 1984), pp. 679–92; (December 1984), pp. 857–68.
8. The economic libertarian view is admirably expressed by Milton Friedman in his many writings. For example, see his recent work (together with Rose Friedman), *Free to Choose* (New York: Harcourt Brace Jovanovich, 1979).

Chapter 2

1. See his influential books *Promise of American Life* (New York: Macmillan, 1909) and *Progressive Democracy* (New York: Macmillan, 1915). For more on the Progressive movement, see Harold U. Faulkner, *The Quest for Social Justice, 1898–1914* (New York: Macmillan, 1951); and Arthur S. Link, *Woodrow Wilson and the Progressive Era, 1910–1997* (New York: Harper & Row, 1954).
2. Ibid., Croly, *Progressive Democracy*, p. 119.
3. Link, *Woodrow Wilson*, p. 19.
4. For the case against Roosevelt's achievements as a trustbuster, see Gabriel Kolko, *The Triumph of Conservatism* (Glencoe, IL: The Free Press, 1963).
5. Obviously these are examples of bills being watered down in the political process by special interest groups or vested interests. In these cases the original bills were tailored or written by the special interest groups involved and were modified by those who sought to protect the public's interests. These cases and other examples in the text are not treated fully or as fully as they deserve because the main focus of this book is on the period after they occurred.
6. Bernard Baruch, *The Public Years* (New York: Holt, Rinehart and Winston, 1960), p. 74.
7. For more details on the economics of wartime finance, see the excellent summary of George Soule, *Prosperity Decade* (New York: Holt, Rinehart and Winston, 1947, reprinted by M. E. Sharpe, Inc., of White Plains, NY, in 1974).
8. Frederick Lewis Allen, *The Big Change* (New York: Harper & Brothers, 1952), p. 131.
9. *Federal Reserve Bulletin* (December 1919), pp. 1107–8.
10. Hearings, U.S. Congress Temporary National Economic Committee, *Hearings on Investigation of Concentration of Economic Power* (Washington, DC: GPO, 1940), pp. 11338–41.
11. William E. Leuchtenburg, *The Perils of Prosperity, 1914–32* (Chicago: University of Chicago Press, 1958), p. 76.
12. Frederick C. Mills, *Prices in Recession and Recovery* (New York: National Bureau of Economic Research, 1936), p. 491.
13. U.S. Department of Commerce, Bureau of the Census, *Long-Term Economic Growth 1860–1965* (Washington, DC: GPO, 1966), p. 167.
14. Ibid., pp. 169, 191.
15. U.S. Department of Commerce, Bureau of the Census, *Historical Statistics of the United States* (Washington, DC: GPO, 1975), pp. 889, 892–93.
16. U.S. Department of Commerce, *Long Term-Economic Growth*, p. 171.
17. Tax Foundation, Inc., *Facts and Figures of Government Finance*, 1973, p. 104.
18. See Milton Friedman and Anna J. Schwartz, *A Monetary History of the United States 1867–1960*, NBER (Princeton, NJ: Princeton University Press, 1963), p. 223, for their judgment.

19. Ibid., p. 239.
20. This view is stressed by Elmus R. Wicker, *Federal Reserve Monetary Policy, 1917–1933* (New York: Random House, 1966), p. 49. Wicker suggests that the model being followed belongs to the type found in the real-bills family of monetary models.
21. Ibid.
22. U.S. Department of Justice, Office of the Attorney General, *Annual Reports of the Attorney General of the United States,* various years.
23. U.S. Department of Commerce, *Historical Statistics,* p. 914.
24. Soule, *Prosperity Decade,* pp. 78–79.
25. U.S. Department of Commerce, *Historical Statistics,* p. 915.

Chapter 3

1. See Frederick Lewis Allen, *Only Yesterday* (New York: Harper, 1931); Mark Sullivan, *Our Times*: VI, *The Twenties* (New York: Scribner's, 1935); and George Soule, *Prosperity Decade* (New York: Holt, Rinehart and Winston, 1947, reprinted by M. E. Sharpe, Inc., of White Plains, New York).
2. Lewis H. Haney, *History of Economic Thought,* 4th ed. (New York: Macmillan, 1949), p. 733.
3. Quoted by Mark Sullivan, *Our Times,* p. 128.
4. For more on this subject, see e e cummings' poem "the first president to be loved by his," in *Poems, 1923–1954* (New York: Harcourt, Brace, 1954), p. 242.
5. Allen, *Only Yesterday,* p. 126. On page 127 Allen quotes Harding whining over a tax problem. "I can't make a damn thing out of this tax problem. I listen to one side and they seem right, and then—God!—I talk to the other side and they seem just as right, and here I am where I started. I know somewhere there is a book that will give me the truth, but, hell, I couldn't read the book. I know somewhere there is an economist who knows the truth, but I don't know where to find him and haven't the sense to know him and trust him when I find him. God! What a job!"
6. William E. Leuchtenburg, *The Perils of Prosperity, 1914–32* (Chicago: University of Chicago Press, 1958), p. 94.
7. Andrew Mellon, *Taxation: The People's Business* (New York: Macmillan, 1924), pp. 29–35.
8. For more details on tariffs, see F. W. Taussig, *The Tariff History of the United States* (New York: Capricorn Books, 8th ed., 1964), pp. 447ff. For more details on taxation, see Sidney Ratner, *Taxation and Democracy in America* (New York: Wiley, 1942); and Roy G. Blakey and Gladys C. Blakey, *The Federal Income Tax* (New York: Longmans, Green, 1940). In matters of taxation I have relied heavily on these two excellent sources.
9. Mellon, *Taxation,* p. 137. The full quotation reveals that Mellon clearly stated what has come to be called supply-side economics in the 1980s.

The adoption of a sound system of taxation will have a favorable effect in many directions. It should help to solve the housing problem, to make possible lower freight and passenger rates by getting the railroads back on an efficiency basis, to increase savings due to the reduction of taxes on earned incomes and the lower brackets and thereby to increase the buying power of the earning class and to raise its standard of living. It will also promote industrial and business activity by diverting into productive enterprise funds which are now going into tax-exempt securities. This should increase the number of jobs and at the same time advance general prosperity.

On pages 16 and 17, Mellon anticipates the so-called Laffer Curve:

It seems difficult for some to understand that high rates of taxation do not necessarily mean large revenue to the Government, and that more revenue may often be obtained by lower rates. There was an old saying that a railroad freight rate should be "what the traffic will bear"; that is, the highest rate at which the largest quantity of freight would move. The same rule applies to all private businesses. If a price is fixed too high, sales drop off and with them profits; if a price is fixed too low, sales may increase but again profits decline. ... The Government is just a business, and can and should be run on business principles.

Experience has shown that the present high rates of surtax are bringing in each year progressively less revenue to the Government. This means that the price is too high to the large taxpayer and he is avoiding a taxable income by the many ways which are available to him. What rates will bring in the largest revenue to the Government experience has not yet developed, but it is estimated that by cutting the surtaxes in half, the Government, when the full effect of the reduction is felt, will receive more revenue from the owners of large incomes at the lower rates than it would have received at the higher rates.

10. Charles O. Hardy, *Tax-Exempt Securities and the Surtax* (New York: Macmillan, 1926).
11. Ibid., pp. 165ff.
12. Ibid., p. 157.
13. In the *Federal Reserve Bulletin* of November, p. 1048, the board stated its theoretical understanding:

Bank credit when granted by commercial institutions upon the strength of, or for the purpose of liquidating, commercial transactions of early maturities, serves as a means of facilitating the flow of commodities from producer to consumer and the return of purchasing power from the consumer to the producer through the various channels of circulation. This process enables goods to act as a means of purchase and payment for other goods, and when the maturity of the average loan granted (or "credit allowed") is no longer than that of the productive processes in which the community is engaged, the effect of it is only that of facilitating and promoting production and distribution.

14. The wording of the *Tenth Annual Report, 1923* is as follows:

But the problem of credit and currency administration implies the use not only of qualitative tests but also of quantitative tests. ... The problem in good administration under the Federal system is not only that of limiting the field of uses of Federal Reserve credit to productive purposes (the qualitative test) but also of limiting the volume of credit within the field of its appropriate uses to such amount as may be economically justified—that is, justified by a commensurate increase in the Nation's aggregate productivity (the quantitative test).

15. See Elmus R. Wicker, *Federal Reserve Monetary Policy, 1917–1933* (New York: Random House, 1966), pp. 91ff.
16. J. M. Keynes, "The Economic Consequences of Mr. Churchill," *Essays in Persuasion* (New York: Norton, 1963), pp. 144–70.
17. The most entertaining of these is J. K. Galbraith, *The Great Crash* (Boston: Houghton Mifflin, 1955).
18. Simon Kuznets, *National Income and Its Compensation, 1919–1938* (New York: National Bureau of Economic Research, 1941), pp. 168ff.
19. Edwin G. Nourse, *America's Capacity to Produce* (Washington, DC: The Brookings Institution, 1934), p. 415.
20. Estimated by Paul H. Douglas, *Real Wages in the United States, 1890–1926* (Boston: Houghton Mifflin, 1930) and in subsequent updates.
21. Frederick C. Mills, *Prices in Recession and Recovery* (New York: National Bureau of Economic Research, 1936), p. 551; and John W. Kendrick, *Productivity Trends in the United States* (Princeton, NJ: Princeton University Press for NBER, 1961), pp. 127–29.
22. Kuznets, *National Income*, pp. 217–18.
23. Maurice Leven, Harold G. Moulton, and Clark Warburton, *America's Capacity to Consume* (Washington, DC: The Brookings Institution, 1934), p. 126.
24. See Soule, *Prosperity Decade*, p. 329.

Chapter 4

1. David Burner, *Herbert Hoover* (New York: Knopf, 1979), p. 10.
2. Ibid., p. 140.

3. Broadus Mitchell, *Depression Decade* (White Plains, NY: M. E. Sharpe), p. 90.
4. See Burner, *Hoover*, p. 252.
5. Quoted by William Manchester, *The Glory and The Dream* (Boston: Little, Brown, 1973), p. 48.
6. Burner, *Hoover*, pp. 259–60. "It is not the function of the Government to relieve individuals of their responsibilities to their neighbors, or to relieve private institutions of their responsibilities to the public, or of local government to the states, or of state governments to the Federal Government."
7. See F. W. Taussig, *The Tariff History of the United States* (New York: Capricorn Books, 1964), pp. 489–526.
8. Burner, *Hoover*, p. 300.
9. Mitchell, *Depression Decade*, p. 12.
10. A mutiny in the navy over pay cuts helped precipitate the crisis.
11. Edwin G. Nourse and Associates, *America's Capacity to Produce* (Washington, DC: The Brookings Institution, 1934), p. 40.
12. See Burner, *Hoover*, p. 271. A similar scheme was devised for railroads. The Railroad Credit Corporation, established in December 1931, collected a tax on freight rates and was to lend to railroads in trouble. It, too, proved ineffective, as the funds available were too meager to meet the railroad's perplexing problems.
13. Lester V. Chandlor, *America's Greatest Depression, 1929–1941* (New York: Harper & Row, 1970), p. 88.
14. Mitchell, *Depression Decade*, p. 89.
15. Ibid., p. 103.
16. Elmus R. Wicker, *Federal Reserve Monetary Policy, 1917–1933* (New York: Random House, 1966), pp. 147–49.
17. Peter Temin, *Did Monetary Forces Cause the Great Depression?* (New York; Norton, 1976), p. 90.
18. Milton Friedman and Anna J. Schwartz, *A Monetary History of the United States 1867–1960* (Princeton, NJ: Princeton University Press, 1963), Chapter 7.
19. Temin, *Monetary Forces*, pp. 170ff.
20. Wicker, *Federal Reserve Policy*, p. 168.
21. See Frederick Lewis Allen, *Since Yesterday* (New York: Bantam Books, 1961), p. 46.
22. Stuart Chase wrote a book with this title.
23. Joseph Alsop, *FDR, 1882–1945* (New York: Washington Square Press, 1982), p. 70.

Chapter 5

1. Had the New Dealers been more radical, they might have seized this opportunity to promote some form of collectivism. Consider the economic

conditions when FDR took office: real output down by 30 percent from 1929; unemployment up by over 638 percent and moving to record highs; firms operating at well below potential capacity; agriculture in shambles; international trade collapsing; state and local governments in financial distress; and the banks closing their doors. Not only was the economy devastated, but there was much sentiment, mainly by intellectuals, for social experimentation.

The banking crisis, with all states observing a banking holiday, would have provided an ideal starting place for public ownership or control of one vital sector of the economy. If ever there was a chance for socialism in the United States, this was it. Measured against this possibility and the later accusations against Roosevelt ("that man in the White House"—"that traitor to his class"), the New Deal could be labeled somewhat conservative. Yet neither the Socialists, led by Norman Thomas, nor the Communists were able to capitalize on this opportunity, despite the interest generated in the search for an alternative system. The occasion passed, perhaps never to return with such obvious promise again.

2. Milton Friedman and Anna J. Schwartz, *A Monetary History of the United States, 1867–1960* (Princeton, NJ: Princeton University Press, 1963), p. 489.

3. It did, however, manage to hurt those countries that were on the silver standard. The program was curiously promoted as a benefit for these nations on the basis that their currencies would increase. Yet, as the price of silver rose, the effect was the loss of silver as it sought the high price abroad. China in particular was hurt as silver was drained, and she had to impose an embargo and nationalize the remaining silver stock. The sharp rise in the price of silver reduced China's ability to export, and thus deflationary pressures had to be imposed. This "benefit" certainly was not sought, and eventually most nations, suffering similar problems, were forced off the silver standard.

4. Friedman and Schwartz, *Monetary History*, pp. 438–9.

5. See Matthew Josephson, *The Money Lords* (New York: Weybright and Talley, 1972), p. 176.

6. Broadus Mitchell, *Depression Decade* (White Plains, NY: M. E. Sharpe, 1975), p. 178.

7. Wassily Leontief, "Helping the Farmer," in Douglas V. Brown et al., *The Economics of the Recovery Program* (New York: Whittlesey House, 1934), p. 141.

8. Mitchell, *Depression Decade*, p. 230.

9. Edward Mason, "Controlling Industry," in Brown, *Economics of Recovery*, p. 58.

10. Mitchell, *Depression Decade*, p. 230.

11. Ibid., p. 240.

12. Lewis Corey, *The Decline of American Capitalism* (New York: Covici, Friede, 1934), pp. 97, 98. Note also this passage on page 495: "Thus monopoly capitalism is wholly reactionary. It means more deliberate and sharper aggression against the newer relations arising out of the

collective forms of production and the international character of modern industry. *The dominant class interests use a bastardized socialism to prevent the coming of socialism, to stabilize the disintegration of the old order.* State capitalism is not a form of transition to socialism but the direct opposite. It is a form of the capitalist struggle to retain power." (Italics in original)

13. Bernard M. Baruch, *The Public Years* (New York: Holt, Rinehart and Winston, 1960), p. 252.

14. Ibid., p. 253.

15. Leverett S. Lyon et al., *The National Recovery Administration* (Washington, DC: The Brookings Institution, 1935), pp. 872–73.

16. Ibid., p. 873. See also Edward Chamberlain, "Purchasing Power," in Brown, *Economics of Recovery*, pp. 22–37. And Adolf A. Berle, *Navigating the Rapids, 1918–1971*. Papers of A. A. Berle, edited by Beatrice B. Berle and Travis B. Jacobs (New York: Harcourt Brace Jovanovich, 1973), pp. 99ff.

17. William E. Leutenberg, *Franklin D. Roosevelt and the New Deal, 1932–1940* (New York: Harper & Row, 1963), p. 106.

18. Ibid., p. 121.

19. Joseph Alsop, *FDR, 1882–1945* (New York: Washington Square Press, 1982), p. 18; also William Manchester, *The Glory and The Dream* (Boston: Little, Brown, 1973), p. 102.

20. Mitchell, *Depression Decade*, p. 315.

21. Ibid., p. 317.

22. Leutenberg, *Roosevelt*, p. 123.

23. Works Progress Administration, *Final Report of the WPA Program* (Washington, DC: GPO, 1946).

24. The Federal Writers Projects turned out thousands of guides to states, cities, and regions. Employed on such projects and others were Conrad Aiken, John Cheever, and Richard Wright. The Federal Art Project employed artists to continue their creative efforts, and teachers were employed to pass on the skills to others. Among those who were involved were Stuart Davis, Willem De Kooning, and Jackson Pollack. Not all the art was meritorious nor all the theatrical productions enchanting, but the amazing part is that the federal government, together with the states, would fund such activities at all. In the past U.S. governmental units paid scant attention to the arts, preferring instead to extol the virtues of business and free enterprise.

25. Mitchell, *Depression Decade*, p. 330.

26. Friedman and Schwartz, *Monetary History*, p. 514. See also Clay J. Anderson, *A Half-Century of Federal Reserve Policymaking, 1914–1964* (Philadelphia: Federal Reserve Bank of Philadelphia, 1965); and Lester V. Chandler, *The Economics of Money and Banking*, 5th ed. (New York: Harper & Row, 1969).

27. In technical terms it could be said that the banks had their own version of liquidity preference, as Keynes had developed for individuals.

28. Friedman and Schwartz, *Monetary History*, p. 533.

29. Manchester, *Glory and Dream*, p. 196.
30. For the evolution of budget concepts, see Alvin H. Hansen, *Fiscal Policy and Business Cycles* (New York: Norton, 1941), pp. 208–22.
31. Roy G. Blakey and Gladys C. Blakey, *The Federal Income Tax* (New York: Longmans, Green, 1940), p. 345.
32. Herbert Stein, *The Fiscal Revolution in America* (Chicago: University of Chicago Press, 1969), pp. 76ff.
33. Hansen, *Fiscal Policy*, p. 68.
34. Ibid.
35. Stein, *Fiscal Reveolution*, p. 68.
36. Sidney Ratner, *Taxation and Democracy in America* (New York: Wiley, 1967), p. 467.
37. Alan Brinkley, *Voices of Protest, Huey Long, Father Coughlin and the Great Depression* (New York: Knopf, 1982), p. 64.
38. Ibid., p. 72.
39. The aim was to prevent the accumulation of large fortunes and with the proceeds of the taxes, provide for the common people: first, by providing everyone with a basic "household estate" of $5,000 to provide for basic necessities; and next, by guaranteeing an annual income for each family of $2,000–2,500 per year. Also, there was to be free higher education, increasing support for veterans, a shortened workweek, old-age pensions, government support of public works, and support for farmers.

   These ideas struck a welcome chord for many, although only a few minutes' thought would have revealed that there was insufficient wealth to support such a massive redistribution scheme. Nevertheless, many were attracted to the spirit of the plan and responded when Long began to organize Share Our Wealth Clubs. Membership grew to about 3 million in 1935, and half that number at least were reading *American Progress*, a newspaper founded by Long.
40. Brinkley, *Voices of Protest*, p. 83.
41. Ibid., pp. 187–88.
42. Blakey and Blakey, *Income Tax*, p. 366. According to the Blakeys, "As this sentence was read, Senator Huey Long of Louisana happened to walking directly in front of the rostrum, with his hands in his pockets. He stopped abruptly, made a grimace, raised his eyes and almost waltzed. When the clerk had finished he alone had a remark to make for the Record: 'Mr. President, before the President's message is referred to the Committee on Finance, I wish to make one comment. I just wish to say Amen'."
43. Ratner, *Taxation and Democracy*, p. 472.
44. Blakey and Blakey, *Income Tax*, p. 402.
45. Ratner, *Taxation and Democracy*, p. 476.
46. Blakey and Blakey, *Income Tax*, p. 429.
47. Ibid., p. 430.
48. Stein, *Fiscal Revolution*, p. 94.
49. Ibid., p. 99.
50. Blakey and Blakey, *Income Tax*, p. 448.
51. Ibid., p. 471.

52. Ibid., p. 472.
53. Stein, *Fiscal Revolution*, pp. 126ff.
54. Larry Berman, *The Office of Management and Budget and the Presidency, 1921–1979* (Princeton, NJ: Princeton University Press, 1979), p. 13.
55. See also Robert A. Gordon, *Economic Instability and Growth* (New York: Harper & Row, 1974), pp. 70–72. And J. K. Galbraith, *The Great Crash* (Boston: Houghton Mifflin, 1954), pp. 173–99.
56. Arthur M. Schlesinger, Jr., "The Hundred Days of FDR," *New York Times*, April 10, 1983, p. 8f, col. 2.
57. Campaign address in Chicago, Illinois, on October 14, 1936.

Chapter 6

1. Charles P. Kindleberger, *The World in Depression, 1929–1939* (Berkeley: University of California Press, 1973), p. 237.
2. Robert E. Sherwood, *Roosevelt and Hopkins* (New York: Harper & Brothers, 1948), p. 128.
3. Harold J. Tobin and Percy W. Bidwell, *Mobilizing Civilian America* (New York: Council on Foreign Relations, 1940).
4. Bernard M. Baruch, *The Public Years* (New York: Holt, Rinehart and Winston, 1960), p. 280.
5. James MacGregor Burns, *Roosevelt: The Soldier of Freedom* (New York: Harcourt Brace Jovanovich, 1970), p. 193.
6. For those interested in the organizations and agencies designed for the war, the best sources are Bureau of the Budget, Committee of Records of War Administration, *The United States at War* (Washington, DC: GPO, 1946), and Bureau of the Budget, War Production Board, *Industrial Mobilization for War*, originally published by the Civilian Production Administration in 1947, Washington, DC, and reprinted by Greenwood Press in New York in 1969.
7. Bureau of the Budget, *United States at War*, pp. 17ff.
8. Bureau of the Budget, *Industrial Mobilization for War*, p. 63.
9. *United States at War*, p. 103.
10. Ibid., pp. 113–14.
11. Ibid., p. 132.
12. *Industrial Mobilization for War*, pp. 961ff.
13. Ibid., pp. 82–83.
14. Ibid., p. 13.
15. *United States at War*, p. 175.
16. Ibid., pp. 479ff. See also *Industrial Mobilization for War*, pp. 411–17.
17. *United States at War*, p. 432.
18. Another solution, proposed earlier, was revived in early 1944—the national service plan. The president, convinced of the gravity of the situation, revived the issue in his January State of the Union message, calling for "a national service law, which for the duration of the war, will prevent strikes, and with certain appropriate exceptions, will make

available for war production or for any other essential services, every able-bodied adult in the nation." Bureau of the Budget, *United States at War*, p. 450). The issue lost its urgency when military needs decreased, and after the spring of 1944, the problem of acute labor shortages lessened considerably. Had the war continued, however, Congress was poised to enact stringent laws on labor mobility, "freezing" labor in certain jobs, assigning draftees to designated jobs, or forcibly transferring workers where they were needed.

19. Ibid., pp. 281–82.
20. While each raw material has a history to follow and each has its peculiarities, perhaps none is more interesting than the case of rubber. Cut off from its suppliers in the Far East, the nation had only a one-year supply at the end of 1941, Rubber was essential for defense purposes, but also very important for civilian use. The situation was critical.

   Dupont had invented a process for making synthetic rubber, but it was largely on paper. The Standard Oil Company had entered into an arrangement with the German chemical and manufacturing trust, I. G. Farber, and they had developed a workable process for making synthetic rubber. In the contract, however, Farber was given exclusive rights over the process. When Germany began its military push, it had no concern for a lack of natural rubber.

   When Standard Oil asked for permission to use the process in 1939, Farber refused, since Germany was then at war. When the United States asked Standard Oil for the process, it refused, citing business ethics and international law. When attacked by Attorney General Thurmond Arnold in March 1942, Standard Oil relented and supplied the patent.

   Yet the problem was not solved, since the rubber could be made from oil or grain alcohol. Petroleum interests wanted to use oil, while farmers foresaw great profits from the use of corn as the base. A struggle ensued; Congress got involved and actually passed a bill requiring grain alcohol, which the president vetoed. Finally Bernard Baruch was asked to investigate, and his commission submitted its report in September 1942. It endorsed petroleum as the base, the immediate construction of new refining plants, and a rationing scheme for tires and gasoline, and a 35-mph speed limit to save rubber. All the proposals were endorsed, and a rubber czar, William Jeffers, was named to control rubber production and use. Output of synthetic rubber rose to nearly 1 million tons for 1943–44, far surpassing forecasts of capacity in the Baruch report. See Baruch, *Public Years*, pp. 301–7; also Cabell Phillips, *The 1940s: Decade of Triumph and Trouble* (New York: Macmillan, 1975), pp. 152–56.
21. *United States at War*, pp. 322ff.
22. Ibid., pp. 350–53.
23. Phillips, *The 1940s*, p. 87.
24. *United States at War*, p. 235.
25. Ibid., p. 137.
26. Baruch, *Public Years*, p. 287.
27. *United States at War*, p. 240.

28. Perhaps the most significant innovation in the act was allowed to pass without controversy. The act permitted subsidies to high-cost producers of commodities deemed essential. Instead of increasing the price ceiling on these commodities so that high-cost, marginal private firms would be able to produce, the price ceilings were maintained, thus preventing inflation, and subsidies were granted to these firms. This provision stabilized production and was regarded as one of the most successful, if unpublicized, wartime programs. See *The United States at War*, p. 246.

29. The Bureau of the Budget responded to the president ten days later: "Bold and concerted action is required. Inflation cannot be stopped as long as wage increases, as well as rising Government expenditures, create additional purchasing power. Wage increases cannot be stopped as long as prices rise. The price rise cannot be stopped unless part of the rapidly increasing purchasing power is absorbed by fiscal measures. Fiscal measures cannot be effective as long as businessmen, wage earners, and farmers can make up for taxes by increasing their incomes. Only simultaneous action on all fronts can stop the inflationary spiral." Quoted in *The United States at War*, pp. 150–51.

30. *The United States at War*, p. 253.

31. J. K. Galbraith, *A Life in Our Times* (Boston: Houghton Mifflin, 1981), p. 165. See also his *A Theory of Price Control* (Cambridge: Harvard University Press, 1952); and Seymour Harris, *The Economics of America at War* (New York: Norton, 1941), pp. 217ff.

32. Samuel I. Rosenman, *Working with Roosevelt* (New York: Harper & Brothers, 1952), pp. 356ff.

33. M. Kalecki, "General Rationing," *Bulletin of the Institute of Statistics* 3, No. 1 (January 11, 1941), pp. 2–6.

34. Henry C. Murphy, *Debt in War and Transition* (New York: McGraw-Hill, 1950), p. 82.

35. Ibid., p. 83.

36. J. M. Keynes, *How to Pay for the War* (New York: Harcourt, Brace, 1940).

37. H. Menderhausen, *The Economics of War* (New York: Prentice-Hall, 1941), p. 142.

38. Murphy, *Debt*, pp. 62ff.

39. Ibid., pp. 104ff. Many of the data in this section come from this source.

40. Ibid., p. 170.

41. See Clay Anderson, *A Half Century of Federal Reserve Policymaking, 1914–1964* (Philadelphia: Federal Reserve Bank of Philadelphia, 1965).

42. Murphy, *Debt*, p. 93ff.

43. Anderson, *Federal Reserve Policymaking*, p. 90.

44. Rosenman, *Working with Roosevelt*, p. 203.

45. Ibid., p. 415.

46. Roy G.Blakey and Gladys C. Blakey, "Two Federal Revenue Acts of 1940," *American Economic Review* 39 (December 1940), pp. 724–35.

47. Sidney Ratner, *Taxation and Democracy in America* (New York: Wiley, 1942), p. 495.

48. Ibid., p. 494.

49. Blakey and Blakey, *Revenue Acts*, p. 729.

50. The excess profits tax applied to all corporations, with rates graduated from 25 percent on net excess profits on the first $20,000 to 50 percent on excess profits over $500,000. The rates were to be applied to excess profits minus a specific exemption of $5,000 and a credit computed by either of two methods, net income or invested capital. If the net-income method was chosen, the credit would be 95 percent of the average base period (1936–39) plus 8 percent of the net capital addition (or minus 6 percent of the net capital reduction) for the taxable year. Corporations that had large profits in those years could earn a large amount of profits before becoming subject to the excess profits tax.

 If the invested-capital basis were chosen, the credit was 8 percent of the invested capital for the taxable year. Only half of the borrowed capital was included in computing invested capital, and capital gains and losses were excluded entirely. Corporations that had small profits in recent years could choose this option and could earn increasing profits before becoming subject to the excess profits tax. Also, corporations could earn large profits on government contracts and smaller profits on private contracts to pull down the average rate and avoid paying excess profits taxes.

51. Clair Wilcox, *Public Policies Toward Business*, 3rd ed. (Homewood, IL: Richard D. Irwin, 1966), p. 689.

52. Murphy, *Debt*, p. 287.

53. Woodlief Thomas, "Lessons of War Finance," *American Economic Review* (September 1951), pp. 618–31.

54. Marriner S. Eccles, *Beckoning Frontiers* (New York: Knopf, 1951), pp. 358ff.

55. Bureau of the Budget, *United States at War*, pp. 461ff. For surplus property disposal, see p. 478; for the preference given to the automobile industry, see Bureau of the Budget, *Industrial Mobilization for War*, p. 925ff.

56. Eccles, *Frontiers*, p. 403.

57. Ibid., p. 400.

58. Alvin H. Hansen, *Fiscal Policy and Business Cycles* (New York: Norton, 1941), p. 439.

59. Ibid., p. 440.

60. *United States at War*, p. 505.

61. Ibid., p. 506.

62. Ibid., p. 519.

63. *Industrial Mobilization for War*, pp. 961ff.

64. Murphy, *Debt*, p. 287.

65. This does not mean to imply that small firms did not benefit from subcontracting.

66. *Industrial Mobilization for War*, p. 927.

67. Murphy, *Debt*, p. 178.

68. Robert J. Lampman, *The Share of Top Wealth-Holders in National Wealth, 1922–56*, NBER (Princeton, NJ: Princeton University Press, 1962), pp. 202, 204. For income data see U.S. Department of Commerce, Bureau of

the Census, *Historical Statistics of the United States* (Washington, DC: GPO, 1975), p. 302.

Chapter 7

1. See Cabell Phillips, *The 1940s: Decade of Triumph and Trouble* (New York: Macmillan, 1975).
2. Paul A. Samuelson, *Economics* (New York: McGraw-Hill, 1948). See also Alvin Hansen, *A Guide to Keynes* (New York: McGraw-Hill, 1953).
3. See, for instance, Seymour E. Harris (ed.), *The New Economics* (London: Dennis Dobson, 1947); and Abba P. Lerner, *Economics of Employment* (New York: McGraw-Hill, 1951).
4. Lerner, *Economics*, p. 3.
5. For some history on these matters, see Robert B. Reich, *The Next American Frontier* (New York: Times Books, 1983).
6. Congressional Quarterly Service, *Federal Economic Policy, 1945–67* (Washington, DC: Quarterly Service, July 1967), p. 24.
7. Perhaps his statement about economists reveals why. He said something like, "I prefer a one-armed economist, so he could not say on the one hand this, and on the other hand that." The exact quote is uncertain.
8. Congressional Quarterly Service, *Economic Policy*, p. 26.
9. Thomas G. Manning, *The Office of Price Administration* (New York: Henry Holt, 1960), pp. 46–49.
10. Marriner S. Eccles, *Beckoning Frontiers* (New York: Knopf, 1951), p. 409.
11. Harold G. Moulton and Karl T. Schlotterbeck, *Should Price Control Be Retained?* (Washington, DC: The Brookings Institution, 1945), p. 12.
12. Congressional Quarterly Service, *Economic Policy*, p. 26.
13. Moulton and Schlotterbeck, *Price Control*, p. 14.
14. U.S. Department of Commerce, Bureau of the Census, *Historical Statistics of the United States* (Washington, DC: GPO, 1975). Other data in this section come from the same source.
15. J. E. Trey, "Women in the War Economy—World War II," *Review of Radical Political Economics* 4 No. 3, (July 1972), pp. 42–57.
16. Closton E. Warne et al. (eds.), *Labor in Postwar America* (New York: Remsen Press, 1949), p. 553.
17. Arthur F. McClure, *The Truman Administration and the Problems of Postwar Labor, 1945–1948* (Madison, NJ: Fairleigh Dickinson University Press, 1969), p. 33.
18. Roosevelt's Economic Bill of Rights detailed the right to a useful and remunerative job ... ; the right to earn enough ... ; the right of every farmer to ... a decent living; the right of every businessman ... to trade in ... freedom from unfair competition ... ; the right of every family to a decent home; the right to adequate medical care ... ; the right to adequate protection from ... fears of old age, sickness, accident and unemployment; the right to a good education. (Taken from McClure, ibid., pp. 11–12.)

19. Ibid., p. 49.
20. Ibid., p. 105.
21. Ibid., p. 172.
22. Council of Economic Advisors, *Economic Report of the President* (Washington, DC: GPO, July 1947), pp. 19–20.
23. Ibid., p. 22.
24. For more details, see A. E. Holmans, *United States Fiscal Policy* (Oxford: Oxford University Press, 1961), pp. 160–84.
25. CEA, *Economic Report of the President*, January 1948, pp. 47–48.
26. Holmans, *U.S. Fiscal Policy*, p. 91.
27. Ibid., p. 100.
28. Ibid., pp. 98–99.
29. Edwin G. Nourse, *Economics in the Public Service* (New York: Harcourt Brace, 1953), p. 215.
30. Eccles, *Frontiers*, p. 427.
31. Wilfred Lewis, Jr., *Federal Fiscal Policy in the Postwar Period* (Washington, DC: The Brookings Institution, 1962), p. 106.
32. See Cabell Phillips, *The Truman Presidency* (New York: Macmillan, 1969), for example.
33. CEA, *Economic Report of the President*, January 1949, pp. 17–19.
34. Lewis, *Federal Fiscal Policy*, makes this point in his careful study.
35. CEA, *The Mid-Year Economic Report of the President*, July 1949, p. 5, contains the following statements: "These facts show that our economy is still operating at high levels of employment and production. The kind of Government action that would be called for in a serious economic emergency would not be appropriate now."
36. Holmans, *U.S. Fiscal Policy*, p. 117.
37. Milton Friedman and Anna J. Schwartz, *A Monetary History of the United States, 1867–1960*, NBER (Princeton, NJ: Princeton University Press, 1963), pp. 577ff.
38. Ibid., p. 581. While it would appear from this explanation that government officials were concerned about inflation in the immediate postwar period, the general public was acting as if it feared deflation. This might also explain the expectations of consumers that led to an increase in the saving rate referred to earlier. Expecting prices to fall and a recession to occur, households became cautious, and despite the pent-up demand for goods, were willing to reduce their savings and security holdings much less than would have been anticipated.

    While there is much to commend this reasoning, it should also be pointed out that the share of cash in portfolios also increased dramatically in the period 1947–54 (up to 17–24 percent of total wealth from 10–12 percent in the 1920s). This is consistent with a liquidity preference view, since yields on bonds were low and pegged, and there might have been expectations of rising prices of goods. This technical issue cannot be settled here, but the peculiar behavior of the velocity and the stock of money are very interesting. See Friedman and Schwartz, *Monetary*

History, p. 584; and Robert J. Lampman, *The Share of Top Wealth-Holders in National Wealth 1922–56*, NBER (Princeton, NJ: Princeton University Press, 1962), p. 143.

39. CEA, *Economic Report of the President*, January 1958, pp. 72–73 and pp. 102–5.
40. Lewis, *Federal Fiscal Policy*, pp. 128–29.
41. Holmans, *U.S. Fiscal Policy*, p. 130.
42. CEA, *Economic Report of the President*, January 1951, p. 35.
43. Congressional Quarterly Service, *Economic Policy*, p. 35.
44. Holmans, *U.S. Fiscal Policy*, pp. 135–40.
45. Ibid., p. 140.
46. Ibid., p. 151.
47. Other provisions were the recognition of the head-of-household category, resulting in a tax reduction for this group by lowering its tax rate; an increase in gross income a dependent could earn from $500 to $600; nonrecognition of capital gains on the sale of a residence if a new residence were purchased within a year; liberalized treatment of family partnerships; subjection of mutual savings banks, S&Ls, and farmers' co-ops to income taxes; and estate tax credit for foreign death taxes paid.
48. *Annual Report* of the Federal Reserve System Board of Governors, 1951, p. 98. For the history of events leading up to the accord, see Friedman and Schwartz, *Monetary History*, pp. 623ff.
49. Phillips, *Truman Presidency*, p. 416.
50. Eccles, *Frontiers*, pp. 412–13.

Chapter 8

1. A. E. Holmans, *United States Fiscal Policy* (Oxford: Oxford University Press, 1961), p. 198.
2. Marty Jezer, *The Dark Ages: Life in the United States 1945–1960* (Boston: South End Press, 1982), p. 20.
3. Harry Magdoff, *The Age of Imperialism* (New York: Monthly Review Press, 1969), p. 126.
4. Samuel Bowles, David M. Gordon, and Thomas E. Weisskopf, *Beyond the Waste Land* (New York: Anchor Press/Doubleday, 1983), pp. 62ff.
5. Congressional Quarterly Service, *Federal Economic Policy, 1945–1967* (Washington, DC: Quarterly Service, July 1967), p. 41.
6. Holmans, *U.S. Fiscal Policy*, p. 200.
7. Congressional Quarterly Service, *Economic Policy*, p. 40.
8. Arthur F. Burns, *Prosperity without Inflation* (New York: Fordham University Press, 1967), p. 56.
9. The date of the trough has subsequently been changed to May 1954.
10. Clay J. Anderson, *A Half-Century of Federal Reserve Policymaking, 1914–1964* (Philadelphia: Federal Reserve Bank of Philadelphia, 1965), p. 118.

11. Council of Economic Advisor, *Economic Report of the President* (Washington, DC: GPO, 1954), p. 52.
12. Robert J. Donovan, *Eisenhower, The Inside Story* (New York: Harper and Brothers, p. 211. See also the *Economic Report of the President*, 1954: "The maintenance of a high and expanding level of output and employment is a definite objective of our society. So also is the maintenance of a reasonably stable level of consumer prices. The pursuit of these twin objectives involves the Government in difficult, yet inescapable, responsibilities." (p. 51)
13. Ibid., *Economic Report*, pp. 20–21.
14. Wilfred Lewis, Jr., *Federal Fiscal Policy in the Postwar Recessions* (Washington, DC: The Brookings Institution, 1962), p. 142.
15. Burns, *Prosperity*, p. 30.
16. CEA, *Economic Report of the President*, 1955, pp. 18ff.
17. Lewis, *Federal Fiscal Policy*, p. 185.
18. Donovan, *Eisenhower*, pp. 282–84.
19. Edward R. Tufte, *Political Control of the Economy* (Princeton, NJ: Princeton University Press, 1978), pp. 16ff.
20. CEA, *Economic Report of the President*, 1956, p. 25.
21. Holmans, *U.S. Fiscal Policy*, p. 258.
22. CEA, *Economic Report of the President*, 1956, p. 25.
23. William Manchester, *The Glory and The Dream* (Boston: Little, Brown, 1973), p. 728. It might be interesting to show some correlations between TV advertising and consumption of consumer durables. The following table gives some data on this score:

Advertising and Consumption Expenditures, 1953–57

Year	Percent Change in GNP	Percent Change in Total Advertising	Percent Change in TV Advertising	Percent Change in Households with TV	Percent Change in Total Consumption	Percent Change in Durable Goods Consumption
1953–54	−6.2	5.2	33.5	27.5	2.3	−1.5
1954–55	9.5	12.6	26.7	18.1	7.9	22.3
1955–56	5.5	7.7	17.8	13.7	4.8	−0.6
1956–57	5.0	4.1	4.8	11.5	5.6	1.4

Source: U.S. Department of Commerce, *Historical Statistics of the United States* (Washington, DC: 1975.

Of course, the date in the table do not prove any relationship between advertising and consumption, but it is interesting to note how consumption seemed to respond to increases in advertising, particularly TV advertising. The boom in consumption in 1954 and 1955 seems to follow the startling increase in TV advertising.

24. Otto Eckstein, "Inflation, the Wage-Price Spiral and Economic Growth," in Compendium of Papers submitted by panelists appearing before the Joint Economic Committee, Hearing on *The Relationship of Prices to Economic Stability and Growth*, March 31, 1958, p. 364.

25. In the same compendium of the foregoing footnote can be found papers by Abba Lerner, "Inflationary Depression and the Regulation of Administered Prices," pp. 257–68, and Gardner Ackley, "A Third Approach to the Analysis and Control of Inflation," pp. 619–49.

26. CEA, *Economic Report of the President*, 1957, p. 49.

27. Lewis, *Federal Fiscal Policy*, p. 194.

28. CEA, *Economic Report of the President*, 1959, p. 122ff.

29. Lester V. Chandler, *The Economics of Money and Banking*, 5th ed. (New York: Harper & Row, 1969), p. 508.

30. CEA, *Economic Report of the President*, 1958, p. 50.

31. Holmans, *U.S. Fiscal Policy*, p. 180. See also Herbert Stein, *The Fiscal Revolution in America* (Chicago: University of Chicago Press, 1969), pp. 330ff.

32. Lewis, *Federal Fiscal Policy*, p. 211.

33. Ibid., p. 200.

34. Ibid., p. 226.

35. Ibid., p. 232.

36. CEA, *Economic Report of the President*, 1960, p. 6.

37. The best way to measure the influence of the budget on economic activity, however, is to remove the effects of the recession from government receipts and expenditures. That is, if the budget is measured as if full employment existed or the economy was performing up to its potential, there would be no loss of revenue or increase in expenditure caused by a recession. The budget then would reflect the impact of the public sector on the economy, with existing tax rates and planned expenditures. The full-employment budget would be what was planned and not what was forced upon it by economic conditions. The procedure was initiated in the *Economic Report of the President* of 1962, but some estimates for prior years were also attempted.

　　The interesting feature of this analysis is that throughout the Eisenhower years, there were full-employment surpluses, even in the recession years of 1958 and 1960. Thus, the federal budget was overly restrictive in these years, with an inappropriate fiscal policy. Instead of offsetting the declines in the private sector, it actually contributed to the declines.

38. Lewis, *Federal Fiscal Policy*, p. 235.

39. CEA, *Economic Report of the President*, 1960, pp. 7–8.

40. Milton Friedman and Anna J. Schwartz, *A Monetary History of the United States, 1867–1960* (Princeton, NJ: Princeton University Press, 1963), pp. 616–18.

41. Ibid., p. 619.
42. CEA, *Economic Report of the President*, 1961, p. 43.
43. Richard M. Nixon, *Six Crises* (New York: Pyramid Books, 1968), p. 333.
44. Ibid., p. 334.
45. U.S. Congress, Senate, Committee on the Judiciary, Subcommittee on Antitrust and Monopoly. *Economic Concentration*, Staff Report of the FTC, Economic Report on Corporate Mergers. Hearings, 91st Cong., 1st sess., on S. Res. 40, Part 8A (Washington, DC: GPO, 1969), p. 184.
46. Ibid., p. 191.
47. See statement of R. J. Arnould, pp. 4679–93 in U.S. Congress, Senate, Committee on the Judiciary, Subcommittee on Antitrust and Monopoly. *Economic Concentration; The Conglomeration Problem*. Hearings, 91st Cong. 2d sess., on S. Res. 40, Part 8 (Washington, DC: GPO, 1969, 1970).
48. U.S. Congress, *Economic Concentration*, p. 5.
49. Holmans, U.S. Fiscal Policy, p. 295.

Chapter 9

1. Arthur M. Schlesinger, Jr., *A Thousand Days* (Greenwich, CT: Fawcett Publications, 1967), p. 123.
2. Richard M. Nixon, *Six Crises* (New York: Pyramid Books, 1968), p. 446.
3. Theodore C. Sorensen, *Kennedy* (New York: Harper & Row, 1965), p. 181.
4. Ibid., p. 118. See also Schlesinger, *Thousand Days*, pp. 65–78.
5. Schlesinger, pp. 115–57.
6. U.S. Department of Commerce, Bureau of the Census, *Long Term Economic Growth 1860–1965* (Washington, DC: GPO 1966), p. 101.
7. Paul A. Samuelson, "Economic Policy for 1962," *Review of Economics & Statistics* 44 No. 1 (1962), pp. 3–6. See also the other commentators in the same issue.
8. For further explanations of these concepts, see Walter W. Heller, *New Dimensions of Political Economy* (New York: Norton, 1967), pp. 64ff. Or James Tobin, *The New Economics One Decade Older* (Princeton, NJ: Princeton University Press, 1974), pp. 6–18.
9. Council of Economic Advisors, *Economic Report of the President* (Washington, DC: GPO, 1962), pp. 185ff. See also Heller, *New Dimensions*, pp. 43–45.
10. The Commission on Money and Credit, *Money and Credit* (Englewood Cliffs, NJ: Prentice-Hall, 1961). The administration adopted them quickly, and they appeared in the *Economic Report of the President*, 1962, pp. 17–21 and 74–76.
11. Heller, *New Dimensions*, p. 30.
12. Samuelson, "Economic Policy," p. 4.
13. Sorensen, *Kennedy*, pp. 610–13.
14. Schlesinger, *Thousand Days*, p. 580. Also see James Tobin, *National Economic Policy* (New Haven, CT: Yale University Press, 1966), pp. 14–24.

15. CEA, *Economic Report of the President*, 1962, p. 90.
16. Ibid., p. 51.
17. Ibid., p. 49.
18. Heller, *New Dimensions*, p. 63.
19. Arthur M. Okun, *The Political Economy of Prosperity* (New York: Norton, 1970), p. 43.
20. Committee for Economic Development, *Fiscal and Monetary Policy for High Employment*, 1961, p. 26.
21. Sorensen, *Kennedy*, pp. 421ff.
22. Ibid., p. 425.
23. The estimates are those of Robert E. Hall, Dale W. Jorgenson, and Charles W. Bischoff, found in Gary Fromm (ed.) *Tax Incentives and Capital Spending* (Washington, DC: The Brookings Institution, 1971), pp. 52 and 117.
24. Tobin, *New Economics*, p. 53.
25. CEA, *Economic Report of the President*, 1963, pp. 17–18.
26. Heller, *New Dimensions*, p. 33.
27. Sorensen, *Kennedy*, p. 432. See also James L. Sundquist, *Politics and Policy: The Eisenhower, Kennedy, and Johnson Years* (Washington, DC: The Brookings Institution, 1968), pp. 40ff.
28. Seymour E. Harris, *Economics of the Kennedy Years* (New York: Harper & Row, 1964), p. 117.
29. CEA, *Economic Report of the President*, 1963, p. 128.
30. David P. Calleo, *The Imperious Economy* (Cambridge, MA: Harvard University Press, 1982), p. 15.
31. CEA, *Economic Report of the President*, 1964, p. 42.
32. John Sheahan, *The Wage-Price Guideposts* (Washington, DC: The Brookings Institution, 1967), p. 90.
33. Ibid., p. 91.
34. Ibid., p. 17.
35. Ibid., p. 36. See also Sorensen, *Kennedy*, pp. 443ff.
36. One of the FBI investigations was of a reporter in the middle of the night, leading to charges of police-state actions. See Sorensen, *Kennedy*, p. 453.
37. His remark, "My father always told me that steelmen were sons of bitches, but I never realized till now how right he was," was misinterpreted to read "businessmen" for steelmen, causing quite a stir. See Sorensen, *Kennedy*, p. 449.
38. Sheahan, *Guideposts*, p. 37.
39. Sundquist, *Politics and Policy*, p. 112.
40. Schlesinger, *Thousand Days*, p. 920. Galbraith's book was published by Houghton Mifflin of Boston in 1958 and Harrington's by Penguin Books of Baltimore in 1963.
41. In addition to his main biographers, see Garry Wills, *The Kennedy Imprisonment* (Boston: Little, Brown, 1981), pp. 255–63, for a more critical assessment; and William Manchester, *Portrait of a President* (New York: MacFadden-Bartell, 1964) for a favorable account.
42. Heller, *New Dimensions*, p. 1.

Chapter 10

1. Johnson's feelings were recorded by Doris Kearns in *Lyndon Johnson and the American Dream* (New York: Harper & Row, 1976): "I took the oath; I became President. But for millions of Americans I was still illegitimate, a naked man with no presidential covering, a pretender to the throne, an illegal usurper. ... And there were the bigots and the dividers and the Eastern intellectuals, who were waiting to knock me down before I could even begin to stand up. The whole thing was almost unbearable" (p. 170); and of Kennedy's men, "I knew how they felt. The impact of Kennedy's death was evident everywhere—in the looks on their faces and the sound of their voices. He was gone and with his going they must have felt that everything had changed. Suddenly *they* were outsiders just as I had been for almost three years, outsiders on the inside" (p. 175).
2. For more on the debate over the effectiveness of fiscal versus monetary policy, see Milton Friedman and Walter W. Heller, *Monetary vs. Fiscal Policy* (New York: Norton, 1969).
3. Arthur Okun, "Measuring the Impact of the 1964 Tax Cut," in W. W. Heller, Ed., *Perspectives on Economic Growth* (New York: Vintage Books, 1968), pp. 25–49. See also Okun's reply to critics in his *Political Economy of Prosperity* (New York: Norton, 1970), pp. 55–59.
4. Walter W. Heller, *New Dimensions of Political Economy* (New York: Norton, 1967), p. 72.
5. Ibid.
6. See the discussion in Herbert Stein, *Presidential Economics* (New York: Simon and Schuster, 1984), pp. 108–13.
7. Lyndon B. Johnson, *The Vantage Point* (New York: Popular Library, 1971), p. 71.
8. Rowland Evans and Robert Novak, *Lyndon B. Johnson: The Exercise of Power* (New York: Signet, 1966), p. 457.
9. For more on the war on poverty, see Johnson, account in *Vantage Point*, pp. 69–87.
10. Mollie Orshansky, "Counting the Poor: Another Look at the Poverty Profile," *Social Security Bulletin* (January 1965).
11. Michael Harrington, *The Other America* (New York: Macmillan, 1962), p. 10.
12. Congressional Quarterly Service, *Federal Economic Policy, 1945–1967,* (Washington, DC: Congressional Quarterly), p. 40.
13. Ibid., p. 67. Martin was accused of forcing the issue in December while there were enough conservative members on the board to pass the increase. Johnson was scheduled to appoint a new, and presumably liberal, member to the board in January. Chairman Martin denied the charge, citing technical conditions for the upcoming Treasury borrowings in January.
14. Okun, *Political Economy of Prosperity*, p. 69.
15. Council of Economic Advisors, *Economic Report of the President* (Washington, DC: GPO, 1966), pp. 58–60.

16. Barry M. Goldwater, *With No Apologies* (New York: William Morrow, 1979), p. 75.

17. Robert W. Stevens, *Vain Hopes, Grim Realities* (New York: New Viewpoints, 1976), p. 75.

18. Ibid. In Johnson's own words, "I knew from the start that I was bound to be crucified either way I moved. If I left the woman I really loved—the Great Society—in order to get involved with that bitch of a war on the other side of the world, then I would lose everything at home. All my programs. All my hopes to feed the hungry and shelter the homeless. All my dreams to provide education and medical care to the browns and the blacks and the lame and the poor. But if I left that war and let the Communists take over South Vietnam, then I would be seen as a coward and my nation would be seen as an appeaser and we would both find it impossible to accomplish anything for anybody anywhere on the entire globe." These words, uttered in 1970, are quoted in Kearns, *Lyndon Johnson*, pp. 151–52.

19. CEA, *Economic Report of the President* 1967, pp. 42–45.

20. Heller, *New Dimensions*, p. 87.

21. Okun, *Political Economy*, pp. 71–72.

22. Ibid., p. 81.

23. CEA, *Economic Report of the President*, 1968, p. 52.

24. Okun, *The Political Economy*, p. 96.

25. See Arthur Okun, "The Personal Tax Surcharge and Consumer Demand, 1968–70" in *Brookings Papers*, Washington, DC, 1971, pp. 167–212; and William L. Springer, "Did the 1968 Surcharge Really Work?", *American Economic Review* 65, No. 4 (September 1975), pp. 644–59; and the subsequent exchange between the two economists in the *American Economic Review* 67, No. 2 (March 1977), pp. 166–72.

26. *New York Times*, December 30, 1975, p. 31.

27. Okun, *Political Economy*, p. 96.

28. U.S. Congress, Joint Economic Committee, *Standards for Guiding Monetary Action* (Washington, DC: GPO, 1968).

29. Others have noted and identified the year 1966 as a crucial one for the U.S. Economy. See, for instance, Samuel Bowles, David M. Gordon, and Thomas E. Weisskopf, *Beyond the Waste Land* (New York: Anchor Press/Doubleday, 1983), pp. 27–28.

30. Consider the reaction that followed these famous quotes: "We should bomb them back to the stone age." (General Curtis Lemay) "It became necessary to destroy the town to save it." (Army Officer)

31. Some of these structural changes are also included in the analysis of the decline of the U.S. economy found in Bowles et al., *Beyond the Waste Land*.

Chapter 11

1. For an excellent description of the delegates and an account of the convention, see Arthur Miller, "From the Delegate's Side," in Walter Schier (ed.), *Telling It Like It Was: The Chicago Riots* (New York: New

American Library, 1969), pp. 43–56. (Reprinted from *The New York Times Magazine*).

2. For more on this period, See Richard M. Nixon, *Memoirs* (New York: Warner Books, 1978), pp. 335–60.

3. See T. H. White, *The Making of the President, 1968* (New York: Atheneum, 1969).

4. Herbert Stein, *Presidential Economics* (New York: Simon & Schuster, 1984), p. 138.

5. Ibid., p. 136.

6. See John E. Schwarz, *America's Hidden Success* (New York: Norton, 1983).

7. Harry G. Johnson, "The Keynesian Revolution and the Monetarist Counter-Revolution," *American Economic Review* 61 (May 1971), pp. 1–14.

8. Milton Friedman's contribution to this field begins with his seminal article, "A Monetary and Fiscal Framework for Economic Stability," *American Economic Review* 38 (June 1948), pp. 145–64, and extends to numerous additions and refinements.

9. Rational-expectation models have been formulated by several economists, among them Thomas Sargent and Neil Wallace, "Rational Expectations and the Theory of Economic Policy," *Journal of Monetary Economics* (April 1976), pp. 241–54; Robert E. Lucas, Jr., "Understanding Business Cycles," in Karl Brunner and Allan Meltzer (eds.), *Stabilization of the Domestic and International Economy* (Amsterdam: North Holland, Carnegie–Rochester Conference Series, Vol. 5, 1977); and Robert Barro, "Anticipated Money Growth and Unemployment in the United States," *American Economic Review* 67, No. 2 (March 1977), pp. 101–15.

10. For an enlightening discussion of the shades of conservatism in the Nixon era, see A. James Reichley, *Conservatives of Change: The Nixon and Ford Administrations* (Washington, DC: The Brookings Institution, 1981), pp. 1–37.

11. Council of Economic Advisors, *Economic Report of the President* (Washington, DC: GPO, 1970), p. 37.

12. According to Herbert Stein, Johnson was reluctant to include the tax surcharge, lest he be saddled with sole responsibility for this unpopular tax measure. See Stein, *Presidential Economics*, p. 169.

13. Reichley, *Conservatives of Change*, pp. 131–43.

14. Adam Smith, *Supermoney* (New York: Popular Library, 1972), p. 44.

15. Arthur Burns, *Reflections of an Economic Policymaker* (American Enterprise Institute, 1978), pp. 103–15.

16. Reichley, *Conservatives of Change*, p. 220.

17. CEA, *Economic Report of the President*, 1971, p. 84.

18. Ibid., p. 80.

19. Reichley, *Conservatives of Change*, pp. 144–49, 157–58.

20. Stein, *Presidential Economics*, pp. 156–58; see also George P. Shultz and Kenneth W. Dam, *Economic Policy beyond the Headlines* (New York: Norton, 1977), pp. 65–69.

21. Stein, *Presidential Economics*, p. 163.
22. Ibid.
23. Reichley, *Conservatives of Change*, p. 209.
24. Shultz and Dam, *Economic Policy*, p.117.
25. CEA, *Economic Report of the President*, 1972, p. 148.
26. Stein, *Presidential Economics*, p. 167.
27. Shultz and Dam, *Economic Policy*, p. 114. The following discussion of international trade developments owes much to this source.
28. Stein, *Presidential Economics*, p. 178.
29. Ibid., pp. 180ff.
30. CEA, *Economic Report of the President*, 1972, pp. 75–82.
31. Ibid., p. 94.
32. Associated Press, *The World in 1971: History As We Lived It* (Western Publishing Co., 1972), p. 218.
33. See, for instance, CEA, *Economic Report of the President*, 1974, pp. 89 and 108.
34. CEA, *Economic Report of the President*, 1973, pp. 68, 90.
35. The Weyerhaeuser Corporation was accused of this action by the IRS. Weyerhaeuser, a friend of Nixon's, denied the charges, but complained against the Price Commission. Nixon shortly thereafter dissolved the Price Commission. The obvious connection was made by a member of the Price Commission, Jack DuVall, in the *Washington Post*, April 22, 1979, p. C5.
36. Stein, *Presidential Economics*, p. 178.
37. CEA, *Economic Report of the President*, 1974, p. 97.
38. CEA, *Economic Report of the President* 1975, pp. 228–29.
39. Robert J. Gordon, "The Response of Wages and Prices to the First Two Years of Controls," *Brookings Papers on Economic Activity*, 1973:3 (Washington, DC: The Brookings Institution, 1972), pp. 777–78.
40. See Gordon's article in the same source as above, "Wage-Price Controls and the Shifting Phillips Curve" (1972:2). See also Edgar L. Feige and Douglas K. Pearce, "Inflation and Incomes Policy: An Application of Time Series Models," in Karl Brunner and Alan Meltzer (eds.), *The Economics of Price and Wage Controls* (Amsterdam: Carnegie-Rochester Conference Series, Vol. 2, 1976). Their conclusion was that the controls worked only during the freeze period.
41. Herbert Stein, "Price-Fixing as Seen by a Price Fixer, Part II," in William Fellner (ed.), *Contemporary Economic Problems, 1978* (Washington, DC: American Enterprise Institute), pp. 133–35; C. Jackson Greyson, Jr., "Controls Are Not the Answer," *Challenge* (November/December, 1974), pp. 9–12.
42. John K. Galbraith, *Economics and the Public Purpose* (Boston: Houghton Mifflin, 1973), p. 196.
43. DuVall, in *Washington Post*, April 22, 1979, p. C5.
44. Galbraith, *Economics*, pp. 312–16. See also the discussion papers on the panel, "Two years of Wage-Price Controls" by R. F. Lanzillotti and Blaine

Roberts, by Barry Bosworth, and by Daniel J. B. Mitchell and Arnold R. Weber, *American Economic Review* 64, No. 2 (May 1974), pp. 82–104.

45. See Herbert Stein, *Presidential Economics*, p. 183.

46. For insights into the administration on these and other economic matters, see John Erlichman, *Witness to Power* (New York: Simon & Schuster, 1982), pp. 244–62.

47. Edward R. Tufte, *Political Control of the Economy* (Princeton, NJ: Princeton University Press, 1978), pp. 45ff.

48. Stein, *Presidential Economics*, p. 190.

49. CEA, *Economic Report of the President*, 1975, p. 48; see Table 7.

50. The other social program, The Family Assistance Plan (FAP), was allowed to die after Nixon found more political advantage in attacking George McGovern's call for a demogrant of $1,000 payable to every person in the United States. McGovern's proposal provoked so much derision that other family assistance programs, by Senator Ribicoff of Connecticut and Casper Weinberger, secretary of HEW, could not rescue the concept after Nixon retreated.

51. Board of Governors of the Federal Reserve System, "Monetary Policy in a Changing Financial Environment," *Federal Reserve Bulletin* (April 1975), pp. 197–208.

52. Robert W. Stevens, *Vain Hopes, Grim Realities* (New York: New Viewpoints, 1976), p. 187.

Chapter 12

1. Nixon has written that his first choice for vice-president was John Connally, but Congress wanted Ford. Richard M. Nixon, *Memoirs* (New York: Warner Books, 1978), p. 481.

2. John Ehrlichman, *Witness to Power* (New York: Simon & Schuster, 1982), p. 197.

3. Galbraith claims that Johnson was misquoted and actually said, "That Gerald Ford. He can't fart and chew gum at the same time." See J. K. Galbraith, *A Life in our Times* (Boston: Houghton Mifflin, 1981), p. 450.

4. U.S. Department of Commerce, Bureau of the Census, *Social Indicators III* (Washington, DC: GPO, 1980), p. 472; J. K. Galbraith, "Inflation: A Presidential Catechism," *New York Times Magazine*, September 15, 1974, pp. 14–15, 87–90; M. Friedman, "Using Escalators to Help Fight Inflation," *Fortune* (May-July 1974), pp. 94–7, 174, 176; and U.S. House of Representatives, 93rd Congress, 2d Session, The 1974 Joint Economic Report, *Report of the Joint Economic Committee on the February 1974 Economic Report of the President*, March 25, 1974.

5. Statement of William E. Simon before House Ways and Means Committee, January 20, 1975, and reprinted in *Treasury News*, January 23, 1975.

6. Alan Blinder, *Economic Policy and the Great Stagflation* (New York: Academic Press, 1979), pp. 164–65. Interestingly, the *Wall Street Journal*

reported on April 2, 1975 (p. 4) that many people were cynical about the tax rebate, but intended to spend it anyway. Later, on July 21, 1975 (p. 1) the *Wall Street Journal* reported that consumers were shaken by the recession and planned to save the rebates.

7. Council of Economic Advisors, *Economic Report of the President* (Washington, DC: GPO, 1977), p. 175.

8. Walter W. Heller, "Ford's Budget and the Economy," *Wall Street Journal*, February 5, 1976, p. 18.

9. U.S. Department of Commerce, *Social Indicators*, pp. 470, 472.

10. Milton Friedman, "Five Examples of Fed Double-Talk," *Wall Street Journal*, August 21, 1975, p. 6. Note the short lag for monetary policy implied in the accusation.

11. This is the view of Alan Blinder from his analysis, *Economic Policy*, p. 197. See also the work of Stephen M. Goldfeld, "The Case of the Missing Money," *Brookings Papers on Economic Activity* 7, No. 3 (1976), pp. 683–730. For a different conclusion from most studies, see R. W. Hafer and Scott E. Hein, "The Shift in Money Demand. What Really Happened?" in Federal Reserve Bank of St. Louis, *Review* 64, No. 2 (February 1982), pp. 11–16. They argue that a one-time shift in the level of the demand for money occurred in 1974, but that the slopes of the money demand curve remained the same; hence the demand for money is considered stable.

12. The Federal Reserve was aware of these changes in velocity as they plotted their course. See for example, "The Implementation of Monetary Policy in 1976," *Federal Reserve Bulletin* 63, No. 4 (April 1977), pp. 323–36. In this same article another suggestion was offered for the decline in interest rates: The market was prepared for a larger deficit, and when that did not materialize, people used their excess funds in money markets and drove down interest rates.

13. This is the title of Chapter 5 of his book, *Presidential Economics* (New York: Simon & Schuster, 1984).

14. For more examples of free-market solutions conflicting with society's interests, see Andrew Schotter, *Free Market Economics* (New York: St. Martin's Press, 1985).

Chapter 13

1. Victor Lasky, *Jimmy Carter, The Man and The Myth* (New York: Richard Marek, 1979), pp. 169–60.

2. For more on the backgrounds of the Carter appointees, see the Congressional Quarterly's *President Carter* (Washington, DC: Congressional Quarterly, 1977), pp. 17–43.

3. Council of Economic Advisors, *Economic Report of the President* (Washington, DC: GPO, 1978), pp. 50–51.

4. Ibid., p. 52.

5. See "Monetary Policy and Open Market Operations in 1977," *Federal Reserve Bulletin* (April 1978), pp. 165–78; and "The Federal Open Market

Committee in 1977," Federal Reserve Bank of St. Louis, *Review* (March 1978), pp. 2–21.

6. Productivity declines, real wages, and the composition of the labor force are covered later in the chapter.

7. CEA, *Economic Report of the President*, 1978, p. 74.

8. "An Uneasy Balance for the U.S. Economy," *Business Week*, December 26, 1977, pp. 52–55.

9. CEA, *Economic Report of the President*, 1979, pp. 78–79.

10. Robert J. Gordon, "What Can Stabilization Policy Achieve?" *American Economic Review* 68 (May 1978) No. 2, pp. 335–41. On the same panel were Charles C. Holt, "Labor Market Structure: Implications for Micro Policy,"; Arthur M. Okun, "Efficient Disinflationary Policies"; and Robert E. Lukas, Jr., "Unemployment Policy." The very composition of the panel shows the disarray in the profession, since the panelists represent nearly opposite views.

11. H. C. Wallich and S. Weintraub, "A Tax-Based Incomes Policy," *Journal of Economic Issues* 5 (June 1971), pp. 1–19. See also, Sidney Weintraub, "TIP: A Tax-Based Incomes Policy to Stop Inflation," and Arthur Okun, "A Reward TIP," as well as other contributors on the same topic in David C. Collander, *Solutions to Inflation* (New York: Harcourt Brace Jovanovich, 1979); also see Arthur M. Okun and George Perry, *Innovative Policies to Slow Inflation* in a Special Issue of *The Brookings Papers on Economic Activity* (Washington, DC, 1978), Vol. 2, and in the same publication but Vol. 1, Martin Neil Baily, "Stabilization Policy and Private Economic Behavior," pp. 11–50.

12. The original bill was watered down as it progressed through the legislative process. The more the bill attempted to alter the direction of the socioeconomic system, and the more specific the expression of goals, the more the give and take of politics modified the original intent. In the original version of the Humphrey–Hawkins bill there were bold initiatives for planning and the extension of government power in the economy.

13. U.S. Department of Commerce, Bureau of the Census, *Social Indicators* (Washingon DC: GPO, 1980), p. 472.

14. "A Proposal for Redefining the Monetary Aggregates," *Federal Reserve Bulletin* 65, No. 1 (January 1979), pp. 13–42.

15. CEA, *Economic Report of the President*, 1980, p. 33.

16. Ibid., 1981, p. 160.

17. Ibid., p. 157.

18. Ibid., p. 40. See for instance, among his other works in the same vein, Robert J. Gordon, "Why Stopping Inflation May be Costly: Evidence from Fourteen Historical Episodes," in Robert Hall (ed.), *Inflation* (Chicago: University of Chicago Press, 1982), pp. 11–40.

19. R. Alton Gilbert and Michael E. Trebing, "The FOMC in 1980: A Year of Reserve Targeting," Federal Reserve Bank of St. Louis, *Review* 63, No. 7 (August/September 1981), p. 4.

20. Jimmy Carter, *Keeping Faith* (New York: Bantam Books, 1982), pp. 91–124.

21. For example, see George P. Shultz and Kenneth W. Dam, *Economic Policy Beyond the Headlines* (New York: Norton, 1977), pp. 186ff.

22. For an excellent short summary of the issues involved in rationing, see Seymour Zucker, "Why More People Are Thinking of Gasoline Rationing," *Business Week*, June 25, 1979, pp. 81–86.

23. Carter's televised speech to the nation on April 18, 1977.

24. U.S. Department of Commerce, Bureau of the Census, *Statistical Abstract of the U.S.* (Washington, DC: GPO, 1981), Table 1006, p. 585.

25. M. A. Adelman, "Oil Import Quota Auctions," *Challenge* 19, No. 6 (January/February 1976), pp. 17–22. See also, Paul Davison, "The Economics of Natural Resources," *Challenge* 22, No. 1 (March/April 1979), pp. 40–46.

26. For instance, see "Is the Worldwide Oil Glut Here to Stay," *Business Week*, May 8, 1978, pp. 78–79.

27. In an interview for *Business Week*, James Schlesinger, the administration's energy czar, gave this estimate of oil supplies: "We can cruise through the rest of our supplies wastefully in the next 20 years. . . . We are just running out [of fossil fuels]." In "The U.S. Can Squeeze Out Waste and Still Grow," *Business Week*, April 25, 1977, pp. 70–71.

28. CEA, *Economic Report of the President*, 1978, pp. 190–93.

29. Carter, *Keeping Faith*, p. 99.

30. Ibid., pp. 108–9.

31. Department of Commerce, *Social Indicators*, p. 41.

32. U.S. Department of Labor, Bureau of Labor Statistics, "Number of Working Mothers Now at Record Levels," USDL 84–321, July 26, 1984. Data from the March *Current Population Survey*.

33. For a discussion of the factors involved, see Victor R. Fuchs, *How We Live* (Cambridge, MA: Harvard University Press, 1983), pp. 99–103.

34. Martin Feldstein, "Temporary Layoffs in the Theory of Unemployment," *Journal of Political Economy* 84, No. 5 (October 1976), pp. 937–57 and "The Importance of Temporary Layoffs: An Empirical Analysis," *Brookings Papers on Economic Activity* 6, No. 3 (1975), pp. 725–44.

35. For more on labor force definitions and problems, see The National Commission of Employment and Unemployment Statistics, *Counting the Labor Force* (Washington, DC: GPO, Labor Day, 1979).

36. See David Gordon, *Theories of Poverty and Underemployment* (Lexington, MA: D. C. Heath, 1972); Peter Doeringer and Michael Piore, "Unemployment and the 'Dual Labor Market'," *Public Interest* 38 (Winter 1975), pp. 67–79. For a survey of the whole area, see Glen G. Cain, "The Challenge of Segmented Labor Market Theories to Orthodox Theory: A Survey," *Journal of Economic Literature* 14, No. 4 (December 1976), pp. 1215–57.

37. President Reagan and many others in his administration have voiced the view that a subminimum wage would help solve the umemployment problem of teenagers. The question is better left to the next chapter.

38. This is the logical result if the natural-rate-of-unemployment concept is combined with the rational-expectations hypothesis, as follows, for

instance, in the work of Thomas Sargent and N. Wallace, "Rational Expectations and the Theory of Economic Policy," *Journal of Monetary Economics* 2, No. 2 (April 1976), pp. 169–84.

39. Harry Magdoff, "Productivity Slowdown: A False Alarm," *Monthly Review* 31, No. 2 (June 1979), pp. 1–12; also the editors, "The Uses and Abuses of Measuring Productivity," *Monthly Review* 32, No. 2 (June 1980), pp. 1–19.
40. Edward F. Denison, "Explanations of Declining Productivity Growth," Department of Commerce, *Survey of Current Business*, August 1979, p. 124.
41. CEA, *Economic Report of the President*, 1979, p. 68.
42. John A. Tatom, "The Productivity Problem," Federal Reserve Bank of St. Louis, *Review* 61, No. 9 (September 1979), pp. 3–16.
43. Samuel Bowles, David M. Gordon, and Thomas E. Weisskopf, *Beyond the Waste Lane* (New York: Anchor Press, 1983), pp. 126–49. For another view on management's role in the decline of U.S. industry, see Robert B. Reich, *The Next American Frontier* (New York: Times Books, 1983).
44. CEA, *Economic Report of the President*, 1981, p. 154.
45. Ibid., pp. 127–30.
46. For example, Victor Fuchs, "Differences in Hourly Earnings between Men and Women," *Monthly Labor Review* 94, No. 5 (May 1971), pp. 9–15; and "Recent Trends and Long-Run Prospects for Female Earnings," *American Economic Review* 64, No. 2 (May 1974), pp. 236–42; the topic was later covered in CEA's *Economic Report of the President*, 1973, pp. 84–112.
47. Wassily Leontief, "What Hope for the Economy," *New York Review of Books*, August 12, 1982, pp. 31–34.
48. CEA, *Economic Report of the President*, 1979, p. 149.
49. See for instance, Jacob A. Frankel, "United States Inflation and the Dollar," in Robert E. Hall (ed.), *Inflation* (Chicago: University of Chicago Press, 1982), pp. 189–209.
50. This is the conclusion of Frankel in the foregoing work.
51. For a more detailed look at declining industries, see Ira C. Magaziner and Robert B. Reich, *Minding America's Business: The Decline and Rise of the American Economy* (New York: Harcourt Brace Javanovich, 1982); see also Reich, *American Frontier* (New York: Times Books, 1983).
52. In addition to the foregoing, see Bowles et al., *Beyond the Waste Land*, Chapter 3, for more on the use of scapegoats to mask the deterioration in U.S. manufacturing.
53. See Reich, *American Frontier*, Chapter 8, for the analysis of what he aptly called "paper entrepreneurialism."
54. Commercial banks increased from 13,705 in 1970 to 14,870 in 1980, an increase of 9 percent; in the same period the number of member banks of the Federal Reserve System fell from 5,767 in 1970 to 5,422 in 1980, a decrease of 6 percent.
55. See CEA, *Economic Report of the President*, 1981, pp. 100-7, for the rationale of regulatory reform and future plans.
56. *Washington Post*, February 18, 1979, p. 66.

57. For a fuller discussion of this congressional shortcoming and an attack on Keynesian economics that fosters it, see James M. Buchanan and Richard E. Wagner, *Democracy in Deficit* (New York: Academic Press, 1977).

58. Walter W. Heller, "Balanced Budget Fallacies," *Wall Street Journal*, March 16, 1979.

59. Herbert Stein, "To Balance or Not to Balance," *Wall Street Journal*, March 12, 1979.

60. See Joseph Schere, "Is the Federal Budget Balanced?" in *Challenge* 22, No. 3 (September/October, 1979), pp. 41–43.

61. See *Business Week*, "Bending on Speculative Loans," May 19, 1980, pp. 32–33.

62. Among the many instances of illegal billings by the oil companies, the most spectacular was the judgment against Exxon in July 1985 for nearly $2 billion in overcharges in the control period.

63. For some ideas, see Otto Eckstein, "The Core Inflation Rate and an Analysis of Stagflation," in Allen R. Sanderson (ed.), *DRI Readings in Macroeconomics* (New York: McGraw-Hill, 1981), pp. 64–78; and in the same source, Otto Eckstein and Sara Johnson, "Energy Inflation and the U.S. Economy," pp. 300–5.

64. See *Business Week*, "The Grain Embargo is Boomeranging" (January 26, 1981), pp. 32–33. Also Clifton B. Luttrell, "The Russian Grain Embargo," Federal Reserve Bank of St. Louis, *Review* (August/September, 1980), pp. 2–8; and his "Grain Export Agreements—No Gains, No Losses," in ibid. (August/September, 1981), pp. 23–29.

65. Carter, *Keeping Faith*, p. 74.

66. A similar point was made by the editors, "The Deficit, The Debt, and The Real World," *Monthly Review* 37, No. 1 (May 1985), p. 5.

Chapter 14

1. Jimmy Carter, *Keeping Faith* (New York: Bantam Books, 1982), pp. 531ff.

2. Ibid., p. 569.

3. See George Katona, "Attitudes toward Fiscal and Monetary Policy," *Public Policy* 18, No. 2 (Winter 1970), pp. 281–88.

4. For instance, see the exchange in *Challenge* 21, No. 6 (January/February 1979) between J. J. Minarik, "Who Wins, Who Loses from Inflation," pp. 26–31, and L. E. Nulty, "How Inflation Hits the Majority," pp. 32–38. See also J. J. Minarik, "The Size Distribution of Income during Inflation," *Review of Income and Wealth* Series 25, No. 4 (December 1979), pp. 377–92 for another analysis written during this period.

5. For more biographical detail, see Lou Cannon, *Reagan* (New York: G. P. Putnam's Sons, 1982); Ronnie Dugger, *On Reagan: The Man & His Presidency* (New York: McGraw-Hill, 1983); and Robert Dallek, *Ronald Reagan: The Politics of Symbolism* (Cambridge, MA: Harvard University Press, 1984).

6. For an excellent analysis of the transformation of Ronald Reagan and the evolution of Republican economic philosophy, see Herbert Stein, *Presidential Economics* (New York: Simon & Schuster, 1984), pp. 135–62. The term "the economics of joy" used in this chapter comes from Stein's chapter title; it is such an apt phrase to describe the approach to economics, much as "the politics of joy" was so appropriate to describe the approach of Hubert Humphrey to politics.

7. Herbert Stein claims authorship of the term, "supply-side." Ibid., p. 241. This is not to imply that Stein agrees with the economic analysis that later used his phrase.

8. See Chapter 3, Note 9.

9. See Walter W. Heller's editorial, "Can We Afford the Costs of Kemp-Roth?" *Wall Street Journal*, February 10, 1981.

10. After championing the supply-side philosophy in *Wall Street Journal*, he published *The Way The World Works* (New York: Simon & Schuster, 1978), which along with George Gilder's *Wealth and Poverty* (New York: Basic Books, 1981) became the standard reference work for supply-side economics. For a view of how supply-side economics affected policymaking in Washington, see Paul Craig Roberts, *The Supply-Side Revolution* (Cambridge, MA: Harvard University Press, 1984).

11. Sometimes the curve is drawn with the axes reversed.

12. See Chapter 3 for a discussion of this point, or Andrew W. Mellon, *Taxation: The People's Business* (New York: Macmillan, 1924), pp. 16–17.

13. Economists refer to the effects as income and substitution effects: As the price of leisure rises (the price for not working rises when take-home pay increases as a result of tax cuts), some people will decide to work more, substitute work for leisure (the substitution effect); some will work less, as the increased income permits more leisure (the income effect); and of course, some will not change their behavior in response to tax cuts.

14. Stein, *Presidential Economics*, p. 261.

15. See Lester M. Salamon and Alan J. Abramson, "Governance, the Politics of Retrenchment," in John L. Palmer and Isabel V. Sawhill (eds.), *The Reagan Record* (Cambridge, MA: Ballinger, 1984), pp. 37–39.

16. Lester M. Salamon and Alan J. Abramson provide a clear description of the governing strategy in *The Reagan Record*, pp. 40ff.

17. *A Program for Economic Recovery*, a White House Report, p. 2.

18. Ibid., p. 10. See also John L. Palmer and Gregory B. Mills, "Budget Policy," in John L. Palmer and Isabel V. Sawhill (eds.), *The Reagan Experiment* (Washington, DC: Urban Institute Press, 1982), p. 7.

19. Stein, *Presidential Economics*, pp. 268–69.

20. For a detailed analysis of the operations of the FOMC in the year 1981, see Daniel L. Thornton, "The FOMC in 1981: Monetary Control in a Changing Financial Environment," Federal Reserve Bank of St. Louis, *Review* (April 1982), pp. 3–22. Also see "Monetary Policy Report to Congress," *Federal Reserve Bulletin* 67, No. 3 (March 1981), pp. 195–208, and 68, No. 3 (March 1982), pp. 125–34.

21. *Federal Reserve Bulletin* 68, No. 3 (March 1982), p. 131.
22. See Daniel L. Thornton, "The FOMC in 1982: De-emphasizing M1," Federal Reserve Bank of St. Louis, *Review* (June/July 1983), pp. 26–35, and "Monetary Report to Congress," *Federal Reserve Bulletin* 69, No. 3 (March 1983), pp. 127–39.
23. William Greider, "The Education of David Stockman," 248, No. 6 *Atlantic* (December 1981), pp. 38–40.
24. Ibid., p. 46.
25. Ibid., pp. 46–47.
26. For a critical analysis of the capital-shortage issue, see S. Bowles, D. G. Gordon, and T. Weisskopf, *Beyond the Waste Land* (New York: Anchor Press, 1983), pp. 53–59. The case for the need to increase capital formation can be found in the CEA's *Economic Report of the President* (Washington, DC: GPO, 1983), pp. 77–95.
27. For estimates of the Reagan policies on investment spending, see Isabel V. Sawhill and Charles F. Stone, "The Economy," in John L. Palmer and Isabel V. Sawhill (eds.), *The Reagan Record* (Cambridge, MA: Ballinger, 1984), pp. 96ff. They conclude: "We estimate that the 1981–1982 recession brought with it a cumulative loss of $112 to $194 billion (1982) dollars of investment, reducing the existing stock of capital by between 1.0 and 2.5 percent relative to what it would have been with a more modest downturn in economic activity."
28. A study by the Citizens for Tax Justice revealed that the corporations that received the largest tax breaks did not invest as much as those that received the smallest or no tax breaks.
29. Lou Cannon, *Reagan* (New York: G. P. Putnam, 1982), p. 324.
30. The CEA in its *Economic Report of the President*, 1983 barely acknowledged that a recession had occurred, but was elated over the fall in prices. The Report began with this sentence: "THE MAJOR ECONOMIC ACHIEVEMENT OF 1982 was a dramatic reduction of inflation to its lowest rate in a decade" (capital letters in original). Considering the severity of the recession, the CEA did not choose to devote much analysis to it, but stressed the nascent recovery.
31. Federal Reserve, "Monetary Policy Report," March 1982, p. 135.
32. Sawhill and Stone, "The Economy," p. 81.
33. Data on prices paid and direct quote from Robert B. Reich, *The Next American Frontier* (New York: Times Books, 1983), p. 147.
34. Robert E. Taylor and Stan Crock, "Reagan Team Believes Antitrust Legislation Hurts Business," *Wall Street Journal*, July 8, 1981, p.1. In that same issue of *Wall Street Journal* is an article, "High Borrowing Costs Fail to Stem Interest in Takeover Activity," by Tim Metz and Bill Paul, p. 1.
35. J. J. Minarik, "Who Wins, Who Loses from Inflation?" *Challenge* 21, No. 6 (January/February 1979), pp. 26–31; and L. E. Nulty, "How Inflation Hits the Majority," in the same issue, pp. 32–38.
36. See the conclusions of the *President's Commission on Military Preparedness* led by General Scowcrof.
37. Sawhill and Stone, "The Economy," p. 82.

38. Ibid., p. 83.

39. Sawhill and Stone have simulated results based on various scenarios, and they generally show more moderate results for gradualism (in monetary policy) than for the cold-turkey approach. See ibid., pp. 84ff, and their *Economic Policy in the Reagan Years* (Washington, DC: Urban Institute Press, 1984).

40. The administration's forecasts were taken from Paul Blustein, "Administration Sees 4% Growth a Year Through '88, Topping Private Forecasts," *Wall Street Journal*, December 31, 1985, p. 3. For additional forecasts, some as optimistic as the administration's, see Lindley H. Clark, Jr., "The Outlook," *Wall Street Journal*, January 6, 1986, p. 1.

41. Barry Bosworth, "Taxes and the Investment Recovery," in *Brookings Papers on Economic Activity* 1, 1985, pp. 1–38. The direct quote is from page 5. Bosworth raises many interesting points in this article, such as what to count as investment in the national accounts. Office equipment, for example, is counted as investment, but much is for home consumption.

42. Data quoted from Gar Alperovitz and Jeff Faux, *Rebuilding America* (New York: Pantheon, 1984), pp. 12–13.

43. Robert Lekachman, *Greed is Not Enough: Reaganomics* (New York: Pantheon, 1982), p. 9.

44. For more of the effects on low-income groups, see Interfaith Action for Economic Justice, *End Results: The Impact of Federal Policies Since 1980 on Low Income Americans* (Washington, DC: IAEN, September 1984), from which some of the data used here were taken.

45. Two such studies, D. Lee Bawden and John L. Palmer, "Social Policy, Challenging the Welfare State," and Marilyn Moon and Isabel V. Sawhill, "Family Incomes: Gainers and Losers," can be found in Sawhill and Stone, *The Reagan Record*. While quarrelling over the definition of fairness in general, Irving Kristol justifies the cuts in social programs, since the Reagan administration "wants to draw a sharper line between those who work and those on welfare in the belief that this will encourage the welfare poor who can work to escape the stigma of dependency and move up into the working poor, while prodding the working poor to work their way out of poverty." From "Fairness and Income Equalizing," *Wall Street Journal*, May 2, 1984, p. 30.

46. The safety net, which always had holes in it, contained most of the New Deal programs, and when asked what constituted it, David Stockman of OMB replied, "It was a happenstance list [of programs] just a spur-of-the-moment thing that the press office wanted to put out"; Martin Anderson, White House policy advisor, said in a speech, "Providing a safety net for those who cannot or are not expected to work was not really a social policy objective. The term 'safety net' was political shorthand that only made sense for a limited period of time." Both excerpts taken from Interfaith Action, *End Results*, p. 3.

47. Ibid., P. 14. The study quotes Margaret C. Simms, *The Effect of Changes in Tax and Transfer Policy on the Economic Well-Being of Minorities* (Washington, DC: Urban Institute, December 30, 1982), p. 5.

48. Lester C. Thurow, "The Disappearance of the Middle Class," *New York Times*, February 5, 1984, pp. 20–29.
49. *Newsweek*, January 2, 1984, pp. 20–29.
50. For more on the labor situation, see Frank Ackerman, *Reaganomics: Rhetoric vs. Reality* (Boston: South End Press, 1982), pp. 101–18.
51. See Steven Greenhouse, "Reshaping Labor to Woo the Young," *New York Times* September 1, 1985, p. F1. See also *Business Week*, July 8, 1985, pp. 72–77.
52. Audrey Freedman, "There's No Recovery in Sight for Unions," *New York Times* January 20, 1985.
53. See Perry D. Quick, "Businesses: Reagan's Industrial Policy," in Palmer and Sawhill, *The Reagan Record*, pp. 237–316; also Murray L. Weidenbaum, "Regulatory Reform under the Reagan Administration," in George C. Eads and Michael Fix (eds.), *The Reagan Regulatory Strategy: An Assessment* (Washington, DC: Urban Institute Press, 1984).
54. FDIC, *Annual Report* (Washington, DC: GPO, 1984), p. 45.
55. Quick, "Businesses," p. 307. See also Paul R. Portney, "Natural Resources and the Environment," in Palmer and Sawhill, *The Reagan Record*, pp. 141–75.
56. Quick, ibid., pp. 307ff. Quick presents some interesting data based on a survey of businesses on the costs of compliance with social regulations. Briefly, businessmen indicated that the costs did not affect profits to any extent and were not as opposed to regulations as the Reagan administration would have predicted. Quick also suggests that the administration grossly overestimated the savings to business by its antiregulation policies.
57. Portney, "Natural Resources," pp. 169–171.
58. See Milton Friedman, "Deficits and Inflation," *Newsweek*, February 23, 1981, p. 70.
59. CEA, *Economic Report of the President*, 1982, p. 102.
60. Ibid., 1983, pp. 16–17.
61. Ibid., 1984, p. 35.
62. Donald Regan, secretary of the treasury, deliberately mispronounced his name, held up a copy of the CEA *Economic Report of 1984*, and told a televised news conference not to read it except for the first nine pages, allegedly written by the president. Inside the administration he was known as Dr. Gloom or Dr. No. Feldstein was gagged in public addresses by having to submit his speeches before they were delivered. He resigned in the summer of 1984; Mr. Reagan was so angered that he failed to replace him, and the CEA for a time had only one member and no chairman.
63. Daniel Patrick Moynihan, "Reagan's Inflate-the-Deficit Game," *New York Times*, July 21, 1985, p. E21.
64. For the administration's analysis of the trade deficit, see CEA, *Economic Report of the President*, 1984 and 1985. Both have an extensive section on the trade problem.

65. See Kenneth N. Gilpin, "The Maze of Latin American Debt," *New York Times*, March 13, 1983, p. F4.
66. For a brief summary of the issues in the banking sector, see Lester C. Thurow, "America's Banks in Crisis," *New York Times Magazine*, September 23, 1984, pp. 48, 72–77, 108–9.
67. For a quick summary of the issue, see *Business Week*, October 8, 1984, pp. 164–76; and the CEA's *Economic Report of the President*, 1984 and 1985.
68. See, for instance, Jeffrey A. Frankel, "The Dazzling Dollar," in *Brookings Papers on Economic Activity* 1 (1985), pp. 199–217. For other views on exchange-rate developments, see the other participants in the symposium in the same source: Peter Isard and Lois Stekler, "US International Capital Flows and the Dollar"; Stephen N. Marris, "The Decline and Fall of the Dollar: Some Policy Issues"; and the discussion papers that follow.
69. For example, Paul S. Samuelson, "Where Iacocca and Common Sense Err," *New York Times*, September 15, 1985, p. F3; and Richard N. Gardner, "Sound Economics, Sound Trade Policy," in the same source, p. E21.
70. Gardner, "Sound Economics."
71. Ibid.
72. See Barry Bluestone and Bennett Harrison, *The Deindustrialization of America* (New York: Basic Books, 1982).
73. Irving Kristol, "Reviewing Reagan's Reviewers," *Wall Street Journal*, September 11, 1985, p. 32.
74. John L. Palmer and Isabel V. Sawhill, "Overview," in *The Reagan Record*, p. 29.
75. Lester M. Salamon and Alan J. Abramson, "Governance,", p. 66.
76. Palmer and Sawhill, "Overview," p. 30.
77. For an excellent summary of some of these tax system proposals and the principles of taxation in general, see Joseph A. Peckman, *A Citizen's Guide to the New Tax Reforms* (Totowa, NJ: Rowman & Allanheld, 1985).

Chapter 15

1. For a short but excellent example, see Andrew Schotter, *Free Market Economics: A Critical Appraisal* (New York: St. Martin's Press, 1985).
2. See the works of J. K. Galbraith, for instance, *The New Industrial State* (1967) and *Economics and the Public Purpose* (1973) both published by Houghton Mifflin of Boston.
3. See Herbert Stein, *Presidential Economics* (New York: Simon & Schuster, 1984), pp. 321ff, for a discussion of some of these points.
4. Ibid., p. 375.
5. See, for instance, George Gilder, *Wealth and Poverty* (New York: Basic Books, 1981) for an influential work espousing these ideas.
6. For the more reasoned arguments against redistribution, see Robert Nozick, *Anarchy, State, and Utopia* (Oxford: Basil Blackwell, 1974).

7. Robert Aaron Gordon, *Economic Instability & Growth: The American Record* (New York: Harper & Row, 1974), p. 196.
8. Friedrich A. Hayek, *Unemployment and Monetary Policy: Government as Generator of the "Business Cycle"* (San Francisco: Cato Institute, 1979), p. xvii.
9. James M. Buchanan and Richard E. Wagner, *Democracy in Deficit: the Political Legacy of Lord Keynes* (New York: Academic Press, 1977), p. 184.
10. Victor Perlo, *The Unstable Economy: Booms and Recessions in the U.S. since 1945* (New York: International Publishers, 1973), p. 151.
11. Edward Boorstein, *What's Ahead? ... The U.S. Economy* (New York: International Publishers, 1984), pp. 22–23.
12. Harry Magdoff and Paul M. Sweezy, *The End of Prosperity* (New York: Monthly Review Press, 1977), pp. 130, 132–33.
13. Walter W. Heller, *The Economy: Old Myths and New Realities* (New York: Norton, 1976), p. 195.
14. Leon H. Keyserling, *"Liberal" and "Conservative" National Economic Policies and Their Consequences, 1919–1979* (Washington, DC: Conference on Economic Progress, 1979), p. 87.
15. Stein, *Presidential Economics*, pp. 307ff.
16. From "The Market as Prison," Southern Political Science Association, *Journal of Politics* 44, No. 2 (May 1982), pp. 324–36. Reprinted in Thomas Ferguson and Joel Rogers (eds.), *The Political Economy* (Armonk, NY: M. E. Sharpe), pp. 3–11.
17. Ferguson and Rogers, ibid., p. 9.
18. This point and many others came from an excellent book by Gar Alperovitz and Jeff Faux, *Rebuilding America* (New York: Pantheon Books, 1984), and although many of the ideas presented here were developed before reading their book, I learned much from their work and they reinforced my own convictions.
19. For specific programs, see ibid., pp. 157–235.
20. One such survey was proposed by S. Bowles, D. M. Gordon, and T. E. Weisskopf in *Beyond the Waste Land* (New York: Anchor Press, 1983), p. 327, to determine household needs, so that real needs could be identified and ranked and so that the planning authority could prepare production targets. The survey proposed here is to determine national concerns in order to set national goals for a planning authority.
21. What might such a survey(s) reveal as major concerns of the nation? Without being presumptuous, the list might contain all or some of the following stated in the vernacular:

    Inflation too great—cost of living too high
    Too much unemployment
    Health care too expensive and not always available
    Housing too costly; decent housing unaffordable for most people
    Not enough public transportation—no alternative to the automobile
    Not enough spent on education
    Not enough spent on highways

Not enough spent on water and sewer systems
Not enough spent on pollution control
More recreation sites needed
Unfair tax system
Poverty too great—distribution of income unjust
Foreigners taking our jobs and buying up our firms
Farmers being forced out of business
Interest rates too high—borrowing for housing, education, farm implements, and so on unaffordable
Energy costs too high
Too much (not enough) spent on national defense—too much waste.

22. Lester Thurow proposed one in his *Zero-Sum Society* (New York: Basic Books, 1980), p. 201, in which he suggested that the distribution of income for the nation should be the same distribution that now exists for fully employed white males. This group was chosen because the incentives for work have never been questioned for it, and so this standard should not affect the incentives to work for other groups either.

23. For instance, see Robert B. Reich, *The Next American Frontier* (New York: Times Books, 1983); Felix Rohatyn is identified with the reconstruction of the RFC in the *New York Times*, April 22, 1982, p. E4; see also *Business Week*, "The Reindustrialization of America," special issue of June 30, 1980; or Lester Thurow, "How to Rescue a Drowning Economy," *New York Review of Books,* April 1, 1982, p. 4. An industrial policy is not without its critics; see, for example, Bowles et al., *Beyond the Waste Land*, or Charles Schultze, "Industrial Policy: A Dissent," *The Brookings Review* 2, No. 1 (Fall 1983), pp. 3–12.

24. See Gordon Tullock, "A Modest Proposal," in Ryan C. Amacher, Robert D. Tollison, and Thomas D. Willett (eds.), *The Economic Approach to Public Policy* (Ithaca, NY: Cornell University Press, 1976), pp. 511–19.

25. Tullock, ibid., pp. 513–14. He went on to suggest (for the CEA), "Further, the fact that this advice would be given publicly would mean that the economists would be subject to pressure not to say things which would look foolish five years in the future. The politicians could hardly maintain that they had not been warned if they chose to disregard the advice" (p. 514).

26. See the interview with Alice Tivlin in *Challenge* 26, No. 6 (January/February, 1984), p. 24.

27. Howard E. Shuman, *Politics and the Budget* (Englewood Cliffs, NJ: Prentice-Hall, 1984), pp. 279ff.

28. Milton Friedman, "Reforming the Fed," *Challenge* 28, No. 3 (July/August, 1985), pp. 4–12.

29. Bowles, Gordon, and Weisskopf, *Beyond the Waste Land*, p. 338.

30. For an analysis of the Swedish system, see John B. Taylor, "The Swedish Investment Funded System as a Stabilization Policy Rule," *Brookings Papers on Economic Activity* 1, 1982, pp. 57–99.

Bibliography

Ackerman, Frank. *Reagonomics, Rhetoric and Reality*. Boston: South End Press, 1982.

Allen, Frederick Lewis. *Only Yesterday*. New York: Harper & Brothers, 1931.

————. *Since Yesterday*. New York: Harper & Brothers, 1939.

————. *The Big Change*. New York: Harper & Brothers, 1952.

Alperovitz, Gar, and Jeff Faux. *Rebuilding America*. New York: Pantheon Books, 1984.

Alsop, Joseph. *FDR, 1882–1945*. New York: Washington Square Press, 1982.

Amacher, Ryan C., Robert D. Tollison, and Thomas D. Willet (eds.). *The Economic Approach to Public Policy*. Ithaca, NY: Cornell University Press, 1976.

Anderson, Clay J. *A Half Century of Federal Reserve Policymaking, 1914–1964*. Philadelphia: Federal Reserve Bank of Philadelphia, 1965.

Anderson, H. Dewey. *Taxation, Recovery, and Defense*. Temporary National Economic Committee, Monograph 20, Washington DC: U.S. Government Printing Office, 1939.

Atkinson, A. B. *The Economics of Inequality*. Oxford: Oxford University Press, 1975.

Baran, Paul A., and Paul M. Sweezy. *Monopoly Capitalism*. New York: Monthly Review Press, 1966.

Baruch, Bernard M. *The Public Years*. New York: Holt, Rinehart and Winston, 1960.

Berle, Adolf A. *Navigating the Rapids*. New York: Harcourt Brace Jovanovich, 1973.

Berman, Larry. *The Office of Management and Budget and the Presidency, 1921–1979*. Princeton, NJ: Princeton University Press, 1979.

Blakey, Roy G., and Gladys C. Blakey. *The Federal Income Tax*. New York: Longmans, Green, 1940.

————. "Two Federal Revenue Acts of 1940." *American Economic Review* 30 (December 1940): 724–28.

Blinder, Alan S. *Economic Policy and the Great Stagflation*. New York: Academic Press, 1979.

Bluestone, Barry, and Bennett Harrison. *The Deindustrialization of America*. New York: Basic Books, 1982.

Board of Governors of the Federal Reserve System. "Survey of Consumers' Finances, 1983." *Federal Reserve Bulletin* 70, No. 8 (September 1984): 679–92; and 70, No. 12 (December 1984): 857–68.

Boorstein, Edward. *What's Ahead? ... The U.S. Economy.* New York: International Publishers, 1984.

Bosworth, Barry. "Taxes and the Investment Recovery." In *Brookings Papers on Economic Activity* 1 (1985): 1–38.

Bowles, Samuel, David M. Gordon, and Thomas E. Weisskopf. *Beyond the Waste Land.* New York: Anchor Press/Doubleday, 1983.

Branyan, Robert L., and Lawrence H. Larsen. *The Eisenhower Administration, 1953–1961.* New York: Random House, 1971.

Brinkley, Alan. *Voices of Protest.* New York: Knopf, 1982.

Brown, D. V. et al. *The Economics of the Recovery Program.* New York: McGraw-Hill, 1934.

Brunner, Karl (ed.). *The Great Depression Revisited.* Boston: Martinus Nijhoff, 1981.

———, and A. Meltzer (eds.). *The Economics of Price and Wage Controls.* Carnegie-Rochester Conference Series 2. Amsterdam: North Holland, 1976.

Buchanan, James M., and Richard E. Wagner. *Democracy in Deficit.* New York: Academic Press, 1977.

Burner, David. *Herbert Hoover.* New York: Knopf, 1979.

Burns, Arthur F. *Prosperity without Inflation.* New York: Fordham University Press, 1957.

Burns, James MacGregor. *Roosevelt: The Soldier of Freedom.* New York: Harcourt Brace Jovanovich, 1970.

Calleo, David P. *The Imperious Economy.* Cambridge, MA: Harvard University Press, 1982.

Cannon, Lou. *Reagan.* New York: G. P. Putnam's Sons, 1982.

Carter, Jimmy. *Keeping Faith.* New York: Bantam Books, 1982.

Chandler, Lester V. *America's Greatest Depression, 1929–1941.* New York: Harper & Row, 1970.

Civilian Production Administration. *Industrial Mobilization for War*, Vol 1, *Program and Administration.* Washington, DC: Bureau of Demobilization, 1947.

Commission on Money and Credit. *Money and Credit.* Englewood Cliffs, NJ: Prentice-Hall, 1961.

Committee for Economic Development. *Growth and Taxes.* New York: Committee for Economic Development, 1961.

———. *Fiscal and Monetary Policy for High Employment.* New York: Committee for Economic Development, 1962.

———. *Reducing Tax Rates for Production and Growth.* New York: Committee for Economic Development, 1962.

Congressional Quarterly Service. *Federal Economic Policy 1945–1967.* 2d ed. Washington DC: Congressional Quarterly.

———. *President Carter.* Washington, DC: Congressional Quarterly, 1977.

Corey, Lewis. *The Decline of American Capitalism*. New York: Covici, Friede, 1934.

Council of Economic Advisors. *Economic Report of the President*. Washington, DC: U.S. Government Printing Office, various years, 1947–1985.

Croly, Herbert. *Promise of American Life*. New York: Macmillan, 1909.

———. *Progressive Democracy*. New York: Macmillan, 1915.

Dallek, Robert. *Ronald Reagan: The Politics of Symbolism*. Cambridge, MA: Harvard University Press, 1984.

Dewhurst, J. Fredrick. *America's Needs and Resources*. New York: Twentieth Century Fund, 1947.

Douglas, Paul. *Real Wages in the United States*. Boston: Houghton Mifflin, 1930.

Donovan, Robert J. *Eisenhower, The Inside Story*. New York: Harper & Brothers, 1956.

Dugger, Ronnie. *The Politician: The Life and Times of Lyndon Johnson*. New York: Norton, 1982.

———. *On Reagan: The Man & His Presidency*. New York: McGraw-Hill, 1983.

Eccles, Marriner S. *Beckoning Frontiers*. New York: Knopf, 1951.

Edie, Lionel D. (ed.). *The Stabilization of Business*. New York: Macmillan, 1923.

Ehrlichman, John. *Witness to Power: The Nixon Years*. New York: Simon & Schuster, 1982.

Evans, Rowland, and Robert Novak. *Lyndon B. Johnson: The Exercise of Power*. New York: New American Library, 1966.

Faulkner, Harold U. *The Quest for Social Justice, 1898–1914*. New York: Macmillan, 1951.

Fellner, William (ed.). *Contemporary Economic Problems, 1978*. Washington, DC: American Enterprise Institute, 1978.

Ferguson, Thomas, and Joel Rogers (eds.). *The Political Economy*. Armonk, NY: M. E. Sharpe, 1984.

Friedman, Milton, and Rose Friedman. *Free to Choose*. New York: Harcourt Brace Jovanovich, 1979.

———, and Walter W. Heller. *Monetary vs. Fiscal Policy*. New York: Norton, 1969.

———, and Anna J. Schwartz. *A Monetary History of the United States 1867–1960*. National Bureau of Economic Research, Princeton, NJ: Princeton University Press, 1963.

Fromm, Gary. *Tax Incentives and Capital Spending*. Washington, DC: The Brookings Institution, 1971.

Galbraith, J. K. *A Life in Our Times*. Boston: Houghton Mifflin, 1981.

———. *A Theory of Price Control*. Cambridge, MA: Harvard University Press, 1952.

———. *Economics and the Public Purpose*. Boston: Houghton Mifflin, 1973.

———. *The Great Crash*. Boston: Houghton Mifflin, 1961.

———. *The New Industrial State*. Boston: Houghton Mifflin, 1967.

Gilder, George. *Wealth and Poverty*. New York: Basic Books, 1981.

Glad, Betty. *Jimmy Carter*. New York: Norton, 1980.

Goldwater, Barry. *The Conscience of a Conservative*. New York: Hillman Books, 1960.

_____ . *With No Apologies*. New York: William Morrow, 1979.

Gordon, Robert A. *Economic Instability and Growth*. New York: Harper & Row, 1974.

Greider, William. "The Education of David Stockman." *Atlantic* 248, No. 6 (December 1981): 27–54.

Hacker, Andrew. "Up for Grabs." *New York Review of Books* (April 1981): 8–16.

Halberstam, David. *The Best and the Brightest*. New York: Random House, 1969.

Hamby, Alonzo L. *Beyond the New Deal: Harry S. Truman and American Liberalism*. New York: Columbia University Press, 1973.

Haney, Lewis H. *History of Economic Thought*. 4th ed. New York: Macmillan, 1949.

Hansen, Alvin H. *Fiscal Policy and Business Cycles*. New York: Norton, 1941.

_____ . *Economic Issues of the 1960s*. New York: McGraw-Hill, 1960.

_____ . *The Postwar American Economy*. New York: Norton, 1964.

_____ . *A Guide to Keynes*. New York: McGraw-Hill, 1953.

Hardy, Charles O. *Tax-Exempt Securities and the Surtax*. New York: Macmillan, 1926.

Harrington, Michael. *The Other America*. New York: Macmillan, 1962.

Harris, Seymour. *The Economics of America at War*. New York: Norton, 1941.

_____ . *Economics of the Kennedy Years*. New York: Harper & Row, 1964.

_____ (ed.). *The New Economics*. London: Dennis Dobson, 1947.

Hart, Jeffrey. *When the Going Was Good: American Life in the Fifties*. New York: Crown, 1982.

Hayek, Friedrich. *The Road to Serfdom*. Chicago: University of Chicago Press, 1944.

_____ . *Unemployment and Monetary Policy: Government as Generator of the "Business Cycle"*. San Francisco: Cato Institute, 1979.

Heller, Walter W. *The Economy*. New York: Norton, 1976.

_____ . *New Dimensions of Political Economy*. New York: Norton, 1967.

Holmans, A. E. *United States Fiscal Policy 1945–1959*. Oxford: Oxford University Press, 1961.

Jezer, Marty. *The Dark Ages: Life in the United States, 1945–1960*. Boston: South End Press, 1982.

Johnson, Lyndon Baines. *The Choices We Face*. New York: Bantam Books, 1969.

_____ . *The Vantage Point*. New York: Popular Library, 1971.

Josephson, Matthew. *The Money Lords*. New York: Weybright and Talley, 1972.

Kalecki, M. "General Rationing." *Bulletin of the Institute of Statistics* 3 (January 1941): 2–6.

Kearns, Doris. *Lyndon Johnson and the American Dream*. New York: Harper & Row, 1976.

Kendrick, John W. *Productivity Trends in the United States*. NBER, Princeton, NJ: Princeton Univesity Press, 1961.

Keynes, J. M. *Collected Writings. Vol 22. Activities 1939–1945, Internal War Finance*. London: Macmillan Press, 1978.

————. "The Economic Consequences of Mr. Churchill." In *Essays in Persuasion*. New York: Norton, 1963.

Keyserling, Leon H. *Liberal and Conservative National Economic Policies and Their Consequences, 1919–1979*. Washington, DC: Conference on Economic Progress, 1979.

Kindleberger, Charles P. *The World in Depression*. Berkeley: University of California Press, 1973.

Kolko, Gabriel. *The Triumph of Conservatism*. Glencoe, IL: Free Press of Glencoe, 1963.

Kuznets, Simon S. *National Income and Its Composition, 1919–1938*. New York: National Bureau of Economic Research, 1941.

Lampman, Robert J. *The Share of Top Wealth-Holders in National Wealth 1922–56*. NBER, Princeton, NJ: Princeton University Press, 1962.

Lasky, Victor. *Jimmy Carter: The Man & The Myth*. New York: Richard Marek, 1979.

Lebergott, Stanley. *Manpower in Economic Growth: The American Record Since 1800*. New York: McGraw-Hill, 1964.

Lekachman, Robert. *Greed Is Not Enough*. New York: Pantheon Books, 1982.

Lerner, Abba P. *Economics of Employment*. New York: McGraw-Hill, 1951.

Leuchtenburg, William E. *The Perils of Prosperity 1914–32*. Chicago: University of Chicago Press, 1958.

Leven, Maurice, Harold G. Moulton, and Clark Warburton. *America's Capacity to Consume*. Washington, DC: The Brookings Institution, 1934.

Lewis, Wilfred, Jr. *Federal Fiscal Policy in the Postwar Recessions*. Washington, DC: The Brookings Institution, 1962.

Link, Arthur S. *Woodrow Wilson and the Progressive Era, 1910–1917*. New York: Harper & Brothers, 1954.

Lisio, Donald J. *The President and Protest: Hoover, Conspiracy, and the Bonus Riot*. Columbia: University of Missouri Press, 1974.

Long, Huey P. *Every Man a King*. Chicago: Quadrangle Books, 1964.

Lowe, Carl (ed.). *Reaganomics: The New Federalism*. New York: H. W. Wilson, 1984.

Lyon, Leverett S., et. al. *The National Recovery Administration*. Washington, DC: The Brookings Institution, 1935.

McClure, Arthur F. *The Truman Administration and the Problems of Postwar Labor, 1945–1948*. Madison, NJ: Fairleigh Dickinson University Press, 1969.

Magdoff, Harry, and Paul M. Sweezy. *The End of Prosperity: The American Economy in the 1970s*. New York: Monthly Review Press, 1977.

————. *The Dynamics of U.S. Capitalism*. New York: Monthly Review Press, 1972.

———. *The Age of Imperialism*. New York: Monthly Review Press, 1969.

Manchester, William. *Portrait of a President*. New York: Macfadden Books, 1964.

———. *The Glory and The Dream*. Boston: Little, Brown, 1973.

Manning, Thomas G. *The Office of Price Administration*. New York: Henry Holt, 1960.

Mellon, Andrew W. *Taxation: The People's Business*. New York: Macmillan, 1924.

Menderhausen, Horst. *The Economics of War*. New York: Prentice-Hall, 1941.

Miller, Douglas T., and Marion Nowak. *The Fifties*. New York: Doubleday, 1977.

Miller, Merle. *Lyndon: An Oral Biography*. New York: G. P. Putnam's Sons, 1980.

———. *Plain Speaking, An Oral Biography of Harry S. Truman*. New York: Berkley Publishing, 1973.

Mills, Frederick C. *Prices in Recession and Recovery*. New York: National Bureau of Economic Research, 1936.

Mitchell, Broadus. *Depression Decade: From New Era Through New Deal*. White Plains, NY: M. E. Sharpe, 1975.

Moulton, Harold G. *The Formation of Capital*. Washington, DC: The Brookings Institution, 1935.

———, and Karl T. Schlotterbeck. *Should Price Controls Be Retained*. Washington, DC: The Brookings Institution, 1945.

Murphy, Henry C. *Debt in War and Transition*. New York: McGraw-Hill, 1950.

Musgrave, Richard A. *The Theory of Public Finance*. New York: McGraw-Hill, 1959.

Myrdal, Gunnar. *Against the Stream: Critical Essays on Economics*. New York: Pantheon Books, 1973.

Nixon, Richard M. *Six Crises*. New York: Pyramid Books, 1968.

———. *Memoirs*. New York: Warner Books, 1979.

Nourse, Edwin G. *Economics in the Public Service*. New York: Harcourt, Brace, 1953.

——— et. al. *America's Capacity to Produce*. Washington, DC: Brookings Institution, 1934.

Nozick, Robert. *Anarchy, State, and Utopia*. Oxford: Basil Blackwell, 1974.

Okun, Arthur M. *The Political Economy of Prosperity*. New York: Norton, 1970.

O'Neill, William L. *Coming Apart*. New York: Quadrangle Books, 1971.

Palmer, John L., and Isabel V. Sawhill (eds.). *The Reagan Experiment*. Washington, DC: Urban Institute Press, 1982.

———. *The Reagan Record*. Cambridge, MA: Ballinger, 1984.

Pechman, Joseph A. *A Citizen's Guide to the New Tax Reforms*. Totona, NJ: Rowman & Allanheld, 1985.

Perlo, Victor. *The Unstable Economy: Booms and Recessions in the United States since 1945*. New York: International Publishers, 1973.

Phillips, Cabell. *The Truman Presidency*. New York: Macmillan, 1969.

————. *The 1940s: Decade of Triumph and Trouble*. New York: Macmillan, 1975.

Projector, Dorothy S., and Gertrude S. Weiss. *Survey of Financial Characteristics of Consumers*. Washington, DC: Board of Governors of the Federal Reserve System, 1966.

Ratner, Sidney. *Taxation and Democracy in America*. New York: Wiley, 1942.

Reich, Robert B. *The Next American Frontier*. New York: Times Books, 1983.

Reichley, A. James. *Conservatives in an Age of Change: The Nixon and Ford Administrations*. Washington, DC: The Brookings Institution, 1981.

Roberts, Paul Craig. *The Supply-Side Revolution*. Cambridge, MA: Harvard University Press, 1984.

Romasco, Albert U. *The Poverty of Abundance*. New York: Oxford University Press, 1965.

Rosenman, Samuel L. *Working With Roosevelt*. New York: Harper & Brothers, 1952.

Salamon, Lester M., and Michael S. Lund (eds.). *The Reagan Presidency and the Governing of America*. Washington, DC: Urban Institute Press, 1984.

Samuelson, Paul A. "Economic Policy for 1962." *Review of Economics and Statistics* 44 (1962): 3–6.

————, and Everett E. Hagen. *After the War*. Washington, DC: National Resources Planning Board, 1943.

Schlesinger, Arthur M. Jr. *The Crisis of the Old Order*. Boston: Houghton Mifflin, 1957.

————. *A Thousand Days: John F. Kennedy in the White House*. Boston: Houghton Mifflin, 1965.

————. *The Politics of Upheaval*. Boston: Houghton Mifflin, 1960.

————. "The Hundred Days of FDR." *New York Times*, April 10, 1983, pp. 8f.

Schotter, Andrew. *Free Market Economics: A Critical Appraisal*. New York: St. Martin's Press, 1985.

Schneir, Walter (ed.). *Telling It Like It Was: The Chicago Riots*. New York: New American Library, 1969.

Schwartz, John E. *America's Hidden Success*. New York: Norton, 1983.

Sheahan, John. *The Wage and Price Guideposts*. Washington, DC: The Brookings Institution, 1967.

Sherwood, Robert E. *Roosevelt and Hopkins*. New York: Harper & Brothers, 1948.

Shultz, George P., and Kenneth W. Dam. *Economic Policy Beyond the Headlines*. New York: Norton, 1977.

Shuman, Howard E. *Politics and the Budget*. Englewood Cliffs, NJ: Prentice-Hall, 1984.

Smith, Adam. *Supermoney*. New York: Popular Library, 1972.

Sorensen, Theodore C. *Kennedy*. New York: Harper & Row, 1965.

Soule, George. *Prosperity Decade: From War to Depression, 1917–1929*. White Plains, NY: M. E. Sharpe, 1975.

Sprinkel, Beryl W. *Money & Markets*. Homewood, IL: Richard D. Irwin, 1971.

Stein, Herbert. *The Fiscal Revolution in America*. Chicago: University of Chicago Press, 1969.

———. *Presidential Economics.* New York: Simon & Schuster, 1984.

Stevens, Robert Warren. *Vain Hopes, Grim Realities.* New York: New Viewpoints, 1976.

Stone, Charles F., and Isabel V. Sawhill. *Economic Policy in the Reagan Years.* Washington, DC: Urban Institute Press, 1984.

Stubblebine, William Craig, and Thomas D. Willett (eds.). *Reaganomics: A Midterm Report.* San Francisco: ICS Press, 1983.

Sullivan, Mark. *Our Times.* New York: Scribner, 1935.

Sundquist, James L. *Politics and Policy: The Eisenhower, Kennedy, and Johnson Years.* Washington, DC: The Brookings Institution, 1968.

Taussig, F. W. *The Tariff History of the United States.* New York: G. P. Putnam's Sons, 1931.

Taylor, John B. "The Swedish Investment Funded System as a Stabilization Policy Rule." In *Brookings Papers on Economic Activity* 1 (1982): 57–99.

Temin, Peter. *Did Monetary Forces Cause the Great Depression?* New York: Norton, 1976.

Thomas, Woodlief. "Lessons of War Finance." *American Economic Review* 40, No. 4 (September 1951): 618–31.

Thurow, Lester C. *Generating Inequality.* New York: Basic Books, 1975.

———. *The Zero-Sum Society.* New York: Basic Books, 1980.

Tobin, Harold, and Percy Bidwell. *Mobilizing Civilian America.* New York: Council on Foreign Relations, 1940.

Tobin, James. *National Economic Policy.* New Haven, CT: Yale University Press, 1966.

———. *The New Economics One Decade Older.* Princeton, NJ: Princeton University Press, 1974.

Tufte, Edward R. *Political Control of the Economy.* Princeton, NJ: Princeton University Press, 1978.

U.S. Bureau of the Budget. *The United States at War.* Washington, DC: U.S. Government Printing Office, 1946.

U.S. Bureau of the Census. *Income Distribution in the United States,* by Herman P. Miller (a 1960 Census Monograph). Washington, DC: U.S. Government Printing Office, 1966.

U.S. Congress. Joint Economic Committee, Compendium of Papers. *The Relationship of Prices to Economic Stability and Growth* (Washington, DC: U.S. Government Printing Office, March 31, 1958).

U.S. Congress, Senate, Committee on the Judiciary, Subcommittee on Antitrust and Monopoly. *Economic Concentration.* Staff Report of the FTC, Economic Report on Corporate Mergers, on S. Res. 40, Part 8A, 91st Cong. 1st sess. Washington, DC: U.S. Government Printing Office, 1969.

———. *The Conglomeration Merger Problem,* Part 8, 91st Cong., 2d sess. (Washington DC: 1969, 1970).

U.S. Congress, Temporary National Economic Committee, *Investigation of Concentration of Economic Power.* Washington, DC: U.S. Government Printing Office, 1940.

U.S. Department of Commerce. *Long-Term Economic Growth, 1860–1965.* (Washington, DC: U.S. Government Printing Office, 1966).

———. *Historical Statistics of the United States* (Washington, DC: U.S. Government Printing Office, 1975).

Wanniski, Jude. *The Way the World Works*. New York: Simon & Schuster, 1978.

Warne, Colston E. (ed.). *Labor in Postwar America*. Brooklyn, NY: Remsen Press, 1949.

Weidenbaum, Murray L. *Economic Impact of the Vietnam War*. Washington, DC: Center for Strategic Studies, Georgetown University, 1967.

Weintraub, Sidney, and Marvin Goodstein (eds.). *Reaganomics in the Stagflation Economy*. Philadelphia: University of Pennsylvania Press, 1983.

White, Theodore H. *The Making of the President, 1960*. New York: Pocket Books, 1961.

———. *The Making of the President, 1968*. New York: Atheneum, 1969.

Wicker, Elmus. *Federal Reserve Monetary Policy, 1917–1933*. New York: Random House, 1966.

Wilcox, Clair. *Public Policies toward Business*. 3rd ed. Homewood, IL: Richard D. Irwin, 1966.

Wills, Garry. *The Kennedy Imprisonment*. Boston: Little, Brown, 1981.

Index

Aaron, Henry J., 536
accelerated depreciation, 288, 302
accord, 176, 222, 226–27
Ackerman, Frank, 524
Ackley, Gardiner, 247, 318
Adelman, M. A., 449–50
advertising: in 1920s, 48; in World War II, 191
Advisory Commission to the Council of National Defense, 157
Agnew, Spiro, 384, 398
agriculture: problems in 1930s, 90–93, 114–16; in World War II, 164–66; in Reagan administration, 526–28; future policies for, 570
Agricultural Adjustment Act (AAA), 114, 115–16, 133, 138, 140
Agricultural Marketing Act, 90–93
Alliance for Progress, 298
American Federation of Labor (AFL), 121, 267
American Enterprise Institute, 22
American Relief Administration, 35
Anderson, John, 449, 484
Anderson, Robert, 257
Atkins, W. E., 49
Auchter, Thorne, 524
automatic stabilizers, 75, 259
automobile industry: post-World War I boom, 29; in the 1920s, 48, 69; in 1950s, 253; in 1970s, 362–66, 403

Baker, Howard, 484
Baker, James, 491

balance of payments: in 1950s, 253, 262–63; in 1960s, 285, 290–92, 325, 333; in 1970s, 429, 463; in 1980s, 513
balanced budgets: as fiscal policy, 54, 491, 505, 509
balanced-budget amendment, 470–72, 505, 509, 528, 567
bank holiday, 103–4, 108–9
Bankhead Cotton Act, 115
Banking Act of 1933, 113
Banking Act of 1935, 113
bankruptcies: from 1920–22, 44; of banks in 1980s, 525–26
Baruch, Bernard, 27, 28, 93, 119, 157, 164, 167–69, 184
Berle, A. A., 107
Beveridge, William, 196
Bischoff, Charles, W., 288
Black, Hugo, 117, 124
Blatnik, John, 297
Blinder, Alan, 401
Blough, Roger, 295
Blumenthal, Michael, 421
Boorstein, Edward, 557
borrowing in World War II, 173–76
Bosworth, Barry, 512
Bowles, Chester, 170, 199
Bowles, Samuel, 576
Bradley, William, 536
Brain Trust, 107
Brandegee, Frank B., 52
Bretton Woods Agreement, 267, 292, 363, 368, 414

About the Author

ANTHONY S. CAMPAGNA is Professor of Economics at the University of Vermont. He is the author of two textbooks in macroeconomics: *Macroeconomics: Theory and Policy* (Boston: Houghton Mifflin, 1974); and *Macroeconomics* (New York: St. Martin's Press, 1981). Dr. Campagna holds B.S., M.A., and Ph.D. degrees from Rutgers, The State University, New Brunswick, New Jersey.